Beijing Spring,1989

CONFRONTATION AND CONFLICT

To our parents,
Israel and Klara Oksenberg,
Virginia and Lawrence Sullivan, Sr.,
Lee and Evelyn Lambert,
and Celia Langert,
whose extraordinary devotion
has nurtured us through the years.

Beijing Spring,1989

CONFRONTATION AND CONFLICT

The Basic Documents

Michel Oksenberg
Lawrence R. Sullivan
Marc Lambert
Editors

Introduction by
Melanie Manion

Featuring
"Death or Rebirth? Tiananmen: The Soul of China"
By Li Qiao et al.
Translated by H. R. Lan and Jerry Dennerline

An East Gate Book

M. E. Sharpe, Inc.
Armonk, New York
London, England

An East Gate Book

Library of Congress Cataloging-in-Publication Data

Beijing spring, 1989 : confrontation and conflict : the basic
   documents/Michel Oksenberg, Lawrence R. Sullivan, Marc Lambert,
   editors : main introduction by Melanie Manion.
      p. cm.
   ''East Gate book.''
   ISBN 0-87332-683-0   ISBN 0-87332-684-9 (pbk.)
   1. China—History—Tiananmen Square Incident, 1989—Sources.
I. Oksenberg, Michel, 1938– . II. Lambert, Marc, reporter.
DS779.32.B45 1990
951.05′8—dc20   0-8077
                                                                   CIP

Printed in the United States of America

ED   10   9   8   7   6   5   4   3   2   1

Contents

Preface

MICHEL OKSENBERG WITH LAWRENCE R. SULLIVAN

Beijing has been the setting for many moments of high drama during the Chinese people's tortuous search for national wealth and righteous rule. As a center of both government and intellectual life, it has witnessed struggles for power by extraordinarily willful politicians, militarists, and popular movements. Its citizens have periodically suffered from invading armies—foreign and domestic—while in this century the city's intellectuals, students, and workers have repeatedly voiced their grievances and hopes for more enlightened and democratic government to transform China into a modern nation.

Politically, the capital embraces a duality. It is physically dominated by the imposing structures from which the Ming (1368–1644), Qing (1644–1911), Republican (1911–1927), and Communist (1949–) leaders and bureaucrats issued their edicts and performed the rituals of rule: the Forbidden City, the Temple of Heaven, the Premier's Office of the Republican government, the Great Hall of the People, the Zhongnanhai headquarters of the Chinese Communist Party (CPC), and the many ministerial offices in the city. But equally important are the memories associated with particular locations where protests and political actions have occurred. Scattered about Beijing, but generally concentrated within or near the Forbidden City, are the places where Kang Youwei and his associates presented their petition to the emperor in 1898; where May Fourth demonstrators paraded for democracy in 1919; where martyrs perished during the 1920s after opposing various warlord oppressors; and where December Ninth movement leaders organized their opposition in 1935–36 to the ineffectual government response to Japanese aggression. Since the Communist revolution in 1949, Tiananmen Square (whose vast space the new regime carved out of the city in 1950) has often been the focal point of mass political activity: from the orchestrated parades of the early 1950s to the massive Red Guard rallies in 1966 when Mao Zedong mobilized youth discontent to attack his political enemies in the CPC. Nearby, in Xidan, is the wall where activists pasted their posters in 1978–79 calling for democracy and freedom of expression, while also denouncing China's Communist system in terms that would reverberate throughout Beijing in the spring of 1989.

The buildings that have housed past and present governments are daily reminders of the glory and power of the state, while recollections of protests and demonstrations that have rocked the capital tenuously exist in people's minds. The former appear powerful, while the latter seem ephemeral. State buildings persist while protests against the state disappear. Yet memories of those outbursts of human energy and thought have often proved just as decisive in shaping the course of Chinese history as have decisions emanating from Beijing's architectural structures.

Thus, the capital's history, as with Berlin, Paris, Moscow, or Washington, and more recently Prague, Budapest, and Bucharest, is encapsulated in both its official buildings and monuments and its public spaces. Activities in these two parts of any capital are usually integrated and interdependent. But occasionally, fissures erupt when large segments of the populace gather to condemn the actions and ideas of officials who occupy state buildings. Many in the street are, in fact, government bureaucrats who have chosen to oppose the very system that employs them. The capital openly divides: political leaders in state buildings versus the public in open spaces.

This is what occurred in Beijing from mid-April through early June 1989. Led by students, a large portion of the city's populace, including some industrial workers, took to the streets in massive demonstrations against their rulers, with Tiananmen Square as the central point of activity. Here was the destination of the huge parades—at times reaching one million—that wound downtown from the university district in the northwestern section of the city. At the western edge of the square, students knelt on the steps of the Great Hall of the People, consciously emulating the way virtuous but loyal censors remonstrated in imperial times to petition the government. In the center of the square at the Monument to the People's Heroes, the newly created Beijing Autonomous Union of Students set up its command headquarters as thousands of students encamped nearby for days on end. Here also the hunger strikers ignited the conscience of the nation, while in the northern portion of the square students later erected the Goddess of Democracy and pointed the statue toward Mao's imposing and stern portrait, which hangs over the tunnel entering the Forbidden City. The square was also the scene for a perfunctory visit by Li Peng, and General Secretary Zhao Ziyang's last tearful farewell to the students, knowing he would soon lose his position.[1] Finally, the square was the destination of the awesome military force that smashed its way into the city after peaceful forays by troops had brought hundreds of thousands onto the avenues to block the army's advance. These

---

[1]Zhao also commented to the students that as a young man he had been involved in student demonstrations against the Guomindang, going so far as to lie on railroad tracks to disrupt rail traffic—an act later emulated by students and workers in several cities after the June 4 crackdown. Zhao's statement in his strong Henan accent that "it doesn't matter what happens to me" (*wusuowei*) was later mimicked by Beijing residents in daily confrontations with authorities.

events are now eradicably embedded in the memories of the city's population as major struggles continue over how future generations in and outside China will recall and judge these events.

This volume presents important documents from the Beijing spring. Together they illuminate several questions: First, how did the populace occupying the public spaces and the political leaders ensconced in state buildings justify their actions? How did each side in this deeply divided city give meaning to their activities? And how did they interpret the motives of their adversaries? Second, since no political rupture of this magnitude occurs suddenly, what were the long-term causes and origins of the demonstrations and protests? What factors explain the enormous gulf that separated the people in the square from the rulers behind the walls of Zhongnanhai and their secret compound west of the city, where they evidently fled in late May?[2] Third, what social, economic, and political forces drove the confrontation toward its tragic end of military suppression and a massacre of several hundred, if not thousands of, Beijing residents? To what extent, indeed, were the participants enmeshed in a struggle that escaped anyone's control? Melanie Manion's introductory essay grapples with these and other questions. In addition, brief introductions to each part provide some guidance to the reader. But the underlying conception of this collection is that the documents speak for themselves.

A central concern of this volume is the origin of the crisis in Beijing. The documents included here do not, however, fully capture the vision, ideals, and yearnings that gripped the students. This important part of the story is only partially captured in Document 1, "Death or Rebirth? Tiananmen, The Soul of China," a moving and detailed account of the first stages of the demonstrations written by several Chinese participants. The voices of student leaders, such as Wu'er Kaixi, are also captured in the transcripts of the student dialogues with Premier Li Peng (Doc. 36) and the poetic testament of the May 12 Hunger Strike Announcement (Doc. 33).[3] Readers interested in the full expression of student, worker, and popular views should, however, consult a forthcoming companion collection of documents, *China's Search for Democracy: The Student and Mass Movement of 1989.*[4]

---

[2]Leaders went to their West Mountain (Xishan) compound for security reasons and also moved their families into Zhongnanhai out of fear of popular reprisals. Unit (*danwei*) leaders and rank-and-file party members were also reportedly frightened that the masses would take revenge on them even before June 3.

[3]Student dialogues with other leaders, such as Beijing Mayor Chen Xitong, were evidently not recorded, and thus transcripts are not currently available. Dialogues were also carried out in other provinces, such as Anhui, and have been described by Western observers. See Jonathan Perry, *Bulletin*, East Asian Studies, University of California, 6, 4 (April–June 1989): 3.

[4]Suzanne Ogden et al., eds., *China's Search for Democracy: The Student and Mass Movement of 1989* (Armonk, N.Y.: M. E. Sharpe, forthcoming).

The primary purpose of the present volume is, instead, to convey the views of the Communist leadership—conservatives and moderates alike—and the establishment intellectuals who have profoundly influenced political debate in China since 1949. Arranged in a rough chronological order of nine parts, these documents provide highly divergent perspectives on the political and economic problems confronting China and, more specifically, the unfolding events of April 15 to June 4, 1989. Part I, "Polarized China," contains two documents with highly contrasting interpretations of the spring movement: "The Soul of China" and the official interpretation on the "quelling of the counterrevolutionary rebellion" given by Beijing Mayor Chen Xitong. The political and economic antecedents to the demonstrations are covered in the next three sections. Part II, "Prelude: Reform and Retrenchment," contains various speeches from 1987 to 1989 by Zhao Ziyang, Li Peng, and others outlining contradictory solutions to China's severe economic problems. An equally contentious debate among party leaders and intellectuals on the political structure of China is presented in part III on "Neo-Authoritarianism," while part IV, "Intellectual Dissent," reproduces the even more radical views of prominent dissidents such as ex–*People's Daily* editor Hu Jiwei and the internationally known astrophysicist Fang Lizhi.

The last four parts cover the movement from the sudden death of Hu Yaobang on April 15, to the declaration of martial law and the crackdown itself, to the aftermath of a divided China. Part V, "The Crisis Begins," provides moving accounts of Hu Yaobang's last days and transcripts of early dialogues between leaders and students. Part VI, "The Political Struggle for Tiananmen," contains various documents on the hunger strike, negotiations, and expressions of support for the students. With Zhao's clear defeat, the government decided on a declaration of martial law on May 19—covered in part VII—that led to the ultimate tragedy of violence and repression on June 3–4, revealed in the documents in part VIII, "Premonitions of Violence." Finally, part IX, "The Aftermath," portrays the deep political divisions and domestic and international outrage produced by the government's decision to resolve the crisis of spring 1989 with bullets and tanks rather than dialogue and compromise.

This volume provides an authoritative record of the most dramatic political struggle in the People's Republic of China since the Cultural Revolution and offers a testimony to its tragic climax.

Introduction: Reluctant Duelists
The Logic of the 1989 Protests and Massacre

MELANIE MANION

Moral outrage at the massacre of protesters and bystanders in Beijing is a natural response to a grossly inhumane act. We reacted all the more acutely because the act took us by surprise: it flatly contradicted the estimates of most China experts and the apparent public defeat of force as a regime option in the first two weeks of martial law. While it may have been naïve to expect a victory for the protesters, even political sophisticates were shocked by the violence of June 4, 1989.

The massacre was a disaster—for the protesters and their supporters most obviously, but also for the Chinese Communist regime and its program of economic reform. What, then, explains this tragic outcome? This introduction reconstructs events of April, May, and June from the inferred perspectives of organized protesters in Beijing and those we now know as regime hardliners. My purpose is to make sense of the narrow rationale of particular acts and to discover how they fit together to produce the massacre of 4 June. Essentially, I conclude that the logic of the 1989 protests and massacre is one of players pressed into a duel. Events unfolded as they did mainly because protesters and hardliners operated on the basis of mistaken and irreconcilable assumptions and estimates about the practical implications of mass political participation. And while the massacre was by no means inevitable from the start, the exchange between protesters and hardliners caused both sets of players to update information in a way that escalated events, to a point at which retreat in the form of compromise was virtually impossible.

Assumptions and Initial Estimates

On April 26 an editorial in the *Renmin ribao*, the Communist Party newspaper, labeled the recent student protests in Beijing "a planned conspiracy and a distur-

I wish to thank the following people for their helpful comments on an earlier draft: Nina Halpern, Abigail Jahiel, Kenneth Lieberthal, John Mueller, Michel Oksenberg, Charles Phelps, and David Weimer.

bance.''[1] On April 27 the Preparatory Committee for a Beijing Autonomous Union of Students responded with an organized protest march and rally. By that time hardliners and protesters had already formed mutually contradictory ideas about what to expect.

Briefly, hardliners took for granted that socialist economic and political development in the People's Republic of China (PRC) require a Communist Party monopoly of leadership and a high degree of social stability. Autonomous organizations such as the nascent student union and large demonstrations obviously challenged both monopoly and stability, and hardliners concluded that protest organizers were deliberately out to ruin them and the system.

At the same time, protesters assumed that the political history of more than a decade provided information on what the regime would tolerate and how it would sanction actions viewed as unacceptable. If that experience was a reliable predictor, then they had good reason to conclude that there was some chance of a positive response to their demands and that the probability of being suppressed was high, but the probable level of suppression relatively moderate.

In fact, policies and protests of the past decade did not provide the most relevant lessons for the protesters. To the extent that they based expectations on those experiences, they were guided by incomplete and misleading information about the norms and costs of unauthorized political action. A main reason is that the size of the movement and forms of protest adopted presented a more serious challenge to the regime than protests of the previous ten years had done. Hardliners reacted less to the content of the protests than to the movement's size and forms of protest, which called up memories of the Cultural Revolution of 1966–1976. The hardliners' perceptions were also conditioned by a particular political context: the protests seemed to be yet another provocation, part of the increasingly radical movement of dissent among nonstudent intellectuals in 1989.

From Mourning to Protests

The catalyst for the Beijing protests was the death of Hu Yaobang on April 15. Hu had been removed from his position as Communist Party general secretary in 1987 for his toleration of an earlier round of student protests, which had begun in late 1986 and were suppressed after he was ousted. Hu's tacit support of the students, his reputation as a defender of political and intellectual freedoms, and his critical stance on official corruption made him a popular leader among liberal intellectuals.

---

[1]Editorial, "It Is Necessary To Take a Clear-Cut Stand Against Disturbances," *Renmin ribao*, April 26, 1989, in Foreign Broadcast Information Service, *Daily Report: China* (hereafter FBIS), April 25, 1989, 24. The editorial was televised nationally on the evening news on April 25. Document 25.

Even before Hu's death, however, student activists at Beijing University had begun organizing a big prodemocracy demonstration for the anniversary of the 1919 May Fourth Movement—the patriotic movement promoting "Mr. Science" and "Mr. Democracy," celebrated annually in the PRC. Some of the same students had earlier organized a "democracy salon," a series of talks by invited liberal intellectuals, held first in a student dormitory room and later (to accommodate a larger audience) on a campus lawn near the statue of Cervantes.[2] In short, some of the students who would later emerge as leaders in the protest movement were already engaging in various forms of unauthorized political activity before the death of Hu Yaobang. Hu's death merely accelerated an ongoing process of political ferment.

Immediately after Hu's death, posters went up at Beijing University, mourning him and also calling for more democracy. Two days later, hundreds of students and teachers marched from the University of Political Science and Law to the square at Tiananmen, located in the center of the city. In the center of the square stands the Monument to the People's Heroes. There the protesters assembled to place wreaths and shout slogans: long live democracy, long live freedom, long live the rule of law, down with corruption! On April 18 thousands of students from Beijing University and People's University marched to Tiananmen. People gathered to listen to informal speeches on political reform. The crowd, including students, numbered about ten thousand. Hundreds of students began a sit-in before the Great Hall of the People, which bounds Tiananmen on the square's west side. Over a thousand assembled outside Zhongnanhai, the elite residential compound about a mile to the west of the square, and demanded a meeting with top leaders. Similar demonstrations took place on April 19 and 20, when the first clashes between students and police occurred.[3] On the morning of April 22, three student representatives knelt for thirty minutes on the steps of the Great Hall of the People, in a vain attempt to present a petition to the government.[4]

---

[2]I was told that Wang Dan was one of the main organizers of the democracy salon. Wang emerged as one of the top student leaders in the protest movement.

[3]I heard several conflicting versions of the clashes, but most students I talked to maintained that students had tried unsuccessfully to enter Zhongnanhai, had dispersed peacefully on April 19, but that there had been violence on April 20. Apparently, some students had thrown things at the police and resisted detention. Police had kicked students with leather shoes and beat them with belts. The authorities denied this version of events. See "Attempted Storming of Zhongnanhai" and "More on Storming of Zhongnanhai," Beijing Xinhua Hong Kong Service, in FBIS, April 19, 1989, 15–16; "Disturbance Disrupts Mourning," Beijing Domestic Service, in FBIS, April 20, 1989, 16–17; "Second Attempt to Storm Zhongnanhai," Beijing Xinhua, in ibid., 24–25; "Beijing TV Carries Dialogue," Beijing Television Service, in FBIS, May 1, 1989, 29–30. Document 27.

[4]The petition was accepted by two members of the funeral committee. Students considered that response inadequate and even humiliating. See the account by one of the students who presented the petition in "Beijing TV Carries Dialogue," 33–36.

Later that morning, while the official funeral ceremony for Hu Yaobang was being held, a crowd of 100,000 gathered in the square to mourn and protest.

Different views and demands were evident in the posters, some of which were openly critical of Deng Xiaoping and Premier Li Peng. But on April 23, representatives of nineteen universities and colleges in Beijing collectively agreed on seven demands: a reassessment of Hu Yaobang, a reassessment of the 1986 student movement and the campaign against bourgeois liberalization that had followed suppression of the movement, increased funds for education, legislation for press freedoms, more measures to combat official corruption, accurate reportage on the protest movement, and an investigation and public disclosure of police violence against students on April 20.[5] Student demands would change frequently in the weeks to come.[6]

By April 24, the students had already presented the authorities with a movement that was bigger, better organized, and with more apparent social support than the protests of 1986. Nineteen schools had united to form the Preparatory Committee for a Beijing Autonomous Union of Students. The committee had decided to promote strikes by students, workers, and shopkeepers and to publish an open letter to the Chinese people, calling for nationwide protests. Students from Shanghai, Nanjing, Wuhan, and Tianjin traveled to Beijing to help plan a nationwide student strike for May 4. Universities and colleges in Beijing sent representatives to other cities to seek

---

[5]See "19 Beijing Universities and Colleges Put Forward a '7-Point Petition' and a '2-Point Provisional Decision', Calling for Strikes by Workers, Shopkeepers, and Students Throughout the Country," Hong Kong *Ming pao*, April 24, 1989, in FBIS, April 24, 1989, 32.

[6]On May 2 the student movement presented a new petition to the government, which dropped the politically sensitive demands for a reassessment of the 1986 protests and the campaign against bourgeois liberalization. The new petition added the following demands: maintaining the constitutional rights of citizens, making public the findings of surveys conducted in ten Beijing universities and colleges, and investigating policy mistakes of recent years so as to discover the reasons for the inflation. These demands were presented as preconditions for opening a dialogue with authorities. On May 6, students dropped preconditions for dialogue and presented a petition that only listed topics for dialogue, as follows: the significance of the student movement, ways to expand political and economic reform, and ways to develop further democracy and the legal system. On May 13, students limited their demands to two: dialogue with the authorities and an affirmation of their movement. After martial law was declared, students again proposed preconditions for dialogue, as follows: the lifting of martial law, the withdrawal of troops, a promise of no reprisals against protesters, and enhanced press freedoms. See "Beijing Student Self-Rule Association Issues Statement at News Briefing," Hong Kong *Hsin wan pao*, May 1, 1989, in FBIS, May 1, 1989, 59; "Students Present Demands," Hong Kong AFP, in FBIS, May 2, 1989, 10–11; "Zhao Aide To Talk with Students," Hong Kong *South China Morning Post*, May 8, 1989, in FBIS, May 8, 1989, 20–21; "Students Stage Hunger Strike," Beijing Xinhua, in FBIS, May 15, 1989, 38; "Authorities, Students Resume Talks," Hong Kong *Hongkong Standard*, May 31, 1989, in FBIS, May 31, 1989, 43–44.

more support for the strike. On April 21, students at Beijing University had begun to boycott classes. By April 24, over twenty universities in Beijing were on an enforced strike, with picket lines surrounding classroom buildings. Students in Beijing were asked to write letters to their friends in other parts of the country to explain the aims of the movement. Public speech groups were established to deliver speeches in the city, to appeal to other sectors of society by talking about problems such as the recent inflation and corruption among officials, both issues on which people tend to have very strong feelings.[7] Students posted pamphlets on street lamps, trees, and bus windows to explain their views. The rudimentary autonomous unions on separate campuses set up independent campus broadcasting stations. Students also began to collect donations to begin an independent newspaper.

Such forms of protest were not without precedent in the history of the PRC. The big-character posters, unofficial student organizations, and link-ups with other units and cities recalled for many older officials the tactics of student Red Guards in the Cultural Revolution. On April 25 Deng Xiaoping concluded: "Now, there are some people doing the same old thing, that is just like the rebellion faction during the Cultural Revolution. They won't be satisfied until all is chaos."[8] Other leaders, too, made references to the Cultural Revolution throughout May and June, in describing the crisis as they viewed it.[9] The association is not surprising: many leaders in the post-Mao regime had been persecuted and toppled from power by Red Guards. Zealous young people defying authority easily raised fears of another such chaotic and threatening movement.[10]

Most of the 1989 student protesters had barely reached the age of ten by the time the Cultural Revolution had ended and been officially repudiated. They did not draw inspiration for their movement from the Red Guards. To the contrary, they believed there was a fundamental difference between the Cultural Revolution and their own protests: the former had been initiated, manipulated, and finally terminated by different groups in the top elite, but theirs was a genuine mass movement.[11]

---

[7]Guomindang failure on those issues contributed to the Communist victory in 1949.

[8]"Text of a Document Circulated Among Senior Party and Government Officials Earlier This Month," Hong Kong *South China Morning Post*, May 31, 1989, in FBIS, May 31, 1989, 35. Document 24.

[9]See, for example, references by Yuan Mu and Yuan Liben in "Beijing TV Carries Dialogue," 26, 32; Yuan Mu in "Yuan Mu Holds News Conference 3 May," Beijing Television Service, in FBIS, May 3, 1989, 23; Editorial, "Safeguard the Overall Interests, Safeguard Stability," *Renmin ribao*, April 28, 1989, in FBIS, May 1, 1989, 13.

[10]Older officials expressed similar fears to me during the 1986 student protests, when I was completing interviews for a study of retirement of revolutionary veterans.

[11]Students and other intellectuals I spoke to greatly resented the comparison of the movement with the Cultural Revolution. This was one reason for the strong reaction to the label "disturbance," the term often used officially to describe the Cultural Revolution. The Chinese press quoted students expressing views on this issue: "The present student

Perspective of Protesters

In a movement that by the end of April could already claim thousands of student supporters and dozens of leaders, there could not be complete unanimity in objectives, motivations, and expectations. But in the seven weeks before the movement was crushed, top protest leaders and elected student representatives managed to make a large number of collective decisions and to obtain active support for those decisions from a large proportion of students. In that sense, despite the differences among them, they presented the authorities with a cohesive student movement, about which several generalizations can reasonably be made.[12]

Obviously and for a number of reasons, protesters estimated initially that a positive response to their demands was not completely unthinkable for the authorities. First, they assumed socialism was a fairly flexible framework, one that could conceivably accommodate their actions and demands. Student protesters had grown up in the most materially prosperous period of Chinese Communist rule. More to the point, they had not been politically socialized in the rigid ideological atmosphere of the Maoist era.[13] They had grown up in a period when the party propagated the view that classics of communism offered no blueprint for building socialism, and that only practical results could reveal the validity of policy. They had seen the boundaries delimiting socialism pushed back by bold economic reforms, such as the decollectivization of agriculture and the opening of special trade zones for foreign investment. They were also familiar with steps toward political reform in other socialist countries—most recently, Poland and the Soviet Union.[14] Indeed, student leader Wang Dan explicitly referred to Eastern European countries such as Poland and Hungary as models.[15] Second, student protesters could justifiably perceive themselves as playing a legitimate role in advancing the political reforms

---

movement is a patriotic democratic movement in which we voluntarily participated after using our brains to think about it seriously. The 'Great Cultural Revolution' was wrongly launched by leaders, and utilized by the counterrevolutionary clique at the upper level, and a disturbance imposed from above. But this is not the case with the current student movement." "Zhao Ziyang's Speech Welcomed by Students," Beijing Xinhua Hong Kong Service, in FBIS, May 6, 1989, 3. Document 32.

[12]Thus, unlike the leaders at the top, whose divisions were translated into different public stances on how to deal with the protest movement, the students presented the authorities with a publicly unified movement.

[13]Indeed, Deng Xiaoping has proclaimed that lack of proper socialization is a main cause for the protests. See " 'Text' of Deng Xiaoping Speech Delivered on 9 June," Beijing Domestic Service, in FBIS, June 27, 1989, 9–10. Document 58.

[14]In addition to learning about events from Chinese news services, many students listen to broadcasts of the British Broadcasting Corporation and the Voice of America.

[15]See excerpts in "Wang Dan Encourages European-Style Reforms," Hong Kong South China Morning Post, September 3, 1989, in FBIS, September 8, 1989, 31–32.

already proposed by the authorities. Many of their demands reiterated the regime's own policies of reform. Corruption among officials, press freedom, and education were major issues on the official reform agenda and extensively discussed in the official Chinese press. In voicing their demands, then, for the most part student protesters were not presenting an inherently subversive program.[16] Indeed, when asked in an anonymous interview with a foreign reporter about the future of the Communist Party, a student leader replied: "There is no other party capable of running the country. We think democratization is possible with the CPC [Communist Party of China] in power."[17] Even after the massacre of June 4 had presumably shattered for protesters the legitimacy of the current regime, in the relative safety of Western Europe student protest leader Wu'er Kaixi affirmed that the next prodemocracy movement would still have the aim of reforming socialism, not fighting it.[18]

Protest leaders made great efforts to signal to the authorities that their aims should be viewed as essentially reformist, rather than counterrevolutionary. They adopted measures to ensure that the demonstration of April 27 was peaceful, orderly, and orthodox. They denounced violent riots that had erupted in Xi'an, tore down posters criticizing party and government leaders, did not shout antiparty or antigovernment slogans, and prevented nonstudent infiltrators from entering their ranks to cause trouble. They confronted police cordons with the slogan "The people love the people's police, the people's police love the people!" They carried banners proclaiming, "Uphold party leadership, adhere to socialism!"

Nonetheless, protesters also estimated that there was a high probability of being suppressed. This view was shared by university administrators and faculty, many of whom pleaded with students not to demonstrate on April 27. The right to post big-character posters had been removed from the constitution, and demonstrations without prior authorization violated Beijing municipal regulations.[19] More generally, dissent is not usually tolerated in the PRC, and previous movements in 1978 and 1986 had been suppressed. The authorities had shown on 20

---

[16]An exception was the demand for a reassessment of the 1986 protests and campaign against bourgeois liberalization, which was politically very sensitive and was dropped on May 2.

[17]"Interview with Unnamed Leadership Member of the Chinese Independent Association of University Students," April 23, 1989 in Beijing, Paris *Libération*, April 24, 1989, in FBIS, May 1, 1989, 9.

[18]"Interview with Exiled PRC Dissidents Wu'er Kaixi and Yan Jiaqi," n.d. in Paris, Paris *Le Monde*, July 11, 1989, in FBIS, July 12, 1989, 29. Not surprisingly, Wu'er has since expressed less orthodox views. For example, in a talk to the American Heritage Foundation on August 4, 1989, he reflected that the students had been naïve to ask for changes from the regime, and that it was now clear that systemic change is needed.

[19]The regulations on demonstrations were issued after the 1986 protests. In a meeting with authorities on 29 April, a student questioned the constitutionality of the regulations: "Some students among us have submitted requests to stage demonstrations, but all their

April that they were prepared to use police force against the protesters. Most important of all, the party newspaper had publicly labeled the movement in serious political terms and threatened to suppress it. It was common knowledge in Beijing that the April 26 *Renmin ribao* editorial had been based on a talk given by Deng Xiaoping on the previous day—and thus had to be taken seriously. The editorial asserted that the protests aimed to "negate the leadership of the CPC and the socialist system." It warned: "All comrades in the party and the people throughout the country must soberly recognize the fact that our country will have no peaceful days if this disturbance is not checked resolutely."[20]

Yet while the protesters were psychologically prepared to be suppressed with force, they also believed with good reason that the level of suppression would probably be moderate. In part, protesters were inclined to be hopeful because of their rather naive assumptions about the flexibility of socialism, their own self-image as legitimate participants in the reform program, and their measures to signal their reformist orthodoxy. But it was also because in recent years protesters had been punished less and less severely with each incident. Under another regime, a 1976 demonstration to mourn Premier Zhou Enlai and protest against the influential Gang of Four had ended with bloody beatings and imprisonment of the more active protesters. The official verdict on that demonstration had been reversed in 1978, when it was labeled a completely revolutionary mass movement.[21] In 1978, under the leadership of Deng Xiaoping, authorities had briefly tolerated a popular pro-democracy movement and then in 1979 had suppressed it, imprisoning its main leaders. Again under Deng, the authorities had ended the late 1986 student protests by criticizing and dismissing from the party three prominent intellectuals—Liu Binyan, Fang Lizhi, and Wang Ruowang—accused of instigating and promoting the movement. Liu, a writer, was permitted to spend the 1988–89 academic year in the United States. The astrophysicist Fang spent 1988–89 on the campus of Beijing University, where he spoke frequently about the failings of the Communists.[22] In short, the costs of protest had decreased with each protest movement. It was entirely reasonable for student protesters to view 1976 as an unlikely worst case scenario and 1979 or 1987 as more plausible ones.

---

attempts have been thwarted by various means. Therefore, my fellow students are of the opinion that even though the ten rules and regulations do not contravene the law, in essence they strictly ban demonstrations because no approval is granted to any request for permission to stage a demonstration." See "Beijing TV Carries Dialogue," 46.

[20]"It Is Necessary to Take a Clear-Cut Stand against Disturbances," 24.

[21]Indeed, when martial law was declared, many protesters expressed to me their conviction that no mattered what happened to them, they were convinced that history was on their side, and that the official verdict on the movement would be reversed as it had been for the 1976 protests.

[22]See, for example, the interviews with Li Yi, "Zhongguo yao jiefang?" *Jiushi Niandai*, no. 10 (1988): 70–77, and Orville Schell, "China's Andrei Sakharov," *Atlantic Monthly* 261, 5 (1988): 35–52. Fang kept a low profile during the movement. Nonethe-

Perspective of Hardliners

Those we now know as regime hardliners viewed the protests and their organizers as deliberately malevolent, because they openly violated the fundamental principle of Communist Party leadership and the post-Mao doctrine of social order as a prerequisite for economic and political development. Yet presumably, a large number of Communist leaders in the post-Mao era share with hardliners those basic normative assumptions. What seems to separate hardliners at the top from other leaders is the hardliners' greater fear of social unrest, greater distrust of intellectuals, and (for some) greater suspicion of Western influences—producing a greater initial willingness to resort to force in the face of actions such as the Beijing protests. Thus, while many at the top may have had similar beliefs, they did not necessarily have similar reflexes. Deng Xiaoping outlined a hard-line response as early as April 25, well before the movement had gained momentum.[23] In this he was undoubtedly influenced by Beijing leaders Li Ximing and Chen Xitong, who provided a crucial briefing on the situation on April 24.[24] Premier Li Peng was also quick to perceive the protests as "antiparty" and "antisocialist"—the conclusion drawn in a meeting he chaired, also on April 24.[25]

Several generations and a set of basic assumptions about what constitutes legitimate political activity separate student protesters and regime hardliners. With some exceptions, protesters' violations of those assumptions did not present themselves in their demands and slogans.[26] Indeed, throughout the movement the authorities stated publicly that they shared with the protesters virtually all of the objectives of political reform that were voiced as issues. The authorities also affirmed that the vast majority of protesters had good intentions. Even the harsh editorial of April 26 stated clearly: "The broad masses of students sincerely hope that corruption will be eliminated and democracy will be promoted. These too are the demands of the party and government."[27] In sum, student protesters were correct in estimating initially

---

less, the regime has recently singled him and his wife out as full participants in the protests, probably in large part because of Fang's role in the 1986 protest movement and because he and his wife fled to the American Embassy in Beijing after June 4. See, for example, "Article 'Exposes' Fang Lizhi's 'Traitorous' Acts," Beijing Xinhua Domestic Service, in FBIS, June 27, 1989, 20.

[23]"Text of a Document Circulated among Senior Party and Government Officials Earlier This Month," 35–36.

[24]See "Beijing Mayor's Report on Quelling Counterrevolutionary Rebellion," Beijing Xinhua, in FBIS, 6 July 1989, 25. Document 2.

[25]Ibid. The meeting was of the Politburo Standing Committee. Party leader Zhao Ziyang was absent, having left the day before for a visit to North Korea.

[26]See note 16 above.

[27]"It Is Necessary to Take a Clear-Cut Stand against Disturbances," 24.

that the regime might find the content of their protest tolerable. Protest in general, however, and the adopted forms of protest in particular, were obviously and utterly subversive. Despite their generally orthodox pronouncements, protesters violated key tenets of post-Mao orthodoxy.

In 1978 party leaders had officially acknowledged economic backwardness as the main obstacle to the PRC's progress toward communism, and, consequently, economic development as the primary task for the current stage of socialism. That decision marked the turning point from Maoism to the post-Mao era of reform, allowing the Chinese, as part of a program to promote socialist development, to introduce practices more common in capitalist market economies.

Reformist leaders had not similarly embraced political pluralism. They had acknowledged, however, that the country could benefit from more consultative politics—encouraging people to voice suggestions and criticism about problems, including mistakes and abuses in leadership. They had reinstated and revitalized a number of organizations and mechanisms for that purpose: party discipline inspection commissions, government supervisory departments, local people's congresses, party and government offices to receive letters and visitors, and "mass organizations" for youth, students, workers, and women. These were the existing legitimate channels of socialist democracy, through which the masses could communicate their views to the authorities.

Post-Mao reformers had also adopted measures to strengthen the rule of law, with one stated rationale that strong rules check strong rulers.[28] In this regard, enhancing rules was enhancing democratic rule. By definition, then, democratic political expression respected the existing framework of rules: "The observance of laws, rules, and regulations constitutes the basic condition for the practice and promotion of democracy. Violating laws, rules, and regulations means undermining democracy and leads inevitably to turmoil."[29]

Yet the underlying objection to the student protests was not that they rejected the existing party-dominated youth league and student unions, nor that their posters and demonstrations violated the constitution and broke the law. These were merely specific instances of the more fundamental challenge to the assumptions on which the post-Mao order had been built: that socialist economic and political development is premised on a Communist Party monopoly of leadership and a high degree of social stability.

Although the authorities had granted the masses the right and provided the means to raise opinions, they had more or less reserved a monopoly on defining and imposing solutions. According to the dominant official view, there was no

---

[28]Ironically, Deng Xiaoping had been one of the most vociferous advocates of building strong systemic checks on arbitrary rule. See especially "On the Reform of the System of Party and State Leadership," *Beijing Review* 26, 40 (1983): 14-22, and 41 (1983): 18–22.

[29]"Safeguard the Overall Interests, Safeguard Stability," 13–14.

need to institutionalize political participation in organizations independent of the Communist Party. It was argued that the party had demonstrated its ability to rectify its mistakes, to lead effectively, and to foster democracy: "Our party is fully capable and bold in giving scope to its strong points, correcting the deviations and mistakes in its work, eliminating negative phenomena of all kinds, and continually advancing the cause of China, revolution and construction. Past history has proved this point."[30]

One major risk of democracy that was not managed by the party was said to be social disorder and its corollary, economic disaster. In Deng Xiaoping's words: "China's main aims are to promote development and eradicate backwardness so that our country will have greater strength and the livelihood of our people will be gradually improved. Without a stable political environment it is impossible for us to do so."[31] The editorial of April 26 warned that protest movements, if unchecked, could develop into "a serious chaotic state." As a consequence: "A China with very good prospects and a very bright future [would] become a chaotic and unstable China without any future."[32]

Authorities could point to the economic successes of authoritarian politics in developing countries in the past several decades. In support of this perspective, some Chinese social scientists had advanced several versions of a theory of neoauthoritarianism, with many arguing that democratization would be most successful as a gradual process of political tutelage, directed by strong, enlightened rulers.[33]

Thus the party had appropriated the responsibility and the exclusive right to solve problems and promote democracy. In principle, both democratization and the economic development that was the main task in the current stage of socialism needed strong party leadership and social stability. These assumptions are not unique to the hardliners: they are the foundation of post-Mao political and economic policy. More radical reformers (including but not limited to party leader Zhao Ziyang, who was from the beginning inclined to be conciliatory toward the protesters) found themselves in a minority among the top elite.

While these basic assumptions help explain the hardliners' revulsion against the protests, the political environment in which the protests took place contributed to a magnified view of the threat they posed. Hardliners lumped all their critics together and perceived the April protests as part of the recent radical

---

[30]Editorial, "Take a Clear-Cut Stand in Upholding the Four Cardinal Principles," *Renmin ribao*, June 23, 1989, in FBIS, June 23, 1989, 15.

[31]"Deng Xiaoping's Expositions on Upholding the Four Cardinal Principles and Opposing Bourgeois Liberalization," *Renmin ribao*, June 24, 1989, in FBIS, June 26, 1989, 54. The quote is from a speech Deng gave on June 29, 1987.

[32]"It Is Necessary to Take a Clear-Cut Stand against Disturbances," 24.

[33]See Liu Jun and Li Li, eds., *Xin quanweizhuyi: dui gaige lilun gangling de lunzheng* (Beijing: Beijing jingji xueyuan chubanshe, 1989).

dissent by older nonstudent intellectuals. This had included a petition to release political prisoners (among them Wei Jingsheng, a protest leader imprisoned in 1979)—signed and publicized by prominent mainland Chinese intellectuals as well as even more radical dissident expatriates in political organizations abroad. Fang Lizhi, who had been blamed for instigating the 1986 student protests, was one of the most outspoken petitioners in 1989. Fang was also living on campus at Beijing University, and his wife was in contact with some of the student activists at the university. The student demand to reverse the verdict on the 1986 protests and the campaign against bourgeois liberalization that had followed suggested a relationship between the 1986 and 1989 movements. Hardliners saw the relationship as direct and organizational.[34] It is not surprising that the hardliners failed to draw fine distinctions among their critics, and that the April protests seemed all the more threatening because of it.[35]

The editorial of April 26 provided the preliminary verdict of the hardliners on the protesters and their movement: "Flaunting the banner of democracy, they undermined democracy and the legal system. Their purpose was to sow dissension among the people, plunge the whole country into chaos, and sabotage the political situation of stability and unity. This is a planned conspiracy and a disturbance. Its essence is to, once and for all, negate the leadership of the CPC and the socialist system."[36]

Exchange and Escalation

By April 26, hardliners and protesters had made public their positions, the former in the *Renmin ribao* editorial and the latter in the decision to protest on the following day. The position of the hardliners did not rule out cooptation: they had focused their attack on protest organizers and had labeled the majority of protesters as confused but essentially well-meaning. The position of the protesters did not rule out compromise: they had adopted as protest objectives many official policies. Given their mutually contradictory assumptions, however, hardliners and protesters could not agree on the answer to a basic question: can

---

[34]Many of the more recent statements about Fang Lizhi's role are obvious attempts to find scapegoats. But there clearly was a perception of the protesters as part of a larger movement of dissent that had not been snuffed out in the campaign against bourgeois liberalization. For example, He Dongchang (vice-minister in charge of the State Education Commission) stated in the April 29 encounter with students: "Some extremists who had shouted the wrong slogans in the past have corrected themselves. This is good, and it is welcomed. But students should be aware of the bearded people—I mean those who are older—and see if they have truly mended their ways. This question requires some deep thought." "Beijing TV Carries Dialogue," 42.

[35]A colleague of mine says he finds this mentality easier to understand when he thinks of an example in the more familiar American context: Richard Nixon.

[36]"It Is Necessary to Take a Clear-Cut Stand against Disturbances," 24.

socialism accommodate institutionalized political forces independent of the Communist Party? Protesters proposed to institutionalize the movement in dialogues with the authorities and autonomous unions; hardliners found this completely unacceptable. Not surprisingly, the exchange between the two from April 27 to June 3 caused the movement not to defuse but to escalate, to a point from which neither hardliners nor protesters could reasonably retreat.

The exchange unfolded in the following way. Responses from the authorities led protesters to update and revise previous estimates: hardliners seemed unable to suppress them and unwilling to grant concessions. The protesters became confident and frustrated. As a result, their positions and tactics became more extreme. At the same time, the bold actions of protesters only confirmed for hardliners the validity of their previous estimates. Their restraint was taken for weakness, their concessions were rejected as inadequate, and the protesters responded with increasingly subversive activities. This convinced hardliners that protest organizers were indeed out to destroy the party monopoly and social stability that they viewed as necessary conditions for development and that sustained them in power.

Zhao Ziyang contributed to the escalation with his signals of an alternative soft line in the top leadership stratum. Zhao's evident willingness to be conciliatory encouraged protesters, initially to hope for meaningful concessions from the authorities and later to call for the political defeat of Li Peng and the hard line. For the hardliners, the tacit coalition of leader and protesters made the movement all the more dangerous and intolerable.

No Repression

For protesters, the demonstration of April 27 provided the information for the first major updating of initial estimates about suppression. Fully expecting to be beaten or detained, about 100,000 university students marched to Tiananmen. Along their route they met hundreds of thousands of citizens who applauded, shouted their support, and offered refreshments.[37] They were joined on the square by more citizens, and the crowd numbered about 500,000. To their surprise, protesters discovered that the overwhelming majority of police along the route and at the square were unarmed. As the crowds jeered and the lines of marchers strained forward, the police cordons yielded easily. Student protest leader Guo Haifeng probably spoke for many when he concluded: ''I am not

---

[37]Students told me they set out on their march feeling like martyrs for a just cause, expecting that the suppression threatened in the April 26 editorial would be realized. Other Chinese told me that virtually everyone expected the regime to use force on that day, and that the courage of the students partly accounts for the massive support they received from the crowds that lined their route to the square.

afraid anymore, this time there are too many of us."[38]

The events of April 27 to June 3 repeatedly confirmed this confident revision of initial estimates. Although hardliners frequently criticized the protests and issued several warnings, they did not take decisive measures to suppress the movement. Even the declaration of martial law on May 20, which at first produced great tension among the protesters and renewed expectations of violent suppression, proved to be a hollow threat for a full two weeks until June 4.[39] Again the Beijing population rallied to support the students and defy the authorities. On the outskirts of the city large crowds of students and citizens surrounded the trucks of more than fifty thousand troops. Officers and peasant soldiers were lectured about the just demands of the movement and scolded for trying to suppress it.[40] The response of the army was to stop, and eventually to retreat. Virtually no incidents of army violence occurred.[41]

For two weeks the troops assigned to enforce martial law held back. Protesters regained their confidence. It was all too easy to conclude once again that the students had won legitimacy, not only among the Beijing population but among those whose job it was to coerce—the police and now the soldiers—and that the movement's moral force had overcome the force of arms. There were also suggestions of high-level military opposition to martial law: for example, on May 21, marshals Nie Rongzhen and Xu Xiangqian had apparently telephoned Deng Xiaoping to urge against the use of force to end the movement, and seven veteran generals had apparently sent a letter to the Military Affairs Commission and the Martial Law Command demanding that the army remain outside the city.[42] Whether or not those rumors are true, they were widely circulated and believed on the square and in the streets.

In the early hours of June 3 the authorities made another major attempt to end the protests. About thirty thousand unarmed soldiers set out on foot from

---

[38]"Student Leader Discusses Issues," Hong Kong AFP, in FBIS, May 1, 1989, 8.

[39]Students on the square expected the troops to suppress them with tear gas, and protest activists had posted notices around the square explaining how to deal with tear gas. Many students and others in the crowd were very frightened, as they were unfamiliar with the gas.

[40]Many students and ordinary citizens displayed great courage in stopping the troops. But from the perspective of the peasant soldiers, the student speeches must also have sounded rather patronizing.

[41]A clash at Fengtai on May 22 produced casualties on both sides, but authorities quickly affirmed that neither students nor soldiers were to blame. Ordinary citizens had become angry when they mistook the army's retreat for an advance into the city. According to the authorities, students had cooperated with troops to reduce tensions. See "Spokesman Holds News Briefing on Confrontation," Beijing Xinhua Domestic Service, in FBIS, May 24, 1989, 39–40.

[42]See "It Is Said that Old Marshals Have Telephoned Deng Xiaoping, Pointing Out that Force Should Not Be Used," Hong Kong *Wen wei po*, May 22, 1989, in FBIS, May

the outskirts of Beijing toward the square. The main force got within several hundred yards of the square but were soon blocked by large crowds, who pushed them and shouted insults. The soldiers were visibly frightened and quickly retreated without resisting. No casualties were reported. An estimated one million people had turned out in the streets to defend the student protesters. Although the troops had nearly managed to reach the square, they had been unarmed and easily overwhelmed by the protesters and their supporters. The incident produced confusion and anger among protesters and their supporters, but ultimately the authorities had again failed to suppress the movement.[43]

It seemed to most protesters and observers that the authorities could not suppress the movement. Hardliners continue to offer a different explanation of their actions: under the circumstances they chose not to suppress the movement. In their account, from the time the movement began until June 3 they acted with great restraint. In retrospect, their version of events is obviously the more accurate one. Nonetheless, it is also true that the massive crowds that came out to support the students at each threat of suppression made it logistically impossible to suppress the movement without using tremendous force, but politically embarrassing to suppress it with such force.

Perspective of Hardliners: Concessions

From the perspective of hardliners, in the three weeks from April 27 to May 20 when they declared martial law, they had responded to the students with concession after concession to end the protests. Each time, protest organizers had rejected the concessions as inadequate, confirming the hardliners' view that the real objective of the movement was to overthrow the party and destroy the system. On May 18 the Minister of the State Education Commission voiced the following opinion on the protesters' demand for dialogue: "We have already held dialogue and consultations between us several times now. It seems that the wishes of our fellow students [sic] can no longer be satisfied merely by holding dialogue."[44] As early as the afternoon of April 27, State

---

22, 1989, 5; "Various Provinces Urged to Express Support for Li Peng's Speech, Hu Qili Changes His Attitude and Supports Zhao Ziyang," Hong Kong *Ming pao*, May 22, 1989, in FBIS, May 22, 1989, 15–16. Copies of the letter by the seven generals were dropped on the square by helicopters.

[43]The incident was confusing because although the soldiers were unarmed, students later discovered trucks and buses with weapons, and a large number of plainclothes police also entered the city center. Many people (myself included) thought the incident was a provocation, to incite the crowds to use violence.

[44]"Li Peng Holds Dialogue with Students," Beijing Television Service, in FBIS, May 19, 1989, 18. Document 36.

Council spokesman Yuan Mu had announced that the government welcomed dialogue with the students: "We are ready for conducting dialogue with the students at any time. At the same time we urge them to return to school immediately and assume a rational and sober attitude in demanding dialogue through normal channels instead of resorting to extremist actions."[45] The All-China Student Federation and the Beijing Student Federation were commissioned to make arrangements for dialogue. On that day the federations set up a reception office and telephone hot line to listen to student views. They began to send representatives to the various universities to solicit opinions and work out conditions for dialogue that would be acceptable to both sides.

On April 28 the state-controlled newspapers and television broadcasts carried fairly detailed coverage of the previous day's demonstration. Accurate and comprehensive reports of the protests were also given in the third week of May.

On April 29 and 30 the All-China Student Federation and Beijing Student Federation organized a "candid dialogue" with Li Ximing (Politburo member and Beijing party leader), Chen Xitong (State councillor and Beijing mayor), Yuan Mu, and other officials and students from sixteen universities. The authorities attempted to respond to a number of student concerns, and the talks were shown on national television. Yuan Mu affirmed the patriotism and good intentions of most of the protesters and identified their objectives as no different from regime objectives: "The broad masses of students, filled with patriotic enthusiasm, hope to promote democracy, strengthen the reform, punish those guilty of embezzlement, and overcome corruption. All those wishes are in complete accord with the wishes of the party and the government."[46] He also assured students that the editorial of April 26 was not directed at the vast majority of student protesters. On the issue of corruption, Yuan Mu enumerated cases of corruption already handled by the courts and welcomed students to provide information on suspected official corruption to centers set up by the Ministry of Supervision. On the issue of press legislation, he reported that State Council departments were currently in the process of drafting a publication law and a law on journalism, which would probably be ready for consideration that year.[47]

In the first week of May leaders in the State Council, the Beijing government, and various government ministries engaged in a number of smaller dialogues with students. These were also arranged by the All-China Student Federation. From May 11 to 13, Hu Qili (Politburo Standing Committee member in charge of propaganda work) and Wang Renzhi (Central Propaganda Department head) went to a number of press offices to hear the views of journalists and editors.

---

[45]See "Deng Xiaoping Talks about Student Unrest and Hu Yaobang," Hong Kong *Ching pao*, May 10, 1989, in FBIS, May 15, 1989, 34.

[46]"Beijing TV Carries Dialogue," 25.

[47]See ibid., 25–49.

On May 13 the government responded to a petition submitted by student protesters by announcing it would hold another dialogue with students on May 15. On May 13 and 14, to counter allegations of insincerity in the offer, Yan Mingfu (Central Committee Secretariat member and Central United Front Department head) and Li Tieying (Minister of the State Education Commission) held informal talks with over forty students, including student protest leaders Wu'er Kaixi and Wang Dan. On May 15 Yan and Li held the formal dialogue with over fifty students from twenty-two universities.

On the morning of May 18, four of the five members of the Politburo Standing Committee (Zhao Ziyang, Li Peng, Qiao Shi, and Hu Qili) paid a nationally televised visit to students who had collapsed during a hunger strike and were being treated in Beijing hospitals. Later in the day, hardliners made another concession: Li Peng invited representatives of the hunger strikers, including Wu'er Kaixi and Wang Dan, to the Great Hall of the People for a dialogue on how to end the strike.[48] The hour-long encounter, shown on national television the same day, was remarkable. Wu'er Kaixi rejected the premier's welcome, asserting that the meeting was "not only a little late, but too late." He went on to put Li in the position of guest rather than host: "In fact, it is not that you asked us to come for discussion, but that the great number of people at the square asked you to come out for a talk. The topics of discussion should be decided by us."[49] Li found himself interrupted by students a couple of times, as they assertively lectured him about the situation and their movement. Obviously angry, Li nonetheless affirmed again the patriotism of the broad masses of students and that they and the government shared many of the same goals. He tried to finesse the demand for a retraction of the editorial of April 26: "Neither the government nor the party Central Committee has ever said that the broad masses of students are creating disorder. We have never said such a thing. We have unanimously affirmed the patriotic fervor of the students."[50] In the same meeting, other officials avoided labeling the student movement per se as a disturbance or turmoil. Instead, they argued that regardless of subjective intentions, the movement had developed to a point beyond student control. Thus, objectively, the protesters were responsible for creating a disturbance.[51]

On May 19 Li Peng and Zhao Ziyang visited hunger strikers who were occupying the square. Again, the event was televised nationally. Later that evening Li and President Yang Shangkun announced that the army had been called on to enter Beijing and restore order. On the following day Li signed the declaration of martial law.

---

[48]Perhaps as an even more subtle sign of concession, the meeting was held in the Xinjiang Hall. Xinjiang is the home of Wu'er Kaixi.

[49]"Li Peng Holds Dialogue with Students," 15.

[50]Ibid., 20.

[51]See especially Li Tieying's comments in ibid., 18.

Perspective of Protesters: No Concessions

From the perspective of student protesters, hardliners had made virtually no meaningful concessions. By contrast, they considered that they themselves had made several concessions, and they grew frustrated by the apparent lack of response.

The visits with hunger strikers in the hospitals and on the square were short encounters, in which the authorities did practically all of the talking. The extraordinary May 18 session between hunger striker representatives and Li Peng was longer and much more of an exchange. It was not, however, the broad dialogue on issues that the protesters had demanded, but rather a crisis session about the hunger strike.[52] At the end of the session a student representative concluded: "This is not a dialogue. This is a meeting."[53] All the other exchanges organized by the authorities were arranged by the All-China Student Federation and the Beijing Student Federation. Most of the student participants in those dialogues were affiliated with those official organizations rather than the newly created autonomous student unions. Many student protesters viewed the federations as puppet unions, because of their organizational affiliation with the Communist Youth League.

By contrast, protest leaders could point to their own important concessions. On May 2 they had petitioned the government with new preconditions for holding a dialogue, dropping the very sensitive demand for a reassessment of the 1986 student movement and 1987 campaign against bourgeois liberalization. On May 5 protesters had ended the boycott of classes in most universities. Only Beijing University students had voted not to resume classes. On May 6 they had presented a new petition with further concessions: they no longer listed specific demands as preconditions for a dialogue, but only discussion topics for the dialogue. They also no longer insisted that the very highest political decision makers participate in the dialogue. Further, they had attempted to take into account the regime's principled objection to holding talks with an "illegal organization." They had formed the University Student Group for Dialogue, an ad hoc group with much overlapping membership but no formal organizational link to the autonomous student union.

Many protesters did not consider the official affirmation of their patriotic intentions as a concession, although they certainly welcomed it. A student representative presented the following argument on the issue to Li Peng on May 18: "The vast majority of students are indeed launching a movement. They indeed are fairly consciously launching a democratic movement, trying to fight for the rights given to

---

[52]Indeed, it was defined as such by both Li Peng and the student representatives.
[53]"Li Peng and Other Comrades Meet Representatives of the Students Who Have Been Fasting To Support Their Petition," *Renmin ribao*, May 19, 1989, in FBIS, May 24, 1989, 23.

them by the Constitution. I would like to have this point clarified. If we today call our action simply an act of ardent patriotism, then there is no way to explain the reason, coolness, orderliness, and observation of law characteristic of the movement. Many things can be done in the name of ardent patriotism.''[54]

Many also rejected the claim that objectively their movement had produced a disturbance. Indeed, students reacted strongly to that label because they had gone to great lengths to be peaceful and orderly in their demonstrations and because the term recalled the official verdict on the Cultural Revolution. One lectured Li Peng: ''A disturbance in a country or society is not caused by student demonstrations, but by the social system in existence, the ills of society. . . . The very purpose of student demonstrations is to expose the ills of society at an early date so that the government can deal with them and overcome the ills without delay. Thus the student movement or the movement to promote democracy will indeed serve to prevent society from falling apart and avoid a real disturbance. The argument is quite simple.''[55]

By May 13 the demands of student protesters were only two. These remained the demands of the movement until the end: dialogue with the authorities and an official affirmation of the protests.[56] On May 18 Wu'er Kaixi explained to Li Peng what these demands specifically implied. Dialogue was to be between regime leaders with major decision-making powers and the unofficially elected student representatives; Chinese and foreign reporters were to be present; and it was to be televised live.[57] Official affirmation of the protests was to consist of a retraction of the editorial of April 26, a statement that the protests were not a disturbance, and a positive evaluation of the movement's place in history.[58]

The stipulated conditions for dialogue provided an opportunity for the students to embarrass the regime while the nation watched and the world listened. To affirm the protests would require Deng Xiaoping personally to concede a serious error and grant the students legitimacy: in Communist systems, those with history on their side are the progressive forces, a major qualification for leadership. But most important, both demands required the authorities to accept a compromise on the basic issues of party monopoly and social stability.

Escalation of Protests

From the perspective of protesters, the response of hardliners from April 27 to June 3 can be summed up as no suppression, no concessions. More confident but

---

[54]"Li Peng Holds Dialogue with Students," 17.

[55]Ibid., 21.

[56]There were, however, preconditions for dialogue. See note 6 above.

[57]While many of the encounters between the authorities and students had been televised, none had been televised live.

[58]"Li Peng Holds Dialogue with Students," 15–16.

frustrated, protest leaders continued to organize demonstrations and adopted more extreme forms of protest, both to promote their demands and to restore momentum to the movement when enthusiasm flagged.[59] Further, after the declaration of martial law, they adopted a more extreme protest agenda—the downfall of Li Peng. Student protesters were also joined by other intellectuals, ordinary citizens, and workers, who formed their own autonomous organizations. The protest movement escalated to a level and kind of mass political participation unprecedented in the history of the PRC.

The most ingenious and successful of the protest tactics was the hunger strike. On May 13 about one thousand students began the strike at Tiananmen to support their demands. By May 16 the number of hunger strikers occupying the square had grown to over three thousand. Tiananmen, normally a rather sterile backdrop for tourist photographs and the stage for rigidly rehearsed celebrations of important events in Chinese Communist history, became the setting for a real drama, featuring students (young enough to be considered by the Chinese as mere children) prepared to die for what seemed to many to be trivial demands.[60] The hunger strike radicalized Beijing society by transforming the protesters into victims. It provided a compelling reason (or pretext) for practically everyone to participate in the exchange between authorities and protesters. Without explicitly opposing the regime by expressing support for the demands of the protesters, people in nearly every social group urged the authorities to engage in dialogue with the students, for humanitarian purposes if nothing else. On both May 17 and 18, over a million people demonstrated with the hunger strikers in the square. Many student protesters wore headbands identifying them by university, department, class, and name. Their boldness seemed justified: how could the hardliners suppress a million people?

During the May demonstrations student protesters were joined on the square by normally submissive journalists from the state-controlled media, secondary school students, cadres from party and government departments, and the Beijing police—as well as other intellectuals, ordinary citizens, and workers. Students from the provinces, about 172,000 from May 16 to 26 alone, traveled to Beijing to show their solidarity and participate in the occupation of the square.[61] Supportive hunger strikes were staged in Shanghai, Xi'an, Chengdu, Shenyang, and Harbin. Demonstrations were held in major cities in every province except Tibet. Li Peng described the situation as one of "complete chaos," in Beijing and throughout the country.[62]

---

[59]The number of demonstrators was relatively low in the second and fourth weeks of May. By the end of May many of the students on the square were from outside Beijing.

[60]Many Chinese expressed to me their dismay at the imbalance between the protesters' objectives and the sacrifices being made to obtain them.

[61]"Xinhua on Railway Travel Difficulties," Beijing Xinhua Domestic Service, in FBIS, May 31, 1989, 62.

[62]"Li Peng Holds Dialogue with Students," 20.

For hardliners, the size and scope of the protests were already a great embarrassment and a grave threat. The timing made them particularly embarrassing for the regime: Soviet leader Mikhail Gorbachev arrived in Beijing on May 15 for the first meeting between top Chinese and Soviet leaders in thirty years. For the event the Chinese had welcomed the largest Western media contingent ever to assemble in Beijing. The hunger strike and massive demonstrations were transmitted by satellite to viewers all over the world, and the protests shunted the summit meeting to second place. But most threatening to the hardliners was the institutionalization of the movement in autonomous organizations—the Beijing Autonomous Union of Students, Local Autonomous Union of Visiting Students, Beijing Autonomous Union of Residents, Beijing Autonomous Union of Intellectuals, Beijing Autonomous Union of Workers, and Headquarters to Defend Tiananmen Square (whose members pledged to defend the square with their lives). In establishing independent mass organizations the protesters upset the party political monopoly. Understandably, hardliners labeled the "illegal organizations" an attempt "to lay a foundation for opposition factions and opposition parties in China."[63]

The earliest of the organizations—the Beijing Autonomous Union of Students—already had a corps of student leaders, functionally specialized departments, elected representatives from more than twenty universities, domestic and foreign financial support, its own flag, an independent broadcasting station at Tiananmen, and a primitive press.

In his talk on April 25 Deng Xiaoping had characterized the Chinese protests as potentially less threatening than those encountered by the Polish Communists, because "China only has [to worry about] students."[64] But on May 19 the newly established Beijing Autonomous Union of Workers issued a declaration supporting student demands and announcing a general strike on May 20 if the authorities did not unconditionally accept those demands. The temporary halt of public transportation (on which many workers depend) in the first few days of martial law makes it difficult to assess support for the autonomous union. Nonetheless, the Polish experience had demonstrated to everyone that independently organized workers presented a serious challenge to the party monopoly.

A final irritant to the authorities was the erection on May 30 of a large plaster "goddess of democracy," obviously resembling the American Statue of Liberty.[65] Students positioned the statue in the place on the square reserved for a

---

[63]"Comrade Li Peng's Speech at the May 19 Meeting of Party, Government, and Military Cadres," *Renmin ribao*, May 20, 1989, in FBIS, May 22, 1989, 8. Document 46.

[64]"Text of a Document Circulated Among Senior Party and Government Officials Earlier This Month," 36.

[65]While a large crowd greeted the unveiling of the statue, many people expressed to me their disapproval of it, for esthetic reasons and because it recalled an American rather than Chinese symbol.

portrait of Sun Yat-sen, father of the republic, and facing the national flag and portrait of Mao Zedong.

When Li Peng declared martial law on May 20, protest organizers made him a public target of the movement. Some protesters also called for the resignation of Deng Xiaoping, but that was never openly part of the organized protest program, and anti-Deng slogans were by far overwhelmed by anti-Li slogans. By conventions established in the Cultural Revolution, naming names amounted to a significantly more extreme protest agenda, and hardliners saw in it indisputable evidence that protest activists were out to topple the regime.[66] Protesters regularly gathered in front of the Great Hall of the People and Zhongnanhai and shouted clever rhyming slogans calling on Li to resign, hang himself, or commit suicide.

Even with the attack on Li Peng, from the perspective of hardliners content was essentially less threatening than the public support for the protesters and the unprecedented forms of protest: for two years the authorities had allowed Fang Lizhi to express to Chinese and foreigners views far more critical and radical than anything promoted by protest organizers.[67] For hardliners, Fang was a serious annoyance. The protests, however, were a pressing crisis.

Zhao's Soft Line

On May 24 President Yang Shangkun delivered the hard-line verdict on Zhao Ziyang, holding him responsible for the continuing protests: "The present problem is that two different voices in the party have been completely exposed in society. The students feel that there is a person in the party Central Committee who supports them and, therefore, they stir up greater trouble."[68]

That accusation to the contrary, Zhao cannot be blamed for the adoption of more extreme protest positions and tactics. Indeed, on at least two occasions his soft line led to immediate concessions from protesters and a brief de-escalation of the movement. After a conciliatory May 4 speech to the Asian Development Bank meeting in Beijing, all schools except Beijing University called off their boycott of classes and formed the ad hoc group for dialogue with the authorities. After Zhao's May 19 visit to hunger strikers on the square, students called off the hunger strike and substituted an ordinary sit-in to continue their protest.

---

[66]In his speech of May 19, Li Peng noted that the spearhead of the protest movement had been directed at Deng Xiaoping. In fact, Deng was far less the target of attack than Li Peng himself. See "Comrade Li Peng's Speech at the May 19 Meeting of Party, Government, and Military Cadres," 8.

[67]See note 22 above.

[68]"Yang Criticizes Zhao," Hong Kong *Ming pao*, May 29, 1989, in FBIS, May 30, 1989, 18.

Nonetheless, during the protests Zhao clearly broke with party discipline to reveal conflict in the top elite. On May 16 he publicly distanced himself from the unpopular inflationary policies of the previous year and from Deng Xiaoping. In a televised discussion with Mikhail Gorbachev, Zhao revealed a secret 1987 party agreement by which leaders had agreed to consult Deng on all major policy decisions.[69] The disclosure caused a sensation among the politically savvy Chinese, because Deng had formally retired from all positions except Chairman of the Military Affairs Commission. While no one had doubted Deng's influence in policy making, the institutionalization of that influence in a secret agreement seemed a cynical act, treating ordinary Chinese as dupes, and another example of the hypocrisy of their leaders.[70]

Clearly, before the declaration of martial law, Zhao's conciliatory stance encouraged protesters to hope for a more positive response to their demands. For example, Zhao's May 4 speech at the Asian Development Bank meeting offered the most conciliatory view of the movement presented publicly by a top leader since the protests had begun. Zhao spoke optimistically of the prospects for accommodating some "reasonable demands."[71] Students who heard the speech broadcast that evening noted the difference in nuance between it and the editorial of April 26, and the favorable student reaction was recorded in the Chinese press the next day. An official news agency quoted a Qinghua University student: "If the government had taken such an attitude right from the very beginning, the mess could possibly have been avoided."[72]

In his May 19 visit to hunger strikers on the square, Zhao was visibly emotional, weeping as he admitted that the visit had come "too late." Again he suggested that the movement's demands would or should be met: "I know your fasting is aimed at obtaining a very satisfactory answer to the issues you put forward to the government and the party. . . . Some issues can be solved only through a process. Some issues—for example, the nature of your action—I feel can be eventually solved. We can reach a consensus."[73]

In short, Zhao did indeed reveal to the general public "two different voices in the party," of which his own appeared to be truly receptive to the demands of protesters. Zhao's views and the negative reception of them among most of the

---

[69]See the account in "Deng Purges Zhao Supporters," Hong Kong *South China Morning Post*, May 22, 1989, in FBIS, May 22, 1989, 6.

[70]The impact of the revelation should not be underestimated. Some people thought at first that Zhao was trying to curry favor with Deng with his references to Deng as the great leader. Only when Zhao revealed the agreement did people begin to understand that Zhao was distancing himself from Deng.

[71]"Students' Reasonable Demands to Be Met through Democratic, Legal Channels," Beijing Xinhua, in FBIS, May 4, 1989, 1. Document 31.

[72]"Zhao Ziyang's Speech Welcomed by Students," 3.

[73]"More on Visits," Beijing Television Service, in FBIS, May 19, 1989, 13.

top political elite were also revealed to student protesters by Bao Tong, Zhao's aide, who kept in touch with protest activists on the square. Obviously, the victory of Zhao's soft line was tied to resolving the elite conflict in his favor. For whatever reasons, Zhao chose to seek his constituency among the people in the streets.[74] In that sense, he made the protest movement even more threatening to hardliners: at the top was a leader who had formed a tacit coalition with the protesters. It was a bold and probably foolish gamble, but a victorious Zhao might have become the Gorbachev of Chinese politics. The potential danger of the situation must surely have been appreciated by Deng Xiaoping, the leader who, more than ten years earlier, had manipulated the 1978 prodemocracy movement to put himself in a position of greater strength to promote reformist policies.

But without underestimating Zhao's role, it is important to point out that the protests were by no means initiated because of Zhao: indeed, Zhao was a target of the movement at the beginning and only gained favor among protesters as he distanced himself from hardliners.[75] Zhao contributed to the escalation of the movement only indirectly, because he presented an alternative to the hard line. Zhao's soft line offered hope to protesters before martial law was declared, and after May 20 hardliners seemed all the more objectionable by contrast. Finally, although the current official interpretation of the protest movement assigns considerable blame to Zhao, it is clear that the regime needs a scapegoat. To overestimate Zhao's importance in the calculus of hardliners is to treat the protests as a mere backdrop for yet another instance of top-level elite struggle and to ignore the obvious: the people on the square and in the streets presented the regime with one of the greatest threats to its power and policies encountered in the forty years since the Communists came to power.

No Retreat

The process of exchange and escalation pushed protesters and hardliners to a point of no retreat. For the protesters, that point probably came soon after the evening of May 19, when Li Peng and Yang Shangkun announced that martial law would be imposed.[76] Martial law signaled the defeat of Zhao Ziyang's soft line, and Zhao was conspicuously absent from that meeting. Protesters expected

---

[74]It seems that Zhao was in disfavor among hardliners even before the protests began. Thus his actions may have been an effort to save his position by appealing to another constituency.

[75]For example, students held up a photograph of Zhao playing golf (as an example of the decadence of top officials) during the April 29 dialogue with authorities. Many people were also critical of the business activities of Zhao's sons.

[76]Two days earlier, following a demonstration by over one million people on May 17, protesters and their supporters were far more optimistic about possible outcomes. For example, among 423 people polled on the square late that night, responses to the question

no concessions from hardliners alone, and consequently they openly took a position to work for the downfall of the Li Peng regime. On May 24 Wang Dan and Chai Ling, leaders of the newly established Headquarters to Defend Tiananmen Square, described the situation as "a decisive battle between light and darkness." They concluded somewhat pessimistically: "We do not want to say that we will never fail but we have no way of retreat."[77]

For a few days it seemed that violent confrontation could be postponed, that a withdrawal from Tiananmen was possible. Six weeks after occupation of the square had begun, enthusiasm for continued occupation was decreasing and the movement was in financial trouble.[78] Protest organizers announced a plan to abandon the square and continue the "battle" through other means. Withdrawal would not mean the end of the protest movement: "This is a long-term movement."[79] But student representatives voted on May 26 to remain at Tiananmen.[80] One explained her rationale as follows: "Some of us wonder if our presence here is very important any more. But I don't want to leave; the wasted effort would be too great."[81]

For hardliners, too, the point of no retreat probably came in the days immediately after the declaration of martial law. For the first time, the protest movement had publicly declared the regime its enemy. A large proportion of Beijing's population had flaunted martial law and openly sided with the protesters. Three days into martial law, over a million people were demonstrating at Tiananmen once again.

On May 22 Li Peng expressed the view that the protests were no longer a matter of one or two months, that the students had made long-term plans. He also observed: "We have come to the stage where there is no retreat. If we retreat still further, we shall have to give China away to them."[82] Two days later Yang Shangkun confirmed Li's view of the situation and drew the logical conclusion

---

"What do you think the outcome of the marches and hunger strike will be?" were as follows: 66 percent chose "the government will agree to the student demands"; 11 percent chose "both sides will compromise"; 2 percent chose "the government will suppress it"; and 11 percent chose "I can't tell clearly." See *Zhongguo qingnian bao*, May 19, 1989. My thanks to Stanley Rosen for sending me this information.

[77]"Beijing Students Set Up Headquarters to Defend Tiananmen," Hong Kong *Ta Kung Pao*, May 25, 1989, in FBIS, May 25, 1989, 26.

[78]At a press conference on May 27, students revealed they were in debt. By their calculations, the movement required fifty thousand yuan daily to maintain itself. See "Beijing Students Urge End to Protest," Hong Kong AFP, in FBIS, May 30, 1989, 66.

[79]"Beijing Students Set Up Headquarters to Defend Tiananmen," 26.

[80]Apparently, students from Beijing were willing to withdraw from the square, but students from the provinces wished to stay.

[81]"Numbers Dip to 'Lowest Level,' " Hong Kong *South China Morning Post*, May 27, 1989, in FBIS, May 30, 1989, 55.

[82]"On 22 May Li Peng Again Stressed that the Student Movement Was a Disturbance," 3. *Ming pao*, May 30, 1989: 1; FBIS, May 30, 1989, 3. Document 49.

for hardliners: "A retreat would indicate our collapse and the collapse of the PRC. . . . We can no longer retreat and must launch an offensive."[83]

Massacre

The official Chinese version of events alleges that no one died at Tiananmen on 4 June, that student protesters marched off the square unharmed.[84] The latter assertion accords with several reports of Chinese and foreign observers, although many facts remain to be clarified and conflicting versions have also been presented. But in the actions of protesters and soldiers on the edges of the square and farther to the east and west, along the broad boulevard leading to the square, there is evidence enough to counter the regime's claim that the massacre is a myth. The army used excessive and indiscriminate violence as it eliminated obstacles preventing it from reaching Tiananmen.

Earlier in the evening, the authorities had broadcast repeated warnings to the public to stay indoors. They had warned that personal safety could not otherwise be guaranteed. Large numbers of people had responded to those warnings by hurrying into the streets, gathering at bridges and intersections, setting up barricades, waiting for the army—as had been done several times in recent weeks in response to similar warnings, one as recently as the previous day.[85]

For the hardliners and the army, the strategically placed buses and concrete and metal barriers were an inconvenience. The crowds, standing between the army and the square, were a major dilemma. For many, presumably, it was a conscious stand in defense of the student protesters. To that end, some had armed themselves with primitive weapons—bricks, rocks, homemade gasoline grenades. But armed or unarmed, militant or simply curious, all were obstacles to an army determined to clear the square. Despite warnings, they had chosen to be in the streets, in front of the army. In that sense, they were indeed forces hostile to the army, preventing it from reaching the square, some prepared to use weapons against the army.

The crowds were hostile, but their hostility was directed at the regime's hardliners and their supporters. On the night of the massacre the crowds waited for the army but for the most part did not prejudge it. As before, they were prepared to lecture, harass, and turn back the soldiers. Certainly, some in the crowd were armed against the army. Undoubtedly, the events of June 3 and

---

[83]"Yang Criticizes Zhao," 17.

[84]See "Yuan Mu Says PRC Not Afraid of World Opinion," Beijing Xinhua, in FBIS, June 8, 1989, 4.

[85]Perhaps because troops had fled from the crowds during the abortive attempt to reach the square on June 3, the atmosphere that night did not initially seem as tense as it had immediately after the declaration of martial law, for example.

previous weeks had left many of the young peasant soldiers feeling humiliated, frightened, and angry. But the ultimate weapon of the crowds was simply their choice to be in the streets—indisputable evidence of the extent of social support for the students. The crowds could stop the army only if the army treated them as inviolable. If the hardliners chose to suppress the movement and if the army cooperated, the streets of Beijing could be cleared.[86]

In what sense can army actions be characterized as a massacre? The regime has retrospectively described the situation as a riot. The failed attempts to end the protest movement since mid-April indicated that the army could not reach the square without using force against the crowds. Clearly, riot control instruments and techniques were required to eliminate the crowds. Yet the army eliminated obstacles in their path with tanks, machine guns, assault rifles, and real bullets. The violence inflicted was excessive, in the sense that more force was used than was reasonably required to execute the order to clear the square that night. Moreover, the violence was indiscriminate. Soldiers shot into the crowds, at chest level, and continued shooting from their vehicles as they moved toward the square. Bystanders were shot and killed.

We know practically nothing about the actual decision making that preceded the massacre. It is almost certainly wrongheaded, however, to consider it as anything but a conscious choice by those who ordered the army to clear the square. Presumably, this includes at least Deng Xiaoping and Yang Shangkun (who were in charge of the Military Affairs Commission), Li Peng, and the other two members of the Politburo Standing Committee who emerged politically unscathed—Qiao Shi and Yao Yilin.[87] Whoever they are, those who ordered the army to clear the square that night, and those who acquiesced in that decision, must have known that force would be required to disperse the crowds. The exercise of June 3, which pitted an unarmed army against the crowds, was only the most recent demonstration of that. Knowing that force would be required to execute the order, they sent in an army armed with weapons of lethal destruction. The outcome was predictable.

It is easy enough to understand why the regime's hardliners ultimately chose to suppress the protest movement with force. But what explains the use of weapons of war rather than simply instruments of riot control? It is not completely inconceivable that the Chinese do not have sufficient riot control forces to deal with a movement of the unprecedented size of the Beijing

---

[86]This is obvious in retrospect but was not obvious at the time. Most people felt safety in numbers.

[87]Deng has also acknowledged the influence of "veteran party cadres," a reference to the very senior veteran revolutionaries who emerged from retirement in the course of the movement. See " 'Text' of Deng Xiaoping Speech Delivered on June 9," 8. See also "Yang Criticizes Zhao," 18.

protests.[88] It is also possible that the Chinese do not have sufficient riot control equipment to put down such a movement.[89] Soldiers trained and equipped to fight a war might have seemed to the hardliners as the only available means to achieve their end.

From another angle, consider the mass response each time the hardliners threatened to suppress the movement: visible support for the protesters grew almost immediately. Judging from this response, I find it highly probable that even had riot control measures cleared the streets on the night of June 3, they would not have ended the protest movement. Large crowds would probably have appeared on the following day.[90] The protests were not a mere riot, they were a mass movement. At a minimum, protesters would have retreated only temporarily, to rally in even greater force at a later date.

This last point is suggestive of the rationale for the massacre: unlike the medium-level suppression of riot control, the force used on June 4 promised to end the movement immediately, certainly, and once and for all. As that was both the point of the effort and its actual outcome, the massacre is in retrospect a logical choice for hardliners—given their assumptions, estimates, and the circumstances they faced. From their perspective, the probable loss of international prestige and foreign investment could conceivably be recouped, but the collapse of their rule would mean irreparable damage. Deng Xiaoping had said as much on April 25: "We must not be afraid of people cursing us, of a bad reputation, or of international reaction. Only if China truly develops, and implements the four modernizations [of agriculture, industry, science and technology, and national defense], can we have a real reputation."[91]

The massacre was effective precisely because the violence was excessive and indiscriminate. The excessive use of force demonstrated that the potential costs of protest were prohibitive: the regime was willing to sanction the killing of protesters in the streets. The indiscriminate use of force demonstrated that those

---

[88]The total numbers in the riot control forces (the People's Armed Police) are much smaller than the army, and they are under the separate operational commands of the provincial governments. Forces as large as the separate armies actually deployed on June 4 could perhaps have been put together from several provinces. But these would not have had experience under a unified command and would have left the provinces without the appropriate forces to handle protests in the localities.

[89]Li Peng has mentioned the shortage of tear gas as one reason for its limited use against the protesters, but that is obviously not sufficient evidence for the hypothesis. See "Why Beijing Used Bullets," *New York Times*, July 3, 1989. Tear gas was used prior to June 4 to disperse smaller crowds and thus was part of the repertoire of the People's Armed Police.

[90]In fact, crowds returned to Tiananmen to do battle with the army on the morning of June 4, many hours after the tanks and troops had installed themselves on the square.

[91]"Text of a Document Circulated Among Senior Party and Government Officials Earlier This Month," 35.

costs would not necessarily be keyed to levels of participation: they could be imposed on mere bystanders. The most prominent and radical of protesters feared for their lives on June 4. But when the army opened fire, any person in the streets had good reason to fear no less. Prior to June 4, people could assume that the potential costs of protest were roughly predictable and that they would vary by degrees of involvement. The massacre invalidated those assumptions. It introduced unprecedentedly high costs and left virtually to chance the question of who would bear them. This combination of severity and near randomness is the essence of political terror.[92]

Conclusion

The logic of the 1989 protests and massacre is one of players pressed into a duel. Protesters and hardliners began with mutually contradictory assumptions and estimates about the implications of mass political participation. Responses from hardliners and the existence of an alternative soft line drove protesters into more extreme positions and tactics; these in turn confirmed the hardliners' view that the protests were deliberately malevolent. With better information about the actual norms and costs of protest, it is almost certain that students would not have chosen to escalate the protests. Although massacre ultimately dominated other choices for hardliners, it is clear that they too were "reluctant duelists."[93]

The protests are often described as a prodemocracy movement, although democracy was only one of many issues aired. Yet it is not an inaccurate characterization of the movement, as it sums up the real point of contention: how do the people rule? The protests assumed the existence of a new and thoroughly unorthodox kind of politics at the same time as protesters borrowed from orthodox notions and rhetoric to voice their demands. Their forms of protest assumed the legitimacy of bottom-up mass politics, institutionalized in real mass organizations, rather than the elite-dominated mass mobilization of the past, the mass consultation of post-Mao reform policy, and the "mass organizations" of the Communist Party.

Could Chinese leaders have offered more significant concessions to the protesters? Obviously, yes—if they had been prepared to abandon basic assumptions and the old politics of elite monopoly for a new kind of leadership. The protesters might be appeased for a time, but the new mass politics would be strengthened. Concessions to end the protests would probably have signaled nothing less

---

[92]Dallin and Breslauer define political terror as "severe and arbitrary coercion or its credible threat." See Alexander Dallin and George W. Breslauer, *Political Terror in Communist Systems* (Stanford: Stanford University Press, 1970).

[93]My apologies to Daniel Ellsberg for using his term for a game rather different than the one he described. See his "Theory of the Reluctant Duelist," *American Economic Review* 46, 5 (1956): 909–23.

than a fundamental change in the nature of Chinese politics—an acceptance of mass initiatives, accountability to the masses, a mass market for solutions to political problems.

In the recent political reforms in Poland and the Soviet Union, we can see examples of what the new mass politics might eventually have become. That Chinese hardliners rejected these models is unsurprising: the Communist leader prepared to legitimate and promote this kind of politics must himself become a new kind of politician. The skill, creativity, and courage that this challenge requires and the crisis of authority needed to force this option onto the agenda should not be underestimated. From the perspective of Deng Xiaoping and other elders who had made revolution and gained power in China, bottom-up politics must have looked far less appealing than it had half a century ago. What we saw in the 1989 protests was the necessarily short-lived practice of new mass politics without a successful elite sponsor.

Beijing Spring,1989

CONFRONTATION AND CONFLICT

Sketch Map of Beijing City Centre

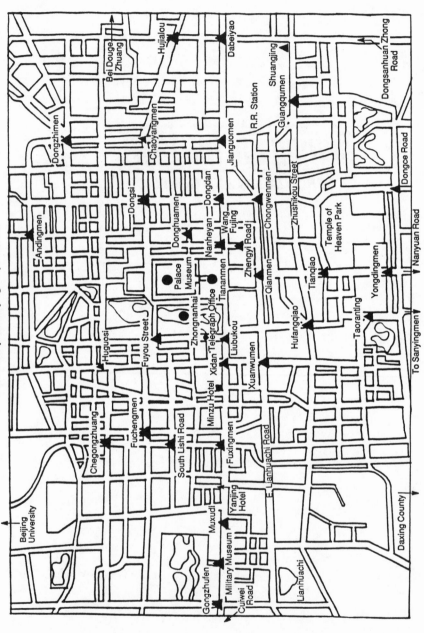

This map shows sites of "disturbances" and confrontation between the public and the PLA as mentioned in a variety of official and non-official descriptions of June 3–4. Clearly, conflict and confrontation was more widespread than initially understood.

Source: Beijing Review, June 26–July 2, 1989, p. 17 (with additions by Marc Lambert).

I
Polarized China
Two ConflictingViews
of Beijing Spring

The two documents in this section provide sharply contrasting perspectives on the events of April and May. Document 1 was written by Li Qiao and several participants in the demonstrations, who took their title, "The Soul of China" (*Zhongguo zhi hun*), from the elegy on Hu Yaobang's Tiananmen funerary wreath. This document presents the student view of developments from the April 15 death of Hu Yaobang until May 16, the third day of the hunger strike. Emphasizing the enormous impact on China of the revolution in international communications, the authors express tributes to Hu Yaobang that contributed to the dismissal of Qin Benli as editor of the liberal Shanghai newspaper *World Economic Herald* after they were published there. In addition, there are vivid descriptions of the public mourning for Hu Yaobang; the galvanizing effects of the provocative April 26 *People's Daily* editorial; the exuberance among participants in the April 27 parade that openly defied CPC and even Deng Xiaoping's authority; and, of course, the dramatic impact of the hunger strike. Also included are texts of the May 2 twelve-point petition from the Beijing Autonomous Union of Students setting forth student terms for a dialogue with the government; the May 16 declaration signed by thirty leading intellectuals who favored student demands for freedom of the press; and a letter to the nation and declaration of purpose by the hunger strikers.

"The Soul of China" clearly portrays the spontaneity, courage, and sense of adventure and optimism that characterized the demonstrators before the May 19 proclamation of martial law. The authors of the document do not, as Communist Party leaders claimed, convey any sense of conspiracy or a plan to bring chaos to China. Their patriotism is palpable. Written before martial law and the massacre on June 4, the documents lack the rage toward the regime that followed the crackdown. For this reason, part IX of this book includes postcrackdown reports from the Hong Kong press that are filled with harsh sentiments and denunciations of the victorious hard-line leaders.

Document 2 stands in sharp contrast to the first. It is the official version of events provided by Beijing Mayor Chen Xitong in his long report to the National People's Congress, twenty-four days after the massacre. Although Chen had engaged in his own dialogue with students, he also played a major role in bringing the leadership to its fateful decision to employ force. He, along with Beijing First Party Secretary Li Ximing and others, had briefed the Politburo Standing Committee on April 24 and Deng Xiaoping on April 25. His descriptions of the demonstrations of the previous week led Deng to issue strident guidelines for the April 26 *People's Daily* editorial, which portrayed an evolving conspiracy against the regime. Chen's report clearly reveals that Beijing security forces—particularly the city party committee's "security bureau" (*anquan ju*)—had monitored the activities of intellectuals and students for some time. Chen pictures these groups as engaged in a conspiracy to stimulate disorder in the capital.[1]

Chen describes the same events covered in Document 1 but attributes them to an organized effort by Zhao Ziyang, his associates, and nefarious internal and external forces, including, by implication, the United States.[2] The victorious hardliners are, in contrast, seen as heroic defenders of national order and integrity, whereas Li Qiao et al. had portrayed the same leadership as corrupt, repressive, and without popular support. To Li Qiao et al., the Communist Party probably merits saving, but not without massive reform; to Chen, the CPC still embodies the future of the nation and guarantees China's national unification. Whereas Li Qiao et al. emphasize the students' patriotism, discipline, and even naïveté, Chen Xitong portrays the same people as treasonous, anarchic, and manipulative. For Li Qiao et al., the students were the harbingers of a new democratic era, but for Chen, they wanted to return China to the Cultural Revolution at the behest of malevolent outside forces seeking to destroy Chinese socialism.

---

[1]Since the mid-1980s, government leaders had become increasingly concerned with possible outbreaks of violence in Chinese cities, especially in reaction to dramatic increases in inflation and the enormous floating population of unemployed workers who have entered the cities in search of jobs. This led to the formation of new security organs, such as the "antiriot squad" (*fanbao dui*), which was especially brutal in its suppression of protesters in the Beijing suburb of Fengtai. Thanks to Robin Munro of Asia Watch, New York, for this information.

[2]For a most revealing condemnation of the purported "involvement" of the United States in the spring movement as part of the West's overall "conspiracy" to bring China to democracy and capitalism, see Beijing First Party Secretary Li Ximing's speech reproduced in this volume (Doc. 45) and *Jiaoxue yu yanjiu (Teaching and Study Monthly)* (September 1989): 46–48, excerpted in *Inside China Mainland* 12, 2, issue no. 134: 1–3.

In sum, these two documents provide a political overview to the volume as a whole. They capture the divergent perceptions between China's rulers and student protesters, not just at the tragic end, but from the beginning, though the gap widened throughout late April and May. Neither document is a dispassionate, objective account of events; each is self-righteous and moralistic. Chen Xitong does greater injustice, however, to the facts as they are currently known. His account contains many purposeful distortions to justify the brutal military actions on June 3–4 and simply overlooks the most damning dimensions of the hardliners' decisions, ranging from the excessive brutality of the police in front of the Zhongnanhai gate on April 20, to the issuance of particularly damaging types of bullets to some soldiers. Chen's version also systematically downplays government harshness and intransigence toward even the most modest student proposals. Li Qiao et al.'s account, on the other hand, understates the sweeping nature of student demands in the May 2 petition and does not accurately describe the disruption to the city brought on by the peaceful protests. Further, neither document prescribes policies for coping with the enormous economic difficulties confronting the country, which are vividly described in part II of this volume. In this sense, the two documents demonstrate the degree to which their main political concerns—maintaining power for the rulers versus initiating reform by protests—came to dominate the evolving situation, while economic issues were shoved, at least temporarily, into the background. The reader cannot, therefore, acquire an accurate account of events simply by combining Chen's and Li Qiao et al.'s documents. What is interesting is the Rashomon-like character of the two.

1
Death or Rebirth?
Tiananmen: The Soul of China

COMPILED BY LI QIAO ET AL.
TRANSLATED BY H. R. LAN AND JERRY DENNERLINE

Compiler's Preface

It is a great pleasure to see "Death and Rebirth" published in English. In April 1989 a spontaneous, peaceful, and far-reaching movement began in Beijing with demands for more freedom and democracy. More than a million people from all walks of life, including students, workers, and intellectuals, took part as the movement developed in Tiananmen Square. The democratic movement was both spectacular and unprecedented. It has stimulated the hearts and minds of all Chinese. Inspired by the events, I was determined to do something to record what was truly a people's democratic movement. To obtain a rich, vivid, and authentic account of the events, I started in early May to organize a group of people for the undertaking. This writing group consisted of some of the best and brightest young people in China. Several of them had themselves been leaders of student movements over the past few years. But, because of the April 26 *People's Daily* editorial, by the time we had finished sixteen chapters, we were still unable to find a publisher in China who would dare to publish our account. As a last resort, at the very beginning of June, at some risk to myself and others I brought the manuscript to the United States. Fortunately, in America our essay has found a publisher through the efforts of Professors Jerry Dennerline and H. R. Lan, who spent a great deal of time and energy translating it into English as well. On behalf of all the writers, I extend my sincere thanks.

At the same time, I regret that we had to leave out many names and details, including the names of the other authors and the whole of one essential chapter of the original manuscript, to preserve the safety of student participants and contributors to the project. My apologies to the readers for this omission.

Li Qiao, August 10, 1989

1. Background

From the looks of it, 1989 was destined to be a very ordinary year. As the new year began, disillusionment covered the vast landscape of China. The mood had spread to every corner of the country and affected every stratum of society. China had known nothing like it in the forty years of the People's Republic. Even during those four decades' most trying, most absurd, and cruelest times—the Anti-Rightist campaign of 1957, the Great Leap Forward of 1958, the Anti-Right Deviation campaign of 1959, the nationwide famine of 1960–61, and the Cultural Revolution that nearly destroyed everyone—the disillusionment was never so deep and widespread as this. In the hearts of many, disillusionment had turned into despair—as far as China was concerned, they no longer had the slightest bit of hope in anyone or anything.

Yet, for the vast majority of the people the past ten years of reform had also been the best years since the founding of the People's Republic. Some say we "take the bowl and enjoy the meat, but then put it down and curse the cook." We Chinese are truly a wretched lot, they say. When there is no meat we only think about eating meat and have no energy for cursing. But when we have eaten enough to gain a little strength, then we get distracted and start complaining. As the ancients put it, "When one's basic needs are met, one's thoughts turn to excessive self-indulgence."[1]

But to be disillusioned and to complain is not to be excessive or self-indulgent. Nor is the complaint due to the improving quality of the meal. As with all social and cultural phenomena there is a greater, deeper cause.

As the world becomes smaller and smaller, it becomes more and more clear that there are two very different ways to compare one's own society and culture with others. Simply put, there are "vertical comparisons" and "horizontal comparisons."

Perhaps because China has such a long history, the traditional Chinese way is to compare vertically. Vertical comparison always gives one a feeling of security. We can always say, "No matter what, the present is much better than the past!" For example, the caveman surely said, "In the past we were apes living in the trees, weather-beaten, and living a hard life. Now we live in a cave. We have become men." Or, for example, the Peking Man might have said, "In the past we ate raw meat. It was hard to bite and hard to chew, and it wasn't very tasty. Now we have fire. We can cook the meat, so it is much tastier. It is both tender and delicious. If we compare the present with the past, what is there to complain about?"

Those who conclude that we "take the bowl and enjoy the meat, but then put

---

[1]The proverb referred to is "Economic sufficiency leads to lust; economic deprivation is the source of goodness" (*bao nuan sheng yin yu; ji han fa shan xin*). See *Shih lin guang ji*. Similar notions are found in Mencius.

it down and curse the cook," are locked into this closed, traditional way of making comparisons.

Comparing horizontally is a more open way, made possible in human society by the development of modern industrial civilization with modern transportation and communication as the basis.

Using this modern horizontal comparative method, we find the widespread mood of disillusionment at the beginning of 1989 not only reasonable but inevitable.

The reform of the past ten years is undoubtedly the greatest accomplishment of the national government under the Chinese Communist Party since the founding of the People's Republic of China. But its greatness, seen from a cultural perspective, depends ultimately on its extension into every aspect of the culture. An eminent Confucian statesman of the late Qing period described the object of reform at that time with the slogan "Chinese learning as the basis, Western learning for practical use."[2] History has proven this idea to be one-sided and self-deluding. In fact, the actual process of reform over the past ten years has also proven this. Reform has brought meat to the bowls of the people in many forms. It has brought the responsibility system in agriculture and a thriving marketplace.[3] It has brought household appliances and the like. But it has also enabled the Chinese people, who were cut off from the outside world for thirty years, to see the world as it really is, to see how "the other two-thirds of the world's people," those "miserable people" whom we were urgently bent on "liberating from fire and water," actually live and work.[4]

After careful observation and reflection, the Chinese people have discovered that if in the world there are indeed miserable people, then the one billion Chinese who have basked in the sunshine of socialism for more than thirty years are conspicuous among them. For those Chinese who were always ready to stand above the waters and save the drowning this discovery was alarming. It was unacceptable. Yet, no matter how hard it is to accept, they cannot wish the reality away. A process has begun and, in time, the reality will be accepted. Stubborn wishful thinking will be smashed. During this process some people try

---

[2]The slogan was espoused by the reformer Zhang Zhidong (1837–1909), who stressed educational reform during the decade before the Republican Revolution of 1911, in his "Exhortation to Learn" (1898). The theme grew out of half a century of efforts by "self-strengtheners" (traditional statecraft thinkers and advocates of *yangwu*, or "foreign studies") to strengthen China by borrowing practical knowledge from the West.

[3]The responsibility system began with the breakup of collective farms, which placed responsibility for agricultural production on individual households, and spread to other state and collective enterprises. Along with the increased role of the market economy, it is the keystone of economic reform.

[4]Phrases that were common in Maoist education.

to revive the stupid slogan of the "Self-strengtheners" of the last century, preaching "Chinese learning as the basis, Western learning for practical use." They have appeared twice already with this banner to launch official ideological campaigns.[5] But in the end, they are destined to lose.

The rational scientific spirit has begun to take root in China, revealing to the Chinese people that China is not a fertile land as we would like to think, but one of the poorest countries in the world. China is the most populous nation in the world, but its natural resources are quite scarce. China is not at all a large land with abundant resources, but a large land with insufficient resources. The Chinese people must swallow their pride and heed the results of a battery of careful statistical studies describing the per capita rates of arable land, forest land, petroleum, grain, vegetables, meat, and fruit, the rate of illiteracy and the present educational situation in China. Suddenly we Chinese have discovered that we are not the favored sons of heaven; we are its disinherited children. Some people even came up with this statistic: if the Chinese land and people were erased from the face of the earth, the living standard of the world's population would increase by a factor of two.

Knowledgeable people predict that even if China had a modernized, highly efficient, democratic government composed of specialists with a complete system of legal checks and balances, it would still take more than fifty years for China to rid itself of poverty and catch up with world development. This prophecy is disheartening enough, but some people still think it is too optimistic, as it totally overlooks China's unique difficulties. The prophecy remains hypothetical in any case, as no one knows if China will ever be able to have a highly efficient democratic government with a complete system of legal checks and balances.[6]

In ten years of reform the leaders of the Chinese Communist Party have succeeded in pushing China out of its isolation of several decades into an ever shrinking and ever more intimate community of nations, thus bringing the majority of the Chinese people unprecedented economic benefits and spiritual freedom that had been denied them for the past thirty years. Even so, this spiritual freedom is not what all the leaders would like to see. There is a great defect in the political structure—perhaps a fundamental defect—and the process of establishing a system of rule of law has led

---

[5]Referring to the Anti–Spiritual Pollution campaign of 1983–85 and the Anti–Bourgeois Liberalization campaign of 1987, both of which were in response to efforts of the prodemocracy movement to establish greater freedom of expression. The latter began by blaming Hu Yaobang for allowing too much freedom, resulting in large-scale student demonstrations in December 1986.

[6]The party has consistently rejected such a system as inappropriate for China. It is considered a tool of the "dictatorship of the bourgeoisie." In August 1989, the point was reinforced with attacks on intellectuals like Yan Jiaqi, who are seen as advocating the overthrow of the dictatorship of the proletariat.

to serious turmoil. Although the Party has constantly launched campaigns to improve its style and has declared success in these campaigns over the past ten years of reform, the problems have in fact gone from bad to worse, until the defect in the structure has finally reached a point that is beyond repair.

A young sociologist says, "All this is historically inevitable. Reform simply must occur in all the socialist countries today." As the Chinese Communist Party's leadership points out, "Reform is the only way out." Yet for what is reform a way out? It is not a way out for socialist principles and communist ideals, nor is it a way out for the system of one-party dictatorship; it is a way out for a society, for a nation, for a people.

The new U.S. secretary of defense, Cheney, said perestroika in the Soviet Union will end in failure, because it will eventually shake and destroy the principles of socialism and the Soviet system of one-party dictatorship. U.S. President George Bush in his May 1 address said even more precisely, "Socialism is not a different economic system, it is economic suicide." The contradictions between reform and the orthodox principles of socialism seem extraordinarily sharp, and the heads of all the socialist states face a serious dilemma.

The leadership of the Chinese Communist Party envisions a unique path of socialist reform with Chinese characteristics. By 1988 this path, which the party leaders described as "crossing the river by groping for the rocks," seemed to be leading into danger, as the rocks in the river could not be found. China's destiny lies in the rushing torrents of the river.

China's ordinary citizens were not in the mood to search for stones in the river. What they were thinking of was much more concrete. Eighty percent of the Chinese population are peasants. After several years of good times (vertical comparison), they face one problem after another—for example, the insufficient supply of pesticides, the shortage of fertilizer, the prohibitively high prices on the black market, constant inflation in the prices of industrial products, and increasing production costs. Although production costs have increased the peasants must still sell their goods to the state at low prices. Urban citizens are also panic-stricken over the unpredictable and uncontrollable inflation. They anxiously see their hard-earned wages (all in native currency) depreciate in value. On the other hand, both in the countryside and in the cities, among officials at all levels and in all departments bribery is rampant and the widespread personal use of public funds is no longer a secret. Nepotism and other sorts of abuses of power are more and more open. Some officials even justify these practices by saying their salaries are insufficient to support their families, and that what they are doing is nothing compared to what their superiors do. The situation of the intellectuals is even worse. The rehabilitation of the "stinking ninth"[7] category

---

[7]In the Cultural Revolution, intellectuals were placed at the bottom of the list of enemies of the people and were commonly referred to as the "stinking ninth" category of such enemies.

(of the Cultural Revolution enemies of the people) is only symbolic. Their real position has not improved at all.

Meanwhile, control of the press, of publication, and of speech is growing tighter. For example, although in 1986 control was loosened slightly the demand of the Chinese people for democracy and freedom became stronger and the suppression was felt even more. Those newspapers that told a little bit of the truth were criticized. When people listened to the news they laughed.

The university students, who are the most energetic and enthusiastic group in Chinese society, grew silent. After the student movement was suppressed in 1986 and General Secretary Hu Yaobang, the most respected and sensible leader of the Chinese Communist Party, was forced to step down, the students lost all interest in Chinese politics and the fate of the country. Many students began to play mahjongg, while others immersed themselves in preparations for TOEFL and GRE exams. Sarcastically they said there are only two student factions: the MA (Marxist) faction and the TO (Trotskyite) faction, where MA stands for mahjongg and TO stands for TOEFL. This development alarmed many observers, who cried out, "A whole generation of students has lost interest in national politics and the fate of the country. This is definitely the decline of the Chinese people." But the sounding of this alarm could not diminish the students' fervent interest in these pursuits.

Such was the mood when the year 1989 arrived.

2. An Untimely Death

May 4, 1989, would be the seventieth anniversary of the May Fourth Movement of 1919, the movement that laid the foundation for China's new culture. Symbolizing patriotic student activism, May 4 has also been made the official youth day.

Early this year I was talking with a friend about what might happen in China on the seventieth anniversary of May 4. The friend wondered if those students who were still full of revolutionary spirit, especially Beijing University students, would do something big to advance the Chinese democracy movement? I was not optimistic. Nothing would happen, I thought. After a series of political farces, the students were weary. Lacking hope they were not enthusiastic, I thought, just wait and see.

Before April 15, all indications were that I was right. This was to be a very ordinary year. Nothing would happen. But at 7:53 A.M.on April 15, 1989, someone died. No one had anticipated it. The Chinese people learned of Hu Yaobang's death on the 7:00 evening news. The former general secretary of the party, Hu had been very close to the student movement of the 1980s. The response of the people showed that they found this death untimely.

It was Saturday evening, a time when people prepare for their weekend relaxation. But this Saturday evening was unusually quiet. The news had set people to thinking.

On April 16, the news appeared on the first page of the *People's Daily* and all the other newspapers in China, along with a photograph and an obituary prepared by the party's Central Committee. On the same day, university students in Beijing, Tianjin, Shanghai, Changsha, Xi'an, and other cities wrote many articles and poems to pay tribute to Hu Yaobang. Of course, all these could only appear in the traditional Chinese form of big-character posters.

The memorial activities for Hu Yaobang might be compared to the popular demonstrations honoring the late Zhou Enlai in 1976.[8] From the outset they showed a strong political tendency. But compared to 1976, people were more direct and outspoken, and their activities more spontaneous.

Hu Yaobang was forced to resign his post as party general secretary in January 1987. The procedure was highly irregular. No one knows the inside story, but according to documents published by the party, Hu had allowed too much bourgeois liberalization in China. By "bourgeois liberalization" the party meant the demonstrations by university students in Beijing, Shanghai, and other places, calling for freedom and democracy, at the end of 1986.

The party's announcement of Hu Yaobang's death said he would be given a state funeral with the highest honors, but students and other citizens were not satisfied. They wanted to pay tribute to this great man, who had died so suddenly, in their own way.

On the afternoon of April 16, five wreaths from Beijing University, Jiaotong University, and other schools were sent to the Monument to the People's Heroes in Tiananmen Square, the symbol of the heart of China. At the same time, in front of the main building of Beijing University, there appeared stacks of black armbands for students. That night more than a thousand students participated in spontaneous demonstrations of mourning in Beijing and Shanghai.

On April 17, thousands of university students in Beijing, Shanghai, Tianjin, and other cities took to the streets shouting slogans, singing the "Internationale," and demanding democracy and freedom. Thousands of citizens turned out to watch, some even participating in the demonstrations.

Nowhere did the police intervene. Although, since 1986, there was a set of ten regulations limiting demonstrations by citizens in Beijing, and there were similar regulations in other cities, the government apparently chose to exercise self-restraint as the citizens spontaneously memorialized the former general secretary.

A wise leader of great integrity, Hu Yaobang was forced to step down. Although he lost power, he gained respect, and his death was most untimely.

---

[8]On April 5, 1976, crowds of people went to Tiananmen Square to lay wreaths and post poems and announcements honoring the recently deceased Premier Zhou Enlai. Beijing party leaders reacted violently and blamed Deng Xiaoping for instigating the affair. This incident came to symbolize the loss of legitimacy by the Maoists and linked Deng and the reformers with the people's conscience.

What would it mean to the China of 1989, where disillusionment was so widespread, the China whose mood verged on despair?

3. Hu Yaobang, the Man

The leader of the nation with the world's largest population and lowest GNP, Hu Yaobang was a man of great integrity. He lived a simple and austere life. Of course, this may not be essential for a national leader. If an American president appeared so poor and plain, people would deride him, but for a backward country like China it is essential for a leader to live an austere life. It is a sign that he has a strong sense of responsibility for the country.

The reason Hu Yaobang could win such respect among the people, especially intellectuals, is not just that he lived an austere life; it was that he made an irreplaceable contribution to the country and its people.

On April 19, the *World Economic Herald* and the *New Observer* jointly sponsored a forum in memory of Hu Yaobang. Among those attending were Li Chang, a member of the Central Advisory Commission (Zhongguwei); the former editor-in-chief of the *People's Daily* Qin Chuan; the scholars Su Shaozhi, Wu Jiang, Yu Haocheng, Yu Guangyuan, and Yan Jiaqi; the writer Dai Qing; and Li Rui, the former vice-director of the Central Organization Department. Their speeches appeared in the April 24 issue of the *World Economic Herald*, which was later shut down by the Shanghai Party Committee. Their evaluations of Hu Yaobang's life were candid and courageous.

A long-time comrade-in-arms and former subordinate of Hu, Li Chang reminisced: "Hu Yaobang was a friend of intellectuals beginning with the Yan'an years. He remained heart-to-heart with young people and he made a great contribution by initiating the discussion of 'Practice as the sole criterion of truth.' "[9]

Qin Chuan said:

> I did not get to know Comrade Hu Yaobang well until I went to work for the *People's Daily*, but I think those past ten years, after the Third Plenum, were the most dynamic and also the most glorious years in his life.[10] We at the

---

[9]The debate over practice as the sole criterion of truth occurred in response to Hua Guofeng's emergence as party chairman after Mao's death. Hua advocated policies based on "whatever" Mao had said, while the opposition argued that policy should be determined by what was learned from practice. The official line then pointed to Mao's early advocacy of "learning truth from facts," a notion traditionally associated with ancient pragmatic Confucian statecraft as opposed to idealistic Confucian self-cultivation and, in Marxism, associated with emphasizing practice over theory.

[10]The Third Plenum of the Eleventh Party Central Committee, held in December 1978, marked the beginning of Deng Xiaoping's reform program. The meeting rejected class struggle and adopted economic reform as key in party planning. It also promised a reevaluation of the role of mass campaigns in the party's history.

People's Daily can never say enough. To us he was not only a great Marxist but also a close friend. Whenever the going got rough for the reforms, it was Hu Yaobang who was most concerned about us at the *People's Daily*. Without his support, there is much we could not have done.

In one incident, the Liaoning journal *The Communist* published an article rehabilitating Zhang Zhixin. Not until one month later did the *People's Daily* try to run the article, and we were criticized immediately. At that point three department heads and two assistant heads in the Central Propaganda Department objected, and the New China News Agency did not release it. At this critical moment, Hu Yaobang spoke out, saying Zhang Zhixin was indeed a heroine in a class with Liu Hulan.[11]

On theoretical issues, Hu Yaobang also gave us much support. The reason I say he was courageous is that he never accepted heresies, nor did he give in to bullying, and nothing was more precious to him than the hearts and minds of the people. After the Third Plenum Hu Yaobang courageously led the people in carrying out the reforms. It would have been impossible without his fearless spirit. A few days ago, the Taiwan correspondent Xu Lu asked me what I thought about Hu Yaobang. I could only answer that he was an extremely good, genuine, and most popular man.

The Marxist who cannot win people's hearts, or who lacks human kindness, or is not genuine, no matter how intelligent he may be, is not a very good Marxist. I have paid Hu several personal visits since he stepped down. Although he was no longer in power, he was still very concerned about the country and the people. He was thinking about the state of the world, and he was very worried. He told me a few things that I believe we should pay attention to in our future ideological work. For example, he asked me how I would evaluate the present work of the party. I said, "Don't we say this is the best time in our history?" He did not respond. In the end he said, "What a pity! Since the Third Plenum of the Eleventh Party Congress we have restored and developed the party work principle of 'seeking truth from facts.' Yet the principle has once again been seriously undermined." This is something we should consider carefully. Another example: After he stepped down, he said several times, "We should never make mistakes in dealing with the intellectuals, and we must not persecute intellectuals. The same is true for youth and for students."

The Marxist scholar Su Shaozhi had this to say:

In 1986 when we discussed the seventh five-year plan for the social sciences Hu Yaobang met with us and said that since the Third Plenum, the party's Central Committee has never used the stick. Many people said, and as I recall Li Honglin was the first to speak up, "What do you mean you never

---

[11]Zhang Zhixin was executed during the Cultural Revolution for refusing to admit that her criticism of party leaders was wrong. Liu Hulan was killed by the warlord and Guomindang ally Yan Xishan in the 1930s. Mao honored her as a revolutionary martyr and had his words engraved on her tombstone: "In life her virtue was great; in death her virtue is glorious."

used the stick? Some people have been expelled from the party.'' Wu Mingyu added that some even lost their jobs. And I also added that some were even expelled from Beijing. But Hu Yaobang did not object to being interrupted by so many people. He took their opinions very seriously, and said, ''Write a report and I'll approve it if it's correct.'' This sort of broad-mindedness is unusual among our leaders. The year before last, when he was treated unfairly, many of us felt sorry for him. That kind of irregular transferring of power is a bad precedent for the party and for the country. But Hu Yaobang himself did not take it grudgingly. He continued to be concerned with affairs of state. ''Work until you die, and when you die it's over.'' Hu Yaobang never abused his power, nor did he seek favors. He was guiltless and always thinking of the people. He will always live in our hearts. Therefore, when he died it was no accident that so many people felt sad and missed him, and felt the injustice that was done him.

Dai Qing said:

Today we should repeat a line (from the national anthem) that we often sing: ''The Chinese people have reached the most critical moment.'' If the reforms do not advance, it will be disastrous for the history of the nation. Today I must emphasize the key point is to democratize politics within the party. As others have said, Hu Yaobang was forced to resign although there was no emergency. Therefore, the decision was contrary to both the principles and the procedures of party organization. He was forced to send a resignation letter and to make self-criticism. I think the most tragic thing in Hu Yaobang's life was that he had to make self-criticism against his will. It is seventy years since the party was founded. Why do we still live under this sort of shadow? The party general secretary represents the party members. He was elected by the members to preside over the party's routine work. But he was ousted under strange circumstances.

This raises a serious question: why is democracy within a party of the proletariat so defective? Su Shaozhi just said that when he was dismissed from his position he was broad-minded about it. I think that when it comes to such irregularities in the party, no matter whether one is an ordinary member, or a middle-level or high-ranking cadre, one should not be so broad-minded as to accept them. I think we should distinguish between right and wrong. Fostering a good style within the party does not depend on the good qualities of individuals, but on a whole set of structural guarantees. We hope the future of China, of the country and of the party, will not depend on the personal qualities of individual leaders, but instead will be founded on structural guarantees.

Yu Guangyuan, the well-known scientist and member of the Central Advisory Commission, revealed the following to Li Chunguang, a correspondent for the overseas Chinese paper *Zhongbao*, in a telephone interview:

When Deng Liqun was interviewed by *Zhongbao*, he said, ''As soon as I learned of Comrade Hu Yaobang's death I rushed to the hospital to pay tribute.

I am very sad. Even though we had some differences of opinion, we have always been close friends. Now that he is gone, I miss him that much more. Hu Yaobang's story is known to everyone. History will remember him. His contributions to the country and the people are obvious. He was noble and aboveboard and he spoke frankly."

Yu continued:

I really doubt what Deng Liqun says.[12] How could he claim to be so close to Hu Yaobang? We know not to insult the living, how could we insult the dead like this! I am no expert on official obituaries. Maybe there are some experts here who can tell me when we should bestow the title "great Marxist" on the deceased. Even Hu Yaobang was not so honored. He was apparently "unqualified" to be called a "great Marxist." In fact, it doesn't mean that much, but the title does exist. In Marxist terms, of course, Hu Yaobang was a Marxist.

Then Yan Jiaqi, the political scientist, spoke:

Some say that China lacks a cohesive force. After I went to Tiananmen Square I felt that China's cohesive force was very strong. The strong feelings of sadness for Hu Yaobang and the sense of justice of the Chinese people are indeed strong cohesive forces. To say that China lacks a cohesive force is to ignore the people.

I also felt very sad at the death of Hu Yaobang. One reason is that he was treated unfairly. People want to express their opinion about this injustice. That is why such a massive expression of mourning has occurred a second time in Tiananmen. This is no accident. Before finishing the manuscript for my book, *A History of the Cultural Revolution*, I wrote this sentence: "A nation that cannot learn from its own disasters is a nation with no future." In fact this sentence was originally Hu Deping's (Hu Yaobang's son). I borrowed it for my preface. But I did not anticipate that six months later Hu Yaobang would be dismissed, in fact, forced to resign.

In Tiananmen Square two phrases are on everyone's lips. The first is, "Remember Hu Yaobang!" The other is, "China needs democracy!" The same two phrases were on everyone's lips in 1976. "Remember Zhou Enlai! China needs democracy!" In my opinion, China's biggest problem is still the lack of democracy. Such a small group of people gathering to make decisions can totally disregard the will and the interests of the whole people.

The resignation of Hu Yaobang was a case in point. The issue concerning democracy is not the quality of the people. Any ordinary peasant, ordinary worker, or ordinary intellectual can easily see that Hu Yaobang made unprecedented contributions to the Chinese people and to China's reform. They can also see clearly that those in charge of ideological work are not qualified to

---

[12]Deng Liqun took the lead in the Propaganda Department in initiating the Anti–Spiritual Pollution campaign of 1983.

pay tribute to him, because they were his persecutors and should be tried by history. I believe history will tell the whole story.

I would also like to give some advice to some people at the Ministry of Public Security. Don't repeat the mistake of 1976. Everything the Beijing Public Security Bureau did on that occasion has been recorded in history. I hope that someday everything the Security Bureau did in that Tiananmen Incident will be publicized. Yesterday at Tiananmen I saw that the police and the soldiers of the PLA were of one mind with the people. Because of the lesson they learned from the Tiananmen Incident, they were unwilling to suppress the people. They simply could not stand up against the people.

Therefore, I think China's future is very clear. The policies at the top must coincide with the people's will. The will of the people is quite simple in this case. Hu Yaobang was unfairly treated. If the evaluation is not corrected more problems will occur. In 1976 it was we the people who spoke up for Premier Zhou Enlai and Deng Xiaoping. We praised them so highly that Deng Xiaoping was able to resume his work. In that case everyone contributed a voice.

Therefore, we still place our hope in the party leadership. For the sake of the people, the country, and the development of democracy in China, we hope they will make a fair judgment of Hu Yaobang and admit their mistake. If they do not admit their mistake, then history will surely repeat itself.

The poet Liu Zhanqiu followed:

At Tiananmen Square when I saw the words, "the soul of China," I cried. If we miss this opportunity and ignore the enthusiasm of the people it would be a grave mistake. I think the unjust evaluation of Hu Yaobang should be reconsidered. It was entirely inappropriate for a vice-chairman of the Central Advisory Commission to announce the dismissal of the party's general secretary. What is happening today will help the party to reconsider the issue.

Then Li Rui said:

This year I was in America for a month and a half. I discovered there was an English edition of Hu Yaobang's biography. The author sent me a copy just before I left along with a draft of the Chinese edition. On April 5 I gave both to Hu Yaobang. That day I talked to him about America and told him about how Liu Binyan was doing there. Hu was still quite concerned about Liu Binyan, and I told him that the Chinese students in America were concerned about Hu. The students were still thinking about the 1987 incident. They mentioned it on every opportunity I had to meet with them. If you can live in people's hearts, you can live forever.[13]

---

[13]The biography, *Hu Yaobang: A Chinese Biography* (Armonk, N.Y.: M. E. Sharpe, 1988), by Yang Zhongmei, makes the case that Hu was the main force behind political reform and that his dismissal was illegal. Liu Binyan, the highly respected journalist and advocate of free expression and political reform, was also blamed for the student unrest and expelled from the party in January 1987. He was writing and lecturing in the United States during the 1988–89 academic year as Nieman Fellow at Harvard University.

Once when Hu Yaobang was visiting Zhangjiajie some two thousand people surrounded him wanting to shake his hand and be photographed with him. Traffic was totally blocked. So, when he reached Nanning he had to stay indoors. He said to me, sighing, "If I had gone out in Nanning and the same thing had happened, what would happen to me if the news got back to Beijing?" The next day a photographer recommended by Qin Chuan went to Hu Yaobang's home to photograph him. As is the custom, the photographer asked him to smile. Hu Yaobang said, "How can I?" Therefore, the photograph showed a forced smile.

He was the youngest among the old Red Army veterans. He served as an Organization Department head in the General Political Department of the army when he was just in his twenties. In Yan'an during the "rectification campaign" [1942–44] his contribution in pointing out mistakes and warning against over-extending the campaign was great. Our party had gone through an ultra-left campaign. To remain clear-headed in the midst of such a leftist campaign and to succeed in keeping it from being over-extended is extremely difficult. Hu Yaobang's most precious political quality was his ability to brave the storms of leftist excesses.

On April 5 as we talked about young people he blurted out, "Young people are our hope. Why are we so afraid of them?!" Another good quality of his is that he always made genuine self-criticisms. In our party's history this quality is rare, and it is an extremely valuable quality. His attitude toward the "anti–spiritual pollution campaign" was very clear. Zhao Ziyang's opinion in his comments on that afterwards included Hu Yaobang's thoughts. As he said many times, "The campaign has gone on for twenty-eight days already. It must stop!" Without his voice who knows what the Anti–Spiritual Pollution campaign might have come to?

Qin Chuan followed:

The night before traveling to Japan he phoned expressly to instruct us, "From now on, shut Deng Liqun out." After the discussion of "the criterion of truth," there was talk of another debate on the purpose of socialism. Once it was reported he put a stop to it. He was endowed with the spirit of humanism and the spirit of democracy. And he regarded humanism and democracy to be goals for the party. This is quite rare among the leadership.

The theorist Wu Jiang said:

Hu Yaobang became an outstanding leader at a critical turning point in our history, the moment when the party and the country started rebuilding. The critical time I refer to is the five years between the Eleventh and Twelfth Party Congresses. It was the period of rectification, especially the early phase. After the Eleventh Congress, when Deng Xiaoping reappeared, the situation was still unclear. In many cases wrong verdicts were not reversed. Those who had already reappeared did not speak up for these comrades. Some sat on the fence and played it cautious. But Hu Yaobang spoke up bravely and, without the slightest hesitation, did the necessary rectification work. When he stepped down he didn't really think about himself, but worried about the fate of the party, the country, and the people. This is probably one of the reasons his health broke down. A very important reason.

Wu Mingyu, deputy director of the Research Center for Economic Development under the State Council, said:

> Hu Yaobang told me two things. All his life he had two regrets. One was the case of Comrade Xiang Nan. He was on the Central Committee of the Communist Youth League when the case came up, and he did not handle it well. He didn't do enough to protect Comrade Xiang Nan. The other regret was his self-criticism in the Anti–Bourgeois Liberalization campaign. He said, "I hurt a certain comrade, but I sent someone to apologize to him."

Sun Changjiang, senior editor of the *Science and Technology Daily*, said:

> A couple of things Hu Yaobang said were especially touching. While we all thought that he was unfairly treated and that he had done a great deal for the people, he said he did not feel that way himself. What he said was, "There are two things I never expected. I did not expect to gain such a high position. And I did not imagine I would still have a good reputation after I stepped down." Looking back, there is a third thing he did not expect: that his death could have such great significance for Chinese history.
>
> That same day he said, "Many years of experience teaches us that there are four kinds of people we must be especially careful about. The first is young students. We must love and protect them. We must be concerned about their growth. The second is the intellectuals. We should try to understand them. We must be magnanimous and tolerant of them. The third is the national minorities, and the fourth is the democratic parties."

Lin Jinyao from the United Front Department added:

> After Hu left office in 1987 I talked to many people and was told by them: although Hu Yaobang did not work long at the Chinese Academy of Sciences, the period he was there was the golden age; comrades in the Propaganda Department said that the period of his tenure as chief was the golden age; when he was vice-president of the Party School and in charge of daily administrative work, people say that was also the golden age; comrades at the Central Organization Department also said the same thing. A leading comrade who could always bring a golden age to the work place must be an extraordinary person.

Mr. Zhang Xianyang, an expert on Marxism-Leninism, said:

> Hu Yaobang's words: "After the success of the revolution the task of the party is still to lead the people in striving for more democracy"; and, "Democracy is never completely won but must constantly be worked on."

People cannot be fooled. As these speeches show, an especially clear and affectionate image of Hu Yaobang has been brought back to life in the people's hearts. Before Hu Yaobang's death, especially while he was party general secretary, he was determined to avoid a personality cult. Because of that the general public knows little about his noble character and great contributions. After he became party chairman he once went to inspect an army and noticed a banner with the words "Long live Chairman Hu" at the entrance to the headquarters. In those days it was the usual thing to say "Long live . . . ," but the first thing Hu Yaobang did when he got out of the car was to tear down that banner.

Hu Yaobang was a most popular and most compassionate leader. During his several years as the party's leader he visited all the poor and remote areas of China, including those places where national minorities still live under tribal rulers, and expressed his concern about conditions there. Hu Yaobang was a genuine Marxist. Of all the Communist leaders of China, he studied the works of Marx and Lenin most earnestly. And he matched words with deeds. But these qualities made him, of all the leaders, the least compatible with the current realities of China.

4. Has Hot Blood Turned Cold?

For several months people had been saying that university students had lost their idealism and, with it, their patriotism and concern for the fate of the country. Then suddenly Hu Yaobang, the symbol of democracy and modernization in the party, passed away. The passions of millions of students who had been numbed by the weight of corruption and the deterioration were rekindled. Had the blood of the young really turned cold so quickly? No. Their answer showed that the pure and unspoiled blood of youth still flowed in their veins.

On April 18 more than 100,000 students and citizens of Beijing gathered spontaneously at the Monument to the People's Heroes in Tiananmen Square to mourn Hu Yaobang. Wreaths and bouquets covered the base of the monument. Essays and poems extolling democracy and freedom appeared all around. People lingered late into the night, quietly singing the "Internationale." Some climbed onto the monument to recite poems in memory of Hu Yaobang. Others made speeches demanding freedom of speech, freedom of the press, and freedom of publication, and they demanded a hastening of reform and of political democratization.

Around 11:00 P.M., about a thousand students mainly from Beijing University and People's University, together with some 10,000 citizens, all under the banner of People's University, arrived at Xinhuamen where the offices of the party's Central Committee and the State Council are located. They demanded a reevaluation of Hu Yaobang and the acceleration of the process of democratization of state politics. They also demanded a dialogue with government officials.

Plainclothes policemen, traffic policemen, armed police, and the Zhongnanhai guards stood arm-in-arm forming a barrier four rows deep, blocking the students. The force of the crowd was so great that the leaders could not stop. In the press of the crowd, some people in the rear threw bottles and shoes at the police. In order to avoid a confrontation and keep to their goal of dialogue, the students in front squatted down upon orders from the student leaders. The police commanders went in and out but brought no official reply to the student's demand for dialogue. Under this pressure some of the plainclothes policemen kicked the demonstrators with leather boots. But thus far there was no greater conflict.

Students shouted the slogan, "Peaceful demonstration!" until two student representatives were allowed to go in to negotiate. As the two students did not return, the students shouted that their representatives should come back. But up to the time the crowd was dispersed in the wee hours of the morning, the two "student representatives" never showed up. Afterwards, participants in the demonstrations claimed they did not know the two students and suspected their true identities.

After 4:00 A.M. the demonstrators became cold and tired, many of them already half-asleep. Suddenly a large number of policemen rushed out from the alleyways around Xinhuamen, formed themselves into rows and drove the students toward the west. One policeman with a walkie-talkie deliberately let the students hear his commander's voice giving orders—if the students were not gone within twenty minutes, they would be dispersed by force. Those who heard the orders later said the police were trying to threaten them.

That night many bicycles that had been parked by the gate disappeared. One witness said that after dispersing the students the police loaded the bicycles onto trucks and took them away.

On April 19 on the evening news Beijing Television and Central Government Television issued a firm warning concerning the conflict of the night before. They also broadcast a close-up of a soldier wounded by a soda bottle.

On the nineteenth, students of the Central Academy of Fine Arts mounted a gigantic portrait of Hu Yaobang, 3 x 2.5 meters, on a pedicab and drove it to Tiananmen Square, where they placed it at the base of the monument. On one side of the portrait were the words, "Where have you gone? Soul come back!"[14]

All day long, people streamed into the square to join the mourners at the monument. Wreaths continuously passed over the heads of people to the base of the monument. Towards evening more and more students, workers, and intellectuals gathered in the square. More than ten thousand of them. More and more stood up to make speeches. Students, professors, and reporters all thought that mourning Hu Yaobang and striving for democracy were closely related activi-

---

[14]The cry "Soul come back!" was shouted from the rooftops by mourners in ancient China at the *hun*, or ethereal aspect of the soul, which was thought to fly up to heaven.

ties. Only at this moment could they say freely what had been weighing on their minds:

> Old ideas and old institutions can no longer satisfy the needs of the people.
> The people want to know the truth. Political power belongs to the people.
> China has been called a sleeping lion. Now we have finally woke up.
> The government uses much foreign exchange to buy fancy cars from Japan and West Germany but spends too little on education.
> Seventy years have passed since the May Fourth Movement. Still we have not got democracy and freedom.

The crowd cheered and applauded every speaker. And on the monument was a small but eye-catching slogan, "Down with dictatorship."

Around 11:00 P.M. two huge balloons rose in front of the monument with banners attached bearing the slogans: "Yaobang is not dead; long live the reform." The slogans were signed by the Economic Reform Research Institute.

Even though the government issued a firm warning on television, crowds of students still came with wreaths and banners to Xinhuamen, shouting at the top of their lungs, "We demand dialogue!" With the crowd pressing forcefully, the students sat down as before. One student sitting on the shoulders of another shouted to the crowd, "Please! Listen! Don't press! We are nonviolent! We want to use peaceful demonstration to urge the government to talk! Please, understand this!"

After midnight, unit after unit of police forces were sent in from both sides of the crowd to try to separate the sitting demonstrators from the spectators. Atop a police car a loudspeaker blared Beijing Municipality announcements. Still the crowds of spectators did not retreat. Skirmishes broke out between them and the police. A plainclothes policeman in his forties, standing in front of the line of armed police, pushed the spectators roughly, then picked up a bicycle and threw it down again. The spectators were enraged. With one voice they shouted, "No beating! No beating!" and the policeman withdrew from the angry crowd.

As a policeman rushed toward some U.S. television correspondents videotaping the events, a young spectator blocked him by shoving his bicycle into his path. The crowd shouted, "Freedom of the press! Freedom of the press!"

Around 2:00 A.M., row after row of police finally succeeded in dispersing the crowd of nearly ten thousand.

By this time, except for a few hundred students who were still sitting in, there were only policemen and plainclothesmen on the scene. The story as to what happened after that is told differently by the two sides.

The official New China News Agency said:

> Around 3:40 A.M. on the twentieth the order that the students must leave within twenty minutes was broadcast. But the students did not leave. At about 4:40 A.M. some were persuaded by school leaders to leave, but at daybreak

more than two hundred remained. Someone shouted, "Whoever leaves is a traitor!" In the interest of public order and for the sake of the normal functioning of transportation, the police had no choice but to remove the students physically. They were carried onto buses and sent back to their schools. Some struggled and refused to board the buses, shouting slogans such as "Down with the Communist Party!" Those already on the buses smashed windows, and there was much shoving and fighting between students and police.

But the students posted leaflets proclaiming "The truth about the tragedy of April 20":

> Around 4:50 A.M., large numbers of police and plainclothesmen surrounded the students. Three or four for each student. They beat the students with belts and kicked them with jackboots. Some students' glasses were broken and blood covered their heads and faces. Some students were badly beaten. Some of the girls' clothes were torn. Some were beaten so badly they begged for mercy. But the police did not let up.

In response to the students' leaflet the New China News Agency said:

> When the students were forced to leave Xinhuamen, both sides suffered minor injuries. It was rumored that police used clubs and wore jackboots. This is false. The policemen on duty those days carried no clubs and were ordered to wear soft shoes. None wore jackboots. Not a single student was badly wounded, and none required hospitalization. Such exaggerations, the use of language like "tragedy," and the demand for "open apology" from the Public Security Bureau, all indicate the degree to which a small number are scheming to confuse and agitate people.

At the "dialogue meeting" of April 29, some students brought up the issue of police beating students during the April 20 incident. Yuan Liben, a member of the Party Standing Committee of Beijing Municipality, said:

> According to regulations, policemen on duty must wear belts. Also according to regulations, armed police must wear army-style sneakers. These policemen did not even wear leather shoes, let alone jackboots. Nor did the traffic police wear jackboots. These days the police are all young people and they like to look good, so they often wear leather shoes. But that night the traffic police didn't wear belts. Now, it is true that someone shouted a reactionary slogan, a girl student, I still remember, with a ruddy face. Our policemen were very angry and wanted to drag her off the bus, but the bus was too crowded, so they let her be. Bus windows were broken and smeared with blood. I must confess that we did not plan well enough. The bus was too crowded. We should have used a bigger one. Still, our police used great restraint.

As for shouting the slogan "Down with the Communist Party!" according to students, the girl who shouted it did so only after being badly beaten by police.

On April 21 more than a hundred people including well-known scholars like Bao Zunxin, Wu Zuxiang, Yan Jiaqi, and Li Zehou, sent an open letter to the party, the National People's Congress, and the State Council, requesting objectivity in news reporting of the memorial activities and of the democracy movement. The letter said:

> It is a constitutional right of the students to criticize the leaders. It may not be considered illegal. The students' demands are as follows. (1) Perpetuate the spirit of Hu Yaobang's ideas and accelerate the reform of the political system. (2) Adopt firm concrete measures to deal with the increasing corruption within the party and the political institutions and to solve the problem of serious social injustice. (3) Solve the problem of weakness and incompetency that exists at all levels of government and implement the responsibility system at all levels and never allow the collective responsibility to obscure the responsibility of individuals. (4) Practice freedom of speech, freedom of the press, and freedom of publication. Guarantee the supervisory functions of the mass media and of public opinion. We think these demands are constructive. They will enable China to overcome its current difficulties, will unify the minds of the people. They are essential policies we must follow. They are the premises for building up a long-term stable social environment. Therefore, we suggest that the party and government leaders learn from the 1976 Tiananmen Incident, listen carefully to the students and engage in a dialogue on equal footing with them. You cannot simply ignore the students. If you ignore the students, this will surely only lead them to more radical action, which would be harmful for the great cause of modernization of China.

Everyone sensed that a great historical moment was about to occur in Beijing.

5. Before the National Emblem, China's Conscience Kneels

The memorial service for Hu Yaobang was to be held in the Great Hall of the People at 10:00 A.M. on April 22. The day before, the Beijing Public Security Bureau issued a notice that Tiananmen Square would be closed to vehicles and pedestrians two hours before the ceremony.

At 8:00 that evening more than 100,000 students marched out through the gates of Beijing's universities carrying banners and heading for Tiananmen Square. Along the way they were cheered on by several hundred thousand citizens, who formed two great walls on either side of the column of marching students. Many chimed in when the students sang the "Internationale," and many were moved to tears. Some emerged from the mass of people to offer the students cigarettes, buns or soda. When someone raised an arm and shouted, "Long live the students!" a chorus of voices responded. One intellectual, wiping away a tear, said to a reporter from the *Peasants' Daily*, "What great students! They say 'the fate of the nation depends on ordinary people.' If everyone had as great a sense of social responsibility as these people, China would be saved! No little bunch of profiteering bureaucrats who ignore what the people think would dare just do as they please!''

Around midnight, after some five hours of marching, the demonstrators, representing all the institutions of higher learning in Beijing and Tianjin's Nankai University finally reached Xinhuamen. They shouted the slogan, "Remember Hu Yaobang," sang the "Internationale" and the national anthem, formed themselves into ranks, and proceeded in orderly fashion to Tiananmen. Contingents of students from Shanghai's Jiaotong University and from Wuhan University joined their ranks. The students' hands raised high their banners with slogans like, "Grieve for the soul of China," "Yaobang—glory (yao) to the country (bang) in life, glory to the country in death!" "Leader of youth, fighter for democracy," "Model of upright government," "Punish the bureaucratic profiteers," "Freedom of the press," "Long live democracy! Long live freedom," etc. By the time the front of the procession reached Tiananmen the rear had not yet left Fuxingmen (some 2.5 kilometers away). The spectacle continued for the entire length of Chang'an Avenue.

At 3:00 A.M. the entire square was filled with students and citizens. Directly across from the Great Hall of the People there waved the eye-catching banner of the Party History Department, People's University.

As it had rained the previous day, it was now cold in Beijing. Standing in the chill of early morning, the lightly clad students shivered in the breeze. Their enthusiasm undaunted, they continued shouting, "Long live freedom! Long live democracy!" and sang the "Internationale" at the top of their lungs. The vast expanse of the square seemed enveloped by a sacred mood.

Around 2:00 A.M., some thirty truckloads of security forces entered the square and took up positions surrounding the Great Hall. By early morning, at Liubukou, Qianmen, Chongwenmen, and Dongdan, curfews were imposed. Soldiers, armed policemen, and security policemen formed three rows in front of the Great Hall of the People. At 7:25 A.M. another troop of armed police entered the square and tried to form a security line against the mourners, but a hundred thousand mourners surged forward, and the troops were forced to the side. People rushed to the edges of the square and the broad way in front of the Great Hall of the People filled up with mourners. Because of the curfew, the tens of thousands of shivering students could not get food, but they remained in high spirits, occupying the square.

On the Monument to the People's Heroes, beside the huge funerary portrait of Hu Yaobang, there appeared a gigantic character, four meters high and three meters across, "Sorrow." The atmosphere in the square became even more solemn. The national flag was raised in the front of the square and the tens of thousands of students and citizens stood up to sing the national anthem, "Build a new Great Wall with our own flesh and blood! The Chinese nation has reached a critical time! Rise up! Rise up! Rise up!''

The boom of the voices shook the square, raising the level of excitement. Their blood warming, the tens of thousands of students were deeply moved for the first time by the resonance of their own voices, and tears like crystals rolled down their cheeks. First the flag was raised to the top, and then lowered to half-mast to pay tribute to the man whose life had renewed the spirit in the young people's hearts.

After the national anthem, the "Internationale" was heard again.

The students' actions won them the understanding and support of the broad masses of the people. The citizens gathered in the square with the students, sang with them, shouted slogans with them, and made the "V" sign with their fingers to wish the students victory. Many gave the students their own breakfasts. Street vendors gave them soda and boxes of apples. Some even offered to raise funds to donate to the students—domestic currency, foreign exchange certificates, ration coupons, postage stamps—whatever they could find to offer. The students were swamped with notes expressing support from workers, peasants, state cadres, small-scale entrepreneurs, intellectuals, antarctic explorers, armed policemen, reporters, soldiers.

Just past 8:00 A.M. on the steps in front of the Great Hall and behind the wall of troops there began to appear those officials and representatives of all walks of life who were invited to the official memorial service. At that moment, two hundred thousand voices joined to sing the "Internationale" and the national anthem once again. The thundering sound penetrated the Great Hall. The officials and representatives on the steps turned to look at the square.

Student organizers selected students to organize a discipline control unit to maintain order among the students. Under their excellent supervision, the student demonstrators sat in an orderly fashion from the beginning to the end. Seeing the degree of order among the students, the commanders of the various kinds of troops ordered them to sit down as well.

The two hundred thousand people who had come spontaneously to participate in the memorial service and the soldiers who formed a broad wall between them and the steps in front of the Great Hall sat facing one another, waiting patiently for the ceremony to begin.

At 9:53 A.M. the loudspeakers in the square began a live broadcast of the proceedings. As those inside the Great Hall paid tribute to Hu Yaobang, the two hundred thousand in the square mourned in silence. The national anthem was played. Those inside the hall stood for a moment of silence, while outside the people sang the words. In the sky above the square banners wept, "Say one more farewell to Yaobang," "Let us see Yaobang one more time."

After twenty minutes, the ceremony came to a close. To the low strains of the dirge the people inside the hall lined up to pay their respects to Hu Yaobang's remains. At 10:30 A.M. the fleet of cars carrying high-ranking officials drove off from behind the police lines. The sea of mourners in the square moved toward the Great Hall.

At 10:40 A.M. the students began to chant rhythmically, "We want dialogue! We want dialogue!" At 11:05 A.M. a few representatives of the students approached the workers from the official mourning office and said, "We want to see Premier Li Peng and deliver a petition. We have no other demands. We just want to have a dialogue with the premier."

Around 11:40 A.M. the student demonstrators again chose four representatives to approach staff people in the Great Hall of the People to demand to see Premier Li Peng. The staff people asked, "How would it be if we delivered your petition for you?" The student representatives did not agree to this, but insisted on seeing Li Peng in person. They were told the request would be forwarded immediately and they would return with a reply. By then it was nearly 12:00 noon, and the students in the square began to chant, "Li Peng come out! Li Peng come out!" The citizens in the square chimed in. For a moment the sound "Li Peng come out!" echoed through the square like a thunderclap.

After 12:00 noon the student representatives returned to the Great Hall and found no one there. After some discussion, they announced, "If we have no reply by 12:45 P.M., the government will be responsible for the consequences." At 12:40 P.M. the staff people reappeared and said, "We would forward your request immediately but Premier Li Peng is not here." The thunderclap, "Li Peng come out!" echoed through the square once more.

At this time, the ten thousand cold and hungry students and citizens, who had been in the square for a whole night, found that they could see the funeral car no more, for it had left the west gate of the Great Hall at great speed toward Chang'an Street and the cemetery at Babaoshan. The people in the square were enraged. Their desire of paying a last tribute to the remains of Hu Yaobang had been totally ignored. They felt cheated and insulted by those arrogant government officials who held the will of the people in contempt.

It was now past 12:45 P.M. The students' only request remained unanswered. Guo Haifeng and two other representatives of the students dashed up the steps of the Great Hall of the People.

Then an extremely touching scene unfolded. There, under the imposing columns of the Great Hall of the People, the solemn symbol of the nation, three warm-blooded young men knelt down, holding a petition over their heads. The square suddenly fell silent. Several hundred thousand pairs of eyes all gazed at the three Chinese youths at the foot of the colossal pillars. They looked like three small figurines from a distance, yet at this moment they seemed huge to everyone in the square because they symbolized the conscience of China.

Then, following that brief moment of silence, came waves of sound, the sound of sobbing. Young women, normally shy, and young men, normally restrained, opened their hearts and cried until the sky was filled with the sound and the heroes' monument and the Great Hall shook with it.

Pearls fall. Listen to the pattering. Hard granite, do you know the strength of human tears?!

As they cried they shouted to the three who were kneeling on the steps of the Great Hall, "Get up! Get up! Get up!"

And all could see that the tears also welled up in the eyes of the soldiers. Guo Haifeng said to those workers who wanted him to get up, "I won't! We knelt for the national emblem, not for some person. The premier is the people's servant. He should have come out to talk with us. We didn't ask for an immediate reply, we only asked that he receive our petition." Chen Mingyuan, the academician from the Academy of Sciences whose poems during the Cultural Revolution were mistaken for Mao's and were widely admired, hugged one of the student representatives and burst into tears.

The conscience of China knelt on those hard steps for forty minutes, but there was no reply.

On May 3, the spokesman for the State Council held a press conference for Chinese and foreign journalists. He Dongchang, the vice-minister of the State Education Commission, said seriously, "On the morning of April 22 some people resorted to the old feudal practice of kneeling at the entrance of the Great Hall of the People."

"Resorted to the old feudal practice"—this was the official response to the Chinese people's expression of their conscience.

6. April 27: A Day that Will Live in History

On the 7:00 P.M. Central Broadcast Corporation news on April 25, anchorman Xing Zhibin solemnly announced that an editorial entitled "Resolutely oppose the instigation of turmoil" would appear in the *People's Daily* the next day. The editorial stated:

> This movement is a well-planned conspiracy; it is intended to instigate turmoil; it fundamentally negates the leadership of the Chinese Communist Party and the socialist system. This is a severe political struggle involving the whole party and the whole nation.

The tone and content of this editorial bring to mind many things that have happened in the past: the Anti–Hu Feng campaign of 1954, the Anti-Rightist campaign of 1957, the Anti–Right Deviation campaign of 1959, and the Tiananmen Incident of 1976. Those Chinese who have been through the worst might be reminded of still other things. Every Chinese could recognize this as a signal, a terrifying signal. Moreover, the experience of the past forty years teaches us that once such a signal is given it can never be revoked. Once the great hand of dictatorship is extended, it will never retract without making its catch.

At this moment countless people froze before their television sets in Beijing,

Tianjin, Shanghai and other large cities. Few were interested in the remaining news. Students, teachers, intellectuals, cadres, and workers alike wondered, "What can we do?"

The most worried were those older professors and teachers who had experienced the humiliation of the political struggles of the last several decades. They knew by their experience that disaster would inevitably descend on their campuses. But they did not know how to protect those brave and innocent students. They were pessimistic—there was nothing they could do.

After the initial shock the students responded quickly. That night several thousand Beijing University students took to the streets in a brief demonstration. Later, they gathered in front of the public address system of the Autonomous Student Association at the university triangle to listen to the speeches of their elected leaders.

The newly established Autonomous Student Association of Beijing University had held formal elections and undergone a reorganization after the events of April 22. In the meantime, because of various differences of opinion, serious divisions had emerged, leading to the abdication of two student leaders who had been especially active from the outset. This division aroused serious concern among many people who knew that internal dissension is especially dangerous for a newly established autonomous student organization.

But on the evening of April 25, the internal division came to an end. Those inexperienced young student leaders understood. The force they confronted was formidable. In China this kind of authoritarian force could smash at will anyone who opposed it.

At the same time, they knew that to retreat was suicide.

They would never retreat. They would stand up and carry on with their peaceful demonstration under the protection of the constitution.

Once again they broadcast the *People's Daily* editorial to their fellow students who gathered at the university triangle. A roar of protest arose from the crowd. Then the Autonomous Student Association declared to the students, "Our peaceful demonstration and demands for democracy are protected by the Constitution. We have no secret plan. We have only an open plan, a plan to accelerate the process of modernization in China."

The determination of the Autonomous Student Association received thunderous applause from the crowd. Students from Qinghua University, Beijing University, the University of Political Science and Law, People's University, and other institutions exchanged information and provided mutual support. The student association of the University of Political Science and Law wrote an open letter to the Autonomous Student Association of Beijing University, saying, "At this moment of darkness, at this crucial juncture for the nation, we the students of the University of Political Science and Law stand resolutely with the students of Beijing University to face this historical baptism of fire."

A tremendous gloom swept over the campuses in Beijing, Shanghai, Tianjin, and elsewhere.

After the event, one young Beijing intellectual said, "No intellectual with a conscience could sleep that night."

On the morning of April 26 the All-Beijing Autonomous Student Association held a press conference for Chinese and foreign correspondents in front of the main building of the University of Political Science and Law. At the news conference student leaders gave a briefing on the work of the association and the donations it had received from people of all walks of life. One leader said, "Today's editorial in the *People's Daily* has only strengthened our fighting spirit." His words won instantaneous support from thousands of students.

In the end the association's chairman announced, "On April 27, that is, tomorrow, there will be a major demonstration of all the institutions of higher learning in Beijing. The demonstration will begin at 8:00 A.M. We hope all our fellow students are fully prepared."

As the students prepared, so did certain government units. That night the CBC and Beijing television rebroadcast the Beijing Municipality's Ten Regulations for Demonstrations and issued a stern warning for students planning to participate in the demonstration.

On April 27 something unexpected happened, beginning at Qinghua University. Students later reported that some "Crown Prince Faction" students (children of high-ranking officials) who had somehow slipped into the Autonomous Student Association tried to stop the demonstration.[15] They said, "According to reliable sources, it would not be to our advantage to hold a demonstration today. The government will respond with very harsh measures. Large numbers of troops have already been despatched to Beijing. All sorts of modern antiriot equipment are at the ready. We're going to suffer heavily today."

At the same time the official Youth League committees and student associations at the various schools were ordered to make the following announcement to their fellow students:

> Teachers and fellow students! According to reliable sources, Qinghua University has decided not to participate in today's demonstration. The other universities will not demonstrate either. We hope that our fellow students will not take to the streets. Today's citywide demonstration has been cancelled.

Could it be true that a demonstration which would decide the fate of this recent student movement and that of China's democratization was going to

---

[15]The term "Crown Prince Faction" (*taizi dang*) is a recent addition to the popular culture, using the traditional term for the heir apparent to the imperial throne to refer to those offspring of high officials who often take advantage of their privileged position to gain wealth and power in the post-Mao era.

abort? And what was awaiting those students? The resolute, mature student leaders had demonstrated an outstanding organizational ability in the midst of crisis. And in the midst of crisis the mass of the students had also proved by their actions that the blood of passionate commitment flowed in their veins. Determined in their beliefs and with a dauntless spirit of self-sacrifice on behalf of the people's fate, they are the most excellent generation of students in Chinese history, the generation of which we can be most proud.

Despite the warnings, the student demonstrators came out. Many left wills on campus behind them, determined to sacrifice their lives for the country. "Remember me, Beijing University!" "Farewell, Beijing Normal University!" One after another the wills were posted on the campuses.

The brigade of students from the western campuses assembled around Huangzhuang, Zhongguancun, and the entrance to People's University.

The police formed a wall five rows deep at the intersection in front of People's University. A crowd of more than ten thousand citizens stood solemnly and watched. A young woman teacher from the Foreign Languages Institute wound her way through the crowd to the line of policemen and said to them one by one, "I beg you! I beg you! Don't beat the students! You are all the same generation! Don't beat them!" The policemen remained silent.

By 10:00 A.M. the students had finished assembling. The brigade of students, with People's University at the head, held high the banners of their schools and departments and chanted:

> People's U.! People's U.! Great are the people!
> For the people! Dare to tell the truth!
> Bleed for them! Sweat for them! Do not fear! Do not fear!

The excited crowd of spectators broke their silence and chanted along with the students, "Police make way! Police make way!" A large crowd of citizens with arms locked together advanced in a wave toward the five rows of police and opened a breach, but the police quickly dispersed them and regrouped.

The People's University demonstrators arrived under their school banner. A large number of citizens again charged in front of the students. The wall of policemen was breached by the combined charge of citizens and students, and the student brigade flowed through.

The huge brigade of Beijing University students went through as the People's University column had done, and chains of students formed on both sides of the demonstrators to prevent outsiders from forcing their way into the ranks. The Beijing University students shouted at the top of their lungs:

> Beijing U.! Beijing U.! We are not afraid! We are not afraid!
> No choice but strike! Equal dialogue!
> Petition for the people! Not afraid to shed our blood!
> Not afraid! Not afraid! We mean it: not afraid!

In the ranks of the students were their own first-aid teams, wearing white headbands or strips of white cloth on their chests with red cross signs and carrying first-aid kits. They were particularly eye-catching. When the spectators saw them they were moved to tears. The dauntless spirit of these young students, daring to face death, shook the boulevards of Beijing.

Between the ranks of People's University and Beijing University and behind the latter came some twenty institutions of higher learning, including Beijing National Minorities Institute, Beijing Jiaotong University, the Foreign Studies University, and Beijing Agricultural University. They shouted:

> Official profiteers! Official profiteers! If we don't attack, they won't fall!
> When the people rise up! With one blow they fall!

> Are we a small handful (of schemers)? No! "A revolutionary party should not fear the voice of the people! The thing to fear is that the people are silent!"—*The Selected Works of Deng Xiaoping*, p. 134.

Their slogans received round after round of applause. Qinghua University brought up the rear, shouting:

> Qinghua, Qinghua! Reared by the people!
> For the people, we will speak the truth!
> Do we have ulterior motives? No! Are we manipulated? No!
> We want rule of law, not rule by man!
> We want science, not sentiment! We want democracy, not dictatorship!
> Guarantee human rights; abolish privilege!
> Long live freedom! Long live democracy!
> Peaceful demonstration is not instigation of turmoil!

Rising to the sky from amidst the ranks of the students were great banners with slogans: "The fate of the country depends on everyone!" "Sincere dialogue; oppose violence!" "Truth in journalism!" "Democracy crippled!" "All men must die; but some die loyally for history to remember! "Humble but loyal to the country!" "Whoever would suppress the student movement is doomed—Mao Zedong!" "The Tiananmen Incident must not be repeated!" "If the old doesn't get out of the way, the new cannot come in!—Deng Xiaoping!"

Most eye-catching were the banners in the student ranks saying, "Support the Communist Party's correct leadership" and "Carry on with the reforms."

Students of about a dozen schools, including University of Political Science and Law, Beijing Normal University, Beijing Aeronautics and Space Technology University, assembled near North Taipingzhuang, marched along Xinwai Street to North Second Ring Road, and from there west to Chegongzhuang, where they joined the students taking the western route. Their ranks were also filled with banners and they marched in high spirits. Leading the Political

Science and Law unit were four strong male students shouldering a large wooden board, 3 x 2 meters, on which were written articles 35, 37, 38, and 41 of the Constitution of the People's Republic of China:

> Citizens of the People's Republic of China have freedom to speak, publish, assemble, associate, parade, and demonstrate.

> Citizens of the People's Republic of China have the right to criticize and make recommendations concerning all national government offices and all official personnel.

> Etc.

Behind this board was a huge banner proclaiming, "We will die to safeguard the Constitution." All the students of Beijing Medical University wore white gowns and carried simple first-aid kits. As they marched they came to the aid of other students and taught them how to aid themselves.

At the Chegongzhuang intersection tens of thousands of spectators gathered. Many offered the students bread, soda, popsicles or ice cream. In front of the students was a wall of policemen in four rows. The spectators shouted continuously, "Police make way! Police make way!" And they flowed in wave after wave toward the police.

Some students who sat in the road, waiting, sent representatives to exhort the citizens not to press the police.

The students taking the western route broke through the blockades at several points and joined the ranks of those coming from Beijing Normal College and others, then marched en masse east to the Chegongzhuang intersection. At the intersection, the two columns merged and the spectacle became even grander. By now the police made way almost automatically. The demonstrators shouted slogans as they marched toward Changan Avenue with the support of tens of thousands of citizens. Well over a hundred thousand strong, the procession of students had not cleared the intersection in the first hour.

One especially eye-catching banner had only four words: "It's been seventy years!" Seventy years have passed since the May Fourth Movement's call for science and democracy spread over the land. What more could one say? The implication of these four words is indeed profound.

On another banner were the words, "Work without pay, life goes astray!"

One young female student held a small banner proclaiming, "Here I am, mom!" The spectators were visibly moved.

Another said, "I'm not wrong, mom!"

On the banner of Beijing Normal College was a couplet: "Haggard and sallow, our teachers starve; its education in crisis, the country's flowers wither."

A male student from People's University held a board wrapped in black cloth with fifty or sixty photos. The title was "Witnesses." The photos were evidence of the confrontation that had occurred between students and police on April 20 and April 22.

All along the route, a wall of spectators expressed admiration and respect for the students. Constantly they offered food and donations to the students. As the students passed under pedestrian overpasses, people tossed food down from above. To express their gratitude the students shouted, "Long live the people!"

At one intersection people held up a traffic sign saying, "Return safely home!" In response the students shouted, "Don't worry! We will come safely home!"

Women cried and men held back their tears. The students, our students, the students who demonstrate for us, they are students who represent the conscience of the nation!

Two Italian students who joined the march said excitedly, "We often have demonstrations in our country, but not like yours. You really do 'have nothing to lose,' and you are not doing it for yourselves but for the people. You are really great!"

At the same time, student demonstrators from Beijing Chemical Engineering Institute, Beijing College of Chinese Medicine and others marched via the eastern route towards Dongdan, shouting slogans and singing songs. Tens of thousands of citizens watched as box after box of popsicles was placed in the students' hands.

When the western column reached Xidan it was blocked by some ten rows of people. It was already after 2:00 P.M. One banner rose from the crowd: "This is the will of the people!" and the spectators cheered enthusiastically.

With the strong support of the people the student demonstrators broke through the blockade and reached Liubukou.

There was already a massive crowd at Liubukou, and the police appeared ready to stand their ground. The crowd chanted continuously, "Police make way! No beating!"

By that time Changan Avenue was jampacked from east to west. The only exception was Tiananmen Square and the area immediately surrounding it, as it had been occupied by PLA troops since morning. As people cheered from their perches in trees, on walls, on signboards and sidewalks on all sides, the students broke through the police blockade at Liubukou, passed by Xinhuamen, and marched toward Tiananmen.

As the column of students pressed through the crowd, they remained well organized. Arm-in-arm, chains of student marshals formed on both sides to hold back the crowd and plead for their help in making way. When the students reached Xinhuamen the slogans echoed even more loudly: "*People's Daily*—a pack of lies! Central Broadcasting—never a word of truth! *Beijing Daily*—so much bullshit! *Guangming Daily*—a bunch of renegades!"

The quotations from Deng Xiaoping's works, the "Internationale," and "Not afraid! Not afraid! We mean it: not afraid!'' emanated from Xinhuamen and filled the air for the entire length of Changan Avenue.

As soon as the students passed Xinhuamen the troops in the square were ordered to withdraw. No sooner had their trucks disappeared than tens of thousands of citizens poured into the square. Many people stopped trucks, whose license plates had been removed, and shouted, ''The people's army loves the people'' and other slogans. Some climbed onto the trucks and read student leaflets taking issue with the *People's Daily* editorial to the soldiers. It was the second time in one day these troops had been stopped by the people of Beijing. Upon their arrival in Beijing that morning, as they reached Fuxingmen, they had been stopped by thousands of citizens including cadres, intellectuals, and workers. Some had climbed onto the trucks and said to the soldiers, ''You cannot beat the students. They are speaking for you, too, in their demonstrations. If you come from the country, you know your parents pay too much for fertilizer and get too little for their grain.'' One old man said to a colonel who had just got off a truck, ''You don't seem so young yourself. How can you think of doing something like crushing these students. Just look at them! They are our hope, our pride and joy!''

Around 4:00 P.M., the students arrived on the north side of the Great Hall of the People and came to a halt. Student marshals went ahead to persuade the people who had climbed onto the trucks to come down and make way for the trucks so they could proceed to Qianmen. Then the students marched across Tiananmen Square toward Jianguomen. It was nearly 5:00 P.M. and the rear of the procession had not yet cleared Fuxingmen, west of Xidan.

On the south side of the Wangfujing intersection there is a huge electronic signboard of the *Beijing Daily*. As the students passed they once again chanted: ''*Beijing Daily*—so much bullshit! *Beijing Daily*—so much bullshit!'' The crowd alongside joined in the chanting.

Countless arms waved from the Beijing Hotel and the Ministry of the Chinese Textile Industry. People also waved from the buses that were parked nearby.

Whenever the students came upon a unit of police they raised their voices and shouted, ''The people's police love the people; the people love the people's police!'' They sang the theme song from the TV series ''Plainclothes Police.'' And tears came to the eyes of many policemen, too. Some extended arms and made the ''V'' sign, wishing the students victory.

On both sides of the road people were talking, ''The police are not so bad today.'' Someone said, ''They don't dare beat the students. Their mothers wouldn't let them in the house!'' One student from Beijing University said, ''When the students and the police were pressing against each other, there were even some policemen who put money in the students' hands!''

Some provincials who stood by the road gasped, ''Only in Beijing!''

As they marched, trying to keep their ranks, some had to run to catch up.

Seeing some of the younger girls exhausted and still running (they had already marched a good ten miles), the spectators urged them, "Students! Slow down a little! Students! There's still a long way to go! Take it easy! Don't overdo it!" Even more people sighed, "Good for them! These kids! What are they doing this for? For us!"

Along the Second Ring Road at Jianguomen, Chaoyangmen, Dongsishitiao, Andingmen, Deshengmen, Huokou, tens of thousands of people waited for the students, saluting them and shouting support. It was already evening, and wherever the students went, loud cheers and slogans were heard. The students had shouted themselves hoarse, but they continued to raise their arms and shout. The massive crowd continued to respond, "Down with corruption! Up with democracy!" The Second Ring Road had become an avenue of triumph, every overpass a gate of triumph.

One spectator commented, "Marx once said, 'Revolution is a festival of the people,' but I never really understood what it meant until today."

On April 27, more than a million citizens watched or joined the student demonstration. It was unprecedented in Chinese history.

It was getting late. In front of all the universities massive crowds waited at the gates for the patriotic students to return.

At Beijing Normal University, teachers and staff members raised a huge banner: "Proud sons of heaven, the people thank you!"

At Haidian, the local people were still waiting for the students to return at 1:00 A.M.

At People's University, younger instructors and staff members joined the students who were ill or otherwise unable to participate in welcoming the students back with firecrackers. The cafeteria prepared a special hot meal and many people donated money on the spot. One private merchant went out of his way to give two cases of beer.

The Beijing and Qinghua University students did not get back until 2:00 or 3:00 A.M., having marched a good thirty miles in the past sixteen or seventeen hours.

White-haired professors, department heads, and staff members greeted them with drums, gongs, and firecrackers. Finally the students had returned. Old professors came up to the students, found their own, and hugged them tightly, tears running down their cheeks.

The next day the old professors at Beijing University put up a poster saying, "The teachers learn from the students, the students are the teachers."

Beijing's millions were happy and proud when the students made it home safely from the demonstration of April 27. Yet little did they know that on that day all of Beijing's hospitals had received an urgent notice: "Be prepared to treat wounded students. If there are no beds free for emergency patients, make some ready. Offer treatment first, arrange for payment later, or treat for free."

According to one inside source who prefers to remain anonymous, "It wasn't until 2:00 P.M. on the 27th that the Central Committee decided not to use military force to crush the students.''

And so it was that April 27 passed without the anticipated violent confrontation. That day was a great day, a historic day. On that day, for the first time in forty years, China's students stood under no one's umbrella. With a clear and concrete political purpose in mind, they appeared on China's political stage as a mature and formidable political force.

7. May Fourth: A Triumph

On April 27, as the student demonstrators passed through Tiananmen toward Jianguomen, the radio broadcast a speech by the State Council spokesman. The tone was quite different from the hard line of the *People's Daily* editorial of the previous day. The spokesman said, "The party and the government welcome the students' demand for dialogue. The party has always believed in direct dialogue with the masses, but dialogue requires a suitable atmosphere and a proper procedure."

On the same day, the New China News Agency in Shanghai reported, "In light of the serious violation of regulations by Comrade Qin Benli, the editor-in-chief of the *World Economic Herald*, the Shanghai Party Committee has decided to remove him from his positions as editor-in-chief and member of the Party Committee, and to assign a rectification team to the newspaper."

According to the New China News Agency, the reason for Qin Benli's dismissal was that the *World Economic Herald* had devoted several pages to a detailed report on the meeting of April 24 in memory of Hu Yaobang, and that some of that reporting was extremely unhelpful to the effort to stabilize the current situation and would confuse the issues in people's minds.

On April 28 and 29, more than a thousand reporters and editors from Beijing and elsewhere around the country sent a telegram to the Shanghai Party Committee supporting Qin Benli and protesting the committee's decision.

On April 28, Qinghua University received a notice from the Beijing United Student Association stating that the State Education Commission, the Beijing Party Committee, and the Beijing city government had agreed to a dialogue with the Qinghua University student representatives. The meeting was set for 2:30 P.M. at the Beijing city government conference hall. After some discussion, the representatives selected by the Qinghua students concluded that because the demand for dialogue had come from the students of all the universities of Beijing, the Qinghua students could not engage in such a dialogue independently, and so they refused the offer for dialogue.

On the morning of April 29, State Council spokesman Yuan Mu, Vice-Minister of the State Education Commission He Dongchang, Beijing Party Committee Standing Committee member Yuan Liben, and others were designated to hold a dialogue with the students from more than a dozen institutions of higher learning in Beijing. Yuan Mu opened the dialogue by conveying Premier Li Peng's words. Li Peng said, "When the *People's Daily* editorial mentioned a small handful of people with ulterior motives this did not refer to the students. The government is in agreement with the students' demands concerning corruption and reform."

When it came time for the students to speak, they all stated that they did not represent the students of their respective institutions because they were not elected, but designated, by the schools. The dialogue lasted three and a half hours of which only slightly more than two and a half hours were televised.

According to students who attended the meeting, during parts of the meeting that were not shown, He Dongchang pounded the table, and Yuan Mu interrupted the last student speaker because he claimed to be the representative of the All-Beijing Autonomous Student Association.

The reactions of different groups of people in the capital varied. Some newspapers, such as *Women of China* and *Economic Daily*, reported some of the reactions.

But the reaction of Beijing's university students was extreme anger. Big-character posters appeared all over, condemning the students who took part in the dialogue as scabs. The poster-writers felt these students had given away at the conference table what all had won on Chang'an Avenue. But their greatest anger was reserved for Yuan Mu and the other officials, whom they thought did not engage in a dialogue but delivered a lecture. The posters touted a popular new piece of doggerel that played on the officials' names:

Climbing Trees to Look for Fish
[Yuan mu qiu yu]

With your ugly faces in charge, how can the country sink its roots?
With this for a dialogue, how can the nation make the East prosper?

[N.B. "Climbing trees" sounds like Yuan Mu; (Yuan) Liben means "sink its roots"; (He) Dongchang means "make the East prosper."]

Around May 1, a large number of students from Beijing's universities fanned out across the country, made contact with universities in the provinces and briefed them on the student movement in Beijing.

On May 2, the All-Beijing Autonomous Student Association was formally established by the process of student elections. The association, which represented the students of more than fifty institutions of higher learning, drafted a twelve-point petition outlining procedures for a dialogue. The petition was delivered to the State Council and the Standing Committee of the National People's Congress at noon on May 2. It reads as follows:

To the Standing Committee of the National People's Congress, the State Council, and the Central Committee of the Chinese Communist Party:

After the April 27 demonstration the government expressed through the news media its willingness to hold a dialogue with the students. We welcome this response. In order to accelerate the process and achieve a genuine dialogue, we, the elected representatives of all the students of Beijing, put forward on their behalf the following demands:

1. The two parties should agree to a dialogue on the basis of complete equality and a sincere desire to solve the problems addressed. In the course of the dialogue, both parties should have equal opportunity to speak and to respond.

2. The students who participate in the dialogue should be recognized by the majority of the students of Beijing's institutions of higher learning (especially those students who participated in the patriotic democratic movement in April) as their official representatives. At the same time, whereas we believe the established student associations of all the undergraduate and graduate institutions were totally ineffective in organizing and advising the students during this movement, we object to the designation of representatives of these student associations, and we refuse to recognize any student representative who has not been approved by the great majority of the students but invited unilaterally by the government side.

3. We propose the following method of selecting the student representatives. Whereas the All-Beijing Autonomous Student Association, which is a product of spontaneous student organization, played a leading role in organizing the movement, and whereas this leadership has been approved by the great majority of the students, let the Association serve as the coordinating body and let the students of each university select a certain number of representatives in proportion to its size, those representatives composing the student delegation. After a full discussion within the delegation, a certain number of representatives will be selected to serve as principal spokesmen for the student side, and the remaining representatives will have the right to observe and to question the spokesmen for the government side.

4. The participants on the government side should come from ranks no lower than members of the Standing Committee of the Politburo, vice-chairman of the Standing Committee of the National People's Congress, vice-premier of the State Council—those who are both familiar with and have decision-making power in all aspects of state affairs.

5. The dialogue must allow both sides to invite private individuals or group representatives to participate and observe, and neither side can for any reason object to or prevent their participation. Anyone thus invited will not have the right to speak at the dialogue but will have the right to comment afterwards on the substance of the dialogue.

6. Spokesmen for both sides will have the same rights concerning the opportunity to speak. Spokesmen for both sides will be subject to a time limit. Answers to queries will be limited to three minutes; the question and answer period for a given speaker will be limited to ten to fifteen minutes, and the spokesmen will be allowed to answer any number of queries within that time.

7. While the dialogue is in progress, foreign and Chinese journalists will be allowed to interview and broadcast live, and Chinese Central Television and Central Broadcasting should carry the entire proceeding live. Both sides have the right to photograph and record the proceedings. No person or group may

for any reason intervene or obstruct the proceedings.

8. The dialogue should be held alternately at places to be designated by the government and the student representatives. The timing will be decided by negotiation.

9. Government participants during the dialogue should answer questions to the best of their ability and, after the dialogue, should do their utmost to solve the problems discussed. If there are questions that cannot be answered immediately, then they should be settled at a second round of discussions to be arranged within a limited time period. Neither side may object to the above for any reason.

10. To guarantee the legal effectiveness of the results of the dialogue, the two sides will issue a signed joint communiqué concerning the results.

11. The physical and political safety of the representatives on both sides should be guaranteed.

12. After each round of talks, the major newspapers and broadcasting stations throughout the country must make a truthful report, publicize the communiqué, and announce the time, the place, and other particulars of the next round of talks.

In connection with the above demands we also make the following statement:

1. To insure the dialogue will be held as soon as possible, we hope to receive a reply to the above demands by 12:00 noon on May 3. Each specific demand should have a concrete response and the rationale for each response should be given in writing.

2. If we receive no reply by 12:00 noon on May 3, we will reserve the right to continue the demonstration on May 4.

3. We suggest that the first round of talks be held at Beijing University at 8:30 A.M. on May 4.

4. A copy of this petition will be sent to the People's Political Consultative Conference.

On the morning of May 3, State Council spokesman Yuan Mu held a press conference for Chinese and foreign journalists at the All-China Journalists' Federation. At this press conference he said of the students' petition, "The true intention of this petition, being essentially an ultimatum, is to threaten us." He went on to say, "Dialogue can only be based on mutual trust and sincerity. There can be no prior conditions." Yuan Mu flatly refused to accept the students' proposal concerning procedures for the dialogue, but still he said, "I hope there will be no large-scale demonstration tomorrow."

That afternoon the All-Beijing Autonomous Student Association held a press conference of its own at Beijing Normal University and announced their decision to hold a demonstration on May 4. Representatives from more than twenty institutions of higher learning all over China (including the Chinese University of Hong Kong) described the state of the student movement at their respective schools and declared their intention to participate in the demonstration of May 4. They also announced that in all the major cities of China, including Hong Kong, there would be a positive response to the Beijing students' decision concerning a general nationwide May Fourth demonstration.

From the very beginning, the May Fourth demonstration was more like a victory celebration than a protest movement. The first-aid teams of the previous marches were replaced by three loudspeaker trucks. There was an even greater variety of banners and leaflets. Although there were fewer demonstrators than on April 27, the broad participation of more than forty institutions from all across the country made it seem even more spectacular. New banners announced the appearance of schools that had not participated before, such as the Academy of Political Science for Youth, the Lu Xun Literary Academy, and Haidian Commuter College.

One banner identified the younger faculty of Beijing University amongst the demonstrators, and the white heads of older professors were also seen among their ranks. The tenor of the slogans on the banners was different from that of April 27. Most noticeable was the absence of banners saying things like "Support the Communist Party." Only one banner proclaimed, "Long live (a) Clean Chinese Communist Party!" Among the banners were new slogans like "M.A.'s, Ph.D.'s have nothing but their consciences," "Dialogue requires sincerity," and "End gerontocracy."

Students also shouted new slogans, such as, "Dialogue! Dialogue! Not a pedant's monologue! Speak sincerely or shut up!" and "Yuan Mu speak up! Who are the 'small handful!' "

A large number of citizens joined the students of their own accord, rapidly swelling the demonstrators' ranks.

By noon, several hundred correspondents from various media in the capital had gathered at the entrance to the New China News Agency. They raised their arms and shouted, "Truth in the media!" and "Freedom of the press!" From there, they proceeded to Fuxingmennei, where they merged with the student procession. The journalists were warmly welcomed by the students and citizens the instant they arrived.

State Council spokesman Yuan Mu swore by his experience of more than twenty years as a journalist that China had no news censorship and that China enjoyed freedom of the press. Now several hundred journalists raised this moving banner: "We want to speak the truth; don't make us lie!"

All along the way these especially visible marchers were continually joined by other news media workers. A retired New China News Agency reporter in her sixties brought a large bag full of bottled yoghurt for her colleagues. Another elderly editor joined the ranks accompanied by his wife. When someone asked, "Hey, who let an old guy like you in here!" He answered, "My conscience is to blame!" Xidan, Liubukou, Xinhuamen, Nanchangjie, Tiananmen. As the marchers progressed loud applause and cheering could be heard all along the way. Everywhere spectators reached out from the crowds to shake the hands of the journalists. Soda bottle after soda bottle, popsicle after popsicle, found their way into the journalists' hands. Even more people raised their arms and made a "V" for victory.

Around 2:00 P.M. the demonstrators entered Tiananmen Square. It was exceptionally hot. Many of the female students suffered sunstroke and had to be carried to the side, including one M.S. student from the Institute of Zoology, Chinese Academy of Sciences.

At 2:30 P.M., tens of thousands of students sat on the ground in Tiananmen Square and read aloud the "May Fourth Declaration": "We have only one purpose—to realize China's modernization."

At 3:30 P.M., at the square, the spokesman for the All-Beijing Autonomous Student Association made the following announcement: "Beginning May 5 all students will return to their classes, but the demand for dialogue will continue!"

8. Chinese Intellectuals Have Stood Up

From the outset of this patriotic democracy movement, China's intellectuals consistently and enthusiastically supported the students. They worried for them, rejoiced for them, and shouted encouragement to them. Some even joined in the processions. This support shows how the role of China's intellectuals as a social elite is maturing and solidifying. As early as April 21, some 140 teachers from Beijing University wrote an open letter to the party Central Committee, the National People's Congress, the Chinese People's Political Consultative Conference, and the State Council asking the government to respond seriously to the students' demands.

Three older senior professors from Beijing Normal University, Liu Liao, Zheng Huazhi, and Dong Yanguo, also sent an open letter to the government on April 24, demanding that it respect the law and restrain itself from using violence against the students. They, too, demanded acceleration of the process of democratization and abolition of unlimited tenure in office. They also pointed out that any attempt to obstruct political democratization would not be accepted by the people.

One thousand and thirteen journalists from thirty news organizations, including the *People's Daily*, New China News Agency, *Guangming Daily*, *Science and Technology Daily*, *Peasants' Daily*, *China's Talent*, *Women of China*, and *Economic Daily*, signed a letter demanding a dialogue with those in charge of propaganda work in the party Central Committee. That letter was delivered to the All-China Journalists' Federation on the afternoon of May 9. Many veteran journalists signed their names.

On May 13, more than thirty scholars, artists and writers jointly drafted a declaration entitled "May Sixteenth Declaration," soliciting signatures of Chinese intellectuals at home and abroad. They urged Chinese intellectuals to enter onto China's political stage and act as a mature, unified, and independent social force on behalf of modernization.

The complete text of the declaration is as follows:

The May Sixteenth Declaration

The "May Sixteenth Directive" of 1966 is universally acknowledged by the Chinese people as a symbol of autocracy and darkness. Today, twenty-three years later, we find democracy and enlightenment strongly appealing. History has finally reached a turning point. At present, a patriotic democracy movement led by young students is rising across the country. Over the short period of less than a month, in one wave after another, large-scale demonstrations have swept through Beijing and other cities. Several hundred thousand students have taken to the streets protesting corruption and calling for democracy and the rule of law. They have expressed the common will of workers, peasants, soldiers, cadres, intellectuals, and all other classes of working people. This is a national awakening which not only draws on the spirit of May Fourth, but also goes beyond it. It is a great historical moment that will determine the fate of China.

Since the Third Plenum of the Eleventh Party Congress, China has embarked on a course of national revitalization. But there are problems. The weakness of political reform has affected the economic reform, when the latter has only begun to show results. The problem of corruption is getting worse and the social contradictions are intensified. The reforms in which the people put so much hope face a grave crisis. At this crucial moment, a moment which will determine the fate of the people, the country, and the ruling party, we, the undersigned Chinese intellectuals at home and abroad, on May 16, 1989, do solemnly and openly declare allegiance to the following principles:

1. We believe that in dealing with the current student movement the party and the government have not been rational enough. This is especially clear in the recent use of pressure tactics and threats of force against the students. We should draw a lesson from history. The Beijing government in 1919, the Guomindang government in the 1930s and 1940s, the Gang of Four in the late 1970s all these dictatorial regimes used force against student movements and in each case it led to their disgrace in the eyes of history. History tells us, "Whoever would crush the student movement is doomed." Recently the party and the government have shown a welcome increase in the use of reason, and the tension has been alleviated somewhat. If we apply principles of modern democratic governance, respect the people's will and respond to changing times, then we will see a democratic and stable China. If we do not, then a very hopeful China will be pushed into an abyss of genuine turmoil.

2. If we want to solve the current political crisis democratically, the first step must be to recognize the legality of the autonomous student organization which consists of the democratically elected representatives of the students. Not to do so is to violate the constitutional right of freedom of assembly. To label the student organization as "illegal" can only lead to intensification of conflict and further crisis.

3. The immediate cause of the current political crisis is the corruption these

young students have rightly opposed with their patriotic movement. The greatest mistake of the past ten years of reform is not the failure of education but the neglect of political reform. Totally untouched, the "official standard" and feudal privileges have infected the world of exchange, and that has led to rampant corruption. This has not only devoured the fruits of economic reform but also shaken the people's faith in the party and the government. The party and the government should take this lesson to heart and, in accordance with the people's will, immediately advance the political reform, abolish official privilege and profiteering and guarantee that corruption will be eliminated.

4. During the student movement, the press, represented by the *People's Daily* and the New China News Agency, have concealed the truth, depriving the people of their right to know. The Shanghai Party Committee dismissed Qin Benli from his position as editor-in-chief of the *World Economic Herald*. These totally wrong measures are greatly contemptuous of the Constitution. Freedom of the press is an effective tool for eliminating corruption, maintaining national stability, and promoting social development. Absolute power corrupts absolutely. If we do not implement freedom of the press, and do not allow unofficial publications, then all the promises of openness and reform are nothing but empty words.

5. It is a mistake to call the student movement antiparty, antisocialist political turmoil. To recognize and protect the right of citizens to express different political opinions is the basic meaning of freedom of speech. Since liberation the true purpose of all the political campaigns has been to suppress and attack different political opinions. A society with only one voice is not a stable society. The party and the government must review the lessons of the "Anti–Hu Feng campaign," the "Anti-Rightist campaign," the "Cultural Revolution," the "Anti–spiritual pollution campaign," and the "Anti–bourgeois liberalization campaign." They must allow a broad expression of opinions and engage in discussion with the young students, intellectuals, and the whole people about state policy. Only then will it be possible for a genuinely stable and unified political system to take shape.

6. It is a mistake to say that there is a "small handful of long-bearded manipulators" behind the scenes. All the citizens of the People's Republic of China, regardless of their ages, are politically equal. All have the political right to participate in discussion about government. Freedom, democracy, and the rule of law are not things that will some day simply be granted to the people from above. All truth-seeking, freedom-loving people must strive to achieve what the constitution promises: freedom of thought, freedom of speech, freedom of the press, freedom of publication, freedom of association, freedom of assembly, and freedom of demonstration.

We have arrived at a historical turning point. We, the long-suffering people, cannot afford to miss this opportunity. There is no place to retreat to.

All patriotic and concerned Chinese intellectuals should realize their inescapable historical mission, step forward to advance the cause of democracy, and strive for a politically democratic, economically developed modern China.

Long live the people!

Long live a free, democratic socialist motherland!

Signed at Beijing
May 16, 1989

Liu Zaifu, Yan Jiaqi, Bao Zunxin, Fan Zeng, Su Shaozhi, Su Xiaokang, Xu Gang, Su Wei, Su Shunkang, Li Tuo, Lao Mu, Lao Gui, Ke Zhilu, Wang Luxiang, Feng Lisan, Chen Lizu, Xu Xing, Wang Runsheng, Gao Gao, Xie Xuanjun, Xia Jun, Shen Dade, Wu Tingjia, Yuan Zhiming, He Huaihong, Zhang Boquan, Chen Xuanliang, Wang Zhaojun, Zhao Yu, Cheng Yi, Liu Ying, Han Hong, Deng Zhenglai, Yazi, He Shaofa, Zhu Shaoping. . .

The signing continues.

9. The Whole World Is Moving Forward

On May 4, just as several hundred thousand citizens attracted by movements in dozens of institutions of higher learning marched as in a victory celebration in Beijing, Party General Secretary Zhao Ziyang returned from a trip to North Korea. In a meeting with the head of a delegation attending the twenty-second annual meeting of the Board of Governors of the Asian Development Bank, he light-heartedly said,

> Although some of Beijing's students and students elsewhere are continuing their demonstrations, I believe the situation will gradually quiet down. There will not be large-scale turmoil in China. I am fully confident about this.
>
> What is needed now is calm, reason, restraint, order, and a solution to the problems arrived at in a way that is consistent with democracy and the rule of law. We also need to open extensive dialogues with students, workers, intellectuals, the democratic parties, and people from all walks of life. In a way that is consistent with democracy and the rule of law, in a rational and orderly manner, we must exchange opinions, promote understanding, and come together to discuss and solve the problems that all are concerned about.

On May 5, Premier Li Peng reiterated the points raised by Zhao Ziyang.

That evening Beijing University students engaged in a debate at the university triangle over whether to return to classes or to continue the boycott of classes. The result was that the majority wanted to continue the boycott. Their reasoning was that none of the demands for which they had begun the boycott had yet been met. If they returned to class now their hard-earned advantage would be lost overnight.

On May 6, the Beijing University Autonomous Student Association sponsored a poll in the dorms to determine whether they should return to class or continue the boycott. The majority still voted to continue the boycott.

Students at Beijing Normal and other universities also continued their boycott.

On May 9, more than three thousand students bicycled to the All-China Journalists' Federation to voice their support for the petition signed by 1,013 journalists demanding a direct dialogue with the leadership of the party Central Committee. The students shouted, "To speak for the people is the most important thing! Unite for a stronger China!'' Then they biked to the offices of the *People's Daily* and shouted more slogans protesting the recent publication of articles bending the truth about the patriotic democratic student movement and the threatening editorial of April 26.

On May 10, tens of thousands of students and some writers in Beijing held a bicycle demonstration. Their slogan was, ''Sell the Mercedes Benzes and pay off the national debt!''

On May 13, some five hundred students from Beijing University, Beijing Normal, and four other institutions formed the Beijing Students' Hunger Strike Group.

On the morning of the thirteenth, some ten thousand students held a solemn ceremony on the Beijing University campus to see the hunger strikers off. The younger faculty of Beijing University used their own meager salaries to throw a banquet for the hunger striking students at the Spring Swallow Garden.

At 2:00 P.M. on May 13, the five hundred hunger strikers assembled at Beijing Normal University, marched via Xinwaidajie, Xinjiekou, Xisi, and Xidan to Tiananmen Square.

Five female students from Beijing Normal raised a banner to send off the hunger strikers: ''Rice is delicious and steak is even better; for the sake of freedom, both can be given up.'' [After a verse by the Hungarian poet Petöfi: ''Life is extremely precious and love is even more so; for the sake of freedom, both can be given up.''] The hunger strikers wore white headbands and white sashes with the words ''No choice but to fast,'' ''We have nothing but the blood in our veins; we want nothing but a strong and prosperous China,'' ''I swear to live or die with democracy,'' ''Give me liberty or give me death,'' ''It is not that I love rice less, but that I love truth more,'' ''The wind blows chill, the Yi River runs cold; I shall achieve my purpose even though I will not return alive [a variation on an ancient poem describing the thoughts of Jing Ke, who sought to assassinate the First Emperor]'' or ''The country belongs to the people, not to 'a small handful.' ''

Wherever the hunger strikers passed, the people in the street showed their respect. Tens of thousands of students escorted the hunger strikers to Tiananmen.

At 4:00 P.M. they entered the square. At 4:30 P.M. the hunger strikers took an oath to fast, and a representative read the hunger strikers' declaration aloud:

> Since the great patriotic democratic movement of April and May began, we have consistently engaged in a series of peaceful activities to promote the process of democratization in China: the April 20 sit-in at Xinhuamen, the April 22 petition at Tiananmen, the April 27 citywide demonstration, the May 4th large-scale demonstration. We have demanded an equal, open, and direct dialogue with the government, but the government has publicly responded to our requests with deception and insults. On May 6 we petitioned the government once again, requesting a definite response by May 8. But on May 11, the government said only that it would do its best to offer a definite response

within the week. We can no longer tolerate this kind of deception by continuous postponement. To express our determination and to vigorously protest, we hereby resort to petition by hunger strike, urging the government to engage in a genuine dialogue with the All-Beijing Autonomous Student Association.

The Hunger Strike Group of the University Students of Beijing
May 13, 1989

Then the five hundred hunger strikers all solemnly raised their right arms, made fists and took an oath together:

I hereby swear that of my own free will, and in order to promote the democratization of China, I will engage in a fast, will abide by the rules of the Hunger Strike Group, and will not give up until our purpose is achieved!

The sound of the oath rolled like thunder over the heads of the assembled crowd, over Tiananmen, over the Great Hall of the People, over the Museum of Chinese History, and over the towering Monument to the People's Heroes.

Old man China, how can this sound thundering from the bottoms of the hearts of these, your fine sons and daughters, not awaken you from your deep slumber of five thousand years! Democracy and science have been pounding at your door for seventy years, and the sound grows steadily faster and louder. Can you really remain silent forever?

Once the oath was taken, the five hundred brave hunger strikers sat silently at the center of the square and began their long, hard life-and-death struggle.

Without the slightest hesitation one student after another joined the ranks of the hunger strikers. As more and more students heard the news, they came from their various schools to take the oath and join the fast. By 10:30 P.M., the number of hunger strikers in Tiananmen Square had increased to more than three thousand. Even more students brought padded quilts, overcoats, and padded sleeping mats, doing their best to contribute to the cause. At 11:00 P.M. some students arrived from Qinghua University to prepare for the arrival of a thousand Qinghua students who had organized a hunger strike group and were on their way to Tiananmen. The same day, a group of petitioners from the universities of Shanghai arrived in Beijing. Also the same day, more than a thousand students from Nankai University in Tianjin braved strong winds and took to the Beijing-Tianjin highway on bicycles to join the petitioners in Beijing.

The whole world is moving forward.

10. The Hunger Strike "Shakes Heaven and Earth and Moves the Gods to Tears"

Hunger strike! Hunger strike! Hunger strike!

With the hunger strike the student movement has reached new heights. Does heaven have feelings? Do spirits exist? If so, how can they not be moved? Impossible that they not be moved. Even heaven and earth are crying, and the spirits must be moved.

China, venerable China, how many times have you been the first in human history and how many times the greatest among civilizations? Yet, along with the pride and the splendor, how often has your greatness brought sorrow and humiliation?

Silent grief, silent sorrow, silent indignation, silent death, silent rebirth.

First ten, then a hundred, then a thousand, and finally more than two thousand. And they fall, one by one, until the ground is covered with their weakening bodies. Another great f⸺ t in the history of human civilization is about to appear! Pay up! Pay up! Pay with your blood, pay with your flesh, pay with your hearts! The world is shocked at the price. Must it always be pay up, sacrifice, and be silent?

China, my motherland, your neighbor India won independence with "non-violence and non-cooperation," and, through fasting, was reborn. Still, she did not pay with the lives of so many of her children. Dear mother, how can you be so cold and callous toward your own flesh and blood? I, a citizen, indict you before the court of human civilization! I testify that I have lost all faith and all hope in you! I, a citizen of the world of the future, curse you! Be dead! May you soon die in labor and may the newborn child survive! My country will be a lovely and vivacious young girl, not an ugly old hag! I can only love the young girl and discard the old woman.

One day, two days, ten days, twenty days. Still no dialogue. The fasting students no longer care for dialogue. They have chosen silence. They have placed their lives on the line before the government, before the people, before history, before the world, and announced: "We will break out of silence, or die in silence!"[16]

A leaflet with this deeply touching letter spread the news of the hunger strikers' silent vigil throughout the country:

Hunger Striker's Letter

In the bright, warm sunshine of May, we have begun to fast. In this precious springtime of our lives, however unwillingly, however reluctantly, we cannot but leave all of life's beautiful things behind.

The state of the nation has come to this: prices are soaring, official pro-fiteering is rampant, power is concentrated at the top, the bureaucracy is filled with corruption, large numbers of dedicated and capable people are forced into exile, and the social order is rapidly deteriorating. At this critical moment of life or death for the nation, fellow countrymen, all of you who have a con-science, hear our plea!

---

[16]Quoting Lu Xun. See "Jinian Liu Hezhen jun" [In Memory of Miss Liu Hezhen] in *Lu Xun quan ji* [Complete Works of Lu Xun](1983), 3:275.

This land is our land, the people are our people, the government is our government. If we do not cry out, who will cry out? If we do not take action, who will take action? Although we are too young and weak to bear the heavy burden of death, we have chosen death and cannot do otherwise, because history demands it of us. Our patriotic feelings are pure, our hearts sincere and loyal, but we have been accused of "causing turmoil," of "harboring ulterior motives," and of "being used by a handful of conspirators."

We plead with every true Chinese citizen, with every worker, peasant, soldier, townsperson, intellectual, dignitary, government official, policeman, and everyone who would accuse us: Put your hand on your heart and ask your conscience, what crime have we committed? Are we causing the turmoil? We boycott classes, demonstrate, fast and dedicate our lives, but for what?! Our feelings have been played with. We starve ourselves in the pursuit of truth, but we are beaten by the police. . . . The student representatives demanded democracy, but they were ignored. The demand for equal dialogue has been postponed again and again, and the student leaders' lives are in great danger. . . .

What should we do?

Democracy is the noblest of basic human needs; freedom is the inalienable birthright of every person. But in order to get them, we have to sacrifice our lives. Is this something for the Chinese people to be proud of?

We have no choice but to fast. Braving death, we will fight for life.

We are only children! We are still so young! Mother China, please look at your children carefully one more time. When hunger ruthlessly destroys us in our youth, when death is so close, how can you not be moved?

It's not that we want to die. We really want to go on living, because these are the best years of our lives. It's not that we want to die. We really want to go on studying, because our motherland is still so poor and we do not want to die and leave her like this. Death is not at all what we seek. But if the death of one of us or a few of us can make life better for many more, and if those deaths can make the country prosper, then what right have we to go on living?

Dear mom and dad, don't grieve because we suffer from hunger. Dear aunts and uncles, don't be heartbroken when death separates us. Hope with us that all may have a better life in the future, and remember always that we did not seek death! As democracy is not just the business of a few people, it requires the efforts of more than just one generation to achieve.

In death we hope for a broad and longlasting response.

"Sad is the cry of a dying bird; good are the words of a dying man."[17]

Farewell, comrades, look after yourselves. The dead and the living are bound together in loyalty.

Farewell, beloved, look after yourself. I hate to leave you, but I have no choice.

Farewell, parents. Please forgive me. Your child cannot serve both you and the country.

Farewell, people. Please allow us to demonstrate our loyalty in this, the only way we can.

---

[17]Quoting *The Analects of Confucius*, trans. D. C. Lau, 8:4. The words are attributed to Zeng Zi.

This pledge, written on our lives, will surely someday brighten the skies of our Republic.

All the student hunger strikers of Beijing University
May 13, 1989

Hunger Strike Declaration

Fellow countrymen:

After several days of continuous massive demonstrations, we gather in Tiananmen Square once more to continue the struggle with a hunger strike.

The reasons for the hunger strike:

1. We protest the government's cold and callous response to the Beijing student boycott.

2. We protest the government's postponement of the dialogue with representatives of the Beijing students' dialogue group.

3. We protest the government's labeling of the students' patriotic movement as "incitement of turmoil" and other serious distortions in the press.

The demands of the hunger strike:

1. We demand that the government engage in a substantial, concrete dialogue with the representatives of the Beijing students' dialogue group on an equal basis.

2. We demand that the government correct its labeling of this student movement, that it make a fair evaluation and affirm the movement as patriotic and democratic.

Time of the hunger strike: May 13 at 2:00 P.M.

Location of the hunger strike: Tiananmen Square.

Immediate redress of the charge of inciting turmoil!

Immediate dialogue; no more delays!

No choice but to fast for the sake of the people!

World opinion, please voice your support for us! Forces of democracy, please support us!

Hunger strikers of the colleges and universities of Beijing
May 13, 1989

Don't Ask Me What My Name Is
(Dedicated to the hunger strikers, who are fighting for Truth)

May is the policeman's busiest month
Like cicadas before emerging they hide at every street corner
Wings fluttering
Under the sun, wings fluttering
Wings covered with spider webs. . . .

Students, don't ask me what my name is
Extend your hand
Extend my hand
Extend our hands
Let us link arms

Like trees, interweave death and hardship
Interweave life and Truth.

On the square in May
We use our own bodies
Weave a great wreath
Everlasting wreath.
Yes, May is the month of lush green trees
The day for breaking ourselves off the Tree of Life
This branch
Countless fresh green branches
Under the Monument
Waiting for the moment to wither and revive.

Students, don't ask me what my name is
Extend your hand
Extend our hands
Let us link arms
Like rocks, pile up darkness and light
Pile up democracy and freedom

Under the sky in May
We use our own souls
Build a great stone relief
Those who came before.

Go, students
Go, brothers
Go, sisters
Go, friends
Extend your hand
Extend my hand
Extend our hands
Come, come, come
Don't ask me what my name is.

A citizen
May 13, 1989

At 6:00 P.M. on May 14, twelve well-known scholars and writers Dai Qing, Yu Haocheng, Li Honglin, Yan Jiaqi, Su Xiaokang, Bao Zunxin, Wen Yuankai, Liu Zaifu, Su Wei, Li Zehou, Mai Tianshu, and Li Tuo jointly signed "An Urgent Appeal Concerning the Current Situation," directed to the students who were fasting in protest at Tiananmen Square: "Last night we learned that you had begun a hunger strike at Tiananmen Square. We understand very well, and we are extremely sad and extremely worried." First they appealed to the students:

Democracy can only develop gradually. We cannot expect it to be achieved overnight. In the interest of China's long-term reform, to avoid hurting friends and helping the enemy, and to ensure that the Sino-Soviet summit progresses smoothly, we urge you to display that noble rational spirit that has characterized this student movement and temporarily withdraw from Tiananmen Square.

Then they demanded that:

1. The central leadership issue a statement affirming that the student movement is patriotic and democratic and that it will not be held against the students in any way whatsoever, now or in the future;
2. The leadership recognize the student organizations formed through the democratic process of election by the majority of the students as legal organizations;
3. Violence against the peaceful hunger striking students not be allowed, for whatever excuse, under whatever name, by whatever means. These twelve scholars and writers declared that if the government failed to meet their demands, they were determined to join the students in their struggle.

The twelve spoke with representatives of the hunger strikers, and the two sides exchanged views on the situation. The scholars and writers read the "Urgent Appeal" to them. After that, they went with the representatives to Tiananmen Square and read the appeal once more to the hunger striking students there, urging them to use their good judgment.

But the appeal of the twelve did not have the desired effect.

On May 15, the hunger strike entered its third day. It is said that nearly a thousand students had joined the hunger strike, and a large crowd surrounded them. More than a hundred people fainted in the square and all received first aid. For three days university professors and administrators had been going to the square urging the students to think about their health and return to their campuses. Others came continuously to support the students.

On the 15th, Beijing's intellectuals marched to Tiananmen Square to voice support for the hunger striking students there.

Yan Jiaqi, Bao Zunxin, Ke Yunlu, Wang Luxiang, and others led the march, carrying a banner saying "China's Intellectuals." Among the marchers were several tens of thousands of professors, lecturers, research workers, advanced graduate students, and staff members of more than sixty units, including some institutes of the Chinese Academy of Sciences, the Chinese Academy of Social Sciences, Beijing University and Qinghua University. They raised banners with words like "Voice support for the students, promote reform," and "fair assessment," and shouted slogans like "the students love their country, we love the students."

Around 4:00 P.M. the demonstrators entered Tiananmen Square, and around 7:00 the crowd of supporters began to diminish. In addition, a group of volunteer medical workers from Union Hospital who had formed a "first-aid team" arrived in the square.

The hundreds of thousands of people surrounding the hunger strikers not only voiced their support for those admirable students who would sacrifice their lives for the people, but also brought them beverages and shouted slogans to put pressure on the government, urging the national leaders to ignore neither the students' lives nor the demands of the people.

On May 16, Yan Mingfu, secretary of the Central Committee Secretariat and director of the United Front Department, appeared at Tiananmen Square and patiently tried to persuade the hunger strikers to return to their campuses. He told the students, "You are the country's future. You have no right to ruin your health." The same day, representatives of the university administrations, the People's Political Consultative Conference, and the democratic parties tried by various means to persuade the students to give up their hunger strike.

Thousands of people from various universities, research institutes, media organizations, democratic parties, and factories appeared at Tiananmen carrying banners and shouting slogans of support for the hunger striking students.

The student hunger strike was already in its fourth day, and by noon more than six hundred people had fainted. Medical personnel from many hospitals and first-aid units did their utmost to provide medicine, transportation and beds in the effort to rescue them. And spectators came to the square in waves.

Large numbers of factory workers also took to the streets to support the hunger striking students and protest the callousness of the party and the government. Lacking any other means to solve the problem themselves, they could only take to the streets a million strong.

The official New China News Agency reported that a spokesman for the Capital Iron and Steel Company denied the rumor that 70,000 workers had declared a strike. The spokesman said, "Capital Iron and Steel is functioning as usual. We are a government contract unit. If we stopped production it would not only damage the national economy, it would also damage the interests of the workers." The report also noted that, according to UPI, the students in Tiananmen Square had announced with their bullhorns, "Of the 220,000 workers at Capital Iron and Steel, so far this week 70,000 have joined the strike" to support the student movement, but that the company spokesman said no such thing had occurred.

This sort of wishful thinking needs no comment. The people know it is like the pirate who buried his treasure and then posted a sign saying "No treasure buried here."

The rate of television viewing in China has reached new heights. Are people looking for something? Although summer has arrived, it is as if people are still waiting for spring. On May 16, the *People's Daily* published this masterpiece by an unknown poet, which captures the mood:

Looking Forward to Spring
Standing on the edge of winter
Looking forward to spring

I feel spring so close to me
Reaching out I can touch it, fragrant aroma
Intoxicates me and compels belief
This vast life momentarily turns many-splendored

In reality spring is so far from me
I cannot tell
The distance from there to here
In the manner of a thousand years ago
At the end of the great plain
Driven by flocks of sheep
At the edge of the horizon
It is being summoned by the dense sunlight

Yet even this is only speculation
In the direction of spring
I see no
Sign of spring's coming
Desolate prairie, a dead silence
In the distance steel blue mountains
Are being pierced by bitter cold

But I still look forward to spring
Above the frozen land
Gazing at the place where heaven and earth meet
A symbol of warmth
Spring begins to spread in my imagination
Beauty beyond words and pain that strains endurance

Yi Dianxuan
May 16, 1989

2
Report to NPC on Quelling the Counter-Revolutionary Rebellion

CHEN XITONG

Source: *Xinhua* (Beijing—in English), July 6, 1989. Translated in Foreign Broadcast Information Service (FBIS), July 6, pp. 20–36; also in *Beijing Review*, July 17–23.

Chairman, vice-chairmen, and members of the Standing Committee,
During late spring and early summer, namely, from mid-April to early June of

1989, a tiny handful of people exploited student unrest to launch a planned, organized and premeditated political turmoil, which later developed into a counter-revolutionary rebellion in Beijing, the capital. Their purpose was to overthrow the leadership of the Chinese Communist Party and subvert the socialist People's Republic of China. The out-break and development of the turmoil and the counter-revolutionary rebellion had a profound international background and a social basis at home. As Comrade Deng Xiaoping put it, "This storm was bound to happen sooner or later. As determined by the international and domestic climate, it was bound to happen and was independent of man's will" [see Doc. 58]. In this struggle involving the life and death of the party and the state, Comrade Zhao Ziyang committed the serious mistake of supporting the turmoil and splitting the party, and had the unshirkable responsibility for the shaping up and development of the turmoil. In face of this very severe situation, the party Central Committee made correct decisions and took a series of resolute measures, winning the firm support of the whole party and people of all nationalities in the country. Represented by Comrade Deng Xiaoping, proletarian revolutionaries of the older generation played a very important role in winning the struggle. The Chinese People's Liberation Army [PLA], the armed police and the police made great contributions in checking turmoil and quelling the counter-revolutionary rebellion. The vast numbers of workers, peasants and intellectuals firmly opposed the turmoil and the rebellion, rallied closely around the party Central Committee and displayed a very high political consciousness and the sense of responsibility as masters of the country. Now, entrusted by the State Council, I am making a report to the Standing Committee of the National People's Congress on the turmoil and the counter-revolutionary rebellion, mainly the happenings in Beijing, and the work of checking the turmoil and quelling the counter-revolutionary rebellion.

1. The Turmoil Was Brewed and Premeditated for a Long Time

Some political forces in the West always attempt to make socialist countries, including China, give up the socialist road, eventually bringing these countries under the rule of international monopoly capital and putting them on the course of capitalism. This is their long-term, fundamental strategy. In recent years, they stepped up the implementation of this strategy by making use of some policy mistakes and temporary economic difficulties in socialist countries. In our country, there was a tiny handful of people both inside and outside the party who stubbornly clung to their position of bourgeois liberalization and went in for political conspiracy. Echoing the strategy of Western countries, they colluded with foreign forces, ganged up themselves at home and made ideological, public opinion and organizational preparations for years to stir up turmoil in China, overthrow the leadership by the Communist Party and subvert the socialist People's Republic. That is why the entire course of brewing, premeditating and launching the turmoil, including the use of varied means such as creating public opinion, distorting facts and spreading rumors, bore the salient feature of support by coordinated action at home and abroad.

This report will mainly deal with the situation since the Third Plenum of the Thirteenth Central Committee of the Chinese Communist Party. Last September, the party Central Committee formulated the policy of improving the economic environment, straightening out the economic order and deepening the reform in an all-round way. This policy and the related measures won the support of the broad masses and students. The social order and political situation were basically stable. A good proof of this was the approval of Comrade Li Peng's government work report by an overwhelming majority (with a mere two votes against and four abstentions) at the National People's Congress in the spring of this year. [This report is excerpted as Doc. 5.] Of course, the people and students raised many critical opinions against some mistakes committed by the party and the government in their work, corruption among some government employees, unfair distribution and other social problems. At the same time, they made quite a few demands and proposals for promoting democracy, strengthening the legal system, deepening the reform and overcoming bureaucracy. These were normal phenomena. And the party and government were also taking measures to solve them. At that time, however, there was indeed a tiny bunch of people in the party and society who ganged up together and engaged in many very improper activities overtly and covertly.

What deserves special attention is that, after Comrade Zhao Ziyang's meeting with an American "ultra-liberal economist" on September 19 last year, some Hong Kong newspapers and journals, which were said to have close ties with Zhao Ziyang's "brain trust," gave enormous publicity to this and spread the political message that "Beijing is using Hong Kong mass media to topple Deng and protect Zhao."[1] In his article entitled "Big Patriarch Should Retire" published in Hong Kong's *Economic Journal*, Li Yi (alias Qi Xin), editor-in-chief of the reactionary *Nineties* magazine, clamored for "removing the obstacle of super old man's politics" and "giving Zhao Ziyang enough power." Another article in the *Nineties* appealed to Zhao to be an "autocrat." Hong Kong's *Emancipation* monthly also carried a lengthy article, saying that some people in Beijing had "overt or covert" relations with certain persons in Hong Kong media circles, which "are sometimes dim and sometimes bright, just like a will-o'-the-wisp," and that such subtle relations now "have been newly proved by a drive of toppling Deng and protecting Zhao launched in the recent months." The article also said that "in terms of the hope of China turning

---

[1]The economist was Milton Friedman, an eminent American economist and an advocate of unfettered market forces.

capitalist, they settle on Zhao Ziyang." To coordinate with the drive of "toppling Deng and protecting Zhao," Beijing's *Economic Weekly* published a dialogue on the current situation between Yan Jiaqi (research fellow at the Institute of Political Science under the Chinese Academy of Social Sciences) who had close ties with Zhao Ziyang's former secretary Bao Tong, and another person. It attacked "the improvement of economic environment and the straightening out of economic order," saying that would lead to "stagnation." It also said that a big problem China was facing was "not to follow the old disastrous road of nonprocedural change of power as in the case of Khrushchev and Liu Shaoqi." It said that "nonprocedural change of power as in the Cultural Revolution will no longer be allowed in China." The essence of the dialogue was to whip up public opinion for covering up Zhao Ziyang's mistakes, keeping his position and power and pushing on bourgeois liberalization even more unbridledly. This dialogue was reprinted in full or parts in Shanghai's *World Economic Herald*, Hong Kong's *Mirror* monthly and other newspapers and magazines at home and abroad.

Collaboration between forces at home and abroad intensified toward the end of last year and early this year. Political assemblies, joint petitions, big- and small-character posters and other activities emerged, expressing fully erroneous or even reactionary points. For instance, a big seminar "Future China and the World" was sponsored by the "Beijing University Future Studies Society" on December 7 last year. Jin Guantao, deputy chief editor of the "Towards the Future" book series and adviser to the society, said in his speech, "attempts at socialism and their failure constitute one of the two major legacies of the twentieth century." Ge Yang, chief editor of the monthly *New Observer* and a party member of dozens of years' standing, immediately stood up to "provide evidence," in the name of "the eldest" among the participants, saying "Jin's negation of socialism is not harsh enough, but a bit too polite."

On January 28 this year, Su Shaozhi (research fellow at the Institute of Marxism–Leninism–Mao Zedong Thought under the Chinese Academy of Social Sciences), Fang Lizhi and the like organized a so-called neo-enlightenment salon at the "Dule Bookstore" in Beijing, which was attended by more than 100 people, among them Beijing-based American, French, and Italian correspondents as well as Chinese. Fang described this gathering as "smelling of strong gunpowder" and "taking a completely critical attitude to the authorities." He also said, "what we need now is action" and professed to "take to the street after holding three sessions in a row."

In early February, Fang Lizhi, Chen Jun (member of the reactionary organization "Chinese Alliance for Democracy"), and others sponsored a so-called winter jasmine get-together of famed personalities at the Friendship Hotel, where Fang made a speech primarily on the two major issues of "democracy" and "human rights," and Chen drew a parallel between the May 4th Movement and the

"Democracy Wall at Xidan."[2] Fang expressed the "hope that entrepreneurs, as China's new rising force, will join force with the advanced intellectuals in the fight for democracy." At a press conference he gave for foreign correspondents on February 16, Chen Jun handed out Fang Lizhi's letter addressed to Deng Xiaoping [Doc. 16] and another letter from Chen himself and thirty-two others to the Standing Committee of the National People's Congress (NPC) and the Central Committee of the Chinese Communist Party (CPC), calling for amnesty and the release of Wei Jingsheng and other so-called political prisoners who had gravely violated the criminal law. [See Doc. 17.] On February 23, the Taiwan *United Daily News* carried an article headlined "Beginning of a Major Movement—A Mega-Shock." It said, "a declaration was issued in New York, and open letters surfaced in Beijing; as the thunder of spring rumbles across the divine land (China), waves for democracy are rising." On February 26, Zhang Xianyang (research fellow at the Institute of Marxism–Leninism–Mao Zedong Thought under the Chinese Academy of Social Sciences), Li Honglin (research fellow at the Fujian Academy of Social Sciences), Bao Zunxin (associate research fellow at the Institute of Chinese History under the Chinese Academy of Social Sciences), Ge Yang, and thirty-eight others, jointly wrote a letter to the CPC Central Committee, calling for the release of so-called "political prisoners." [See Doc. 19.]

Afterward, a vast number of big- and small-character posters and assemblies came out on the campuses of some universities in Beijing, attacking the Communist Party and the socialist system. On March 1, for example, a big-character poster entitled "Denunciation of Deng Xiaoping—A Letter to the Nation" was put up at Qinghua University and Beijing University simultaneously. The poster uttered such nonsense as "the politics of the Communist Party consists of empty talk, power politics, autocratic rule and arbitrary decision," and openly demanded "dismantling parties and abandoning the four cardinal principles (adherence to the socialist road, to the people's democratic dictatorship, to the leadership by the Communist Party and to Marxism-Leninism and Mao Zedong Thought)." A small-character poster entitled "Deplore the Chinese" turned up in Beijing University on March 2, crying to overthrow "totalitarianism" and "autocracy." On March 3, there appeared in Qinghua University and other universities and colleges a "Letter to the Mass of Students" signed by the "Preparatory Committee of the China Democratic Youth Patriotic Association," urging students to join in the "turbulent current for democracy, freedom and human rights under the leadership of the patriotic democratic fighter, Fang Lizhi." On the

---

[2]The May 4th Movement of 1919 was a major turning point in modern Chinese history. Its adherents advocated a cultural renaissance based on democracy and science. The Democracy Wall at Xidan refers to where Beijing youths pasted wall posters in December, January, and February 1978–79 calling for democracy.

campuses of Beijing University and other schools of higher learning on March 29, there was extensive posting of Fang's article "China's Disappointment and Hope" written for the Hong Kong *Ming Pao Daily News*. In the article, Fang claimed that socialism had "completely lost its attraction" and there was the need to form political "pressure groups" to carry out "reforms for political democracy and economic freedom." But what he termed as "reform" actually is a synonym of total Westernization. The big-character poster, "Call of the Times," that came out in Beijing University on April 6, questioned in a way of complete negation whether there is any rationale now for socialism to exist and "whether Marxism-Leninism fits the realities of China after all." On April 13, the Beijing Institute of Post and Telecommunications and some other schools received a "message to the Nation's College Students" signed by the "Guangxi University Students' Union," which called on students to "hold high the portrait of Hu Yaobang and the great banner of democracy, freedom, dignity, and rule by law" in celebration of the May 4th Youth Day.

Meanwhile, so-called democratic salons, freedom forums, and various kinds of seminars, conferences, and lectures mushroomed in Beijing's institutions of higher learning. The "democratic salon" presided over by Wang Dan, a Beijing university student, sponsored seventeen lectures in one year, indicative of its frequent activities. They invited Ren Wanding, head of the defunct and illegal "Human Rights League," to spread a lot of fallacies about the so-called new-authoritarianism and democratic politics. At one point they held a seminar in front of the statue of Cervantes, openly crying to "abolish the one-party system, force the Communist Party to step down and topple the present regime." They also invited Li Shuxian, the wife of Fang Lizhi, to be their "adviser." Li fanned the flames by urging them to "legalize the democratic salon," "hold meetings here frequently," and "abolish the Beijing municipality's ten-article regulations on demonstrations."

All this prepared, in terms of ideology and organization, for the turmoil that ensued. A *Ming Pao Daily News* article commented: "The contact-building and petition-signing activities initiated by the elite of Chinese intellectuals exerted enormous influence on students. They had long ago planned a large-scale move on the 70th anniversary of the May 4th Movement to express their dissatisfaction with the authorities. The sudden death of Hu Yaobang literally threw a match into a barrel of gunpowder." In short, as a result of the premeditation, organization and engineering by a small handful of people, a political situation already emerged in which "the rising wind forebodes a coming storm."

2. Student Unrest Was Exploited by Organizers of the Turmoil from the Very Beginning

Comrade Hu Yaobang's death on April 15 prompted an early out-break of the long-brewing student unrest and turmoil. The broad masses and students mourned Comrade Hu Yaobang and expressed their profound grief. Universities and colleges provided facilities for the mourning on the part of the students. However, a small number of people took advantage of this to oppose the leadership of the Communist Party and the socialist system under the pretext of "mourning." Student unrest was manipulated and exploited by the small handful of people from the very beginning and bore the nature of political turmoil.

This turmoil found expression first in the wanton attack and slanders against the party and the government and the open call to overthrow the leadership of the Communist Party and subvert the present government as contained in the large quantity of big- and small-character posters, slogans, leaflets and elegiac couplets. Some of the posters on the campuses of Beijing University, Qinghua University, and other schools abused the Communist Party as "a party of conspirators" and "an organization on the verge of collapse." Some attacked the older generation of revolutionaries as "decaying men administering affairs of the state" and "autocrats with a concentration of power." Some called the names of Chinese leaders one by one, saying that "the man who should not die has passed away while those who should die remain alive." Some called for "dissolving the incompetent government and overthrowing autocratic monarchy." Some cried to "abolish the Chinese Communist Party and adopt the multiparty system" and "dissolve party branches and remove political workers in the mass organizations, armed forces, schools and other units." Some issued a "declaration on private ownership," calling to "sound the death knell of public ownership at an early date and greet a new future for the republic." Some went so far as to "invite the Guomindang back to the mainland and establish two-party politics," etc.[3] Many big- and small-character posters used disgusting language to slander Comrade Deng Xiaoping, clamoring "down with Deng Xiaoping."

This turmoil, from the very beginning, was manifested by a sharp conflict between bourgeois liberalization and the four cardinal principles. Of the programmatic slogans raised by the organizers of the turmoil at the time, either the "nine demands" first raised through Wang Dan, leader of an illegal student organization, in Tiananmen Square or the "seven demands" and "ten demands" raised later, there were two principal demands: one was to reappraise Comrade Hu Yaobang's merits and demerits; the other was to completely negate the fight against bourgeois liberalization and rehabilitate the so-called wronged citizens in the fight. The essence of the two demands was to gain absolute freedom in China to oppose the four cardinal principles and realize capitalism.[4]

---

[3]The Guomindang, now the ruling party on Taiwan, was the ruling party on the mainland from 1927 until its defeat by the Communists in 1949.

[4]The four cardinal principles: uphold the socialist road, the dictatorship of the proletariat, the leadership of the Communist Party and Marxism–Leninism–Mao Zedong Thought.

Echoing these demands, some so-called "elitists" in academic circles, that is, the very small number of people stubbornly clinging to their position of bourgeois liberalization, organized a variety of forums during the period and indulged in unbridled propaganda through the press. Most outstanding among the activities was a forum sponsored by the *World Economic Herald* and the *New Observer* in Beijing on April 19. The forum was chaired by Ge Yang and its participants included Yan Jiaqi, Su Shaozhi, Chen Ziming (director of the Beijing Institute of Socioeconomic Science), and Liu Ruishao (head of Hong Kong *Wen Hui Po* Beijing office). Their main topics were also two: one was to "rehabilitate" Hu Yaobang; the other was to "reverse" the verdict on the fight against liberalization. They expressed unequivocal support for the student demonstrations, saying that they saw therefrom "China's future and hope." Later, when the Shanghai municipal party committee made the correct decision[5] on straightening things out in the *World Economic Herald*, Comrade Zhao Ziyang who consistently winked at bourgeois liberalization, refrained from backing the decision. Instead, he criticized the Shanghai municipal party committee for "making a mess of it" and "landing itself in a passive position."

This turmoil also found expression in the fact that, instigated and engineered by a small handful of people, many acts were very rude, violating the Constitution, laws and regulations of the People's Republic of China and gravely running counter to democracy and the legal system. They put up big-character posters en masse on the campuses in disregard of the fact that the provision in the Constitution on "four big freedoms" (speaking out freely, airing views fully, holding great debates and writing big-character posters) had been abrogated and turned a deaf ear to all persuasion. They staged large-scale demonstrations day after day in disregard of the ten-article regulations on demonstrations issued by the Standing Committee of the Beijing Municipal People's Congress. Late on the night of April 18 and 19, they assaulted Xinhuamen, headquarters of the party Central Committee and the State Council, and shouted "Down with the Communist Party," something which never occurred even during the "Cultural Revolution." They violated the regulations for the management of Tiananmen Square and occupied the square by force several times, one consequence of which was that the memorial meeting for Comrade Hu Yaobang was almost interrupted on April 22. Ignoring the relevant regulations of the Beijing Municipality and without registration, they formed an illegal organization, "Solidarity Student Union" (later changed into "Federation of Autonomous Student Unions in Universities and Colleges"), and "seized power" from the lawful student unions and postgraduate unions formed through democratic election. Disregarding law and school discipline, they took by force

---

[5]Qin Benli, editor of this newspaper and well known for his backing of reform and opening to the outside world, was dismissed from his post on April 26.

school offices and broadcasting stations and did things as they wished, creating anarchy on the campuses.

Another important means that the small number of turmoil organizers and plotters used was to fabricate a spate of rumors to confuse people's minds and agitate the masses. At the beginning of the student unrest, they spread the rumor that "Li Peng scolded Hu Yaobang at a Political Bureau meeting and Hu died of anger." The rumor was meant to spearhead the attack on Comrade Li Peng. In fact, the meeting focused on the question of education. When Comrade Li Tie-ying, member of the Political Bureau, state councilor and minister in charge of the State Education Commission, was making an explanation of a relevant document, Comrade Hu Yaobang suffered a sudden heart attack. Hu was given emergency treatment right in the meeting room and was rushed to a hospital when his condition allowed. There was definitely no such thing as Hu flying into a rage.

On the night of April 19, a female foreign language student of Beijing Teachers' University was run down by a trolley-bus on her way back to school after attending a party. She died despite treatment. Some people spread the rumor that "a car of the Communist police knocked a student to death," which stirred up the emotions of some students who did not know the truth.

In the small hours of April 20, policemen whisked away those students who had blocked and assaulted Xinhuamen and sent them back to Beijing University by bus. Some people concocted the rumor of "April 20 bloody incident," alleging that "the police beat people at Xinhuamen, not only students, but also workers, women and children," and that "more than one thousand scientists and technicians fell in blood." This further agitated some people.

On April 22, when Li Peng and other leading comrades left the Great Hall of the People at the end of the memorial meeting for Comrade Hu Yaobang, some people perpetrated a fraud with the objective of working out an excuse for attacking Comrade Li Peng. First they started the rumor that "Premier Li Peng promised to come out at 12:45 and receive students in the square." Then three students knelt on the steps outside the East Gate of the Great Hall of the People in order to hand in a "petition." After a while they said, "Li Peng went back on his word and refused to receive us. He has deceived the students." This assertion fanned strong indignation among the tens of thousands of students in Tiananmen Square and came very close to leading to a serious incident of assaulting the Great Hall of the People.

Rumor-mongering greatly sharpened students' antagonism against the government. Using this antagonism, a very small number of people put up the slogan: "The Government Pays No Heed to Our Peaceful Petition. Let's Make the Matter Known Across the Country and Call for Nationwide Class Boycott." This led to the serious situation in which sixty thousand university students boycotted class in Beijing and many students in other parts of China followed suit. The student unrest escalated and the turmoil expanded.

This turmoil was marked by another characteristic. It was no longer confined to institutions of higher learning or the Beijing area; it spread to the whole of society and to all parts of China. After the memorial meeting for Comrade Hu Yaobang, a number of people went to contact middle schools, factories, shops and villages, made speeches in the streets, handed out leaflets, put up slogans and raised money, doing everything possible to make the situation worse. The slogan "Oppose the Chinese Communist Party" and the big-character poster "Long Live Class Boycott and Exam Boycott" appeared in some middle schools. Leaflets "Unite With the Workers and Peasants. Down With Despotic Rule" were put up in some factories. Organizers and plotters of the turmoil advanced the slogan "Go to the South, the North, the East and the West" in a bid to establish ties throughout the country. Students from Beijing were seen in universities and colleges in Nanjing, Wuhan, Xi'an, Changsha, Shanghai, and Harbin, while students from Tianjin, Hebei, Anhui, and Zhejiang took part in demonstrations in Beijing. Criminal activities of beating, smashing, looting, and burning took place in Changsha and Xi'an.

Political forces outside the Chinese mainland and in foreign countries had a hand in the turmoil from the very beginning. Hu Ping, Chen Jun and Liu Xiaobo, members of the "Chinese Alliance for Democracy" which is a reactionary organization groomed by the Guomindang, wrote "an open letter" from New York to Chinese university students, urging them to consolidate the organizational links established in the student unrest and ''strive to carry out activities effectively in the form of a strong mass body.'' The letter told the students to "effect a breakthrough by thoroughly negating the 1987 movement against liberalization," "strengthen contacts with the mass media," "increase contacts with various circles in society," and "enlist their support and participation in the movement."

Wang Bingzhang and Tang Guangzhong, two leaders of the "Chinese Alliance for Democracy," made a hasty flight from New York to Tokyo in an attempt to get to Beijing and have a direct hand in the turmoil. A number of Chinese intellectuals residing abroad who stand for instituting the Western capitalist system in China invited Fang Lizhi to take the lead, and cabled from Columbia University a "declaration on promoting democratic politics on the Chinese mainland," asserting that "the people must have the right to choose the ruling party" in a bid to incite people to overthrow the Communist Party.

Someone in the United States, using the name of "Hong Yan," sent in by fax "ten pieces of opinions on revising the Constitution," suggesting that deputies to the National and local People's Congresses as well as "judges in all courts should be elected from among candidates without party affiliation," in an attempt to keep the Communist Party completely out of the organs of power and judicial organs.

Some members of the former *China Spring Journal* residing in the United States hastily founded a "China Democratic Party." They sent "a letter addressed to the entire nation" to some universities in Beijing, inciting students to "demand that the conservative bureaucrats step down" and "urge the Chinese Communist Party to end its autocratic rule."

Reactionary political forces in Hong Kong, Taiwan, the United States, and other Western countries were also involved in the turmoil through various channels and by different means. Western news agencies showed unusual zeal. The Voice of America, in particular, aired news in three programs everyday for a total of more than ten hours beamed to the Chinese mainland, spreading rumors, stirring up trouble and adding fuel to the turmoil.

Facts listed above show that we were confronted not with student unrest in its normal sense but with a planned, organized, and premeditated political turmoil designed to negate the Communist Party leadership and the socialist system. It had clear-cut political ends and deviated from the orbit of democracy and legality, employing base political means to incite large numbers of students and other people who did not know the truth. If we failed to analyze and see the problem in essence, we would have committed grave mistakes and landed ourselves in an extremely passive position in the struggle.

3. *People's Daily* April 26 Editorial Correctly Determined the Nature of the Turmoil

From the death of Comrade Hu Yaobang on April 15 to the conclusion of the memorial service on April 22, Comrade Zhao Ziyang all along tolerated and connived at the increasingly evident signs of turmoil during the period of mourning, thus facilitating the formation and development of the turmoil. In face of the increasingly grave situation, many comrades in the central leadership and Beijing Municipality felt that the nature of the matter had changed, and repeatedly suggested to Comrade Zhao Ziyang that the central leadership should adopt a clear-cut policy and measures to quickly check the development of the matter. But, Zhao kept avoiding making an earnest analysis and discussion of the nature of the matter. At the end of the memorial meeting for Comrade Hu Yaobang, comrades in the central leadership again suggested to Zhao that a meeting be held on April 23 before his visit to the Democratic People's Republic of Korea. Instead of accepting this suggestion, Zhao went golfing as if nothing had happened. Because he took such an attitude, the party and the government lost a chance to stop the turmoil.

On the afternoon of April 24, the Beijing Municipal Party Committee and People's Government reported to Comrade Wan Li. At his proposal, members of the Standing Committee of the Political Bureau met that evening, with Comrade Li Peng presiding, to analyze and study earnestly the development of the situation. A consensus of view was reached that all signs at that time showed we were confronted with an antiparty and antisocialist political struggle which was conducted in a planned and organized way and manipulated and instigated by a small handful of persons. The meeting decided that a group for stopping the turmoil be established in the central leadership, and at the same time requested the Beijing Municipal Party Committee and People's Government to arouse the masses fully, try to win over the majority and isolate the minority in a bid to put down the turmoil and stabilize the situation as soon as possible.

The following morning, Comrade Deng Xiaoping made an important speech, expressing his full agreement with and support to the decision of the Political Bureau Standing Committee and making an incisive analysis of the nature of the turmoil. He pointed out sharply that this was not a case of ordinary student unrest, but a political turmoil aimed at negating the leadership by the Communist Party and the socialist system. Deng's speech greatly enhanced the understanding of the cadres and increased their confidence and courage in quelling the turmoil and stabilizing the overall situation.

The *People's Daily* editorial on April 26 embodied the decision of the Political Bureau Standing Committee and the spirit of Comrade Deng Xiaoping's speech, and pointed to the nature of the turmoil. [See Doc. 25.] At the same time, it made a clear distinction between the tiny handful of persons who organized and plotted the turmoil and the vast number of students. The editorial made the overwhelming majority of the cadres feel sure about the matter and pointed out the direction of their action, enabling them to work with a clear-cut stand.

After the editorial was published in the *People's Daily*, the Beijing Municipal Party Committee and People's Government, under the direct leadership of the Chinese Communist Party Central Committee and the State Council, convened in quick succession a variety of meetings inside and outside the party, upholding the principle and seeking unity of understanding; cleared up rumors and set people's minds at ease through various forms; supported school leaderships, party and youth league members and backbone students by encouraging them to work boldly, and advised and dissuaded those students who took part in demonstrations and worked hard to win over the masses by conducting a variety of dialogues. The dialogues, between the State Council spokesman Yuan Mu and other comrades and students, between leaders of relevant central departments and students, and between principal leaders of the Beijing Municipal Party Committee and People's Government and students, achieved good results.

Meanwhile, earnest work was done in the factories, villages, shops, primary and secondary schools, and neighborhoods to stabilize the overall situation and prevent the turmoil from spreading to other sectors of society. Various provinces, municipalities and autonomous regions did a good job in their respective localities according to the spirit of the editorial to prevent the situation in Beijing from influencing other parts of the country.

The clear-cut stand of the April 26 editorial forced the organizers and plotters of the turmoil to make an about-turn in strategy. Before the publication of the editorial, large numbers of posters and slogans were against the Communist

Party, socialism and the four cardinal principles. After the publication of the editorial, the illegal Beijing "Federation of Autonomous Student Unions in Universities and Colleges" issued on April 26 "No. 1 Order of the New Student Federation" to change their strategy, urging students to "march to Tiananmen under the banner of supporting the Communist Party" on April 27 and setting such slogans as "Support the Communist Party," "Support Socialism," and "Safeguard the Constitution." It also, at the suggestion of Fang Lizhi, changed such subversive slogans as "Down With the Bureaucratic Government," "Down With the Corrupt Government," and "Down With the Dictatorial Rule" into ones like "Oppose Bureaucracy, Oppose Corruption and Oppose Privilege"—slogans that could win support from people of various circles.

The Japanese JIJI News Agency then dispatched from Beijing a news story entitled "Young Officials Form a Pro-Democracy Group," describing some figures in the so-called "Zhao Ziyang's Brain Trust" as "young officials of the Chinese Communist Party Central Committee and the Government," and saying that they "made frequent contacts with representatives of the new autonomous student unions in Beijing's universities and colleges including Beijing University, Qinghua University, People's University, and Beijing Teachers' University, which took part in the demonstrations, and offered advice to the students." It also said that during the mass demonstration on April 27, the students held "placards of 'supporting socialism' and 'supporting the leadership by the Communist Party.' They did so at the instruction of the group."

Leaders of the student unrest originally planned to stage "a hundred-day demonstration and a student strike of indefinite duration." But they lost such enthusiasm after the publication of the editorial.

Compared with the demonstration on April 27, the number of students taking part in the one held on May 4 dropped from over thirty thousand to less than twenty thousand, and the onlookers also decreased by a big margin. After the May 4 demonstration, 80 percent of the students returned to class as a result of the work done by party and administrative leaders of various universities and colleges. After the publication of the *People's Daily* April 26 editorial, the situation in other parts of the country also tended to be stabilized quickly. It was evident that with some more work, the turmoil, instigated by a small handful of persons by making use of the student unrest, was likely to calm down. A host of facts show that the *People's Daily* April 26 editorial is correct and indeed played its role in stabilizing the situation in the capital and the whole country as well.

4. Comrade Zhao Ziyang's May 4 Speech Was the Turning Point in Escalating the Turmoil

When the turmoil was close to subsiding, Comrade Zhao Ziyang, who was the general secretary of the Chinese Communist Party, adopted a changeable attitude of contradicting himself. At first, when the Political Bureau Standing Committee solicited his opinions during his visit to [North] Korea, he cabled back explicitly expressing "full agreement with the policy decision made by Comrade Deng Xiaoping on handling the current turmoil." On April 30, after he returned home, he once again expressed, at a meeting of the Politburo Standing Committee, his agreement with Comrade Deng Xiaoping's speech and the determination of the nature of the turmoil as made in the April 26 editorial, maintaining that the handling of the student unrest in the previous period was appropriate.

A few days later, however, when he met with representatives attending the annual meeting of the Asian Development Bank on the afternoon of May 4, he expressed views diametrically opposed to the decision of the Politburo Standing Committee, to Comrade Deng Xiaoping's speech and to the spirit of the editorial. [See Doc. 31.] First, when the turmoil had already come to the surface, he said "there will be no big turmoil in China." Second, when a host of facts had proved that the essence of the turmoil was the negation of the leadership by the Communist Party and the socialist system, he still insisted that "they are by no means opposed to our fundamental system. Rather they are asking us to correct mistakes in our work." Third, although facts had shown that a tiny handful of people was making use of the student unrest to instigate turmoil, he merely said that it was "hardly avoidable" for "some people to take advantage of this," thus totally negating the correct judgment of the party's Central Committee that some people were creating turmoil.

This speech of Comrade Zhao Ziyang's was prepared by Bao Tong beforehand. Bao asked the Central Broadcasting Station and CCTV to broadcast the speech that very afternoon and repeat it for three days running. He also asked the *People's Daily* to frontpage the speech the following day and carry a large quantity of positive responses from various sectors. Differing views were held up and even not allowed to appear in confidential reading. Comrade Zhao Ziyang's speech, publicized through the *People's Daily* and certain newspapers, created serious ideological confusion among the masses and the cadres while inflating the arrogance of the organizers and plotters of the turmoil.

The vast difference of Comrade Zhao Ziyang's speech from the policy of the party Central Committee evoked much comment at home and was also discerned by the media abroad. A Reuter dispatch said Zhao's remarks constituted a sharp contrast to the severe reproof to students a week before and was a major revision in the judgment in the previous week. An article in *Le Monde* of France on May 6 stated that the party chief (referring to Zhao Ziyang) seemed to make development of the situation favorable to himself.

The dish-out of the speech resulted in ideological confusion among leading officials at various levels, party and youth league members and the backbone of the masses, particularly those working in universities and colleges. They were at a loss in their work and many voiced their objection. Some people asked, "There are two voices in the central leadership. Which is right and which is wrong? Which are we supposed to follow?" Some queried, "We are required to be at one with the central leadership, but with which one?" Others complained, "Zhao Ziyang plays the good guy at the top while we play the bad ones at the grass roots." Cadres in universities and colleges and backbone students generally felt being "betrayed" and with a heavy heart, and some even shed sad tears. Work at the universities and colleges was bogged down in a completely passive situation.

At that time, the Beijing Municipal Party Committee and People's Government were also in a difficult plight. Although they knew opinions differed in the central leadership, against their will they had to tell the lower levels that the central leadership was of one opinion with some stressing this and others stressing that. They had to ask the central leadership for instructions on many things, but Comrade Zhao Ziyang, as the general secretary, was reluctant to call a meeting. Under the strong demand of the Beijing Municipal Party Committee and People's Government, a meeting was convened on May 8. However, he refused to hear the briefing by the Beijing authorities. At the meeting some comrades said Comrade Zhao Ziyang's speech on May 4 did not accord with the spirit of the April 26 editorial. Zhao retorted, "I'll bear the responsibility if I made wrong remarks." At another meeting, some comrades said that comrades working at the grass roots complained that they "had been betrayed." Comrade Zhao Ziyang rebuked, "Who has betrayed you? It was only during the Cultural Revolution that people were betrayed." In those days, quite a few people echoed with Hong Kong and Taiwan newspapers, repeatedly attacking the Beijing Municipal Party Committee and People's Government and comrades working at the grass roots. Demonstrating hooligans yelled, "The Beijing Municipal Party Committee is guilty of making false reports to deceive the central leadership." In face of the worsening situation, certain measures under consideration could not be implemented.

In contrast, organizers and plotters of the turmoil were encouraged by Comrade Zhao Ziyang's speech. Yan Jiaqi, Cao Siyuan (director of the Research and Development Institute of the Stone Company), and others said that "things have turned for the better. It is necessary to mobilize the intellectuals to support Zhao Ziyang." Zhang Xianyang said, "Aren't we advocating making use of the students? Zhao Ziyang is now doing just this." Egged on by Comrade Zhao Ziyang and plotted by a few others, leaders of the "Autonomous Student Unions" of Beijing University and Beijing Teachers' University declared to resume the class boycott that night. Many other universities followed suit and organized "pickets" to prevent students willing to resume class from going to the classroom.

After that, a new wave of demonstrations surged ahead. On May 9, several hundred journalists from more than thirty press organizations took to the streets and submitted a petition. About ten thousand students from a dozen universities including Beijing, Qinghua, and People's universities, Beijing Teachers' University, and the University of Political Science and Law, staged a demonstration, supporting the journalists, distributing leaflets and calling for continued class boycott and a hunger strike.

Henceforth, the situation took an abrupt turn for the worse and the turmoil was pushed to a new height. Influenced by the situation in Beijing, the already calmed situation in other parts of China became tense again. Shortly after Comrade Zhao Ziyang's speech, a large number of student demonstrators assaulted the office buildings of the Shanxi Provincial Party Committee and provincial government in Taiyuan on May 9 and 10. They also assaulted the ongoing international economic and technological cooperation fair, the import and export commodities fair and the folk arts festival. This exerted very bad influence both at home and abroad.

5. Use Hunger Strike as Coercion to Escalate the Turmoil

Good and honest people asked if the lack of understanding, consideration and concession on the part of the government had brought the students to make so much trouble?

The facts are just the opposite.

From the very beginning of the turmoil, the party and government fully acknowledged the students' patriotism and their concern about the country and people. Their demands to promote democracy, promote reform, punish official profiteers, and fight corruption were acknowledged as identical with the aspirations of the party and government, which also expressed the hope to solve the problems through normal democratic and legal procedures.

But such good aspirations failed to win active response. The government proposed to increase understanding and reach consensus through dialogues of various channels, levels, and forms.

Yet the illegal student organization put forward very strict conditions as terms of the dialogue. They demanded that their partners to the dialogues "must be people holding positions at or above the Standing Committee member of the Political Bureau of the party Central Committee, vice-chairman of the NPC Standing Committee and vice premier"; "a joint communique on every dialogue must be published and signed by both parties"; and dialogues should be "held in locations designated in turn by representatives of the government and students."

These were nothing like a dialogue but were setting the stage for political negotiations with the party and government.

Especially after Comrade Zhao Ziyang's speech on May 4, the very small number of people took this as an opportunity, regarding the restraint on the part of the party and government as a sign of weakness. They put forward harsher terms, adding increasing heat to the turmoil and escalating it.

Even under such circumstances, the party and government still took the attitude of utmost tolerance and restraint, with the hope to continue to maintain the channels for the dialogue in order to educate the masses and win over the majority.

At 2:00 in the early morning of May 13, leaders of the "Federation of Autonomous Student Unions in Universities and Colleges" raised the demand for a dialogue, which was accepted two hours later by the General Office of the party's Central Committee and that of the State Council.

However, the students ate their own word and cancelled the dialogue at daybreak.

On the morning of May 13, the Bureau for Letters and Visits of the General Offices of the Central Committee, the State Council, and the NPC Standing Committee again notified them of the decision to hold the dialogue with students on May 15.

Despite their agreement, the students began their maneuvering on the number of participants in the dialogue.

After the government agreed to their first proposed namelist of twenty people, they then demanded the number be raised to two hundred.

Without waiting for further discussion, they went to accuse "the government's insincerity for dialogue." Only four hours after they were informed of the dialogue, they hastily made public the long-prepared "hunger strike declaration," launching a seven-day fasting that involved three thousand people and a long occupation of Tiananmen Square since.

May 13 was chosen as the starting date of the hunger strike "to put pressure on them by way of Gorbachev's China visit," said Wang Dan, leader of the "Federation."

The very small number of people who organized and plotted the turmoil used the fasting students as "hostages" and their lives as a bet to blackmail the government in vile means, making the turmoil more serious.

During the student hunger strike, the party and government maintained an attitude of utmost restraint and did everything they could in various aspects. First of all, staff members of various universities and leading officials at all levels and even party and state leaders went to Tiananmen Square to see the fasting students on many occasions and gave them ideological advice.

Second, efforts were made to help the Red Cross Society mobilize one hundred ambulances and several hundred medical workers to keep watch at the fasting site day and night; fifty-two hospitals were asked to have more than two thousand beds ready so that students who suffered shock or illness because of the hunger strike could get first-aid and timely treatment.

Third, all sorts of materials were provided to alleviate the sufferings of the fasting students and ensure their safety.

The Beijing Municipal Party Committee and People's Government mobilized workers, officials, and vehicles to provide the fasting students with drinking water, edible salt and sugar via the Red Cross Society day and night.

The municipal environment sanitation bureau sent sprinklers and offered basins and towels for the fasting students.

Adequate supplies of medicine preventing sunstroke, cold, and diarrhea were provided by medicine companies and distributed by the Red Cross Society.

The food organizations sent a large amount of soft drinks and bread to be used during emergency rescue of the students.

A total of six thousand straw hats were provided by commercial units and one thousand quilts were sent by the Beijing Military Area Command, in response to the city authorities' request, to protect the fasting students from heat in the day and cold at night.

To keep the hunger strike site clean, makeshift flush toilets were set up and sanitation workers cleaned the site at midnight. Before the torrential rain on May 18, seventy-eight coaches from the public transport company and four hundred thick boards from the materials bureau were sent to protect the fasting students from rain and dampness. No fasting student died in the seven-day hunger strike.

But all this failed to get any positive response. Facts told people time and again that the very small number of organizers and plotters of the turmoil were determined to oppose us to the very end and that the problem could not be solved even with tolerance on a thousand occasions and ten thousand concessions.

It needs to be pointed out in particular that Comrade Zhao Ziyang did not do what he should have done when the situation quickly deteriorated, but instead stirred up the press with a wrong guidance for the public opinion, making the deteriorated situation more difficult to handle.

In his May 6 meeting with Comrades Hu Qili and Rui Xingwen, both then in charge of propaganda and ideological work in the Central Committee, Comrade Zhao Ziyang said that the press "has opened up a bit and there have been reports about the demonstrations. There is no big risk to open up a bit by reporting the demonstrations and increasing the openness of news." He even said, "Confronted with the will of the people at home and the progressive trend worldwide, we could only guide our actions according to circumstances."

Here, he even described the adverse current against communism and socialism as "will of the people at home" and "progressive trend worldwide."

His instructions were passed on to major press units in the capital the same day and many arrangements were made afterward.

As a result, the *People's Daily* and many other national newspapers and periodicals adopted an attitude of full acknowledgement and active support to the demonstrations, sit-in, and hunger strike, devoting lengthy coverages with no less exaggeration. Even some Hong Kong newspapers expressed their surprise over this unique phenomenon.

Under the wrong guidance of public opinion, the number of people who took to the streets to support the students increased day by day as their momentum grew since May 15. The number of people involved grew from tens of thousands to a hundred thousand and several hundred thousand in addition to the two hundred thousand students who came from other parts of the country to show their support for the fasting students.

For a time, it looked as if refusal to join in the demonstrations meant "unpatriotic" and refusal to show support was equal to "indifference to the survival of the students."

Under such circumstances, the fasting students had begun to ride the tiger and found it difficult to get off. Many parents of the students and teachers wrote to or called leading organs, press organizations, radio and TV stations, asking them not to force the fasting students onto the path of death and show mercy in saving the children and stopping this kind of "killing public opinion."

But this did not work. The students' hunger strike and the residents' demonstrations threw social order in Beijing into a mess and seriously disrupted the Sino-Soviet summit which was closely followed worldwide, forcing some changes on the agenda with some activities even cancelled.

Meanwhile, demonstrations in various major cities throughout China and even all provincial capitals registered a drastic increase in the number of people involved, while people also took to the streets in some small and medium-sized cities, producing a large scale of involvement and a serious disturbance never seen since the founding of the People's Republic.

To back up the students and add fuel to the flames of turmoil, some so-called elitists, who took a stubborn stand for bourgeois liberalization, threw away all disguises and came out to the front.

On the evening of May 13, the big-character poster "We can no longer remain silent" appeared at Beijing University. It was written by Yan Jiaqi, Su Shaozhi, Bao Zunxin, and others, and it urged intellectuals to take part in the big demonstrations they had sponsored to support the students' hunger strike.

On May 14, "Our urgent appeal for the current situation" was jointly made by twelve people including Yan Jiaqi, Bao Zunxin, Li Honglin, Dai Qing (reporter with the *Guangming Daily*), Yu Haocheng (former director of the Mass Publishing House), Li Zehou (research fellow at the Philosophy Institute of the Chinese Academy of Social Sciences), Su Xiaokang (lecturer at the Beijing Broadcasting Institute), Wen Yuankai (professor at the China University of Science and Technology), and Liu Zaifu (director of the Literature Institute under the Chinese Academy of Social Sciences). They demanded that the turmoil be declared a "patriotic democracy movement" and the illegal student organization be declared legal, saying that they would also take part in the hunger strike if these demands were not met.

This appeal was published in the *Guangming Daily* and broadcast on China Central Television. These people also went to Tiananmen Square many times to make speeches and agitate. They slandered against our government as "an incompetent government," saying that through the fasting students, "China's bright future can be envisioned."

Then the people formed the illegal "Beijing Union of Intellectuals" and published the "May 16 declaration," threatening with counter charges that "a promising China might be led into the abyss of real turmoil" if the government did not accept the political demands by the very small number of people.

As the situation became increasingly serious, Comrade Zhao Ziyang used the opportunity of meeting Gorbachev on May 16, deliberately directing the fire of criticism at Comrade Deng Xiaoping and making the situation even more worse. [See Doc. 34.]

Right at the beginning of the meeting, he said, "Comrade Deng Xiaoping's helmsmanship is still needed for the most important issues. Since the Thirteenth National Party Congress, we have always reported to Comrade Deng Xiaoping and asked for his advice while dealing with the most important issues." He also said that this was "the first" public disclosure of the "decision" by the party of China.

On the following day, Yan Jiaqi, Bao Zunxin and others published their most furious and vicious "May 17 Declaration." They made such swears: "Because the autocrat controls the unlimited power, the government has lost its own obligation and normal human feelings"; "despite the Qing dynasty's death seventy-six years ago, there is still an emperor in China though without such a title, a senile and fatuous autocrat." "General Secretary Zhao Ziyang declared publicly yesterday afternoon that all decisions in China must be approved by this decrepit autocrat," they said without any disguise. In their hoarse voices they shouted "gerontocratic politics must end and the autocrat must resign."

Some newspapers and periodicals in Hong Kong and Taiwan echoed their reactionary clamor. The Hong Kong newspaper *Express* published an article on May 18 entitled "Down with Deng and Li but not Zhao." It said "Zhao Ziyang's speech was full of indications that the foul atmosphere at home now was caused by Deng Xiaoping's helmsmanship. . . . At present the masses are eager to get rid of Deng and Li, while Zhao's role is almost open upon calling." It also added, "It is good news for Hong Kong if Deng could be successfully ousted and China's reforms embark on the path of legal-rule with the realization of democracy."

Against the backdrop of such screams, slogans smearing Comrade Deng Xiaoping and attacking Comrade Li Peng were all around. Some demanded "Deng Xiaoping step down" and "Li Peng step down to satisfy the people," while still others asked "Where are you China's Walesa?" Meanwhile, slogans like "Support Zhao Ziyang," "Long live Zhao Ziyang," and "Zhao Ziyang [should] be promoted [to] chairman of the Central Military Commission" could be seen and heard in the demonstrations and at Tiananmen Square.

Plotters of the turmoil attempted to use the chaos as an opportunity to seize power. They distributed leaflets, proclaiming the founding of the "Preparatory

Committee to the People's Conference of all Circles in Beijing" to replace the Municipal People's Congress. A case was made to establish a "Beijing Regional Government" to replace the legal Beijing Municipal People's Government. They attacked the State Council, which was formed in accordance with the law, as "pseudo-government." They also made rumors saying that the Foreign Ministry and a dozen other ministries already had "declared independence" from the State Council and that about thirty countries in the world broke diplomatic relations with our country. After the rumor that "Deng Xiaoping has stepped down" was made, some went to demonstrations carrying a coffin, burned Comrade Xiaoping's effigy and set off firecrackers on Tiananmen Square to celebrate their "victory."

The situation in Beijing became increasingly serious, with anarchism viciously spreading and many areas sinking into complete chaos and white terror. If our party and government did not take resolute measures under such circumstances, another vital chance would be missed and further great irredeemable damages could be done. This end would by no means be permitted by the broad masses of the people.

6. The Government Had No Alternative but to Declare Martial Law in Parts of Beijing, a Correct Measure

To safeguard the social stability in the city of Beijing, to protect the safety of the life and property of the citizens and ensure the normal functioning of the party and government departments at the central level and of the Beijing Municipal Government, the State Council had no alternative but to declare martial law in parts of Beijing as empowered by Clause 16 of Article 89 of the Constitution of the People's Republic of China and at a time when police forces in Beijing were far inadequate to maintain the normal production, work, and living order. This was a resolute and correct decision.

The decision on taking resolute measures to stop the turmoil was announced at a meeting called by the central authorities and attended by cadres from the party, government and military institutions in Beijing on May 19. Comrade Zhao Ziyang, persisting in his erroneous stand against the correct decision of the central authorities, neither agreed to speak at the meeting together with Comrade Li Peng, nor agreed to preside over the meeting. He didn't even agree to attend the meeting. By doing so, he openly revealed his attitude of separating himself from the party before the whole party, the whole country, and the whole world.

Prior to this, members of the Standing Committee of the Politburo of the party's Central Committee met to discuss the issue of declaring martial law in parts of Beijing on May 17. On the same day, a few people who had access to top party and state secrets gave the information away out of their counter-revolutionary political consideration. A person who worked at the side of Comrade

Zhao Ziyang said to the leaders of the illegal student organization, "The troops are about to suppress you. All others have agreed. Zhao Ziyang was the only one who was against it. You must get prepared."

On the evening of May 17, Bao Tong summoned some people from the Political Structural Reform Research Center of the party Central Committee for a meeting. After divulging the secret on declaring martial law, he made a "farewell speech" in which he warned the attendants not to reveal the schemes worked out at the meeting, saying that anyone who revealed them would be a "traitor," a "Judas." On May 19, Gao Shan, deputy bureau director of this Political Structural Reform Research Center, hurried to the Economic Structural Reform Institute to pass on to those who were holding a meeting the so-called instructions from "above." After that, the meeting, presided over by Chen Yizi, the institute director, drafted a "six-point statement on the current situation" in the name of the Economic Structural Reform Research Institute, the Development Institute of the China Rural Development Research Center under the State Council, the Institute on International Studies of the China International Trust and Investment Corporation and the Beijing Association of Young Economists. The statement, which was broadcast at Tiananmen Square and distributed widely, demanded "publicizing of the inside story of the decisionmaking of the top leadership and the divergence of opinions" and "convening of a special session of the National People's Congress and a special congress of the Chinese Communist Party." It also urged the students on Tiananmen Square to "end their hunger strike as soon as possible," hinting that the government "would adopt extreme measures (military control)."

Soon after that, some people, who identified themselves as employees of the State Commission for Restructuring the Economy, went to Tiananmen Square to deliver a speech in which they said, "With deep grief and extreme anger, we now disclose a piece of absolutely true news—General Secretary Zhao Ziyang has been dismissed from the post." The speakers called on the workers, students, and shopkeepers to carry out nation-wide strikes and instigate the masses to "take immediate actions to fight a life-and-death struggle." The speech was soon printed in the form of a *People's Daily Extra*, which was widely distributed. On the same evening, leaflets entitled "Several Suggestions on the Tactics of the Student Movement" were found at the Beijing railway station and other public places. It said that "at present, hunger strikes and dialogues should no longer be our means and demands. We should hold peaceful sit-ins and raise clearcut new political demands and slogans: (1) Comrade Ziyang must not be removed; (2) a special national congress of the Chinese Communist Party [should] be convened immediately; (3) a special session of the National People's Congress [should] be held immediately." It also said that people "shouldn't be terrified by the coming troops" and that "this attitude should be explained time and again to the students before their coming." Some leaders of the Autonomous Students Union of Beijing Universities and the Beijing Autonomous Workers Union who had been arrested also confessed that at about 4:00 P.M. on May 19, someone holding a piece of paper and identifying himself as a staff worker of a certain organization under the party Central Committee, went to the "Tiananmen Square Headquarters" and revealed the news that martial law was about to be declared.

As a result of the close collaboration between a small number of people who had access to top party and state secrets and the organizers and schemers of the turmoil, the organizers made a timely adjustment to their tactics. That night, forty-five minutes before the meeting called by the central authorities and attended by cadres from the party, government and military institutions in Beijing, they changed the hunger strike to a sit-in in a bid to give people the false impression that since the students had already ended their hunger strike it was not necessary for the government to declare martial law. By so doing they also gained time to organize people and coerce those who were in the dark to set up roadblocks at major crossroads to stop the advance of the troops and to continue to mislead public opinion and confuse people's minds. While viciously cursing Comrade Deng Xiaoping and other proletarian revolutionaries of the old generation, saying that "we don't need Deng Xiaoping's wisdom and experience," they lavished praise on Comrade Zhao Ziyang by saying that "The country is hopeless without Ziyang as the party leader" and "Give us back Ziyang." They also plotted to rally forces for greater turmoil, claiming that they were going to mobilize two hundred thousand people to occupy Tiananmen Square and to organize a citywide demonstration on May 20. Concerting with Comrade Zhao Ziyang's three-day sick leave which started on May 19, they spread the word that a "new government" would be established in three days.

Under the extremely urgent circumstances, the party Central Committee and the State Council decided resolutely to declare martial law in parts of Beijing, starting from 10:00 A.M., May 20, to prevent the situation from worsening and grasp the initiative to stop the turmoil so as to give support to the broad masses who were opposed to the turmoil and longed for stability. However, as the organizers and schemers of the turmoil had learned of our decision before it was implemented, there were tremendous difficulties and obstacles for the troops to enter the city.

On the eve of declaring martial law and on the first two days after it was declared, all major crossroads were blocked. More than 220 buses were taken away and used as roadblocks. Transportation came to a standstill. Troops to enforce the martial law were not able to arrive at their designated places. The headquarters of the party Central Committee and the State Council continued to be surrounded. Speeches inciting people could be heard anywhere on the street. Leaflets spreading rumors could be seen anywhere in the city. Demonstrations, each involving thousands of people, took place in succession, and Beijing, our capital city, fell into total disorder and terror. In the following few days, the martial law troops managed to enter the city by different ways. Meanwhile, the armed police and [the regular] police continued to perform their duties by overcoming tremendous difficulties. Urban and suburban districts organized workers, residents, and government office workers, as many as 120,000 people altogether, to maintain social order. The outer suburban counties also sent out militiamen. The concerted efforts of the troops, police, and civilians helped improve the transportation, production, and living order in the capital and people felt much at ease. But the very small number of people never stopped for a single day their activities to create turmoil and never changed their goal of overthrowing the leadership of the Communist Party. Things were developing day by day toward a counter-revolutionary rebellion.

One of the major tactics of the organizers and schemers of the turmoil after martial law was declared was to continue to stay on Tiananmen Square. They wanted to turn the square into a "center of the student movement and the whole nation." Once the government made a decision, they planned to make "strong reaction" at the square and form an "antigovernment united front." These people had been planning to stir up blood-shedding incidents on the square, believing that "the government would resort to suppression if the occupation of the square continues" and "blood can awaken people and split up the government."

To ensure that the situation on the square could be maintained, they used funds provided by reactionary forces both at home and abroad to improve their facilities and install advanced telecommunications devices, spending 100,000 yuan a day on an average. They even started illegal purchases of weapons. By using the tents provided by their Hong Kong supporters they set up "villages of freedom" and launched a "democracy university" on the square, claiming they would turn the university into "the Huangpu Military Academy of the new era."[6] They erected a so-called goddess statue in front of the Monument to the People's Heroes. The statue was formerly named the "Goddess of Freedom" but its name was later changed to "Goddess of Democracy," showing that they took American-style democracy and freedom as their spiritual pillar.

Fearing that the students who took part in sit-ins could not hold on, Liu Xiaobo and other behind-the-scene schemers went up to the front stage and performed a four-man farce of a 48–72 hour hunger strike so as to pep the students up. They said, "As long as the flags on the square are still up, we can continue our fight and spread it to the whole country until the government collapses."

---

[6]The Huangpu (Whampoa) Military Academy was established in 1924 in Guangzhou by Sun Yat-sen, with Chiang Kai-shek as first commandant and Soviet advisers as political instructors. Prior to the 1926 disruption of the United Front, many Guomindang and Communist military leaders received their training at Huangpu. Students who later joined the Guomindang came to be known as the "Whampoa Clique."

Taking advantage of the restraint that the government and the troops still exercised after martial law was declared, the organizers and plotters of the turmoil continued to organize all kinds of illegal activities. Following the establishment of the "Autonomous Students Union of Beijing Universities," the "Beijing Autonomous Workers Unions," the "Fasting Contingent," the "Tiananmen Square Headquarters," and the "Union of Capital's Intelligentsia," they set up more illegal organizations such as the "Patriotic Joint Conference of People from All Walks of Life in the Capital for Upholding the Constitution" and the "Autonomous Union of Beijing Residents." In the name of the Research Institute for Restructuring the Economic System, the Development Institute of the China Rural Development Research Center under the State Council, and the Beijing Association of Young Economists, they openly sent telegrams to some of the troops in an attempt to incite defection. They were engaged in such underground activities to topple the government as organizing a special team in charge of molding public opinion and making preparations to launch an underground newspaper.

They organized their sworn followers in taking a secret oath, claiming "under no condition should we betray our conscience, yield to autocracy and bow to the emperor of China in the 1980s." Wan Runnan, general manager of Stone Company, listed the following six conditions for retreating from Tiananmen Square when he called together some leaders of the Autonomous Students Union of Beijing Universities in the international hotel: "To withdraw the troops, cancel martial law, remove Li Peng, ask Deng Xiaoping and Yang Shangkun to quit, and let Zhao Ziyang resume his post." During the meeting, they also planned to organize "a great march to claim victory at midnight." Moreover, as they believed that there was almost no hope to solve problems without the party after Comrade Zhao Ziyang asked for sick leave, they pinned their hope on an emergency meeting by the Standing Committee of the National People's Congress.

Yan Jiaqi, Bao Zunxin, and others sent a telegram to the leaders of the NPC Standing Committee, saying that "as the Constitution is being wantonly trampled by a few people, we hereby make an emergency appeal to hold an emergency meeting by the NPC Standing Committee immediately to solve the current critical problems."

Inspired by a certain member of the NPC Standing Committee, the Stone Research Institute of Social Development issued an opinion-collecting letter on the suggestion to convene such an emergency meeting. After getting the signatures of several members of the NPC Standing Committee, it sent urgent telegrams to NPC Standing Committee members outside Beijing. Conspiratorially, they said nothing about their true purposes in those letters and telegrams in an attempt to deceive those comrades who did not know the truth. They even went so far as to usurp the names of those comrades to serve their ulterior motives.

After doing all this, Yan Jiaqi and Bao Zunxin published an article in Hong

Kong's *Ming Pao Daily News*, entitled "Solve China's Present Problems in a Democratic and Legal Way—Also a Letter to Li Peng," which called "every member of the NPC Standing Committee and every deputy to the NPC to cast a sacred vote to abolish martial law and dismiss Li Peng as premier." [See Doc. 51.]

Organizers and instigators of the turmoil also unbridledly agitated and organized actions of violence. They hooked up local hooligans, ruffians, and criminals from other parts of the country, ex-convicts who did not turn over a new leaf and people who have deep hatred of the Communist Party and the socialist system to knock together the so-called Dare-to-Die Corps, Flying Tiger Teams, Volunteer Army, and other terrorist organizations, threatening to detain and kidnap party and state leaders and "seize state power by means of attacking the Bastille." They distributed leaflets to stir up counter-revolutionary armed rebellion, advocating "a single spark can start a prairie fire" and called for establishing "armed forces that might be called the people's army," for "uniting with various forces including the Guomindang in Taiwan" and for "a clear-cut stand opposing the Communist Party and its government by sacrificing lives."

They declared their desire to settle accounts with the party and the government after the event and even prepared a blacklist of officials to be suppressed. The Hong Kong-based *Ming Pao Daily News* published a "dialogue" on June 2 between Liu Xiaobo, one of the organizers and planners, and "a mainland democratic movement leader," in which Liu said, "We must organize an armed force among the people to materialize Zhao Ziyang's comeback."

The activities of the instigators of the riots have strong financial backing. In addition to the materials worth some hundreds of thousands of yuan from the Stone Company, they also got support from hostile forces overseas and other organizations and individuals. Some people from the United States, Britain, and Hong Kong offered them nearly one million U.S. dollars and millions of Hong Kong dollars. Part of the money was used for activities to sabotage the martial law enforcement. Anyone who took part in establishing obstacles to stop traffic and block army vehicles could get thirty yuan a day. Also they set high prices to buy off rioters to burn military vehicles and beat soldiers, promising to offer three thousand yuan for burning one vehicle and more money for capturing or killing soldiers.

A high-ranking official from Taiwan launched a campaign to "send love to Tiananmen" and took the lead of donating 100,000 Taiwan dollars. A member of the Central Committee of the Guomindang in Taiwan suggested that 100 million Taiwan dollars be donated to establish a "Supporting Mainland Democratic Movement Fund." Some people of the Taiwan arts and cultural circles also launched "a campaign supporting the democratic movement on the mainland." A letter by the Autonomous Students Union of Beijing Universities to "Taiwan Friends in Art Circles" said that "we heartily thank you and salute to you for your material and spiritual support at this crucial moment. . . ."

All this shows that the turmoil planned, organized and premeditated by a few people could not be put down merely by making some concessions on the part of the government or just issuing an order to impose martial law, contrary to the imagination of some kind-hearted people.

They [had] made up their minds to unite with all hostile forces overseas and in foreign countries to launch a battle against us to the last. All one-sided good-will would lead only to their unscrupulous attack against us and the longer the time the greater the cost.

7. How Did a Small Minority of People Manage to Stir Up the Counter-Revolutionary Rebellion?

The Chinese People's Liberation Army undertakes not only the sacred duty of "strengthening national defense, resisting aggression and defending the mother-land," but also the noble responsibility of "safeguarding the people's peaceful labor, participating in national reconstruction and working hard to serve the people," which are provided for in Article 29 of the Constitution of China. It was exactly to carry out the tasks entrusted to them by the Constitution that the troops entered the city proper and safeguarded social order.

After the announcement of martial law in some areas of the capital on May 20, the troops, despite repeated obstructions, were mobilized to march toward the city proper in accordance with a deployment plan and by different ways to take up appointed positions.

The handful of organizers and plotters of the rebellion were well aware that they would have no way to continue their illegal and counter-revolutionary activ-ities and their conspiracy would come to nothing if the martial law troops took up positions in the center of Beijing. Therefore, they started to create trouble deliberately and did their best to aggravate the unrest, which eventually devel-oped into a counter-revolutionary rebellion.

On June 1, the Public Security Bureau detained a few of the ringleaders of the illegal organization known as the "Federation of Autonomous Workers' Unions." The agitators of the rebellion then took advantage of this opportunity to incite some people to surround and attack the offices of the Beijing Municipal Public Security Bureaus, the municipal party committee and government, and the Ministry of Public Security.

On the evening of June 2, a police jeep on loan to the Chinese Central TV Station was involved in a traffic accident in which three people died. None of the victims was a student. This was deliberately distorted as a provocation by martial law troops. The conspirators attempted to seize the bodies and parade them in coffins, stirring up the people and making the atmosphere extremely tense. After this incitement and uproar they lit the fire of the counter-revolutionary rebellion.

Just after midnight on June 3, while the martial law troops were heading for their positions according to schedule, agitators urged crowds to halt military and other motor vehicles, set up roadblocks, beat soldiers, and looted trucks of materials at Jianguomen, Nanheyan, Xidan, Muxudi, and other road crossings. Some twelve military vehicles were halted by crowds near Caogezhuang. Soldiers marching past the Yanjing Hotel were stopped and searched by rioters, and military vehicles parked in front of the Beijing Telegraph Office had their tires slashed and were surrounded with road dividers.

About dawn, military vehicles on the Yongdingmen Bridge were overturned, others at Muxudi had their tires slashed and a group of four hundred soldiers in Caoyangmen were stoned. In the Liubukou and Hengertiao areas, military vehicles and soldiers were surrounded by unruly crowds.

Around 7:00 A.M., some rioters swarmed over military vehicles which had been halted at Liubukou and snatched machine guns and ammunition. From Jianguomen to Dongdan and in the Tianpiao area, martial law troops were surrounded and beaten. On the Jianguomen overpass some soldiers were stripped and others severely beaten.

Later in the morning, troops in the Hufangqiao area were beaten by rioters and some were blinded. The mob prevented injured soldiers from reaching hospitals by deflating ambulance tires and the victims were dragged from the vehicles. From Hufang Road to Taoranting Park, twenty-one military vehicles were surrounded and halted. Policemen escorting the soldiers were beaten by the rioters.

From noon onward, many of the soldiers trapped by mobs and barricades at the Fuyoujie, Zhengyilu, Xuanwumen, Hufangqiao, Muxudi, and Dongsi crossroads were injured and their equipment was stolen. At Liubukou, policemen tried several times to recover a military truck loaded with arms and ammunition from an enraged mob but failed. They were then forced to use tear gas to disperse the rioters and recapture the dangerous cargo.

About the same time, mobs began to surround and assault buildings housing state organizations and establishments of vital importance, including the Great Hall of the People, the Propaganda Department of the CPC Central Committee and the Ministry of Radio, Film and Television, as well as the West and South Gates of Zhongnanhai, the seat of the party Central Committee and the State Council. Dozens of policemen and guards there were injured.

As the situation rapidly deteriorated, the instigators of the upheaval became more vicious. At about 5:00 P.M., the ringleaders of the illegal organizations known as the "Beijing Federation of Autonomous Students' Unions of Universities and Colleges" and "Federation of Autonomous Workers' Unions" distributed knives, iron bars, chains, and sharpened bamboo sticks, inciting the mobs to kill soldiers and members of the security forces. In a broadcast over loudspeakers in Tiananmen Square, the "Federation of Autonomous Workers' Unions" urged the people "to take up arms and overthrow the government." It also broadcast how to make and use Molotov cocktails and how to wreck and burn military vehicles.

Mobs organized about one thousand people to push down the wall of a construction site near Xidan and stole tools, reinforcing bars and bricks, ready for street fighting. They planned to incite people to take to the streets the next day, Sunday, to stage a violent rebellion in an attempt to overthrow the government and seize power at one stroke.

At this critical juncture, the party's Central Committee, the State Council, and the Central Military Commission decided to order troops poised on the outskirts of the capital to enforce martial law and quell the counter-revolutionary rebellion.

8. How Did the Counter-Revolutionary Rebels Injure and Kill People's Liberation Army Soldiers?

Since the enforcement of martial law in Beijing, the martial law troops heading for Beijing proper tried their best to avoid conflicts, exercising great restraint. After the June 3 riot happened and before the troops entered the city, the Beijing Municipal Government and the Headquarters of the Martial Law Enforcement Troops issued an emergency announcement at 6:30 P.M., which said, "All citizens must keep off the streets and not go to Tiananmen Square as of the issuing of this notice. Workers should remain at their posts, and other citizens must stay at home to ensure their security." The announcement was broadcast over and over again on TV and radio.

About 10:00 P.M. on June 3, most of the martial law troops heading for Beijing proper from various directions had been halted at barricades set up at the main crossroads. Even so, the troops were still quite restrained, while the counter-revolutionary rioters took advantage to beat and kill soldiers, to steal military materials and burn military vehicles.

From 10:00 P.M. to 11:00 P.M. the same day, at Cuiweilu, Gongzhufen, Muxudi, and Xidan, twelve military vehicles were burned. Some people threw bricks at soldiers. And some rioters pushed trolleybuses to the crossroads, set them on fire and blocked the roads. When fire engines got there, they were also smashed and burned.

Around 11:00 P.M., three military vehicles were wrecked and one jeep was overturned at Hufangqiao, and military vehicles on Andingmen flyover were surrounded. In Chongwenmen Street, a regiment of soldiers was surrounded, and on Jianguomen flyover, thirty military vehicles were halted by barricades, and another three hundred military vehicles were halted near the Beijing Mining School.

Trying to persuade the rioters to let them through, PLA men from warrant officers to generals were beaten or kidnapped.

To avoid conflicts, the barricaded military vehicles in Nanyuan and Sanyingmen made a detour. When they reached the South Gate of the Temple of Heaven, they were halted again and many of these vehicles were wrecked and burned. One military vehicle was halted in Zhushikou and a group of people swarmed over it. When a man looking like a cadre came up and tried to persuade them to leave it alone, he was severely beaten and no one knows whether he died or not.

Just after dawn June 4, more military vehicles were burned. Several hundred military vehicles on dozens of road crossings in Tiantan Dongche Road, North Gate of Temple of Heaven, Qianmen Donglu, Fuyou Street, Liubukou, Xidan, Fuxingmen, Nanlishilou, Muxudi, Lianhuachi, Chegongzhuang, Donghuamen, Dongzhimen, Dabeiyao, Hujialou, Beidougezhuang, and Jiugongxiang in Daxing County were attacked with Molotov cocktails. Some soldiers were burned to death, and some others were beaten to death. In some areas, several dozen military vehicles were burning at the same time.

At the Shuangjing crossroad, more than seventy armored personnel carriers were surrounded and machine guns ripped from twenty of them.

From Jingyuan crossroad to Laoshan crematorium, more than 30 military vehicles were burning at the same time. Some rioters with iron bars and gasoline drums, waiting on the crossroads to burn passing motor vehicles. [as received] And many military vehicles carrying food, bedding and clothing were hijacked.

Several mobs drove stolen armored personnel carriers along the Fuxingmen flyover area firing the guns. The "Federation of Autonomous Workers' Unions" claimed in their own broadcast that they had stolen a military transceiver and a cipher code book.

The mobs also assaulted civilian installations and public buildings. Shop windows including those of the Yanshan Department Store in Xicheng District were broken. Pine trees in front of Tiananmen gate and the western part of Chairman Mao's Memorial Hall were burned. Some public buses, fire engines, ambulances and taxis were also wrecked and burned. Some people even drove a public bus loaded with gasoline drums toward the Tiananmen rostrum and attempted to set fire to it. They were stopped by martial law troops on the southern side of Gold Water Bridges.

The mobs also murdered soldiers in various bestial ways. About dawn June 4, some mobs beat up soldiers with bottles and bricks at Dongdan crossroad. In Fuxingmen, a military vehicle was surrounded and twelve soldiers were dragged off the vehicle. They were searched and severely beaten. Many of them were badly injured. In Liubukou, four soldiers were surrounded and beaten, and some were beaten to death. In the Guangqumen area, three soldiers were severely beaten. One was rescued by some bystanders and the other two have not been found yet. In Xixingsheng Lane of the Xicheng District, more than twenty armed policemen were beaten up by mobs; some were badly injured, and the whereabouts of the others are unknown. In Huguosi, a military vehicle was halted, and soldiers on it were beaten up and detained as hostages. Submachine guns were snatched. A truck full of bricks was driven from Dongjiao Minxiang to Tiananmen Square, and people on the truck shouted, "If you are really Chinese attack the soldiers."

After dawn, a police ambulance was carrying eight injured soldiers to a hospital when it was halted by mobs. They beat a soldier to death and shouted that they would do the same to the other seven. In front of a bicycle shop in Qianmen Street, three soldiers were severely beaten by hooligans, who threatened anyone who tried to rescue them. On Changan Avenue, a military vehicle broke down suddenly and was attacked right away by about two hundred rioters. The driver was killed inside the cab. About 30 meters to the east of Xidan crossroad, another soldier was beaten to death. Then the mob poured gasoline over his body and set fire to it. In Fuchengmen, another soldier's body was hung over the flyover after he had been savagely killed. In Chongwenmen, a soldier was thrown from the flyover and burned alive. Near the Capital Cinema on West Changan Avenue, an officer was beaten to death, disemboweled and his eyes plucked out. His body was then strung up on a burning bus.

In the several days of the rebellion, more than 1,280 military vehicles, police cars and public buses were wrecked, burned or otherwise damaged. Of the vehicles, over 1,000 were military vehicles, more than 60 were armored personnel carriers and about 30 were police cars. More than 120 public buses were destroyed as well as more than 70 other kinds of motor vehicles. During the same period, arms and ammunition were stolen. More than 6,000 martial law soldiers, armed police and public security officers were injured and the death toll reached several dozens. They sacrificed their blood and even their precious lives to defend the motherland, the Constitution and the people. The people will remember their contributions forever.

Such heavy losses are eloquent testimony to the restraint and tolerance shown by the martial law troops. The PLA is an army led by the Chinese Communist Party and serves the people whole-heartedly. They are ruthless to the enemy but kind to the people. They were able to defeat the eight million Guomindang troops armed by U.S. imperialism during the war years and able to defeat U.S. imperialism, which was armed to the teeth, effectively safeguarding the sacred territory and territorial waters and air space of our country. So why did they suffer such great casualties in quelling the counter-revolutionary rebellion? Why were they beaten and even killed, even when they had weapons in their hands? It is just as Comrade Deng Xiaoping pointed out that "it was because bad people mingled with the good, which made it difficult for us to take the firm measures that were necessary." It also showed that the PLA loves the people and is unwilling to injure civilians by accident. The fact that they met death and sacrificed themselves with generosity and without fear fully embodies the nature of the PLA. Otherwise how could there be such a great number of casualties and losses? Doesn't this reflect that the army defends the people at the cost of its own life?

To quell the counter-revolutionary rebellion and to avoid more losses, the martial law troops, having suffered heavy casualties and been driven beyond forbearance, were forced to fire in the air to open the way forward after repeated warnings.

During the counter-attack, some rioters were killed. Because there were numerous bystanders, some were knocked down by vehicles, and some were trampled on or were hit by stray bullets. Some were wounded or killed by ruffians who had seized rifles.

According to the information we have so far gathered, more than three thousand civilians were wounded and over two hundred, including thirty-six college students, died during the riot. Among the nonmilitary casualties were rioters who deserved the punishment, people accidentally injured, doctors and other people who were carrying out various duties on the spot. The government will do its best to deal with the problems arising from the deaths of the latter two kinds of people.

Due to a rumor spread by the "Voice of America" and some people who deliberately wished to spread rumors, people talked about a "Tiananmen bloodbath" and "thousands of people massacred." The facts are that after the martial law troops reached Tiananmen Square at 1:30 A.M., the Beijing Municipal Government and the martial law headquarters issued an emergency notice, which stated, "A serious counter-revolutionary rebellion occurred in the capital this evening" and "all citizens and students in Tiananmen Square should leave immediately to ensure that martial law troops will be able to implement their tasks." The notice was broadcast repeatedly for three hours through loud-speakers. The sit-in students gathered around the Monument to the People's Heroes in the southern part of the square. At around 3:00 A.M., they sent representatives to the troops to express their desire to withdraw from the square voluntarily and this was welcomed by the troops.

At 4:30 A.M., the martial law headquarters broadcast the following notice: "It is time to clear the square and the martial law headquarters accepts the request of the students to be allowed to withdraw." At the same time, another notice on quickly restoring normal order to the square was issued by the municipal government and the headquarters and broadcast. After hearing this, the several thousand students organized hand-in-hand pickets and started to leave the square in an orderly manner, carrying their own banners and streamers.

At about 5:00 A.M., the troops vacated a wide corridor in the southeastern part of the square to ensure the smooth and safe departure of the students. At the same time, a few students who refused to leave were forced to leave by martial law troops. By 5:30 A.M., the clearing operation of the square had been completed.

During the whole operation no one, including the students who refused but were forced to leave, died. Tales of "rivers of blood" in Tiananmen Square and the rumor-mongers themselves "escaping from underneath piles of corpses," are sheer nonsense.

The counter-revolutionary rebellion was put down with Tiananmen Square returning to the hands of the people and all martial law enforcement troops taking up their assigned positions.

During the quelling of the counter-revolutionary rebellion, the PLA and the police fought valiantly and performed immortal feats. And many people gave first-aid to the wounded and rescued besieged soldiers, rendering their cooperation and support to the martial-law enforcement troops.

Due to the counter-revolutionary rebellion, Beijing has suffered heavy losses in its economy, and losses in other fields that cannot be counted with money. Workers, peasants and intellectuals are now working hard to retrieve the losses. Now, order in the capital has fundamentally returned to normal and the situation throughout China is also tending to become smooth, which shows that the correct decision made by the party Central Committee has benefited the Chinese people of all nationalities. Yet, the unrest and the rebellion are not completely over, as a handful of counter-revolutionary rioters refuse to recognize defeat and still indulge in sabotage, and even dream of staging a comeback.

To achieve thorough victory, we should mobilize the people completely, strengthen the people's democratic dictatorship and spare no effort to ferret out the counter-revolutionary rioters. We should uncover instigators and rebellious conspirators, and punish the organizers and schemers of the unrest and the counter-revolutionary rebellion, that is, those who obstinately stuck to the path of bourgeois liberalization and conspired to instigate rebellion, those who colluded with overseas and other foreign hostile forces, those who provided illegal organizations with top secrets of the party and state, and those who committed the atrocities of beating, smashing, grabbing and burning during the disturbances. We should make a clear distinction between two different types of contradictions and deal with them accordingly, through resolute, hard, and painstaking work. We must educate and unite people as much as possible and focus the crackdown on a handful of principal culprits and diehards who refuse to repent. On this basis, we will retrieve all the losses suffered in the unrest and the counter-revolutionary rebellion as soon as possible. For this, we must rely on the people, try to increase production, practice strict economy and struggle arduously.

Chairman, vice-chairmen, and Standing Committee members, our country's just struggle to quell the unrest and the counter-revolutionary rebellion has won the understanding and support of governments and people of many countries. We extend our wholehearted gratitude for this. However, there are also some countries, mainly the United States and some West European countries, which have distorted the facts, spread slanderous rumors and even uttered so-called condemnations and applied sanctions to our country to set off an anti-China wave and wantonly interfere in our country's internal affairs. We deeply regret this. As for the outside pressures, our government and people have never submitted to such things, not this time nor any time. The rumors will be cleared away and the truth and facts will come out.

Our country will unswervingly take economic construction as the central task and persist in the four cardinal principles and in economic reform and opening up to the outside world. Our country will, as always, adhere to our independent foreign policy of peace, continue to develop friendly relations with all countries in the world on the basis of the Five Principles of Peaceful Coexistence, and make our contributions to the safeguarding of world peace and the promotion of world development.[7]

---

[7]*Wuxiang yuanze*, from a 1954 agreement between China and India: (1) mutual respect for territory and sovereignty; (2) nonaggression; (3) noninterference in internal affairs of other states; (4) equality of states and work for mutual benefit; (5) peaceful coexistence.

ANTECEDENTS

II

Prelude

Reform and Retrenchment

This section outlines the political and economic background to the crisis of April to June. It conveys the complex policy issues that confronted and seriously divided the leadership in the late 1980s. Despite, or some might say because of, the success of economic reform during the previous years, China's top leaders were split over the future course of economic reform. Four important documents are presented here that capture the complex issues of these political, economic, and environmental challenges.

The first document excerpts General Secretary Zhao Ziyang's report on October 25, 1987, to the Thirteenth Party Congress (Doc. 3). The passages selected here deal with the need for political reform. This speech was drafted by members of several proreform think tanks established in Beijing, many of whom, such as Bao Tong and Yan Jiaqi, became vociferous supporters of the students in the spring of 1989 and figured in Chen Xitong's harsh indictment in Document 2. Although advocating sweeping changes in the structure of state and party—such as expanding the authority of representative assemblies, strengthening the role of law, and expanding press freedoms—this document evidently had Deng Xiaoping's explicit endorsement. Not surprisingly, Zhao rejects a parliamentary or multiparty system and falls short of proposing reforms similar to those Mikhail Gorbachev initiated in the Soviet Union in 1989–90.[1] Despite attacks on

---

[1]Deng's visceral hatred for the American system of separation of powers led Zhao to make proposals for reform that did not appear American. Yet Zhao supported many fundamental changes, namely, increased democracy in labor unions—indicated by his appointment of the liberal ex-propaganda chief, Zhu Houze, vice-chairman of the All-China Federation of Trade Unions—and proposals for open elections at the grass roots. In February 1987, during a party seminar on Gorbachev's reforms, Zhao reportedly berated his aides for not raising the issue of citizens' rights. In asserting that "people should get

"bourgeois liberalization" following Hu Yaobang's dismissal in early 1987, Zhao's program clearly reveals that some leaders still supported keeping political reform on the CPC's agenda.[2] One sentence in the section on "Establishing a System of Consultation and Dialogue" merits stress: "Different groups of people may have different interests and views, and they too need opportunities and channels for the exchange of ideas."[3] This embryonic concept of a plural system would allow the formation of *voluntary* associations, a heresy in the Leninist tradition that, nevertheless, has been overturned in Eastern Europe and most recently the Soviet Union. Zhao, however, indicates his unwillingness to challenge the basic structure of power in China by refusing to extend the reforms that far in his discussion of mass organizations.

Document 4 is a sobering account of the cataclysmic population and environmental problems facing China. Written at the prestigious Academy of Sciences and published in a widely circulated magazine, the article highlights the pressures that confront both urban and rural populations: severe environmental degradation, overcrowding, unemployment and underemployment, water shortages, and soil erosion. The author, Xiao Jiabao, believes these problems can be resolved but insists that time cannot be lost. Appropriate measures must be undertaken immediately, he says, including reform. "The Chinese people . . . must have a sense of crisis for survival, a sense of apprehension for their nation, a sense of urgency for reform, and a sense of responsibility for history. The decision makers, the intellectual circles, and the masses must form a consensus and a new, enduring, and strong cohesiveness." Continuation along the current path, the author implies, is insufficient and will lead to national disaster. In this, he reflects the view of many scientists, social scientists, and humanists that China's very survival is at stake.

Similar issues are addressed in Li Peng's March 21, 1989, report to the NPC

---

more freedom in their real life," Zhao was appealing to widely popular demands to eliminate the "dossier system" (*dang'an*) and terminate such other government intrusions into personal lives as the monitoring of personal telephone and mail communications. Wu Guoguang, "The Issues of Participation in the Political Reform: Pressures and Limitations," paper presented to the Conference on "China: Crisis of 1989—Its Origins and Implications," SUNY Buffalo, February 16–18, 1990.

[2]Several former provincial first party secretaries had, indeed, called for greater internal party democracy in reaction to the secretive and highly centralized manner in which the decision on the campaign against "spiritual pollution" had been made. These complaints by Liu Jie (Henan), An Pingsheng (Yunnan), Chi Buqing (Guizhou), and Zhou Hui (Inner Mongolia) may help explain the rapid decision to terminate that campaign in 1985. The party's Organization Department also aired and partially implemented proposals for electing officials through mass discussion and recommendation. Ibid.

[3]Zhao's legitimation of "different interests" in the political system reflects similar ideas formulated by Soviet theorists in the years preceding Gorbachev's reforms. Ronald J. Hill and Peter Frank, *The Soviet Communist Party*, 3d ed. (Boston: Allen and Unwin, 1986), p. 14.

(Doc. 5). Although full of positive and optimistic assessments, the speech also portrays a strained economy, as production of grain and cotton—China's major crops—fell by 2.2 percent and 1 percent, respectively, in 1988. The rate of inflation, according to Li, was 18.5 percent, an understatement for urban areas, where the effective rate probably hit 30–40 percent. The government was also experiencing major budget deficits and excessive growth in money supply, problems the conservative Li attributes to hasty and ill-considered reform. Implicitly pointing his finger at Zhao, Li asserts: "We had made an overoptimistic estimation of the 1987 economic situation. . . . We did not give full consideration to the capacity of the state. . . . We relaxed and readjusted the prices of some commodities." Li thus offers a remedy—already adopted the previous September—of readjustment and retrenchment that essentially postpones further economic reform and, of great importance to the students, halts significant political changes.

The final document in part II (Doc. 6) contains two versions of remarks delivered by Zhao on April 12, roughly three weeks after Li's NPC report. The first comes from the New China News Agency (Xinhua), and the second from Beijing Television. Together, they sharply contrast with Li's conservative approach. Zhao sought to salvage important components of the reform program, especially price reform and changes in the enterprise management system. Noting the profound changes in the economy wrought by ten years of reform, Zhao insisted that the reimposition of controls favored by Li would not restore economic balance. Although Li and Zhao agreed that the economy was not in good shape, the two leaders were now openly advocating two fundamentally different policy positions. Zhao essentially believed that persistence in reform with some retrenchment was the proper remedy, while Li wanted a complete return to a centralized command economy.

3
Report to the Thirteenth CCP National Congress [Excerpts on Political Reform]

ZHAO ZIYANG

Source: *Beijing Review* 30, 45 (November 9–15, 1987): 37–43.

V. Reforming the Political Structure

The deepening of the ongoing reform of the economic structure makes reform of the political structure increasingly urgent. The process of developing a socialist commodity economy should also involve the building of a socialist democracy. Without reform of the political structure, reform of the economic structure cannot succeed in the end. The Central Committee of the party believes that it is high time to put reform of the political structure on the agenda for the whole party. Comrade Deng Xiaoping's speech, "On the Reform of the System of Party and State Leadership," delivered to an enlarged meeting of the Political Bureau of the Central Committee in August 1980, is a guide to reform of the political structure.

The purpose of reforming both the political and economic structures is, under the leadership of the party and the socialist system, to better develop the productive forces and to take full advantage of the superiority of socialism. In other words, we shall catch up with the developed capitalist countries economically and, politically, we shall create a democracy that is of a higher level and more effective than the democracy of those countries. We shall also try to produce more and better-trained professionals than they do. The merits of the reform should be judged on the basis of whether these objectives are attained.

China is a socialist country under the people's democratic dictatorship, and its basic political system is good. However, there are major defects in our system of leadership, in the organizational structure and in our style of work. Chief among these defects are overconcentration of power, a serious degree of bureaucratism, and feudal influences that are far from eliminated. The purpose of reforming the political structure is to promote what is beneficial and eliminate what is harmful and to build a socialist democracy with Chinese characteristics. The long-range goal of reform is to build a socialist political system with a high degree of democracy and a complete set of laws, a system that is effective and full of vitality. And that is something which cannot be achieved without sustained effort.

Like the development of a socialist commodity economy, the building of a socialist democracy is a gradual, cumulative process. Confronted as we are with the complicated social contradictions that arise in the drive for modernization, we need a peaceful social and political environment. We shall never again allow the kind of "great democracy" that undermines state law and social stability. The system of the people's congresses, the system of multiparty cooperation and political consultation under the leadership of the Communist Party, and the principle of democratic centralism are the characteristics and advantages of our system. We shall never abandon them and introduce a Western system of separation of the three powers and of different parties ruling the country in turn. In the reform of the political structure, we must handle properly the relationship between democracy and stability and between democracy and efficiency. We must overcome bureaucratism and feudal influence so as to promote the reform of the economic structure and the policy of opening up both internally and externally. The immediate objective of reform is to institute a system of leadership that will help to raise the efficiency, increase the vitality and stimulate the initiative of all sectors of society. Every measure taken in the reform should serve this objective and help to solve those problems for whose solution conditions are ripe.

1. Separating Party and Government

The Communist Party is the leading force in building socialism in China. In the new situation the party's leadership can be strengthened only by improving the system, methods and style of leadership. In the last few years we have worked hard to improve the party's leadership and have achieved some progress. But one long-standing problem has not yet been completely solved: the lack of distinction between the functions of the party and those of the government and the substitution of the party for the government. Until this problem is solved, party leadership cannot be really strengthened and other reform measures cannot be smoothly carried out. Therefore, the key to reforming the political structure is the separation of party and government.

This means the separation of the functions of the party and the government. It was under the party's leadership that a Constitution was drawn up for the country and laws were enacted, and the party must conduct its activities within the limits prescribed by that Constitution and those laws. . . . It should respect mass organizations, enterprises and institutions and not monopolize the conduct of their affairs. The party exercises political leadership, which means that it formulates political principles, points the political direction, makes major policy decisions and recommends cadres for the key posts in organs of state power. . . .

Separating the functions of party and government is a major reform in the system of party leadership. It must be pointed out that when there is no distinction between party and government, the party's position is in fact lowered and its leadership weakened; only when the two are separated is it possible for the party to ensure its leadership and improve its methods. . . . When there is no distinction between party and government, the party has to bear the burden of administrative work and may easily become one opposite of a contradiction or even the focal point of many contradictions; only when the two are separated is it possible for the party to handle contradictions with ease, assume overall control of a situation and coordinate the work in all fields. . . .

2. Delegating Powers to Lower Levels

Overconcentration of power is manifested not only in the concentration of all power of administrative, economic and cultural departments and mass organizations in the hands of leading organs of party committees, but also in the concentration of all power of grass-roots units in the hands of leading organs at higher levels. On the one hand, our leading organs have taken charge of many matters which they should not and cannot handle, or cannot handle efficiently, getting bogged down in routine work. On the other hand, the grass-roots units lack the power to make decisions, and it is hard to fully arouse the initiative of the people. The way to solve this problem is to delegate power to lower levels. This devolution of power has proved effective in rural reform and should be carried out in all other fields. . . .

3. Reforming Government Organs

Bureaucratism remains a serious problem in the political life of our party and the state. For economic, cultural, social, and historical reasons, our struggle against it will last a long time. Separating the functions of the party from those of the government, delegating more powers to lower levels and developing socialist democracy will all help overcome bureaucratism. It should be noted that the overstaffing, overlapping, and unwieldiness of government organs, confusion of their responsibilities and buck-passing are also major causes of bureaucratism. . . .

4. Reforming the Personnel System Relating to Cadres

We cannot stimulate the cadres' energy, efficiency and initiative without reforming the personnel system. Over the past few years we have taken some important measures and accumulated some useful experience in this regard, but serious defects still exist in the personnel system relating to cadres. These are mainly as follows: The concept of the "state cadre" is too general and lacks a scientific classification; the power of cadre management is overconcentrated and the people who handle personnel affairs lack professional knowledge; the methods are outdated and simplistic, which hinders the intellectual growth of talented people; the management system is flawed and there are no laws governing the way personnel are used. As a result, we have for a long time been faced with two major problems: First, it is difficult for promising young people to fully display their talents; and second, it is difficult to avoid malpractices in the use of people. . . .

The emphasis of the current reform of the personnel system relating to cadres is on establishing a system of public service. This means formulating laws and regulations for the scientific management of government personnel who exercise the administrative power of the state and perform official duties. . . .

5. Establishing a System of Consultation and Dialogue

To correctly handle contradictions and reconcile various social interests is an important task in a socialist society. Only when the leading bodies at all levels listen attentively to the views of the masses can they gear their work to actual conditions and avoid mistakes. And only when they let the people know what they are doing and what difficulties they face can they secure the people's understanding. There should be channels through which the voices and demands of the people can be easily and frequently transmitted to the leading bodies, and there should be places where the people can offer suggestions or pour out any grievances they may have. Different groups of people may have different interests and views, and they too need opportunities and channels for the exchange of ideas. It is therefore imperative to develop a system of consultation and dialogue, so that what is going on at higher levels can be promptly and accurately be made known to lower levels and vice versa without impediment, thus enabling people at all levels to understand each other.

The basic principle for establishing a system of consultation and dialogue is to carry on the fine tradition of "from the masses, to the masses"[1] and to make public the activities of the leading bodies, letting the people know about important events and discussing important issues. The first thing to do now is to formulate regulations regarding consultation and dialogue. These should clearly define which problems are to be solved by which units or organizations, through consultation and discussion. The consultation and discussion on issues that are important at the national, local, or grass-roots level should be conducted at that

---

[1]Mao Zedong's principle of "mass-line" politics whereby cadres maintain close interaction with the masses in order to formulate and disseminate more acceptable policies.

level. Leading bodies at all levels should make this a top priority in their work. While opening new channels for consultation and dialogue, we should make better use of existing ones. We should provide wider coverage of the activities of the government and the party through all forms of modern mass media, to give scope to the supervisory role of public opinion, to support the masses in their criticism of shortcomings and mistakes in work, to oppose bureaucratism and in general to combat all unhealthy tendencies.

6. Improving a Number of Systems Relating to Socialist Democracy

The essence of socialist democracy is that the people are masters of the country, genuinely enjoying all citizens' rights and the power of administering the state, enterprises, and institutions. In building socialist democracy at the present stage, we should place emphasis on practical results and on arousing the initiative of the grass-roots units and the people. We should start with things we are able to do, concentrating on improving a number of basic systems.

The system of people's congresses is the fundamental system of government in China. In recent years the people's congresses at various levels have made much progress in their work. In the years ahead, they and their standing committees should continue to improve the way they function and to strengthen their work of legislation and supervision through law. They should maintain closer contact with the people in order to be better able to represent them and be supervised by them. Meanwhile, the National People's Congress, and particularly its Standing Committee, should be strengthened organizationally, and the committee members should gradually become younger in average age and serve full time. . . .

The trade unions, the Communist Youth League, the Women's Federation and other mass organizations that have always been a bridge linking the party and government with the working class and other sections of the people have an important role to play in the implementation of socialist democracy. It is essential for party and government departments to maintain harmonious relations with these mass organizations so that the latter can carry out their work independently in light of their own characteristics. This will enable them to better express and defend the specific interests of the masses they represent, while safeguarding the overall interests of the people throughout the country. The mass organizations, too, should undertake organizational reform, changing their pattern of functioning by actively participating in consultation and dialogue, democratic management and democratic supervision and focusing their attention on the grass-roots units. And if they want to win the trust of the people, especially those at the grass-roots level, they should also rid themselves of their official airs and overcome the tendency to become mere administrative institutions.

In the past few years China's elections have become more and more democratic. However, the electoral system has not been fully and effectively implemented and needs to be improved. We should respect the will of the voters and ensure that they have more options in elections. We should continue the practice of holding elections with more candidates than posts, as prescribed by law, and improve procedures for nominating candidates and methods of publicizing them. For instance, the present practice of setting rigid quotas for different geographical areas when nominating candidates for the election of deputies to congresses at various levels tends to prevent the election from fully reflecting the will of the voters. In order to have candidates who represent broader sections of the people, therefore, we shall introduce the practice of electing deputies not only from geographical areas, as is done at present, but also from different walks of life.

Institutionalizing democracy in grass-roots units provides the foundation for ensuring that the working class and other sections of the people are masters of the country, as well as for mobilizing the initiative of people in all quarters and maintaining stability and unity in society. Since from time to time the rights of the masses are encroached upon, we should enact laws governing the press, and establish a people's appeals system, so as to guarantee the citizens' rights and freedom as stipulated by the Constitution. At the same time, we should put an end to abuses of those rights and freedoms. It must be pointed out that leadership characterized by feudal, patriarchal practices is still found in some departments and grass-roots units. To eliminate the conditions that allow such practices to persist, we should formulate rules and regulations promoting a rational flow of personnel, build a labor arbitration system, and promote the socialization of public welfare services. . . .

7. Strengthening the Socialist Legal System

Socialist democracy is inseparable from a socialist legal system. Without stability and unity throughout the society, we can succeed neither in economic development nor in the reform of economic and political structures. In exercising democracy and dictatorship in all spheres of activity—political, economic, and social—we should see to it that there are laws to abide by, that laws already enacted are observed and enforced to the letter, and that violators are brought to justice. . . .

Our current political structure, which took shape during the revolutionary war years, was basically established in the period of socialist transformation. It developed in large-scale mass movements and in the process of constantly intensified mandatory planning. It is no longer suited to our drive for modernization in economic, political, cultural, and other fields under conditions of peace, or to the development of a socialist commodity economy. We should make an historical analysis of this state of affairs. The political structure was the product of the historical conditions of the time, but today things have changed. The cause of the party has progressed, and it is therefore necessary to reform this structure. This is a difficult and complex task, so we must adopt resolute yet cautious policies, trying to implement them in a guided and orderly way and to advance the reform as steadily as possible. In this period of transition from the old structure to the new, we should make special efforts to ensure that work is coordinated and conflicts are avoided. In pursuing reform, we must stress experimentation, encourage exploration, seek practical interim methods and measures and advance one step at a time. . . .

The immediate objective for the reform of the political structure is limited. However, when that objective is achieved, it will lay a sound foundation for socialist democracy and for the realization of our long-range objective. . . .

4
Four Major Crises China Will Face and Countermeasures

Xiao Jiabao

Source: *Liaowang Overseas Edition* (Outlook Weekly) (Hong Kong), no. 10 (March 6, 1989): 7–8, and no. 11 (March 13): 12–15; FBIS, April 19, pp. 28–34.

I

After analyzing and studying population, natural resources, environment, grain, and other major factors which limit China's long-term development as components of productive forces, the National Situation Analysis and Research Group of the Chinese Academy of Sciences maintains that China will face serious crises in four areas:

Population Crisis: By the Year 2000 China's Population May Top the 1.3 Billion Mark, the Latent Unemployed Population in the Countryside Will Exceed 300 Million, and the Population Will Be Aging Fast

The first crisis China faces is that of a continuously expanding and aging population and unemployment. It is forecast that China's population will top 1.1 billion in 1990 and 1.3 billion by 2000, of which about 1 billion will be in the countryside.

China's population explosion in the mid-2000s will be further complicated by an aging problem. Compared with the developed nations, China's aging population is characterized by a larger base figure, faster speed, and heavier burdens.

Unquestionably China ranks first in the world in the aging population base figure. The number of Chinese aged 60 and above may top the 100 million mark by 1990, and exceed 300 million and reach a peak of 320 million by 2040. This last figure will, in 2025, equal the total number of people aged 60 and above in all developed nations.

The Chinese population's low income and heavier burden is a phenomenon seldom seen in the world. When the population of a developed nation begins aging, its per capita income will have either approached or already exceeded ten thousand dollars. Even then, developed nations believe that the welfare burden of old people is too heavy. Because the Chinese population is entering the aging stage when per capita income is still low, the welfare burden for China's old people will be much heavier than the world average. At present, the number of old people without families cared for by China's rural collectives is only 4 percent of the total rural population, while the other 96 percent is being cared for by peasant families. It is anticipated that this situation will continue for a long time to come. Raising social welfare funds for several hundred million old people and making arrangements for their lives will be a most difficult issue for China in the future.

A fast population expansion, which is expected to bring the total number of working-age people to around 1 billion by 2020, will exert a great pressure on employment. This pressure will mainly come from the rapid growth of surplus manpower in the rural areas. By 2000, the number of working-age people 15 to 59 years of age in the rural areas will be about 660 million. Some 595 million of them will be actually seeking employment. But the actual demand for rural laborers will only be about 279 million. Thus, about 316 million individuals will actually be unemployed. By the early 2000s, the latent rural unemployment figure will be from 300 to 350 million. By then, a situation in which "three people compete for one job" will emerge.

Natural Resources Crisis: With Population Expanding and Farmland Shrinking, Some Localities and a Large Number of Cities Will Experience Water Shortages; by 2030, China's Natural Resources Will Be Stretched Far Beyond What They Can Bear

The second crisis will be the daily dwindling agricultural resources which will be stretched far beyond their capability. According to estimates and actual surveys, China today has 20.89 billion *mu* of farmland, 1.73 billion *mu* of forests, 4.3 billion *mu* of natural grassland, 430 million *mu* of water areas, 2.7 trillion cubic meters of water flowing through its rivers and streams, and 830 billion cubic meters of underground water. Although China ranks far above many other nations in absolute figures of natural resources, its per capita use of farmland is less than 2 *mu*, forest 1.7 *mu*, grassland 4.1 *mu*, water resources 2,600 cubic meters—all lower than the world average.

It is anticipated that by the end of this century, China's total population will reach 1.3 billion. If it should further expand to 1.5 billion by 2020, the consequences will be as follows:

The per capita use of farmland will be 1.46 *mu* by 2000 and 1.27 *mu* by 2020, a continuous drop of the absolute figure in both areas.

But the per capita use of forest areas and the percentage of land covered by forests will increase slightly. By 2000, forest areas will increase to 2.16–2.3 billion *mu*, and the percentage of areas covered by forest will increase to 15–16 percent. By then, the per capita use of forest areas will be about 1.7 *mu*, and the annual lumber supply will be short by 30–50 million cubic meters.

The total area of grassland will increase slightly, the per capita use of grassland area will decrease. The total area of grassland may reach 4.8 to 6 billion *mu*, and the per capita use of grassland area will be 3.75 to 3.91 *mu*.

The per capita amount of river water will drop further and the water resources crisis is drawing near. By that time, the country's total water demand will be 820 billion cubic meters; the per capita demand will be 634 metric tons, which is still below the per capita demand of 900 metric tons in developed countries. However, the per capita available amount of water will drop to 2,200 cubic meters, and the total amount of developed water resources will be 660 to 670 billion cubic meters, with a water shortage of 48 to 106 billion cubic meters. The country as a whole will enter the initial stage of a water resources crisis, and some areas and most cities will enter the immediate stage of a water resources crisis. For this reason, people throughout the country should strive to alleviate the pressure on our resources and not let the situation worsen. At present, however, a considerable number of regions are still excessively consuming available resources, and are in fact using what belongs to future generations. Such a situation poses a constant threat to the material foundations for the survival and development of the entire Chinese nation.

Environmental Crisis: By the End of the Century, 70 Percent
of the Fresh Water Resources Will Be Seriously Polluted

The third crisis is that of environmental pollution. At present, environmental pollution has spread in China and the ecology is becoming worse with each passing day:

—The area of soil erosion is increasing. Since the founding of the People's Republic, we have improved the conditions of 410,000 square kilometers of land with soil erosion, but the total area of land with soil erosion has increased to 1.53 million square kilometers now from the 1.16 million square kilometers in the early post-liberation years. About 5 billion metric tons of silt, together with some 40 million metric tons of [word indistinct], phosphorus and potassium are washed away each year. The loss in chemicals equals China's annual chemical fertilizer output. One-third of the cultivated land is damaged by soil erosion.

—The forest area is decreasing and grassland is deteriorating. At present, our annual timber consumption exceeds annual forest growth by nearly 100 million cubic meters, and the total area of deteriorated grassland has reached 770 million *mu*.

—More land is being eroded by sand. From the 1950s to the end of the 1970s, the area of land eroded by sand in China increased at an average annual rate of 1,500 square kilometers. Up to now, 1.09 million square kilometers of land, about 11.4 percent of China's total area, has been eroded by sand. An analysis of the causes shows that 90 percent of the erosion is caused by human error.

—The total area of inland rivers and lakes is shrinking. Since 1954, the water area of rivers on the middle and lower reaches of the Yangtze has decreased by about 13,000 square kilometers.

—Environmental pollution has extended from cities to rural areas. At present, more than 80 percent of the sewage is drained, without any treatment, into rivers and lakes. Sulphur dioxide exceeds the permitted amount in one-fourth of the cities in northern China. Serious acid rain occurs in some southern regions and particularly in the southwestern region, and as a result many people are drinking polluted water there. Agricultural, animal husbandry, and fishery products are slightly contaminated. Nearly 300 million *mu* of cultivated land has been polluted, and one-seventh of it is polluted by insecticides.

Unless we take resolute and effective measures right now, the per unit output of grass in major animal husbandry provinces and regions will drop 15 percent by 1990 and 30 percent by 2000 from the present output. By the end of the century, the total area of desertified land will increase to 251,300 square kilometers, from 176,000 square kilometers in 1980; 70 percent of the fresh water resources in China will become too polluted for use; and 65 million *mu* of the cultivated land and 26 million *mu* of the grassland will become polluted.

Food Grain Crisis: By the End of the Century, It Will Be Almost Impossible for Each of the 1.3 Billion People to Have 800 *Jin* of Grain a Year

After initially meeting the basic needs in food and clothing and increasing per capita income, the per capita consumption of agricultural produce, including grain, will increase rapidly in China in the future. According to a forecast, because of population growth, the demand for grain as food will exceed 890 billion *jin* in the year 2000. From 1985 to 2000, consumption of other foods will also increase sharply; pork consumption will double, beef and mutton consumption will increase 130 percent, poultry consumption 160 percent, and egg consumption 80 percent.

With such a huge demand for food in the future, what are the prospects for China's grain production? At present, the major ways for China to increase grain production are to increase the area of grain crops, increase the irrigated area, improve the soil, apply more chemical fertilizer, practice intensive farming, promote mechanization, increase labor input, promote intensive cultivation, cultivate superior strains, and adopt advanced agricultural techniques. However, the present and future situation will be as follows:

The area of cultivated land will decrease year by year and the area of grain crops will shrink drastically. From 1978 to 1987, cultivated land in China decreased by 52.51 million *mu*, the area of farm crops decreased by 77.21 million *mu*, and the area of grain crops decreased by 13,979 *mu*. In 1988, as compared with 1987, the area of farm crops shrank by 11.196 million *mu*, of which 21.746 million *mu* [as published] were grain crops. At this rate of reduction, the area of grain crops will drop to 1,487.28 million *mu*, with a per capita area of 1.14 *mu*, in the year 2000. In order to have a per capita grain level of 800 *jin*, per *mu* yield must be raised to over 700 *jin* by then, from the per *mu* yield of 485 *jin* in 1987.

One fact is worth pointing out. On the one hand, our arable land reserves are insufficient and difficult to reclaim, urban and rural construction is taking more and more land year by year, and the decrease of grain crop area is conspicuous. On the other hand, with a fixed total area of cultivated land, the increase in the area of grain crops will inevitably reduce the area of other crops, such as cash crops, fodder, and green manure. As a result, the structure of crop cultivation, aquaculture, and processing industry will become even more nondiversified, unable to satisfy the people's daily increasing and diversified consumption needs, and detrimental to readjustment of the rural production structure and to further economic development.

The area of irrigated land shows a tendency to decrease, and water shortage is a major factor obstructing the increase of grain output. In the last 30 years or more, increasing the area of irrigated land has always been an important measure China has taken to raise grain output. From 1979 to 1987, the area of irrigated land in China did not increase; on the contrary, it decreased by 9 million *mu*. In northern China, groundwater was generally put to use in rural areas, while surface water was yielded to industry due to its price. During water shortage seasons in recent years, Beijing Municipality had to "abandon agriculture and restrict industry to ensure the residents' livelihood." Grain and agricultural production is facing a serious water shortage challenge.

Additional chemical fertilizer plays an important role in increasing grain production, but its effect is lessening year by year. According to a calculation made by the Statistics and Analysis Department of the Rural Development Research Center of the State Council, in China, chemical fertilizer occupies a one-third share in increasing grain production; its role is next only to increasing the area of grain crops. In 1952, the ratio between grain output and the amount of chemical fertilizer used was 2,101.5 to 1. Later, it dropped rapidly, became 34.5 to 1 in 1978, and 25.3 to 1 in 1980. Then the change slowed down, showing diminishing returns.

Peasant capital accumulation is very low, agricultural investment is evidently decreasing, and grain production lacks a sufficient basis for further development. First, state investment in agriculture has decreased not only in terms of relative value, but also in terms of absolute value. During the Fifth Five-Year-Plan period, the state invested 24.6 billion yuan in agricultural capital construction, accounting for 10.6 percent of its total investment. During the Sixth Five-Year-Plan period, China's total capital construction investment was up 50 percent from the Fifth Five-Year-Plan period, but its investment in agricultural capital construction was reduced by nearly one-third. State investment in agricultural capital construction during those five years was 17.3 billion yuan, accounting for 5.1 percent of the total capital construction investment, averaging 1.5 yuan per year per peasant. At the same time, state investment in state-owned industry averaged 1,243 yuan per worker.

In the meantime, peasants also reduced their investment in agriculture. Grain prices were on the low side, while the cost of grain production rose steadily, with the cost in 1984 doubling that of 1978. Economic returns of grain production were very low. In 1984, the net profit on 1 *jin* of grain was 3.7 cents, lower than that of cash crops and much lower than income from industry and sideline undertakings. As a result, it dampened the peasants' enthusiasm for growing grain, and their investment in land decreased year by year. According to a sample survey, labor investment in land sown to six kinds of grain crops decreased by one-third in 1980. More than 70 percent of the peasants' investment was made in nonproductive projects, of which more than 65 percent was in housing. In 1985 and 1986, per capita investment in housing among peasants was 56.6 yuan and 67.6 yuan respectively, while per capita investment in productive projects was 15.2 yuan and 18.1 yuan. The per capita expenditure for grain production was even less.

II

The basic conditions in China and the fierce international competition have determined that the Chinese people in this and the next few generations must have a sense of crisis for survival, a sense of apprehension for [their] nation, a sense of urgency for reform, and a sense of responsibility for history. China's modernization is a grand national undertaking, which is deeply rooted in the people's understanding and practice. For the modernization campaign to succeed, the decision makers, the intellectual circles, and the masses, including workers and peasants, must form a consensus and a new, enduring, and strong cohesiveness, and establish an overall national mentality for long-term hard work and struggle. This is where China's basic hope lies.

That China's future is faced with four major crises does not mean prospects for its development are bleak. While analyzing and studying the crises, the experts on the national conditions at the China Academy of Sciences also delve into China's potential and prospect for future development and come up with the countermeasures.

Bright Prospects for Economic Development

Experts hold that as long as China persists in reform and opening to the outside world, places its total population under strict control, makes no major policy errors, and suffers no other unexpected incidents (such as serious natural disaster or war), it has bright prospects for development.

From now till 2020, China's economy will enter a stage marked by a continuous high rate of growth. China will shift from low-income level to medium-income level. The notable characteristics of this stage are as follows: The per capita GNP will increase from $300 to $1,700. The economic growth rate is estimated at between 6 and 7 percent. Calculated in terms of GNP, China will rank ninth in the world in 1995 and fifth in 2000, overtaking Italy, Canada, France, and Britain. By 2020, China will surpass the Federal Republic of Germany and draw close to the Soviet Union, and can be regarded as a great world economic power. However, due to a sharp rise in population, China's per capita GNP in 2000 and 2020 will stand at only $763 (calculated according to prices in 1980) and $1,724 respectively, which are 63.3 percent and 85.6 percent of that of the nations of medium-income level at the time. At this stage, China's accumulation rate and savings ratio will also stay at a higher level. The urban population growth rate will be pretty high, but population reproduction will gradually move into a phase of low birth, death, and natural growth rates. The economic system and social structure which support a continuous economic growth and efficient economic operations will be formed basically.

If the economy can sustain the high-rate growth, China will enter a modern economic stage marked by stable growth from 2020 to 2050. The marked characteristics of the stage: GNP will steadily increase at a rate of 4 to 5 percent. By 2050, China will outstrip the Soviet Union and rank only after the United States and Japan in national strength. However, the per capita GNP will reach only $3,800, still falling short of the average level ($4,350) of the low- and medium-income nations at the time. At this stage, China's economic structure will undergo the first step of modernization, with the tertiary industry employing more people than the secondary industry and its output value correspondingly surpassing that of the secondary industry. In secondary industry, the capital- and technology-intensive industry, which reflect the scientific and technological progress, will rise quickly to become the leading industries. Agriculture will basically realize mechanization and modernization. After hitting its apex at 1.5 billion in 2030, the total population is likely to begin entering a period of zero growth.

Experts on Chinese conditions at the Chinese Academy of Sciences expressed their belief that many factors can become a great potential for the future development in China. These factors include a strong force that the central government can muster in mobilizing and utilizing all kinds of resources in the society as a whole, relatively all-around industrial and national economic systems, and all kinds of forces that support our economic progress, such as the ones we have developed and accumulated in social, economic, and cultural fields since the implementation of the reforms.

Agriculturally, China has a considerable potential in natural resources, labor force, investment, science, and technology. In the existing farmland in China, the proportions of first, second, and third grades are 41.5 percent, 34.4 percent, and 20.3 percent respectively. In terms of high, middle, and low yields of this farmland, its proportions are 22.3 percent, 56.8 percent, and 20.9 percent respectively. About 20 million *mu* of middle-yield land is of the first grade, with good soil quality, but has not yet reached its potential yield level. This land, as long as we put more investment into it and strengthen our management of it, will be transformed into high-yield land. As far as most of the second grade land is concerned, if we adjust the crop structure or adopt some improvement measures, we can achieve the result of higher production. After a suitable amount of capital was invested in the three experimental areas of Fengqiu, Henan Province; Yucheng, Shandong Province; and Nanpi, Hebei Province, by the Chinese Academy of Sciences to change the soil content and improve irrigation conditions, the unit grain production increased from 100 to 200 kg in 1964 to 800 to 1,400 kg in recent years.

In addition, China has an abundance of solar and thermal resources. We can create various conditions and fully utilize multi-crop systems, such as intercropping. In this way, we can increase the multi-crop rate from 147 percent at present to 155 percent in 2000 and 160 percent in 2050. A 1 percent increase in the multi-crop rate represents an increase of 15 million to 20 million *mu* of farmland. In other words, in 2000 and 2025, China will have another 120 million *mu* and 190 million *mu* of land respectively. At present, China's agricultural science and technology transfer rate is only 30 to 40 percent. If we can effectively overcome various obstacles in technical development and extension and improve the technical extension system to make the rate grow to 50–60 percent or higher, then there will be a great development in China's agriculture.

China has a sufficient and ample labor resource. Although it constitutes a tremendous obstacle and pressure to agricultural development at present, it also represents a most important potential resource for agricultural production in China. If we solve the problem of educational investment in labor resources, we can fully release tremendous potential of various resources (including material and labor resources) that support the long-term development of China's agriculture.

Countermeasures: Six Systems and Four Measures

Experts on Chinese conditions at the Chinese Academy of Sciences expressed their belief that, in order to have a stable and rapid development in the economy and release the potential of abundant resources in China, we must establish a production system which is low in terms of consuming resources, a livelihood system with proper consumption, an economic system that ensures a continuing and stable economic growth and increasing economic results, a social system which guarantees social results and social fairness, a technological system which can fully absorb new technologies and new crafts, and an international economic system that can have close contacts with world markets in trade and nontrade affairs. Meanwhile, China must strictly control the growth of its population, reasonably develop and utilize resources, prevent pollution, and guarantee ecological balance.

Judging from China's conditions, our strategy for long-term development should be the one that guarantees existence and continuing development. By guaranteeing existence, we mean to guarantee the existing conditions and space for the Chinese nation as a whole; by continuing development, we mean a kind of development that will satisfy the needs of our contemporaries and also not constitute a destruction of and obstacle to the foundation upon which our future generations depend for existence and development. For this purpose, we must adopt proper measures to deal with the crisis in population, resources, environment, and food aspects.

For a considerably long period of time in the future, China must resolutely and conscientiously implement its present family planning policy; that is, to vigorously promote one child per couple, strictly control the growth rate of two children per couple, and resolutely stop the trend of three children per couple.

Since the Third Plenum of the Eleventh CPC Central Committee [December 1978], China has taken its population policy as its basic national policy, with "strictly controlling population size, vigorously improving population quality, and gradually adjusting population structure" as its basic content.

At present, China should focus on the following points to improve its population quality: popularizing elementary education for peasants, eliminating illiteracy, and promoting production skills through professional training. It is necessary to impose a compulsory education on peasants to realize the goal of eliminating illiteracy or semi-illiteracy by the end of this century and to struggle to achieve the goal, by the early period of the twenty-first century, of making high school the average educational level for peasants. In terms of the aging population problem, it is not suitable for China to adopt a high birth rate policy to dilute the population rate of the elderly because of the capacity of China's resources. Instead, we must develop the economy, promote cultural standards, and implement a social security system for the elderly to balance the cost that we must pay for an aging society, and to gradually establish a system of social service and social guarantees for the elderly.

The Chinese government should strictly supervise the enforcement of various laws on environmental protection, shoulder its responsibilities in this respect, and regard environmental protection as a major item in assessing the achievements of government leaders at various levels.

While acting on the principle of stressing the prevention of environmental pollution, China should increase its investment in improving the environment. In structure, it is necessary to do away with management by many departments, with each performing only certain limited functions; to establish a united, authoritative organization for ecological and environmental protection; and to improve the quality of managerial personnel in this field. Emergency plans should be worked out as soon as possible to cope with possible accidents in environmental pollution. It is essential to set up a special fund for research on recycling of polluted materials and to establish an industrial-agricultural recycling system for multipurpose use of materials at various levels.

It is necessary to make people understand the importance of the environment and to strengthen their supervision in this regard. This is the key to solving problems concerning the environment. The names of factories which use and discharge poisonous or harmful materials should be made public, and the percentages of harmful materials in products and their harmfulness should be put on their labels. This will make it easier for the people to understand the pollution or harmfulness of such materials and to exercise supervision over them. Correct guidance should be given to village and town enterprises with regard to their production and distribution in order to avoid environmental pollution caused by their short-term measures. Environmental protection should be included in all contract systems and in the appraisal of such systems. Efforts should be made to prevent soil deterioration; to strictly forbid people to wantonly use farmland for other purposes; to protect areas producing marketable grain; to prevent pollution of the sources of drinking and irrigation water; and, in particular, to avoid major pollution accidents that are difficult to treat and are rather harmful to the people. While strictly implementing the environmental evaluation system and the system of fees for pollution, it is necessary to institute step by step a system of issuing licenses for pollution treatment and to use the process of natural purification following pretreatment in order to control the total amount of pollutants.

In utilizing natural resources, China should lay down a resources-protecting policy to economize on the use of its existing natural resources and to rationally develop them. China should use administrative controls and economic levers to regulate the behavior of enterprises and peasant households in order to make them conscientiously increase the rates of reuse or multipurpose use of natural resources, reduce production costs, and improve their economic results. A system of evaluation of natural resources should be instituted in order to control the utilization of natural resources and the rates of such utilization. Technological and economic policies should be coordinated so as to promote technical transformation.

Solution of water and land problems should be stressed in China's strategy for the development of natural resources. To this end, China should adopt drastic measures to put an end to or reduce using farmland for other purposes, to have people pay for the use of water or land, to economize on the use of water in industrial and agricultural production, and to increase the water-reuse rate. Vigorous efforts should be made to develop agricultural ecological engineering with a view to making multipurpose use of materials and energy. Modern technology should be used to make crop cultivation, breeding, and processing a coordinated process in order to raise the resources-utilization rate.

China's structure of crop cultivation should continue to take grain crops as the main ones and fodder and industrial crops as the auxiliary ones. For a fairly long period of time to come, the system of rationing (meeting basic needs in) grain, meat, and cooking oil for city residents should be practiced in connection with market regulation. Grain prices should be readjusted step by step in order to reduce the financial burden on the state. China should adopt measures to control grain prices and to raise tax rates on cigarettes, foodstuffs, and alcohol.

Experts hold that agriculture is the most difficult problem in China's economic development, and the key to agricultural development lies in grain production. For a fairly long period of time to come, China should coordinate its efforts to readjust the structure of rural production and the agricultural structure and to develop a diversified economy as well as village and town enterprises with its efforts to support and promote grain production. The government should use economic means as the main methods and administrative means as the auxiliary ones to regulate or intervene in the variety of crops planted by peasants to ensure that an adequate area, or no less than 1.6 billion *mu* of farmland, is sown to grain crops. This will ensure a sufficiency of marketable grain. At the same time, the Chinese government should support peasants with investment funds, technology, and basic means of agricultural production.

In land policy, China should further define the land property right in order to promote land annexation and large-scale farming. No time should be lost in promoting appropriately large-scale farming in developed areas, especially in areas near cities and areas producing marketable grain. Management should be strengthened in purchasing, storage, transport, and marketing of grain crops so as to reduce grain waste. Financial means should be used to reduce risks in agricultural production. It is necessary to set up land records and conduct national farmland surveys as soon as possible.

On the premise that China is basically self-sufficient in grain, it should gradually increase grain imports, from 20 billion *jin* at present to 70 billion *jin*. Various parts of the country should be allowed to readjust their structures of crop cultivation according to the principle of benefit comparison so that they may be able to exchange industrial crops and processed products for more grain from the international market.

5
Report on the Work of the Government

LI PENG

Source: Speech delivered by Li Peng at the Second Session of the Seventh National People's Congress in the Great Hall of the People [March 20, 1989]. Beijing Domestic Television Service—live; FBIS, March 21, pp. 11–31 (excerpts).

Fellow deputies,

Improving the economic environment and rectifying the economic order is the focus of China's construction and reform this year and next year and it is also the focus of government work. Therefore, on behalf of the State Council, I now concentrate on this issue in the report on the work of the government for examination and approval by this session.

I. Wholeheartedly Carry Out Improvement and Rectification

The year 1988 was the tenth year of our reform and opening up. Over the past ten years, tremendous and historic changes have taken place in all fields. The social productive forces have developed greatly, the national economic strength has markedly increased, and the people's living standards in both town and country have markedly improved. Practice has proved that the CPC's line since the Third Plenum of the Eleventh CPC Central Committee is correct. The year 1988, which has just passed, was a year in which China's socialist modernization cause continued to forge ahead.

The national economy grew steadily. The 1988 GNP reached 1,385.3 billion yuan and, calculated in terms of comparable prices, showed an increase of 11.2 percent over the previous year. The national income reached 1,153.3 billion yuan and, calculated in terms of comparable prices, showed an increase of 11.4 percent over the previous year. Given that natural disasters were frequent and fairly serious in the country as a whole, grain output dropped by 2.2 percent and cotton output by 1.1 percent. But with further growth in many other farm products and diversified undertakings, the gross value of agricultural production still registered an increase of 3.2 percent. To support state construction, the vast number of peasants energetically sold grain to the state. The nation's grain purchase task was basically completed.

Industrial production, transport and communications, and post and telecommunications developed steadily. . . . New successes were scored in key construction projects. . . .

Economic restructuring continued to deepen. The enterprise-contracted management responsibility system gradually improved and enterprise vitality further increased. By optimizing labor formation, many enterprises improved their labor productivity. Commodity, capital, technology, labor service, and foreign exchange regulatory markets made new developments. In the field of macroregulation and macrocontrol, we gradually conducted structural reforms in planning, investment, materials, finance, and foreign trade and initially strengthened management over finance, taxation, banking, prices, auditing, customs, and industrial and commercial administration.

The policy of opening up to the outside world was further expanded. The total volume of imports and exports topped $100 billion, an increase of 24.4 percent over the previous year. The proportion of exported industrial goods rose. Some $8.94 billion in foreign capital was actually used, an increase of 16.4 percent over the previous year. A total of 5,896 enterprises using foreign investment were approved, the most numerous in the past 10 years. We earned nearly $1.3 billion in the contracting of projects abroad and labor service cooperation and $2.22 billion in international tourism, a substantial increase over the previous year.

On the basis of economic growth, new achievements were made in science and technology, education, culture, public health, and sports. The correct positioning of a practical telecommunications satellite over the equator, the successful collision of Beijing's electron-positron collider, and the successful conclusion of the first space exploration rocket test in the low-altitude area showed that our country made remarkable headway in some aspects of high technology.

The building of socialist democracy and the socialist legal system was strengthened. In keeping with the plan approved by the First Session of the Seventh National People's Congress [NPC, 1988], the structural reform of the State Council was basically completed.

Public security, security, judiciary, and other departments did much to safe-guard public order. The people's army played a tremendous role and made outstanding contributions by defending the motherland, aiding and supporting the socialist modernization drive, rushing to deal with the emergencies, and providing disaster relief.

While scoring successes in all fields of endeavor, we also faced many prob-lems and difficulties. The most outstanding ones were the emergence of marked inflation and the excessively steep price increases. The nation's general index of retail sales prices rose by 18.5 percent over 1987. Such steep price increases exceeded the capacity of the masses, the enterprises, and the state to withstand the strains and the actual living standards of a considerable number of urban residents dropped to some extent.

All this has aroused the common concern of society and serious uneasiness of the masses and has affected social stability and the people's confidence in re-form. If we do not adopt resolute measures to curb inflation, not only will our economy be unable to be stabilized and developed, but also our reform in various fields cannot be further deepened. The aggravation of inflation is a result of the overheated economy, the expansion of both the investment and consumption demands, and the fact that the general social demand is higher than general social supply. The number of fixed-asset investment projects now under con-struction in our country is excessively high and their scope is too wide, which has gone beyond our reasonable bearing capacity and possibility. As consump-tion demand is too great, the social purchasing power has been growing faster than commodity supply.

In state finance, expenditure is greater than revenue. The scope of credit is too wide and there has been an excessive issuance of money. Under the situation of imbalance between general demand and general supply, there are dislocations in the economic structure. Agricultural development has lagged behind. An exces-sively high proportion of the limited resources have been thrown into the pro-cessing industry and nonproductive projects. Under the situation that industrial production has been growing at a high speed, the shortage in energy and raw materials supply and the difficulties in transport have been aggravated. In order to seek private gains, some units and individuals have engaged in illegal activi-ties such as reselling goods at a profit, driving up prices level by level, and making and selling false and inferior products. All this has further accelerated price increases and aggravated disorder in the economic field.

The above-mentioned situation is inseparable from the fact that in the period of replacing the old structure with the new, it is impossible to establish a new mechanism of self-regulation and self-restraint very quickly. However, there are also shortcomings and mistakes in our work guidance. Generally speaking, there does exist a trend of being overanxious for quick results in economic construc-tion and social development. Our country is a developing country. We need to have a certain speed of economic development. But we have often neglected the fact that our country has a large population but relatively insufficient natural resources and that our economic development is very uneven. In work guidance, we have not paid sufficient attention to prevent and rectify phenomena such as blindly expanding construction scope, onesidedly pursuing output value and output, and vying with one another for a higher speed of development. The orientation of reform is correct and, in general, reform is also successful. But in offering concrete guidance, we have often failed to gain a sufficient understanding of the arduousness and complexity of reform and have not paid sufficient attention to the comprehensive and harmonious development of things. . . .

At the beginning of last year, we worked out the policy of stabilizing the economy and deepening reform. But later, as we had made an overoptimistic estimation of the 1987 economic situation, we did not take resolute action and effective measures to implement the policy. Although we understood the important position of price reform in the economic structural reform as a whole, in practical work we did not give full consideration to the bearing capacity of the state, the enterprises, and the masses. When the situation of inflation was already quite clear, we did not adopt effective measures immediately to stabilize finance and control prices. Instead, we relaxed and readjusted the prices of some commodities, making the masses of people more panic-stricken over price increases. In many places, there was panic buying among the people, and savings deposits dropped.

The Third Plenum of the Thirteenth CPC Central Committee, which was held last September, made a correct analysis of China's economic situation; put forth the policy of improving the economic environment, rectifying the economic order, and deepening reform in an all-around way; and drew up a plan for laying the stress of construction and reform on improvement and rectification in the next two years. In order to implement this policy and plan, it is necessary to unify stability, reform, and development, and necessary to promote reform and seek development in a situation of stability. Beginning this year, we must use two or more years to strive for the realization of the targets of improvement and rectification:

1. To eliminate overheated economic development and reduce the speed of development to a comparatively rational level.

2. To curb inflation so that price increases in 1989 will be obviously lower than those in 1988 and price increases after 1990 will be further reduced.

3. To reduce the scope of investment in fixed assets so that it can suit the bearing capacity of the national strength, and to control the excessive growth of consumption funds so that it can suit the growth of national income.

4. To gradually alleviate the contradiction that the general social demand is greater than the general social supply so that a basic balance can be achieved among finance, credit, materials, and foreign exchange.

5. To conscientiously readjust the economic structure so that the output of grain, cotton, oil, and other major agricultural products can be increased by a comparatively wide margin and so that the shortages in energy and raw materials supply and difficulties in transportation can be improved to a certain extent.

6. To establish and perfect necessary economic laws and regulations as well as a macroeconomic regulation and control system and supervision system, and to actively promote the building of a new order of socialist commodity economy.

Only when we attain these targets can we greatly improve the quality of our country's economy and increase our economic returns and can we ensure a long-term and stable development of the national economy. . . .

Through our work in the past half year, a cooling in the overheated economy has begun. The momentum of rising prices has weakened. The people's nervous sentiments toward commodity prices have eased somewhat. Urban and rural markets are basically stable. . . .

In order to firmly carry out improvement and rectification, we must further solve the following three problems of ideology and understanding:

1. Governments and government personnel at various levels, particularly responsible personnel, must resolutely safeguard the leadership authority of the CPC Central Committee and the State Council's leadership authority in terms of government work. We must ensure the enforcement of orders and prohibitions. Historical experience has repeatedly proved that it is simply impossible to readjust the economy and overcome difficulties without necessary centralization and uniformity and without rigorous organizational discipline.

2. To carry out improvement and rectification, it is inevitable to make necessary readjustment of the existing interests pattern. All localities, departments, and units must take the interests of the whole into account and must firmly establish the concept that partial interests should be subordinated to the interests of the whole. Otherwise, if everybody does not give up the vested interests which affect the interests of the whole, improvement and rectification will become idle theory.

3. While improvement and rectification is being carried out, both the government and the people should be ideologically prepared to live a hard life for a few years. Governments and departments at various levels, the broad masses of cadres, leading cadres in particular, should take the lead in being industrious and thrifty, arduously working hard, and resolutely overcoming extravagance and waste. So long as we set a good example, and explain clearly to the masses the objective demand to live a hard life, we believe the broad masses of the people will understand and support it.

In short, the State Council demands that responsible persons of governments and departments at various levels further increase their understanding, unify their ideology and deeds on the basis of policies and principles formulated by the CPC Central Committee and the State Council, unite the masses together, grasp improvement and rectification with one heart and one soul, and make unremitting efforts to stabilize the economy and deepen reform. . . .

II. The Current Focus of Improvement and Rectification Is, as Before, to Cut Social Demand

Inflation in our country in recent years has been triggered mainly by an over-heated economy and high demand. In improving the economic environment and rectifying the economic order, efforts should of course be made to cut social demand and increase social supply. But first of all, we must firmly cut the excessive aggregated social demand. The reduction of the scale of investment in fixed assets is an important measure having a decisive bearing on cutting aggre-gate social demand. It is also the most important task to curb inflation and to stabilize the overall economic situation. . . .

The key to retrenching and controlling the scale of investment in fixed assets is to check up on projects under construction. Only by resolutely cutting a large number of ongoing projects can the scale of investment be really reduced. . . .

It is necessary to strengthen macrocontrol and regulation over investment activities in fixed assets in the entire society, to use economic and legal methods as well as the necessary administrative means to exercise good management over investment activities planned and arranged by the state, and to attach particular importance to controlling investment activities outside the plan and budget. Bank loans for investment should be put under mandatory planned management, and nonbanking monetary organs are forbidden to engage in investment and credit activities. Strict control must be exercised over the attempt to expand the scale of investment in fixed assets by collecting funds from society. . . .

We should try all possible means to stabilize the financial situation, to strengthen planned management over all kinds of bank loans, and to control the credit scale in the entire society. . . .

VI. Closely Link Improvement of the Economic Environment and Rectification of the Economic Order with the Deepening of Reform

The improvement of the economic environment and rectification of the eco-nomic order is carried out on the premise of persisting in the general direction of reform. We will not return to the old economic mode marked by overcentralized, excessive, and rigid control. Neither will we take the road of negating the social-ist system and the road of privatization.

The current measures we have adopted to improve the economic environment and rectify the economic order are in themselves an important content of our efforts to deepen reform. Doing well in improving the economic order and recti-fying the economic order is inseparable from deepening reform.

Stressing improvement of the economic environment and rectification of the economic order does not mean putting a stop to reform. If the work of improving the economic environment and rectifying the economic order is done well, it will, from the macroeconomic point of view, create a relatively good environment for deepening reform and better promote the development of the socialist commodity economy....

VIII. Strive to Create a Good and Stable Social and Political Environment

Giving full play to our political advantage and striving to create a good and stable social and political environment are important guarantees for successfully carrying out the mission of improving the economic environment and rectifying the economic order.

In accordance with the plan of the Thirteenth National Congress of the CPC, China's political restructuring is advancing soundly and steadily. Notable progress has been made in separating party and government and reforming government departments. The system of consultation and dialogue with the masses is extensively being practiced. The existing unsound legal system is being changed step by step.

In the course of improving the economic environment and rectifying the economic order, we must further strengthen socialist democracy; improve the socialist legal system; safeguard the democratic rights of the masses of people; improve the system of multiparty cooperation and the system of political consultation under the leadership of the CPC; give full play to the role of democratic parties, nonparty patriotic personages, and people's organizations in participating in government and political affairs and in exercising democratic supervision over government departments; strengthen the organization of basic level political power in urban and rural areas; and consolidate and develop the political situation of stability, unity, democracy, and harmony.

Any social turbulence and chaos which will hamper the advancement of reform and construction and gravely impair the fundamental interests of the people of all nationalities throughout the country runs counter to the aspirations of the masses of people. We should deepen education to enhance the people's awareness of law. On the basis of implementing the Constitution and the law, we should strive to improve our administrative statutes and rules and regulations and strictly enforce laws.

Governments at all levels must take the lead in abiding by laws and discipline and at the same time see to it that supervisory, judicial, and administrative departments exercise their functions according to law. By strengthening democratic supervision and law enforcement, we shall restore law and discipline; strictly deal with criminals who disrupt the economy; resolutely punish criminals who disrupt social order; and resolutely crack down on hooliganism, prostitution, and other criminal activities such as trading in human beings.

Governments at all levels must mobilize and organize the masses and draw up a comprehensive program to improve social order and create good order in production, work, study, and daily life.

The reform of departments under the State Council has been basically accomplished as planned. The main tasks in this respect for this year are as follows: To consolidate our reform achievements; further straighten out the relations between departments and the relations within the departments themselves; gradually transform their functions in practical work; and raise work efficiency. To concentrate our forces on carrying out the campaign to improve the economic environment and to rectify the economic order, we shall postpone the reform of government organs at the provincial, municipality, and autonomous region levels scheduled to start this year as planned.

To ensure economic development, the government must be honest in carrying out its duties. The State Council and governments at all levels must take the lead in implementing the rules and regulations for promoting clean administration formulated by the party Central Committee and the State Council. It is necessary to strictly deal with relevant leaders and those directly involved in discriminately distributing bonuses and materials to workers, giving lavish dinner parties and presents, touring places of interest, and building private homes with public funds in violation of state regulations; it is necessary to strictly deal with government functionaries, especially leading cadres, regarding their bureaucratic behavior and dereliction of duty; it is necessary to strictly enforce administrative statutes and decrees, resolutely punish anyone who disregards orders and prohibitions.

In dealing with matters directly concerning the masses, it is necessary to institute an open work method and make public the results of work. It is necessary to increase the visibility of government activities, intensify self-restraint, and ensure that powers are exercised in accordance with statutes and regulations and under the supervision of cadres and the masses. . . .

We should energetically intensify the education on patriotism, national self-respect, and revolutionary traditions; properly carry out ideological and political work under the new situation; adhere to the course of serving socialism and the people; and firmly implement the principle of ''letting a hundred flowers blossom and a hundred schools of thought contend.'' Through creating the necessary conditions for the development of material civilization and a proper environment for the public opinion, we should draw up and implement economic policies in the cultural sector. We should intensify the development and management of the cultural market in order to ensure a healthy cultural and artistic development. We should give full scope to the positive roles played by the press, publishing business, radio broadcasts, movies, and television in spiritual construction.

In connection with the actual state of reform, opening to the outside world, and modernization drive, the vast number of theoretical workers should deepen their theoretical study on building a socialist society with distinctive Chinese characteristics, use new results obtained from theoretical study to answer the questions emerging from actual life and persistently combat undesirable habits and customs in rural and urban areas. Things which are reactionary, obscene, and ugly must never be allowed to disseminate unchecked. Feudalistic, superstitious, and gambling activities which disturb public order and are harmful for people's physical and mental health must be banned according to law. . . .

China has consistently adopted a foreign policy for peace and for maintaining independence and keeping the initiative in our own hands and supported the just cause of the people in the world. China opposes hegemonism, safeguards world peace, and promotes common development. . . .

Deputies, on the whole, the current domestic and international situation is conducive to China's construction and reform. The difficulties we face in domestic economic construction are by their nature issues that arise in the course of progress and development. As long as the leadership and the rank and file are of one mind and we pool our wisdom and efforts, we can definitely pull through the difficulties and achieve the anticipated goals in the course of improving the economic environment and rectifying the economic order. We should work together with one heart to greet the fortieth anniversary of the founding of the PRC with outstanding achievements and to advance the magnificent cause of building socialism with Chinese characteristics [applause].

6
Zhao Ziyang on Economic Retrenchment and Reform at Enterprise Forum

Source: Speech of April 11, 1989, in Xinhua Domestic Service; FBIS, April 12, pp. 13–14; Beijing Television Service, April 11; FBIS, April 12, pp. 15–16.

Speaking to the representatives attending the national forum on enterprises' contractual operation at the Huairen Hall in Zhongnanhai today, Zhao Ziyang, general secretary of the CPC Central Committee, said: The current economic retrenchment is different from the several previous economic readjustments, and only when we fully understand the differences can we succeed in improving the economic environment and rectifying the economic order, and achieve the anticipated results. The previous readjustments were carried out when productivity was undermined, whereas the current readjustment is being carried out when productivity has grown substantially and the economy has relatively developed.[1]

Zhao Ziyang said: The current economic retrenchment is being carried out during the course of reform. In other words, it is being carried out under the situation where the old system is being replaced by a new one and where there is a two-tier price system. Aside from making economic retrenchment more complex and more difficult, it sets new and even higher demands on us. Certain readjustment measures useful in the past can hardly be effective today because we have decontrolled large areas in the economic sector in the past several years. For those areas that have been decontrolled, they cannot be steered by means of old measures. However, we must not reimpose a rigid control on the rejuvenated economy. On the contrary, during the current economic retrenchment we should consolidate what we have achieved in reform and create conditions for further reforms. This being the case, we must actively explore new measures to resolve retrenchment problems and facilitate reform. To say the least, these new measures should not create problems for our reform in the future. Certain measures adopted during economic retrenchment looked regressive, but they are contingent measures meant to buy time for solving other problems. This is a price we have to pay for the time being. We have to be mentally prepared for this, and we must also work actively to create conditions so that these measures can be gradually replaced by new ones. Instituting new macroscopic control mechanisms to keep pace with the new development of the socialist planned commodity economy is a major issue confronting us today. Whether we can properly resolve this issue has a close bearing on the success or failure of our economic retrenchment.

Zhao Ziyang said: The current economic retrenchment is being carried out when the country is opening to the outside world. This is in our interest. China has abundant and relatively inexpensive manpower; our fairly strong industrial foundation, including the defense industries, have relatively strong processing capacity; and our scientific and technological strength is quite strong. These are the resources with which we can take part in international economic cooperation and exchange. The world situation is now heading toward relaxation, and international exchange and cooperation are developing. This is an opportunity. Under the condition of opening to the outside world, we do not have to fully depend on balancing the needs at home to deal with our "shortages." We should rather solve the problem through international exchange and promote development. This is

---

[1]This sentence was reported by the Beijing Television Service but was omitted in the otherwise more extensive Xinhua account.

different from the time when our country was closed to the outside world. Not only is this true in the coastal areas, it applies to all other parts of the country as well. This has been proven by the development in the past ten years, especially in the last few years when China's economic cooperation and exchange with foreign countries have developed substantially. Our exports have grown rapidly, and gratifying changes have been observed in our export structure. It seems that much can be accomplished in this area.

While studying our development strategy, we should fully consider how to exploit the opportunities provided by the policy of opening to the outside world. We have our own strengths, and we can bring them into play. Thus, there is no reason to be pessimistic about the future of our economic development. The important thing is we must stand on a higher plane, see farther ahead, continue to carry out reform and open to the outside world, seize the opportunities, do our jobs properly, and push economic retrenchment and the four modernizations forward.

Zhao Ziyang said: Since the convocation of the Third Plenum of the Thirteenth CPC National Congress, we have achieved preliminary success in our economic retrenchment, which must go on and not stop halfway. Zhao Ziyang also stressed, in particular, that special efforts must be made to strengthen enterprise reform during economic retrenchment. He said: We must uphold and improve the contract system and improve scientific management on that basis. While we must earnestly implement the "Enterprise Law" and give enterprises the power to make their own decisions, enterprises must use this power from the state to tap their potentials and achieve better economic performance so as to contribute more to the state.

Commenting on improving the economic environment and rectifying the economic order, Zhao Ziyang said: Thanks to the measures adopted by the State Council, initial successes have been achieved in this regard. Economic retrenchment must proceed firmly and not stop halfway.[2]

---

[2]From Beijing Television report.

III

Neo-Authoritarianism
Debates on China's Political Structure

The following seven documents outline major differences among political reformers, all of whom rejected the totalitarian monopoly of the CPC. This fascinating debate focused on several issues, including the relationship between economic and political reform, the free-market requisites for successful economic reform, and the immense obstacles and difficulties in implementing reform. Despite its academic character, this debate was not without political relevance. Zhao Ziyang presumably envisioned himself as the reform-oriented strongman who, proponents of neo-authoritarianism suggested, should be given extraordinary authority similar to that of leaders in South Korea and Taiwan. The creation of a market economy in China required temporary strong leadership from the top. Otherwise, the effort to reform would simply lead to a fragmented and chaotic political and economic system, the direction in which advocates of neo-authoritarianism now saw China headed. Despite their ultimate commitment to democracy, they called for recentralizing power by retrieving the authority transferred to local officials over the past decade. Neo-authoritarianism would be a transitional system, leading to democracy after the full implementation of a free-market economy—a process increasingly successful in both Taiwan and South Korea.

Arrayed against the neo-authoritarians, though cloaking their views to various degrees, were advocates of immediate democratization. These reformers argued that political and economic reform must proceed in tandem. Recentralizing power, irrespective of intent, would, they argued, simply sustain China's totalitarian system.[1]

---

[1]Earlier debates on the same issue, articulated in historiographical terms, are analyzed in Lawrence R. Sullivan, "The Controversy over 'Feudal Despotism': Politics and Historiography in China, 1979–82," *The Australian Journal of Chinese Affairs,* no. 23 (January 1990): 1–32.

Economic reform would never take place and the political system would never become democratic, while the debilitating power struggles that had gripped China over the previous forty years would continue.

Zhao's identification with the neo-authoritarian argument made him vulnerable to attack from both liberal and conservative directions. Support for a "transition" to democracy made the old guard suspicious of Zhao's commitment to a Leninist state structure. But in endorsing neo-authoritarianism, Zhao also raised the ire of liberal intellectuals, who concluded that the general secretary was seeking a formula to justify his assumption of dictatorial powers. Ironically, if Zhao had not favored neo-authoritarianism, it probably would have lost Deng Xiaoping's support, as is revealed in Deng's statement in Document 7.

A swift overview of the debate, which flourished in Beijing and Shanghai in late 1988 and early 1989, is provided in Document 8. Documents 9 and 13 are written by Wu Jiaxiang, one of the leading exponents of neo-authoritarianism. Wu's position is attacked in documents 10, 11, and 12. Appearing in three widely read and influential Beijing papers in February and March 1989, these three articles—a small sample of the many published—reveal in somewhat elliptical language a vigorous call for democracy. Noting the serious erosion of the populace's confidence in the CPC's political leadership, all three advocate immediate popular participation as the only solution to China's problems.

7
Deng Xiaoping on Neo-Authoritarianism

Source: Zhongguo Tongxun She (China news organization) (Hong Kong) (April 7, 1989); FBIS, April 7, p. 15.

It is known that the controversial theory of neo-authoritarianism on the mainland has recently been noticed by CPC leader Deng Xiaoping. This 85-year-old statesman held that the modernization process in a backward country needs strongman politics with authority rather than Western-style democracy as a driving force.

According to sources concerned, since the debate on neo-authoritarianism developed in the mainland press last January, scholars have been continuously discussing this issue which has a bearing on the orientation of China's political structural reform. In late February, the influential Beijing Young Economists' Association and the China Economic Structural Reform Research Institute, when mentioning China's political reform, explicitly announced in the "Summary of the Symposium on the National Economic Situation" that "China needs an authoritative supreme leading group which can rally the social elite and the nation in this complicated environment to firmly and rhythmically advance this historic reform." Today, the debate has attracted attention from the top CPC leadership.

According to informed sources here, on March 6, when talking about work arrangements, Zhao Ziyang told Deng Xiaoping that there is a theory about neo-authoritarianism in foreign countries, and that domestic theoretical circles are now discussing this theory. The main point of this theory is that there should be a certain stage in the modernization process of a backward country wherein the driving force should come from strongman politics with authority and Western-style democracy should not be adopted.

Deng Xiaoping then said: This is also my idea. However, Deng Xiaoping had reservations about the term neo-authoritarianism. He said that the specific word for this notion can be reconsidered.

It is learned that the rumor about Deng Xiaoping's support for the theory of neo-authoritarianism has been quietly circulated among intellectuals in Beijing but it has not been officially confirmed. People here hold that the debate in mainland theoretical circles on neo-authoritarianism will not stop due to Deng Xiaoping expressing his attitude. The debate will continue in depth in connection with China's political realities.

8
Concerning Controversial Views on Neo-Authoritarianism

DENG ZIQIANG

Source: Originally published in *Shenzhen tequ bao* (Shenzhen Special Economic Zone news); reprinted in *Ta Kung Pao* (Hong Kong) (April 17, 1989): 2; FBIS, April 19, pp. 26–28.

I

The debate on neo-authoritarianism first began among some young and middle-aged scholars in Beijing and Shanghai, and recently spread to ideological and theoretical circles. Here, I would like to summarize the latest developments in the debate and the main viewpoints on this controversial issue.

What Is Neo-Authoritarianism

At present, there is not yet a commonly accepted definition of this term. People who uphold neo-authoritarianism say that neo-authoritarianism, being different from the old authoritarianism, is oriented toward modernization. In political terms, it is not autocracy, but only semi-autocracy; in economic terms, its target is market-oriented restructuring. Wu Jiaxiang, a young scholar, holds that human history inevitably undergoes three stages of development, namely, the stage of old authority, the stage of new authority, and the stage of liberal democracy. Neo-authoritarianism is a transitional stage between traditional society and modern society. Economically, it is characterized by the semi-market economy, which is a transitional form between the natural economy (or product economy) under the rule of the old authority and the free economy (or market economy), and politically, it is characterized by enlightened autocracy, which is also a transitional form between the old authority's autocracy and the democratic polity.

According to another scholar, Xiao Gongqin, neo-authoritarianism is a transitional form of authoritarianism, or a special political mode in the initial stage of the modernization process in some Asian, African, and Latin American non-socialist countries and regions, such as the "four little dragons." It appeared as a reaction against early-stage parliamentary democracy in Third World countries, and took the form of authoritarian politics built by modernization-minded military or political strongmen.

According to Beijing University's Zhang Bingjiu, neo-authoritarianism is semi-power centralism. The essence is to realize the separation of the economy from politics and to realize dualism in social life. The short-term objective is two-fold: In the economic field, non-economic power should withdraw from the economic realm and economic life should be organized on the basis of the market, and in the political field, political power should be limited to the political realm and must not interfere directly in economic life.

Points Used to Support Neo-Authoritarianism

Hu Jiwei, former editor-in-chief of *Renmin ribao*, opposes the thesis of neo-authoritarianism. He said: We attach importance to authority, but we will establish the authority of democracy rather than the authority of autocracy. Qin Xiaoying, a theoretical worker in the CPC Central Propaganda Department, holds that those who advocate neo-authoritarianism are either ignorant about history or trying to produce a sensational effect. They argue that the general public in China lacks the capacity for democratic participation in government affairs, so they prefer the option of sacrificing a certain degree of political democracy so as to prevent the "disorder" which may be brought about by democracy. They hold that a perfect social structure based on rule by law should first be formed and that order should be established in economic activities. However, according to Qin, this will only cause a vicious cycle in history. Law expert Yu Haocheng said: The advocates of neo-authoritarianism lump together democracy and anarchism. In fact, only autocracy will cause disorder, and only democracy will ensure unity and stability.

Wu Jiaxiang said: The most urgent and imperative step that China should take now is to turn the principle of democracy into applicable concrete steps. He justified neo-authoritarianism according to the following points: Social development cannot transcend the stage of rule by new authority and step directly into the stage of liberal democracy from the stage of traditional autocracy. Democracy must be based on the development of the market, because the market will reduce the amount of public decision-making and the number of people chasing power to a minimum. Under non-market conditions, people tend to seek economic benefit through chasing political power.

Market economy represents a force balancing supply and demand, so it will also lead to a balance between political forces, promoting the formation of political contracts. In a certain sense, democratic politics itself is a kind of contract politics. Democracy must be based on the market, while the operation of the market needs a new authority. Market economy has a prerequisite, that is, the separation of economy from politics. This relies on the emergence of a new rational authority with power and strength of will. Such rational and enlightened authoritarian politics will ensure order and stability for the whole process of social development, and will provide a relatively stable social environment for the growth of an independent middle class along with the development of the economy.

Wu Jiaxiang stressed that the new authority exists only during a certain stage. To prevent the new authority from degenerating, it is necessary to maintain four pressures on it, namely the pressure from the democratic movement among the public, the existence of a middle class composed of independent property owners, healthy state finances, and a democratic atmosphere in the outside world.

Xiao Gongqin said that the checks and balances of power are a necessary factor for the success of China's reform. He said: A disorderly social condition in which laws are not strictly observed and enforced and people are becoming more apathetic continues to develop. This is because authority is being weakened. So it is now necessary to strengthen the authority in the administrative system, deal severe blows at crimes and corrupt phenomena according to the law, overcome political romanticism in the economic field and the overanxious mentality which is reflected in the viewpoint of "system determinism," and make advances step by step so as to dualize the economy and politics.

II

Wang Yizhou, a research assistant at the Institute of Marxism-Leninism of the Chinese Academy of Social Sciences, pointed out some of the flaws of neo-authoritarianism, namely: placing the hopes of reforms on an enlightened individual, putting economic efficiency above all else and not hesitating to sacrifice political freedom and democracy; using its viability as a rationale to seek only quick successes and instant benefits to the detriment of long-term interests; the premise for the successes of the "four little dragons" laid in economic liberalization and not in a market created out of authoritarianism; the thesis that "the development of a market economy ends where democracy begins" does not apply to the reality of simultaneous political and economic developments in the Guangdong coastal regions.

Focusing on the view advanced by proponents of neo-authoritarianism that the present stage of democracy in China lacks viability and that emphasis on democracy would create chaos, Huang Wansheng pointed out that democracy is divided into different levels. One level is idealism vis-à-vis democracy which, in the ultimate sense of the word, affirms that every entity in society is a free person and recognizes the equality of all persons. Denial of this idealism will cause the disappearance of the goal in the implementation of realistic political structural reforms. A second level concerns the structure. It creates an effective social system where the common will of members of society gains statistical majority, thus preventing the dominance of the will of any one person over that of the people. The third level is the practice of democracy in society. Some people claim that the Chinese people know nothing about democracy. This is a ridiculous statement. Democracy does not involve preliminary tests; rather, it is a process of practical exercise. Only by practicing democracy can it be mastered and applied. Because neo-authoritarianism treats democracy as a means, it also excessively emphasizes its viability.

Zhou Wenzhang believed that contrary to the views of those advocating neo-authoritarianism, the problem of loss of authority and the need for its reassertion do not exist in China. Rather, the key lies in how to exercise those authorities scientifically; neo-authoritarianism tends to take the one-sided view that centralized authority is a magic weapon and ignores the core issue, that is: On what basis should "neo-authoritarianism," which is the politics of centralized power, be established and maintained? Failure to consider and resolve these questions as well as vague calls for "strongman politics" and "politics of centralized power" are tantamount to the return of social politics and economy to the old path taken before the implementation of reforms.

As the economist Yan Yining pointed out, neo-authoritarianism advocates the rule by an "enlightened" person, but what we need is the authority of law.

A Middle-of-the-Road Point of View

Xiao Guoliang of Beijing University agreed with the view that neo-authoritarianism is a stage in the development of history, but added that it cannot save China. He maintained that the promotion of political democratization does not mean the discarding of authority; instead, it favors authority identified through a democratic order. Yuan Zhimin, who has a doctorate degree in philosophy from the Chinese People's University, believed that both advocates and opponents of neo-authoritarianism share the goal of establishing a broad social democracy in China, and that this goal carries implications of political pluralism and market economy. He expressed his concurrence with neo-authoritarianism's proposal to achieve this goal through the centralization of state power in the hands of "an elite." But how is this centralization of power in the hands of "an elite" to be carried out at the moment? The choice of a mechanism to train this "elite" is a matter that must be given due consideration by proponents of neo-authoritarianism.

Sun Liping of Beijing University deemed that the arguments from both sides reflected two kinds of concerns: those in favor of neo-authoritarianism are worried about the chaotic state of social life in view of the deepening crises in China's social and economic problems; on the other hand, those opposed to it are concerned that neo-authoritarianism would put an end to the just-unfolding process of democratization. He himself has a third concern: if we cannot make a wise choice and decision, it is possible that two kinds of social conditions, characterized by the lack of order and democracy, will prevail. Consequently, he believed that it is imperative to build up the authority of the law before anything else and steadily promote the process of democratization and legalization.

9
Commenting on Neo-Authoritarianism

WU JIAXIANG

Source: *Shijie jingji daobao* (World economic herald) (Shanghai) (January 16, 1989): 12; FBIS, February 1, pp. 33–35.

Sensitive people may have already noticed that a strange soul is flapping its wings in the ideological forest. That strange soul is neo-authoritarianism.

At the outset the strange soul was only an ambiguous shadow. In 1986 when the democrats in Beijing felt discontented with their achievements, in Shanghai, I heard a lot of young scholars talking about competent political leaders, the role played by the centralization of state power in the process of modernization, the situation in various East Asian countries, and Samuel P. Huntington. Later on, I read a report written by a young scholar named Wang Huning, who strongly advocated the centralization of state power in the process of reform. However, Wang Huning's views were misunderstood as hindering the process of democratization.

Almost at the same time Beijing University and the Central Party School jointly held a "Salon Forum" in Beijing. Zhang Bingjiu, a young scholar who is doing research for his doctorate, delivered a speech at the "Salon Forum." In his speech, Zhang Bingjiu said that at the present stage China should adopt a semi-centralized political system commensurate with the development of China's commodity economy.

Understandably, these premature views of Zhang Bingjiu were given the cold shoulder. Later on, conscientious discussions on such new views were also suspended. It was not until the beginning of 1988 when the Thirteenth CPC National Congress was convened that these new views began to be revived. However, the stalemate in which the new structure and the old structure of our country were locked plunged our country into some new social and economic crises. This new situation of our country made people think deeply. As a result, the theory of neo-authoritarianism was revived again. When I wrote my article entitled "Seeds and Transplantation: The Historical Road Along Which Individual Power Grows" in February 1988, I surprisingly discovered that the earliest guardian of British modernization was the King of Great Britain [most likely a reference to Henry VIII]. The miracle the King of Great Britain created in pulling down 100 castles overnight laid a solid foundation for the building of British modernization. My simple conclusion was: before democracy and freedom "get married," there should be a period in which autocracy "flirts with" freedom. If democracy is regarded as the lifelong companion of freedom, then autocracy should be regarded as the premarital "lover" of freedom.

At a forum held by the CPC Central Committee Propaganda Department's Research Office in June of 1988, Zhang Bingjiu reiterated the idea he put forward two years before. Zhang Bingjiu held that under the present circumstances, it is more feasible and realistic for China to let some powerful leaders forcibly push ahead with the process of modernization than to thoroughly implement democracy at once. Zhang Bingjiu believed that the pressing matter of the moment was to dualize the social life, which means that China should economically practice a free enterprise system and politically practice the centralization of state power. At the Forum Commemorating the 90th Anniversary of the Meiji Restoration of Japan, which was held in September of 1988, Lady Dai Qing put forward an idea which shocked the audience. Lady Dai Qing believed that the reform and modernization going on in mainland China were calling for the emergence of a political strongman who was as capable as those politically strong men who have emerged in many countries and regions in East Asia over the past decades. At the forum, I put forward two hypotheses concerning the two-way development of political power in a traditional society in the course of modernization. I asserted that the centralization of state power at the top level of society and the development of individual freedom at the bottom level of society are just two aspects of one process.

At a small-scale symposium on the relations between the political reform and the economic reform, which was held in October of 1988, Rong Jian reexpounded his views which had once been misunderstood by others. Rong believed that in the course of China's modernization, the transformation from the natural economy to the commodity economy objectively calls for not only the relative centralization of political power but also the rapid transformation from centralized politics to democratic politics. At the symposium, Rong Jian also distributed to the audience his thesis entitled "Does China's Modernization Call for Centralized Politics?" which he planned to publish at the "Pacific Forum." It has been learned that at the current Symposium on Theories of Modernization, the question of centralized politics is a focal point of discussion. The people who are both for and against centralized politics have expressed their views at the current symposium.

People may indignantly ask the following question of those who are for centralized politics: "You think that the old highly centralized structure has already been dismantled, don't you? You don't think that China once suffered a lot from the centralized autocracy, do you? Is it true that you think the centralized autocracy practiced by Hitler, Stalin, and some others resulted in the development of freedom?" I fully understand and sympathize with these people's indignation. However, we should first of all make clear what the people who are for centralized politics really advocate before we condemn them.

In my view, what the people who are for centralized politics advocate is completely different from traditional centralism. As a matter of fact, what the people who are for centralized politics advocate is neo-authoritarianism. Why should we call it neo-authoritarianism? This is because neo-authoritarianism is not an autocratic authority established on the basis of deprivation of individual freedom. Neo-authoritarianism is aimed at removing the obstacles to the development of individual freedom and at safeguarding individual freedom. Depriving individual freedom or safeguarding individual freedom is the watershed between old authoritarianism and neo-authoritarianism. It is true that there are numerous examples which show that the application of authority can either lead our society to a success or lead our society to a disaster. Nevertheless, once we carry out a more detailed analysis of these examples, it will not be difficult for us to discover that the new authority is aimed at safeguarding all types of individual freedom whereas the traditional autocratic authority is aimed at suffocating all types of individual freedom and thus causes one disaster after another.

Is it impossible to safeguard individual freedom with[out] democracy? The answer depends on to what type of society you are asking this question. If you ask this question to a mature modern society, then the answer will be yes. On the contrary, if you ask this question to a transitional society in which individual freedom has not yet fully evolved, then the answer will be: it is not that democracy will foster freedom but that freedom will promote the development of democracy. Insofar as I know, social development undergoes approximately the following three stages: the stage characterized by traditional autocratic authority, the stage characterized by the development of individual freedom under the protection of neo-authoritarianism, and the stage characterized by the integration of freedom with democracy. Why is it impossible to jump from the stage characterized by traditional autocratic authority into the stage characterized by the integration of freedom with democracy? No society has yet been able to make such a super jump. This is because along with the decline of the old authority, there is bound to be a process in which a former highly centralized power is gradually decentralized. However, it is impossible for the past highly centralized power to be decentralized to the hands of ordinary citizens because such power, in the process of its decentralization, will be grabbed by the intermediate social structure created by the old authority. The grabbing of power by the intermediate social structure created by the old authority will inevitably plunge the society into a state characterized by a lack of authority and freedom. As a result, in such a society there will be no necessary centralization and no necessary democracy but only decentralization. Decentralization destroys not only centralism but also democracy. Consequently, the measures of developing democracy and freedom will become the measures of accelerating decentralization while the measures of enforcing centralization will become the measures of further reducing individual freedom. Under such circumstances, a new authority is needed to destroy the old social structure created by the old authority and to enable power, which expands at the intermediate level, to develop in the following two ways: to develop individual freedom, on the one hand, and eliminate obstacles to the development of individual freedom by virtue of the necessary centralization of power, on the other, so as to maintain the social stability in the course of the development of freedom.

Who can guarantee that the newly created authority will not be transformed back into the traditional autocratic authority? No one can guarantee this except the ever intensifying social crisis itself. The decline of the old authority is the natural result of the continued intensification of the traditional social crisis. The restoration of the old autocratic authority will only result in the intensification of the social crisis. The ever intensifying social crisis will diminish all efforts aimed at rebuilding the old authority. So long as a society or a nation does not perish, the ever intensifying social crisis will eventually select a new authority capable of overcoming itself. From this, we can see that neo-authoritarianism does not stress the political structure but the political leader. Like the autocratic political system, the democratic political system can produce an authoritative leader. However, it is also possible that, like the autocratic political system, the democratic political system can produce no authoritative leader at all. As a matter of fact, there are myriad ways of selecting a great leader who is capable of leading a country to successful modernization. These measures include election, heredity, appointment, and coups. We can find countless examples of these measures in the history of the modern world.

Neo-authoritarianism stresses individual freedom, which is actually economic freedom. There is absolutely no economic freedom in a society in which the officials carve up and monopolize the economic interests by dint of their monopoly of the state power. The absence of economic freedom means that individuals cannot freely carry out capital accumulation and cannot fairly trade in commodities, labor force, and property right on the market. Developing the commodity

economy under such circumstances will only result in astonishing social catas-
trophes, including corruption in society, price increases, and great disorder in
society. If such an eventuality does happen, a powerful authority is needed to
separate the official circles from the market.

This is the "political and economic dualism" repeatedly advocated by Rong
Jian. Rong Jian repeatedly called for nonintervention in the market by political
power and stressed the implementation of free competition on an equal footing.
Nevertheless, a new authority should be capable of providing the objective conditions which the economy itself cannot provide to ensure the free development
of the economy. These objective conditions include those aimed at enhancing
capital accumulation and effective disposition of resources as well as the laws
and order indispensable to the commodity trade. In this sense, neo-authoritarianism is similar to conservative economic liberalism. History has attested that
without authority, there would be no healthy development of freedom.

Neo-authoritarianism stresses not only the leader but also the decision-making
group which is closely associated with the leader—on the brilliant and far-
sighted views, on resolute and decisive actions, on the force of overcoming
obstacles, and on the capability of adapting to changing situations.

The above-mentioned is the image of the soul of neo-authoritarianism that we
have imagined. Due to the lack of theoretical study, neo-authoritarianism is still
rather young and immature. Because it sounds similar to autocracy and is suspected of encroaching upon freedom, neo-authoritarianism has understandably
been given the cold shoulder. However, this owl has taken off, through the early
dawn. I hope this article can help it open its wings wider and fly even higher.

10
Neo-Authoritarianism:
An Impractical Panacea

Zhou Wenzhang

Source: *Gongren ribao* (Workers daily) (Beijing) (February 3, 1989): 3; FBIS, February
28, pp. 25–26.

Although it does not offer a well-knit, systematic, theoretical exposition, the
influence of "neo-authoritarianism" is now spreading because of some scholars'
enthusiastic efforts to publicize it. The core of this theory is the hope placed on a

small number of "political elite" or "political strongmen" who are expected to form a highly authoritative and centralized government to ensure the free development of the economy, to cope with the loss of macroeconomic control at home, and to extricate the country from predicaments. It is said that the reason this theory bears the name "neo-authoritarianism" is because it advocates the use of authority to remove obstacles to the free development of the individual and to safeguard personal freedom—this is different from the traditional centralism that tends to build autocratic authority on the basis of deprivation of personal freedom. Its implication is quite clear: the reason China's economic development has suffered repeatedly from chaos and loss of control is the lack of a highly centralized authority (a leader or a leading group) in a position to play a balancing role. We could ignore neo-authoritarianism for the moment if it appeared as a purely academic theory. However, now that it is put forth as a "panacea," we just cannot keep silent any longer in anticipation of the negative effects that may come out once it is implemented. So we think we must study the basis, feasibility, and rationality of this theory.

There is no doubt that the role of authority is indispensable in every society. Nobody would doubt the necessity of establishing the necessary power and authority of the central government in China today, where reform has landed in a predicament. The Chinese people have a long-standing tradition: whenever they are in difficult times or at a crucial stage, they all look to effective measures presented by the highest authorities to lead them out of the predicament or to bring about a historical turning point. Furthermore, to date China's reform has been proceeding under centralized leadership, coordinated and controlled by the central authorities. Even some major powers that are not kept by the central authorities at present have been "delegated" or "given up" on a voluntary basis since the central authorities have realized the disadvantages of a high degree of centralism and the practices of intervening in everything. It is almost certain that if the central authorities decide to regain all the powers that have been delegated or all the interests that have been given up, or if they want to put some "mandates" into force or to impose some "bans," they can readily do so at any time. Is it not true that expenditure has been cut throughout the country as soon as the central authorities ordered an economic deflation?! This indicates that the central government still keeps the power and remains the core of the whole power mechanism in China. The loss of authority and the necessity of rebuilding authority are just irrelevant. In fact, the key issue here is the scientific way to use the power. Therefore there is little ground for resorting to "neo-authoritarianism." This is the first fault of the proponents of the theory.

Nevertheless, there is no denying the fact that the public's confidence in the government has decreased even though the government still maintains its authority. In other words, the prestige of the authorities has declined. Nowadays, strategic goals, development modes, ideal blueprints, and so on that the top decision-making stratum has taken great pains to work out can hardly inspire the public and will no longer be accorded enthusiastic support. It has been quite common for people to feel indifferent to, take a passive attitude toward, or even make a mockery of, the decisionmakers. How can we change this situation? Will it be possible to raise or maintain prestige by simply relying on political centralization and the intensification of the government's authority? We did believe this in the past and Chinese society has had much experience with this. As a result, however, China has now arrived at a point where it has no choice but to introduce an overall reform. The second fault of the proponents of "neo-authoritarianism" is that they have blindly worshipped centralization as a magic weapon but have ignored an essential point: on what basis are we going to establish and maintain the "new authority" of political centralization? If one simply vaguely calls for "strongmen's politics" or "centralist politics" without carefully pondering and resolving this problem, one will bring the social, political, and economic setups back onto the prereform track and push for an overall retreat.

In seeking a solution to extricate China from the present predicament, of course we must learn from our predecessors' theories and foreign experience. But, no matter how, we certainly must take China's national conditions into consideration. One of the important arguments that the proponents of "neo-authoritarianism" have cited is the economic takeoff of the "four little dragons of Asia" which was achieved under highly autocratic political conditions. Extrapolating from this fact, they believe that economic development through political centralization is the only way for China's reform to progress. However, the proponents of "neo-authoritarianism" have never pondered the following questions thoroughly: what are the special characteristics of the political centralism practiced by the "four little dragons of Asia"? How does this political centralism operate? What are its economic functions and how does it perform these functions? And, in particular, what is the economic structure that faces this political centralism and what is its operational mechanism like? In brief, is the political centralism and free economy practiced by the "four little dragons of Asia" suited to China's realities? Needless to say, the answer is no. Therefore, the third fault of the proponents of "neo-authoritarianism" is that they have indiscriminately copied foreign experience and modes without making specific analyses. As everybody knows, we have suffered bitterly enough from this kind of fault in the past.

A sober analysis of China's reform process and its predicament shows that the crux of the problem lies not in the lack of authority on the part of the central government and the diversification of power, but in excessive interference in the economy by the power and in the lack, on the part of the government, of all the indispensable qualities for modern economic management, such as science, democracy, high efficiency, honesty, and so on. Economic development is governed by its own intrinsic objective laws. It is normal that the operation of objective economic laws may give rise to one problem or another or even some awful dilemmas during the transition from the old structure to the new one. It is these problems and dilemmas that embody good opportunities for economic development and offer the possibility of a switch from an abnormal economic state to a normal one. If the government can provide appropriate guidance at this moment, problems can be turned into good opportunities and a predicament can become a possibility of development. However, we used to make a big fuss, rush to exercise political power and the government's force, intervene recklessly, or even enforce some incorrect measures, whenever we came across a problem. The centralized administration and control that "neo-authoritarianism" proposes have always existed in China. While the central government has, in the past, exercised a kind of macroscopic "unitary" centralized control that "demands uniformity in everything," a tendency of "diversified" or "decentralized" command in the microscopic aspect has developed within the government: it is quite common that leading cadres overstep their authority and give arbitrary instructions without making thorough investigations and studies. This is one of the factors contributing to chaos in and loss of control over economic operation. If we also take corruption, poor efficiency, and bureaucracy of the government into account, we will be able to see the shortcomings of the current political structure more clearly.

Therefore, for the present stage of reform, the only way for China to extricate itself from its predicament is not to carry on the centralist politics under which the Chinese society and people have endured all kinds of suffering but to consolidate the current reform, continue to storm the existing highly centralized political structure, readjust the power structure and system, and thus develop a political structure which can be free from overall economic turbulence resulting from faults made by a small number of people.

China needs a "political elite" or "political strongmen" along with the central government's unified leadership. But political elite or government leadership must represent the spirit of science and democracy and must be the crystallization of science and democracy. If one emphasizes only "centralization" and ignores the reform of political power itself, one is actually attempting to restore the traditional government controlling system. That is by no means a "good program" for either the state or the people.

11
Establish Democratic Authority

HU JIWEI

Source: *Jingjixue zhoubao* (Economic studies weekly) (Beijing) (March 5, 1989): 5; FBIS, March 17, pp. 16–18.

We always attach importance to authority, and attach importance to the authority of the leading party, the leading organs, and the leading people. In both the revolutionary period and the construction period, we [needed] such leadership authority. However, what we need to establish is democratic authority rather than autocratic authority.

The authority we [now] need is one with prestige and popular trust. However, autocratic authority is built on the basis of despotic and dictatorial power. It is easier for one person to hold power than to establish prestige and popular trust. At present, there are many problems in reality. In my view, a serious problem is the lack of prestige and popular trust. The prestige of the party and the government in the minds of the people is declining rather than rising.

In the period of reform, it is necessary to establish authority with high prestige in order to exercise effective leadership over reform and to carry on economic structural reform focused on the development of the commodity economy and political structural reform focused on democratic construction.

With respect to political structural reform, real authority can only be built on the basis of democracy. There are fundamental differences between democratic authority and autocratic authority. The characteristics of democratic authority can be summarized into the following points:

First, the establishment of democratic authority requires a democratic and scientific decision-making system. When formulating the guiding principles for making policy decisions, the leading organs and leading people should first carefully and thoroughly investigate and study the actual conditions, listen to various opinions with an open mind, and especially pay attention to skeptical and opposing opinions. Only in this way can the correctness of the policy decisions be ensured to the largest possible extent.

Second, the establishment of democratic authority requires that leading people be elected strictly according to the democratic procedures prescribed by the relevant law. The nomination of candidates and the election should be carried out on the basis of full discussions, comments, and election campaigns, and the number of candidates should be greater than the posts to be filled. Democratic elections may not necessarily choose leaders of the best quality, but they do ensure that bad leaders will not be able to remain in power. Democratic elections also put an end to various means of seizing power and contending for power in violation of democratic procedures, and this will raise the prestige of the leaders among the masses.

Third, the establishment of democratic authority requires the maintenance of democratic centralism. When policy decisions are made, people must strictly abide by the principle of the minority submitting to the majority. At the same time, the minority of people who hold different opinions, must also be respected and protected. The leaders will then win greater support and esteem from the masses as they show a broad-minded and magnanimous attitude.

Fourth, the establishment of democratic authority requires that leaders not only have broad knowledge and superb leadership skills, but also strictly abide by law and discipline and remain incorrupt and honest in performing their official duties, thus becoming ideal leaders and trustworthy public servants in the minds of the masses.

Fifth, the establishment of democratic authority should find expression in the smooth implementation of major policy decisions. The correctness of the contents of these decisions, the democratic procedures for making these decisions, and the exemplary role of the decision makers in the implementation of these decisions will help prevent such phenomena as no final decision being made after prolonged and repeated discussions, or a decision proving impractical after it is made. This will also help prevent, reduce, and correct such abnormal phenomena as the orders and bans issued by the upper authorities being defied by those at the lower levels.

Sixth, the establishment of democratic authority must adhere to the democratic system for selecting and appointing cadres on their merit. Leaders must be good at enlisting able and upright people and be good at correctly judging the ability and talents of the people and giving full play to able and talented people, especially those who oppose their opinions. Only in this manner can we prevent such corrupt phenomena as favoritism in cadre appointments, toadyism, abuse of power, graft, racketeering, and nudging able and talented people from power.

Seventh, the establishment of democratic authority requires the openness of policy making and administrative work. This will subject the leading organs and leading people to thorough supervision by the masses, and will ensure the people's right to get information, to comment on the government's work, and to participate in political activities. The major activities of the party and the state must be regularly reported to the masses in good time to ensure that the masses have full opportunity to discuss major domestic and foreign affairs.

Eighth, the establishment of democratic authority requires that the change of leading people strictly follow the democratic procedures prescribed by the relevant laws. This will prevent the occurrence of some sudden events which damage the condition of rule by law, and will reduce unstable factors that may cause social unrest. In addition, this will also help eradicate autocratic and patriarchal leadership and terminate the system of ensuring cadres' lifelong tenure in office, thus preventing feudal autocracy from firmly holding a ruling position under a revolutionary disguise.

Ninth, the establishment of democratic authority requires a transition from rule by man to rule by law through the development of a perfect legal system. Thus, our country and society will be governed according to the laws, and all people will be equal before the law. That is, if any people, including leading cadres and their relatives, violate laws or discipline, serious sanctions must be applied against them. Only thus can an incorrupt and enlightened style of government based on the observation of law and discipline take shape from top to bottom.

Only when the above mentioned characteristics are formed will leading organs and leading cadres enjoy high prestige and will real democratic authority be realized. In my view, this is the main point that differentiates democratic authority from autocratic authority.

In the era of feudal dynasties, there were some comparatively enlightened and wise autocratic monarchs. They indeed made positive contributions to the prosperity of the country and to the well-being of the people by exercising their dictatorial power. In some modern countries, there have also been some dictators and autocrats who played a positive role in economic development by iron-handed means. If we draw a conclusion from these facts and hold that we need such autocratic authorities in our present effort to improve the economic environment and rectify the economic order, if we call it by a fine-sounding name of "neo-authoritarianism," then we will make a big mistake. This is because what is required by our socialist system is not a wise monarch who can set himself above the people, nor a dictator who rides roughshod over the people and even suppresses the people wholeheartedly. Our Constitution stipulates that all powers belong to the people. The people have the right to manage state affairs, manage economic and cultural affairs, and manage social affairs. Therefore, leading organs and leading people can only be the people's public servants, and must subject themselves to the people's supervision. Their authority must be built on the basis of the democratic system.

People who uphold "neo-authoritarianism" argue that our current political structural reform cannot be oriented to an all-around advance of political democratization; instead, necessary power centralization and political monopoly should be realized. Some comrades even use the "four little dragons," including South Korea, as an example to show the necessity of developing a free economy (or a market economy, a commodity economy) through authoritarian politics. They hold that this should be the orientation of our reforms.

In my view, this opinion includes at least two major misunderstandings: the first is a misunderstanding of the government's function in economic management in a capitalist country. Take South Korea as an example. A rather developed export-oriented free economy has taken shape there, and in the period of economic takeoff, its government heads were rather autocratic. However, the government played a small role in economic management. The commodity economy there was able to develop at a high speed mainly because the country's basic policy was to give free rein to the development of the commodity economy—the state formulated laws for managing the economy according to this basic policy. The government interfered little in specific economic entities. However, in our country, although the government is democratic, its control over the economy is very strict. At present, we are carrying out an economic structural reform focused on the development of a commodity economy, and our policy is being changed from one of restraining the commodity economy to one of promoting the commodity economy. Our government is trying to reduce administrative interference in the business activities of the economic entities to promote the change from a long-standing product economy to a commodity economy. If we stop the process of political democratization and return to the old system, characterized by a high degree of power centralization in economic management, rather than weakening and reducing the government's economic control, then we will not be able to promote the development of the commodity economy—this will go diametrically against the purpose and principle of our reforms. This misunderstanding fails to see the real picture in the "four little dragons," and also fails to see the real conditions in our country. As a matter of fact, the automatic systems in the "four little dragons" are now also facing the challenge of the new democratic trend, and the world-wide democratic trend is irresistible.

The second is a misunderstanding of the relationship between the formulation of policy decisions and the implementation of policy decisions. When making policy decisions, we pursue a system of democratic centralism and stress the necessity of in-depth investigation and study of the actual conditions and the necessity of giving consideration to different opinions. A final decision should then be made according to the principle of the minority submitting to the majority. At the same time, the minority's right to reserve their opinions should be protected. However, after the democratic decision-making process and after democratic elections, the policies must be implemented by various administrative departments under the leader responsibility system, and there must be a centralized and powerful government to perform its administrative function and implement the policies with high efficiency. In routine work, the government leader must hold unified command of all government work and need not submit every concrete affair for discussion or vote. The government must make public all its administrative activities and completely subject itself to mass supervision. The masses can freely criticize the government's work and put forward proposals, but they must respect the government and obey the government head's orders and must not defy these orders, act in their own ways, and practice anarchism. This is exactly the principle of "free discussion and unified action" advocated by Lenin. This shows that democratic centralism in the decisionmaking process and the leader responsibility system in the implementation of policy decisions belong to two different categories and should not be confused. If we replace the system of democratic centralism in the first realm with the leader responsibility system, then we will just restore an autocratic and patriarchal system and our democratic politics will degenerate into autocratic politics again.

"Neo-authoritarianism" stressed the authority of leaders rather than an authoritarian polity. This opinion holds that under the present conditions, we need some powerful leaders to advance modernization in an arbitrary way, and that the pressing task of the moment is to realize a dual society which is characterized by a free enterprise system in the economic field and a power centralization system in the political field.

A document of the Thirteenth CPC Congress explicitly stipulates that a major problem in our political system that we must resolutely solve through reform is the high degree of power centralization in the political field. The document points out that in our country, "excessive power centralization is not only reflected in the party committees holding too much power over various economic, administrative, cultural institutions, and mass organizations, but is also reflected in too much power of the grass-roots units being held in the hands of the upper leading organs. On the one hand, the leading organs manage many things that they cannot manage properly or they should not interfere in, and they are consequently mired in routine affairs; on the other hand, the grass-roots units lack decision-making power and it is hard to fully arouse the initiative of the masses." In our country, authoritarian politics represent a time-honored tradition, so the great reform will encounter many obstacles and difficulties.

If we use "neo-authoritarianism," a medicine which may cause a fever, to cure our nation's chronic fever, this is similar to using gasoline to extinguish a fire. What result will this achieve? Is it hard to imagine?

12
"New Authority" Going Astray

LI WEI

Source: *Jingjixue zhoubao* (Economic studies weekly) (Beijing) (March 26, 1989): 7; FBIS, April 7, pp. 15–16.

In Western political science, authoritarianism and totalitarianism are two vastly different terms. Authoritarianism means that one dictator or a clique of such people concentrates and controls the power of a political system, except that they do not monopolize power in such areas as economy and culture. Totalitarianism refers to a system of government which puts all aspects of social life under strict control using coercive measures, opposes any form of constitutional separation of powers, calls for the absolute obedience of individuals to the state, and propagates absolute collectivism. It seems that in the eyes of the proponents of "new authoritarianism," what our country practiced in the past and is practicing at present is "old authoritarianism." In our country there has never been authoritarianism, still less a difference between so-called new and old authoritarianism. In real life, in the absence of ownership reform and political and economic dualization as prerequisites, and when the government intervenes in everything, any view and theory claiming to be "authoritarianism" can but only be totalitarian in essence and substance.

In Western political science there is a strict distinction between the two terms power and authority. Power means that the subject subjugates the object through coercion, while authority means that the object voluntarily submits itself to the subject under noncoercive conditions. "New authoritarianism" confuses power and authority, and thus fails to grasp the essence of the issue. In reality, the government already has very great power, but inadequate command of authority. "New authoritarianism" confusedly equates the government's lack of authority with its lack of power. Our government once commanded great authority and possessed a strong legal status. However, after experiencing excessive setbacks and frustrations in the previous numerous movements and the Great Cultural Revolution, the government's legal status and authority have undeniably been reduced. Awakened, people found the contrast between reality and their expectations of the government too vast. Therefore, the reason the government lacks authority lies in the inadequate effectiveness of the government's behavior, rather than in the degree of power in its hands. The way to heighten the authority of the government lies in making the government's behavior more effective, especially putting policy making on a scientific and democratic basis, while striving to foster the image of a clean government, rather than enhancing the power of the government.

"New authoritarianism" places particular stress on political stability and social order. This is understandable. However, the previous political upheavals following the founding of the PRC were the product of power struggles and political corruption, rather than the result of political participation going awry. In China, the forces of people's participation in political affairs are very weak. Our country has conducted much political mobilization (movements from top to bottom) but what it lacks is political participation. The fundamental way to achieve political stability is to reform the power structure and political system and to update systems and organizations. A stable and effective society with good order is bound to be organizationally developed. Nevertheless, over nearly four decades in the past, we have always replaced all other organizations with administrative organizations. Market, enterprise, educational, and cultural organizations were run in the way administrative organizations were operated, grouped into the government's administrative ranking system, and put under its firm control. Consequently, the numbers of all organizations other than administrative ones have shrunk. This organizational shrinkage has resulted in universal disorder and inefficiency in society. For example, the market organizational shrinkage has brought disorder and inefficiency to society. "New authoritarianism" neglects reform of the existing power structure and political system and updating of systems and organizations; but it favors increasing the power of the government while maintaining the existing political power structure (in fact, it means giving more power to several particular individuals in the government—"new authoritarianism" admires strongman politics). In this way, power struggles will surely become more acute the further it goes; the situation in which society lacks order and rallying capability will worsen; and the objectives, such as political stability, which new authoritarianism seeks, will be lost.

The key to getting rid of this disorderly state of affairs lies in standardizing the power of the government so that the government can take charge of what it ought to do. Failure to do so will lead to a structural restoration or more deep-seated disorder.

13
Commenting Again on Neo-Authoritarianism—Pushing Democratization Forward through the Market

WU JIAXIANG

Source: *Shijie jingji daobao* (World economic herald) (Shanghai) (April 10, 1989): 12; FBIS, April 19, pp. 24–26.

Young academic Wu Jiaxiang has been a "central figure" in the theoretical debate over neo-authoritarianism conducted by people in academic circles. This newspaper has published quite a number of articles airing different views. Feeling that his "opponents" did not completely understand his ideas and concepts, Wu Jiaxiang has written another article to explain his views.

Democracy Cannot Be Separated from the Market

Keeping aside primitive democracy, we will discover that democratic politics has risen in the company of a market mechanism and that the range and quality of democracy have always fallen into line with improvement of the market mechanism.

—The market has reduced public rights and public decisions to the minimum limits (this viewpoint was suggested by Mr. Pan Kang). Through reducing political rights, the number of people seeking political rights is also reduced. These two reductions also cause a drop in the dealing costs of democratic political bodies. These dealing costs form a direct ratio with public rights, public decisions, and the number of people seeking political rights and participating in decision-making. When there is no market, when the market is imperfect, or, in particular, when politics is mixed with the economy, there will be excessive public rights and public decisions. In such cases a large number of people will seek political rights (because they cannot gain economic interests through the market, they have to strive for official posts to achieve this end). As a result, the costs for democratic participation will rise to such an excessive extent that effective consultations are difficult. Under such circumstances, the best method of economizing political dealing costs is to exercise a high degree of centralism. It can thus be seen that there is democracy above the market but what lies above the natural and product economies is autocracy.

—The market helps separate politics from the economy. The separation of these "two powers" has laid a foundation for the separation of three powers and will prevent the centralization of powers from turning into autocracy, and local powers from becoming local separatist regimes. All of this will fundamentally prevent democracy from turning into autocracy or separatism.

—The market system explicitly defines individual interests and risks, strengthens one's sense of responsibility for democratic rights and reduces the possibility of politicians practicing bribery during elections. But under the non-market public ownership system it costs little to canvass for candidates because the voters do not know where their interests lie and do not care much about who is being elected.

—As a contract economy, the market economy enables politics to take on a contract nature and turns democratic procedures into contracts that must be implemented or that do not allow unilateral alteration. As a matter of fact, democratic politics is contract politics.

—The development process of the market is a diversification process of economic interests. The diversification of economic interests is the basis of political diversification and also of the modern party system. Without this basis, people can only choose between autocracy, anarchy, underworld gangs, and warlord politics.

—The popularization of the market system enables people to build mutually beneficial relationships. Under these relationships people will get rid of their naïve ideas, free themselves from dogmatism, and improve their sense of coexistence and mutual accommodation. This is an indispensable condition for the emergence and development of democratic politics.

—The market serves as a stabilizer for manufacturers and consumers. As long as there is no major fluctuation in the market it is difficult for excessive remarks and actions (from either the upper or lower social strata) to disrupt the entire society. This will increase people's sense of safety in society and enable society to contain radical ideas and actions. Radical ideas and actions serve as a necessary condition for preventing the emergence of rigidity in society. They suggest the original meanings of democratic politics.

—The operation of the market can turn out middle class people who account for the majority of the population. This will prevent the principle of subordinating the minority to the majority from becoming a principle that deprives people of their private property. It will also prevent a clash between democratic principles and the principles of economic growth.

A healthy market obviously serves as a basis for establishing democratic politics. Without this basis it will be very difficult to form a democratic political system. Even if it could be formed, no one can guarantee that it will not change. Hitler, a rare dictator in history, was elected through normal procedures. But a new government that arises without a market system or a perfected market system (be it elected through revolutionary violence or a democratic election) will only be a tool in the change of regimes.

Of course, the market also produces corrosive effects on democracy. Economic inequality caused by the market constitutes a threat for equal civil rights. However this problem will not be discussed now because it belongs in a higher category.

Introduction of the Market System Requires Neo-Authoritarianism

Since the market system is so important to democracy, a backward country must make major efforts to introduce this system if it really wishes to practice democracy. During this process some democratic radicals first turn their feelings for democratic politics into enthusiasm to promote the implementation of the market system. As I see it, this is an expression of ideological maturity. It is really surprising to say that some people feel strange about this situation.

What we should study are the political conditions for ensuring smooth implementation of the market system. To solve this problem there is a need to know the relevant basic conditions and the obstacles that may be encountered during implementation of the market system.

The separation of politics from the economy is a precondition for and a result of the implementation of the market system. In nonsocialist backward countries the mixing of politics with the economy does not constitute a prominent problem. In these countries, this mixing finds expression in excessive government intervention in economic activities and in government officials running enterprises. In socialist countries this manifests itself in the government being the owner of the enterprises. The government is deeply involved in economic activities, so deeply that it cannot get out of this involvement. This indicates that it is much more difficult to implement the market system in socialist countries than in nonsocialist backward countries. What is the method for tearing politics away from the economy? Can the expansion of political participation help solve this problem? I do not think so. The expansion of political participation will not lead to the separation of politics from economy but will instead increase the participants' portion in sharing the "fruit" of the combination of politics with economy. What about introducing general elections? This will be good if the head of state elected has the power to separate politics from economy. But it is quite possible that his accommodation of the interests of the voters and social groups will make him powerless in preventing the following two kinds of misconduct from undermining the market system:

One is evading the market. During the initial stage of the market system almost everyone tries to evade the market. Consumers are trying to evade high market prices and look for low market prices or obtain commodities and labor free of charge. This was where China's "unitary economy" and "manor economy" originated. Whether a consumer can succeed in his attempt to evade the market depends on how much power he possesses. Laborers try to evade the labor force market. Producers try to evade the production materials and capital markets; they are seeking low price raw materials and nonrisky government loans.

The other is carving out the market. The "duke [fiefdom] economy" Mr. Xia Yulong was talking about and the "territorial economy" referred to by Mr. Lu Zhongyuan are the results of government departments carving out the market.

Obviously, if these actions are not stopped it is impossible for the market mechanism to develop and mature. Both economic and political methods should be applied in stopping this misconduct. Economic methods include "waging a protracted war" against the government. In other words, producers who do not have the power to carve out the market should gradually be allowed into the market and efforts should be made to monetize all rights that obstruct market operation, so that these rights will be converted into something that circulates in the market. This is a long process of transforming the traditional political structure. Apart from being long, this process will encounter government corruption. Even a modern country finds it difficult to endure the slow process of the "natural death" of the old social structure. An example is the occurrence of all kinds of bourgeois revolutions.

Newly emerging modern countries generally use political means to speed up implementation of the market system. Some of them maintain that it was necessary first to set up a parliamentary democratic political structure under which economic development could be speeded up and the market system implemented. But so far no country has provided any successful experience. Some weak parliamentary political structures turned into military dictatorships and others fell into political and economic confusion. Why? Because a parliamentary democratic political structure cannot exist without the market or the influence of the old political structure that evades and carves out the market. It is precisely this influence that controls parliamentary activities and the elections for heads of state. There are two choices facing the elected head of state: one is to be very weak and allow all political forces (local interest groups and trade unions) to evade and carve out the market; the other is to be a hardliner who is free from the control of any forces and is ready to abolish general elections for the effective introduction of the market system. The former may lead his country into confusion and disaster, whereas the latter may become a new authority. In this sense, a new authority can avoid detours and speedily bring about democratization through the introduction of the market system.

Some people will probably cite India and the United States to prove that a parliamentary democratic political structure can directly be formed without establishing a new authority or introducing the market system. As a matter of fact, British colonialists were playing the role of a new authority in setting up the parliamentary democratic political structure. The privileges of the old society basically did not exist in the United States. The United States, a society of immigrants enjoying equality, could transplant directly the market system from Britain. As a result of this difference in historical development, the United States cannot appreciate the significance of establishing a new authority in the course of modernization.

It Is Necessary to Impose Democratic Pressure on a New Authority

Some people are worried and even indignant about neo-authoritarianism because they are afraid that it may ignore democracy. This is a misunderstanding which has resulted from their different explanations concerning the concept of democracy. In my opinion, democracy can be divided into the following three forms: democracy as a short-term movement, democracy as a normal activity, and democracy as a political system. The most frequently asked questions are: How can neo-authoritarianism be formed? How can it be prevented from turning into old authoritarianism? My views are basically as follows: historically, neo-authoritarianism generally emerged in the course of a short-term democratic movement and withstood certain pressures from the democratic movement. Eventually a democratic political system was established on the basis of the introduction of the market system and the trial-implementation of democracy. On this point, [U.S. President Woodrow] Wilson remarked explicitly: "The constitution is not the source but the expression of our freedom." Democracy occurred first and the system is only an expression.

Therefore, as soon as neo-authoritarianism comes into being, it is necessary to impose pressure on it by carrying out regular democratic movements. I agree with Mr. Cao Siyuan's views: there should be places and rules for democratic activities. According to China's specific conditions, ideal places for democratic activities are not the streets but the sessions of the National People's Congress [NPC] and the Chinese People's Political Consultative Conference [CPPCC]. To allow democratic activities during these sessions, it is necessary to reduce the number of deputies and members so as to facilitate discussions and consultations and to economize on costs. To enhance deputies' and members' sense of responsibility in making suggestions, it is necessary to select deputies and members from people who meet the age and political requirements. I agree with the views of many comrades: places for democratic activities should be distinguished from places where veteran comrades rest and display their exploits. To improve the effectiveness of policy appraisals and democratic consultations and to reduce unrealistic unanimity that was common in the past, it is necessary to hold activities for party and Communist Youth League members. There are many ways to impose democratic pressure. Apart from meetings, there is also a need to encourage the openness of public opinion.

In preventing neo-authoritarianism from turning into old authoritarianism it is also necessary to impose proprietary, financial, and social pressures. If neo-authoritarianism ignores these kinds of pressure it will run into financial deficit. As everyone is aware, the British Tudor dynasty took the throne from the manor lord back to a free land. This was the result of financial pressure. In our country, if an enterprise that mixes politics with economy is providing less and less revenue and an independent proprietor is providing more and more revenue, there is no reason for the government to ignore this pressure. In conclusion, amid the wave of world democratization and economic liberalization, and in a country that has not achieved modernization, the possibility of neo-authoritarianism turning into old authoritarianism is smaller than that for the early introduction of political diversification. Viewed from modern Chinese history, political diversification prior to the introduction of the market system generally led to separation, confusion, underworld politics, and separatist warlord regimes. If future practice proves this to be wrong, I am willing to revise or give up this viewpoint at any time.

IV

Intellectual Dissent

This section turns to the explicit expression of dissent by Chinese intellectuals and their direct petitions to the party leadership. The opening salvo (Doc. 14) is by Su Shaozhi, former director of the Institute of Marxism–Leninism–Mao Zedong Thought in the Chinese Academy of Social Sciences (CASS). Su delivered his address to a December 1988 symposium that evaluated the historic Third Plenum of the Eleventh Central Committee, held in December 1978. This plenum marked the reascendancy of Deng Xiaoping (following his second purge in 1976); more important, it initiated the reform era. Despite his proreform views, Su's attendance at the December 1988 session (at which conservative party leaders tried to avoid open criticism of recent political and economic retrenchment) was controversial: several prominent dissident intellectuals had not been invited, while others decided not to attend, apparently out of displeasure. Su's invitation was surprising since he had been criticized for his excessively prodemocratic views along with others excluded from the symposium. His appearance and talk were courageous acts—especially his defense of Yu Guangyuan and Wang Ruoshui, leading moderate theoreticians who had drawn the ire of such conservative ideologues in the party as Deng Liqun and Hu Qiaomu. Su was now once again pitted against old political enemies, particularly Deng Liqun, who had failed to dislodge him in the 1983–85 "anti–spiritual pollution" campaign. Su was even more daring in condemning the campaigns against "humanism and alienation" (1978–1983), "bourgeois liberalization" (1987), and "spiritual pollution," because each had had the explicit imprimatur of Deng Xiaoping.

Even more radical views were expressed by Fang Lizhi, an internationally recognized astrophysicist who had been unceremoniously tossed out of the CPC by Deng Xiaoping in early 1987. Placed under police surveillance (*genzong*), Fang nonetheless was able to meet with friends and write tracts that reached the outside world, where they were published and then returned to China for dissemination, especially among students at Beijing University. Three of his essays, from January–February 1989, are presented here. The first, Document 15, summarizes Fang's views, specifically his prescient prediction that 1989 would be a turbulent year of consequence in Chinese history. Document 16 is a bold petition that Fang submitted to Deng Xiaoping seeking a general amnesty for political prisoners and the release of Wei Jingsheng, a leading dissident during the 1978–79 Democracy Wall movement who has been incarcerated ever since, sometimes in solitary confinement. The third document (Doc. 18) represents Fang's effort to draw the world's attention to the abuses of human rights in China. In so doing, he departed from a previous tendency of Chinese intellectuals to work within the system rather than appeal for outside support on behalf of universal principles—an act that undoubtedly outraged Deng Xiaoping but also contributed to Fang's reputation as China's principal human rights advocate.[1]

Documents 17 and 19 are petitions from leading Chinese intellectuals to CPC leaders indicating support for Fang Lizhi's effort to win the release of Wei Jingsheng and advance political reform. The later also calls for increased government budgetary support for education. Taken together, they reveal both the relaxed and relatively open political atmosphere in which such challenges could be expressed and the increasing boldness of intellectuals concerned with the slow pace—and even retrogression—of China's political reform. Despite the leadership's ostensible proreform rhetoric at the 1987 Party Congress (Doc. 3, above), few real institutional changes had been effected.[2] With intellectuals increasingly prepared to air their grievances and openly petition the leaders, the situation was now ripe for polarization and confrontation.

Among top CPC leaders, divisions and tensions intensified. This is clearly revealed in the transcript of Zhao Ziyang's February 27 meeting with President George Bush during his trip to China (Doc. 20). Referring to the difficulties being encountered in the reforms, Zhao acknowledged opposition from two quarters: conservative opponents of reform, and liberal advocates of immediate democratization. (The latter group implicitly refers to the intellectuals cited in Documents 14–19.) Aware that President Bush had invited Fang Lizhi to the U.S. Embassy barbecue planned for that evening, Zhao elliptically warned that the fact "that some people in American society support those who are not satisfied with the Chinese Government will be detrimental not only to China's political stability . . . but to the progress of its reform." Zhao was telling Bush, in other words, that the invitation was giving Zhao political problems at home.[3]

---

[1] Fang Lizhi was the recipient of the 1989 R. F. Kennedy Award for Human Rights.

[2] Zhao's proposal at the congress to begin dismantling the party's pervasive apparatus of "small groups" (*xiaozu*) in state and mass organizations evidently had gone nowhere, though the influence of local party secretaries over policy had diminished considerably.

[3] Yang Shangkun purposely arrived at the barbecue twenty minutes late, after he was sure that Fang had been prevented from attending, thereby avoiding a face-to-face meeting with the dissident.

Two additional articles from a well-informed Hong Kong journal further describe the political struggles erupting in Beijing in February and March. Documents 21 and 22 suggest, as other Hong Kong sources also claimed, that Zhao was under heavy fire from conservative party elders, especially Chen Yun and Bo Yibo, who were evidently now pressuring Deng Xiaoping to remove him. Deng had already succumbed to similar efforts from the same quarter two years earlier in forcing the dismissal of Hu Yaobang. This time, the party elders were particularly incensed by the open advocacy of democracy during the neo-authoritarianism debate, and the bold petitions from intellectuals. Document 21, by Lo Ping, notes with considerable foresight that just as Hu Yaobang had become particularly vulnerable when a student movement arose, so too would Zhao since he had also protected intellectuals whose ideas were purportedly motivating the students.[4] Document 22, written a month later by the same Beijing-based Hong Kong correspondent, asserts that Zhao's position had weakened even more in the intervening month. Indeed, Li Peng's report to the NPC (Doc. 5) proved that his conservative coalition had seized the initiative from Zhao, while Deng Xiaoping's support for the general secretary was beginning to waver. The leadership was thus unable to confront the upcoming crisis in a unified manner. Each leader would, instead, calculate how the situation would affect his power and personal political position.

---

[4]Student leaders, such as Shen Tong, hotly deny the direct influence of Chinese intellectuals like Fang, citing instead the impact of student movements in South Korea, democratization in Taiwan, and the philosophical ideas of Westerners such as Karl Popper.

14
Speech at the Theoretical Discussion Meeting Marking the Tenth Anniversary of the Third Plenary Session of the Eleventh CPC Central Committee [Excerpts]

SU SHAOZHI

Source: *Shijie jingji daobao* (World economic herald) (Shanghai) (December 26, 1988): 3, 15; FBIS, January 13, 1989, pp. 19–23.

I come here to attend this theoretical discussion meeting marking the third plenary session of the Eleventh CPC Central Committee [of December 1978] because I firmly support the spirit of the third plenary session, and also because I hope that unity among theoreticians will be achieved. My speech today is also for the purpose of enhancing unity.

Drawing Lessons and Unity Among Theoreticians

I was one of the participants in that meeting ten years ago to discuss theoretical principles. That meeting was the freest and most lively one to be held since the founding of the PRC. It was during that meeting that some principles which are universally accepted nowadays, for example annulment of the life tenure system for leading posts, were put forward. However, the participants in today's meeting are strongly encouraged to concentrate on more practical issues and not touch theoretical problems. We are also asked "not to quibble over the past." In fact, history should not and cannot be cut apart. Our purpose in summing up our past experience is to draw lessons from it so that we can do a better job in the future. Why don't people want to mention that discussion meeting on theoretical principles? Why should we not discuss theoretical principles? How can we make progress without discussing theoretical principles, summing up our experience, and drawing lessons from our theoretical studies prior to and, in particular, since the third plenary session of the Eleventh CPC Central Committee?

The "Double Hundred Principle" has been mentioned at every meeting on theoretical work but has been violated all the time.[1] The principle has never been implemented to the letter. The divorce between theory and practice in this regard can be counted as a chronic malady. Some people may say that we should not quibble over the past anymore because opinions vary on the drive to "eliminate spiritual pollution" and the "opposition to bourgeois liberalization." But I would say that "eliminating spiritual pollution" and "opposition to bourgeois liberalization" are the most important issues for theoretical circles in the past ten years, and many comrades have been demanding that these questions be clarified. In particular, these issues involve many theoretical and academic disputes on humanism, alienation, the evaluation of Bukharin, the theory on the stages of socialist development, the elimination of the pernicious influence of feudalism, and so on. All these issues concern academic and theoretical viewpoints but over the past ten years a unitary theory or even a single person's views have been applied in judging academic and theoretical issues while other views have been repudiated. What is more, criticism has been made against some people because of their different views on certain academic and theoretical problems and political labels have been attached to them. In this connection, unfair political punishment has been imposed on many scholars. All this cannot be solved simply by urging people "not to quibble over the past." Now that we are attending a theoretical discussion meeting held by the party it is high time for us to thoroughly discuss all these theoretical and academic issues and to draw a lesson from the old practice of attacking others because of their different theoretical and academic views. All these issues, if they remain unsolved, will hinder the enhancement of academic freedom, the development of theoretical studies, and unity among theoreticians.

With regard to unity, I have met quite a few enlightened comrades and also quite a few young theoreticians at this meeting. But most of the pioneer theoreticians who were known as vanguard thinkers at the time that theoretical discussion meeting was held ten years ago, and during the past ten years, and some newly emerging young scholars, are unable to attend today's meeting. I am not quite clear about the inside story as I have just returned from abroad. But I have been told: "Fifty people are attending the meeting by special invitation . . . among them are, in particular, some comrades who hold to different theoretical and academic views. You will notice this if you have a glimpse at the name list." I have also seen a document explaining how those specially invited participants were selected, which addresses them as "comrades

---

[1]"Let a hundred flowers bloom, let a hundred schools of thought contend"—lines from a classical poem used by Mao Zedong to launch the "open" criticism campaign of May–June 1957.

who have been criticized and dealt with." I believe that both this style and the guiding concept behind it are wrong.

First of all, the existence of different views in the theoretical and academic fields is a normal and good phenomenon. Do you prefer varying opinions or a centralized public opinion? Do you prefer to see a hundred schools of thought contending with each other or would you rather have a single school of thought dominating all the others? Now that everybody agrees that there is no need to seek a uniform public opinion, why should people be forced to worship a single theory? Should the people in this country be forced to worship a single theory, I am certain that this country would be lifeless. We are now attending this theoretical discussion meeting. If the guiding ideology for this meeting is to seek uniformity in the theoretical and academic fields, if the sponsors of the meeting just cannot tolerate different theoretical and academic views, (I am very sorry but I have good grounds for saying this—that document, in explaining how the theses were selected, noted: "By the way, also selected are some theses which represent different theoretical and academic views." This remark seems to be telling us that the selection of theses representing different theoretical and academic views is a great grace! Isn't that very ridiculous, my God?) and if the purpose of this theoretical discussion meeting is to place a view in command of everything, then I think we had better cancel this meeting since it will be meaningless or even will fail to live up to its name—"A Theoretical Discussion Meeting." While this meeting is a "theoretical discussion," some people still regard different theoretical and academic views as heresies. Is this not a great mockery?

If one links the title of this meeting to the style "comrades who have been criticized and dealt with," one can find a second mistake. What I mean is, the fact that people were criticized and dealt with because of their different theoretical and academic views is in itself a violation of the "Double Hundred Principle" and academic freedom. As everybody knows, among those on the list of specially invited participants in this meeting, Li Shu, Yu Guangyuan, and Wang Ruoshui have suffered unfair treatment in the drive to "eliminate spiritual pollution" and "oppose bourgeois liberalization." Comrade Li Shu passed away recently and we deeply regret his death. A Marxist historian, he had been unfairly treated since the drive to "eliminate spiritual pollution." He was invited to attend this meeting but was styled a comrade who had been criticized and dealt with. Such a practice is bitterly disappointing. Now that he has just passed away and our scholars still have not recovered from grief over his death, we are reminded to have a look at the name list lest we forget his disgraceful status. Can such a strong hostility be interpreted as an expression of the spirit of unity? The views of Yu Guangyuan and Wang Ruoshui are above criticism. Their only mistake was that their views did not suit the taste of the leading people in theoretical circles at that time. Even if their academic views were wrong, their being punished because of their different academic and theoretical views was in itself a violation of the provisions of academic freedom laid down in the Constitution, and of the principle of "letting a hundred schools of thought contend." Since they are listed by the sponsor of this meeting as specially invited participants with such a status, it is quite natural that they refused to attend. Based on the above analysis, can we say the remarks and practice of the meeting sponsors are conducive to internal unity in theoretical circles?

On Contention of a Hundred Schools of Thought

Conscientiously letting a hundred schools of thought contend and ensuring academic freedom is the problem with which people in academic and theoretical circles are most concerned.

Let us first of all talk about something which happened before the Great Cultural Revolution. The "Double-Hundred Policy" was put forward in 1956, but it was never conscientiously implemented. It is, of course, right to say that it was due to the " 'leftist' mistake in the guiding thinking of the party" that we failed to implement the policy. However, this kind of view is too abstract and is not at all specific. The reason why we failed to implement the "Double-Hundred Policy" was mainly that we failed to respect the article contained in our Constitution: "Citizens enjoy freedom of speech, the press, assembly, and association," namely, political freedom. There is no stipulation in the Constitution that political issues cannot be discussed. According to the principle of the science of law, pursuing something which is not banned by the law cannot be regarded as violating the law. If discussions on political problems are prohibited, any measures aimed at encouraging the contention of a hundred schools of thought are of no avail. Those who aired certain divergent views in academic discussions were very often regarded by certain leaders as making political mistakes, and were therefore punished. The antirightist struggle in 1957 is a striking example. Almost all the cream inside and outside the party was overthrown. Before the Great Cultural Revolution, the policy of "letting a hundred schools of thought contend" could not be implemented because, under the guidance of the principle of "taking class struggle as the key link," it was stressed that proletarian dictatorship must be exercised in each and every field, including the ideological and theoretical fields. As a result, political campaigns were launched in turn and "academic mass criticism" was carried out in various circles. This kind of "mass criticism" which was carried out on a grand scale without letting the victims defend themselves, developed to the extreme in the Cultural Revolution, and became a cultural autocracy. This "mass criticism" completely ran counter to the articles on academic freedom contained in the Constitution and to scientific spirit, and severely damaged our theories, science, and culture. According to statistics, "academic mass criticism" has been carried out on thirty-four occasions in the natural sciences field since the founding of the PRC. None of these were correct. The situation in the social sciences field was more serious. Many scholars were criticized and punished and a number of subjects of learning were abandoned, such as psychology, political science, sociology, and even some parts of the science of law. We should now reiterate that the articles on various kinds of freedom contained in our Constitution must be respected and that political problems can be discussed. In the meantime, we should take measures to avoid the recurrence of the mistake of "academic mass criticism."

Since the third plenary session of the Eleventh CPC Central Committee, the principle of "letting a hundred schools of thought contend" has been implemented in a better way. Drawing a lesson from the past, the broad masses of intellectuals strive to free themselves from spiritual trammels, and to enhance their capability in thinking independently and distinguishing right from wrong. In particular, due to the fact that cultural autocracy, "academic mass criticism," wielding big sticks, pinning on political labels, and so on do not enjoy popular support, the number of people who follow the baton of power and influence has [been] greatly reduced. This has created favorable conditions for letting a hundred schools of thought contend. However, during the past ten years not everything has progressed smoothly. Campaigns, which were not called campaigns, or academic mass criticism which was not called academic mass criticism, still happened. The two most prominent campaigns were "eliminating spiritual pollution," and "opposing bourgeois liberalization." Actually, they were a refurbished version of "academic mass criticism." A small number of leaders in the theoretical field regarded themselves as the embodiment of the party and proclaimed themselves fighters defending the purity of Marxism. They made subjective judgments on right and wrong, and, relying on administrative and coercive measures and false reports, they criticized divergent academic views from the high plane of principle, regarded them as political mistakes, and punished those who advocated the views. The Wang Ruoshui incident was a notable example.

It was not all wrong for Wang Ruoshui to put forward his ideas on humanism and alienation. Progressive personages throughout the world now regard humanism as one of the basic characteristics of socialism. Alienation has existed in China and in socialist countries in reality. Are not various kinds of corrupt phenomena, "government profiteering," privileges, and so on, which people hate very much, typical examples of alienation? Even if the ideas were wrong could they not be discussed as academic problems? Are socialist countries and communist countries in practical reality not discussing these problems? However, there is a person [Hu Qiaomu] who maintains that both humanism and alienation are antisocialist, but regards his own "On Humanism And Alienation" as teaching material. If he took part in the discussion on an equal basis as a member of the theoretical field, we would welcome him regardless of the acuteness of his views. However, he announced that academic discussion on the above-mentioned two issues was a forbidden zone, and regarded Wang Ruoshui's problem as a political one and punished him repeatedly. The punishment escalated from depriving him of his post to expelling him from the party. Although Yu Guangyuan was not punished, he was treated unfairly. Ten meetings of so-called criticism and self-criticism were organized to criticize him. The participants did not know in what capacity they attended the meetings. The speeches delivered at the meeting and the methods adopted were no different from mass criticism. It was finally decided that he had committed ten mistakes.

What is surprising is that a small number of leaders say that no incident of wielding a big stick has occurred during the past ten years, and that only personal persecution can be regarded as the practice of wielding big sticks. Their views not only cover up the actual mass academic criticisms during the past ten years, but have also absolved many academic mass criticisms before the Great Cultural Revolution from blame. Actually, even if we follow the "harsh" criterion set by these leaders, mass academic criticism has occurred during the past ten years. Why is Comrade Zhou Yang still confined to date? We should think about this. Is this not directly connected with the unfair criticism of him in 1983? It has been ten years since we advocated the spirit of seeking truth from facts in the third plenary session. On this occasion marking the tenth anniversary of the third plenary session throughout the country, a small number of leaders have still failed to pursue the spirit of seeking truth from facts. Such being the case, is it difficult for people in theoretical circles to avoid a "lingering fear" or an "anticipatory fear"?

We need warmest enthusiasm and sufficient space to stress the necessity of protecting the enthusiasm of theoretical workers in making explorations and blazing new trails so that they will have the necessary freedom and sense of security. We should fully explain that if the necessary protection is not provided for theoretical studies and exploration, development in the practice of reform will be greatly hampered. A guarantee must be given to resolutely discard the previous arbitrary, rude, and coercive practice of "mass criticism." Leaders must not block criticism using the pretext that the theoretical field must "oppose the practice of wielding a big stick."

On Marxism

One of the reasons why we fail to provide academic freedom is that we are not able to understand Marxism correctly. The problem is that certain leaders in the theoretical field consider themselves to be Marxists. Actually, they subjectively judge what is right and what is wrong using Marxist viewpoints which were oversimplified, dogmatized, ossified, and sanctified in the 1930s to 1940s.

1. With regard to the crisis of Marxism, we should frankly admit that at present Marxism is in crisis. If we fear the word "crisis," it will do no harm for

us to use the phrase "at a turning point." We should fully recognize the current grim situation in Marxism. Because Marxism was dogmatized and sanctified for a long time and was supported by power, Marxists were able to rest content with the hackneyed and stereotyped expressions in textbooks. They neglected to study the new situation and new problems. Therefore, their vigor and capability in observing and criticizing things was weakened. Contemporary Marxism lags behind the reality of modern capitalism and socialism and also behind the reality of reform in China.

The fundamental reason for the existence of the crisis is that due to previous leftist mistakes and dogmatism and subjectivism in theoretical work, we clung to ossified dogmas. We were unable, unwilling, and not allowed to get in touch with new problems arising in the development of reality. What is more serious is that we completely followed what the people in high authority said. We regarded their views as "new developments," or "milestones." We neglected their harm to practice. All this greatly corrupted the prestige of Marxist theories and brought them to crisis so that people treated them coldly. Instead of criticizing people for their frigid attitude toward Marxism, it is better for us to ponder the crisis, so that we can invigorate Marxism in the course of pondering the crisis and promoting reform.

2. On adherence to and development of Marxism. Under the above circumstances, in order to adhere to and develop Marxism we should first of all lay stress on the development of Marxism. Without achieving the development of Marxism it is impossible for us to adhere to Marxism. To date, we still adhere to the outdated notion we held thirty or forty years ago, which is: "Marxism is a scientific truth repeatedly proved by practice." Is it true that Marxism cannot develop any further? According to this outdated notion, Marxism cannot develop any further. Obviously such a notion is not commensurate with the spirit of the Thirteenth CPC National Congress [of October 1987]. When commenting on scientific socialism, the Thirteenth CPC National Congress stressed the necessity of discarding the utopian factor and the dogmatic understanding of Marxism as well as all the erroneous views forced on Marxism. When we say that Marxism still contains the utopian factor we mean that Marxism has yet to turn its utopian factor into a scientific one and that Marxism has not yet become a scientific truth. Therefore, we should point out that according to the spirit of the documents of the third plenary session of the Eleventh CPC Central Committee, the sixth plenary session of the Twelfth CPC Central Committee [of September 1986], and the Thirteenth CPC National Congress, Marxism is not a dogma but a point of departure and a method in our theoretical study. We should try to understand that Marxism is a science that is constantly developing and that the development of Marxism is commensurate with the development of the times and practice. Whether Marxist truth and Marxist viewpoints are correct or not, outdated or not, and should be developed or not, will therefore be judged con-

stantly by practice. Marxism should also explore new situations and new questions, and critically absorb the achievements of the modern natural and social sciences to put forward new conclusions in the course of practice. Only by adhering to practice, development, and creation will we be able to adhere to Marxism.

3. On various schools of thought inside and outside Marxism. Are there any other schools of thought inside Marxism? Apart from Marxism are there any other schools of thought in the academic circle? Is it possible for the various schools of thought to contend with one another?

Here, the fundamental issue is that we should recognize the pluralistic nature of Marxism. This is not only a theoretical reflection but also a specific practice, a reflection of the attitude toward the specific practice, and an inevitable outcome of opposing Stalin's legally constituted authoritative theory of great unity and the sole model. The Marxist ideology is a great and profound one. No one has ever had such great power as Stalin in monopolizing Marxist ideology. No one has ever had such great power as Stalin in judging who is and who is not a Marxist. We should recognize that there are various schools of thought inside Marxism and that, apart from Marxism, there are other schools of thought in academic circles. Therefore it is wrong to force scholars to accept Marxism. We should let various schools of thought contend with one another so that we can pursue truth in the course of such contention. The practice of cracking down on theories which run counter to the views of certain leaders is not only unscientific but also dangerous. Personality cult and despotism once caused us much suffering, impaired the development of Marxism, and even plunged Marxism into crisis. In the future we must make every possible effort to prevent such a situation from repeating itself.

All in all, in order to carry out academic study, vigorously promote academic contention, guide and support the reform with theories, and unswervingly implement the policy of reform and opening up to the outside world, we should oppose all ideological prejudices, bureaucratism, sectarianism, Zhdanovism, and cultural autocracy and break through all the forbidden zones in our academic and theoretical studies.

It has already been confirmed that there are no forbidden zones in academic circles, but, as a matter of fact, although many sweeping promises have been made, a lot of forbidden zones still remain in our academic and theoretical studies. Recently, it has been ruled that writers must refrain from writing about the Cultural Revolution, that publishing houses must refrain from publishing articles and literary works on the Cultural Revolution, that reportage regarding some leaders must be submitted for examination before being published, and that writers and scholars must refrain from commenting on certain questions about the CPC's history, certain questions about the history of the international communist movement, and certain questions concerning international relations.

In the past, writers were banned from carrying out explorations on these questions. To this day our academic contention has yet to succeed in breaking through these forbidden zones. For instance the ban on carrying out explorations on the Asian mode of production, agricultural socialism, alienation under socialism, and some other questions has not yet been lifted. We need answers, particularly specific answers, to these questions now. The saying that "there are no forbidden zones in academic contention" seems unable to nullify all the forbidden zones that exist in our academic and theoretical studies.

Today, I have come to this symposium because I want to see unity. The speech I am making is also aimed at achieving unity. The mainstream of the broad masses of our theoretical workers is unity. In the past, some theoretical circle leaders proclaimed themselves Marxist, discriminated against those comrades who held views that were not commensurate with theirs, raised academic and theoretical differences to the higher plane of politics, divided theoreticians and anti-Marxists, artificially split the theoretical circles, and frequently delivered reports similar to those on the "history of the struggle between the two lines," which they themselves delivered zealously during the Cultural Revolution. It is such erroneous practice, not the academic and theoretical differences that presently exist in our theoretical circles, that has impaired stability and unity. Therefore, only by putting an end to such erroneous practice will our theoretical circles become more united than before and will we be able to bring about a real spring in our theoretical circles.

15
China Needs Democracy

FANG LIZHI

Source: *Libération* (Paris) (January 17, 1989): 5; FBIS, January 27, pp. 14–16.

In China, 1989 is the year of the snake. Though it is not certain that this snake will present any great temptations, the following is at least to be expected: The year will prompt the Chinese to examine their past more thoroughly and to take a more penetrating look at the present. The year will mark both the seventieth anniversary of the May 1919 Movement (an intellectual and political movement of prime importance against a background of nationalism and Western cultural influence) and the 40th anniversary of the founding of socialist China. These two anniversaries can serve as eloquent symbols of China's hope and despair.

These forty years of socialism have left the people in a state of dependence. In the fifties, watchwords such as "only socialism can save China" or "there is no New China without the Communist Party" were as readily accepted as laws of physics. Now a glance at the "New" China suggests that the naïve sincerity of those years and the people's enthusiasm have been betrayed.

Of course, the past forty years have not been entirely devoid of change or progress. However, the comparative criterion for measuring the failure or success of a society should be this: Has the distance between China and the world's most advanced societies increased or not? In light of this question, not only have the forty years of Maoist China been a failure but even the past ten "years of reform" have produced nothing to justify a chorus of praise.

The failure of the past forty years cannot be attributed—at least not entirely—to China's cultural tradition. The facts clearly show that almost all of the other nations proceeding from bases similar to China's have already joined, or are about to join, the ranks of the developed countries.

Nor can this failure be attributed to China's overpopulation. First, we must recognize that this overpopulation is itself one of the "political successes" of the Maoist years. It was Mao's policy in the 1950s to oppose birth control (regarded as a "bourgeois Malthusian doctrine") and to encourage rapid population growth. Furthermore, as everyone knows, one of the major factors retarding China's economic development has been the great succession of "class struggle" campaigns and large-scale political persecutions. Are we to believe that every overpopulated society necessarily produces such struggles and persecutions? Such a view is clearly illogical.

Logic leads to only one conclusion: the disappointments of the past forty years must be attributed to the social system itself. This is why in China today the pursuit of modernization has replaced faith in ideology. Socialism, in its Lenin-Stalin-Mao version, has been entirely discredited. At the same time, the May 4th Movement slogan "science and democracy" is being reintroduced and becoming a new source of hope for Chinese intellectuals.

The reforms of the past years, undertaken within the context of this ideological transition, have considerably changed China, which is no longer that of the Maoist period. We must regard these changes as positive. The emphasis now being placed on the economy in domestic policy and on ending "the exporting of the revolution" in foreign policy are two important instances of progress. Having said that, the banning of the "wall of democracy" nine years ago created the depressing feeling that when it comes to political reforms the authorities do not intend to do much.

Although the Chinese Constitution guarantees freedom of speech and other human rights, the Chinese Government has hitherto not always adhered to the UN human rights charter. In current practice, even a basic right such as the right to knowledge, which has little political impact, is frequently held in contempt. There are cases—some very recent—of natural science courses being banned for political reasons.

Chinese education, which for years suffered the ravages of Mao's anti-intellectual and anti-cultural political principles, has left China with a population in which the proportion of illiterates is the same as forty years ago. Nevertheless current education spending, as a proportion of China's GNP, is exactly the same as under Mao—30–50 percent lower than in countries on an economic par with China.

In recent years the authorities have stepped up their appeals for "stability" and "unity," especially since the emergence of signs of political unrest. Stability and unity seem to have been elevated to the status of supreme principles. However, when it comes to one of the prime causes of the instability in Chinese society— the state of civil war maintained with Taiwan—this supreme principle no longer applies. In its attempt to end the forty-year-old state of war, the Chinese Government has hitherto refused—at least in theory—to accept the principle of relinquishing the use of military force against Taiwan.

These various problems have created a constant conflict under the surface of Chinese society. The 1986 student demonstrations openly demanding freedom and democracy only brought these conflicts to the surface. In their efforts to minimize the impact of these demonstrations, the authorities were forced to resort to the following arguments: (1) Chinese culture lacks a democratic tradition and therefore cannot tolerate a democratic system. (2) Economic development does not necessarily require a democratic system. Indeed, a dictatorial system can be more efficient in this regard. What would suit China best is a dictatorial policy plus a free economy.

The brandishing of these arguments revives public awareness that what we have now is not a democracy but a dictatorship. If this is so, however, how can Marxism retain its place in China's orthodox ideology?

The first of these arguments could be called "the law of conservation of democracy." It implies that a society's "maximum level of democracy" can be fixed. If there is no democracy to start with there will be none subsequently either. Of course nobody has tried to prove this law because there are too many examples to the contrary. The argument cannot save the dictatorship in China but it can provide some comic relief.

The second argument does seem to be better corroborated by the facts. There really do seem to be some societies that have succeeded in combining political dictatorship with a free economy. However, there are also some examples of failure among them. It follows that the issue cannot be decided simply by listing precedents but must be treated specifically in China's own particular case. Can a free economy be compatible with the specifically Chinese form of dictatorial government? A glance at the China of 1988 proves that, broadly speaking, the answer is "no."

First, China differs from other countries in that its system of dictatorship cannot accept an entirely free economy. This is because the socialist dictatorship is entirely bound to a system of "collective ownership" (actually official ownership) and its ideology is fundamentally antithetical to the kind of rights of ownership required by a free economy. Furthermore, it has already been shown—twice, rather than once—that China's dictatorial system lacks efficiency. It is enough to consider the corruption within the Communist Party itself to realize this. The ten years of "correction of party conduct" have in fact produced only an annual increase in the numbers of "unhealthy tendencies." Our minimum conclusion could be as follows: we need the public to be able to perform a greater role and we need a more independent judiciary. In practice this means more democracy.

China's hope for the present lies in the fact that more and more people have abandoned blind faith in the government. They have realized that the only way to social progress depends on the public's adopting a "supervisory" role. It should have the right to openly express criticisms of the authorities. The editor of a Canton journal recently wrote that his journal's role is to speak not on the Communist Party's behalf but on behalf of an emergent Cantonese middle class. The old idea that "you must not oppose your superiors" is losing ground. Democratic awareness is making headway. Democracy is more than a slogan; it is exerting its own pressure. The aim of this pressure is to force the authorities, gradually and by nonviolent means, to accept changes in the direction of political democracy and a free economy.

Since the period of the May 4th Movement in 1919, China's history (including the forty years since 1949) has proved this idea that democracy cannot be promulgated from above but that it is necessary to fight to gain it. We must not expect this to change in the decades ahead. However, it is precisely because democracy comes from below that, despite the many frustrations and disappointments of our present situation, I am still hopeful about the future.

16
Letter to Deng Xiaoping

FANG LIZHI

Source: *News from Asia Watch*, March 15, 1989.

January 6, 1989
Central Military Commission, Chairman Deng Xiaoping:

1989 is both the fortieth anniversary of the founding of the PRC and the seventieth anniversary of the May 4th Movement. Many activities are expected to mark the two anniversaries. However, more people are concerned about the present than about recollections of the past. They are hoping that these important dates will bring new hope.

Therefore, I would like to suggest sincerely that a general amnesty be granted nationally, and in particular, that Wei Jingsheng and all other political prisoners be released.

No matter how Wei Jingsheng himself should be evaluated, I think it will be a humanitarian act to release a prisoner who has already spent ten years in prison. This will promote a better social atmosphere.

1989 is also the 200th anniversary of the French Revolution. Liberty, Equality, and Fraternity embodied thereby is now generally respected by mankind in every sense. Here I earnestly request that you would be kind enough to consider my suggestion so that our future will be blessed with more hope.

Very truly yours,
Fang Lizhi

17
Open Letter to the Party and Government from Thirty-three Famous Chinese Intellectuals

Source: *News from Asia Watch,* March 15, 1989.

February 16, 1989
We have heard about Mr. Fang Lizhi's letter to Chairman Deng Xiaoping on January 6, 1989, and we are deeply concerned.

We think that to release political prisoners, especially Wei Jingsheng and others on the occasion of the fortieth anniversary of the People's Republic of China and the seventieth anniversary of the May 4th Movement is helpful in creating a harmonious atmosphere, which is good for the reform; and it also conforms to the universal trend for human rights in the world today.

These are the first thirty-three signers of the open letter from Beijing:

Bei Dao (poet and playwright), Shao Yanxiang (poet and writer), Niu Han (writer), Lao Mu (editor), Wu Zuguang (playwright), Li Tuo (playwright), Xie

Bingxin (writer, 89 years old), Zong Pu (writer), Zhang Jie (writer), Wu Zuxiang (professor, Chinese literature), Tang Yijie (professor, Chinese philosophy), Yue Daiyun (professor, literature), Zhang Dainian (professor, Chinese philosophy), Huang Zipeng, Chen Pingyuan, Yan Wenjing (writer), Liu Dong, Feng Yidai (writer), Xiao Qian (writer), Su Xiaokang (writer), Jin Guantao (theorist), Liu Qingfeng (theorist), Li Zehou (research fellow, philosophy), Pang Pu (professor, Chinese philosophy), Zhu Wei, Wang Yan, Bao Zunxin (research fellow, Chinese philosophy), Tian Zhuangzhuang (movie director), Wang Ke, Gao Gao (research fellow), Su Shaozhi (research fellow, political science), Wang Ruoshui (theorist, philosophy), Chen Jun (artist).

18
On Human Rights Abuses

FANG LIZHI

Source: *Hong Kong Sunday Standard* (China Today Supplement) (February 26, 1989): 2; FBIS, February 27, p. 45.

For their narrow purposes, some politicians have adopted a double standard in regard to human rights. Specifically, they have adopted a double standard by holding different attitudes toward human rights events in the Soviet Union and Eastern Europe, on the one hand, and China, on the other.

When dealing with the former, they have openly expressed concern and have even made the issue a paramount condition in matters of their foreign policy.

But, when dealing with the latter, they have said and done very little. This has not only shown a wrong attitude, but has hardly been in the spirit of human rights themselves.

China is currently in the process of implementing social reforms of both an economic and political nature. One of the most important aspects of these reforms should be the improvement of the Chinese human-rights situation.

After embracing the dogma of class struggle, just like the Soviet Union and the various socialist countries of Eastern Europe, China has found itself host to a whole series of occasions where human rights in China were violated on a very wide scale.

In 1957 during the political persecutions of the antirightist movement alone, some 500,000 people were purged because of their thoughts and opinions. Some lost their jobs, while others were shipped off for "reform through labor."

To this day the fates of many of them are still unknown. And, as for our record of disrespect for religious rights and the rights of minority peoples, China has been no different than any other socialist country.

Compared to the era of Mao Zedong, the situation of this past decade has indeed shown some improvement. However, the way in which present Chinese authorities continue either to disregard or to simply ignore the question of human rights makes for a grave situation.

First and foremost, Chinese authorities have still not completely acknowledged that the human-rights violations alluded to above were wrong in principle.

For example, to this day they still proclaim the antirightist movement of 1957 as necessary and "correct." Since then, the suppression and persecution of people with differing beliefs and opinions has never ceased.

Obvious examples of this policy are the suppression on the Democracy Wall Movement in 1979, the campaign against "spiritual pollution" in 1983 and the movement against "bourgeois liberalization" in 1987. And lest the world forget, Democracy Wall activist Wei Jingsheng and other similar political prisoners have now been in jail for ten years.

Throughout this truly grim period, efforts by some on behalf of human rights never ceased, gaining the support of rights activists and organizations elsewhere in the world.

There should, in fact, be a universal standard for human rights everywhere. Just as the International Declaration of Human Rights has stated, the rights and freedoms that all men ought to enjoy should not be denied.

19
Intellectuals' Open Letter to Leaders [February 26, 1989]

Source: *Ming Pao* (Enlightenment) (Hong Kong) (March 7, 1989): 10; FBIS, March 7, pp. 18–19.

General Secretary Zhao Ziyang, Chairman Wan Li, Chairman Li Xiannian, Premier Li Peng, the CPC, the NPC Standing Committee, the CPPCC, and the State Council:

Since the third plenary session of the Eleventh CPC Central Committee, our country's modernization drive, which is guided by ideological liberation and based on the national policy of opening up and reform, has attained achievements that have attracted worldwide attention. Though some complications and deviations have appeared, the general direction of development is in conformity with the people's opinions and the historical trend of the world. This decade is indeed the best period since the founding of the state. Today, however, the reform is facing serious hindrances in its progress: the corruption trend, the rampant "bureaucrat speculation," price hikes, the fact that people have become lax in spirit, and the serious crisis faced by educational, scientific, and cultural undertakings. China's intellectuals, who have inherited the tradition that "every man has a share of responsibility for the life and death of the country," cannot but worry about these problems. In order to avoid a premature end of the modernization drive, and motivated by a sense of social responsibility to the state and the people, we, the old- and middle-aged intellectuals who have been fighting a long time in the frontline of science, technology, education, and culture, eagerly wish to raise the following suggestions out of sincere patriotic feelings:

1. Under the prerequisite of insisting on opening up and reform, we should try with every effort to carry out the political structural reform (in other words, political democratization) in step with the economic reform. The reason is that world historical experiences and China's reality have already told us that political democratization (including rule of law) is a necessary guarantee of the economic reform and the whole modernization drive. Only with the realization of democratization can the people fully display their initiative and enthusiasm, so that the people throughout the country will be willing to jointly undertake the inevitable difficulties during the reform. With joint efforts and intelligence, all difficulties can be overcome. Moreover, "clean and honest administration" can only be achieved if we realize democracy under conditions of the commodity economy, and when it is under the supervision of the broad masses of people and effective media supervision. On the contrary, regimes not supervised by the people are unable to end corruption. This inevitable historical law has been known to everyone for a long time.

2. The major condition for political democratization is to give a realistic guarantee of the basic rights of citizens as stipulated in the constitution, especially regarding the freedom of speech and the freedom of the press. If people can speak freely, all kinds of different opinions can be publicly expressed, and criticisms against leaders will not be repressed or retaliated against. Then, the whole country will become active, happy, and harmonious, and the citizens' democratic consciousness can be fully enhanced. This is the only reliable guarantee of stability and solidarity, and in this way the reform can be successfully pushed forward.

3. We should prevent the historical tragedies, when people were punished for expressing views or publishing articles holding different political views, from happening again. So please instruct the relevant departments to release all the

young people who have been imprisoned or are being given reeducation through labor for ideological problems. If people are no longer sentenced for ideological reasons, it will open a new political era for our country.

4. We should give necessary support to the educational and scientific undertakings that do not produce direct economic benefits but are decisive for the country's future. We should try our best to increase the proportion of funds for education and scientific research (especially for fundamental research) in the total output value of the national economy, and increase the pay of intellectuals (including old, middle-aged, young, and retired intellectuals), so that they do not have to lead a difficult life forever. At present, some people who were grade one professors in the 1950s have applied for the difficulty allowance. Recently, a 78-year-old grade two senior engineer committed suicide due to problems of livelihood by jumping from an apartment. This is obviously unfavorable to the modernization drive and will spoil the country's image.

It will be a great fortune to the country if the above suggestions can be accepted. Also, democracy and science, which were advocated by the leaders of the May 4th Movement seventy years ago, will thus be really developed on this great land of China, and a joyous atmosphere will be created on the fortieth anniversary of the founding of the state.

With best regards,
Qin Linzhao, Wang Ganchang, Shi Yafeng, Xu Liangying, Guo Xingguang, Xue Yugu, Ye Duzheng, Huang Zongzhen, Hu Shihua, Zhu Zhaoxiang, Zhou Mingzhen, Xu Guozhi, Jiang Lijin, Sun Keding, Wang Rong, Liu Yuanzhang, Mao Yushi, Hu Jimin, Yan Rengeng, Zhang Xuansan, Du Ruji, Yu Haocheng, Zhang Xianyang, Li Honglin, Bao Zunxin, Liu Shengji, Shao Yanxiang, Wu Zuguang, Wang Laidi, Gu Zhiwei, Ge Ge, Liu Liao, Zhang Zhaoqing, Liang Xiaoguang, Zhang Chonghua, Hou Meiying, Wu Guozhen, Cai Shidong, Cao Junsi, Xiao Shuxi, Zhou Liquan, Liang Zhixue

20
Zhao Ziyang at a Meeting with President Bush

Source: Beijing Television Service, February 26, 1989; FBIS, February 27, pp. 26–27.

[Video opens with shots of Bush and Zhao walking toward each other, surrounded by photographers and delegation members from both sides. The two meet, shake hands, and exchange brief greetings. After a short delay, the two walk from the meeting hall, together with their respective delegations.]

Zhao Ziyang, general secretary of the CPC Central Committee, met with U.S. President Bush and principal members of his entourage this afternoon in the Great Hall of the People.

The two sides exchanged views on international issues of common interest. Both expressed willingness to continue developing the friendly and cooperative relations in various fields between the two countries.

Touching on China's reform, Zhao Ziyang said: Reform is a very difficult and complicated process, which cannot be completed in a short time, especially in a big country like China. It can only be pushed forward step-by-step in a realistic way. [Video cuts to closeups of first Zhao and then President Bush, zooming back to show them seated side-by-side, separated by a low table.]

He said: We often mention two basic factors when analyzing China's reform: first, the Chinese people are both participants and beneficiaries of the reform and generally support the reform. Second, quite a few among them are not sufficiently prepared mentally for the difficulties that may be encountered in the reform. The first factor is a favorable condition, and the second is an unfavorable condition. The unfavorable condition is easily covered up when the reform is going smoothly, but will become obvious when difficulties are encountered in the reform.

[Video zooms back and begins to pan the meeting room, showing members of the two delegations seated in a semicircle facing the two leaders. Wu Xueqian (state councillor and former minister of foreign affairs) and Qian Qichen (current minister of foreign affairs) are seen seated just off the center, facing Zhao. Video then begins to intercut between various medium and pan shots of the room and President Bush and Zhao.]

There are two extreme viewpoints, which affect each other. One viewpoint is that the reform has gone on a wrong track and should be reversed. This enjoys no public support. The other viewpoint attributes difficulties in the economic structural reform to political reasons. [Video cuts to show photographers and press area, cutting back to interspersed pan and medium shots.] People with this viewpoint advocate the importation from the West of multiparty and parliamentarian politics. Of course, only a few people hold this viewpoint. The basic problem of this viewpoint is that it ignores China's national conditions, not to mention the issue of ideology, so it is unrealistic. [Video shows President Bush smiling, offering his hand to Zhao. The two leaders shake hands, after which they remain seated, each surveying the room. Video resumes intercutting between various pan and medium shots of the meeting.] As for their role in real life, these people are not promoting the reform, but providing an excuse to reverse the reform and stir up social unrest. At the least, this increases obstacles to the reform or even causes setbacks, leading to serious consequences.

Zhao Ziyang said: A country can only be run according to its own situation. We will neither export our own system to other countries nor copy the system of any other country. Some people in the American media probably like to depict themselves as being close to those Chinese who are advocating importation of a political system from the West, including the United States, in an attempt to influence the U.S. Government's current and future Chinese policy. However, the real motivating force pushing China's reform is the Chinese Government and people, who are acting in line with China's characteristics. Therefore, the fact that some people in American society support those who are not satisfied with the Chinese Government will be detrimental not only to China's political stability and the progress of its reform, but also to Sino-U.S. friendship.

At the meeting, President Bush spoke highly of China's ongoing reform.

21
Three Attacks Aimed at Overthrowing Zhao

Lo Ping

Source: *Chengming* (Contending) (Hong Kong), no. 137 (March 1, 1989): 6–9; FBIS, March 3, pp. 22–25.

Shortly after the emergence of "Chen Yun's Eight Opinions" directed against Zhao Ziyang, Bo Yibo wrote a letter to Deng Xiaoping launching a second attack. Recently, a group of intellectuals submitted a joint letter to the authorities urging the release of political prisoners like Wei Jingsheng and others. This gave the old-man party an excuse for overthrowing Zhao. This reminds people of the success of the old men two years ago in ousting Hu Yaobang from office by using the opportunity of student unrest and opposing "liberalization."

The year 1989 should be a peaceful year in the world, but it absolutely will not be a peaceful year inside the CPC.

According to news from Zhongnanhai, a group of political old men are launching a "spring attack" on Zhao Ziyang.

"Overthrowing Zhao" Duet by Chen Yun and Bo Yibo

Some people say that this New Year's Day Zhao Ziyang found things very difficult and was in a very bad mood. First of all, the horrible "Chen Yun's Eight Opinions" were concocted and second, Bo Yibo, a political old man who has been promoted to vice-chairman of the Central Advisory Commission of the CPC Central Committee due to his success in "ousting Hu from office" two and one-half years ago, "submitted a letter" to Deng Xiaoping. These two matters might echo and coordinate with each other and become an "overthrowing Zhao" duet.

Three of "Chen Yun's Eight Opinions" accuse Zhao Ziyang of completely abandoning the socialist economy on the mainland, namely the "planned economy," in the name of reform. This means that Zhao Ziyang is pursuing a "capitalist commodity economy" and that he has deviated from the major direction of socialism. Chen also accused Zhao of "turning Chinese agriculture into a mess and ignoring the life and death of the 800 million peasants." Regarding current ideology Chen Yun stressed, "The entire ideological front is occupied by the bourgeoisie and nothing proletarian is left." He also pointed out, "A regime can be subverted because of the failure of doing public opinion, ideological, and theoretical work properly." Therefore, he emphasized that we must be strongly determined to "recover the lost ideological front."

Bo Yibo Wrote a Letter to Deng Xiaoping
Lodging a Complaint Against Zhao

The above-mentioned opinions of Chen Yun completely negate Deng Xiaoping and Zhao Ziyang's line. Some people say that it is actually a call condemning Deng Xiaoping and Zhao Ziyang.

If we say that the emergence of "Chen Yun's Eight Opinions" is the first attack launched by the old men on Zhao Ziyang, Bo Yibo's letter to Deng Xiaoping lodging a complaint is the second attack.

Bo Yibo launched his attack by making use of the following "incidents": Su Shaozhi's speech at the theoretical discussion meeting marking the 10th anniversary of the third plenary session of the Eleventh CPC Central Committee criticizing the "eliminate spiritual pollution" and "oppose bourgeois liberalization" campaigns launched from Zhongnanhai and wanting the verdict on Wang Ruoshui reversed; Shanghai's *Shijie jingji daobao* [World economic herald] used one and a half pages to publish the speech. Bo Yibo said that this was an "attack on the party Central Committee" by mainland intellectuals. He also mentioned recent speeches and articles by Yan Jiaqi, Ge Yang, and Yu Haocheng. After that, he came to the conclusion that it was necessary to "criticize those elements who oppose the party, Marxism, and Mao Zedong thought." According to Bo

Yibo's proposals, measures must first of all be taken to punish the editor-in-chief of *Shijie jingji daobao*, Qin Benli, and to suspend publication of this newspaper which "discards the classics and rebels against orthodoxy." This political old man also cannot tolerate Yu Haocheng's article on the issue of human rights entitled "Defending Human Rights is a Just Cause Marking the Progress of Mankind" published in *Shijie zhishi* [World affairs], no. 23 (1988). The subtitle of the article is: "Written to Mark the Fortieth Anniversary of the Publication of the United Nations 'Declaration on Human Rights.'" Bo Yibo seized on the incident to exaggerate the seriousness of the matter, saying that the article and Professor Fang Lizhi's letter written to Deng Xiaoping urging a special pardon for Wei Jingsheng echoed each other, and that the case should be "handled" seriously.

At the Critical Moment, Deng Xiaoping Refused to Change His Trusted Subordinate

Chen Yun and Bo Yibo went into action personally in order to "overthrow Zhao." Besides, they had a "special detachment" comprising Yao Yilin and Li Peng. They repeatedly lodged complaints against Zhao, saying that the general secretary had extended his reach too far and wide in economic affairs and that the general secretary should keep himself within the bounds of his power. This special detachment cooperated closely with Chen and Bo to give an impetus to the "overthrow Zhao" drive.

However, things did not develop as the ultra-conservatives wished and planned. In the face of the attack launched by Chen Yun, Bo Yibo, and others around New Year's Day, Deng Xiaoping discovered that this was undoubtedly another action to "force Zhao to abdicate" by inventing an excuse to compel Deng to change his trusted subordinate. It seems that Deng realized his unwise move in ousting Hu Yaobang from office two years ago. He definitely did not want to "cut off his other arm." Deng Xiaoping originally planned to strike back at Fang Lizhi and Yu Haocheng. However, after rethinking this matter soberly he understood that under the current delicate situation he must avoid falling into a trap. At this critical moment the revered Mr. Deng soberly endorsed Zhao Ziyang's opinions on handling "Chen Yun's Eight Opinions" and the letter of complaint written by Bo Yibo.

Zhao Ziyang Withstood the Pincer Attack by Chen Yun and Bo Yibo

Regarding "Chen Yun's Eight Opinions," Zhao Ziyang suggested it should not be "transmitted throughout the country." A similar decision was later made by the central authorities. With regard to Bo Yibo's letter of complaint, Zhao

Ziyang said: "Intellectuals have their own understanding of problems. What is there to be surprised at?" He added, "Just ignore it (Su Shaozhi's speech) and there is no need for us to handle the case." This means that the leaders should adopt a lenient attitude toward intellectuals who hold unique views. They should refrain from flying into a rage, let alone coming down with the big stick upon divergent views. Bo Yibo and his collaborators in the central secretariat originally intended to expel Su Shaozhi from the party. However, after Zhao Ziyang had replied to Bo Yibo's views Su Shaozhi retained his party membership.

In recent years the revered Mr. Deng has been most disgusted by the phrase "human rights." However, after considering the overall situation and weighing the advantages and disadvantages of handling the case he gave Yu Haocheng, a jurist, a way out, and no longer insisted on investigating his case.

Deng Xiaoping and Zhao Ziyang Stress:
Do Not Take the Road Back

What is more noticeable is that Deng Xiaoping keeps a look out for and is worried about "taking the road back."

On January 17 (or January 20 according to another report), Deng Xiaoping delivered an important speech to a restricted audience to the effect that "we have made great achievements during reform over the past ten years but we have also encountered numerous difficulties. At present, we should not fear inflation or price hikes. We should not fear panic buying or unhealthy trends. We should not only persist in the policy of reform and opening up but also greatly promote it. There is currently a trend toward taking the road back. This is definitely not allowed!" His speech strongly backed Zhao Ziyang so that the general secretary has a "symbol of high authority."

At a meeting of the Politburo and Secretariat of the CPC Central Committee, Zhao Ziyang boldly talked about the issue of preventing the two erroneous trends. He said, "At present, there are two erroneous trends. First, faced with difficulties some people intend to take the road back. Second, seizing the opportunity of the current serious situation, some others preach the parliamentary politics of the West and multiparty or two-party systems. The first trend is leftist whereas the basis of the second is rightist." To put it bluntly, those wishing to take the road back are those who have gained vested interests like leftists, high-ranking officials, and so on. Those who advocate the multiparty system and parliamentary politics are intellectuals and common people who have lost confidence in the CPC. Some people who heard Zhao Ziyang's relayed report said: When the CPC finds itself in a predicament facing crises everywhere, is there any way which can help it change the situation except pluralistic politics aimed at uniting the one billion people?

Is the Situation Favorable or Unfavorable to Zhao?

The current economic situation on the mainland is favorable to Zhao in spite of the fact that Chen Yun, Yao Yilin, and Li Peng's line has a profound basis and vigorous roots. Not long ago, because economic decline, stagnation, and fluctuation in production occurred throughout the country, common people began to weigh the advantages and disadvantages of restoring the planned economy to a considerable extent and persisting in a commodity economy. They thought fondly of the "overheated economic development" which was criticized recently. In addition, when General Secretary Zhao was besieged on all sides, Deng Xiaoping resolutely supported him and revealed that he would not "change this trusted subordinate" arbitrarily. The situation is therefore favorable to Zhao.

March will probably be the month during the first half of the year in which the greatest number of meetings will be held. A plenary session of the CPC Central Committee or a central work meeting will be held in mid-March. It will be followed by the NPC session, CPPCC session, a national conference on education, a national conference on united front work, and so on. All these meetings are very important to Zhao Ziyang's power and position. The diehards might seize on Zhao's braid—the problem of feeding the people. At present it seems that nothing can be done to further promote rural reform (if the cooperative system is pursued again this will lead to disastrous results). In the past, the emphasis in numerous reports and propaganda was focused on Sichuan and Anhui provinces which were respectively governed by Zhao Ziyang and Wan Li. As the problems in the rural areas are particularly serious, this gives the diehards an opportunity to launch their attack. It was reported that Chen Yun had ordered the relevant state departments to form a group to investigate practical problems in the rural areas. Therefore, the road Zhao Ziyang must traverse is by no means smooth.

A Major Test to Be Passed: The Upcoming
Plenary Session of the CPC Central Committee

Of course, the NPC and CPPCC National Committee sessions have a more important bearing on Li Peng. At the meetings, some critical people's deputies (or CPPCC members) might deliver speeches addressing inquiries to Li. Some non-party personages might also discuss government affairs and some of them might be like Qian Jiaju, who dares to criticize the evils of the times. At that time, Li Peng might have a taste of criticism from the non-party personages.

However, as far as Zhao Ziyang is concerned, the most important test he must pass is the fourth plenary session or central work meeting. However, from the meeting's agenda we know that it is mainly aimed at solving educational problems. Of course, the issue of nationwide "education in current affairs" will also be discussed, namely, propaganda on the "achievements made over the past ten years." The meeting will also touch upon agricultural production, which is not progressing well, and the new historical stage confronting united front work. Decisions might be made on these issues in order to provide a guide for the subsequent meetings of the NPC and CPPCC National Committee. If Zhao Ziyang can successfully pass the major test of the fourth plenary session, or central work meeting, and defeat the diehards, it is believed that he might reiterate the "big international circle" and "plan for coastal economic development" strategies, and restore the measures "delegating power to the lower level."

Zhao Ziyang's Brain Trust Has Become Active Again

When Zhao Ziyang makes slight progress in his counterattack on the diehards during the spring, his brain trust becomes active again. It has always been reported that Zhao Ziyang supports *Shijie jingji daobao*, whereas the diehards hate it very much. Of late, the newspaper has repeatedly urged the people "not to take the road back!" It took over the slogan from Deng and Zhao. On January 23, this newspaper, which is of a very high professional level, published on the front page speeches by members of Zhao's brain trust: Chen Yizi, director of the Institute for Restructuring the Economy; Wang Xiaoqiang and Li Jun, deputy directors of the institute; and others. They said that great achievements have been made over the past ten years in the reform and that no serious mistakes were made with regard to the direction and strategy of the reform. They pointed out, "If we say that we have made great achievements in the reform over the past ten years and that we have made serious mistakes with regard to the direction and strategy of the reform, that view is logically contradictory. Using our current views on certain issues to negate the reform over the past ten years is as groundless as an adult completely negating things he did when he was a child. The occurrence of these new difficult problems has precisely revealed the defects of the traditional systems. This will help us understand reform more profoundly, so that we can set a higher demand on promotion of the reform." This is the voice of the members of the brain trust and also that of Zhao Ziyang himself. There is no mistaking what the remarks are aimed at. We can discern from them the disputes and new developments in the power struggle among the highest leadership stratum of the CPC.

"New Authoritarianism" Emerges as the Times Require

Wu Jiaxiang, a middle-aged theoretician, published an article in this year's first issue of *Huaren shijie* [Chinese world] advocating the "development of new authoritarianism" to solve the problems caused by multipolar politics and the chaotic situation. At present, who can become the "new authority?" The revered

Mr. Deng is too old. Chen Yun is old and can only sing the old leftist tune. Obviously, it is only General Secretary Zhao Ziyang who can become the new authority. Zhao has made well-conceived arrangements in this regard. On the upper level he is supported by Deng, chairman of the Military Commission, and on the lower level he is supported by scholars and intellectuals. It seems that he can stage a comeback and retrieve himself from an inferior position.

Intellectuals in Beijing are disgusted with the slogan of establishing a certain leader's authority in a "large and particular way." If the "new authority" does not keep himself within the bounds of his power, or is not put under the supervision of the people, the unfortunate history of the past will definitely repeat itself. Many people are not satisfied with the indiscreet criticisms of those Marxist old men. But they do not place too great hopes, or expect too much, of Zhao Ziyang's openness. Even if the "era of Zhao Ziyang" has come, they will still adopt a "wait-and-see attitude" toward it.

"The Rebellion of the Scholars" and the Third Attack Aimed at "Overthrowing Zhao"

It is not easy for the occurrence of such an era and it will probably never happen.

Over the past few days various kinds of stories have been pouring out. Bei Dao, a famous obscure[!] poet during the "Beijing Spring" period who published the magazine *Jintian* [Today], suddenly jumped off his small world of nihilism to cooperate with Chen Jun, an activist in the democratic movement, to launch a signature drive urging the CPC to release Wei Jingsheng. More than thirty noted writers and scholars jointly signed their names to the letter. Xiao Qian, a party-member writer who was previously regarded as a writer of the first loyalty, was among them. This was the first story to spread in Beijing. The second was that the masters and lords in Zhongnanhai were surprised and angry about this matter, in particular Bo Yibo and his collaborators. They said that this was another "attack on the party" which was much more "furious" than the previous ones. They believed that the fire might spread far and wide, and that this matter must not be treated lightly. The third story was that Zhao Ziyang was severely criticized at an urgent meeting of the Political Bureau but this cannot be confirmed for the time being. According to well-informed sources, some of the intellectuals urging the release of Wei Jingsheng were once protected by Zhao Ziyang.

In the meantime, some CPC leaders believe that the bold activities of "rebellion" and "bourgeois liberalization" by these scholars are connected with Zhao Ziyang's policy of opening up. This is a braid which the old men can seize upon. In any case the third attack by the political old men will be more vigorous than the previous two. This reminds us of the success of Bo Yibo and his collaborators in ousting Hu Yaobang by taking the opportunity of student unrest and "bourgeois liberalization."

Deng Xiaoping's attitude will play a decisive role under the present situation. Analysts in Beijing say that Deng Xiaoping is absolutely dissatisfied with the "rebellion of scholars." They doubt whether he will continue to protect Zhao amid continuous attacks aimed at "overthrowing Zhao." They believe that Deng's stratagem is as follows: He might protect Zhao if it is still possible for him to do so. Otherwise, he will give him up. It is believed that the Zhao Ziyang problem will become clear at the fourth plenary session (or even the next Beidaihe meeting).

22
Li Xiannian Urges Changing the General Secretary

LO PING

Source: *Chengming* (Contending) (Hong Kong), no. 38 (April 1, 1989): 6–8; FBIS, April 3, pp. 39–41.

The fact that the fourth plenary session of the Thirteenth CPC Central Committee yielded the way to the National People's Congress [NPC] and the Chinese People's Political Consultative Conference [CPPCC] is due to an intensifying inner-party power struggle. An inner-party group aiming to topple Zhao Ziyang has taken form and frequently exerted pressure on Deng Xiaoping. This group has seized on Zhao Ziyang's three major problems. The old watchdogs of the conservatives are most resentful of the campaign for democracy initiated by the intellectuals. Li Xiannian proposed to Deng Xiaoping that Zhao Ziyang should make a self-criticism at the fourth plenary session of the Thirteenth CPC Central Committee, resign from the office of general secretary at the central conference to be held later this year, and temporarily take charge of the Central Military Commission.

The government work report Li Peng submitted to the NPC reveals signs of the fierce inner-party struggle; the grip of the nation's economy and politics will be still more tightened.

Why Was the Fourth Plenary Session of the Thirteenth CPC Central Committee Postponed?

"Oddities were rare in past years, but there have been many this year." The song is as good today as it was forty years ago, when it was very popular among the people.

According to usual practice, the CPC Central Committee calls a meeting prior to the opening of the NPC and the CPPCC. It was originally planned that the fourth plenary session of the Thirteenth CPC Central Committee would be called prior to the "two sessions," but it was called off quite unexpectedly. Such an unusual and odd alteration has surprised all politically conscious people. Why should the fourth plenary session of the Thirteenth CPC Central Committee have been postponed? It is said that the education plan, the theme of the session, was not yet ready. However, I am not convinced, and I think there must be some important trends that are worth tracking. This is why I have been trying to find out what is going on behind the scenes.

The result is that inner-party struggle, especially the fate of General Secretary Zhao Ziyang, explains the postponement of the fourth session of the Thirteenth CPC Central Committee.

A Group Aiming to Topple Zhao Ziyang Has Taken Shape

As personalities who know the inner workings of the top echelons of the CPC have disclosed to me, an opposing group aiming to topple Zhao Ziyang has taken shape. It includes Bo Yibo, Wang Zhen, Li Xiannian, and Deng Yingchao, as well as Yao Yilin and Li Peng, with Chen Yun as the central figure. This group actually came into being by establishing ties and colluding with each other when Deng Xiaoping was out of Beijing some time ago. They listed ten charges against the reform faction, to topple Zhao Ziyang with their joint forces, and planned to "correct the course of China's revolution."

Seizing on Zhao Ziyang's Three Major Problems

The group planning to topple Zhao Ziyang has seized on Zhao Ziyang's three major problems; namely, the 1988–89 drop in agricultural output nationwide, inflation, and errors in decision making on "relaxing macrocontrol" economically, and the problem of intellectuals as well as the ideological and political line. The old watchdogs of the conservatives have been most resentful of the democracy campaign started by the intellectuals. Zhao Ziyang personally gave Fang Lizhi the green light to go abroad. Some of the intellectuals who have recently taken the lead to "start trouble" and proposed "political pluralism" have been under Zhao Ziyang's umbrella. Therefore, Zhao has been under great pressure in this regard. Bo Yibo, Wang Zhen, and Hu Qiaomu have all spoken against him.

Bo Yibo Says the Party Is Under Violent Attack

Bo Yibo said: A number of rightist intellectuals, with Fang Lizhi as their representative, have launched violent and vicious attacks on the party under the pretext of fighting for democracy, petitioning for the people and showing concern for reform since the end of 1988. Bo Yibo made this statement when he was receiving relevant leading members of the People's Liberation Army General Political Department and the Chinese Communist Youth League Central Committee in the Great Hall of the People in late February. The fortieth anniversary of the founding of the PRC falls this year. Chen Yun has said that our party and nation are facing a new, critical life and death juncture! I am all for Comrade Chen Yun's view.

Wang Zhen: The General Secretary's Line Is a Little to the Right

Wang Zhen's remarks were even more to the point. He said: The general secretary's ideological and political lines are basically a little to the right. This is tantamount to determining the character of the general secretary's thinking. In the history of the CPC, "being inclined toward the right" and having "rightist tendencies" were accusations by which leaders were overthrown.

In early February, Hu Qiaomu wrote a letter to Bo Yibo, Wang Zhen, and others to enumerate Zhao Ziyang's major mistakes.

Hu Qiaomu: Zhao Ziyang Suppresses Comrades Adhering to Marxism-Leninism

Hu Qiaomu criticized Zhao Ziyang for "suppressing comrades adhering to the Marxist stand." "The political differences between ourselves and Comrade Zhao Ziyang came to light in May 1987. Whether or not we should oppose bourgeois liberalization and whether or not a tendency toward bourgeois liberalization exists within the party are major matters of political principle. If we had acted strictly in accordance with Comrade Deng Xiaoping's instructions two years ago, the situation within the party and in the country, I think, would not have become so chaotic."

Zhao Ziyang Is in Danger of Getting Drowned

Of the three persons' remarks, those by Wang Zhen carry the greatest weight. Wang Zhen's remarks were passed on to a "nongovernmental" news agency through unofficial channels. To fully understand the spirit of the message from the central authorities, this news agency formally asked the Central Propaganda Department about it. The Central Propaganda Department replied, "In the future, you will act in accordance with the spirit of the official documents passed down from the central authorities. At present, the format of propaganda regarding the major central leaders, including Comrade Zhao Ziyang, will remain unchanged."

This reply basically confirmed that Zhao Ziyang is in danger of being drowned. *Renmin ribao* [People's daily], *Jiefangjun bao* [Liberation Army daily], *Guangming ribao* [Enlightenment daily], and other units received similar replies at the same time.

Chen Yun Is the Backstage Boss

Bo Yibo and Wang Zhen have been most active in the campaign to pull Zhao down. However, Chen Yun is the backstage boss behind all this. To make Li Xiannian join the campaign to pull down Zhao, Bo Yibo, Wang Zhen, and Hu Qiaomu personally called on Li Xiannian at his home and told him about their resentment. Finally, Li Xiannian boldly stepped in and flew to Shanghai to hold secret talks with Deng Xiaoping. During their talks, Li Xiannian suggested that Zhao Ziyang be told to resign as general secretary and that efforts be made to radically change the chaotic economic and political situation in China.

Li Xiannian Raised Three Suggestions to Deng Xiaoping

It is said that Li Xiannian raised several basic suggestions to Deng Xiaoping: First, Zhao Ziyang should hold himself responsible for the failure of the economic reforms, criticize himself and take responsibility for it at the fourth plenary session of the CPC Central Committee. Second, even if Deng Xiaoping resigns as the chairman of the Central Military Commission, he will remain the chief architect of China's reforms and China's highest leader. Third, Zhao Ziyang should resign as the party general secretary at a central conference to be held in the second half of this year. There can be a transitional period during which he will be in charge of the work of the Central Military Commission. However, a new Central Military Commission chairman will be elected at the next central plenary session of the Central Committee.

It is said that Deng Xiaoping asked Li Xiannian: Is this your own view or the common view of the old comrades? Who would you like to be the general secretary?

Deng Xiaoping Decided to Put Off the Fourth Plenary Session of the Central Committee

Following Li Xiannian's return to Beijing, Deng Xiaoping sensed something was wrong. Therefore, he decided to put off the fourth plenary session of the CPC Central Committee. Deng Xiaoping first asked the opinions of Jiang Zemin, secretary of the Shanghai Municipal CPC Committee, and the secretaries of some provincial party committees regarding his decision. After learning this, the Shanghai branch of Zhongguo Xinwen She [China News Service] passed on to the head office the news that the Fourth Plenary Session of the Central Committee would be put off, saying that according to the principal leaders on the Shanghai municipal party committee, the fourth plenary session might be put off. However, Zhongguo Xinwen She regarded this piece of news as a serious matter and something falling within the jurisdiction of Xinhua News Agency. Therefore, it did not transmit it, nor did it ever question the accuracy of this piece of news.

Immediately on his arrival in Beijing, Deng Xiaoping summoned Zhao Ziyang and held a two-hour meeting with him. Subsequently, he summoned Wan Li, Yang Shangkun, and others.

In the Face of Three Difficult Problems, Deng Stresses the Need to Stabilize the Situation

However, shortly after his return to Beijing, Deng Xiaoping ran into three difficult problems. First, George Bush invited Fang Lizhi to a banquet. Deng Xiaoping ordered people to stop him by force, thus arousing the displeasure of the Americans. Second, the situation in Tibet was becoming increasingly tense and the antagonistic sentiments among minority nationalities in Xinjiang, Inner Mongolia, and other parts of the country were growing. And third, the signature campaign started by intellectuals was gathering momentum, like a snowball. Therefore, Deng Xiaoping sternly ordered that every necessary measure be adopted to stabilize the domestic situation. He said, "We must never be afraid of foreign opinions. Still less should we let foreigners lead us by the nose. We have our own sovereignty and our own criteria. The most important thing to do at present is to stabilize the domestic situation. The whole party should remain united in overcoming this difficulty."

Zhao Ziyang's Political Future Will Be Decided This Coming Summer

Apart from these three major problems, Deng Xiaoping is also preoccupied with the Sino-Soviet summit to be held in May. Some intellectuals in Beijing have suggested that Deng Xiaoping would not easily agree with the conservatives to have a reshuffling before the Sino-Soviet summit. If Deng Xiaoping lets Zhao Ziyang step down, not only would he find it difficult to explain to the people, he would also be too embarrassed to meet the more liberal-minded Gorbachev. In addition, he also believes that Chen Yun and others would take the overall situation into consideration. Therefore, they think that Zhao Ziyang will not step down before the Sino-Soviet summit. However, since both sides will have several months to make behind-the-scenes preparations at central conferences to be held after the summit, such as the Beidaihe conference, something interesting is going to happen.

Yao Yilin and Zou Jiahua Might Get Promotions

However, according to some people in the know, one must not take Zhao Ziyang too lightly. To protect the reform, which is the main direction, and to hold on to his own power at a crucial moment, Zhao Ziyang will not easily step down voluntarily.

People are interested to know who will replace him when the general secretary steps down. It is said that his replacement will be Yao Yilin, one of Chen Yun's henchmen and a staunch advocate of the restoration of the socialist planned economy. He is a vice-premier of the State Council and a Standing Committee member of the Politburo. According to people in the know, Yao Yilin himself will be replaced by Zou Jiahua, son of Zou Taofen and minister of electronics industry.

Yao Yilin and Li Peng Will Backtrack

At present, intellectuals in Beijing are generally worried about the "replacement" of a high-level CPC leader. Although they are also critical of Zhao Ziyang because of his strong dislike for the democratic movement started by the intellectuals, which might produce a damaging effect on his power and position and give the conservative old people something to capitalize on, they strongly feel that if the general secretary is replaced by Yao Yilin, with Li Peng continuing to head the government, the pursuit of the policy of opening up will come to an abrupt halt and the reform will become nothing more than a token. Yao Yilin has his own systematic views on backtracking. He is used to the bird-cage economy based on the Soviet model. Some people have gone so far as to suggest that the use of "coupons" will soon be resumed in mainland China.

Li Peng's Report Reflects a Fierce Power Struggle

It is very likely that the high-level struggle within the CPC will be reflected at the "sessions" of the NPC and the CPPCC. Problems were revealed throughout the course of the drafting and finalizing of Li Peng's government work report. It is said that the draft was mainly prepared in accordance with the instructions of Li Peng and Yao Yilin. Members of Zhao Ziyang's think tank were excluded. Policy making and guidance mistakes in economic work are stressed and illustrated with the example of the price reforms in many parts of the draft. Both Deng and Zhao were not happy with it. Later, some parts were deleted. In the last paragraph of its first section, the report points out the need to uphold the authority of the CPC Central Committee and that of the State Council (over government work). According to analyses, Li Peng and Yao

Yilin put this in so they could prevent Zhao Ziyang from minding economic work too much.

According to people in the know, the inner-party struggle was extremely fierce on the eve of the NPC session. Li Peng's report has confirmed this. It was also evident from this report that there would not be a democratic atmosphere at the NPC and CPPCC sessions and that political and economic control would become tighter.

BEIJING SPRING

SPRING SPIRITS

V

The Crisis Begins

The next set of documents covers the period from the April 15 death of Hu Yaobang to the beginning of the hunger strike on May 13. Readers should note that the documents above by Li Qiao et al. (Doc. 1) and Chen Xitong (Doc. 2) also cover this period in some detail. Provided here are ancillary materials referred to in the Li and Chen accounts.

The first document (Doc. 23) is Hong Kong correspondent Lo Ping's account of Hu Yaobang's death. It claims that Hu suffered a heart attack during a heated Politburo meeting on April 8 when either Zhao Ziyang or Li Peng asserted that Hu had "no right to speak" to the policy issue of education then under review.[1] This charge was explicitly repudiated, however, in Chen Xitong's report, and by knowledgeable sources inside China. Yet the regime still has not provided a detailed account of Hu's last days. Hu's family and relatives have had difficulty contacting foreign friends and have suffered harassment since June 4. Although Document 23 may not be totally accurate, the conflicting versions of Hu's death all agree that he died of heart failure on April 15, and that he had suffered attacks earlier, in 1987–88. This document thus exemplifies the lively gossip network at the time, which, irrespective of its possible distortions, made Hu into a folk hero and indicated how willingly people accepted reports of villainous behavior by Li Peng and Yao Yilin. The article's possible authenticity is further strengthened by its credible descriptions of procedures at Politburo meetings, which coincide with the way former Politburo members have privately described them. Chen Xitong's explicit condemnation of the rumors surrounding Hu's death also reveals a sense of vulnerability among the postcrackdown leadership to charges they had mistreated Hu.

Document 24 reports on the April 25 meeting of Deng Xiaoping with Li Peng and Yang Shangkun. The intervening events of April 15–25 are fully described

---

[1]This information comes from sources inside the PRC, who also suggest that Hu Qili—later deposed—was the offending party.

in part I and in the long transcript of the first major dialogue between some students and government spokesman Yuan Mu (Doc. 27). These include the mourning for Hu Yaobang; the bloody incident of April 20 between students and police in front of the Xinhua gate entrance to Zhongnanhai; and the refusal of the leadership on April 22 to drive the hearse bearing Hu's body around the square to enable the amassed public to pay their last respects.[2] Following the massive demonstration of April 22, Zhao Ziyang refused requests to convene a Politburo meeting to discuss the situation, instead departing for a trip to North Korea. In his absence, Beijing Mayor Chen Xitong and First Party Secretary Li Ximing briefed the Politburo on April 24, followed by Li Peng's and Yang Shangkun's decisive meeting with Deng a day later.

Deng's instructions on April 25 set the leadership's course for the remainder of the crisis. In his characteristically succinct and blunt fashion, Deng concluded that the people allegedly behind the students were seeking to create chaos throughout China, similar to the Cultural Revolution, and were trying to overthrow the CPC. Deng thus called for the immediate publication of a forceful editorial and for preparations to crush the movement. He acknowledged that confrontation was probably inevitable, and he foresaw that terminating the "conspiracy" might involve bloodshed.

The April 26 *People's Daily* editorial (Doc. 25) reflected Deng's thoughts of the previous day. It was drafted rapidly, evidently by Beijing Vice-Mayor Xu Weicheng, another member of the conservative Beijing city government who, as editor of *Beijing Daily* in the mid-1980s, had launched frenzied attacks on intellectuals using harsh Maoist rhetoric.[3] Zhao Ziyang, then in Pyongyang, approved a draft of the document, to which subsequent changes were made. Precisely who approved the final version is not known, though Li Peng was certainly involved. The document's critical sentence accused a small number of people involved in the demonstrations of a "planned conspiracy" whose "essence is to negate the leadership of the CPC and the socialist system." Unequivocally tough and, most ominously, reviving such terminology of the Cultural Revolution era as "tur-

---

[2]It must be noted, however, that an elaborate state funeral for Hu was somewhat beyond protocol, as he had lost his preeminent position of general secretary in 1987. Some people in China believe that Deng Xiaoping was actually trying to placate public criticism by agreeing to such a ceremony, though to no avail.

[3]During the 1970s, Xu was a rabid leftist supporter of the Gang of Four. This was indicated by his involvement in the notorious Huang Shuai incident in 1975, when a small girl, purportedly forced to study and work hard by her parents and teachers (at the time a "revisionist" crime), was encouraged by Jiang Qing to denounce them. Xu's leftist background may also explain the harsh Cultural Revolution–style rhetoric of the April 26 editorial. See "A Word of Advice to the Politburo: Text by He Xin, Translated, Annotated, and Introduced by Geremie Barme," *The Australian Journal of Chinese Affairs*, no. 23 (January 1990):65–66.

moil'' (dongluan), it signaled the intent of conservative leaders to crack down. But as Melanie Manion's introductory essay stresses, it did not have an intimidating effect. On April 27, the largest rally yet occurred in Beijing's streets.

Document 26 represents the reaction to the blistering editorial among many leading intellectuals, including long-time party theoreticians committed to Deng's reform program, such as Wang Ruowang.[4] A veteran journalist who had run afoul of Mao in the 1950s, Wang had initially been restored to honor in the Deng era but then was expelled in 1987. Like Su Shaozhi, he numbered among his long-time enemies conservative ideologues such as Hu Qiaomu and Deng Liqun. Wang saw in the editorial the same mentality as earlier *People's Daily* editorials of the Mao era, such as the one of June 8, 1957, which ushered in the disastrous antirightist campaign prosecuted by none other than Deng Xiaoping. Wang realized that this latest example of the profound anti-intellectualism in the CPC provided the basis for yet another political movement to suppress China's intellectuals.[5]

Perhaps as a reaction to the enormous expression of popular support for the students following the editorial, the government agreed to a dialogue with some students. Document 27 reproduces a considerable portion of the April 29 meeting between four government officials, including State Council spokesman Yuan Mu and State Education Commission Vice-Minister He Dongchang, and students from sixteen Beijing universities. Excerpted in a broadcast on Beijing Television on May 1, this text merits careful reading as it enumerates student grievances more clearly than any document in the collection so far. Corruption, nepotism, inadequate funding for education, and the abuse of power are among the major complaints voiced by the students. They were also agitated by the way the government had handled the demonstrations; they especially protested the April 20 beatings in front of Zhongnanhai, the failure of Li Peng to meet with them (something that a lower-level official evidently had promised), and the editorial's challenge to their patriotism. The students' derogatory references to leaders playing golf was a clear slap at Zhao Ziyang, whose delight with the game—a symbol of Zhao's excessive attraction to expensive Western ways—was openly publicized throughout China.[6]

Zhao Ziyang's futile efforts to defuse the situation upon his return from North

---

[4]Even He Xin, postcrackdown supporter of Deng, considered the editorial ''stupid''—an indication that perhaps Deng Xiaoping was not responsible for the document, since He Xin would never have used such harsh language to characterize an authoritative instruction by Deng. Ibid., p. 72.

[5]He Xin described the general reaction to the editorial among intellectuals as ''panic and resistance.'' Ibid.

[6]Workers' organizations established during the popular movement also complained of Zhao's golf and of gambling by Deng Xiaoping's son in Hong Kong—symbols of the leadership's corruption. Suzanne Ogden et al., eds., *China's Search for Democracy: The Student and Mass Movement of 1989* (Armonk, N.Y.: M. E. Sharpe, forthcoming).

Korea—actions that figured prominently in Chen Xitong's later indictment of the general secretary—are captured in Documents 29 through 32. Zhao not only spoke to a May 3 commemoration meeting of the seventieth anniversary of the 1919 May Fourth Movement, but also also addressed the first meeting of the Board of Governors of the Asian Development Bank held in Beijing on May 4, a meeting made noteworthy by the unprecedented attendance of an official from Taiwan, Minister of Finance Shirley Kuo. On both occasions, Zhao struck a conciliatory tone, praising the spirit of China's youth and calling for a solution to the crisis by "legal and democratic" means. Without even mentioning the April 26 editorial, Zhao foresaw no major turmoil in China and predicted that the situation would soon calm down. Documents 28 and 31 reproduce the lengthy versions of Zhao's statement on May 3 and 4, while briefer summaries of Zhao's remarks carried in national newspapers and television are presented in Documents 29 and 32. Although this coverage was quite favorable and positive, State Council spokesman Yuan Mu threw in a discordant note (Doc. 30) on May 3 by dismissing as unreasonable the student preconditions for dialogue. (The preconditions are contained in Doc. 1, above.) As Melanie Manion's essay concludes, these documents from April 26 and May 4 reveal that the leaders were sending divergent messages to the populace. At a minimum, some students sensed that the leadership was seriously divided, while at a maximum, they concluded that many high-level leaders were not prepared to crack down. Similar signals had also been implicitly sent by the leaders' tolerance of the massive parades and their failure to follow the April 26 editorial with any concrete harsh measures.

The period from May 5 to May 10 saw a lull both in demonstrations and in dramatic actions by the leadership. Looming ahead was Mikhail Gorbachev's arrival in Beijing on May 15. The international press converged on the city to cover the first major summit between the two major Communist powers' heads of state in three decades. For student protesters, the challenge was to sustain the momentum they had generated in the previous three weeks, which seemed to have faltered somewhat after May 4. The April 26 editorial had provided them a strong incentive to do so, since the organizers were now on notice that they were vulnerable to arrest. Safety, some evidently thought, could be found in rallying additional support, and using the presence of Gorbachev and the international press as temporary safeguards against a harsh government crackdown.

To regenerate the movement, some students came up with the idea of launching a hunger strike in Tiananmen Square. The origin of this symbolic act of peaceful resistance was diverse, drawing inspiration generally from outside Chinese history—from Gandhi and Martin Luther King, Jr. Students from several universities were involved in the decision, and there is no indication that influential intellectuals provided any guidance. The hunger strikers gathered for a final banquet on May 12, when their sense of history led them to record the event on videotape. On May 13, they went to the square and immediately ignited the conscience of the nation by risking slow death. Popular beliefs that university students were spoiled and self-centered—beliefs that government propaganda consciously fostered after the 1986–87 demonstrations—rapidly dissolved. Document 33 is the students' heartfelt announcement (also reproduced in Document 1). It marks the emergence of a fundamental, and perhaps irreconcilable, division between the students and the conservative, hard-line leaders.[7]

Soviet President and General Secretary Mikhail Gorbachev thus came to a deeply divided Chinese capital. His visit was intended as a crowning achievement of Deng Xiaoping's foreign policy. The Soviet leader had accepted, though not fully, the three conditions that Deng had imposed a decade earlier for normalization of Sino-Soviet relations: reduction of Soviet forces along the border between the two countries; withdrawal of Soviet forces from Afghanistan; and cessation of Soviet support for the Vietnamese occupation of Cambodia. With Sino-Soviet reconciliation and the continuing improvement of relations between the mainland and Taiwan, for the first time since the nineteenth-century Opium Wars China did not face an immediate, predatory military threat from any direction. In Deng's eyes, the protesters and their throngs of supporters occupying the square denied him the ability to savor this triumphant moment. Gorbachev was unable to tour the Forbidden City, and the arrival ceremony, which in recent years has been held for visiting dignitaries in Tiananmen, was moved to the airport. Regular access to the Great Hall of the People was also blocked. Western television cameras, meanwhile, spent more time focusing on the square than on the Sino-Soviet summit.

Two documents are reproduced here from the Soviet-Chinese meetings. Ignoring foreign policy, they deal with how Zhao Ziyang and Gorbachev—the father of perestroika and demokratiia—used the occasion to discuss political reform. Chinese domestic television coverage of the meetings (Doc. 34) reported Zhao's continuing commitment to political reform, while Zhao openly revealed to Gorbachev that Deng Xiaoping remained China's preeminent leader despite his nominal "retirement" in 1987. Though Zhao's comment could be seen as communicating Deng's backing of political reform, Zhao's detractors subsequently claimed that he was signaling that any popular displeasure with China's governance should be directed at the aging strongman.

---

[7]Beijing citizens reacted to the hunger strike, and to the students' deteriorating health, by vowing to protect "our university students" (*women de da xuesheng*). The effects of food deprivation on the strikers further polarized the situation, however, as their increasingly frenzied state of mind led to highly emotional reactions. Student leader Chai Ling, for example, purportedly threatened to blow herself up on the Monument to the People's Heroes unless the government yielded.

Document 35 summarizes Gorbachev's adroit speech to the Chinese people on May 17 in which he implicitly acknowledged the demonstrations—"popular aspirations often run ahead of reforms"—while also issuing a gentle warning—"some are not hiding their hopes that the introduction of . . . democracy will lead to a mixed form of social order, if not the restoration of capitalism." With Gorbachev's departure from Beijing on May 18, China's hardliners could now concentrate on dealing with both the crisis in the streets and with Zhao Ziyang. Meanwhile, the demonstrators lost the protective umbrella provided by the international news coverage of Gorbachev's visit.

23
The Last Eight Days of Hu Yaobang

LO PING

Source: *Chengming* (Contending) (Hong Kong), no. 139 (May 1, 1989): 6–10; FBIS, May 2, pp. 20–24.

My First Interviewee in the Course of Finding Out the Cause of Hu's Death

In a country shrouded in mystery, many things remain unsolved. Since the death of Hu Yaobang, some people said that his death was also a mystery. I tried to probe the "bewildering" mystery to its depths.

I tried to trace the clues among some people. My first interviewee was a friend of mine, a scholar who visited Hu Yaobang at the hospital three days after he suddenly fell ill at a Politburo meeting on April 8.

When my friend visited Hu, his condition was improving. My friend was entrusted with the task of taking Hu some books and magazines he wanted to read. Some were newly published magazines on social science. At that time, Hu looked good. After greeting the visitor, and asking him to take a seat, Hu put on his glasses to look over the books and magazines. My friend told Hu Yaobang: We all hope you will recover soon. You look good today. Thank goodness!

Hu Yaobang said cordially: Since I am only suffering from a minor illness, I should not take a long rest. I will leave in a few days. If I lie in bed all the time, I will truly become ill. Hu then asked a nurse to bring in some fruit to entertain his visitor.

Hu Yaobang was a person who always kept himself busy. He rapidly turned the topic of conversation to the domestic political situation. Due to the change of the topic of conversation, Hu no longer looked relaxed. He said: As long as the party and the people unite closely as one, no difficulty is insurmountable. Saying so, he pondered the problem. It seemed as though he was not lying in bed. It seemed as if he was addressing an audience of tens of thousands, as he did in the past. My friend told Hu Yaobang: Now the problem of the workers is not merely loafing on the job. They simply do not work. The intellectuals' confidence in the state has increasingly weakened. Listening carefully to what he said, Hu Yaobang said in a deep tone: We must arouse the enthusiasm of our national spirit, and our country can never collapse!

Three Kinds of Information and Three Kinds of "Possibilities"

When Hu Yaobang had just touched upon the subject, a nurse asked the visitor to go out for a while and told him, "The central leaders have issued instructions to let Comrade Hu Yaobang have a good rest. Don't discuss this subject with him. Let him calm down."

After the visitor had returned to the ward for several minutes, Hu Yaobang's secretary entered the room. He told Hu in a low voice: Comrades Qiao Shi and Ding Guangen will come to visit you in fifteen minutes. Hearing this, Hu Yaobang shook his hand in disapproval, and told his secretary, "They must be very busy with their work. Ask them not to come. Ask Comrade Ziyang not to come either. I will leave the hospital soon." When Qiao Shi and others came to visit Hu Yaobang, my friend stood up and left. Hu told his secretary, "Show the guest out on my behalf." He also told my friend, "You must not only work well, but also take good care of yourself."

This scholar provided me with three kinds of information: (1) Hu Yaobang may have to stay in the hospital for a long time, and he was not suffering from a "minor illness," as he himself said. (2) Judging from what the nurse said, that the "central leaders have instructed . . . we should let him calm down," one knew that even after staying in the hospital Hu Yaobang had probably not calmed down. (3) Hu's condition possibly had something to do with his being unable to calm down.

These three "possibilities" truly give us much food for thought.

My Second Interviewee Was Enlightened at Hu's Residence

The second interviewee, a writer, also is a friend of mine. He personally went to Hu's residence, located at 25 Kuaijishi Lane, to express sympathy to Hu's family. He was familiar with the family members, and talked with one of them.

My friend: We hear that you personally suggested to Zhao Ziyang that the central authorities pass judgment on Comrade Hu Yaobang's personal history. Is that true?

Hu's family member: Before the publication of the obituary, they solicited our opinions on it. The central authorities truly showed concern for us. You can rest assured.

My friend: It was said that Comrade Yaobang fell ill suddenly at a meeting of the Politburo. Did he fall ill because he was so angry?

Hu's family member: We had better not talk about this now.

My friend: Judging from the pictures in the newspapers, Comrade Yaobang looked pretty good. Why did he suddenly fall ill? It was really strange. People are saying a lot about this.

Hu's family member: He truly was not in a good mood during a period of time. But he felt better recently. What some people said was groundless.

My friend: Did Comrade Deng Xiaoping come to see you?

Hu's family member: Every central leading comrade is showing concern for his sudden death. . . . But it is too late.

Hu's family member spoke as if they were following the instructions of the authorities. But it did imply something. I paid special attention to the sentence: "We had better not talk about this now." If Hu Yaobang did not suddenly fall ill at a meeting of the Politburo because he was angry, my friend, who is a writer, would not have heard the sentence, and Hu's family member would [not] have advised him "not" to talk about the matter.

After drawing a deep breath, I said to myself: It is time for me to trace the news.

Four Kinds of Grapevine News on Hu's Death

At that time, I heard the following news through the grapevine.

—At the Politburo meeting held on April 8, members of the Standing Committee of the Politburo Li Peng and Yao Yilin bitterly attacked Hu Yaobang for the mistakes which occurred when he was in power. (1) Educational work was neglected. (2) "Right deviationist" political and ideological mistakes gave rise to the current disastrous effect of "bourgeois liberalization." This meant that Hu Yaobang must be held responsible for this year's political crisis (continuing dissident views of the intellectuals, people's complaints about "stagflation," and so on), although he had fallen out of power two years before.

—A female Chinese People's Political Consultative Conference [CPPCC] National Committee member who is close to Zhongnanhai affirmatively told her friends: Hu Yaobang was overexcited when he heard that the CPC supreme leadership stratum was considering appointing him to an important position again. This caused the heart attack.

—At the Politburo meeting, Hu Yaobang argued bitterly with Zhao Ziyang. Hu said that Zhao must be responsible for the chaotic social situation in the mainland. He was also resentful of Zhao's unprincipled accommodation to and his fawning on veteran cadres. Zhao defended himself, saying that chaotic phenomena are normal and cannot be avoided during the reform and opening up. Hu fell ill because of the dispute.

He Provided Me with Reliable Information

News from the grapevine is not necessarily groundless. An empty hole invited the wind. With regard to the above-mentioned grapevine news, which one truly tallied with the facts? Some friends completely dismissed the third one, saying that this was a smoke screen of certain people with ulterior motives, because they tried to cover up the true cause of Hu's illness. I thought what they said was right. To further dig up facts, I looked for a friend who had contacts with people in the supreme leadership stratum (Hu Yaobang liked to make friends; some ten years ago, when *Chengming* was just published, some young people in Beijing liked to go to "Uncle Hu's" home to read the magazine). I must heartily thank this friend, and I was also so lucky that I eventually got from him the information which I wanted to obtain.

The meeting of the Politburo of the CPC Central Committee held on April 8 was an official meeting. It was different from a routine "brief meeting" or an enlarged "urgent brief meeting." A decision was made earlier to hold the meeting, and the main theme of the meeting was to discuss the current very serious education problem.

After he was forced to resign two years ago, Hu Yaobang rarely attended the meetings of the Politburo. Even if he attended the meetings, he only stayed for a while, or did not say anything.

Hu's Decision to Speak at the Politburo Meeting Shocked Everyone

Before the Politiburo held its April 8 meeting, like all other members of the Politburo, Hu Yaobang received a notice on the convocation of the meeting, which was jointly issued by the Secretariat of the Politburo and the General Office of the CPC Central Committee. The Secretariat of the Politburo and the General Office of the CPC Central Committee stipulate that Politburo members should give one week's notice if they decide to take leave and not to attend a Politburo meeting and that the Politburo members should submit the key points and major topics of their speeches to the Politburo beforehand if they decide to speak at a Politburo meeting. For instance, if it is decided that an upcoming Politburo meeting will focus on the agricultural question, then all Politburo members and all the other leading comrades who are invited to attend the Politburo meeting will not be permitted to talk about the question of family planning or any other questions which are irrelevant to the agricultural question. This is one of the Politburo's long-standing regulations. In the last two years, each time Hu Yaobang received an official notification on the convocation of the Politburo meeting, he always signed his name in the leave column, indicating that he would take leave and would not attend the meeting. However, this time Hu Yaobang decided not only to attend the Politburo meeting but also to speak at it!

Zhao Ziyang personally made a telephone call to Hu Yaobang, asking about the topics Hu Yaobang would talk about at the Politburo meeting, and reiterated that the upcoming meeting would focus on the question of education.

Apart from Zhao Ziyang, Hu Qili, Li Peng, Qiao Shi, and some other leaders

were also very concerned about Hu Yaobang's decision and personally telephoned Hu Yaobang's secretary, asking him, "What are the key points Comrade
Hu Yaobang is going to talk about at the upcoming Politburo meeting?" Hu
Yaobang's secretary replied, "I have no idea." Before the meeting was held, the
news that Hu Yaobang would speak at the meeting had already spread among all
the Politburo members.

This news greatly shocked the conservative elements among the Politburo,
particularly those who were eager to see the thorough downfall of Hu Yaobang.

Before the meeting was held, other members of the Politburo had no idea
what Hu Yaobang was going to talk about at the meeting. It has been learned that
on April 6, Wan Li also telephoned Hu Yaobang. Only Wan Li had known that
Hu Yaobang was going to talk about something concerning party style.

Hu's Wife Li Zhao Asked Hu to "Speak Less" at the Meeting

Because of Hu Yaobang's decision to attend and speak at the Politburo meeting,
this routine meeting was shrouded in a tense and serious atmosphere even before
it was actually held.

On the night of April 7, Hu Yaobang stayed up very late. Hu Deping told
others: My father had almost no rest the whole night through. He paced back and
forth in his room, smoked cigarettes, and read materials. My mother asked him
to go to bed to have a rest several times. My father just said, "I cannot sleep even
when I lie in bed."

On April 8, before driving to attend the Politburo meeting, Hu Yaobang
talked with his wife in his study for a short while. Hu Deping disclosed: My
mother asked my father to "speak less at the meeting," but my father did not say
anything.

Hu Yaobang arrived at the venue on time: the No. 1 Conference Room of the
Politburo of the CPC Central Committee in Zhongnanhai. The venue was only
100 meters from the location of the Secretariat of the CPC Central Committee.

Zhao Ziyang and Li Peng Tried to Prevent Hu
from Speaking at the Meeting and Yao Yilin Stood Up
and Left the Conference Room

Only Li Ruihuan and another Politburo member did not attend the April 8
Politburo meeting. Members of the Secretariat of the CPC Central Committee
and the responsible leaders of the State Education Commission, the State Science
and Technology Commission, the PLA General Political Department, and some
other relevant departments were invited to attend as nonvoting delegates.

From the outset, the atmosphere at the meeting was very tense. After arriving
at the No. 1 Conference Room, the Politburo members casually greeted one

another. The meeting was presided over by Zhao Ziyang. The Politburo members sat in the front row around a huge oval conference table. The leading cadres who were invited to attend the meeting as nonvoting delegates sat behind the Politburo members. Behind Zhao Ziyang were three conference note-takers.

Zhao Ziyang first briefed the attendees on the major topic for discussion at the meeting and then talked about some questions concerning education. Li Peng also spoke at the meeting. The third speaker at the meeting was Hu Yaobang. Hu Yaobang asked for the floor.

At the very beginning, Hu Yaobang spoke very calmly. Hu said that he would like to spend a little time on the question of party style. Hu Yaobang pointed out that nowadays, party style had seriously deteriorated, which had already given rise to social disorder. However, before Hu Yaobang finished his speech, Zhao Ziyang interrupted him, saying that the current meeting was devoted to the study of the question of education, and asked those in attendance to discuss a certain document. Zhao Ziyang was clearly reminding Hu Yaobang not to deviate from the central topic for discussion at the meeting.

Hu Yaobang turned a deaf ear to what Zhao Ziyang said and went on speaking. It seemed that Hu Yaobang was "defying" Zhao Ziyang's authority.

The atmosphere at the meeting became very tense.

The second man who stood up to interrupt Hu Yaobang's speech was Yao Yilin. Yao Yilin asked: Is this meeting devoted to the study of the question of education? If it were a meeting devoted to the discussion of principles and ideological guidelines, I would talk about the question of commodity grain. If it is not, I will have to leave the meeting because I have another meeting to attend! Yao Yilin clearly showed his strong aversion to Hu Yaobang's speech. At this time, the atmosphere at the meeting became more tense than before.

Li Peng intervened and told Yao Yilin: You can discuss the grain question at the next meeting. The grain question is also a pressing issue at the moment. However, we'd better concentrate on the study of the question of education at this meeting. What Li Peng meant was obvious to everyone at the meeting.

At this time Hu Yaobang stood up and said in agitation: Education problems and grain problems are equally important. But most important of all is the problem of party style. . . .

Meanwhile, Yao Yilin was impatient to leave his seat. He whispered something to Li Peng and requested leave from Zhao Ziyang to chair another meeting.

Then Hu Yaobang could no longer restrain [himself] and said in greater agitation: Some of the comrades may not like to hear me talking about this problem, but I must insist. As of now, if the party still does not care about party style, does not deal with corruption, then our party and our country. . . . [as received] Hu Yaobang also said: Where are the root causes? The root causes lie within our party! Chaotic situations have appeared in our country, and responsibility lies with our party, with the party's Central Committee! With the Politburo! . . .

He Was Carried Away with Indignation, and He Flopped onto the Desk

Hu Yaobang became overagitated while making his speech. While he was talking, he was banging the desk with his fists, and he fainted away leaving the speech unfinished. All of a sudden he fell onto his desk. The time was 9:40 A.M., just forty minutes into the meeting.

The whole meeting was thrown into chaos. Medical personnel and security guards rushed to the scene immediately. Those familiar with Hu Yaobang's physical state produced two tablets and shoveled them into the mouth of the now unconscious Hu Yaobang. Fifteen minutes later the doctors arrived. The experts made a joint spot diagnosis and determined the case as a sudden massive myocardial infarction, and administered emergency aid right in the Politburo conference room. At 4:00 P.M. his electrocardiogram did not show any signs of deterioration, and only then was Hu sent to the hospital. There was nothing to do except postpone the meeting. At the same time, several people, including Wan Li, Qiao Shi, and Wu Xueqian, hurried to the hospital. Twenty minutes later Li Peng and Hu Yaobang's wife, Li Zhao, and other people also arrived at the hospital. . . .

After emergency treatment by anxious doctors, Hu Yaobang soon regained consciousness. He said in a weak voice to the people present, "The meeting is not yet over. . . . My speech is not yet finished . . . " People beside him, such as Wan Li, all consoled him, "Take a good rest first. The meeting has been temporarily called off."

Hu Yaobang also told them, "Don't stop the meeting because of me . . . " Central leaders who had come to visit Hu Yaobang personally gave instructions to the hospital authorities and the responsible persons of the related departments "Comrade Hu Yaobang must be cured!"

After the emergency treatment by the doctors, Hu Yaobang was out of danger.

Doctor's Saying

At 7:00 P.M. on April 15, Hu Yaobang asked for water and watermelon. He also asked to sit up, but the doctors did not let him. At 7:30 P.M., Hu wanted to excrete. The doctors found him constipated. They administered glycerine and found his heartbeat quickened. But they thought it a normal response for exerting pressure. However, in no more than ten minutes, at 7:40 P.M., Hu suffered from ruptures of blood vessels occasioned by myocardial infarction. By then every emergency treatment was of no avail. Hu passed away without saying a final word.

By 8:00 P.M. the news of Hu's death had reached the media, but very few important central organs had yet learned the news. Wang Guangmei only learned it when she received at noon a Hong Kong telephone call from her elder brother, Wang Guangying. That afternoon high-ranking personnel were already paying their last respects to Hu's family, among whom included Zhao Ziyang's sons and daughters. At night, many renowned figures in the intellectual field visited Hu's family, including persons like Yu Guangyuan and Sun Changjiang. Many wept.

A doctor told me that Hu died of blood vessel ruptures occasioned by myocardial infarction. The attack may have taken place as early as the April 8 Politburo meeting, except that the bleeding was minor then, and it was not until April 15 that massive bleeding occurred.

When human brains sustain severe shock, there is often minor bleeding, but the patient may still be conscious and able to carry out normal activities as usual. It will take a lapse of time before a sudden coma occurs. Therefore, it was the quarrels at the Political Bureau meeting that triggered Hu's attack.

On the Eve of His Death, Hu Requested the Party to Make Conclusions on His Case

Late on the night of April 14, Hu Yaobang told his wife, who had been beside him all this time, something to the following effect: If one day I really die, then ask the central authorities to make a fair judgment on me. Make my funeral simple, and don't make too much of a fuss. . . . This of course was not the official will. But no one could have guessed that these would be his last words.

At 5:00 P.M. on April 15, Hu's eldest son, Hu Deping, went to see Zhao Ziyang. He made three requests: One, there must be a statement that Hu Yaobang died while working. Two, to make conclusions (in effect a request to rehabilitate) on the 1987 forced resignation. And third, the funeral must be simple. Zhao stated that there must be a solemn funeral; that there must be a public funeral to be held in the hall of the National People's Congress. That same night the General Office of the Central Committee issued a red-headed memorandum for the memorial service arrangements and the agenda and forms of the ceremonies.

On the night of April 16, Li Zhao received in grief the preliminary draft of the memorial speech sent over by the Secretariat, which actively evaded criticism of Hu and his forced resignation by circumstances in 1986–87. Li Zhao was dissatisfied with the speech and reserved her opinions.

"The Conclusion of Anti–Bourgeois Liberalization Cannot Be Changed"

But the sender of the draft said "the conclusion of anti–bourgeois liberalization cannot be changed." That very night Li Zhao became ill. She was immediately admitted into a hospital and received transfusions.

Hu Yaobang's death was not only a great shock to the proreform faction within the party, but also a great shock to the tens of thousands of Chinese people. Its depth of influence and degree of impact will surpass that of Zhou Enlai's death. For Hu Yaobang was viewed as the chief banner-waver of the firm political reform faction within the CPC. And in the latest development, the reform line advanced by Deng Xiaoping had received setbacks, and with Zhao Ziyang caught in a dilemma, there was an urgent need for Hu Yaobang to shake off the status of being merely an empty Politburo member and truly return to the Chinese political arena. It was not expected that just when the CPC needed Hu most, Hu would go down for good.

For many years, among high-ranking CPC officials, Hu had won hearts by having integrity, by being "clean," enlightened and open, and by firmly upholding reform. People thought, "Those who should have died did not, while those who should not, died first." (A couplet pasted on the wall of a courtyard at Beijing University.) These moods, which requested fair judgment of the victim of injustice, and incensed by the harsh acts committed by the octogenarian party members, erupted like volcanoes, pushing the present democratic movement to a new height. If Hu Yaobang knew this, he would be happy about the students' new awakening, and the new start of the democratic movement.

24
A Document Circulated among Senior Party and Government Officials Earlier This Month [April 25, 1989]

Source: *South China Morning Post* (Hong Kong) (May 31, 1989): 12; FBIS, May 31, pp. 35–36.

On the morning of April 25, 1989, (Prime Minister) Li Peng and (President) Yang Shangkun reported to Deng Xiaoping on the situation in Beijing. The Beijing Municipal Party Committee requested that the Central Committee give them the authority to broadly mobilize the masses to struggle with the opposing force, that is, the people behind the students.

Deng Xiaoping said, "This is not an ordinary student movement, but turmoil.

So we must have a clear-cut stand and implement effective measures to quickly oppose and stop this unrest. We cannot let them have their way.

"Those people who have been influenced by the liberal elements of Yugoslavia, Poland, Hungary, and the Soviet Union have arisen to create turmoil. Their motive is to overthrow the leadership of the Communist Party and to forfeit the future of the country and the nation.

"We must move quickly to adopt preemptive measures in order to gain time. Shanghai's attitude was clear and they won time. We must not be afraid of people cursing us, of a bad reputation, or of international reaction. Only if China truly develops, and implements the four modernizations, can we have a real reputation.[1]

"The Four Basic Principles are indispensable. Comrade Yaobang was weak and retreated; he did not truly carry through the campaign against bourgeois liberalization. At the end of 1986 [*sic*?], the purge against spiritual pollution petered out after only twenty-odd days.

"If we had effectively acted at that time, then the state of mind of the general public would not have developed into what exists today. It is impossible to avoid minor turmoil. That could have been handled separately, and would not have developed into what exists today. Now the Central Committee is forced to interfere and resolve the problem from the center.

"Among the Four Basic Principles, there is one—the people's democratic dictatorship. We need to use this one. Of course, we want to use it appropriately and minimize the crackdown.

"Now, we must be especially careful to prevent the unrest from spreading to middle schools. Maintaining stability in middle schools is very important. The workers are stable. Of course, there are some unstable factors. There is no problem with the peasants. We also must pay attention to the stability of other sectors of society. We must keep Beijing informed of this.

"This turmoil is entirely a planned conspiracy to transform a China with a bright future into a China without hope. The major harm is to negate the leadership of the Communist Party and to negate the socialist system. A dialogue can be held, but we cannot tolerate incorrect behavior. Pretending to overlook the problem will not solve it. That will only fan the flames.

"We must do our best to avoid bloodshed, but we should foresee that it might not be possible to completely avoid bloodshed. In Georgia, the Soviet Union made a few concessions but failed to solve the problems. There was turmoil in Moscow, and the result was that they still have to arrest people. Other places in the Soviet Union could still erupt.

"The suggestions of the Beijing Municipal Party Committee is correct. The

---

[1]The four modernizations are agriculture, industry, science and technology, and national defense—a development strategy advocated by Zhou Enlai in 1975 and subsequently promoted as central to Deng Xiaoping's program.

attitude of the Central Committee should be clear, and then the Beijing Municipal Party Committee's task would be easier. The turmoil this time is definitely national in scope, and we must not underestimate it. We must issue a forceful editorial and make use of the law.

"It is a shame that we have wasted time. They (the students) are using the rights of democracy and freedom in the Constitution to impose restrictions on us. Beijing has ten regulations concerning demonstrations—let's use these ten points to restrain them. We must prepare ourselves to enter into a nation-wide struggle, and resolutely crush the turmoil. Otherwise, there will be no peaceful days, indeed peace will be lost forever.

"I told (American President George) Bush, if China allows demonstrations with so many people in such a big country, how can we talk of stability? If there is no stability, nothing can be achieved.

"Now, there are some people doing the same old thing, just like the rebellion faction during the Cultural Revolution. They won't be satisfied until all is chaos. They would burst the bubble of China's hope, and prevent us from continuing economic development and the open door policy, thereby bringing immediate ruin.

"There are 60,000 students boycotting classes, but there are 100,000 who are not. We must protect and support the 100,000. We must lift the threat from their heads. Worker and peasant cadres support us. The democratic parties are good. We also have several million PLA [soldiers]. What are we afraid of? Of the 60,000 (students), many have been forced. The (student organized) monitors are illegal.

"Communist Party and Communist Youth League members should play an active role. The Communist Party organization should play an active role. We must reaffirm the discipline within the party. Party cells in factories, universities, middle schools, and state organs should hold meetings. If it is only students who stir up trouble, that is not a big deal. The main thing is not to let them stir up society as a whole.

"We need to strengthen the Public Security Ministry's work to maintain social order. Comrade Yaobang did make mistakes, but when someone has died, one should say good things about him. Indeed, he did many good things. For example, he supported reform and openness. But he was weak in the face of bourgeois liberalization. Nor was his attitude toward the economy correct. The high speed double digit approach will only produce greater inflation. Now the posthumous evaluation is too high.

"Some people struggle to evaluate him as a great Marxist, but he was not qualified enough. None of us are. After I die, I do not want to be given that title.

"Now the character of the student movement has changed. We need to quickly use a sharp knife to cut the tangled weeds in order to avoid even greater turmoil.

"Concessions in Poland led to further concession. The more they conceded, the more chaos. The opposition faction in Poland is very strong. They have two strong forces, religion and unions. China only has students. The other sectors are better. Your Standing Committee decisions are correct; you have a consensus. Only if you maintain a clear attitude and staunchly carry out measures and support the local leadership by allowing them to handle things, can we then stop this turmoil.

"We should not simply administer the economic environment, we should also administer the political environment. We may have more struggles like this in the future. We have said in the past that of the Four Basic Principles, we can talk less about implementing the people's democratic dictatorship, although we have said that we cannot do without it.

"But now don't you think we need it? In focusing against the Four Basic Principles, the students have grabbed the major point. Without the Four Basic Principles they will become unbridled and brazen, they will run wild.

"Both the Central Committee and the Standing Committee need two different groups—one to focus on construction, another to focus on turmoil. We need to focus our main energy on construction. We can't sink too many people into the other, although in the short term it is all right. Our action cannot be slow, otherwise it will involve more and more people."

In the document, Hu Qili added, "Normally, Xiaoping would revise his own words before putting it into a document, but because time is short, we will first circulate the spirit of his speech."

25
It Is Necessary to Take a Clear-Cut Stand Against Disturbances

Source: *Renmin ribao* (People's daily) editorial (printed April 26, 1989), Beijing Domestic Service reported 0930 GMT, April 25; FBIS, April 25, pp. 23–24.

In their activities to mourn the death of Comrade Hu Yaobang, communists, workers, peasants, intellectuals, cadres, members of the People's Liberation Army and young students have expressed their grief in various ways. They have also expressed their determination to turn grief into strength to make contributions in realizing the four modernizations and invigorating the Chinese nation.

Some abnormal phenomena have also occurred during the mourning activities. Taking advantage of the situation, an extremely small number of people spread rumors, attacked party and state leaders by name, and instigated the masses to break into the Xinhua Gate at Zhongnanhai, where the party Central Committee and the State Council are located. Some people even shouted such reactionary slogans as, Down with the Communist Party. In Xi'an and Changsha, there have been serious incidents in which some lawbreakers carried out beating, smashing, looting, and burning.

Taking into consideration the feelings of grief suffered by the masses, the party and government have adopted an attitude of tolerance and restraint toward some improper words uttered and actions carried out by the young students when they were emotionally agitated. On April 22, before the memorial meeting was held, some students had already showed up at Tiananmen Square, but they were not asked to leave, as they normally would have been. Instead, they were asked to observe discipline and join in the mourning for Comrade Hu Yaobang. The students on the square were themselves able to consciously maintain order. [Beijing Xinhua Domestic Service in Chinese at 1400 GMT on April 25, reporting on the April 26 Renmin ribao editorial, deletes this sentence.] Owing to the joint efforts by all concerned, it was possible for the memorial meeting to proceed in a solemn and respectful manner.

However, after the memorial meeting, an extremely small number of people with ulterior purposes continued to take advantage of the young students' feelings of grief for Comrade Hu Yaobang to spread all kinds of rumors to poison and confuse people's minds. Using both big- and small-character posters, they vilified, hurled invectives at, and attacked party and state leaders. Blatantly violating the Constitution, they called for opposition to the leadership by the Communist Party and the socialist system. In some of the institutions of higher learning, illegal organizations were formed to seize power from the student unions. In some cases, they even forcibly took over the broadcasting systems on the campuses. In some institutions of higher learning, they instigated the students and teachers to go on strike and even went to the extent of forcibly preventing students from going to classes, usurped the name of the workers' organizations to distribute reactionary handbills, and established ties everywhere in an attempt to create even more serious incidents.

These facts prove that what this extremely small number of people did was not to join in the activities to mourn Comrade Hu Yaobang or to advance the course of socialist democracy in China. Neither were they out to give vent to their grievances. Flaunting the banner of democracy, they undermined democracy and the legal system. Their purpose was to sow dissension among the people, plunge the whole country into chaos and sabotage the political situation of stability and unity. This is a planned conspiracy and a disturbance. Its essence is to, once and for all, negate the leadership of the CPC and the socialist system. This is a serious political struggle confronting the whole party and the people of all nationalities throughout the country.

If we are tolerant of or conniving with this disturbance and let it go unchecked, a seriously chaotic state will appear. Then, the reform and opening up; the improvement of the economic environment and the rectification of the economic order, construction, and development; the control over prices; the improvement of our living standards; the drive to oppose corruption; and the development of democracy and the legal system expected by the people throughout the country, including the young students, will all become empty hopes. Even the tremendous achievements scored in the reform during the past decade may be completely lost, and the great aspiration of the revitalization of China cherished by the whole nation will be hard to realize. A China with very good prospects and a very bright future will become a chaotic and unstable China without any future.

The whole party and the people nationwide should fully understand the seriousness of this struggle, unite to take a clear-cut stand to oppose the disturbance, and firmly preserve the hard-earned situation of political stability and unity, the Constitution, socialist democracy, and the legal system. Under no circumstances should the establishment of any illegal organizations be allowed. It is imperative to firmly stop any acts that use any excuse to infringe upon the rights and interests of legitimate organizations of students. Those who have deliberately fabricated rumors and framed others should be investigated to determine their criminal liabilities according to law. Bans should be placed on unlawful parades and demonstrations and on such acts as going to factories, rural areas, and schools to establish ties. Beating, smashing, looting, and burning should be punished according to law. It is necessary to protect the just rights of students to study in class. The broad masses of students sincerely hope that corruption will be eliminated and democracy will be promoted. These, too, are the demands of the party and the government. These demands can only be realized by strengthening the efforts for improvement and rectification, vigorously pushing forward the reform, and making perfect our socialist democracy and our legal system under the party leadership.

All comrades in the party and the people throughout the country must soberly recognize the fact that our country will have no peaceful days if this disturbance is not checked resolutely. This struggle concerns the success or failure of the reform and opening up, the program of the four modernizations, and the future of our state and nation. Party organizations of the CPC at all levels, the broad masses of members of the Communist Party and the Communist Youth League, all democratic parties and patriotic democratic personages, and the people around the country should make a clear distinction between right and wrong, take positive action, and struggle to firmly and quickly stop the disturbance.

26

The Student Movement and Hu Yaobang Represent the Banner of Justice—Thoughts on Reading the April 26 *Renmin ribao* Editorial

WANG RUOWANG

Source: *Pai hsing* (Commoners) (Hong Kong), no. 192 (May 16, 1989): 17–19; FBIS, May 19, pp. 43–47.

It Is Only Just that "Officials Are Driven Out of Power by the People"

After reading the April 26 *Renmin ribao* editorial, I was so amazed and indignant that I attacked the table and rose to my feet. My tenacity having been aroused, I immediately wrote a letter to Deng Xiaoping, chairman of the Central Military Commission, to criticize this article. Feeling that I have not exhausted what is in my mind, I now refute some of its preposterous arguments as follows:

The editorial says: "After the memorial meeting, an extremely small number of people with ulterior motives continued to take advantage of the young students. . . . This is a planned conspiracy and a disturbance. Its essence is to once and for all negate the leadership of the CPC." According to Marx's historical materialism, mass riots and wars are generally divided into two clearly opposite kinds—the just and the unjust. Take "the people are driven to rebellion by tyranny" as an example. Historical books in our country always say that it is just, while suppression by government troops and police is unjust. Similarly, it is only just that "officials are driven out of power by the people." For example, Prime Minister Noboru Takeshita recently announced that he was going to step down. This comes under the category of officials being driven out of power by the people. It is also just for the common people in our country to inform against "official profiteers" perverting the law for a bribe. Can we change its progressive and just character just because an extremely small number of people with ulterior motives have sneaked into the ranks of the people driven to rebellion by tyranny?

Since it is a mass movement spontaneously joined by millions upon millions of people, it is inevitable that there are thirty, fifty, and even one or two thousand people with ulterior motives (they can also be called opportunists). Just as the saying goes, when mud and sand are carried along, the good are mingled with the bad. It is impossible to make clear the political motives and family backgrounds of all participants. There are no exceptions to these regular phenomena in history just because our socialist system has a special character. We may as well cite the anti-imperialist struggle staged by the Boxers:[1] There were indeed individuals with ulterior motives (such as Yehonala [Ci Xi] and her minister of defense) behind the movement. But all Marxist-Leninist historians in our country do not, on this account, define it as a riot. Take as another example the gang of hero-bandits of Liangshan Lake, which is known to every household.[2] All the 108 heroes maintained political unanimity with the ringleader of the fortified mountain village and united as one. These people can be regarded as extremely pure. Only Mao Zedong, a Marxist revolutionary teacher, suddenly ferreted out a capitulationist from among them. It was none other than Song Jiang, the spiritual leader of Liangshan. On the strength of this unique discovery, he totally negated the justness of the people driven to rebellion by tyranny. In an article written in 1980 [Mao was quoted as saying:] "Song Jiang was said to be a capitulationist. However, if this matter cannot be summed up as 'negating one's words because of his character,' it should be said that 'a person has written off 108 heroes' " (*Xinguancha* [New observer], no. 4, 1980).

To Whom Does "People with Ulterior Motives" Refer?

It was only after Mao's death that we were able to comment on his absurd arguments. Perhaps because he felt bored after attacking all old cadres and intellectuals, he suddenly had a very fantastic idea, namely, to vent his spleen by finding the spiritual leader of the peasant uprising and putting a label on him. It was a morbid mental characteristic of a person suffering from sadism in his later years. But how could his successors take his ravings as supreme instructions and look up to them as the standard? Some phrases in Mao Zedong Thought are still useful to us. He said, "Whoever suppresses a mass movement will come to no good end." This should be regarded as the cream of Mao Zedong Thought. However, his bludgeoning and labeling of Song Jiang is dross devoid of cultural accomplishment.

Given that the "editorial" is entitled "It Is Necessary to Take a Clear-Cut Stand," I think the concept "people with ulterior motives" is very hazy and generalized. It is not clear-cut as the most crucial point. If the meaning of this

---

[1]A group of martial artists thought invulnerable to modern weaponry who instigated antiforeign uprisings in North China (1898–1900) under the motto, "Preserve the dynasty; destroy the foreigners."

[2]These hero-bandits are Robin Hood–type characters found in the literary classic *The Water Margin*, or *The Outlaws of the Marshes* (Shuihuzhuan).

special phrase, which defines the target of attack, is ambiguous, it will lead to a large number of people being attacked and make it convenient to wrong good people, to wantonly infringe upon human rights, and to fabricate unjust, false, and erroneous cases. This kind of phrase, which is used to determine the nature of an offense or a case and which has extensive meanings, is neither a legal nor a political term. Like other phrases, such as "people unacceptable to the government," "people who are dissatisfied with the party and the government," and "a handful of bad people," this phrase can lead to serious consequences, bringing calamity to the country and the people. First, obviously, the writers of this editorial did not take part in the study and examination of legal knowledge in 1986 and, even if they did sit for the examination, they must have failed. (This refers to the nationwide study movement to popularize legal knowledge which the National People's Congress called on party and government cadres at all levels to take part in.) Second, they have not drawn bitter lessons from millions of unjust, false, and erroneous cases that occurred during the Mao era. Third, they do not have the grammatical level of a middle school pupil. As a result the whole article does not read smoothly and is illogical in reasoning.

From the whole text of the "editorial" I try to find out who the "people with ulterior motives" refers to. In this editorial, the words "some people even shouted such reactionary slogans as 'down with the Communist Party' " have been cited twice. The persons shouting the slogan are perhaps the extremely reactionary people "with ulterior motives." But I cannot but suspect the veracity of this statement. You cannot blame me for distrusting the party because this is our exclusive news and all its reports are one-sided and are exclusively reported in the government's favor. For example: The students shouted a dozen or so slogans. Why didn't you carry any of the others and why is it that you happened to hear this reactionary slogan? Precisely because the press serves exclusively as a mouthpiece of the party, people distrust it, giving rise to an opposition mentality and suspicion among the readers. Even I have become a person with "ulterior motives." Isn't my reaction caused by government monopoly of the news?

**Telling Somebody for What It's Worth and Putting
This Down as Public Record**

I still remember Ge Peiqi, a veteran teacher of People's University who has made many contributions to the party. Using a banner headline, the self-same *Renmin ribao* reported that he publicly stated his intention to "kill the Communist Party with a knife." As a result, the man was labeled as an extreme rightist and imprisoned for over ten years. It was later made clear that he had never uttered such a remark and that he had been framed. At that time, in an effort to create public opinion and arouse the deep hatred of the workers, peasants, and soldiers for the rightists, the People's University CPC Committee, which was under the Anti-Rightist Office led by Deng Xiaoping, imposed the false, frame-up remark on Comrade Ge. Old people like to recall and make comparisons. Linking the past with the present, I have this suspicion. I have no proof whether or not some people in the student processions have shouted such a slogan, but the editorial seems to have no real proof either when it says that "some people even shouted . . . ." It is only that I cannot suppress the thought or recollection that has flashed through my mind in connection with the above-mentioned words "ulterior motives" and, therefore, I cannot but put this down as a public record.

I also think that, in the late twentieth century, when the "Emperor of the Last Generation" became a hot item in our country, it is entirely possible that some people with ulterior motives, who have sneaked into the crowd, have shouted such a slogan.[3] Party leaders may as well examine themselves and find out why some people dare to shout such a slogan. If they regard this as an alarm bell, then this is an expression of people feeling happy when told of their errors, demonstrating a higher spiritual quality and a democratic manner. Unfortunately, with the tone of someone sharpening a sword, the "editorial" regards these people with ulterior motives as reactionary or as "people with a planned conspiracy." This is an attitude of bullying people by dint of one's power. I recall a matter which I heard in northern Shaanxi many years ago and which I shall never forget my whole life. When it was reported that a peasant cursed Chairman Mao, saying that he wanted to "kill Chairman Mao," the comrades present at the meeting were stupefied. But Chairman Mao said, "You should try to find the peasant, but you should neither frighten nor blame him. Ask him what complaints he has for the party. The peasant must be in a fit and want to vent his spleen. He has never seen me and he cursed me because he has grievances." (I have only jotted down the main idea. The story is available at the Exhibition Hall of Revolutionary History and there is no harm in finding it for people to study.)

The story was passed along through word of mouth in the base areas with general approval. It is a glorious tradition of great benevolence and virtue which enabled our party to win power. It is a pity that, after winning power, it has acted in a diametrically opposite way. It has time and again punished the so-called antiparty and antisocialist elements. And eventually, even Liu Shaoqi, Peng Dehuai, and others could not escape by sheer luck. The people not only turn the "story passed on with approval" into a curse, but they dare to vent their spleen on

---

[3]Wang is apparently referring to CCTV's production of ''The Last Emperor'' (not to be confused with the Western film by the same name) describing the life of Puyi, the last Qing ruler. This long, popular series evidently led viewers to draw comparisons between the Qing emperor and Deng Xiaoping as the ''last emperor of the Communist dynasty.'' In this sense, the TV show played the same political role as the early 1960s play, *Hai Rui Dismissed from Office*, which, in drawing parallels between a Ming emperor and current Chinese politicians, provoked Mao's ire against its author, Beijing Vice-Mayor Wu Han.

the Communist Party only behind closed doors. The prestige of our party has also dropped correspondingly. When I recall this, I am overcome with grief.

Why is it that the leaders of our party have always turned a deaf ear to some criticism or words unpleasant to the ear? The root cause of the trouble is that, following the exercise of power by the party, they have developed an air of self-importance, thinking of themselves as the only revolutionaries and considering themselves unbeatable in the world. This has given rise to various reversals. For example, a customer has to give presents to a shop assistant when buying a commodity in great demand. By the same token, when masters become slaves, public servants naturally become very cocky and use the power in their hands to do whatever they like. The editorial is also like this. With great difficulty, it has found a pretext, saying that some people have shouted an anti–Communist Party slogan and have attacked state leaders by name in big-character posters, as if it has reasons to clamp down on all demonstrators. They do not know that if an equal, genuinely democratic multiparty system is instituted, there should not be a sharp confrontation in the eyes of the Communists, even if some people have shouted "Down with the Communist Party." Nor will they utter in alarm such remarks as "the reactionary students want to engage in rioting!"

One-Party Dictatorship and Supremacy for All

The *Renmin ribao* editorial, "It Is Necessary to Take a Clear-Cut Stand Against Disturbances," is like a notice of critical illness, indicating that the CPC leading body is heading for self-destruction. Instead of frightening the people, it has laid bare its cruelty and brutality and showed that it has returned to the old path of using political labels and the dictatorship of the proletariat to persecute citizens and intellectuals, as was characteristic during the Mao era. The editorial can be regarded as "full of nonsense." The "meticulously written" article has brought galling shame and humiliation to the great CPC!

Here I would like to specifically deal with the words "a clear-cut stand" in the title of the editorial, which seems familiar. In early 1987 we heard this blustering tone, characterized by blind faith in a supreme power, in the form of an editorial entitled "It Is Necessary to Take a Clear-Cut Stand against Bourgeois Liberalization." (Please refer to *Renmin ribao*.)

What on earth is meant by the "bright-colored banner," which has been held high on two occasions? It happens that on both occasions it has been waved under the same guiding idea. It is a banner calling on the whole party to make an example of young students and the intellectuals who are standing in the forefront of the reform. On the first occasion, it took "a clear-cut stand" in overthrowing Hu Yaobang, who represented the banner of democracy and opening up; on the second occasion, it threatens the younger generation, forbidding them to hold high the banner of Hu Yaobang!

The Failure of Those Having Blind Faith in the "Banner"

Why is it that the *Renmin ribao* editorial is so partial to the word "banner"? Judging by etymology, it is because in previous ages most Chinese were illiterate, simple-minded, and ignorant. The "banner of the dragon" represented the imperial power to which people knelt three times and kowtowed nine times. When it was changed into the five-color flag of the Republic, which was later changed into the flag of the blue sky and white sun [i.e., the Guomindang flag], the people of the country invariably saluted it according to the customs. When it was changed into the banner of Mao Zedong, not only should people prostrate themselves before it in admiration and repeatedly shout "Long live," but they should also sing: "You are our great savior!" Because the people of the country have the tradition of "being awed by the sight of the banner" and "subjugated by the sight of the banner," the 800 million people seem to be in a constant state of anxiety, like bees losing the queen bee, if they do not hold high the banner of somebody. Like those who were quite familiar with the art of emperors and kings, Comrade Hua Guofeng, realizing that he did not have ample political capital, found it necessary to hold high "with a clear-cut stand" the banner of Mao Zedong during the period of his "short-lived cabinet" as a successor. When Deng Xiaoping returned to power in 1978, he also had to hold high the banner of Mao Zedong. However, he was more brilliant than Hua Guofeng in that he, together with Chen Yun, Hu Yaobang, and Ye Jianying, began to criticize Mao Zedong, albeit very superficially. Being aware that the banner of Mao Zedong had paled into insignificance in the eyes of the people, Deng used the method of repair. He created the banner of "Mao Zedong Thought" in a collective manner and mended Mao's dilapidated banner so that it would not fall. And, fearing that the common people remained unconvinced, he incorporated his invention into the general principles of the "Constitution [of 1978]," turning it into one of the four cardinal principles.

In the above paragraphs I have briefly recalled the history of "king's flags changing hands on top of the city wall" (Lu Xun's poem). From here we can see that, since the banner of Mao Zedong became as insupportable as A Dou [the infant name of Liu Shan, last emperor of Shu Han, known for his want of ability and weakness of character], the Chinese people are no longer satisfied with having a banner in the sky. They are no longer colorblind or illiterate. Now they want to see clearly the color of the banner before making a decision. This is a great enlightenment of ideological emancipation and a great awakening surpassing that of the May 4th Movement. This time, however, the leaders of our ruling party still have blind faith in the "banner." They can neither see the great enlightenment of the people, nor do they know that the charm and appeal of the "banner" does not lie in the "king's banner" but in the different political contents it may represent. The fact that on both occasions the *Renmin ribao* editorial was entitled "It Is Necessary to Take a Clear-Cut Stand . . . " is a reflection of the mentality of deviating from the times and the masses.

Hu Yaobang Was a Bright-Colored Banner

The antibourgeois campaign in early 1987 and the incident of forcing General Secretary Hu Yaobang to step down, which were followed by perverse acts and retrogression of the reform, served as an enlightening lesson for the people of the whole country. There are two different kinds of banners: one that is in keeping with the trends of the world, such as democracy, freedom, honesty, and civility, and another representing autocracy, decadence, and acts of riding roughshod over the people. Being as incompatible as fire and water, the two banners are really bright-colored! Hu Yaobang represented the former kind of Communist Party leaders. But he was suddenly overthrown, without being allowed to defend himself or discussing it in the plenary session of the CPC Central Committee. This ugly practice, which was characteristic of the Mao era, showed that the side overthrowing him was not in the right. If they did not represent the banner of autocracy and decadence, why did they want to fell the banner representing democracy, progress, honesty, and civility? The practice of the past two and one-half years also tells the people of our country that, as soon as the banner of Hu Yaobang fell, corruption and bribery prevailed, prices and confusion rose simultaneously, the conditions of intellectuals became worse. . . . Isn't this caused by the other banner, which claims to have a clear-cut stand, getting the upper hand?

Precisely because *Renmin ribao* carried an editorial entitled "It Is Necessary to Take a Clear-Cut Stand . . . " the people of the whole country have thought things out for themselves and made a clear-cut choice. The people, especially college students and intellectuals, have chosen the banner represented by Hu Yaobang and resolutely cast aside the banner representing conservative ideas, autocracy, retrogression, and hypocrisy. This is the choice of history; this is the will of the people across the country! When coming to the end of their tether, our party and state leaders have resorted to the dilapidated banner of "it is necessary to take a clear-cut stand," which was also held high in early 1987, in an attempt to use this hastily-tied scarecrow to frighten the surging masses in their hundreds of thousands. Did not this add fuel to the flames and arouse the tide of indignation across the country?

Who Provokes the Disturbance?

A paragraph in the "editorial" reads: "This is a planned conspiracy and a disturbance. Its essence is to once and for all negate the leadership of the

CPC." Those having a little knowledge of the causality of dialectics know that those provoking the disturbance are not "the extremely small number of people with ulterior motives," as referred to in the editorial. (They are called "a handful of people" in the "announcement" issued in Shanghai. But the meanings are the same because "a handful" is a political term consistently used by Mao before he went all-out to attack people. The Beijing authorities avoid using it. This shows that the level of the party Central Committee is higher than that of Shanghai. However, Shanghai is more clear-cut than Beijing because even a lie detector finds it hard to detect whether a person with "ulterior motives" has a flitting idea to sing a different tune.) There are three reasons for this: First, the banner of Hu Yaobang was erroneously felled but the party Central Committee refused to admit this after his death. Second, over the past two years, false talks, boasts, and empty talk have flooded the press. After comparing practical life with a series of actions against democracy and human rights, people are indignant. Third, the party adopts various measures to guard against and stifle the students, such as threatening them, making things hard for them, causing them to disintegrate, or luring them by promise of gain. The result is that the students have lost faith in the ruling party. The tide of going abroad that has developed over the past two years serves as a serious warning to the authorities and a silent protest!

From these three points we can see who has provoked the current angry tide of the student movement. At this late hour, instead of carrying out self-examination, ideological transformation, and self-criticism, the editorial again used the much-abused terms of the Mao era to label and threaten the citizens. It has shifted the contradiction into "a handful of bad people" or "an extremely small number of people with ulterior motives" and used the pet phrase "class struggle" to prepare public opinion for the use of force. Realistically speaking, the editorial also serves as an "open conspiracy" to provoke more serious disturbances. (By using "disturbance" [*dongluan*] instead of "trouble-making" [*daoluan*], the editorial has not only raised the student movement to the higher plane of principle, but also confused it with the decade of disturbances by the "Gang of Four" in an attempt to arouse the people's strong aversion.) The wording of the editorial is a well-known trick of reversing cause and effect and putting the blame on somebody else. There is no need to talk more about it here.

Pragmatism on the Part of the Ruling Party

On the other hand, the editorial is ambiguous or tries to smooth things over where it should take a clear-cut stand. For example, there are indeed people, words, and deeds obstructing and sabotaging the reform, but the editorial dares not criticize or touch them. It even forbids people from mentioning the word "conservatives." Before 1986, the ruling party still stressed the need to criticize leftism. After that, even this was no longer mentioned. Instead, it was changed into "ideological ossification." Nobody knows whether this refers to the ideological ossification of old people or whether it is mentioned for the sake of personal interest. This process of making the concept more and more unclear is a reflection of the increasingly growing force of the conservatives (including ultra-leftists) in leading departments. Take as another example the campaign to eliminate spiritual pollution. What does spiritual pollution mean?

The phenomena of people wearing jeans or trousers with narrow trouser legs, growing long hair, engaging in social dancing, playing video tapes imported from Hong Kong and Taiwan, using pictures of beautiful girls as book covers, and the phenomena of novels describing females going to a temple to burn incense or two young people embracing each other were all labeled as spiritual pollution. This was not a clear-cut stand. Later, Hu Yaobang exerted great efforts to curb this frenzied political movement. As a result, instead of extending throughout the entire country, as the Great Cultural Revolution did, it came to an end in a short time. People say that the campaign to eliminate spiritual pollution was a counter-current aimed at attacking reform and opening up. But inside and outside the party, it is forbidden to criticize this preposterous thing, which "deprived the country of peaceful days." This is another example of failing to distinguish between right and wrong and to take a clear-cut stand. A study of the above-mentioned two examples in relation to the two "editorials" will enable the Chinese people to be more clever. When people cry for "a clear-cut stand," this is a signal to get ready to attack the "class enemy" (illusory or framed up); when people want to cover up their errors or pursue an unpopular policy, they need not "take a clear-cut stand" and, the more muddleheaded they are, the better. We can thus see that whether or not it is necessary to "take a clear-cut stand" is nothing more than pragmatism on the part of the ruling party. Out of a moment's political need, the ruling party sometimes shows its hand and sometimes covers up its hand.

I dare to predict that the words "it is necessary to take a clear-cut stand" will still appear in the newspapers several times. Nobody can guarantee that among the one billion people there are no people with "ulterior motives" "hatching a big plot." However, if this remark is used indiscriminately, it will lose its deterrent function. This prediction will also come true.

27
Yuan Mu and Others Hold Dialogue with Students [April 29, 1989]

Source: Beijing Television Service, April 29, 1989; FBIS, May 1, (excerpts), 25–49; corrections in FBIS, May 3, p. 48.

[Meeting between Yuan Mu, spokesman for the State Council; He Dongchang, vice-minister in charge of the State Education Commission; Beijing Municipality officials Yuan Liben and Lu Yucheng; and student representatives from sixteen Beijing institutions of higher learning, held at the conference room of the All-China Students Federation in Beijing on April 29—recorded.]

[Video opens with caption reading: "Yuan Mu and Others Hold Dialogue with Students"]

[Announcer:] This afternoon the All-China Students Federation and the Beijing Municipal Students Federation have invited some students from 16 schools of higher learning in the capital to take part in discussion and hold a dialogue in the conference room of the All-China Students Federation. Yuan Mu, spokesman of the State Council; He Dongchang, vice-minister in charge of the State Education Commission; and Yuan Liben [member of the Standing Committee of the Beijing Municipal CPC Committee] and Lu Yucheng [vice-mayor of Beijing], responsible persons of Beijing Municipality, will take part in the discussion. Yuan Mu will speak first.

[Yuan Mu:] Entrusted by the State Council and Comrade Li Peng, I and concerned comrades of the State Education Commission and Beijing Municipality have come here to hold a discussion, a dialogue, with you today.

Leading comrades of our party and state are showing great concern for the broad masses of students. They asked me to speak to you and through you to speak to the broad masses of students of schools of higher learning in the capital. They hope that the broad masses of students will return to their classes as quickly as possible. If you have any opinion on state affairs and social problems, you can present those opinions through normal channels. They, particularly Comrade Li Peng, asked me especially to tell you and through you to tell the broad masses of students in Beijing that, regarding the political struggle against those who negate the leadership of the Communist Party of China and negate the socialist system as mentioned in the *Renmin ribao* editorial, the question is directed against the illegal behavior of a very small handful of people and is not aimed at the broad masses of students. The broad masses of students, filled with patriotic enthusiasm, hope to promote democracy, strengthen the reform, punish those guilty of embezzlement, and overcome corruption. All those wishes are in complete accord with the wishes of the party and the government.

The leading comrades of the party and the state hope that you students will fully understand your important social responsibility. Our young people, especially the university students, are our country's future and hope. They hope that you will fully understand your own social responsibility, think about the situation in a sober and reasonable way, maintain social stability, and support the party and government to tide over our present difficulties.

We can say that at present our country is faced with many difficulties, and it would be even more difficult to overcome those difficulties if there are disturbances and instability. They hope that you students and people of all circles in the society will strive to support the party and the government, adhere to the four cardinal principles, keep to the general policy of reform and opening to the outside world, carry out the reform and open policy, and promote socialist modernization through to the end and achieve our desired victories. Before I came here, the leading comrades of the party and state asked me to make these remarks to you students.

Now if you have any questions, please ask them.

I want to make one more point clear: As the sponsor has just said, because we, and I, in particular, lack experience in this form of dialogue, and also because we cannot possibly be very familiar with problems in various areas, it is possible that we will be able to address your questions, but we may not be able to answer some of your questions at this moment. What shall we do if we are unable to answer your questions? I want to ask you students to permit us to go back and think about your questions and to return to talk with you again when there is an opportunity. I think this way there will be a harmonious atmosphere. [Yuan Mu laughs.] You don't have to corner us and put us on the spot. [Unidentified person laughs, then Yuan Mu laughs again.] Is this good? [Yuan Mu laughs.] Let us begin in this way, okay?

[Unidentified student:] I am a student from [Beijing Aerospace University?]. I enrolled as a student in its foreign language department in 1986. Among the demonstrators, I heard a student shouting the slogan, "Official profiteering, official profiteering, it is impossible to strike it down if we don't strike [i.e., boycott classes]." From this and other slogans, I have come to realize that a problem exists, namely, there exists in our party, state, and society a fairly serious phenomenon of corruption. Many who engage in activities of corruption are children of cadres. With regard to the measures taken by the Central Committee, it can be said that the Central Committee talks a lot about this problem, but no firm measures have been taken. The students resent this very much. Therefore, the students have strongly demanded that in handling this problem, the central authorities see to it that policies are firmly implemented so as to let the students and people see the results. Moreover, I think the central authorities should take resolute measures to close those companies that should be closed and to lock up those people who violate discipline and the law. Thank you.

[Yuan Mu:] I bitterly hate official profiteering. However, I think if we adopt the method of striking down official profiteering, we may not necessarily achieve our objective. I am afraid we should rely on two measures. The first measure: We should fully expose wrongdoing in accordance with the evidence. Anyone who has data in his hands is welcome, including people of all walks of life, including the masses of students. Now, the Ministry of Supervision, procuratorial departments, and nearly all cities throughout the country have set up crime-reporting centers, and democratic parties also have crime-reporting centers. All people can report wrongdoing to these centers in accordance with the facts. Of course, we should not report something without evidence, but it is all right if you report that you suspect somebody of wrongdoing, and investigations will be conducted according to the facts.

I trust that the party and the government will have a serious attitude when investigating and meting out punishment. Regarding this, it is necessary to further improve the system. So far, we have promoted a system of handling cases of corruption, making their results public, and welcoming public supervision. Of course, the work in this field has not progressed quite satisfactorily or quickly. Further legislation is needed to promote the system. . . . I would like to state that, with all sincerity, the party and government intend to solve problems with the masses of people. However, I feel that it will be rather difficult to overcome such practices through toppling [*da dao*] in one stroke. If things go wrong, they may lead to a recurrence of the Cultural Revolution, which we do not want to happen. Moreover, things should not be handled hastily and incorrectly for fear of unjust, false, and wrong cases. Some of the cases are still being redressed, and they constitute a factor for instability. Therefore, the work should be carried out according to the procedures. Once again, on behalf of the State Council, I sincerely invite people from all walks of life, including the vast number of young students, to report cases of corruption involving any officials. They will be investigated thoroughly [applause].

[Student Xiang Xiaoqi:] I am Xiang Xiaoqi, a postgraduate student in the study of international law at the University of Political Science and Law. My statement has two points.

First, dialogue is being held between the State Council and the representatives of all the students of the institutions of higher learning in the capital. However, the students present here today do not represent all the students in the capital. Students from only sixteen universities and colleges are here. Students here have not been selected through general elections. Therefore, students here today cannot represent all the students in various universities and colleges in the capital.

Thus, the meeting today can only be regarded as a preliminary one aimed at creating a tranquil atmosphere and smoothing out the channels for dialogue. This is not the official form of dialogue demanded by the broad masses of students. This is the first point of my statement.

The second point of my statement involves a three-point proposal which we would like to make concerning dialogue. On April 27, a State Council spokesman issued a statement welcoming the students' demand for dialogue. He said that dialogue should be carried out in a proper atmosphere and in a suitable form. I believe that the students of various institutions of higher learning in the capital welcome the positive attitude adopted by the State Council and are willing to create a tranquil atmosphere for dialogue as soon as possible and develop a form of dialogue with a realistic attitude so that dialogue may be sincerely and openly held on the basis of equality. It is for this reason that we would like to offer the following three-point proposal:

1. A general election should be immediately held in each institution of higher learning in the capital to elect two representatives, and a delegation to participate in the dialogue should be formed of members elected by all the representatives.

2. Preparatory dialogue should be held before dialogue of a substantive nature takes place. During this preparatory dialogue, negotiations should be carried out concerning the location, the number of representatives, and the topics and form of dialogue.

3. We may consider resuming classes when dialogue of a substantive nature begins. This is our three-point proposal.

[Yuan Mu:] With regard to this statement, I would like to express my views. The form of dialogue can be varied, I think. Our dialogue is not a negotiation between opponents. There is no negotiation existing between opponents. There is no negotiation existing between the government and the students. Today's form of dialogue is fine, if the students wish to express their views. Dialogue can be conducted even on a small scale, among two to three or among eight to ten people, in various forms and through various channels. Dialogue means getting together and engaging in conversation, exchanging ideas, and deepening understanding. So long as we conduct dialogue in this manner without setting preconditions, today's dialogue will certainly help facilitate the exchange of views, I think. We have a fine meeting today. I would like to make this meeting a success. We may also convene similar meetings in the future. Perhaps other comrades will talk with you the next time instead of me. For example, the ministers of various ministries may conduct dialogue with students in schools under their administration. Right? All the people get together to discuss various issues. I think this is a better way to do things. Also, in the face of reality, I think it will be quite difficult for institutions of higher learning in the capital to immediately conduct general elections for representatives in the current atmosphere. Who wants to be a representative? Was the last dialogue aborted because of a lack of representatives? We were unable to achieve our goal. This will not benefit us. It will be better for us to do things calmly and according to the actual situation. This conforms with the guidelines laid down by the party and government. This will further improve the situation in the capital and create a stable environment conducive to the implementation of reform and the open policy. This is my view.

[Student Yang Hongzheng:] I am Yang Hongzheng from Qinghua University's Computer Department. My question is this: We feel that an unhealthy party style and corruption are now rather serious, as everyone can see. There is also hearsay at the school. For instance, a few days ago all sorts of relationship charts appeared in the school, charts which claim that many children of cadres have acquired high positions because of their connections. Of course, some of them may have acquired these positions because of their genuine talents. But it is true that some mediocrities have attained such positions through connections. We would like to hear your reply to this. Also, is it possible to correct this situation by improving the system? That is all I want to say.

[Yuan Mu:] . . . Indeed, we have many problems with party style. But first we must undertake a basic assessment of our party. I admit that the problems in party style have tended to become more serious in recent years. This is a fact. Even as we hold talks here today, I still think that, on the whole or for the most part, our party cadres and members are good. However, serious problems exist. During their march, students shouted slogans in support of the Communist Party. This is the basic premise. If the party has become thoroughly corrupt from within, if it has become degenerate, then it will not have the students' support, nor will it have mine. We will have to reconsider whether we should stay in the Communist Party.

I believe that, on the whole or for the most part, our party is good. Since the third plenary session of the Eleventh CPC Central Committee ten years ago, our party has followed the basic line of our center and two basic points. This direction is correct in principle. No matter how you look at it, our country has undergone tremendous historical changes in all areas in the past ten years. No one can deny this absolute fact. Today's achievements would have been impossible without the party's efforts and the party members' struggle. But due to social, political, economic, historical, and ideological reasons, and due to our lack of resolution in opposing bourgeois liberalization, the problem of party style has grown more serious.

I think that our party has the determination and confidence to overcome this problem. . . .

Comrades may recall events several years back. Some of you may have forgotten the Great Cultural Revolution, or may not be familiar with it because of your ages. However, comrades over thirty will still recall it. This approach was also used when the Great Cultural Revolution first started. The so-called figure of a hundred ugly persons was one of them. It is not an effective approach, nor does it promote stability. It only increases destabilizing factors. It is not good to spread this approach widely. I do not know whether the students agree or not. ...

[Student Chang Weijun:] I am Chang Weijun of the College of Architectural Engineering. I would like to ask Comrade Yuan a question. To lead an austere life, we need the proper atmosphere. We should share weal and woe. Some people golf every Sunday in the company of their wives. Is there not a big gap between this practice and the material life of the whole people as well as the spirit of working together to tide over difficulties [applause]?

I have with me issue No. 2 for 1989 of the magazine *Jiankang zhinan* [Guide to health]. On page 48 is a report on an excellent golfer. There is also a color picture here.

[Yuan Mu:] Is it true that golf was played each week?

[Chang Weijun:] Yes. You can read this. Weekly exercise includes golf practice. [Another student holds up a copy of *Jiankang zhinan*, showing a page which reads: "Excellent golfer—Zhao Ziyang." The page also shows four color photos of Zhao Ziyang playing golf.]

[Yuan Mu:] I will forward this student's opinion to the leading comrades concerned. There are still very few golfers in China. Students think it is unnecessary. Sometimes, however, for the sake of international intercourse, it is permissible to golf a little. But do not overdo it. But I do not know the actual situation and cannot tell if golf was played every Sunday. If this is true, I will convey this message to the leader. This is one thing.

On the other hand, I would like to pass on a piece of information to you. The central authorities have considered the masses' reactions on this issue. The government has also taken note. In his report at the Second Session of the Seventh National People's Congress [NPC], Premier Li Peng also mentioned that government agencies at all levels should take the lead in leading an austere life in order to obtain the masses' understanding. I am fully in favor of it.

Here I would like to tell you one thing. In the past, the party Central Committee and the State Council used to work in Beidaihe because of the summer heat. While there, some leaders were vacationing and working at the same time. This has increased financial expenditures and strained transportation. Now, in view of the fact that this is not appropriate and does not conform with the requirements to improve the economic environment, rectify the economic order, and lead an austere life, it has been formally announced that we will not go there anymore. I think we will not go there in the future. In addition, it has been decided that no more deluxe sedans will be imported from now on [applause].

[Student Wang Chong:] I am Wang Chong, a student of the Architectural Engineering Department of North Industrial University, admitted in 1987. First of all, I wish to make a request. I request that news media give a true report on this meeting, and that no restriction or demand whatsoever be imposed on journalists either before or after the meeting. Second, I wish to ask Comrade Yuan Mu a question: You have said that anyone involved in embezzlement should be investigated and dealt with. I wish to ask whether any phenomenon of embezzlement exists among the children of cadres at the central level and, if so, whether their cases have been investigated and dealt with. Please make the facts public.

[Yuan Mu:] I can say with full responsibility that the party Central Committee and the State Council have decided that if any cadre at any level has been involved in embezzlement or has received bribes, he must be investigated and dealt with. But if you want me to say here clearly which leading comrades or their children have this kind of problems or which leading comrades or their children have no such problems, it is very hard for me to do so. It is hard not only because I do not understand the situation entirely, but also because under the circumstance of stressing the legal system, if I confirmed or denied anything here and what I said were found not in accord with the facts, I would be held legally responsible. I am a government spokesman, not an individual who can speak carelessly [laughter]. . . . If we do want to expose this kind of problem, I think this should be investigated by a procuratorial department. If a case is filed and there really is a criminal act, the case should be tried by the court. If I am asked to talk about this question while the above procedures are not followed, it is very hard for me to do so. Please understand my situation.

[Student Wu Gen:] I am Wu Gen, a student of Beijing Foreign Studies College. The general opinion of the students is that requesting the news media to tell the truth is one of their strongest appeals in this student unrest. This request has won extensive support from the broad masses of people. The students have strongly appealed that the news media tell the truth and act as a genuine mouthpiece of the people, not merely a mouthpiece of the party. Regarding this incident, from April 15 to 25, various news media did not give a complete and true report. The few reports they made were very lopsided. For instance, the orderly parades held by the students were not reported; those that were reported were not composed exclusively of students, and were held in a comparatively disorderly way. Not until April 26 did principal news media carry some reports, but the reports were still not very comprehensive. The students generally felt the news blackout was one of the factors that contributed to the growing scale of this student unrest. News reports must tell the truth. On no account should they cover up the facts, nor should they make arbitrary comments, add something or delete something as they please. As demanded by all students, there should be a true, comprehensive report on this student unrest and the report should be made public. Also, there should be a fair appraisal of this student unrest, and all untrue reports published previously should be corrected, so that people will know the true facts that have occurred in our country. Meanwhile, making news media tell the truth is also a way to supervise the government organs and their leaders. In sum, the demand to be placed on news reporting is comprehensiveness, truthfulness, and promptness. The students unanimously believe that this demand constitutes part of the work of building up a democratic system. If there is no freedom of the press, no other things about building up a democratic system can be discussed. May I ask if such a demand can become a reality, and what measures will the central authorities take to realize this demand?

[Yuan Mu:] In principle, news reports should objectively, genuinely, and thoroughly report matters of concern to the people. I am completely for this principle. Moreover I can tell you that the State Council departments concerned are in the process of drafting a publication law and a law on journalism. I think the publication law and the law on journalism will be ready for submission to the NPC Standing Committee for examination and approval this year. . . .

Some people have suggested that press censorship be lifted and the press deregulated. I can assure you in a responsible manner—since my official duties also involve supervising the press and I was a Xinhua reporter for more than twenty years—that as far as I know, press censorship does not exist in our country. China's system holds chief editors responsible for their newspapers. When a chief editor is not quite sure about publishing a certain report, article, or editorial, he or she may send it to the relevant authorities for advice. This does happen. So-called press censorship, which young students today may not be aware of, did exist in the old society, where newspapers had to be examined by Guomindang press officers before publication. When a press officer did not like a certain item, he would cross it out. This left a blank space in the newspaper published the next day, since the paper did not have the time to find another item to fill the space. This practice does not exist today.

[He Dongchang:] I believe that there can be no absolute freedom of the press, which should be bound by the law. For example, libel is not allowed in newspapers, and they cannot make up their own rules.

[Yuan Mu:] Overall, I feel that journalists and newspapers today enjoy the freedom of the press prescribed in the Constitution. At the same time, the Constitution and laws restrict them to a certain extent. As media for the masses, they must fulfill the social responsibilities required of them. Every article and report they publish will exert a certain influence on their readers. Therefore, they must hold themselves responsible to society. They should be selective in publishing materials, and should not publish just anything that happens in society at will. This is a common practice, which probably exists in all countries.

[Unidentified student:] I am a student of the Department of Management of the Beijing Aeronautical Engineering Institute, admitted in 1986. I have a few remarks to make. First, this meeting must be called a discussion meeting. Second, the students' representatives here represent only individuals. They do not represent any schools. Third, the most important questions that need to be answered today are the questions we raised in the student strike. Therefore, our dialogue must be held with the party and state leaders. However, no party and state leaders are present here today; thus, today's dialogue cannot answer any questions raised in the student strike. So this is not the dialogue we students asked for. So I, representing myself, have decided to leave this meeting room. Fellow students who support my opinion, please also leave. I have another thing to say: After a meeting held by students of each institute of higher learning, a statement should be issued. Now I decide to leave the meeting room. [Video shows student leaving alone, while other students raise their hands asking for the floor.]

[Student Han Chenchong:] I am Han Chenchong of the communications engineering specialty of Beijing Post and Telecommunications Institute. I would like to ask Yuan Mu a few questions: First, Article 35 of the Constitution stipulates that citizens enjoy freedom of speech, of association, of procession, etc. However, Beijing Municipality's regulations on procession and demonstration set various restrictions on processions and demonstrations. The local regulations have gone against the Constitution. Which should we follow? Second, a *Renmin ribao* editorial inappropriately linked the procession activities of some students of institutes of higher learning in Beijing with what happened in Xi'an and Changsha.[1] May I ask why? Also, on April 22, when students asked for a dialogue with Premier Li Peng, was Premier Li Peng informed of it at that time? Moreover, people thought Comrade Hu Yaobang's hearse would go around Tiananmen Square, which is the usual practice. However, it actually went out from the West Gate. Why?

[Yuan Mu:] The Constitution indeed stipulates that citizens enjoy freedom of assembly, of association, of procession, and of demonstration. [Yuan turns to He Dongchang] Is demonstration not included? And procession?

[He Dongchang:] Procession and demonstration are included, but not strikes.

[Yuan Mu:] No worker strikes or student strikes. Citizens enjoy freedom of speech, of association, of assembly, of procession, and of demonstration. In addition, the Constitution also stipulates that when citizens exercise their rights, they should not violate the interests of the state or the collective. Nor should they hamper the freedom of other people. The Constitution also stipulates that local people's congresses at all levels have the power to formulate necessary regulations and laws in accordance with the Constitution to protect the implementation of the Constitution and regulations. I believe the Beijing Municipal People's Congress Standing Committee did not go against the Constitution when it set some necessary stipulations on procession and demonstration in accordance with these principles. Fellow students may ask legal experts for their opinion on this question.

Furthermore, should the regulations have contradicted the Constitution and laws promulgated by the state, the NPC and its Standing Committee would have

---

[1]For a description of the demostrations and violence in Xi'an, see Suzanne Ogden et al., eds., *China's Search for Democracy: The Student and Mass Movement of 1989* (Armonk, N.Y.: M. E. Sharpe, forthcoming).

annulled them. Yet the regulations have not been repealed. Beijing residents, including the massive number of students, therefore, are all obliged to abide by the demonstration regulations drawn up by the Standing Committee of the Beijing Municipal People's Congress.

Now, let us get to the second question. . . . Let Comrade Dongchang answer this question [laughs]. I'll take a break for now [laughs].

[He Dongchang:] At present, I do not remember the exact wording of the editorial. I have to state this right at the beginning, as I did not take part in either the discussion or the formulation of the editorial. I only learned of it as an ordinary reader. I noticed one thing, that Beijing students, whether during their demonstrations at Tiananmen Square or in any other activities, did not take part in any beating, smashing, or looting. In Xi'an and Changsha, however, when students held group mourning activities at squares or other places, beating, smashing, and looting did occur for a variety of reasons, although students were not mainly responsible for them. There is a distinction here. It reminds us of one thing. That is, when students take action, if there are no policemen to maintain order or students do not maintain discipline, it is very easy for bad guys to penetrate under the current social circumstances and serious beating, smashing, and looting will result. An example in point is the incident in front of the Xinhua Gate [at Zhongnanhai]. The number of students there at the time was small, yet onlookers on the sidelines numbered 8,000. At that time, if there had been no policemen and soldiers to maintain order, beating, smashing, and looting would very likely have occurred. The danger did exist.

According to comrades of Beijing Municipality, the municipality has a huge migrant population of . . . [he pauses; Yuan Liben is heard from off camera saying "1.3 million"] 1.3 million. For a period of time quite a number among this population—here, I don't want to name names—directed their attention to Wangfujing and Dasha Building. Why? They can rob and loot at those fairly wealthy places. But there were no bad consequences, because the police and military units paid special attention to those areas. While you students were busy with your mourning activities, demonstrations, and other things, there was a danger of chaos. If no police and military personnel are there to maintain order, the consequences would be grave should chaos occur. This is the point I want to make.

The editorial should not be construed as having hinted that Beijing students had engaged in beating, smashing, and looting. No such thing. As for other, following issues, I don't remember them.

[Yuan Mu:] I would like to add a few words to what Comrade Dongchang has just said: First, from the beginning I have conveyed to you the words party and government leaders have for you. To put it explicitly, the political struggle against the negation of party leadership and negation of the socialist system mentioned in the *Renmin ribao* editorial was directed at a small handful of lawbreakers, and therefore has nothing to do with the masses of students. The masses of students are patriotic and desire reform and democracy. Their desires are identical to those of the party and the government. Therefore, I express here the earnest and sincere hope that our students will consciously divorce themselves from that small handful of people and from law-breaking activities. The party and the government had no intention of saying that all of the students were bad elements and that all the demonstrating students were engaged in beating, smashing, and looting. Nobody is so muddle-headed and stupid as to say such a thing. Impossible!

Here I want to remind you that you should think rationally and calmly. I feel that those who plot behind the scenes in the schools of higher learning in Beijing may be more dangerous than those who directly engaged in beating, smashing, and looting in Changsha and Xi'an. The disturbances they want to create may be serious. For example, the demands they have put forward are aimed at thoroughly negating the four cardinal principles.

They also want complete redress for the fight against spiritual pollution and against bourgeois liberalization. What does this mean? This means that there is serious political significance in opposing spiritual pollution and bourgeois liberalization. This political meaning is that negation of the four cardinal principles is not permitted. There is no need to demand redress, since this is negating the correct principles and correct direction. As far as I know, no citizen has been deprived of his rights during the campaigns against spiritual pollution and bourgeois liberalization. Therefore, a question of redress for the citizens who were supposedly wrongly charged and who consequently suffered injustice does not exist. As for Fang Lizhi, Wang Ruowang, Liu Binyan, and a few other party members who were expelled from the party, that was because they violated our party discipline and party constitution. The party dealt with them in accordance with the party constitution and its organizational principles. This is a normal thing for the party to do.

If this is denied and no one is allowed to say anything about opposing the opposition to liberalization and opposing the opposition to the four cardinal principles; that is, if full right of freedom is given to those who are opposed to the four cardinal principles, then what will become of our country? I ask comrades and students to think this over. As another example, in the course of parades by students of educational institutions of higher learning in Beijing, the capital, the slogans "Down with the bureaucratic government" and "Down with the corrupt government" have been shouted and displayed. I am not saying that all students taking part in the parades agreed to these slogans. I do not hold and approve of that view. It seems that such parades are not needed for any communist party or socialism [laughter]. Such parades are not needed. I do not know whether or not this change means that those making the plan have sincerely changed their stand. Isn't this worth thinking about on the part of the students? Also, if we make an analysis of various types of conduct and phenomena and compare many things that have occurred at present with what happened in the Great Proletarian Cultural Revolution, the matter is well worth our deep thought. Today, I have seen something written by a Red Guard, a veteran Red Guard. He says that many practices today have alarming similarities with the Great Cultural Revolution in those years. Then, for example, big-character posters could be seen here and there. Now, there are big- and small-character posters everywhere in educational institutions of higher learning. Another example is "establishing ties."[2] At that time, ties were established. Now, although ties have not yet been established, they are being established, albeit not on such a large scale as in those years.

[He Dongchang:] Ties are being established with middle schools.

[Yuan Mu:] Establishment of ties is underway. In Beijing, ties are being established among schools, with factories, and rural areas, and people have been sent out to other localities to do this.

[He Dongchang:] Fourteen middle schools.

[Yuan Mu:] For example, in those years, there was a famous slogan of kicking out the party committee to make revolution. Now, in our educational institutions of higher learning, someone has proposed that party leadership be abolished.

For instance, during the Great Cultural Revolution there were two, three, or more factions. Now the students are forming various kinds of organizations to gain legal rights for their own organizations, and they want to seize various units. Is this not somewhat similar to the situation during that period? If we let those things continue to develop, what will the outcome be? In my own judgment, the scale of social disturbances will be greater than simply smashing a few motor vehicles, and the consequences will be more serious. This is my view. Whether my view is correct or not, today I just wish to express it in exchanging views and having a heart-to-heart talk with you students. Some students present here may agree with my view, and some may disagree. I do not want to impose my view on you. However, I hope that you comrades will keep your senses and be calm. We were young people once [laughs]. I do not intend to display my seniority. I do not mean that. When we were attending universities, Comrade Dongchang and I also took part in campus upheaval, albeit under the rule of the Guomindang reactionaries.

[He Dongchang:] Please let me say a few words. Regarding our students of schools of higher learning in the capital as well as students of the entire country, I, myself, and staff members of the State Education Commission, adult comrades, teachers and presidents of various schools all have the same frame of mind, that is, they want to love students as they love their dearest children. Even if the students make mistakes, we will help them correct their mistakes. In other words, if there are 160,000 students in the capital, we have such feelings toward more than 99 percent of them. However, we must guard against those who hide

---

[2]*Chuan lian*, the practice whereby Red Guards, allowed free travel to "exchange revolutionary experiences," formed factions and alliances during the Cultural Revolution.

behind you and whom you students don't know. Those people are only a small handful, but it merits our attention to watch them. You students are now expressing your wishes out of genuine desire and good intentions. As I can recall, when the Great Cultural Revolution started, I was overthrown from my post. Nevertheless, I was quite understanding toward those young pathbreakers, including those who had beaten me. Some of the Red Guards at that time, to show their loyalty toward Chairman Mao, pinned Chairman Mao's badge on their flesh. They did this out of genuine enthusiasm. As to the consequences, you comrades all know about that.

[Student Fu Haifeng:] I am Fu Haifeng, a student of the 1988 class of the Department of International Politics at Beijing University. I was one of the representatives who went down on their knees in front of the Great Hall of the People on April 22. [Video shows Fu being interrupted by noise from unidentified sources.]

[Unidentified speaker:] You may continue your questions.

[Fu Haifeng:] I was one of the three representatives who went down on their knees. As a participant and witness of history, I would like to raise several questions regarding the circumstances at that time. First, according to the customary practice for state funerals, Comrade Hu Yaobang's casket should have come out from the main gate and been carried around the square before heading toward Babaoshan cemetery. In view of the orderly manner of the 100,000 students at that time, the parade would not have caused any disturbance or disorderliness. Why couldn't the 100,000 students fulfill their modest request to eulogize Comrade Hu Yaobang? This is my first question. Second, according to *Renmin ribao*, even before the memorial service was over, we had raised questions which had nothing to do with the mourning activity. Nevertheless, when we representatives made the request to submit the petition, the 4,000 party, government, and army leaders had already come out of the Great Hall of the People and stood on the stairs, watching us. Moreover, in our seven-point demand, we requested, first of all, that Comrade Hu Yaobang's rights and wrongs, merits and demerits, be reevaluated, and that his views on democracy, freedom, political relaxation, and harmony be affirmed. This request is directly related to the official mourning activity. What is the government's answer to this question? Third, the 100,000 students sat quietly for several hours and the three representatives went down on their knees for thirty minutes, expressing our strong desire to hold a dialogue with the government.[3] Why didn't the government send an official to talk to the students and their representatives? Instead, only two staff members of the funeral committee showed up. As is known, the funeral office was an ad hoc organization. What is the government's answer to this question? Those are my three questions.

---

[3]Kneeling was the traditional posture of deference required when presenting a memorial to the emperor.

[Yuan Mu:] As for the petition made by the students at the stairs in front of the Great Hall of the People on April 22, the course of events was published in newspapers. Yesterday or the day before?

[He Dongchang:] Yesterday.

[Yuan Mu:] The entire course of events was published in the newspapers yesterday. Here I do not want to repeat, and only would like to add one point, that this, Comrade Li Peng had already left the Great Hall of the People at that time. He had not been aware of the students' action and petition. . . .

[Fu Haifeng:] But why didn't the coffin go through the main gate?

[Yuan Liben:] I have not talked about that yet [laughs]. As for which gate Comrade Yaobang's coffin should go through, I don't know, because I was not a member of the funeral committee. I have inquired about this, however. It was already decided before the students reached the square on the night before the funeral. It was decided that Comrade Yaobang's coffin would go through the Xidan Gate of the Great Hall of the People. This was originally arranged. The night before the funeral, at 9:00. . . .

[He Dongchang, interrupting:] The slope at the Xidan Gate is a gentle one.

[Yuan Liben:] Right, it is a gentle slope. This is one circumstance. Another is that during a discussion with the student representatives, our representatives asked whether the students could help maintain order, because the student representatives requested that Comrade Yaobang's coffin pass through the square. Two of you who are present here can verify this. Our representatives replied that we could comply with all demands except the one requesting Premier Li Peng to appear.

[Fu Haifeng:] I want to elaborate.

[Yuan Liben:] You had better listen until I finish what I have to say. In accordance with this circumstance, it was decided the coffin would proceed as originally planned. This is the issue. Now, let's talk about the three students who knelt down at the square. In fact, the student representatives had several contacts with our workers. This was seen clearly by all. After the few representatives entered the first line of blockade, they moved here and there. They could be seen clearly. Later, there was a rumor that Premier Li Peng was prepared to receive the representatives. However, later we were unable to find out which one of our functionaries said this.

The problem reflected by the students was merely a rumor and did not reveal who was responsible for it. Finally, it was understood that a *Fazhi bao* [Legal system news] reporter transmitted the news. We later found the reporter but he categorically denied the matter, saying he never said such a thing. Therefore, we don't know yet which student transmitted the message from which public functionary. According to our understanding, not a single public functionary said such a thing. I am convinced that no public functionary would be so audacious. Furthermore, they do not have the authority to say that Li Peng could receive the students. They are just common public functionaries. This is one thing.

As to the kneeling by the students' representatives, as a public functionary of the Municipal CPC Committee, I can frankly tell you comrades that after the three representatives went forward, other students immediately wanted to submit their petition. The public functionaries said that they would transmit the petition to the higher authorities, but the representatives rejected the offer and insisted on handing it to Li Peng personally. After the representatives knelt, the public functionaries at the Great Hall of the People had to study the matter because some of the public functionaries were staff members there, namely service and management personnel, and some of the public functionaries were staff members of the funeral committee and their mission only involved funeral activities. Therefore, I think it was possible that there was a delay. Later, those common public functionaries were quite worried about the situation, so they came out to say that they would transmit the petition to the higher authorities. Under such circumstances, Fu Haifeng and two other students said that they must hand the petition to Li Peng personally. This was the actual situation.

Another thing was that, shortly after the funeral activities, Comrade Li Peng had left the area. The functionaries thought that they had clearly answered the students' questions and held that it was not necessary to report the matter to Comrade Li Peng. Besides, those public functionaries were very common public functionaries. Right? It was impossible that they could directly report those problems to Comrade Li Peng. This was the situation at that time. Now, we can say that some students' problems have been clearly answered. Due to the large number of students, we did not know their ideas about some other problems. However, there was some misinformation which generated confusion in the minds of students. For example, it included the misinformation about Li Peng wanting to receive students. Of course, now both sides cannot find the people who said those things. Which student said what, who transmitted the information, which public functionary said such a thing? We have asked all the public functionaries and no one admitted saying anything such as Li Peng would receive the students.

One more thing: The three students' kneeling down, to tell the truth, surprised everyone. Under such circumstances, those common public functionaries could not help but wonder what to do because they are just common public functionaries. I think you should understand this point. Those public functionaries finally went out to accept the petition and said that they would deliver it to Li Peng. However, the three students refused to get up. I think this was the situation. It should be said that this was the only true scenario. If you still want to find out more about this matter, I think it is not really necessary, right? Compared with the main demands of our students, including the slogans at the demonstration such as supporting the Communist Party, supporting socialism, opposing embezzlement and opposing corruption, I think this was just a very small incident. We already have clearly explained the events. . . .

[Unidentified student:] I would like to raise a question, not on behalf of the People's University, but myself. The purpose of dialogue is to solve problems. However, as you know, this purpose can be accomplished only when dialogue is held between student representatives of the schools of higher learning in Beijing and the central leaders. Since Comrade Yuan Mu has just said that the time for such a dialogue is not ripe yet, I would like to know whether there are any specific conditions regarding the appropriate atmosphere for this dialogue, which has been called for by the central authorities. For example, should the students go back to school, or should the Autonomous Union be disbanded? We hope we will get clear answers from the central authorities [applause].

[Yuan Liben:] Before Comrade Yuan answers this question, let me have a few words first. I feel that regardless of the form of dialogue and regardless of whether or not the participants are representative of the students, dialogue is comprehensive only when it serves to help understand the thinking of people from all strata and all walks of life. Let me illustrate this point by citing an example. I am a graduate of Beijing Aerospace University. I was a graduate student of the class of 1966. About a month ago, I discussed with the school leadership this plan: As an alumnus, I will visit my alma mater before May Day, where I will join a class and, from the afternoon to the evening, I will get together with the students, see what they do, and chat with them. Any class will do, although the size of the class should not be too large. We will chat on any subject. The purpose is to find out what is in the students' minds, what kind of problems they have. As the municipal party committee is still a grass-roots unit as far as the central party committee is concerned and many concrete problems are handled and resolved at the municipal level, we would like to find out what the problems are, what problems we should tackle first, what problems we should make greater efforts to resolve. We made definite plans in this regard.

However, the plan was aborted by what is going on right now, and I did not make the trip to the school. Although I did not go to the school according to the plan, I made my position known to the school leadership. I told them that I still wish very much to go to the school in a day or two to have this dialogue in the capacity of an alumnus and member of the leadership of the municipal party committee. I would not go if someone puts forward preconditions and insists that I must have dialogue with so and so and with a certain number of participants. Don't you agree? This is because dialogue itself is to understand things in all respects. In the past, dialogue was held frequently. When we visit the counties, we have dialogue, even with only a few people. We have dialogue when we meet with a certain unit. This being the case, I suggest that we not make the dialogue too rigid in form.

For instance, today we have understood the views of many students and the problems they have. As for solutions, I agree that the purpose of dialogue is to find solutions. However, we must not be metaphysical. We must not think that all problems have solutions once dialogue is held. If we think like this, then we are guilty of holding an oversimplified view of our country's entire modernization process. Some of the questions raised by the students can be answered, especially certain specific questions raised to clarify certain facts. Some questions can be explained to the students. Some questions need to be reported and further studied. Certain questions, in particular, require a legal process.

Take legislation on the press, for example. Comrade Yuan Mu has touched on this question. However, if I was asked this question, I would not dare to say: Students, there is no problem and we will enact a press law immediately. Frankly speaking, I personally have suffered deeply from inaccurate reports. This is because how our work is reported has something to do with how the reporter views a particular issue and how he approaches the issue in general. Their views are sometimes different from ours and sometimes their reports greatly encumber our work. This is why I also wish to enact a press law. However, the question can only be referred to the legislative departments. The law can be enacted only through due process after soliciting the views of all sectors, especially the views of the legal experts. The ultimate goal is to find solutions. I believe it is somewhat difficult to find on-the-spot solutions and give specific answers to all questions in this dialogue. This sort of demand is somewhat unreasonable, is it not? This is all I have to say before we hear from Comrade Yuan Mu.

[Yuan Mu:] As far as this question is concerned, I have already given my thoughts, and I do not wish to further elaborate, as Comrade Yuan Liben has also added his views. When I said that a suitable atmosphere and necessary conditions are needed for holding dialogue, I mean that both sides must be sincere and willing to sit down and talk, exchanging views with no strings attached. In addition, as the sponsor has said earlier, there must be a harmonious, democratic, tolerant atmosphere [laughs]. For example, my words may be hard for you to swallow, but you still listen; what you say may not be agreeable to me, but I also listen. This should be the attitude. . . .

[Student Zhang Zhaohui:] I am Zhang Zhaohui from the Department of Chinese at Beijing Teachers University. Leaders have often said that we should draw a line of demarcation between troublemaking by a handful of people and the good will of the vast number of students. Now I would like to ask: What is the central authorities' assessment of the recent student movement joined by over 100,000 students in Beijing, and how will the central authorities deal with the student organizers of the movement?

[Yuan Mu, turning to He Dongchang:] You answer. Comrade Dongchang will answer your questions [laughs].

[He Dongchang:] In giving equal stress to democracy and the legal system, we handle problems in the spirit of democracy and according to the law. So long as one does not violate the provisions of state laws and decrees, he or she is innocent. This applies to people in general, including students, teachers, and other citizens. Even before the student movement took place, I, as an official of the Education Commission, believed that young students who engaged in improper behavior or speech out of excitement should be totally forgiven. This is still my attitude [applause].

[Yuan Mu:] I completely endorse Comrade He Dongchang's suggestion [applause]. And I shall inform the State Council of his suggestion. We shall do our work in line with this spirit [laughs].

[Student Huang Dingzhong:] I am Huang Dingzhong, a student from the Beijing University of Science and Engineering. I have a question; that is, official profiteering has emerged in China. Is the emergence of official profiteering an inevitable phenomenon in the course of reform in a socialist country, or is it caused by some erroneous economic policies adopted by the State Council or the party Central Committee? In addition, who should be responsible for the mistakes in economic policies? What procedures are involved when the party Central Committee adopts economic policies? Could Teacher Yuan Mu answer my question, please?

[Yuan Mu:] Speaking of the emergence of official profiteering in our society today, if we explore it carefully, it will become a major theoretical issue. We can make a long analysis. To talk about it in simple terms, I think, first, there are social, economic, and political reasons. The economic reason: First of all, the productive forces in our country are still underdeveloped. The commodity economy is still in the initial stage of development. The market is not only underdeveloped but also gravely chaotic. This is our current economic situation. Talking about the political situation in China, we want to create socialist democracy, but we have to exert long-term efforts to achieve this objective. In some of our organs of state power, because of the lack of necessary legality and restrictions, we must painfully admit that there exist the phenomena of exchanging power for money, of buying power with money, and of integrating power with money. This is a fact nobody can deny. We must make unyielding efforts to solve this problem. Talking about the ideological reason, there is also the influence of feudal ideology and the influence of decadent capitalist ideology. Moreover, some people will do anything, including ignoring personal honesty and the interests of the state, for money; they either use money to buy power or use power to buy money. All of us bitterly hate these phenomena. All students hope for the solution of this problem, and the party and the government also hope for the solution of this problem.

There is another important factor: We still need to gradually perfect our legal system. If we do not rely on the perfection of the legal system and only rely on the methods of parades and demonstrations, we cannot solve our problems. Of course, the masses have expressed their dissatisfaction with those things and urged the government to pay greater attention and asked the party and government to take a more positive attitude in solving those problems. With regard to those wishes, therefore, we can say that the wishes of the students are in accord with the tasks to be implemented by the party and the government. This is my view of this problem. I wonder whether I am right or not.

There was also another question; I cannot remember. Could you remind me? Ah? Oh, policy decision. I have overlooked one thing in my answer, that is, besides those reasons, there were mistakes in the work of the government. This should also be considered a factor. This is also a factor that has caused some confusion in our economic life, especially in the field of circulation. We have encountered various phenomena such as speculation, profiteering, exploitation by middlemen, reselling of commodities for profit, and collaboration of bureaucratic and private racketeering. Those things are, to a certain extent, related to the mistakes in our work. The errors in our work mainly include our being overanxious for quick results in economic work and failure to meet the total demand with the total supply, which in turn leads to a relatively apparent inflation. The relatively apparent inflation also exists amid the dual-track price system, which provides opportunity and conditions for speculative activities and profiteering. Speculative activities and profiteering in turn have promoted the increase of commodity prices. Therefore, we can see that inflation, speculative activities, and profiteering promote each other, and thus the situation has deteriorated. This is indeed related to the mistakes in our work. Concerning the mistakes in the work of the government, Comrade Li Peng already made self-criticism in his report on the work of the government at the Second Session of the Seventh NPC, held this year. As to his self-criticism, the deputies to the NPC expressed their satisfaction, and the session adopted Comrade Li Peng's report.

[He Dongchang:] There were two votes against it. . . .

[Unidentified student:] Both sides have touched on official profiteering, an issue that has indeed aroused strong public resentment. Since Comrade Yuan Mu has indicated the government's strong determination to tackle this problem, I would like to address my question to him: Who do you think is the biggest profiteering official in China [Yuan Mu chuckles] and what progress and results have been made in rectifying this profiteering official since an effort was launched to tackle this problem? [Video shows Yuan Mu; the student is not seen.]

[He Dongchang, seen whispering:] [Words indistinct] We cannot identify who is the biggest, as we cannot line them up in order.

[Yuan Mu, chuckling:] In fact, I have just answered your question. It is difficult for me to identify the biggest profiteering official. However, I can discuss a few issues of keen interest to you. One of the issues is the work of screening and reorganizing companies, which I am sure is an issue of great concern to you. The Auditing Administration has had a fairly large work team auditing and examining the economic activities of the Kanghua Corporation, Chinese International Trust and Investment Corporation, Everbright Corporation, and China Agricultural Investment Corporation for a long time. Based on my work with the State Council, and by attending its meetings, I have learned that some of the preliminary results in auditing have already been obtained. It has been decided that after further verification in various fields, the results will be made public. In addition, according to Premier Li Peng's work report, in order to guard against perfunctoriness in the work, departments and localities should publish the results of screening and reorganizing companies through various forms, including publication in the press, so the public may make comments and exercise supervision. . . .

[Lu Yucheng, vice-mayor of Beijing Municipality:] Improving the economic environment and rectifying the economic order are currently the primary tasks of our party and the people throughout the country. This work also includes the important task of investigating official profiteering. The work of improving the economic environment and rectifying the economic order has just begun. We learn from newspaper reports and the report on the work of Beijing Municipality that initial success has been achieved since the work began more than six months ago. The biggest profiteering official, as I understand, will be exposed in the ordinary course of events as the work of improving the economic environment and rectifying the economic order deepens. I am confident that the biggest profiteering official will be exposed. On the other hand, as Comrade Yuan Mu has pointed out, we need an environment of political stability and unity for this. At the same time, we need the support of the people throughout the country, including the support of the students, to help us expose these things. . . .

[Student Zhu Mei:] I am a student from Beijing Normal University. My name is Zhu Mei. Many students who participated in the march raised a question about paying more attention to education. I think that the central authorities have pointed out that the major mistake of reform in the last ten years was the lack of attention to education. Why was this the case? Now that this is known, what specific measures have been planned and how will they be implemented? For example, what specific methods will be adopted and when? I would like to cite a few concrete examples. One concerns the issue of the education funding being too low. According to our understanding, the state appropriates education funds to schools according to the number of students. In the case of teachers colleges, the amount of funds appropriated includes the amount of financial aid to the students. In other words, if the financial aid to the students is deducted, the amount of funds allocated to the teachers colleges is actually lower than that allocated to other universities and colleges. We feel that we cannot accept the statement that more attention has been paid to education. Another point is that we demand legislation on education which will ensure that more attention is truly paid to education so that the statement will not remain mere words. [Speaker is not shown on video during the entire course of the statement.] . . .

[Student Jia Jie:] I am Jia Jie, a student from the class of 1988 of the Department of Management Science at Beijing Normal University. In order to help Comrade Yuan Mu and Teacher He Dongchang understand even more distinctly the issue which we have raised, I would like to discuss it in even more detail. Please hear me out. I believe that there is really a crisis in the field of education in China. The consequences of this crisis will perhaps be gradually noticed in the 1990s. There are many reasons for this crisis in the field of education. However, there are three main reasons: First, there are not enough education funds, and the teachers' pay is too low. At the same time, such funds have not been put to their best use. Second, there is the issue of educational legislation which was just mentioned by our fellow student Zhu Mei. Third, teachers and their successors need to improve themselves in terms of quality. However, there are not many facilities which they can use to improve themselves. In addition, the amount of financial aid to students in teachers' colleges has not been changed since the 1950s. Right now, it is still twenty yuan per student. Also, I would like to publicize a statistic. Although this figure may not be accurate, it at least reflects the problem of only 4 percent of the students in our college being willing to work as teachers. Has the government given this issue some thought and tried to increase this percentage and encourage more students to become teachers? This is my view.

[Zhu Mei:] I have some additional remarks that I would like to make. It will be difficult to remedy our nation's defects in the field of education, even if the educational funds are increased. I think that the government should take the situation in the educational field into consideration when it appraises its achievements, because education represents a long-term interest of the people. This is my view.

[He Dongchang:] Since the question of education was brought up just now, let me speak again. In accordance with the decision of the Politburo of the CPC Central Committee, a research group of the State Council was set up last April and has been in operation for a year now. The Politburo has already discussed the draft decisions on the question of education and is soliciting views from the democratic parties, the intellectual circles, and the various provinces and municipalities. For the first time since the founding of the PRC, a full session of the Central Committee will be held at an appropriate time to discuss the question of education. This is the first thing I want to say. Second, I believe that what the students said just now with regard to facts is completely true. There is no discrepancy regarding the facts. With regard to facts, what they said is true. Let me say a few words about what we should do. Regarding our mistakes in education, this is the way we speak of our mistakes: The biggest mistake of the last ten years is in the area of education. When we say in the area of education, the meaning is twofold. First, it refers to the areas of ideology, moral character, and spiritual civilization. In recent years, the social atmosphere has not been good. Among the students, the moral character in certain basic aspects is not very good either. The responsibility for this does not lie with the students— college students, primary students, or middle school students. They have been subject to the influence of the social environment. Thus, this is a question of improving our moral education, a question of moral and ethical education of the entire society. We made mistakes in this area. Second, it refers to educational undertakings. This is the area of education the students have asked about. Solutions must be found for both areas. As far as I know, the draft decision has not been finalized. It will be finalized by the Central Committee. We believe that the mistakes in education are mistakes in the overall arrangements in socialist construction. To overcome the problems in education, we therefore need to readjust the overall arrangements. The way we presented this question is very significant. This is the first point. Arrangements include the readjustment of the structure of financial input; that is, how much money will be spent and who will spend it. The structure must be readjusted. The teachers' pay must be raised, the ideological and moral education must be improved, and so on. For the Communist Party, the first thing is to increase the entire party's understanding of education. We must understand education anew. Our understanding of education in the past is not enough. With regard to primary and middle school education, the progress is not enough. There has not been enough progress in primary and middle school education during the last ten years, or even during the last forty years. We must do some soul-searching. Only by so doing can we truly resolve the problem ideologically. This is the first thing. The second thing concerns the emphasis on educational development. Higher education is very important. However, for our country to raise the quality of our entire nation, primary and middle school education and vocational education should come first. Equally important is vocational and technical education for primary and middle school graduates who cannot continue their education. A person must have skills to obtain employment. Education in these two areas is the emphasis and foundation of our education in general. Teachers colleges are very important; however, they are not the only ones which are important.

Third, teachers' pay should be increased, and their status should be raised. This is true, but there is the problem of money to be resolved. This means the government must readjust its financial structure. Beijing has already done so, and its educational expenditures have reached 20 percent of its budget, as compared to 18.1 percent last year. This means that if the Beijing government has 100 yuan, it will spend 20 yuan on education. Later, Vice-Mayor Lu will answer the question concerning your school. . . .

[Lu Yucheng:] Being concerned with education means being concerned with the quality of our people and the future of our country. I fully agree with the views you students have put forward.

Comrade He Dongchang said that the central authorities are formulating the relevant guidelines, and the Beijing government has implemented these guidelines in its plans for this year and the future. You all can see this in the government work report Mayor Chen Xitong made during the recent Beijing Municipal People's Congress. As far as the education budget is concerned, Beijing's educational budget for 1989 is 1.1 billion yuan, but with other input, the actual amount will be a little over 1.3 billion yuan this year. Our total budget is 5.2 billion. This means that 20 percent of the total budget will be spent on education. Beijing spends 3.2 billion yuan on subsidies—including subsidies for meat—for schools of higher education, including those of the central authorities. The subsidies may be even higher this year. Last year, the subsidies were a little over 3.25 billion yuan. You can see that, after spending 3.25 billion and 1.1 billion yuan, not much is left. We really have made the greatest efforts to increase the education budget. We must realize the relatively large size of various projects. This is why many of your requests cannot be fulfilled. While more time is needed for fulfilling your requests, you can see our determination. . . .

[Yuan Liben, interrupting:] Allow me to interpose. The supply of meat, eggs, and vegetables, public transportation, public parks, and the supply of soap and so forth are all subsidized in Beijing. You students may not realize this. You heard just now that subsidies amounted to 3.2 billion yuan. This is to say that large amounts of money in our budget have been used for subsidies. The subsidy was only a small percent of our budget in [1956?] and increased year by year, and now it has reached 60 percent and more money is needed for subsidies. I hope you will tell other students about this. You see, in Beijing, the purchasing price of cabbage is 11 fen, but the selling price is 3.5 fen. This means the government spends about 7 fen for subsidizing each *jin* of cabbage. Thus, the task of stabilizing commodity prices and protecting the farmers' interests is a formidable one. The prices of certain commodities have gone up only 1 fen. The price of matches, for example, has gone up from 2 fen to 3 fen per box, and this price has been the same for several years. Why has there not been another price rise? We would like you to tell the other students of the formidable problems we face in commodity price reform.

[Lu Yucheng:] You ask, why is the construction of laboratories still unfinished after so many years? In Beijing, budgets for educational construction projects have been increasing every year. In 1986, over 20 percent of the education budget was spent on construction. In 1987, it was over 30 percent. In 1988, it was over 40 percent. In 1989, the percentage will be even higher. Why is it that the Shangri-la Hotel can be built and your laboratories cannot? This is because of the different sources of capital. Money spent for educational purposes can only be drawn from tax revenues and profits various enterprises turn over to the municipal government, whereas hotels like the Shangri-la are built with foreign capital or bank loans. We cannot borrow money from banks to build laboratories because we cannot afford the repayment. I think you can understand this. The construction of laboratories will be expedited. This is a decision that has been made.

I would also like to comment on teachers. Secondary and primary school teachers are indeed the key factor for improving the quality of our education. We often say that good teachers are essential for educational development. This is why the burden of teacher training colleges is a heavy one. To encourage more outstanding middle school graduates to study in teacher training colleges, Mayor Chen said in his government report that stipends for students studying at teacher training colleges will be increased. A plan in this regard has also been drawn up. With the many reports concerning student parades recently, there is no room for our news release concerning the increase in stipends for students of teacher training colleges [laughter]. Therefore, I hope you will calm down and go back to study as soon as possible so that all the problems can be resolved more efficiently. This is my reply to your question. . . .

[Student Jiang Jingcheng:] I am Jiang Jingcheng, a student from the Beijing College of Leadership and Economic Management, admitted in 1987. I wish to point out that two large-scale student demonstrations were held on April 21 and 27. The demonstrators were cheered and assisted by hundreds of thousands of Beijing residents who lined the procession route. Some people carried weaker students on bicycles and trishaws, while others offered money, cigarettes, and food, shouting "Long live college students," "The people support you," and other slogans. Some people even broke into tears and were moved by the students' enthusiasm and sincerity. Doesn't this show that the students' movement should be affirmed and that it accords with popular sentiments? What is the government's explanation of these incidents?

[Yuan Mu:] We addressed this question at the very beginning of this meeting, as well as in many of our replies to other questions. Out of patriotic enthusiasm, most students wanted to express their desire to promote democracy, to deepen reform, to punish corrupt officials and official racketeers, and so on. This is completely understandable to the party and the government, both of which consider the students' desire to be entirely in accord with the goal that the party and government should strive to achieve in their work.

Now, we hope that the students who have not resumed class will do so as soon as possible. I hope that our young comrades will treasure their right, opportunity, and time to study. Wasting time is a regrettable thing. Students can improve their knowledge and talents while in school and make great contributions to the country after they graduate.

[He Dongchang:] I would like to say a few more things about the question raised by the student from the College of Leadership. Students support the Communist Party, the socialist system, and the Constitution, and they oppose corruption, official racketeers, and others. All this truly reflects popular sentiments, as well as our party's desire. We share a unanimous view on this point. Students should be aware of one thing. If our parades did not follow this line, or if some people, even a few of them, had sneaked into the ranks and shouted slogans that oppose the four cardinal principles and call for the redress of the chieftains who practice liberalization, would they then have received so much support? This is another question. Why did some people change the slogans? This was because most students and residents did not approve of them. Some extremists who had shouted the wrong slogans in the past have corrected themselves. This is good, and it is welcomed. But students should be aware of the bearded people—I mean those who are older—and see if they have truly mended their ways. This question requires some deep thought. . . .

[Student Wu Junjie:] I am a student in the Department of Law at the University of Political Science and Law. My name is Wu Junjie. I have come to today's consultative discussion meeting as a guest at the invitation of the All-China Students Federation. . . .

First, I would like to talk about the views put forward by the editorial of *Renmin ribao* on April 26. At present, the broad masses of fellow students are of the opinion that they cannot agree with the term "disturbance." We are not creating a disturbance. Second, my fellow students do not agree with the term "a handful of people." Most students have taken part in this activity. The editorial, the broad masses of students believe, is a calumniation and smear against the students. Third, they do not agree with the editorial's determination of the nature of the students' demonstration as an activity that advocates opposition to the party and the government. The broad masses of fellow students still love their country. Shortly before this consultative discussion meeting began, Comrade Yuan Mu said something to the effect that the editorial of the central authorities is not directed against the broad masses of college students but against only a handful of people among them. This I have clearly heard. What, then, do fellow students think about it? My fellow students believe that the editorial of the central authorities gives a final conclusion to the whole incident. Since the college students present as a whole constituted the main body of the incident, a question arises as to whether the final conclusion should be directed against the handful of people or against the mainstream and the majority of the movement [applause]. . . .

My second topic deals with the real situation on April 22. Though some students may blame Li Peng for not having come out, and feel themselves cheated, students are now saying that Li Peng actually did not say he wanted to come out, no matter what replies are offered by the government and no matter how the real situation stands. If that is the case, why is a premier unable to come out to meet his people? Can one be qualified to be the people's premier if he is afraid of meeting the people? This is what is actually on the minds of my fellow students. I am stating their views here as they really are. If the excuse was offered that Li Peng did not know about this matter, then something must be really wrong with our system. A call raised in unison by 100,000 college students in the square asking Li Peng to come out and the petition they were submitting should be conveyed to Li Peng through an unobstructed channel.

Third, fellow students stress that if the real situation of the beating during the April 20 incident is admitted, and if policemen did slash demonstrators with leather belts, they hope the government will apologize and find out and deal with the culprits guilty of beating, particularly the culprits who assaulted Huang Zhiyong of our school. This is what is on the minds of my fellow students.

[Yuan Liben:] What should be addressed here is what to do. Comrades Yuan Mu and He Dongchang, I think that many rumors about the April 20 incident have been spread in various schools not only in Beijing but also in other places over the past few days. To be frank, I do not understand what the truth of the April 20 incident means. [An unidentified individual interrupts, saying that it means seeking truth from facts.] I happened to be on the scene when the April 20 incident occurred. Let me first remind you what had occurred in front of the Xinhua Gate on April 20. The incident here lasted from 11:30 P.M. to 4:50 A.M. Some students on the scene also said that police exercised great restraint. After the participants left the scene, smashed soft-drink bottles were seen everywhere in front of the Xinhua Gate. I believe students also saw this. As police were maintaining order and persuading the participants to disperse, some people were throwing rocks from behind, although they did not throw too many rocks. Did students know this? Rocks are not usually seen on the streets. Where did the rocks come from? Then, there were many soft-drink bottles, which was something very strange. Seven or eight armed policemen were injured by soft-drink bottles. Students on the scene should have been able to see that armed policemen also exercised great restraint. . . .

Now, I would like to say something that might not be appropriate. While we permit cadres and students to make mistakes, we must also understand that some of the young armed policemen had just joined the police force. Although we have time and time again educated them, can we guarantee that not one single armed policeman among the several thousands will not violate the rules governing their discipline? I believe the student [who was beaten up] can understand this. We will never tolerate such a policeman because he represents the image of the government and the image of all other public security personnel and armed policemen. . . .

Students should think this over. I would like to tell you that the government has its own difficulties. There have been all kinds of hearsay. Some people want the hearsay to be published in the newspaper. Can this be done? I can only talk about the general situation. If the mainstream is harmonious—that is, if the armed police had exercised restraint—the students should consider what the attitude of the government and public security fighters was in handling these incidents. This is one thing.

Next, I think we cannot deny the fact that in every student demonstration, there are always a few bad elements, as well as the idlers in the society. For instance, those who were engaged in beating, smashing, and looting in Xi'an and Changsha were idlers.

[He Dongchang:] There were also some perverts.

[Yuan Liben:] . . . Students should know that the government is not opposed to them. Although we disapprove of some of your actions, from the bottom of our hearts, we still regard you as children, and you are our students. This is the basic idea. I hope students will go back and convey this idea to other students. You can also calmly analyze the two demonstrations. This much I have to say. . . .

[He Dongchang:] We have different views on some problems. It depends on how you look at it. I think we can take our time. We should seek truth from facts. Regarding the matters involving the University of Political Science and Law, the armed police, and Tiananmen, students may check with the armed police. I think we should seek truth from facts by conducting studies and investigations. We should not handle things based on our feelings. There is a song called "Move Ahead by Following Our Feelings." We cannot move ahead by simply following our feelings.

I think we can call it a day at this point. We will talk again in the future when an opportunity arises.

28
Make Further Efforts to Carry Forward the May 4th Spirit in the New Age of Construction and Reform

ZHAO ZIYANG

Source: Beijing Television Domestic Service, May 3, 1989; FBIS, May 3, pp. 16–19.

Young friends, students, and comrades: The seventieth anniversary of the May 4th Movement is a great festival for Chinese youth and the entire Chinese nation. It is of vital significance for us to commemorate the seventieth anniversary of the

May 4th Movement and make further efforts to carry forward the May 4th spirit today, when the fortieth anniversary of the founding of the People's Republic of China is forthcoming, when it has been ten years since the beginning of China's new age of socialist modernization and all-around reform opened by the third plenary session of the Eleventh CPC Central Committee, and when the people and youth throughout the country are required to unite more closely and work with one mind to overcome difficulties, safeguard social stability, and promote construction and reform.

First of all, the May 4th Movement was a great patriotic movement against imperialism and feudalism. The most general and profound reasons that the broad masses of youth and people of all walks of life were attracted to this movement were their deep concern about the peril of our country and the destiny of our nation, and their warm yearning for building a new China that is truly independent, free, prosperous, rich, and strong.

The May 4th Movement was also a great new cultural movement, a great ideological enlightenment, and an emancipation movement. The broad masses of youth at that time began to see themselves, China, and the world in a new perspective under the banner of democracy and science. Some of the most enlightened young intellectuals finally chose the Marxist truth and, in 1921, founded the Communist Party of China through exploration and comparison of various social and political theories, planned to save the nation from extinction.

The Chinese people and Chinese youth carried out a new, long and extremely arduous democratic revolutionary struggle under the leadership of the Communist Party of China. The process of this great revolution of the people was a process which combined Marxism with the practice of the Chinese revolution and a process in which the May 4th spirit of patriotism, democracy, and science was carried forward continuously.

The victory of the people's revolution opened a new page in Chinese history. During the one hundred years between the old democratic revolution and the new democratic revolution, our central task was destruction, which was directed at the old system that obstructed China's advance. After the founding of the People's Republic of China, our central task has become one of construction to build a socialist New China. This transition from destruction to construction represented a most profound change in the historic mission for the Chinese people. In the past, we were not able to realize this change effectively and with full consciousness. The chaotic decade of the Cultural Revolution represented an all the more catastrophic destruction that went diametrically against what was called for by history.

The entire party and the people of the entire country have embarked on the correct road of building socialism with Chinese characteristics and unswervingly shifted the focus of work to the drive for socialist modernization after summing up historical experience and lessons since the third plenary session of the Eleventh CPC Central Committee. In addition, centered on the cause of construction, we have decided to carry out the task of reforming the political and economic systems. Thus, we have entered a new era, an era for socialist modernization and comprehensive reform.

As we commemorate the May 4th Movement now, we should conform with the need of the new era, or, in other words, the need for construction. We should inherit and carry forward the patriotic, democratic, and scientific spirit of the May 4th Movement, add new meaning to it, and elevate it to a new height. Our purpose in stressing patriotism today is to build China well, realize the four modernizations, and invigorate the Chinese nation. Our purpose is to focus attention on the development of the productive forces and use this as the pillar to promote the prosperity of the socialist planned commodity economy by carrying out reforms of the economic, political, science and educational systems, establish socialist democratic politics and develop scientific culture—that is, socialist spiritual civilization guided by Marxism.

When we said that the Chinese people had stood up, at the time of the founding of the PRC, we were referring to the fact that the Chinese people were no longer dominated politically by imperialism or ruled by the reactionary classes. The people themselves had become the masters of their country. What we want to add now is that the Chinese people have not completed the final phase of the task of standing up. Only after arduous struggle by the people of several generations to come and the realization of the goal of socialist modernization will China be able to completely stand up in the development of its economy, culture, science and technology, and society, and in its overall strength vis-à-vis the world. It is only through this course of struggle can socialist superiority gradually and fully manifest itself in the land of China.

We must carry forward the patriotic spirit to turn it into a powerful rallying force to inspire young people in their hundreds of millions to display a spirit of devotion, to inspire the masses of workers, peasants, technicians, teachers, students, reporters, physicians, scientists, writers and artists, entrepreneurs, civil servants, officers and men of the People's Liberation Army, and other laborers of various trades and departments to display a spirit of devotion, to strive to build a powerful, democratic, civilized, great socialist modern country.

Likewise, when we stress democracy and science today, we should do so by keeping the focal point of construction and using democracy and science to serve it. China's great project of socialist modernization inevitably will be a great project in transforming the entire society and raising the quality of the whole nation. We must transform our backwardness, break free from poverty, overcome ignorance, and eliminate step-by-step all sorts of undemocratic and unscientific ideas and habits existing in social life and the people's minds.

In a large country with a population of 1.1 billion, we should, in all aspects of social life and all our reform and construction work, carry on the spirit of democracy, build up a system of democracy, develop a scientific spirit, do everything with a scientific attitude in light of the actual conditions, and gradually and greatly promote science and education. We will not have socialism and socialist modernization without democracy and science. We must study and develop democracy and study and respect science in our building of socialist modernization and in the course of all-around reform. This is an extremely important task facing the Communist Party of China. This is also an extremely important task facing the people and all youth of the entire country.

Comrades, our grand and arduous tasks of socialist modernization and reform can only be successfully carried out in a stable social and political environment, instead of a time of turmoil. We have been able to implement the party's correct principles and policies and achieve tangible results in reform and construction in the ten years following the third plenary session of the Eleventh CPC Central Committee. The most important reason is because we have kept social stability. This is the result of concerted efforts by people of the entire country. The workers, peasants, intellectuals, young students, people of all nationalities, all parties, and people of all circles in the country have made efforts to promote stability and have enjoyed the benefits of stability. On the issue of stability, which is related to the entire situation of the country, we must have a common understanding and work in full cooperation and with unity of purpose. This is not an easy thing. When people are living in a state of stability, they sometimes do not realize the importance of stability. However, if one day stability disappears, it will be too late to repent. We will not be able to accomplish even one of the things desired by all of us. Even our achieved results will be lost in a single day.

If we destroy stability, what do we have? Can we win democracy and achieve progress in science? Can we enjoy the fruits of the reform and construction? Can we revitalize the motherland? No, we cannot do any of this. All we will have is turmoil. Were there only a few cases of turmoil in our country? From 1840 to this year, over a period of about 150 years, we have only had less than 30 years of peace and stability. For more than 120 years, our country was in a muddle caused by imperialism, feudalism, and bureaucratic capitalism. The other 10 years and more were ruined by Lin Biao, the Gang of Four and our own mistakes in subjective guidance.

What makes everyone feel gratified these days is that we have had a good life since the third plenary session of the Eleventh CPC Central Committee. If large-scale unrest and social conflict take place again, if anarchy occurs, which will cause disorder among the people—disturb social order, production order, study order, and work order; create confusion among the people themselves; and cause disquiet for the entire country—then China, a country with a very promising and bright future, will turn into a country of unrest and instability, a country with no future. If this situation takes place, then national construction, reforms, democracy, and science, which have been hoped for by the people of the whole country, including the vast numbers of youths and students, will all go up in smoke. Moreover, all kinds of antidemocratic and antiscientific things and all kinds of ignorant and even [words indistinct] matters will begin to spread. The whole party, people of the whole country, and youths of the whole country are all opposed to unrest in a clear-cut manner and are determined to maintain the political stability and unity we have earned through hard work. Maintaining stability does not mean that we do not want democracy; it means that we want to promote democracy in an orderly manner and embody democracy in the form of law.

While we develop a new order of socialist commodity economy, we should also develop a new order of socialist democracy. This new order of democracy is one built on the basis of the four cardinal principles. It is a requirement for carrying out modernization and reforms, and a requirement for maintaining a stable social and political environment. Stability, [words indistinct], reason, order, and rule by law are requirements for carrying out construction and reforms and are also requirements for promoting democracy and science. If we think and do our work according to these requirements, then we will succeed in carrying out our undertakings. Our great and arduous tasks of modernization and reform can advance steadily only under the correct and powerful leadership of the Chinese Communist Party. Our party is a party that upholds Marxism and develops it in a creative manner, a party that respects knowledge and people of knowledge, and a party that relies on the people and on youth. In the past 68 years, our party, in addition to having made great historical contributions to the Chinese people, has committed many major and minor mistakes of all kinds. However, history has proved and will continue to prove that our party is a party with a spirit of self-criticism and strong vitality. The vast numbers of youth, including the vast numbers of students, hope to promote democracy and call for punishing people who commit bribery and are guilty of corruption. This is also the exact intention of our party.

The heart of the Communist Party of China is linked with the hearts of the people and the youth. Let us exchange ideas and have mutual understanding. Let us do a better job in our future tasks amid an atmosphere of stability and unity and in the spirit of crossing a river in the same boat. While transforming the objective world, we must transform our own subjective world. In the course of construction and reform, our society and the entire nation are undergoing a profound transformation. Our party is also undergoing a profound transformation. The purpose of this transformation is not to change the nature of our party and its inherent superiority. It is to enable our party to better assume the heavy task of leading the people to build socialist modernization with Chinese characteristics. The construction, reform, democracy, and science of our country will vanish if they become divorced from the leadership of the Communist Party of China. Without the leadership of the Communist Party of China, we could not have achieved the victory of the Chinese revolution, could not have today's socialist China, cannot achieve socialist modernization in China, and will not have a good future and hope for our country.

Concerning the patterns of the historical development in China since the May 4th Movement, this is precisely the most important pattern. By understanding and respecting this law, we will be able to win success in our cause.

Comrades, the predecessors of the May 4th Movement repeatedly expressed their confidence that the building of a youthful China would rely solely on the awakening of the young people. Their confidence in and hope for the young people and their far-sighted views and optimism are still extremely important things in judging the Chinese young people and China's destination.

When we commemorate the seventieth anniversary of the May 4th Movement, we must review the past and look to the future. The party and the people have placed their hope on the youth.

Comrade Deng Xiaoping has shown great concern for and loves the young generation. He has ardent expectations concerning the important role of the young people of the contemporary era in carrying out the reform and construction work. He said: The growth of the young generation is precisely the dependable hope for developing and succeeding in our cause.

In the ten years since the third plenary session of the Eleventh CPC Central Committee, socialist modernization and the reforms have been the main tasks of our times. We have invariably called on the young generation to follow the party in making progress in the great historical cause [applause].

Young people should foster the spirit of continuing to advance and make explorations in the course of construction. Without explorations, there will be no creation. Without creation, it is impossible for construction and reform to advance. The young people's initiative to demand that their potential ability be put into play and their own value be turned into reality should be safeguarded. This way they will be able to overcome difficulties and temper themselves and improve themselves in carrying out the cause of modernization. The value of young people lies in that they like to think deeply and dare to explore new knowledge. Without thinking, how can young people make progress? Without different fields of new knowledge, it is impossible to enrich themselves and to make comparisons. In the course of thinking deeply, partiality and perplexity are unavoidable. However, as long as they are patriotic, integrating their duty with the destiny of the state; as long as they possess a democratic spirit, integrating the role of the individual with the strength of the collective; as long as they possess a scientific spirit, integrating good ideals with practical conditions, through their own thinking and explorations the young people will certainly be able to overcome their shortcomings and defects, to understand the people's genuine interests and needs, to understand the calls and trends of the times, and to understand that their efforts and those of their predecessors are connected and that they have a noble mission to perform for the future of the country. In this way, young people will certainly better understand the historical necessity of adhering to the socialist road, adhering to the people's democratic dictatorship, adhering to the leadership of the Communist Party of China, and adhering to Marxism–Leninism–Mao Zedong Thought. They will better understand the historical necessity of adhering to the general policy of reform and opening to the outside world, and from the future of the country as a whole they will clearly understand which road they must take.

Young people should foster a spirit for down-to-earth struggle in the course of construction. To build this big country of ours—a country with a large population and a backward economy and culture—into a modern socialist country is a great, protracted, extremely arduous, and complicated cause, which calls for sustained efforts by several generations of our entire nation. The young people of this generation are destined by history to be a generation of people who must immerse themselves in hard work for China's drive for socialist modernization in a pioneering spirit. There is no short cut to reform and construction. Every advance we make is inseparable from the labor and struggle on the part of the people, particularly young people. What we need to do is to wage a firm and indomitable, down-to-earth and protracted struggle. We have to have a clear understanding of our historical mission, be clear-minded, rational, persistent and steady, seek truth from facts and work hard. These are the most valuable and necessary qualities for the young people of China in the contemporary era.

The Communist Youth League [CYL] is the mass organization of the advanced young people of our country. In the course of development in the youth movement during the past seventy years, in the course of creating a new situation in youth work in an all-around way during the ten years of reform and open policy, it has played an irreplaceable and tremendous role. In the new historical period, our party should attach greater importance to, be more concerned about, and give greater support to the work of the CYL.

For its part, the CYL should make sure it does not fail to meet the party's expectations and join the youth organizations, including youth federations, and students' federations, in maintaining close and dynamic ties with the broadest masses of young people. It should make even better efforts in playing its role as the party's assistant and reserve force—the role of bridge and bond between the party and the government on the one side and the masses of young people on the other—as well as its role as social representative of young people's interests and demands, and truly build the CYL into a big school for young people to study communism in the course of practice.

In another eleven years from now we will enter the twenty-first century. The future belongs to young people. The younger generation that stands astride these two centuries is shouldering a glorious and arduous mission. The party pins its hope on you. The people pin their hopes on you. All young people across the country, all compatriots of the whole country, let us work with one heart and one mind, work hard, surmount all difficulties and make joint efforts to invigorate the Chinese nation.

29
Zhao Urges Nation
to Maintain Stability

Source: *China Daily* (Beijing—in English) (May 4, 1989): 1.

The leader of the Chinese Communist Party (CPC) called on the entire nation to firmly oppose social unrest and maintain stability and unity, essential to reform and modernization.

Addressing a meeting yesterday commemorating the seventieth anniversary of the May 4th Movement, Zhao Ziyang, general secretary of the CPC Central Committee, asked the Chinese people to appreciate the hard-won stable situation since the third plenary session of the Eleventh Central Committee of the CPC.

"We have lived ten good years since then," Zhao said. But if social unrest returns with large-scale social conflict and disruption of production, study and work, a country of promise will be turned into a country of hopelessness and turbulence, he added.

Zhao's speech was amid the two-week-old campus unrest in Beijing, which culminated last Thursday in a mass student demonstration crying for democracy, press freedom, and the elimination of corruption following an eleven-day boycott of classes at some universities.

If social disturbances arise, there will be no room for the economic construction, reform and the development of democracy and science that are expected by the whole country, including the vast majority of students, Zhao said.

"When we have stability we sometimes aren't aware of its value," he said to the more than 8,000 young people, including university students, who attended the meeting at the Great Hall of the People. "But once we lose it we feel deep regret."

Recalling modern Chinese history since 1840, when China was first defeated by the Western powers in the "Opium War," the party leader asked, "Haven't we had enough of social turmoil?" Since that time China has had only about twenty years of stability.

Zhao said stability does not mean the elimination of democracy, but democracy should be channeled into order and legality.

"Stability, sober-mindedness, order and legality are not only required for economic construction and reform, but also for democracy and science," he said.

The May 4th Movement of 1919 was hailed as a new cultural movement that strongly urged the introduction of democracy and science into traditional China. The meeting was also attended by other party and state leaders, including President Yang Shangkun, Premier Li Peng, Chairman of the National People's Congress Wan Li, and Qiao Shi, Hu Qili, and Yao Yilin.

Also present were Deng Yingchao and other veterans who took part in the May 4th Movement seventy years ago.

Zhao also said that the demands of students and other people for promoting democracy, combating corruption, and developing education and science correspond with the aims of the party.

He said the hearts of the party, of youth, and of other people are linked to one another.

"Let's understand one another in the future, do a better job and cross rivers in the same boat in stability and unity," Zhao said.

He said the party has made "great historical contributions" to the Chinese people since it was founded sixty-eight years ago. It has made some errors, but history has proved and will continue to prove that the party is vigorous and full of spirit of self-criticism.

He said the party is changing greatly in the country's construction and reform.

"The transformation aims to improve the party's ability to do an even better job in leading the Chinese people in their modernization drive, instead of changing the party's nature and weakening it."

Zhao said China's construction and reform, as well as its democratic and scientific progress, cannot be separated from the leadership of the party.

He said efforts should be made to encourage young people to demonstrate their potential, to appreciate their own value, and to develop their character.

Zhao said it is inevitable that young people should make some errors or be indecisive in their thinking and pioneering.

He encouraged young people, by displaying the spirit of patriotism, democracy and science, to combine personal responsibility with the destiny of the nation, the individual's role with the collective, and great ideals with actual conditions.

There is no shortcut in reform and construction, Zhao said. No step in the cause can be divorced from the efforts and struggle of the people, the young in particular.

At the meeting, seventy young people were commended by the Communist Youth League Central Committee and the All-China Youth Federation for their outstanding contributions to socialist construction and reform.

30
State Rejects Students' List of Demands

Source: *China Daily* (Beijing—in English) (May 4, 1989): 1.

State Council spokesman Yuan Mu yesterday expressed government willingness to continue dialogue with striking students but rejected as "unreasonable" the preconditions set by students in a petition.

In a morning press conference televised repeatedly throughout yesterday, Yuan said that discussions between government officials and students should be based upon sincerity and mutual trust and "should not be turned into a negotiation between adversaries."

Students on Tuesday had submitted their revised list of ten demands to the National People's Congress (NPC) Standing Committee, the Party Central Committee and the State Council. The act followed three weeks of campus unrest, student demonstrations, class boycotts and two government-organized dialogues.

Yuan said the government sincerely protects students, and cherishes and respects their patriotic enthusiasm. And the government has been dealing with the student problems with great care, he said.

The students said they would take to the streets again today if the government failed to agree to their demands by noon yesterday.

The government spokesman described the students' main preconditions for talks as "unreasonable, emotionally impulsive and menacing to the government in the form of an ultimatum."

He said students were unreasonable to demand that their unregistered Autonomous Union of Beijing Colleges and Universities be an organizer and participant in the dialogues, replacing the All-China Students' Federation, the Beijing Students' Federation, student associations and post-graduate associations in colleges and universities.

Yuan said that if the Government recognizes other student organizations "set up in special conditions" and has dialogue with them, "it will only make the disunity among the students more serious."

Yuan said the students' deadline, the demand for an equal standing with the government and even a status above the government, the claim that students should decide who on the government side should attend the dialogue, were all harsh terms.

Yuan said this showed that a small minority of people were inciting the students behind the scenes.

"Many signs and facts have proved that a handful of people are organizing the student movement," Yuan said, adding that he believes most of them are not students although a few students are involved. He said that the U.S.-based Alliance for Democracy, proclaimed by China to be a reactionary organization, had been playing a role.

He said he hoped the majority of students would separate themselves from so-called inciters, resume classes and stop demonstrations.

"I hope that tomorrow there will be no mass demonstration, but maybe my hopes will not come true," he said, adding that central authorities would continue to adopt the correct measures and attitude toward the students in the event of a protest.

He said he was confident that the students would not disrupt the annual meeting of the Asian Development Bank and activities marking the May 4th Movement to be held in the Great Hall of the People and at Tiananmen Square respectively today.

Responding to foreign concerns about political unrest in China, Yuan reaffirmed that the reform and open policy would remain.

31
Students' Reasonable Demands to Be Met through Democratic, Legal Channels: Zhao

Source: Xinhua (Beijing—in English), May 4, 1989; FBIS, May 4, p. 1.

There will be no big riots in China and the ongoing student demonstrations will gradually calm down, said Zhao Ziyang, general secretary of the Chinese Communist Party Central Committee, here today.

Reasonable demands from the students should be met through democratic and legal means, through reforms and through various other means in line with reason and order, the general secretary said. But what are needed most at present are calm, reason, restraint, and order.

At a meeting with some governors of the Asian Development Bank (ADB) now attending the twenty-second annual meeting of the ADB's board of governors in Beijing, the general secretary said that the recent demonstrations by some university students did not indicate political instability in China. And the demonstrators meant in no way to oppose the fundamental system of China, but to correct the errors in the work of the party and the government.

Zhao said that the slogans of the demonstrators reflected their fundamental attitude toward the Chinese Communist Party and the government: both satisfaction and dissatisfaction. The slogans included "support the Communist Party," "support socialism," "support the Constitution and reform," and "advance democracy" and "oppose corruption."

The students are satisfied with the achievements of China's ten-year reform and economic construction, and with the progress and development of the country. What they are most dissatisfied with are errors and mistakes in the party and the government's work. However, Zhao said the students' demands for correcting errors so as to march forward coincide with those of the party and the government.

"It is inevitable that some people want to take advantage of the students' demonstrations for their ulterior motives as China is so large. And it would be unimaginable not to have such a tiny number of people doing so," Zhao said. However, he added, vigilance is needed to guard against this minority, and "I think the overwhelming majority of the students will be aware of this."

"Though demonstrations are still underway in Beijing and some other big cities in the country, I still believe there will be no big riots and the demonstrations will gradually calm down," he said. "I'm very confident about this."

The reasons why students are dissatisfied with the amount of corruption, which the party and the government have been tackling over the past few years, stem from imperfections in the socialist legal system and democratic supervision, and lack of openness in the system of work, which gives rise to rumors and exaggerations. There does exist the phenomenon that some people seek privileges and violate laws and discipline, he admitted, but the number is not as large as people say and the cases are not so serious as hearsay has it.

As a matter of fact, most of the officials working at the party and government institutions have no other income except their monthly salaries, Zhao said. Neither have they legitimate privileges.

Corruption will definitely be eventually wiped out, but this has to keep pace with the improvement of the legal system and democratic supervision, and the implementation of other reform measures. In this way, the crackdown on corruption is linked to the building up of the country's legal system.

The issue of student demonstrations should also be handled through legal and democratic means in an orderly and reasonable atmosphere, Zhao said.

In order to exchange views, promote mutual understanding and explore settlement of issues of public concern, the general secretary urged that extensive consultations and dialogues be pursued with students, workers, intellectuals, non-Communist parties and leading personages from all walks of life.

Sober-mindedness, reason, restraint, order, and devotion to democracy and legality are most essential for resolving the problems, he stressed. The party and government are ready to take such measures, and "I believe students and people of various walks of life will take the same attitude," he said.

"If we all do things this way, we can surely maintain stability and thus enjoy unity at a new and higher level," the general secretary explained.

Based on such stability and unity, the country's political and economic restructuring and the modernization drive will advance more smoothly, Zhao said. While showing optimism about the future of China's reform and political stability, Zhao promised a better environment for foreign investment.

32
Zhao Ziyang's Speech Welcomed by Students

Source: Xinhua (Hong Kong Service), May 5, 1989; FBIS, May 6, pp. 3–4.

The speech made by Zhao Ziyang while meeting with guests from the Asian Development Bank's annual meeting and broadcast by the Central Television Station at 1900 yesterday has produced wide repercussions in universities and colleges in Beijing.

Renmin ribao and *Zhongguo qingnian bao* [China youth daily] today report students' responses to the speech.

According to a report, when students of the Chinese University of Political Science and Law were listening to the broadcast of Zhao Ziyang's speech in the campus at 10:00 P.M. yesterday, they widely discussed it. When the speech finished, the audience applauded. A student of the department of economics and law of the class of 1986 said, "Zhao Ziyang's speech is fairly objective and practical. I agree with the four words he mentioned: soberness, reason, restraint, and order. This is what we need now. It is the wisest method to solve the problems along the track of democracy and the legal system." A student added, "We earnestly hope that the party and government will truly strengthen the building of democracy and the legal system, go about things in accordance with law, and increase openness."

In a student dormitory of Beijing University, several students studying for Ph.D.s said: Zhao Ziyang's speech is much fairer. The present student movement is a patriotic democratic movement in which we voluntarily participated after using our brains to think about it seriously. The "Great Cultural Revolution" was wrongly launched by leaders, and utilized by the counterrevolutionary clique at the upper level, and was a disturbance imposed from above. But this is not the case with the current student movement. It is incorrect to compare it with the "Great Cultural Revolution."

More than 1,000 people in Beijing University got together to listen to the broadcast of Zhao Ziyang's speech. A young teacher who taught economics told our reporter, "This is a moderate speech which shows the sincerity of the party and government. It will play a positive role in solving the current problems." A student who was more active in the demonstration said, "We welcome such an attitude for solving problems, but the key lies in the dialogue to be conducted in the next stage, and in whether practical problems can be solved."

On the second floor of the student dormitory of the Chinese People's University, several postgraduate students talked with our reporters. They had just come back from the demonstration and knew the contents of Zhao Ziyang's speech. One of them said, "Both leaders and students must have reason, and Ziyang's speech is reasonable enough." A postgraduate student of the department of statistics said, "Let us funnel problems through normal channels. But guarantee must, first of all, be made that the channels are truly unimpeded. Otherwise, how can we funnel the problems?"

Some students of the Chinese People's University who were interviewed pointed out: Zhao Ziyang's speech is permeated with the spirit of full understanding. We are not only "juniors," but also citizens. The government must be the government of the citizens, but not the government of children. When it is conducting a dialogue with students, it must not take a patriarchal attitude.

Several postgraduate students of Qinghua University said: Zhao Ziyang's speech earnestly affirms students' patriotic enthusiasm and affirms the main trends of the movement. This tallies with reality. If the government had taken such an attitude right from the very beginning, the mess could possibly have been avoided. Another student added: We and the government and the state are on the same boat. We always have the desires of "repairing the boat." Our reporters found out that the campus of the Qinghua University was quiet, and students participating in the demonstration had returned to the university. A number of students were reviewing their lessons. A student of the automotive department of the 1987 class said, "We can accept Zhao Ziyang's speech. Students' patriotic enthusiasm must be understood." Some students, who had just finished watching a videotape on the May 4th Movement in the studio, told our reporters, "Boycott classes, don't boycott study" has actually affected our study. Now everyone must remain calm. Anyway, it is time to resume classes.

After listening to Zhao Ziyang's speech, students of Jiaotong University in the north decided to resume classes on May 5.

At Beijing Normal University, President Wang Zikun, who had just come out of a student dormitory, told our reporters: "Ziyang's speech is more comprehensive. He affirms the achievement in reform and construction over the past ten years and points out the existing serious problems such as corruption, corrupted phenomena, and so on. The actions of students have reflected that a fairly large number of the masses are dissatisfied with the corrupted phenomena. I just visited students at their dormitory. I want them to do two things: first, read carefully Ziyang's speech tomorrow, and second, resume classes as early as possible."

Our reporters have also learned that some university and college students have taken exception to certain things in Zhao Ziyang's speech.

33
Hunger Strike Announcement

Source: Originally printed at Tiananmen Square in *Xinwen daobao* (News express), May 12, 1989; reprinted in *Zhongguo zhichun* (China spring) (New York) 75 (August 1989): 11–12.

In this bright sunny month of May, we are on a hunger strike. In this best moment of our youth, we have no choice but to leave behind us everything beautiful about life. But how reluctant, how unwilling we are!

However, the country has come to this juncture: rampant inflation; widespread illegal business dealings by corrupt officials; the dominance of abusive power; the corruption of bureaucrats; the fleeing of a large number of good people to other countries; and the deterioration of law and order. Compatriots and all fellow countrymen with a conscience, at this critical moment of life and death of our people, please listen to our voice:

This country is our country,

The people are our people.

The government is our government.

Who will shout if we don't?

Who will act if we don't?

Although our shoulders are still tender, although death for us is still seemingly too harsh to bear, we have to part with life. When history demands us to do so, we have no choice but to die.

Our national sentiment at its purest and our loyalty at its best are labeled as "chaotic disturbance"; as "with an ulterior motive"; and as "manipulated by a small gang."

We request all honorable Chinese, every worker, peasant, soldier, ordinary citizen, intellectual, and renowned individuals, government officials, police and those who fabricated our crimes to put their hands over their hearts and examine their conscience: what crime have we committed? Are we creating chaotic disturbances? We walk out of classrooms, we march, we hunger strike, we hide. Yet our feelings are betrayed time after time. We bear the suffering of hunger to pursue the truth, and all we get is the beatings of the police. When we kneel down to beg for democracy, we are being ignored. Our request for dialogue on equal terms is met with delay after delay. Our student leaders encounter personal dangers.

What do we do?

Democracy is the most noble meaning of life; freedom is a basic human right. But the price of democracy and freedom is our life. Can the Chinese people be proud of this?

We have no other alternative but to hunger strike. We have to strike.

It is with the spirit of death that we fight for life.

But we are still children, we are still children! Mother China, please take a hard look at your children. Hunger is ruthlessly destroying their youth. Are you really not touched when death is approaching them?

We do not want to die. In fact, we wish to continue to live comfortably because we are in the prime years of our lives. We do not wish to die; we want to be able to study properly. Our homeland is so poor. It seems irresponsible of us to desert our homeland to die. Death is definitely not our pursuit. But if the death of a single person or a number of persons would enable a larger number of people to live better, or if the death can make our homeland stronger and more prosperous, then we have no right to drag on an ignoble existence.

When we are suffering from hunger, moms and dads, please don't be sad. When we bid farewell to life, uncles and aunts, please don't be heart-broken. Our only hope is that the Chinese people will live better. We have only one request: please don't forget that we are definitely not after death. Democracy is not the private matter of a few individuals, and the enterprise of building democracy is definitely not to be accomplished in a single generation.

It is through death that we await a far-reaching and perpetual echo by others.

When a person is about to die, he speaks from his heart. When a horse is about to die, its cries are sad.

Farewell comrades, take care, the same loyalty and faith bind the living and the dead.

Farewell loved ones, take care. I don't want to leave you, but I have to part with life.

Farewell moms and dads, please forgive us. Your children cannot have loyalty to our country and filial piety to you at the same time.

Farewell fellow countrymen, please permit us to repay our country in the only way left to us. The pledge that is delivered by death will one day clear the sky of our republic.

The reasons of our hunger strike are: first, to protest the cold and apathetic attitude of our government towards the students' strike; second, to protest the delay of our higher learning; and third, to protest the government's continuous distortions in its reporting of this patriotic and democratic movement of students, and their labeling it as "chaotic disturbance."

The demands from the hunger strikers are: first, on equal basis, the government should immediately conduct concrete and substantial dialogues with the delegation of Beijing institutes of higher learning. Second, the government should give this movement a correct name, a fair and unbiased assessment, and should affirm that this is a patriotic and democratic students' movement.

The date for the hunger strike is 2:00 P.M., May 13; location, Tiananmen Square.

This is not a chaotic disturbance. Its name should be immediately rectified. Immediate dialogue! No more delays! Hunger strike for the people! We have no choice. We appeal to world opinion to support us. We appeal to all democratic forces to support us.

Beijing, China

34
Zhao Ziyang Meets Mikhail Gorbachev

Source: Beijing Television Service, May 16, 1989; FBIS, May 17, pp. 13–15.

[Announcer-read report with video on meeting between General Secretary Zhao Ziyang and General Secretary Mikhail Gorbachev at the Diaoyutai State Guesthouse.]

[Video opens with the caption: "Important News," followed by shots of Zhao and Gorbachev speaking through interpreters.] General Secretaries Zhao Ziyang and Mikhail Gorbachev held a friendly meeting at the Diaoyutai State Guesthouse at 1740 [0840 GMT] today.

Gorbachev expressed great pleasure at meeting with Zhao Ziyang. He said:

Major changes are taking place in the relations between our two countries. I had a meeting with Comrade Deng Xiaoping this morning, a meeting which was rich in content. We had a good conversation. We are both very satisfied.

Gorbachev noted: Both the Soviet Union and China are carrying out reforms. These reforms are of great significance to our two countries, and even to the entire world. The Soviet people are very much concerned about China's reforms and they highly appreciate the achievements of the Chinese people under the leadership of the CPC. Reform at the present time is no easy job. One cannot expect reform to succeed overnight.

Gorbachev also briefed Zhao Ziyang on the necessity and progress of reform in the Soviet Union, as well as the progress made in developing its legal system.

Zhao Ziyang stated: Through the joint efforts of the two sides, the summit between you and Comrade Deng Xiaoping was realized this morning. As recognized at home and abroad, Comrade Deng Xiaoping has been the leader of our party since the third plenary session of the Eleventh CPC Central Committee. Comrade Deng Xiaoping stepped down from the Central Committee and the Standing Committee of the Politburo of his own accord at the Thirteenth CPC Congress. However, all the comrades in our party hold that in the interests of the party we still need Comrade Deng Xiaoping, his wisdom and his experience. This is of vital importance to our party. Therefore, the first plenary session of the Thirteenth CPC Congress made the solemn decision that we still need Comrade Deng Xiaoping at the helm when it comes to most important questions. Since the 13th CPC Congress, we have always made reports to and asked for opinions from Comrade Deng Xiaoping while dealing with most important issues. Comrade Deng Xiaoping also always fully supports our work and the decisions we have made collectively.

The summit signified natural resumption of relations between the Chinese and Soviet Communist Parties. Normalization of relations between the two parties is in accordance with the interests of the Chinese and Soviet peoples, as well as in the interest of world peace. We are happy about this. Zhao Ziyang stated: I hope that relations between the Chinese and Soviet Communist parties will develop on the basis of the following four principles; namely, independence, full equality, mutual respect, and noninterference in each other's internal affairs. These are also the principles we follow when we handle our relations with Communist parties of other countries. Our party holds that only when relations between parties are based on the above four principles can they be mature, normal, and steady. This is our summary of historical experience.

Zhao Ziyang talked to Gorbachev specifically about the question of socialist reform. He said: The socialist movement in all countries has come to a crucial period indeed; it is faced with many problems that require profound thinking and that need a solution. Some people, particularly young people, have always raised the following question: Does a socialist system have superior qualities? I think that this doubt is primarily the result of two factors. On the one hand, some comrades do not quite understand the basic historical fact that countries which have established a socialist system through revolution were not the most developed countries in the first place. Old China was a very underdeveloped country. Our starting point was much lower as compared with the developed countries in Western Europe and North America. We will not arrive at a correct conclusion if we neglect the basic fact about the different stages of economic and cultural development. This is one aspect. On the other hand, we were not experienced in how to build socialism. In addition, we did commit the mistake of staying in a rut. This was not an inherent malady of the socialist system; it was a mistake in our own subjective guidance.

Following World War II, many major capitalist countries have constantly tried their best to readjust their systems and policies to meet the need for the adoption of new science and technology. To a certain extent, they have eased their internal contradiction among the social classes. But in our case, we have stuck to our original formula. This formula was precisely the special formula developed under a special historical condition in those years when the Soviet Union was experiencing armed foreign intervention, encirclement, and war. Since there are two aspects to this question, our work should also have two aspects. On the one hand, we should effectively conduct ideological education among the masses. On the other hand, it is imperative to reform the original system and policies. Basically speaking, only through reform can we make the masses personally feel the superior qualities of socialism. Without undertaking reform, there is definitely no way out. Socialism is faced with serious challenges. To meet these challenges, we have no other choice but reform. We should make the inherent superior qualities of the socialist system fully shine through by undertaking reform. This is the historical mission of contemporary Marxists.

He asserted: Since the conditions of all countries are different, we cannot demand uniformity in reform. China has conducted economic reform for ten years. Almost all the more easily solved problems have been tackled to varying degrees, and the results have been good. The most difficult thing now is how to develop the role of the law of value under the system of public ownership. Without a market, the law of value is meaningless. If the prices of most commodities are not liberalized, then the law of value cannot play its part. But in the situation when commodities are in short supply, it will be hard to curb price increases if prices are liberalized. A shortage economy is precisely the inevitable result of the old system. This is a great contradiction. It seems that it is hard to resolve this contradiction within a short time. We should be prepared to fight a protracted war and we should strive to be more meticulous in doing our work in all fields in the course of reform.

Now we are improving the economic environment, rectifying the economic disorder, curtailing the scale of capital construction, readjusting production and enterprise structure, and improving macroeconomic control. Through our efforts in these areas, we plan to better coordinate the general supply and the general demand to create a more favorable condition for deepening reform.

Zhao Ziyang stated: China's political reform should keep abreast with the development of the economic structural reform. It should be neither faster nor slower than the economic reform. Without political reform, the economic reform will not succeed. At Comrade Deng Xiaoping's suggestion in 1986, we conducted a fairly systematic study of the question of political reform and worked out a tentative plan. The seventh plenary session of the Twelfth CPC Central Committee [October 20, 1987] and the Thirteenth CPC National Congress held that the key to restructuring the political system in China is, above all, the separation of party from government functions. We are not for the multiparty system as practiced in the West, nor for establishing new political parties. The CPC's leadership role among the Chinese people has evolved through history. Without the CPC leadership, China cannot adhere to its socialist system nor can its socialist reform succeed. Like the economic reform, China's political reform must proceed from its own conditions.

There are nine political parties in China—the CPC and eight democratic parties. The relationship between these parties is not that between the ruling party and the opposition parties as in the West, but is one of mutual cooperation, consultation, and supervision. The CPC plays the leadership role in the multiparty cooperation system. Some people have asked whether it is possible to give expression to democracy and to exercise effective supervision over the negative, unhealthy, and even corrupt practices within the party and government organs while adhering to the one-party leadership. I believe that this is not an unsolvable question. Our party has led the people in working out a Constitution in line with socialist principles and imbued with democratic substance. There are two keys to ensure such supervision: one is to stick to the principle that the party must carry out its activities within the scope of the Constitution and the laws as stipulated in the party's Constitution, and the other is to actively formulate and strictly enforce various substantive laws and procedural laws. With these two keys, I believe that Chinese citizens can enjoy genuine democracy and freedom under one-party leadership. Of course, this cannot be accomplished overnight. We must start to solve problems that are already ripe, and we must make relentless efforts to carry out a great deal of solid work. I am convinced that China's political structural reform will advance, in a prudent and active way, on the track of democracy and the legal system, thereby further harnessing the enthusiasm and creativity of the hundreds of millions of the masses and making our reform and construction undertakings genuinely serve the vital interests of the masses of people.

Zhao Ziyang added: Reform involves many important but complex theoretical and conceptual issues. Therefore, what counts is to proceed from the basic tenets of Marxism in continuously developing theory and updating concepts along with changes in the situation.

During the meeting, Gorbachev suggested that the CPSU and the CPC carry out exchanges at different levels for discussing and studying questions. Zhao Ziyang agreed with this suggestion.

Gorbachev invited General Secretary Zhao Ziyang to visit the Soviet Union, and the latter accepted the invitation with pleasure.

After the meeting, Zhao Ziyang hosted a banquet for General Secretary Gorbachev and his entourage in the Diaoyutai State Guesthouse. [Video opens with shots of Zhao Ziyang shaking hands and exchanging greetings, through interpreters, with Gorbachev and Shevardnadze. It cuts to show closeup shots of Gorbachev and Zhao, both seated, alternately for two minutes. While the announcer continues to read the report, video shows Zhao's still picture for seven minutes. It ends with medium-range shots of a garden where Zhao, Qiao Shi, Hu Qili, Wu Xueqian, and other unidentified Chinese officials are shaking hands and chatting with Gorbachev and his wife Raisa, Shevardnadze, Yakovlev, and other unidentified Soviet officials.]

35
Gorbachev Speaks on Reform Issues

Source: Xinhua (Beijing—in English), May 17, 1989; FBIS, May 17, p. 21.

Comprehensively democratizing the Soviet Union's political system implies greater responsibility of all members of society for its healthy development and social and political stability, said Soviet leader Mikhail Gorbachev here today.

"Without this a normal process of change is inconceivable," said Gorbachev, citing this argument to support the importance the Soviet leadership attaches to strengthening law and legal order and to creating other conditions for building a socialist state based on the rule of law.

Reform was a major topic of Gorbachev's speech. He stressed that economic reform would not work unless supported by a radical transformation of the political system.

The Soviet leader said the Soviet Union follows the implementation of China's reforms very sympathetically. "One has to respect the courage of the party and the people who have embarked on a profound transformation of the social mechanism to modernize their vast country with a difficult legacy of centuries-old isolation and semi-colonial backwardness.''

''We are aware of your major accomplishments on this road as well as of the difficulties you face,'' Gorbachev said, adding a note to wish China steady progress toward its primary objective of turning itself into a developed modern socialist state.

He pointed out that difficulties are only natural in a complex undertaking such as the creation of a new socialist state. ''We know that full well from our own experience,'' he added.

After briefing the audience about reforms in the Soviet Union, Gorbachev went on to say, ''It would go against the truth if I said that all those changes proceed smoothly and without complications.''

He noted that popular aspirations often run ahead of reforms since glasnost and the pluralism of views have laid bare problems, which were piling up for decades without a solution.

Although attempts to put history on a galloping course prove costly, he said, things cannot be allowed to drift without political or economic control. ''After a mechanism has been turned up, it gains a momentum of its own. But it will take a lot of effort to set it in motion. We need a well-considered and balanced strategy of change. And the role of the party assumes special importance under such circumstances,'' Gorbachev stressed.

Initiating perestroika for radical economic and political reforms, he said, the Soviet Communist Party today ''is the only uniting force capable of bringing socialist renewal in our country to successful completion. People in the West who show tremendous interest toward our perestroika, the reforms in China and similar processes in other socialist countries are wondering to what extent these processes represent a development of socialism, and to what extent they constitute a retreat from it,'' he noted.

He also pointed out, ''Some are not hiding their hopes that the introduction of cost-accounting, market incentives, glasnost, and democracy will lead to some mixed form of social order, if not to the restoration of capitalism.''

He said that such expectations are based on a mistaken assumption that economic incentives and democracy belong exclusively to capitalism.

''We are convinced that socialism can and, indeed, will ensure the harmonious combination of economic and political democracy, social protection of man and his freedom,'' he added.

The Soviet leader noted that the Soviet Union and China could also share each other's experiences in economic, social, and socio-political reforms.

VI

The Political Struggle for Tiananmen

The hunger strike had an extraordinary effect. Public sympathy went overwhelmingly to the students, who, by risking death, had captured the high moral ground from a political leadership that seemed more concerned with preserving their power and providing business opportunities for their relatives than with "serving the people."[1] Order in the city was disrupted as traffic around the square was halted and some cars and buses were commandeered. Support for the hunger strikers was also expressed in other cities, where some hunger strikes were also initiated.[2] The government was under great pressure to ensure that no harm would come to the hunger strikers, as the Central Committee ordered the Beijing Party Committee to mobilize hospital staff against such a possibility. But the divided leaders confronted a massive problem: how to terminate the hunger strike while reestablishing their authority, which was now rapidly eroding, even among workers. The latter now joined the demonstrations in force.[3] From the start of the hunger strike, conservative leaders worked behind the scenes to decide upon a response, which soon included a decision to impose martial law and send military forces into the capital (see part VII).

---

[1]This phrase, emblazoned on the entrance to Zhongnanhai, is Mao's old dictum to cadres, which the pervasive corruption of recent years had blatantly violated. Some protesters thus nostalgically carried pictures of Mao and Zhou Enlai.

[2]Hangzhou, in Zhejiang Province, witnessed a supportive hunger strike by local students. Keith Forster, "Impressions of the Popular Protest in Hangzhou, April/June 1989," *The Australian Journal of Chinese Affairs*, no. 23 (January 1990): 103.

[3]See Suzanne Ogden et al., eds., *China's Search for Democracy: The Student and Mass Movement of 1989* (Armonk, N.Y.: M. E. Sharpe, forthcoming), for a full discussion and analysis of worker involvement. Participation of party cadres and even some elements of the army in demonstrations also undoubtedly frightened the leadership, which relies on these institutions to maintain their power.

The five days from May 14 to May 19 were critical. This period included a televised May 18 meeting with Li Peng, several of his leading associates, and the student leaders. Dressed in hospital garb and showing the psychological effects of going without food, the students, especially Wu'er Kaixi (a charismatic student leader from the Uighur minority), showed little respect for Li Peng, who reciprocated by treating their demands with scorn and derision. Televised nationally, the gripping meeting, as revealed in Document 36, ended in a stalemate. The conversation was essentially a futile effort by the leaders to garner public support.[4] Meanwhile, the suddenly uncensored media published the outpourings of public sympathy for the hunger strikers, which were immediately communicated to the students on the square, undoubtedly bolstering their confidence. Six such statements (Documents 37–42) are selected here from among literally dozens of significant expressions of concern for the welfare of the students and support for their "just and reasonable" demands. Significantly, these documents came from influential political sectors: the military, the mass media, government-sponsored trade unions, and individual members of the National People's Congress.[5] In recognizing the students' patriotism, they implicitly rejected the government's, and more specifically Deng Xiaoping's, arguments in the April 26 editorial regarding a "planned conspiracy" against the CPC and socialism.

On the morning of May 19, Zhao Ziyang and Li Peng suddenly called upon the hunger strikers. Perhaps responding to the open letter of Beijing press units (Doc. 38), the two leaders pleaded with the students to end the hunger strike. Documents 43 and 44 are two accounts of the moving visit, when the tearful Zhao stated, "We came too late. . . .You have the right to criticize us. We do not come here to ask you to excuse us." What Zhao failed to tell the students was that he had just lost the struggle to avert a harsh crackdown, and that martial law would be proclaimed the next day. The event proved to be Zhao's farewell address.

---

[4]Anecdotal evidence from foreigners who viewed the televised confrontation in various parts of China indicates that some Chinese viewers praised Wu'er Kaixi for standing up to Li Peng, while others criticized the young student's impetuosity.

[5]Some insiders from the PRC also suggest that the party center at this time was overwhelmed by telegrams from provincial party leaders encouraging the central leadership to yield on many of the students' most reasonable demands.

36
Li Peng Holds Dialogue with Students

Source: Beijing Television Service, May 18, 1989; FBIS, May 19, pp. 14–21. Students' names are from *Renmin ribao* (May 19: 1, 4) version in FBIS, May 24, pp. 19–23.

[Video report, captioned "Li Peng and Others Meet Representatives of the Fasting Students" on meeting between Li Peng, member of the Standing Committee of the Poltiburo of the CPC Central Committee and premier of the State Council, and fasting students at the Great Hall of the People "this morning."]

[Unidentified announcer:] Li Peng, member of the Standing Committee of the Politburo of the CPC Central Committee and premier of the State Council, and others met with representatives of the students, who have been fasting at Tiananmen Square, at the Great Hall of the People this morning.

[Video opens with a long shot of Li Peng entering a large conference room, zooming in to focus on Li Peng shaking hands with each student as he or she is introduced to Li by an unidentified official carrying a namelist of the students. Li is seen shaking hands and briefly chatting with a total of eleven students. Most conversation is inaudible, except for the sixth and seventh students who are identified as Wang Dan, wearing a headband, and Wu'er Kaixi, in hospital pajamas. Next, camera cuts to show Li Peng, seated on a sofa and with Li Tieying on his left and Yan Mingfu on his right.]

[Li Peng:] Delighted to meet you. This meeting came a little late. I apologize for this. Some of your fellow students are now waiting for you at the east side of the Great Hall, making me feel as if under siege [laughing]. I hope that we will have a frank conversation instead of [indistinct]. I would like to discuss only one topic today and shelve other topics until some time in the future. The topic I would like to discuss is how to relieve the fasting comrades of their predicament as soon as possible. The party and the government are very much concerned about the students. Therefore, I would like to exchange views with you mainly on this question, and on how a solution can be found so that we can discuss other questions. It is not that we do not want to [indistinct], but that we are mainly [indistinct]. Frankly, I guess that the oldest of you is about 22 or 23. My youngest child is even older than you. None of my three children is engaged in official profiteering. None. They are all older than you. We look at you as if you were our own children, our own flesh and blood.

[Wu'er Kaixi:] The time is pressing. We can sit down and have a drink here, but the students are sitting on the cold ground and starving on the square. I'm sorry I had to butt in. We hope we can enter into a substantial dialogue as soon as possible. Sorry I have to interrupt. Yes, you are like our elders to us.

[Li Peng:] It does not matter [if you wished to be the elder?] . . .

[Wu'er Kaixi:] It certainly does matter. You have just said that this meeting is a little late. The fact is that we asked for a meeting with you as early as April 22 at Tiananmen Square. Therefore, this meeting is not only a little late, but too late. However, it doesn't matter because you have already met us [indistinct]. You said we are going to discuss only one question. In fact, it is not that you asked us to come here for discussion, but that the great number of people at the square asked you to come out for a talk. The topics of discussion should be decided by us. Fortunately, we share an identical view that there is only one, just one question that needs to be discussed. Therefore, let us discuss just this question.

Many students have already fainted. But this is not my point. What is important is to solve the problem. How can the problem be solved? I think that it is good that you have finally come out and shown your sincerity to resolve the problem. We read and listened to Comrade Zhao Ziyang's written statement yesterday and the day before. Why didn't the students leave? Why did we stay? You should know the reason, I believe. We regard the written statement as insufficient. It is not enough to meet our demands. Moreover, I believe you are aware of the prevailing atmosphere at the square. If such an atmosphere continues, then it is likely that there will be no room for discussion here. Premier Li, it may sound like I am exaggerating a bit. Please think about this: Should the slightest error occur at the square, or should a student . . . I do not want to elaborate further. [Wu'er Kaixi motions to Wang Dan, seated next to Wu'er, to speak.]

[Wang Dan:] [Indistinct] So far, some 2,000 have fainted. [Indistinct] On the contrary, the students' emotion is rising to a high level. It is necessary to [indistinct] so that the students will leave the scene. Moreover, several million people [indistinct] in order to solve the problem as soon as possible. Therefore, our stand is clear [indistinct].

[Wu'er Kaixi:] Let me tell you, Teacher Li. First of all, the problem now lies not in dissuading us—a handful of student representatives. We have already stated clearly that you need not dissuade us because we too wish very much for the students to leave the square. Second, even if you succeed in utterly rebuking us here, it is still useless. The situation at the square now is dictated by 99.9 percent of the students who rule over the remaining 0.1 percent. If a student refuses to leave, then thousands of others will also stay.

[Wang Dan:] [Video shows shots of Wang Dan speaking, then being interrupted by the arrival of Li Ximing and some college teachers. Li Peng and others stand up to greet them, shake hands, and introduce them to those present; one of the teachers walks up to shake hands with Wu'er Kaixi.] [Indistinct] We have agreed to discuss just one question: that is, how to persuade the students to leave the square [indistinct]. I would like to take this opportunity to clearly state once again our demands. First, the current student movement should be evaluated as a democratic, patriotic movement and not unrest. Second, [indistinct].

[Wu'er Kaixi:] I would like to add my explanation to the above two demands. We hope that the verdict will be reversed and that the editorial will be negated immediately. First, we demand that the current student movement be given a positive assessment and that the April 26 *Renmin ribao* editorial be negated. So far, no one has declared that the student movement is not unrest. Second, we demand that the actual meaning, or the great significance, of the May 4th Movement be defined. As for concrete measures to be taken, we suggest that Comrade Zhao Ziyang or Li Peng—better if it were Comrade Zhao Ziyang—make a speech to the students at the square and not in the official residence.

Another point: There is another solution to the problem: that is, the use of the *Renmin ribao* editorial. As Minister Li has just said, and Director Yan has stated before, an immediate solution to the problem, a resolution of the problem within a very short time, is impossible. In that case, I have a question: Was the decision to publish the April 26 editorial made after a very big meeting had been called? If that was not the case, then I sincerely request that *Renmin ribao* quickly publish an editorial today or tomorrow to negate the one on April 26, that it offer a full apology to the people of the entire country, and that it immediately recognize the great significance of the student movement. Only by so doing, I think, by fulfilling this point, can we try our best, I mean the *Renmin ribao* editorial, to persuade our fellow students to change their hunger strike to a sit-in. Only under this condition can we continue to solve the problem. We will try our best. We dare not guarantee that we will surely be able to persuade them. But if it cannot be done, then it will be hard to say what will happen later.

With regard to dialogue, we mean an immediate, open, equal, direct, and sincere dialogue with the real representatives of the broad masses of students [indistinct]. Is there any need to go into such trouble? I can answer for several thousand people who have fainted at the square: There is such a necessity. Regarding equality, I think that leading comrades in real decision-making power should hold a dialogue with representatives directly elected by the students. This indeed is the meaning of equality. I think that I must mention one thing. Such things as saying that I cannot answer this or that question, that this is only my personal opinion, and so forth, should not occur again in a dialogue. If problems that have not been discussed at Politburo meetings are pointed out by us, then a meeting should be called immediately to study them. This is the attitude that must be adopted to really solve the problem. This is my view [indistinct].

[Wang Dan:] We can discuss these technical problems he has just raised later. Now we, the representatives, have come here while our fellow students are fainting one after another. In fact, we have come here bearing in mind that we are responsible for their lives. Therefore, we hope that you leaders, who are present here, will quickly and explicitly make known your position regarding the demands we have submitted. I say that you should explicitly make known your position because the situation is very serious. While we are here as initiators and organizers, we are worried about the safety of the students. I think that some individual leaders may think along similar lines. If they do, then there is a need for quick solution to the problem. It is not very hard to resolve these two problems. Do other students have different opinions?

[Wu'er Kaixi:] I think that if other students have something to add to these opinions, then they should say so quickly because we do not have much time left.

[Zhen Songyu, University of Political Science and Law:] I want to say something. I am one of the representatives of the students who are participating in the current hunger strike [indistinct]. I have taken part in the hunger strike directly. I have witnessed our students being carried away on stretchers, one after another. I think that you have heard about this. One student after another has been carried away on a stretcher continually since last night, or since the day before yesterday, or even the day prior to the day before yesterday. Therefore, I hope that a discussion will be held as quickly as possible. I have nothing else to say.

[Xiong Yan, Beijing University:] I want to say a few words. We hold that whether it is recognized by the government or other sectors of society as a great patriotic democratic movement or not, history will recognize the current student movement as a great patriotic democratic movement. But why do students still want the government to particularly recognize it as a patriotic democratic movement? I think that their desire is the same—all want to see whether our own government is still our own government. In fact, herein lies the problem. This is the first point. Second, comrades, we all are fighting for communism. To save one life is already a job of prime importance, let alone saving thousands of lives. Many of our students have fainted. We are all people of good conscience. We are human beings. To solve this problem, we should forget face and other things of secondary importance. Even if the people's government admits its own mistakes, the people will still support it. I think that the masses of people will do so. This is the second point. Third, our criticism of Premier Li Peng is not directed at you personally. We criticize you because you are the premier of the Republic. In fact, you have just said that your coming out is too late. I have nothing more to say.

[Wu'er Kaixi:] Fellow students, I think that if you have any essential questions to discuss, you had better discuss them quickly.

[Unidentified student:] Quickly ask the leaders to make their position known.

[Wang Chaohua, China Academy of Social Sciences:] I agree with what my fellow student has just said. I just want to add the following: It has just been said that even if we adopt a resolution here, it is of no effect if we cannot persuade our fellow students. But the detailed points expressed by Wu'er Kaixi just now are not entirely meaningless. If they can be carried out, then we might be able to persuade the students to withdraw.

[Wang Xuezhen, secretary of the Party Committee of Beijing University:] I work at Beijing University. I think I understand the students of Beijing University. As teachers, we are very deeply distressed when we see the students of Beijing University taking this kind of action at Tiananmen Square. I believe that our students are patriotic. They hope to advance democracy in our country. Therefore, I hold that our students are not trying to create unrest. I hope our government will affirm this point—that our students are not engaged in creating unrest. The second point is that I hope our government leaders and even our general secretary will go to the square to talk to the students to show that they understand the students' feelings. With regard to the matter of official profiteering and corruption, I think that our government has indicated on many occasions that it is determined to solve these problems. These problems must be solved. The government should make up its mind to solve these problems.

In addition, as a functionary, as a responsible person of the school, and as a teacher, I also hope that the government will cooperate with the students and persuade them to return. If this continues, it will have an adverse effect on the health of the students. The burden of developing China and of promoting democracy in China in the future all falls on the shoulders of our young people. It is bad to ruin your health. This is my three-point view. I hope that you give it consideration.

[Li Peng:] Any other student who wants to . . . .

[Wang Zhixin, University of Political Science and Law, interrupting:] If this is put off any longer, not only the students but also citizens in general will not be able to control themselves. [Video shows Li Peng nodding his head.] I think that these questions should be clarified. First, the current movement is no longer simply a student movement; it has become a democratic movement. The movement concerns the slogan of democracy and science, which was shouted out seventy years ago. However, this goal has not been achieved in the last seventy years. Now the slogan is being shouted out once again, with much more force than it was in the past. Today's situation is this: since May 13, many students have joined our ranks. This is not something that the students are in a position to control. I want to point this out first of all. Besides, we are not obligated to assume responsibility for maintaining order in the square.

I have another question to ask the government. On April 22, we went down on our knees for a long time to present our petition. However, you did not show up despite our repeated request for you to do so. Another question. We began the hunger strike on May 13, a strike which now has entered its sixth day. There is a practice in the world that when a hunger strike enters its seventh day, the governments in general will respond. This is true even in the case of countries like South Africa. I wonder if the Communist Party and a great country like ours can restore and cultivate our original image. One more question. I wonder how the government is going to respond to this. At present, different types of people, including aunties, grandpas, and whole families, have joined our ranks. I wonder what the government thinks of this. There are people as old as eighty and as young as just a few years old. Small children formed a line marching in an orderly way, shouting slogans, and crying: Big brothers, big sisters, drink some water, eat something.

[Wu'er Kaixi:] Fellow students, fellow students. I feel that we are almost finished with things of a practical nature. With a sense of responsibility toward the students in the square, we must try to make it as brief as possible.

[Li Peng:] Any other student? Since you are here, speak as much as possible.

[Wang Chaohua:] I am sorry. This leading comrade just now . . .

[Li Peng, interrupting:] He is the secretary of the Party Committee of Beijing University.

[Wang Chaohua:] Oh, Comrade Wang Lizhi [Xuezhen, sic]. How are you? I feel that the leading comrades seem to agree with the views expressed by him. That is, that the vast number of students are not acting to create disturbances. Am I right? The leading comrades here seemed to nod their heads just now. However, I would like to point out that the vast number of students are indeed launching a movement. They indeed are fairly consciously launching a democratic movement, trying to fight for the rights given to them by the Constitution. I would like to have this point clarified. If we today call our action simply an act of ardent patriotism, then there is no way to explain the reason, coolness, orderliness, and observation of law characteristic of the movement. Many things can be done in the name of ardent patriotism.

[Li Peng:] Is there anyone else?

[Unidentified voice:] No one else. Please go ahead.

[Li Peng:] If there is no one else, I will make this demand. Please do not interrupt as we speak. We have already fully . . . If you interrupt when we speak, then it will be difficult for us to continue. . . .

[Yan Mingfu, interrupting:] If you do not have any more questions . . .

[Li Peng, interrupting:] If you still have questions, then I hope that you will continue to speak. Since you have this many representatives here, fully air your views.

[Wu'er Kaixi:] Does this mean that when you finish talking, we can no longer talk? Is that what you mean?

[Li Peng:] What I mean is that when we are talking, do not interrupt us.

[Shao Jiang, Beijing University:] Yes, yes. We hope that the current state of affairs will not become more serious, for China really should maintain a stable social order to develop itself and to become prosperous. At this stage, however, the student movement has already begun to change directly. Perhaps it has become a movement of the whole people. The student movement itself, as the central authorities have admitted, is relatively reasonable. However, we cannot guarantee that this movement of the whole people is a reasonable one. Thus, I would like to ask you gentlemen to calm this situation down as soon as possible by meeting our two demands.

[Li Peng:] Finished? Li Tieying, you say something about this.

[Li Tieying:] As the minister of the State Education Commission, I have talked with everyone twice before. I already expressed my views [on the first issue] the last time; that is, the State Education Commission from now on will develop more channels for dialogue to listen to the views of those in the education field, as well as those of the broad masses of teachers and students, and hear, through you, the opinions of all sectors of society with regard to our work and problems. On this issue, we at the State Education Commission were unable to establish a regular multilevel or multichannel system through which everyone has the opportunity to speak and to express his views on state affairs. If we have not done enough in this regard, then we should sum up our experience.

On the second issue, the student strike has already become a major nationwide event. We should [make it clear?]. Moreover, the demands of the students not only involve students, but also include some political issues. Therefore, all these issues have created enormous repercussions. The state of affairs is still developing. This event is still developing. Therefore, we call the student parades and demonstrations a student strike. I have already expressed my views on this issue in two previous official talks with you people. I am sure that those students who are present here today understand my views clearly. It should be said that the broad masses of students have demonstrated the spirit of patriotism, have voiced their criticisms and opinions, have offered many suggestions, and have expressed their patriotic aspirations during this event. However, many things do not develop in a way that accords with our own subjective views and wishes. The development of such an event in one way or another can only be verified by the final result of the development itself and by history. Right now, the state of affairs is spreading. We are quite worried.

I myself am very worried about what is going on now. Things may possibly develop in such a way that they will turn out to be inconsistent with what our fellow students thought and wished in the beginning. We oppose it, and so do the students and people throughout the country. Moreover, we all wish to have a stable situation. In today's China, if we do not have a stable situation, if we do not have a situation of stability and unity, then, in my opinion, everything will go down the drain. If there is not a stable situation in the country, if we cannot continue to establish through the reform a stability mechanism for a lasting period of peaceful rule, if there is not a stable and peaceful international situation, then, whatever it may be, whether it is economic construction, or reform of the economic and political structure, or any other cause that we are undertaking, or the four cardinal principles, in short, our wish to invigorate the Chinese nation, in my view, will remain only a wish or empty talk. So, we must stay within the confines of the legal system and democracy in discussing or arguing among ourselves about all problems, no matter how numerous they are. We have National People's Congress deputies, don't we? We have the NPC and all kinds of mechanisms, don't we?

If you want to show the greatest love and care for the students who are at the square now, as well as for all other students, then I think that they wish we could undertake joint efforts to create, on the basis of the legal system and gradually in the course of the reform, a kind of system that will really enable us to realize the goal of invigorating the Chinese nation. This is our historical mission. It is also the goal set forth by the Thirteenth CPC Congress for us to attain in the initial stage of socialism.

Well, the way things are developing now may not be decided entirely by the subjective wish of our fellow students, by their fine and warm patriotic sentiments. Things have already evidenced further developments in various aspects. Take yesterday, for instance. Parades and demonstrations at different levels and to varying degrees took place in about nineteen cities across the country. There are many students from various cities who have ridden into Beijing. Already, not all the students now at the square are from Beijing alone. There are some students who have come from other localities. So, we now have a kind of order, a kind of situation, that is no longer completely in accordance with our subjective wishes.

As for solving the problems pointed out by our fellow students, we have already held dialogue and consultations between us several times now. It seems that the wishes of our fellow students can no longer be satisfied merely by holding dialogue. Do you not think that we should now study the most important, the most pressing problem? There is no problem that we cannot discuss and study. We can solve all problems by resorting to the means of democracy and the legal system. It is hoped that our fellow students will keep to reason and think seriously in order for the students here today to be able to do their work and for the students at the square to leave and return to their schools as soon as possible.

[Yan Mingfu:] Let me say a few words. I will speak very briefly. In the past ten days or so, I have had many contacts with our students. My primary concern is to save the lives of the students who have been on a hunger strike at the square for many days. They have become very weak. The lives of these children are in danger. I think the final solution to the problem must be separated from saving lives, that is, must be apart from the saving of lives. Do not take . . . [changes thought] in particular those students who are not on a hunger strike, should not take the lives of . . . [changes thought] should care about the lives of their fellow students who are on a hunger strike. I believe that the problems will be solved in the end. However, now we must immediately send these very weakened students to the hospital. I think that we should reach an agreement on this problem. Let us solve these two problems separately. As I mentioned to Wu'er Kaixi and Wang Dan on the night of May 13, the development of the situation has already overtaken the good intentions of those who initiated the event. The event has gone beyond the control of the students. When I went to the square that day to exchange views with the students, I proposed three things. I said: First, I want you to immediately leave the square; that is, the students on a hunger strike should go to the hospital as quickly as possible to receive medical care. Second, I announced on behalf of the CPC Central Committee—that is, I was empowered by the CPC Central Committee—that the central authorities will absolutely not persecute the students; in other words, I addressed the problem of later punishment raised by the students. Third, if the students do not believe me, I offered to go with the students to their schools before the opening of the NPC session. After I left the square, I heard that Wang Dan and others presided over a discussion. Some agreed with my views, but the majority of the students disagreed. Due to the circumstances, central leading comrades, who on several occasions have wanted to visit students at the square, have been unable to enter the square because of the inability to get in touch with you students. Perhaps you know about this. Now more and more signs show that [the three organizations spontaneously set up by] the students are having less and less influence on the situation. More and more of the masses will not follow your intention to continue your action. How the situation will develop worries us. The only thing you can influence is to decide when the hunger strikers will leave the scene. The CPC Central Committee and the State Council are sincere and determined to solve the problems raised by the students. The problem people care about right now—and the crux of the matter—is the lives of these children. This is one of the most important issues. Do not take the lives of these children . . . [changes thought] not attach high importance to it . . . [changes thought] someone will have to take responsibility for the lives of these children. This is all I want to say.

[Li Peng:] Will Comrade Xitong say a few words?

[Chen Xitong:] I came to this meeting on short notice. We could not drive our car over here for this meeting. Finally, we came here by holding a Red Cross flag. This made me feel that it was very difficult to come here. This is why I am late. I was the last one to arrive here.

[Li Ximing:] Eighteen teachers were frustrated. I had to bring them here.

[Chen Xitong:] Comrade Li Peng wants me to say a few words. I would like to say something in my capacity as a mayor. The students have seen the development of events in the last few days. The broad masses have also seen them. At present, many people are very concerned about this. Our workers, peasants, intellectuals, and cadres of various organs are all very concerned about the events that have occurred. Many city residents, workers, and peasants, as well as workers in Xi'an, Hunan, and other localities, have telephoned the municipal government and party committee, asking us to convey their opinions. They hope that the issue can be solved along the track of democracy and the legal system, as mentioned by Comrade Zhao Ziyang. This is one opinion. Another point is that traffic throughout the city is now paralyzed, or is basically paralyzed. Production has been seriously affected. Some factory workers have come out in support of the students, but many workers now hope that the present situation will not continue but will calm down. Only in this way will it be possible to better solve the issue. If the traffic in the whole city remains paralyzed and supply is discontinued, there will be a serious impact on our people and the country. The students are very clearly aware of this. I have conveyed the opinions people want me to convey. This is the first thing.

Another thing is the deep concern about the students on a hunger strike. Medical workers, doctors, and staff members of the Red Cross are very concerned about the health of those students who are on a hunger strike. These people request that they be provided with the greatest cooperation so that they can get assistance in transporting to the hospital all weak students among the hunger strikers. They presented a demand to me: The political question is the political question, but the lives of our children, the students, should not be played around with or used in exchange for something—these are their exact words. Comrades of the Red Cross Society, many other people in society, and city residents have all expressed this opinion. I hope that this will be understood by the students.

First and foremost, it is necessary to guarantee the health of our children and the students of the whole municipality. By holding this hunger strike, you may adversely affect your health or even sacrifice your lives. What is the advantage to you? What will you gain by doing so? In my opinion, if you do not use this method, you can still solve many problems. Isn't this so? You can solve problems in accordance with the law and democratic procedures. As mayor, I would like to convey these two points. I hope that the students will give more assistance so that the Red Cross Society can fulfill its humanist duty and responsibility and ensure that not a single student's life is threatened. The municipal government is determined to provide all the necessary means to help the students, including provisions against rain and equipment to protect against cold. We have now made full preparations for this. Thank you.

[Li Ximing:] I do not have much more to say. Right now, our major task is to ensure that nobody's life is in danger. Let us unite as one to tackle this issue first. This issue brooks no delay. I hope that all of us will pool our efforts to tackle this issue. There is nothing else I would like to talk about. This is the most urgent issue.

[Li Peng:] I would like to express my views on several points. Everyone is interested in discussing essential issues. First I want to discuss one essential issue. I propose that the China Red Cross Society and its chapter in Beijing responsibly and safely send those on hunger strike to various hospitals. I hope that all other students at the square would help and support this operation. This is my concrete proposal. At the same time, I urge the medical workers in Beijing Municipality and in all units under the central government to join this rescue operation, care for our students on hunger strike, save their lives, and ensure their maximum safety. No matter how many common views we share and how much we differ in views, our primary task at present is to save lives. This is the government's duty. The government is responsible for doing this. All the students at the square must show comradely concern for the students on a hunger strike. My proposal does not mean that only those comrades on a hunger strike who are critically ill should be sent to the hospital. What I mean is that all of them should be sent to the hospital right now. I have already instructed all major hospitals to vacate more beds and spare the necessary medical facilities to take care of these students. During the past few days, our medical workers had already worked very hard. For days and nights, they had meticulously taken care of fasting students. Myself, Comrade Ziyang, and other comrades visited some of the students this morning.

Another point is that neither the government nor the party Central Committee, has ever said that the broad masses of students are creating disorder. We have never said such a thing. We have unanimously affirmed the patriotic fervor of the students. Their patriotic aspirations are good. Many of the things they have done are correct. A considerably large number of their complaints are also problems that our government seeks to solve. I will tell you in all honesty that you have played an excellent role in helping us solve these problems. We plan to solve these problems, but there will probably be many obstacles. Some of the problems are difficult to solve. The students have actually helped the government overcome the difficulties on our road of advance by pointedly bringing up these problems. Therefore, your efforts are positive. Nevertheless, things often develop independently of your good will, fine ideas, and patriotic fervor. No one is able to control this objective law.

There is complete chaos in Beijing. Moreover, chaos has spread throughout the country. I can tell you students that yesterday our lifeline, our railway lifeline, was blocked for three hours in Wuhan, suspending our important means of transportation. At present, many urban students have come to Beijing. Others who are not students but who are people without fixed duties in society have also come to Beijing under the banner of students. I can state that during the past few days, Beijing has been in a state of anarchy. I hope you students will think for a moment what consequences might have been brought about by this situation. The government of the People's Republic of China is a government responsible to the people. It is impossible for us to be indifferent to this phenomenon. It is impossible for us not to protect the safety and lives of students, not to protect factories, and not to protect our socialist system. Whether or not you are willing to listen to what I have to say, I am really pleased to have the opportunity to say it. I want to tell you that it is absolutely not my intention to impose anything on you, because some things are independent of man's will. Much unrest has occurred in China. Many people did not want unrest to occur, but it occurred anyway.

The third point is that currently there are many personnel from government departments, workers, and even staff members of some of the State Council departments who have taken to the streets to demonstrate to show their support. I hope you will not misunderstand their support. They have done so out of concern for you. They do not want any harm done to your health. However, I do not totally agree with the actions taken by many people. In other words, if people advise you to eat some food and drink some water to maintain your health, or if they advise you to quickly leave the square and hold a discussion with the government, then this is entirely correct. However, many people have come to encourage you to continue your hunger strike. I cannot say what their motives are, but I do not agree with this action. As head of a responsible government, I cannot but make my position known regarding this matter. I have not finished yet. Some . . . [changes thought] of course, two questions have been raised by students. We are very concerned about these questions, and we understand them. As the premier of the government and a member of the Communist Party, I do not hold back my viewpoints; however, I do not want to talk about these questions today. I will talk about these questions at an opportune time, but I think I have already talked quite a lot about my point of view.

Yes, I have made my point of view clear now. If we insist on endless quibbling over this issue today, in my view, this is inappropriate. This is unreasonable. I want to appeal to you for the last time: if you think that you comrades present at this meeting cannot, well, either command or—however you may describe it—your partners, if you cannot have complete control over their actions, then I would like to appeal, through you, directly to our fellow students on the hunger strike in the square. I hope that they will stop their hunger strike and go to the hospital for treatment as soon as possible. Once again, on behalf of the party and the government, I extend cordial greetings to them. I hope that they will be able to accept this very simple, but also very pressing, request made to them by the government. I have finished what I wanted to say.

[Wu'er Kaixi:] Premier Li, I am very sorry for having written you a note a while ago telling you that in case you do not get to the essential matters I may have to cut you short. Respecting our agreement, I did not do so. I would like to remind you about the question of quibbling about which we have just heard. In the view of us students, we are only seeking a solution to the problem from the standpoint of humanitarianism. As for quibbling, that is about some specific questions. This has nothing to do with us. It is not us, the representatives of the students, who are quibbling.

I have another point to make. I first thought that there was no need to repeat what I said right at the beginning of this meeting. However, it seems that some of you leading comrades still do not understand me. Therefore, I am now willing to repeat what I said once more. The key to solving the problem now does not lie in convincing those of us present at this meeting. The key lies in how to make the students leave. The conditions for them to leave . . . [changes thought] I have, well, I have already made it very clear just a while ago about the conditions for them to leave. There is only one possibility, and this is objective reality, objective fact. If there is even one last person who does not leave the square and who continues his hunger strike, then it will be very difficult for us to guarantee that the thousands of people who choose to remain will leave. Furthermore, with regard to the issue of the Red Cross, I believe, well, I want to ask Premier Li and other leading comrades present here to consider its feasibility. Moreover, Premier Li, let me repeat once again what I have just said: Let us avoid endless quibbling. We also think this should be avoided. Please quickly respond to the conditions we have presented, because our fellow students in the square are suffering from hunger right now. If this meeting leads nowhere, and if we continue to quibble on this question, then, in our view, the government does not have any sincerity, not the slightest sincerity, to solve the problem. In this case, there is no need for we representatives of the students to remain sitting here any longer.

[Wang Dan:] Let me add one point. If Premier Li believes that this will create a disturbance or have a very adverse effect on society, then I can speak for the vast numbers of students that the government should take absolute, full responsibility.

[Xiong Yan:] I will repeat once more. Dear Comrade Li Peng, just now you brought up the point that there are signs of a disturbance in society. I have spoken for three miniutes, explaining in the most simple way the difference between a student movement and a disturbance. If a disturbance occurs in a country or a society, does it have a direct cause-and-effect relationship with a student demonstration? I say no. A disturbance in a country or society is not caused by student demonstrations, but by the social system in existence, the ills of society. It does not have a direct cause-and-effect relationship with student demonstrations. The very purpose of student demonstrations is to expose the ills of society at an early date so that the government can deal with them and overcome the ills without delay. Thus, the student movement or the movement to promote democracy will indeed serve to prevent society from falling apart and avoid a real disturbance. The argument is quite simple. This is what I want to say.

[Yan Mingfu:] I would like to ask your view on this. Someone just gave me a note, saying that the students of the provisional headquarters of the fasting students are in danger of losing control of the situation and they hope that you will return immediately. At today's dialogue, you have presented your views to the party Central Committee and the State Council. On behalf of the State Council and the party Central Committee, Comrade Li Peng has expressed our views on these issues. The most pressing issue that needs to be resolved at present is to have fasting students go to the hospital for treatment with the help of the Red Cross. Regarding other problems, there will be enough time to resolve them. Shall we end our dialogue here? Comrades of the provisional headquarters of the fasting students are asking Comrades Wang Dan and Wu'er Kaixi to return as soon as possible . . .

[Unidentified student, interrupting:] I want to make one point. At the beginning it was said that this is a meeting, not a dialogue.

[Li Peng, interrupting:] Yes, it is a meeting. See you again.

[Yan Mingfu:] Premier Li Peng is having talks with a foreign delegation in the next hour. . . . [Video shows Li Peng standing up and shaking hands with the students.]

37
Some PLA Officers Send Open Letter to Central Military Commission

Source: Zhongguo Tongxun She (China news organization) (Hong Kong) (May 18, 1989); FBIS, May 18, pp. 38–39.

At 6:00 this morning, the Tiananmen Square broadcasting station of the student hunger strikers broadcast an open letter from a number of People's Liberation Army [PLA] officers to the Central Military Commission. The main points of the letter were as follows:

1. We absolutely cannot suppress the students and the masses by armed force. We must teach the whole body of PLA officers and men to love the people and protect them; to carry forward the people's army's glorious tradition of identity of army and people; and to strictly follow Central Military Commission First Vice-Chairman Comrade Zhao Ziyang's demand for reason, calm, restraint, and order in properly handling our relations with the masses. Under no circumstances may we act like family members drawing swords on each other, which would give joy to our enemies.

2. As quickly as possible, urge the government and the student representatives to hold a public and fair dialogue. The lives of the hunger-striking students in Tiananmen Square are in danger and we hope you will be able to persuade the government leadership to go among the students and accept their reasonable demands to attain genuine stability and unity.

3. Immediately take part in rescuing the students who are going without food and water. We ask you to immediately order the major PLA hospitals in Beijing to send medical personnel to Tiananmen Square to take part in rescue work and to display revolutionary humanitarianism and the spirit of healing the sick and succoring the dying, to ensure the safety of the students' lives.

4. Beginning with the armed forces, actively promote all reforms in the units, cut military spending, streamline the organs and the units, and reform the armed forces setup. The armed forces leaders at all levels should take the lead in giving up their imported cars, share weal and woe with the masses, and spend on education the money thus saved, to accomplish the invigoration of the economy and culture of the whole nation.

38
Fourteen Beijing Press Units Send Open Letter to CPC Central Committee and State Council

Source: Zhongguo Tongxun She (China news organization) (Hong Kong) (May 18, 1989); FBIS, May 18, p. 70.

At 10:00 yesterday evening, thousands of journalists from 14 Beijing press units issued an open letter to the CPC Central Committee and the State Council on the student demonstration.

The text of the open letter is as follows:

"The students are in imminent danger! The situation is critical! The country is in a desperate situation! We sincerely hope that the responsible comrades of the CPC Central Committee and the State Council will take the overall situation and interests of the state into account, go with the tide of popular feeling, and make efforts to prevent the situation from turning for the worse. We hope that General Secretary Zhao Ziyang and Premier Li Peng will go to see the hunger-striking students in Tiananmen Square and meet their reasonable demands. The central authorities should hold a genuine dialogue participated in by responsible persons of the CPC Central Committee and the State Council."

The journalists who signed the open letter are from *Renmin ribao*, *Gongren ribao*, Xinhua News Agency, *Zhongguo qingnian bao*, *Nongmin ribao* [Farmers daily], *Keji ribao* [Science and technology daily], *Jingji ribao* [Economic daily], *Guangming ribao*, *Zhongguo funü bao* [Chinese women's newspaper], *Beijing ribao*, Central Broadcasting Station, China Television Station, International Broadcasting Station, and *China Daily*.

39
Personnel from Nineteen Overseas and Home Media Send Letter to Zhao Ziyang and Li Peng

Source: Zhongguo Xinwen She (China News Agency) (Hong Kong) (May 18, 1989); FBIS, May 18, p. 70.

Nineteen overseas and home news media this afternoon sent a letter to CPC Central Committee General Secretary Zhao Ziyang and State Council Premier Li Peng in which they called on the highest-ranking leaders to open dialogue with students on an equal basis as quickly as possible.

The letter said: "The student hunger strike in Tiananmen Square has entered its sixth worrisome day! The situation has reached a very critical point. It is of concern to the whole country and is being focused on by the whole world. Yesterday, in Beijing the number of citizens participating in the call to support the students reached millions! This demonstrates that the student prodemocracy movement has received extensive support from the broad masses."

"We have just learned from a news broadcast that you made a trip to the hospital this morning to visit the hunger-striking students currently under medical treatment. We sincerely urge you to make use of the opportunity of this visit to arrange a direct meeting, in the fastest possible way, with students on hunger strike in Tiananmen Square, in which substantial dialogue can be conducted. Both the government and the students have repeatedly stated that the fundamental goals of both sides are identical. Both agree on eliminating corruption, making reform a reality, and launching China on the path of democracy and legal rule. We therefore have full reason to believe that the dialogue will achieve success.''

"Messages from all over the world show that the current events in China have caused deep concern among the wide masses of overseas ethnic Chinese, Chinese compatriots in Hong Kong and Macao, and foreign friends. The hearts of the majority of the descendants of Chinese ancestors living overseas and foreign friends are linked with the hearts of Chinese people. They all hope for an early conclusion of the present events. They all hope to see China continue on its path of reform and reconstruction in an environment of stability and solidarity."

The letter to Zhao Ziyang and Li Peng was jointly signed by the following nineteen news media: Zhongguo Xinwen She, *Hua sheng bao* [Chinese voice], *Beijing Review, People's Pictorial, China Reports*, Chinese Literature Publishing House, Foreign Languages Press, New World Publishing House, Hong Kong *Wen wei po, Ta kung po, Hsin wan po, Macao Daily News, Meizhou Huaqiao ribao* [U.S. Chinese daily news], Apple Television New York, *Huafu xinwen bao* [Washington news], *Meihua luntan* [U.S. and China forums], and the *Los Angeles Herald*.

40
All-China Federation of Trade Unions Issues Statement

Source: Beijing Domestic Television Service, May 18, 1989; FBIS, May 22, p. 80.

[From "Night News"]

The statement says: The vast number of students' patriotic, democratic, and progressive demands for promoting democracy and law, combating corruption and government profiteering, and expediting economic and political reforms have received widespread sympathy from the working masses. The All-China Federation of Trade Unions strongly urges the principal leading members of the party Central Committee and the State Council to make prompt arrangements for face-to-face dialogues with representatives of students, and to take effective measures and actual steps to put an end to the students' hunger strike as soon as possible.

The face-to-face dialogues with workers in the capital—dialogues sponsored by the All-China Federation of Trade Unions and attended by leading comrades of central authorities—should continue. Earnest efforts should be made to hear the voices, requests, views, and proposals of the working masses and trade union workers. Effective measures should be adopted to wipe out corruption, control inflation, achieve fair distribution, and improve public order to promote economic reform and expedite political reform.

The vast number of workers are very worried about the current economic situation, which is very severe. The development of the current situation has already seriously affected normal production routine and social and economic life. The vast number of workers thoroughly realize that all the problems cannot be resolved without a stable social environment. They do not want to see the future of the country overshadowed by any interruption or stoppage of the progress in reform, opening up, and modernization. We believe the vast number of workers fully understand their responsibilities, hold fast to their posts, persist in production and work, and join the vast number of students to maintain stability and unity and achieve their patriotic, democratic, and progressive objectives.

41
Shanghai Municipal Trade Union Council Cable

Source: Shanghai City Service, May 18, 1989; FBIS, May 18, p. 69.

The Shanghai Municipal Trade Union Council today cabled a message to the All-China Federation of Trade Unions. The following is the text of the message.

To the All-China Federation of Trade Unions for forwarding to the CPC Central Committee and the State Council:

The hunger strike of the more than 3,000 students in Tiananmen Square has entered its seventh day, and the hunger strike of the students in Shanghai has also entered its third day. Their young lives are in imminent danger. The workers are distressed by the students' hunger strike. Workers in Shanghai are extremely concerned about this, and activities in support of the students are spreading. This has already affected production and life. To swiftly stop the further worsening of the situation, we urge Comrades Zhao Ziyang and Li Peng to go to the students as soon as possible to hold dialogue with the students without conditions. We urge the Central Committee to take the overall situation into consideration, have the courage to assume responsibility, and forthwith adopt decisive measures or make a specific reply to the just and reasonable demands made by the students and workers.

42
Twelve NPC Members' Letter of Appeal for an Emergency Meeting

Source: Zhongguo Xinwen She (China news agency) (Beijing), May 18, 1989; FBIS, May 18, p. 72.

Twelve Standing Committee members today made an emergency appeal, calling on the NPC Standing Committee to hold an emergency meeting to discuss the current grave situation in China. The full text of the emergency appeal is as follows:

Today, the hunger strike staged by some young students at Tiananmen Square has entered its sixth day. So far, nearly 1,000 people have fainted because of physical weakness. If the situation continues, the problem will become more complicated and more serious. We are deeply worried about the grave situation and about the health of the hunger striking students. Therefore, we have decided to make this emergency appeal:

1. We think that the current student activities, including hunger strikes, demonstrations, and petition, are a patriotic student movement. Out of their love for their motherland and their enthusiastic support for the CPC, the students have put forward such slogans as "Supporting the Constitution," "Promoting Democracy," "Opposing Corruption," "Punishing Official Profiteering," and so on, which conform with the stand of the party and the government and have received understanding and support from all walks of life in the society. Therefore, we appeal to the principal leaders of the CPC and the State Council to meet the students and hold talks with them as soon as possible and to pragmatically handle the reasonable demands made by the students within the orbit of democracy and the legal system.

2. We earnestly request the hunger-striking students to immediately end their current hunger strike in the interests of the great cause of developing our motherland and for their own health. Students, your parents, families, and the broad masses of the people are concerned about you from the bottom of their hearts.

3. We suggest that the NPC Standing Committee hold an emergency meeting

as soon as possible to discuss the current grave situation and seek a solution to the problem.

NPC Standing Committee Members: Ye Duzheng, Feng Zhijun, Jiang Ping, Xu Jialu, Wu Dakun, Chen Shunli, Lin Lanying, Yang Jike, Hu Daiguang, Tao Dayong, Peng Qingyuan, and Chu Zhuang.

43
Zhao Ziyang and Li Peng Visit Fasting Students at Tiananmen Square

Source: Beijing Television Service, 23:30 GMT, May 18, 1989; FBIS, May 19, pp. 13–14.

[Video report, captioned "Important News: Zhao Ziyang and Li Peng Visit Fasting Students at Tiananmen Square"]

[Announcer] Zhao Ziyang, general secretary of the CPC Central Committee, and Li Peng, premier of the State Council, at 4:45 this morning [19:45 GMT, May 18] went to Tiananmen Square to see students who are on a hunger strike and to sincerely urge them to end their fast in order to protect their health.

[Begin recording] [Video report begins by showing Zhao Ziyang and Li Peng shaking hands with fasting students seated on a bus. Zhao and Li extend regards to the students.]

[Li Peng] Where do you go to school?

[Unidentified student] I am from Teachers' University.

[Li Peng] And you?

[Second unidentified student] Teachers' University.

[Li Peng] You are all students at Teachers' University.

[Third unidentified student] [Video shows one of the students maintaining order asking fellow students to make way for Zhao Ziyang and Li Peng to step off the bus.] Back up, please.

[Zhao Ziyang] [Video shows a very tired Zhao Ziyang, speaking through a small megaphone handed to him by a student.] I want to say a few words to the students. We have come too late.

[Fourth unidentified student] You have finally come.

[Zhao Ziyang] I am sorry, fellow students. No matter how you have criticized us, I think you have the right to do so. We do not come here to ask you to excuse us. All I want to say is that the fasting students are physically very weak now. Your fasting has entered its seventh day. This simply cannot go on. If the fasting lasts longer, the damage to the students' health will be irremediable, and their lives will be in danger. This is understood by everyone. The only thing—the most important thing—to do now is to immediately terminate this fasting.

I know your fasting is aimed at obtaining a very satisfactory answer to the issues you put forward to the government and the party. I think that a satisfactory answer is obtainable because the channel for our dialogue is still open. Some issues can be solved only through a process. Some issues—for example, the nature of your action—I feel can be eventually solved. We can reach a consensus. As you all know, many things involve complicated situations. It takes a process to solve them. You just cannot fast for six or seven days and adhere to the idea that your fast will not be terminated unless you receive a satisfactory answer, because if you end your fast only when you receive a satisfactory answer, it will be too late.

Your health will be irreparable. You are still young, fellow students. You still have ample time. You should live healthily and live to see the day when China completes the four modernizations. You are not like us, who are old. It is not easy for the state and your parents to nurture you and send you to college. How can you, at the age of only eighteen or nineteen, or in your twenties, sacrifice your lives like this? Just use your head and think. I am not here today to hold a dialogue with you. Today I just want you fellow students to use reason and try to understand what a serious situation is now facing us.

You all know the party and the state are now very worried. The entire society is [words indistinct]. All of Beijing is talking about your action. Moreover, as you all know, this situation in Beijing simply cannot go on anymore. This city of ours, the capital of China, is facing more and more grave situations every day. You comrades all have good intentions to do something good for the country, but this strike which has happened and is out of control, has affected everything—communications, transport, work, and the regular patients who want to see doctors.

In short, when you end your fast, the government will never close the door to dialogues, never. If you have questions, we will solve them. Despite what you say and the fact that we are a little late, we are getting closer to solving the problems. We are getting there step-by-step. That is all for now. My main purpose is to see the comrades here and express my feelings. I hope you comrades soberly think about this question. Those comrades who have organized the fast should also think soberly. Fasting is not something that can go on without reason.

We were once young, and we all had such a burst of energy. We also staged demonstrations, and I know the situation at that time. We did not think of the consequences. You should soberly think of things in the future. The sixth day is gone and the seventh day is here. Will the fasting really go on for the eighth, ninth, and tenth days? I say many things can eventually be solved. If you want to wait for that day, the day you receive a satisfactory answer, then you should end the fast early. Thank you, comrades. I just wanted to see you all. [Video shows students surrounding Zhao Ziyang and asking for his autograph; Zhao is shown signing his name on a handkerchief, a notebook, and a piece of cloth handed to him by students.] [End recording]

[Announcer] Also visiting students at Tiananmen Square were Wen Jiabao, alternate member of the Secretariat of the CPC Central Committee, and Luo Gan, secretary general of the State Council. The Tiananmen Square students' hunger strike has entered the seventh day. Many of the students are physically very feeble and weak. Yesterday evening and this early morning, many fasting students fainted and were rushed by medical personnel to hospitals for treatment.

44
Zhao, Li Visit Hunger Strikers in Tiananmen

Source: *China Daily* (Beijing—in English) (May 20, 1989): 1.

Communist Party General Secretary Zhao Ziyang and Premier Li Peng visited hunger-striking students in Beijing's Tiananmen Square shortly before dawn yesterday.

The more than 1,000 hunger strikers had moved into ninety buses the day before to seek shelter from the rain.

When Zhao and Li approached the students' buses, many students applauded and others stretched their arms out windows and shook hands with the leaders.

"I came too late, too late," Zhao said as he boarded a bus holding students from Beijing Normal University. "We deserve your criticism and we are not here to ask for your forgiveness."

Students said that Zhao had tears in his eyes as he spoke with them and signed students' hats and shirts.

Speaking through a loudspeaker, Zhao said to the students that their intentions were good.

"You all want our country to become better," he said, adding that the problems they had raised will eventually be solved. But, he said, things are complicated and there must be a process to resolve these problems.

Most students complained that the leaders' visit, which came as a surprise, was too short. They told *China Daily* that Li stayed at the square for only two minutes.

The party and government hope that the students could calm down and stop fasting immediately, Zhao said.

He promised the students that the party and government will continue to hold dialogues with them after the hunger strike is over.

Some students shouted, "Give us substantial answers," referring to the students' demands for a positive assessment of the movement and equal dialogues between senior leaders and student representatives.

Zhao said he knew that the students launched the hunger strike in an attempt to obtain satisfactory answers from the party and government. But, he said, channels for dialogues were wide open and as to the nature of the student unrest, the government and students would eventually reach agreement.

He urged the students to stop fasting, saying that it could become too late if they insist on getting a satisfactory answer before ending the hunger strike. "You should live to see the realization of the four modernizations in China," he said.

The worsening situation in Beijing, with mass demonstrations and traffic jams, must not go on, Zhao said.

"I am not here to hold dialogues with you," Zhao said. But he told students, "We are getting closer and closer with regard to some questions."

By 3:00 A.M., most of the student fasters had ended their hunger strike on Tiananmen Square, some had gone back to schools and homes as the loudspeakers repeatedly broadcast speeches made by Premier Li Peng and President Yang Shangkun.

The square is still packed with thousands of students including some continuing their eight-day hunger strike. They have abandoned 80 buses provided by the Beijing Red Cross. The drivers and technicians from the bus companies are preparing to check out the buses and drive them back.

VII

Martial Law

An extraordinary meeting was convened at midnight on May 19 to announce martial law. Document 45 presents the opening speech by Beijing First Party Secretary Li Ximing. Unlike the speeches by Li Peng and Yang Shangkun that follow, Li Ximing's briefing to the gathered political and military leaders was not broadcast on central television, though the same speech is part of the June 3 *People's Daily* article reproduced in part VIII. Although acknowledging the large scale of the movement, Li Ximing agreed with Deng Xiaoping's earlier characterization of it as a "conspiracy" against the CPC and socialism. For Li, the evidence of conspiracy was everywhere: big-character posters at the universities attacking Deng Xiaoping, socialism, and Marxism; the democratic salons organized by students; and, of course, the purportedly instigating role of Fang Lizhi—the real "culprit" in the eyes of hard-line leaders—who had praised the students' democratic ideas and supposedly exhorted them to take to the streets.[1]

Like Chen Xitong's later report to the NPC, Li Ximing also discounts the allegations that Li Peng had provoked Hu Yaobang's death, and even the wild rumor that Deng Xiaoping's bodyguards had shot the ex–general secretary. Li stresses the students' attacks on leaders as proof of a conspiracy, but he also recognizes—and denounces—their call for fundamental change, such as the creation of a democratic system and the dismantling of party branches in state institutions—curiously a decision already taken by the Thirteenth Party Congress. For Li and the hardliners, the true cause of the crisis was not the institutional deficiencies of CPC rule, but the machinations of internal enemies, particularly Fang Lizhi, and external agents, such as the Taiwan government and even the United States. The "turmoil" in Beijing—traffic jams, lack of food deliveries, and halts in factory production—was evidence of a giant

---

[1]Fang had consciously stayed out of the student movement to avoid tainting it, though his wife, Li Shuxian, evidently did get involved.

conspiracy against the PRC for which the young, naïve students were only unwitting tools.[2]

Li Ximing's address was immediately followed by Li Peng's announcement of martial law (Doc. 46). Dressed appropriately in conservative Mao tunic, the premier reinforced the "conspiracy" theory by focusing his ire not on the mass of students, but on "a handful of persons" who, if left unchecked, would bring down the entire PRC. Li Peng also noted a most ominous development: the spread of the demonstrations to other cities and the growing involvement of workers and even peasants.[3] Similar to Li Ximing, Li Peng also projected a "benevolent" concern for the health of the student hunger strikers—a cynical claim in light of the subsequent use of overpowering lethal force on June 3 and 4.[4] Arguing that cataclysmic consequences would befall the regime if the protests continued, Li then declared martial law for Beijing and called on Yang Shangkun to make a few supporting comments, which are also included in this document.

Zhao Ziyang pointedly absented himself from the meeting, despite instructions to attend. His absence again revealed to the world that the leadership was divided.

The proclamation of martial law, however, raised as many questions as it settled. Was this simply another effort to intimidate the students? When and how would military rule be enforced? Would the troops enter the city? How could this escalation be used to terminate the hunger strike? How could the hardliners rally support among the upper echelons in the Party and government to support the crackdown? Perhaps ever more important, what would the army's reaction be to this assignment? Would all commanders and soldiers welcome their assignments? And would students resist the crackdown? Could bloodshed be minimized or avoided? Such questions dominated thoughts in the days following the proclamation.

---

[2]Li's description of the various problems in the city are exaggerated, but not fundamentally untrue. Beijing journalists, however, accused the government of deliberately stopping food deliveries and engaging in other disruptive action, often by undercover agent provocateurs, to create an atmosphere of crisis that could justify the crackdown. See Suzanne Ogden et al., eds., *China's Search for Democracy: The Student and Mass Movement of 1989* (Armonk, N.Y.: M. E. Sharpe, forthcoming).

[3]See the detailed and frank descriptions of the spring movement throughout China in the internal (*neibu*) study, *Jingxin dongpo de wushiliu tian* (An astounding fifty-six days), by the Ideological Work Bureau of the State Education Commission (Beijing: Dadi Publishing House, 1989). This study has now reportedly been withdrawn.

[4]A witness on Tiananmen Square on June 3 and 4, Robin Munro asserts that army troops would certainly have used lethal force on the students occupying the Monument to the People's Heroes if they had not voted to leave. Apparently, very few students, if any, were killed on the square itself, though many people, mostly "commoners" (*laobaixing*) died in other parts of the city. See Amnesty International, *People's Republic of China: Preliminary Findings of Killings of Unarmed Civilians, Arbitrary Arrests and Summary Executions Since June 3, 1989* (N. Y.: August 1989) and Robin Munro, "The Real Story of the Slaughter in Beijing," *The Nation*, June 11, 1990.

Document 47 is the formal declaration of martial law adopted by the State Council. Most noteworthy is its brevity, as the declaration contained virtually no specific instructions to the citizens, nor an announcement of a curfew.[5] In reaction to this martial law declaration and the obvious defeat of Zhao Ziyang's forces, student leaders immediately sought out support from China's two remaining PLA marshals (*yuanshuai*), Nie Rongzhen and Xu Xiangqian. Although nominally retired, both men retained sufficient stature as revolutionary heroes to challenge Deng Xiaoping. Despite Yang Shangkun's and Li Peng's promise that the military would not attack the students, the army's entry into the capital led some students, perhaps encouraged by Zhao Ziyang's aides, to seek the marshals' moral backing, which, the documents indicate, they generally received.[6]

Yet if the students could get support from old marshals, so could Deng Xiaoping bring his old-guard supporters back into the political fray. As Documents 49 and 52 make clear, the hard-line coalition of Deng, Li Peng, and Yang Shangkun now sought crucial political backing from other "retired" leaders to launch an attack against Zhao Ziyang. Presenting an equally apocalyptic view of unfolding events, the hardliners blamed Zhao Ziyang for creating a "split in the party"—the real cause, they argued, for the growth and spread of the demonstrations.[7] Yang Shangkun agreed and blamed the second "high tide" of the movement after April 26 not on the provocative impact of Deng's editorial, but on Zhao Ziyang's machinations (Doc. 50). In Maoist fashion, hard-line leaders were deliberately polarizing the political situation by making the crisis into a Manichaean struggle between socialism and capitalism, and by raising the specter of the revolution's complete defeat. Yang thus declared that "retreat would indicate our collapse and the collapse of the PRC," which, he claimed, would be followed by the "comeback for capitalism" in China as originally planned by John Foster Dulles!

Yang also agreed with Deng Xiaoping in blaming the present crisis on Zhao Ziyang's and Hu Yaobang's earlier resistance to the anti–spiritual pollution and anti–bourgeois liberalization campaigns. The events in the streets all could have been avoided, Yang averred, if the leadership had protected China's young minds from the polluting effects of Western, "bourgeois" culture. Yet before

---

[5]Neither in this decision nor through the media were Beijing citizens informed of just what the declaration prohibited, nor were specific areas of the city, other than the square, declared off-limits. The leadership retained arbitrary discretion, a situation strengthened by the fact that many Beijing residents did not even know what the term "martial law" (*jieyan*) really meant.

[6]Since June, reportedly neither of the two old marshals, nor General Zhang Aiping, have acquiesced to demands that they write self-criticisms.

[7]To heighten the sense of crisis, Li Peng put the May 4 demonstration at one million, while Li Ximing, in contrast, gave a much smaller figure of ten thousand to prove the purported stabilizing effects of the April 26 editorial.

launching another "reeducation" campaign, Yang had to deal with the immediate situation. Defending Deng Xiaoping's individual decision ordering troops into the city, Yang declared, "we must launch an offensive," though he continued to claim that the army would not assault the students.[8] Virtually admitting disarray in the military's ranks, he then issued a harsh warning to wavering elements by promising that "if any troops do not obey orders, I will punish those responsible according to military law."[9]

Document 51 presents a totally different perspective on these events from two Zhao Ziyang supporters, the political scientist Yan Jiaqi and the philosopher Bao Zunxin. The student movement, they claimed, was not a "disturbance" but had "announced to the whole country the basic principle of democratic politics: all the power of the country belongs to the people." Chanting the slogan "down with Li Peng" was not a criminal act, they asserted, but the inherent right of any people to condemn their government and call for a leader's resignation—a right made all the more prominent by the recent resignation under fire of the Japanese prime minister. Reflecting the reformers' support for following legal procedure, Yan and Bao quoted chapter and article of the state constitution to justify their call for Li Peng's resignation, and for the convening of an extraordinary meeting of the NPC to challenge Li's "illegal" declaration of martial law.[10]

The last two selections in this section come from veterans Chen Yun and Deng Xiaoping. In a speech to the Central Advisory Commission Standing Committee (Doc. 52), Chen—the architect of China's orthodox economic planning system—endorsed his elderly colleagues' apocalyptic view by suggesting that nothing less than the previous "sacrifice of more than twenty million people" in the Chinese revolution was at stake. In addressing Li Peng and Yao Yilin, Deng Xiaoping then focused on the future policies and leadership group that would follow the ousted Zhao Ziyang (Doc. 53). Ostensibly heeding public opinion, Deng insisted that new leaders must not be "mediocre." The policy of reform, he asserted, must continue, though not along the lines of Zhao's alleged "capitalist liberalization"—a term remarkably similar to the charge against Deng as a "capitalist roader" during the Cultural Revolution. Deng seems to have had no apprehension about the events looming ahead; he gave no hint of the military action to

---

[8]Yang's curious defense of Deng's right to order the troops personally was probably a response to complaints by the commander of the 38th Army, Li Jijun, who evidently demanded that such a crucial decision be made by "collective" (*jiti*) procedures in the Central Military Commission, where Zhao Ziyang—still a formal member—could have opposed the order.

[9]Yang's order that he would personally punish troops apparently reflected widespread fears that rank-and-file soldiers might fire on their commanders, as evidently occurred in the early 1970s. Anonymous interview.

[10]The assertion by Yan and Bao that, according to the constitution, one-fifth of the NPC membership could call for an extraordinary meeting is an example of the long-standing controversy over procedures for convening meetings of state and party bodies.

come nor did he refer to the amassing of army units then underway. Rather, Deng was preoccupied at this meeting with succession reform, and rallying support for a cohesive new leadership following Zhao's dismissal.

Deng also agreed with other hard-line leaders that the students' intense criticism of corruption within party ranks was basically correct. Once and for all, Deng insisted, the problem must be rooted out, though any suggestion that this required institutional changes, such as a free press, was not forthcoming. Deng also confidently asserted, as if the massive demonstrations had not even occurred, that the "people are basically satisfied with this collective [leadership] of ours," and he virtually guaranteed that the opening to the outside world would continue: "China cannot possibly return again to the previous closed era." Unlike Hu Yaobang's and Zhao's regime, however, the new leadership collective would not waver "in opposing bourgeois liberalization." In a curiously defensive tone, Deng then denied he was "a perfect man" and insisted that "I have never formed a small coterie." On the verge of his most fateful decision, it was as if Deng felt compelled to defend his entire political career, perhaps against the great leader who, lying in state in the mausoleum at the center of Tiananmen, might have found repugnant Deng's plan to crush the people with the People's Army.

45
Report on the Situation of the Student Movement in Beijing

LI XIMING

Source: Fax of speech on May 19, 1989, translated by L. N.

The student movement (*chao*) that broke out in Beijing during April and May is a movement with the most serious effect, with the largest scale and with the longest duration since the founding of the People's Republic of China.[1] Here is a brief report on this student movement in terms of the political struggle situation it has reflected, and the losses it has brought to various aspects of politics, economy, and social life.

Most of the ordinary people and young students supported the decision on the administration, rectification, and deepening of the reform made by the party Central Committee at the third plenary session of the Thirteenth Party Central Committee held in September last year. And, basically speaking, social order and the campus atmosphere on the whole were stable. It's a normal phenomenon for some students to disagree with the corruption that has occurred in some places, the unfairness of social [i.e., income] distribution, and the allocation of college students to jobs after graduation. However, in the meantime, we have been clearly aware of the fact that a very few people had plotted inside and outside some schools of higher learning to take the opportunity of the seventieth anniversary of the "May 4th Movement," the fortieth anniversary of the People's Republic of China, and the bicentennial of the French Revolution to incite student unrest and make trouble.

In early March this year, some anonymous big- and small-character posters in Beida, Qinghua, and other schools of higher learning directly attacked the party's leadership and the socialist system. For instance, somebody wrote a so-called denunciation of Deng poster, which publicly clamored to "Abolish the

---

[1]Li's term for "movement" (*chao*) carries a more negative connotation than *yundong*, the usual term in Chinese Communist terminology for a political movement.

party and the four cardinal principles." It also called [on people] to "angrily denounce Deng," pointing directly at Comrade Deng Xiaoping. Another small-character poster entitled "Grieve for the Chinese people" described the current government as a "dictatorship" and called on people to "fight for freedom." Raised in another big-character poster, entitled "The call of the times," were the questions of "whether or not there is still reason for the existence of socialism" and "what philosophic system should substitute for Marxism." A "Letter to the masses of students," posted at the triangle on the Beijing University campus, called for fighting for "democracy, freedom, and human rights" under the leadership of Fang Lizhi.[2] And there appeared in succession some "salons" with a strong political color that held meetings and all kinds of activities. Fang Lizhi praised those meetings for "adopting a totally resistent and thoroughly critical attitude toward the authorities" and as "having a strong smell of gunpowder." He also predicted that "after three successive meetings [people] will take to the streets." When Comrade Hu Yaobang passed away on April 15, some people, believing that their time had come, were determined to indulge in creating disturbances.

It's certain that most of the ordinary people and the young students mourned Comrade Hu and sincerely expressed sorrowful feelings toward him. The universities and colleges provided various kinds of convenient facilities for students to hold activities for grieving over Comrade Hu Yaobang. But some very few people used this chance to spread rumors, which for a time emerged everywhere. The atmosphere was abnormal. At that time, there were many rumors as to the cause of Hu Yaobang's death. The most popular one was that "Hu died out of anger caused by Li Peng who cursed Hu bitterly at the Politburo meeting." One rumor even claimed that "Hu Yaobang was shot dead by Deng Xiaoping's bodyguards." Many students got very excited, having heard these rumors, and there was a rapid increase of small- and big-character posters on campuses of various universities. Many of the posters and elegiac couplets were not about mourning over Comrade Hu Yaobang. On the contrary, they attacked the Communist Party leadership and the socialist system. . . . On April 15, the day Comrade Hu died, there appeared a big-character poster in Beida entitled "Praising Yaobang—and to some other people." It claimed that the Central Committee criticism of Hu amounted to "calling the other person lascivious because he himself is impotent."[3] In Qinghua and some other universities there appeared slogans calling for "Li Peng to resign" and advocating "Replacing and dismissing the incompetent government and overthrowing the autocratic monarch." On April 16 at People's

---

[2]This phrase was changed in the June 3 editorial to "under the leadership of a certain scholar who had advocated bourgeois liberalization."

[3]Liu Xiaobo also used this sarcastic phrase to describe the impotence of Chinese society, in his Ph.D. thesis written at Beijing Normal University.

University, there also appeared a poster entitled "Crying over Yaobang," which attacked and hurled invectives at the Central Committee leaders [Deng] Xiaoping, [Zhao] Ziyang, Li Peng, [Yang] Shangkun, Wan Li, [Li] Xiannian, and Wang Zhen. Someone in the Central Minority College wrote a big-character poster entitled "Express News," which said, "There is a wave of attacks on the three people (Deng Xiaoping, Zhao Ziyang, and Li Peng) at Beida, Qinghua, and some other universities and colleges in Beijing. . . ." On the same day, there appeared a big-character poster at People's University entitled "A few suggestions," which called for "elegiac couplets and floral wreathes to be placed at Tiananmen Square and to set up a Committee for Arranging Funeral Arrangements made up of several universities and colleges in the capital to reevaluate Hu Yaobang's work, to abolish dictatorial politics, and thus establish a democratic political order." On April 18, a "Letter to all compatriots" posted in the Beijing Aerospace University demanded that the "Communist Party system be abolished and a multiparty system be introduced," and that "party branches and political work cadres in the army, schools, and others units be eliminated." There was another request to "invite the Guomindang to come back to the mainland to establish a two-party political system." There were many small- and big-character posters cursing Comrade Deng Xiaoping in vile language and advocating "Down with Deng Xiaoping; finish the old-man politics." The student movement developed rapidly in only two or three days. There were more and more demonstrations and assemblies in and out of the campuses, with more and more impetus, and the political watchwords became more and more explicit. Being provoked by the few, thousands upon thousands of students came out onto the streets to hold a sit-in on Tiananmen Square. At midnight on April 18 and 19, there happened in succession two violent incidents in which Xinhuamen—the place where the Central Committee is located—was attacked. Such attacks have never occurred since the founding of the People's Republic of China. During the attack, some shouted "Down with the Communist Party." And some students on campus held the horizontal banner of [unreadable]. Then there appeared the rumor of the "April 20 tragedy." On April 22, the night before Comrade Hu Yaobang's funeral, thousands upon thousands of students occupied Tiananmen Square. And on the day of the funeral, there was a rumor that "Comrade Li Peng refused to meet the students, and this brought great dissatisfaction among the students." After the funeral, some people proposed the slogan of "Announcing to all students in China to carry out a class boycott," and thus there was created the situation in which sixty thousand students boycotted their classes. In the meantime, the May 4 demonstration started. The Central Committee, the State Council, the Beijing Party Committee, and the Beijing Municipal Government, out of concern for most of the young students, adopted a very restrained attitude during the funeral arrangements for Comrade Hu Yaobang so as to guarantee the success of the mourning activities. No major incidents had occurred by then, though there happened the attacks [of the previous days].

Kind-hearted people thought that the students would put an end to their activity and that everything would be back to normal after Hu Yaobang's funeral. On the contrary, the student movement continued to develop in a more intensified direction. Its characteristics included the following:

1. The movement had a tendency of spreading to the whole society. On April 23, a big-character poster like the following was put up: "We will not only boycott classes, we will also sing the victory song and unite the workers and peasants to overthrow the tyrannical politics with true action." After that, some people went to the middle schools, factories, and commercial outlets to establish ties, and they sent out and put up leaflets aimed at making things more serious. Big-character posters in some middle schools advocated "Down with the Chinese Communist Party." Many university students went out on the streets to give lectures, distribute leaflets, and ask people to donate money. They also held mobile mass rallies. On April 25, there were 150 such activities held by students from twenty-eight universities. . . .

2. After that, some people carried out the organized and well-planned "grabbing power" (duoquan) activities in some universities.[4] On April 19, some Beida students publicly announced the abolition of the [government-run] students' union and the postgraduates' union, both of which are elected by the students. They also announced the establishment of the "Preparatory Committee of the New Students' Organization." On April 20, they elected and established the illegal "United Students' Union Preparatory Committee." There appeared a big-character poster at the Political Science and Law University calling for "elimination of the present chairman of the students' union." Many universities organized illegal student "autonomous" organizations. This happened in more than ten universities where offices and [radio] broadcasting stations were seized. In the evening of April 23, students from twenty-one universities and colleges established the illegal "University Temporary Committee" at Yuan Ming Yuan. Later, this committee was changed into the "University Students' Autonomous Association in Beijing" (abbreviated as Gao Zilian). It has become the command center of this student movement and engaged in uniting [student] slogans, organization, and action.

3. They proposed the slogan of "Going down south and going up north," which was aimed at carrying out a movement to establish ties all over China. Students coming from Beijing were found in universities in Nanjing, Wuhan, Xi'an, Changsha, Harbin, Shanghai, etc. Students from Tianjin, Hebei, Anhui,

---

[4]"*Duoquan*" was used by Red Guards to attack CPC leaders; thus, Li's use of the term was another example of the current leadership's attempt to compare the student movement to the Cultural Revolution. Observers of the student movement, however, claim this term was never used—and in fact conspicuously avoided—throughout the spring.

Shanghai, and so forth, came to Beijing to take part in the demonstrations. In line with the above three aspects, the provocative, aggressive small- and big-character posters developed to a higher degree. Some students proclaimed the "Announcement of a private ownership system" and advocated "Let's strike the funeral bell of the public ownership system as soon as possible and welcome the new tomorrow of the Republic." Some shouted slogans to overthrow the present government and proposed that "the latest goal is to make Li Peng, who is derelict of duty, resign." The Standing Committee of the Politburo made a correct analysis of the situation and an accurate judgment on the nature of this student movement at the time when the scale of the movement was growing daily and conditions became so complicated that it was nearly out of control. The April 26 *People's Daily* issued the editorial "It is Necessary to Take a Clear-Cut Stand Against Turmoil." The editorial exposed the nature of the very few people who intended to create turmoil by provoking the students. Here one thing that should be emphasized is that for most of the students who have taken part in the student movement, their patriotic enthusiasm and their heart of concern about the country and the people are treasurable. And most of their requests for promoting democracy, deepening the reform, and clearing up corruption are reasonable. Thus, they are still understandable, though some of their words and action went too far. The word "turmoil" in the editorial does not refer to the majority of the students. It actually refers to the very few who aim at using the student movement, using the excitement of the students, using some of our errors, and using some of the existing problems. They have actually provoked a political struggle aimed at opposing the party leadership and the socialist system, and they intend to spread this struggle from Beijing to all over China to create turmoil everywhere. This should not be denied.

The *People's Daily* April 26 editorial exposed the nature of the problem and has stabilized the situation in the whole country. It forced the very few to withdraw their rampant arrogance by changing their strategy, though many of the students who have taken part in the movement misunderstood it. In the meantime, the radicalism of the slogans diminished rapidly. In the demonstration of more than thirty thousand students from thirty-eight universities and colleges on April 27 (those who followed the demonstration troops and those who were there watching are not included), invectives hurled at the leadership suddenly disappeared. Instead, there were slogans of "Support the Chinese Communist Party" and "Support the socialist system." And there were proposals to "oppose bureaucracy, oppose corruption, and oppose privileges," and to "stabilize prices." They were supported by ordinary people on the streets. The dialogue between the State Council spokesman Yuan Mu and the student representatives, and the dialogues between the directors of various ministries and committees of the State Council with the student representatives, had a very good result. In the demonstration on May 4, there were fewer students involved (only about ten thousand), and they were not as excited as before. After having made the May 4 announcement, the organizers of the movement proclaimed that the demonstration had come to an end, and that they would go back to their classrooms and would start having a dialogue with the government.

At that time, the majority of the students agreed to restore normal order. Most of them had gone back to their classrooms. They expected to solve the problems through democracy and law. But because there were two ways of evaluating the student movement among the central leaders, the direction of public opinion changed explicitly. There was a tone contrary to the April 26 editorial. This made most caring and good people misunderstand the situation, and they did not know what to do. The very few who were concerned about the restoration of order thought that there was a chance to resume their activities. [But] the situation retrogressed suddenly. The student movement, which had diminished, rose up again. There were more and more small- and big-character posters that launched attacks. And there were more and more requests for dialogues with the government. Major requests proposed at that time included: (1) To thoroughly repudiate the April 26 editorial; to deny the claim that the turmoil was created by the very few in the guise of the student movement; and to admit that this student movement is a great patriotic democratic movement. (2) To recognize the student autonomous organizations established during the movement, even though the government can only have dialogue with the legal student organization representatives. (3) Restore the editor-in-chief Qin Benli of the *World Economic Herald*. (4) Abolish the ten regulations on demonstrations issued by the Beijing Municipal Government Standing Committee of the People's Congress. Later on, these requests concentrated on the first two, especially the first. In the meantime, the very few played a double-faced game, that is, on the one hand, they appeared to be willing to have dialogue with the government; on the other hand, they proposed the hunger strike announcement, which was prepared earlier, and pushed the so-called volunteer hunger-striking students to the front line. At that time, no effective result was achieved, even though our party and government had done a lot to work things out.[5]

In the afternoon of May 13, more than 200 students from about as many universities and colleges, protected by more than 100 people, came to Tiananmen Square to hold the sit-in hunger strike. There were more and more people getting involved in the strike, 3,000 at most. And there were [unreadable] who were aside watching. Up to the 19th, 3,500 students had fainted from the hunger strike and been sent to the hospital; 2,500 of them stayed in the hospital to have further medical treatment. This large-scale hunger-strike movement drew great attention from the whole society. Most ordinary people expressed their sympathy.

---

[5]Literally, "to channel the waters"—a reference to the Chinese government's traditional role of dike construction and maintenance.

Our party and government has done a great deal with anxious feelings throughout the hunger strike. First came ideological persuasion work. Comrades Ziyang, Li Peng, Qiao Shi, Qili, [Li] Tieying, and [Yan] Mingfu, the party secretary of the Beijing Party Committee, members of the Standing Committee of the Beijing Party Committee, and the vice-mayor of the Beijing municipal government have all gone to the hunger-strike site and visited hunger-striking students in hospitals and have made very patient, responsible, and benevolent persuasions. Second, in the name of the Red Cross, we sent more than 100 ambulances and a few hundred doctors to stay at the site of the hunger strike day and night. We also mobilized some fifty-two hospitals to reserve about 2,000 hospital beds for the students, and we made sure the students who had fainted and those who were sick from the hunger strike received immediate medical treatment. Third, we supplied all kinds of materials to reduce the pain of the hunger-striking students and to guarantee their safety. The Beijing Party Committee and the Beijing Municipal Government sent carriers, workers, and vehicles and, also in the name of the Red Cross, transported water, salt, and sugar to the students day and night. The Environmental Sanitary Bureau in Beijing provided water-spreading vehicles, basins, and towels to the hunger-striking students. Medical suppliers sent ample anti–heat stroke, anticold, and antidiarrhea medicine through the Red Cross, which distributed the medicine to the students. Food stores and department stores sent ample beverages and bread to be used for the students' immediate rescue. The Commercial Industry Bureau in Beijing sent 600 straw hats, and the Beijing military region sent 1,000 cotton quilts to make sure that the students would avoid getting heat stroke in the daytime and would have protection against the cold at night. We also built temporary toilets that are usually only set up for holidays. And sanitary workers cleaned the hunger-strike site at night. Before the heavy rain on the 18th, we sent seventy-eight buses from the Public Transportation Corporation and more than 400 thick wood flats from the Materials Bureau to the hunger-strike students. Faculty members of the schools and from various fields of society gave intensive care to the hunger-strike students. Many older professors, university presidents, and university party secretaries went to the hunger strike site themselves to persuade the students to stop the strike, accept medical treatment, and return to school. They were so deeply affected that they wept when they spoke. With the hard work of the medical workers, the lives of the hunger strikers were saved. People from various walks of life also made emergency appeals to both the central leaders and the students, asking the former to hold a dialogue with the students and the latter to have restraint in order to prevent the situation from worsening. All of these actions demonstrate the concern, love, and responsible attitude of the party, the government, and society.

Despite these efforts, the student movement failed to diminish. On the contrary, because of the strong encouragement of erroneous opinion, the continued agitation by a few people, the extreme sentiments of some students, and the masses' ignorance of the true situation, the student movement rapidly gained in intensity. It suddenly became ''unpatriotic'' not to participate in the demonstrations.

Starting on [May] 15, more and more people took to the streets, with the numbers growing from tens of thousands to hundreds of thousands, and finally to one million. Demonstrators included not only students but also workers, peasants, government functionaries, staff members of democratic parties, children from kindergartens and elementary schools, and officers and men of judicial departments and even military academies. About twenty thousand outsiders rushed into Beijing to support the demonstration. The situation was such that the students were obviously being pushed to a ''dead end.'' Instead of giving correct guidance, the media did its best to fan the flames even higher. The [students] proposed many political slogans that attacked and cursed the Communist Party and socialism. Those slogans centered on and were pointed at Comrade Deng Xiaoping. Some even said, "Deng Xiaoping step down," "[We] strongly demand that Deng Xiaoping withdraw from the party," . . . [and] "Oppose monopoly control and put an end to old-age politics." Some slogans even said, "Deng Xiaoping is cruel-hearted and Zhao Ziyang is cunning," and "Li Peng step down so that the country and the people are stable." One horizontal scroll publicly questioned, "Where are you, the Chinese [Lech] Walesa?" All these indicate that this student movement, which has spread out to the whole country, is by no means an ordinary movement. It is a serious political struggle provoked by some people who have used the student movement.

In addition to this, the fact that various kinds of political groups both at home and abroad have been involved indicate that this struggle has a profound social and political background.

Ren Wanding, director of the illegal organization "League of Human Rights," who was put into prison for four years, was active from the very beginning of this student movement. He gave speeches in some universities and colleges many times, saying, "[We] started this student movement by exploiting the death of Hu Yaobang." He attacked the forty-year leadership of the Chinese Communist Party, saying, "Politics is corrupt; the people are leading a hard life; and popular discontent is boiling." He attacked the slogan of "All rights belong to the people," guaranteed by the constitution, as a "sheer fraud." He also slandered the [policy of] opening to the outside world, reform, and strengthening the nation as "a painted pan-cake hung on the wall" [i.e., useless]. And he reminded the students that "The reason why the 1987 student movement failed is that there was no alliance with the workers." He therefore advocated that the workers' union "should break away from the leadership of the Communist Party and establish a true workers' union." He also provocatively said that "students should combine with the working class and unite and fight in blood." In another speech, he brazenly proposed that "the Communist Party and eight big democratic parties are unable to lead the Chinese people." And he called for establishing a "Free Democratic Party." The "Student Autonomous Preparatory Association" of one of the universities broadcast these slanders, attacks, and provocative sayings to the campuses.

On April 22, members of the "China Democratic League" (which we have declared to be illegal) Hu Ping, Chen Jun, etc., together sent a letter entitled "An open letter to the college students in China" from New York City in the United States. It not only showed support to the student movement, but also made suggestions to the students. It asked the students to pay attention to "consolidating the ties established in their current activity and to strive to carry out effective activities with a strong union." It also asked the students to "make basic concrete requests," and to "take the request of thoroughly negating the antibourgeois movement in 1987 as a starting point." "If those requests cannot get the relevant response, [you] should go on with your protest." They thought that only by doing this could they change "the cyclical situation of change where there is impetus but no solution," which has characterized previous movements. In the meantime, they suggested that students should "step up contacts with various newsmedia"; "strengthen ties with all circles of society . . . to win their support for and participation in the movement"; "try your effort to implement freedom on campus"; "found independent publications"; "establish various kinds of social clubs with real autonomy"; and "reinforce freedom of speech on campus." They also provoked the students to "prepare to struggle with us by way of big-character posters and demonstrations, etc." Besides this, two chieftains of the "China Democratic League," Wang Bingzhang and Tang Guangzhong, hurriedly flew from New York to Toyko in an attempt to interfere in Beijing and have a hand in the movement. Some of the overseas Chinese intellectuals who advocated instituting a Western-style democratic system suggested that Fang Lizhi take the lead. They sent back an "Announcement of Sincerely Supporting Democratic Politics in Mainland China," preaching that "China is China of the whole people, it is not the possession of one party"; "now it's time for the people to actively stand up to express their own political requests"; and "the fundamental point is that people must have the right to choose the party that holds the reins of government."

Some Chinese who live abroad and who hold a different political point of view sent a letter "To all compatriots" in the name of the "Temporary Acting Committee of the Chinese Democratic Party" in April this year. It said that Comrade Hu Yaobang is "the victim of the autocratic system of the Chinese Communist Party," and then, exploiting the mourning for Comrade Hu Yaobang, it provoked the students to unite and "demand that the conservative bureaucrats step down."

The Standing Committee of the Guomindang held its Central Standing Committee conference on April 26 and discussed the situation of the student movement on the mainland. It was thought that "the movement requesting democracy which was started by mainland students recently has kindled the torch of complaints that have accumulated for a long time among our mainland fellow countrymen toward the Chinese Communist Party. Our government and people should support them in a more active way so as to bring democracy and freedom to the mainland soon." The [unreadable] of the Guomindang and the Central Agency also wrote articles and published articles taken from some Western publications to cheer up the student movement. They said something like this: "Experience has proven that communism is impossible in this place and in other socialist countries."

The American government also used every ounce of its strength to interfere in this democratic political affair. On April 28, White House spokesman [Marlin] Fitzwater made a speech supporting the protest held by the Chinese students. He said that the American President Bush believes in the principle of freedom and the right of assembly expressed by China. He also said, "We hold a supporting attitude to the protest since the Chinese students have a right to hold demonstrations and have a right to express interest in striving for democratic actions and freedom."

This student movement outnumbered all other movements that have occurred before, in terms of the length of time, its impetus, the scale of society's involvement, and the serious harm it has brought. They attacked the Xinhua Gate twice and occupied Tiananmen Square many times. Such a thing never happened in the ten-year turmoil [i.e., the Cultural Revolution, 1966–76]. It is the first time that more than a thousand people have gone on hunger strike in Tiananmen Square. This has never happened in any of the previous student movements since the founding of the People's Republic of China. The fact that they chose to start the hunger strike during Gorbachev's visit to China has seriously interfered in our country's important foreign affairs and has damaged our country's image. The demonstration of more than a hundred thousand or even a thousand people caused by the hunger strike is much more serious than the linking-up movement of the Red Guards in the Cultural Revolution. This allowed anarchism to spread everywhere and made laws and regulations useless. The social turmoil it has caused is severe. The effect of rumors, slander, and personal assaults that are antidemocratic and illegal is awful, especially when they reach a climax.

The student movement has seriously destroyed normal production, work, and living order in the capital. There have been many traffic jams in the city since May 17; more than sixty lines of trolleys and buses were halted; and traffic in the busy district [of the city] was paralyzed. Most workers have had trouble going to work, and it has directly influenced production. Among the 425 important and big medium-sized enterprises that are under the Municipal Economic Committee

System, 35 were in a condition of semiproduction, and 16 actually stopped production. Banks couldn't clear accounts in time every day, and this has caused some financial disorder. Some gas stations were in trouble. Liquified gas and coal for everyday use were prevented from being supplied in time. Newspapers and mail were prevented from being delivered. Street cleaning, garbage clearing, and transportation were also prevented from operating normally. The delivery of oxygen to hospitals could not be done on time. All these have directly influenced the people's everyday life. Only 2 million *jin* of vegetables could be transported to the city, and this has caused a rise in vegetable prices. The price of cucumbers went up from 0.50 *kuai* per *jin* to 1.00 *kuai*. The delivery of meat, soy sauce, vinegar, etc., was hindered. The total sales of some of the big department stores in Wangfujing, Xidan, and Longfusi [Beijing shopping areas] dropped rapidly—20 percent, 27 percent, and 30 percent respectively since April 27. Social order has been disrupted. Bank robberies have occurred, customers have refused to pay at restaurants, and gas stations. Some people even tried to hijack cars. Unlawful elements have gathered in busy districts and proclaimed their intentions to smash up everything. The threat of fighting, looting, and arson is very real.

More importantly, the movement has not only undermined the political, economic, and social order of the capital, but also undermined political stability and unity in the nation. Throughout the country, demonstrations have recently occurred in over twenty large and medium-sized cities. They range in scale from several thousand to tens of thousands of people. Hunger strikes have also occurred in Shanghai and Taiyuan. All this demonstrates the gravity of the situation. There is a high probability that the movement will develop into national turmoil, creating an irremediable situation. It threatens to change China, whose future is very hopeful, into a chaotic, hopeless country.

At this critical point, in consideration of the fate of the party, the nation's future, the interest of the people, and in order to protect the college students who are participating in the movement, we have decided, under the direct leadership of the party's Central Committee and the State Council, to adopt decisive and prudent measures to quiet down this student movement. At the same time, we must also punish corruption and decadence to win popular support. We must do our best to succeed in our work, unite to preserve stability and unity in the capital and throughout the country, and dedicate our efforts to promoting reform and the four modernizations.

46

Li Peng Delivers Important Speech on Behalf of Party Central Committee and State Council

Source: Beijing Television Service, May 19–20, 1989, 15:27 GMT; FBIS, May 22, pp. 9–13.

[Video report, captioned: "Li Peng Delivers Important Speech on Behalf of Party Central Committee and State Council," at a meeting of cadres from party, government, and army organs of the central and Beijing municipal levels convened by the CPC Central Committee and the State Council on May 19—place not given; *live or recorded* [*sic*]; report is preceded by caption: "Important News"]

[Unidentified announcer] A meeting of cadres from the party, government, and army organs at the central and Beijing municipal levels was convened by the CPC Central Committee and the State Council on the evening of May 19. On behalf of the party Central Committee and the State Council, Li Peng made an important speech. [Video begins with a close-up of Li Peng in a Mao suit, reading from a prepared speech. During his address, video shows medium-length shots of Yang Shangkun, Qiao Shi, Hu Qili, Wang Zhen, and Yao Yilin seated, and pan shots of a conference hall with an audience of approximately 1,000 people. Video focuses on Yang Shangkun while he follows Li Peng in making a speech.]

[Li Peng] Comrades, in accordance with a decision made by the Standing Committee of the CPC Central Committee, the party Central Committee and the State Council have convened a meeting here of cadres from party, government, and army organs at the central and Beijing municipal levels, calling on everyone to mobilize in this emergency and to adopt resolute and effective measures to curb turmoil in a clear-cut manner, to restore normal order in society, and to maintain stability and unity in order to ensure the triumphant implementation of our reform and open policy and the program of socialist modernization [applause].

The briefing by Comrade Li Ximing, secretary of the Beijing Municipal Party Committee, a little while ago indicated that the current situation in the capital is quite grim. The anarchic state is going from bad to worse. Law and discipline have been undermined. Prior to the beginning of May, the situation had begun to cool down as a result of great efforts. However, the situation has become more turbulent since the beginning of May. More and more students and other people have been involved in demonstrations. Many institutions of higher learning have come to a standstill. Traffic jams have taken place everywhere. The party and government leading organs have been affected, and public security has been rapidly deteriorating. All this has seriously disturbed and undermined the normal order of production, work, study, and everyday life of the people in the whole municipality. Some activities on the agenda for state affairs of the Sino-Soviet summit that attracted worldwide attention had to be canceled, greatly damaging China's international image and prestige.

The activities of some of the students on hunger strike at Tiananmen Square have not yet been stopped completely. Their health is seriously deteriorating and some of their lives are still in imminent danger. In fact, a handful of persons are using the hunger strikers as hostages to coerce and force the party and the government to yield to their political demands. In this regard, they have not one iota of humanity [applause].

The party and the government have, on one hand, taken every possible measure to treat and rescue the fasting students. On the other hand, they have held several dialogues with representatives of the fasting students and have earnestly promised to continue to listen to their opinions in the future, in the hope that the students would stop their hunger strike immediately. But, the dialogues did not yield results as expected. The square is packed with extremely excited crowds who keep shouting demagogic slogans. Right now, representatives of the hunger-striking students say that they can no longer control the situation. If we fail to promptly put an end to such a state of affairs and let it go unchecked, it will very likely lead to serious consequences which none of us want to see.

The situation in Beijing is still developing, and has already affected many other cities in the country. In many places, the number of demonstrators and protesters is increasing. In some places, there have been many incidents of people breaking into local party and government organs, along with beating, smashing, looting, burning, and other undermining activities that seriously violated the law. Some trains running on major railway lines have even been intercepted, causing communications to stop. Something has happened to our trunk line, the Beijing-Guangzhou line. Today, a train from Fuzhou was intercepted. The train was unable to move out for several hours.

All these incidents demonstrate that we will have nationwide major turmoil if no quick action is taken to turn and stabilize the situation. Our nation's reforms and opening to the outside world, the cause of the four modernizations, and even the fate and future of the People's Republic of China, built by many revolutionary martyrs with their blood, are facing a serious threat [applause].

Our party and government have pointed out time and time again that the vast numbers of young students are kindhearted, that subjectively they do not want turmoil, and that they have fervent patriotic spirit, wishing to push forward reform, develop democracy, and overcome corruption. This is also in line with the goals which the party and government have strived to accomplish. It should be said that many of the questions and views they raise have already exerted and will continue to exert positive influence on improving the work of the party and government. However, willfully using various forms of demonstrations, boycotts of class, and even hunger strikes to make petitions have damaged social stability and will not be beneficial to solving the problems. Moreover, the situation has developed completely independent of the subjective wishes of the young students. More and more it is going in a direction that runs counter to their intentions.

At present, it has become more and more clear that the very, very few people who attempt to create turmoil want to achieve, under the conditions of turmoil, precisely their political goals which they could not achieve through normal democratic and legal channels; to negate the CPC leadership and to negate the socialist system. They openly promoted the slogan of negating the opposition to bourgeois liberalization. Their goal is to gain absolute freedom to unscrupulously oppose the four cardinal principles. They spread many rumors, attacking, slandering, and abusing principal leaders of the party and state. At present, the spearhead has been focused on Comrade Deng Xiaoping, who has made tremendous contributions to our cause of reform and opening to the outside world. Their goal is precisely to organizationally subvert the CPC leadership, overthrow the people's government elected by the People's Congress in accordance with the law, and totally negate the people's democratic dictatorship. They stir up trouble everywhere, establish secret ties, instigate the creation of all kinds of illegal organizations, and force the party, the people, and the government to recognize them. In doing so, they are attempting to lay a foundation and make a breakthrough for the establishment of opposition factions and opposition parties. If they should succeed, the reform and opening to the outside world, democracy and legality, and socialist modernization would all come to nothing, and China would suffer a historical retrogression. A very promising China with a very bright future would become a hopeless China without a future.

One important reason for us to take a clear-cut stand in opposing the turmoil and exposing the political conspiracy of a handful of people is to distinguish the masses of young students from the handful of people who incited the turmoil. For almost a month, we adopted an extremely tolerant and restrained attitude in handling the student unrest. No government in the world would be so tolerant. The reason that we were so tolerant was out of our loving care for the masses of youths and students. We regard them as our own children and the future of China. We do not want to hurt good people, particularly not the young students. However, the handful of behind-the-scenes people, who were plotting and inciting the turmoil, miscalculated and took the tolerance as weakness on the part of the party and government. They continued to cook up stories to confuse and poison the masses, in an attempt to worsen the situation. This has caused the situation in the capital and many localities across the country to become increasingly acute. Under such circumstances, the CPC, as a ruling party and a government responsible to the people, is forced to take resolute and decisive measures to put an end to the turmoil [applause].

It must be stressed that even under such circumstances, we should still persist in protecting the patriotism of the students, make a clear distinction between them and the very, very few people who created the turmoil, and not penalize students for their radical words and actions in the student movement. Moreover, dialogue will continue in an active way through various channels, in different forms, and at different levels between the party and the government on one hand and the students and people from other walks of life on the other, including dialogue with those students who have taken part in parades, demonstrations, class boycotts, and hunger strikes, in order to take full heed of opinions from all segments. We will not only give clear-cut answers to the reasonable demands raised by them, but will also pay close attention to and earnestly accept their reasonable criticisms and suggestions, such as punishing profiteering officials, getting rid of corruption, and overcoming bureaucratism as well as promoting democracy, developing education, and so forth, so as to earnestly improve the work of the party and the government.

Under extremely complicated conditions in this period, many responsible comrades and the masses of teachers and students have taken pains and done a great deal of work to try to prevent demonstrations and keep order on campuses. They have been called campus traitors for their efforts. Public security personnel and armed policemen have made great contributions in maintaining traffic, social order, and security under extremely difficult conditions. Government offices, factories, shops, enterprises, and institutions have persisted in production and work, and made strenuous efforts to keep social life in order. The party and the government are aware of all this and are grateful; the people will never forget [applause]. Now, to check the turmoil with a firm hand and quickly restore order, I urgently appeal on behalf of the party Central Committee and the State Council: First, to those students now on hunger strike at Tiananmen Square to end the fasting immediately, leave the square, receive medical treatment, and recover their health as soon as possible. Second, to the masses of students and people in all walks of life to immediately stop all parades and demonstrations, and give no more so-called support to the fasting students in the interest of humanitarianism. Whatever the intent—I will not say that their intent is ill—further support will push the fasting students to desperation [applause].

Comrades, on behalf of the party Central Committee and the State Council, I now, at this meeting, call on the whole party, the entire army, and people of all nationalities throughout the country to unite, to pull together, and to act immediately at all their posts in an effort to stop the turmoil and stabilize the situation. Party organizations at all levels must unite the broad masses, must carry out thorough and painstaking ideological and educational work, and must fully play the role of core leadership and fighting fortress in stabilizing the situation. All Communist Party members must strictly abide by party discipline. They should not only stay away from any activities harmful to stability and unity, but they should also provide an exemplary vanguard role in uniting the masses and curbing the turmoil.

Governments at various levels must enforce administrative discipline and law, conscientiously strengthen leadership and control over their regions and departments, and earnestly carry out the work of stabilizing the situation, of reform, and of economic construction.

All government functionaries must stick to their own posts and maintain normal work order. All public security personnel should make greater efforts to maintain traffic and social order, to intensify social security, and to resolutely crack down on criminal activities of all kinds that have emerged. All industrial and commercial enterprises and institutions should abide by work discipline and persist in normal production. Schools of various kinds and at various levels should maintain normal teaching order. Those on strike should resume classes unconditionally.

Comrades, our party is a party in power and our government is a people's government. To be responsible to our sacred motherland and to all people, we must adopt firm and resolute measures to end the turmoil swiftly, to maintain the leadership of the party as well as the socialist system. We believe that our actions will surely have the support of all members of the Communist Party and the Communist Youth League, as well as workers, peasants, intellectuals, democratic parties, people in various circles, and the broad masses [applause]. We believe that we will certainly have the backing of the People's Liberation Army [PLA], which is entrusted by the Constitution with the glorious task of safeguarding the country and the peaceful work of the people [applause]. At the same time, we also hope that the broad masses will fully support the PLA, the public security cadres, and the police in their efforts to maintain order in the capital [applause].

Comrades, under the conditions of resolutely safeguarding stability and unity, we must continue to adhere to the four cardinal principles, to persist in the reform and opening up to the outside world, to strengthen democracy and the legal system, to eliminate all kinds of corruption, and to strive to advance the cause of socialist modernization [applause].

[Qiao Shi] Will Comrade Shangkun please make a speech? [applause]

[Yang Shangkun] First of all, I fully support the report and the various demands that Comrade Li Peng has made on behalf of the Standing Committee of the Political Bureau. Beijing of late is actually in an anarchistic state. Basically, the work of government organs, classes in schools, transportation, industry, and so forth have all been thrown into a confused state. This confused state is, in reality, a state of anarchy. Comrade Li Peng has just said that with regard to such a historic event as the Sino-Soviet talks, we could not hold the welcoming ceremony at Tiananmen. The location was changed to the airport at the last moment. Several discussions that should have been held at the Great Hall of the People were compelled to take place at Diaoyutai Guest House. In addition, some activities previously scheduled were canceled. Such a state of affairs....

[Unidentified person, interrupting] Even the wreath could not be presented.

[Yang Shangkun] Even the originally scheduled presentation of a wreath at the Monument of the People's Heroes could not be held. This has produced a very bad effect on our foreign relations. Even you had no freedom in driving here for this meeting. You had to make many detours to arrive here. You had to depart from your place one hour or more earlier in order to arrive at this meeting place in time. If this state of affairs is allowed to continue, then our capital will not be a capital. The work of the Beijing Municipality cannot be carried out, and the work of the State Council cannot be carried out. This is extremely serious.

To restore normal order, to restore public order, to stabilize the situation in Beijing Municipality, and to restore normal order [as heard] there is no choice but to move a group of the PLA to the vicinity of Beijing [applause; pan shots show presence of several uniformed men seated in the hall, also applauding].

The military vehicles on the road which you saw just now are those of the PLA troops entering the vicinity of Beijing Municipality a short while ago. This was done out of absolute necessity. It is because the police force in Beijing Municipality has been unable to maintain order in the municipality. In addition, nearly all the armed police and public security cadres and police in Beijing Municipality have been working hard day and night for the past month. Many comrades have been sick, yet they have had no choice but to stand on duty day and night, some without sleep for two or three days. Thus, without a group of PLA entering here to maintain public order in Beijing Municipality, order, we believe, would be very difficult to restore.

The arrival of PLA troops in the vicinity of Beijing is definitely not aimed at dealing with students. They have not come here to deal with the students. Their aim is to restore the normal order of production, of life, of work in Beijing Municipality. At the same time, they aim to protect a number of important departments and major government organs. Therefore, the stationing of the PLA troops in the capital is aimed at maintaining public security. They are, by no means, directed at the students. Everyone will be able to clearly see their activities in the next few days [applause].

That is to say that the PLA troops are compelled to enter the capital in order to restore the normal order in Beijing, maintain public security, and prevent important government organizations from being affected or stormed. I would like to explain this point clearly to all those who are present here. The PLA troops' arrival is definitely not aimed at dealing with the students. It is hoped that all trades and professions, people in various circles, and particularly people of the various democratic parties will support the PLA troops for their action to safeguard the capital and maintain public security. I hope that you will give them your full understanding and support [applause].

This is the point that I wanted to explain to you comrades here. I have nothing else to say. That is all [applause].

[Announcer] Attending the meeting were the president and vice president of the state, members of the Standing Committee of the Political Bureau of the CPC Central Committee currently in Beijing, and responsible comrades from the CPC Central Committee, the State Council, the National People's Congress, the Central Military Commission, the Central Advisory Commission, the National Committee of the Chinese People's Political Consultative Conference, and Beijing Municipality.

At the beginning of the meeting, Li Ximing, secretary of the Beijing Municipal Party Committee, briefed the meeting about the current situation in Beijing Municipality.

47
The Order of the State Council
on Enforcing Martial Law
in Part of Beijing Municipality

LI PENG

Source: *Renmin ribao* (People's Daily) (Beijing) (May 21, 1989): 1; FBIS, May 24, p. 24.

The order of the State Council of the People's Republic of China on enforcing martial law in part of Beijing Municipality:

In view of serious turmoil in Beijing Municipality, which has disrupted social stability, normal life and public order, and in accordance with Item 16 under Article 89 of the Constitution of the People's Republic of China, the State Council has decided to enforce martial law in part of Beijing Municipality from 10:00 A.M. [0100 GMT] on May 20, 1989, so as to check the turmoil with a firm hand, maintain Beijing Municipality's public order, protect citizens' lives and property, defend public property, and protect the central state organs and the Beijing Municipal Government doing day-to-day official business.

The Beijing Municipal People's Government will be in charge of the enforcement of the martial law and adopt specific martial law measures according to actual needs.

[Signed] Li Peng
Premier of the State Council
May 20, 1989

48
Students Visit Marshals Nie Rongzhen and Xu Xiangqian

Source: Beijing Domestic Service (unscheduled news report), May 21, 1989; FBIS, May 22, pp. 51–52.

According to our sources, eleven students of the Chinese Science and Technology University including Zhu Zhongji and Luo Zhiqiang made a call to the residence of Marshal Nie Rongzhen at 7:00 P.M. May 21. They asked to meet Marshal Nie and presented a letter to him.

The letter says: This afternoon, Comrade Li Peng presided over a meeting at which a four-point decision was adopted:

1. It claims that the students are engaged in a rebellion;
2. They purport to crack down on the 200,000 college students in Tiananmen Square;
3. The major jails in the capital have been cleared out; and
4. All sanitation workers will report to duty at 5:00 A.M. tomorrow to sweep Tiananmen Square.

The situation is extremely desperate. We request that Marshal Nie say something fair about this.

The students implored Marshal Nie to answer them immediately.

Marshal Nie answered:

1. These four points are a groundless rumor. Students, please do not believe them;
2. The troops are moving into Beijing to execute martial law for the sole purpose of safeguarding social order and stability in the capital. It is hoped that students will help the Liberation Army in carrying out this work well.
3. It is hoped that the students will leave Tiananmen Square as quickly as possible for the sake of national prestige, order in the capital, the livelihood of

the citizens, and their own health and study. I hope that students of the Science and Technology University will take the lead in returning to campuses and resuming classes.

Students Call on Marshal Xu

At about 9:00 P.M. on May 21, seven students of the Science and Technology University called on Marshal Xu Xiangqian at his residence. They were received by Marshal Xu's staff workers.

A representative of the students said: The troops are going to suppress the students, and it is highly possible that a bloody incident will occur tonight. They asked Marshal Xu to say a few words.

A staff worker of Marshal Xu told the students: The troops are carrying out the martial law tasks to restore the capital's normal order and safeguard the situation of stability and unity. These tasks are by no means targeted at the students. Army comrades are, under no circumstances, willing to see a bloody incident and will do everything to avert such an incident. Please do not listen to rumors. It is hoped that the students will return to school as quickly as possible and help the government to calm down the situation with a rational attitude.

The staff worker reported to Marshal Xu what he had told the students, and Xu agreed with what he told them. After hearing the staff worker's words, the students left Marshal Xu's residence immediately.

49
On May 22 Li Peng Again Stressed That the Student Movement Was a Disturbance

Source: *Ming pao* (Enlightenment) (Hong Kong) (May 30, 1989): 1; FBIS, May 30, pp. 3–4.

Three days after speaking at the party, government, and army cadre meeting on May 19, Chinese Premier Li Peng gave another internal speech, stressing that the recent student movement was an organized, planned, and premeditated disturbance. He also held that there were indeed trouble makers, with some directing at the frontline and others at the second and third lines. Li also said that they would by no means engage in this for merely one or two months but had made long-term plans.

The main points of Li Peng's internal talk were as follows:

Although the Political Bureau of the CPC Central Committee has not held a meeting recently, the Standing Committee has held numerous meetings, which have been attended by almost all of the old comrades. It is generally held that the April 26 [*Renmin ribao*] editorial is correct and that the present incident is a disturbance—an organized, planned, and premeditated disturbance—aimed at negating the socialist system and the leadership of the CPC. This can be seen more clearly now. Therefore, those old comrades with the highest prestige in the party, such as Comrades Xiaoping, Chen Yun, Li Xiannian, Peng Zhen, Yang Shangkun, and Wang Zhen, and most comrades of the Standing Committee of the Political Bureau of the CPC Central Committee hold that we should never retreat from the position of the April 26 editorial. Of course, the editorial could have been better written and the two different types of contradictions could have been written more clearly. This is a question of summing up experience, which can be completely and clearly explained. But the editorial itself is not wrong. If it is negated, this will mean that we have lost the spiritual pillar as a whole.

Viewed from the causes at a deeper level, these events are the result of the long-standing, unchecked spread of liberalization and are aimed at practicing the so-called democracy, freedom, and human rights of the West. Now backtracking will lead nowhere. If you take a step backward, he will take a step forward; if you take two steps backward, he will take two steps forward. We have come to the stage where there is no way to retreat. If we retreat still further, we shall have to give China away to them. Some old comrades in the party unanimously hold that we cannot retreat, but they agree that it is necessary to strictly distinguish between the two different types of contradictions. That is why in my speech on May 19 I made a point of repeating the words "a small handful" twice. There are indeed such people, with some directing at the frontline and others at the second and third lines. They are quite brilliant. They will by no means engage in this for merely one or two months but have made long-term plans.

We do not want a split within the party and we are very willing to unite as one. We would still be able to reach a consensus through discussion if this were an ordinary issue and there were differences of opinion on policy. But this case is different. After returning from Korea, Comrade Ziyang made a speech to the Asian Development Bank on May 4. He prepared the speech himself, without consulting any other member of the Standing Committee. The tone of the speech was completely different from that of the April 26 editorial. The speech was publicized widely and with great momentum. Since then we have discerned at least one problem, i.e., there are two differing views in the party. Anyone with political experience can discern this, and those involved in the disturbances can naturally discern this too. Comrade Ziyang's speech on May 3 marking the seventieth anniversary of the May 4th Movement was sent to us in advance. Several of us suggested that it was necessary to put in the words "opposing bourgeois liberalization," but he rejected this. In the wake of his speech marking the May 4th Movement, the student unrest escalated, with 1 million people taking to the streets. Many people from other places also came to Beijing to take part in the demonstrations. Eventually, the central authorities decided to impose martial law.

There is still another question that merits our attention: Who is the key leader of our party and who represents reform and opening up? Is it Comrade Ziyang or Comrade Xiaoping? On this count, all people must keep a clear head. All major principles and policies have been put forward by Comrade Xiaoping since reform was conducted ten years ago. Comrade Xiaoping is the general designer of the reform and the open policies. Comrade Xiaoping represents China's reform and opening up as far as the world is concerned. Naturally, Comrade Ziyang has also done a lot of work, but he has also implemented what Comrade Xiaoping has said. He has also made quite a few mistakes in his work. In his talks with Gorbachev, he first said that Comrade Xiaoping was the highest decision maker in our party, that this was decided at the first plenary session of the Thirteenth CPC Central Committee, and that we consulted him on all major issues. What did this mean? He put Comrade Xiaoping to the fore. As a result, the slogan chanted during the demonstration the following day was "Down with Deng Xiaoping." If we want to uphold party unity and the unity of the party nucleus, I think we should defend Comrade Xiaoping with a clear-cut stand.

Let me brief you on something else: The speech I made at the meeting of responsible comrades of the central and Beijing party, government, and army organizations on May 19 was approved by the central authorities. The Standing Committee decided to hold the meeting and to impose martial law. Comrade Ziyang should have attended the meeting if he wanted to uphold party unity. But he asked for sick leave. As general secretary, it was all right for him not to speak if he did not feel well, but he should have been able to preside over the meeting, which he did not do. It was all right for another person to preside over the meeting instead, but he should have attended the meeting. However, he didn't want to do this either. Who has disrupted party unity and who has sabotaged the party principle of democratic centralism? His speeches, including the one he gave when he called on the students at Tiananmen in the small hours of May 19, have laid bare to the people of the whole country the differences of opinion within the party.

This struggle is indeed very complicated and the problem lies precisely within the party. If this were not so, it would not have developed to such an extent.

These events have very profound causes. Unless the problem is solved from within the party and from the root, the problem cannot be solved at all.

50
Main Points of Yang Shangkun's Speech at Emergency Enlarged Meeting of the Central Military Commission

Source: *Ming pao* (Enlightenment) (Hong Kong) (May 29, 1989): 1–2; FBIS, May 30, pp. 17–20.

([*Ming pao*] editor's note: This is a speech given by Yang Shangkun, executive vice chairman of the Central Military Commission at an emergency enlarged meeting of the Military Commission on May 24. It was originally entitled, "Main Points of Comrade Yang Shangkun's Speech at Emergency Enlarged Meeting of Central Military Commission on May 24, 1989, Edited from the Transcript." The subheads are ours.)

Is This State of Affairs Still Not a Disturbance?

The Military Commission has decided to convene an emergency enlarged meeting and ask the principal responsible comrades of all major units to attend. The principal aim is to tell you one thing: that the present situation in Beijing is still chaotic. Although martial law has been declared, some of the martial law tasks have in fact not been carried out. Some army units enforcing martial law have been blocked, and they have not forcibly passed through, in order to avoid direct confrontation. Through great effort, most units have not entered their predetermined positions. The situation was even more chaotic a few days ago. No vehicle bearing a military plate could pass through. Is this state of affairs still not a disturbance? The situation in the capital is precisely a disturbance. This disturbance has not subsided.

There have been ups and downs in the student movement in the past month and more. Generally speaking, it is moving upward. Since Comrade Yaobang's death, the slogans in the streets have changed several times. When Comrade

Yaobang died, the slogans were about rehabilitating Comrade Yaobang and "Down with the Communist Party," "Down with the bureaucratic government," and "Down with the corrupt government." At that time, the slogan "Down with Deng Xiaoping" was not common, and was only shouted in a small number of places. After *Renmin ribao* carried the editorial, "It is Necessary to Take a Clear-Cut Stand Against Disturbances" on April 26, the students changed their slogans. They no longer shouted "Down with the government" and "Down with the Communist Party," but changed the slogans to "Eliminate corruption," "Down with bureaucrats," "Support the correct CPC," and "Support the four cardinal principles." After May 4, some of our comrades suddenly said that the current movement was patriotic and reasonable. This immediately started another high tide, which later developed into a hunger strike. In Comrade Li Ximing's speech, he talked about these things in great detail. The party Central Committee has distributed the material to you, and I am not going into detail about it here. The party Central Committee has always tried to ease the feelings of the masses and calm the situation. But they have stirred up greater trouble, and now Beijing is out of control. Moreover, for a time it was calm in other provinces, but now trouble has been stirred up again there. There is now trouble in almost every province and city. In short, every time we take a step backward, they take a step forward. At present, they are focusing on one slogan: "Down with Li Peng." This is what they have decided internally, and they have discarded other slogans. Their objective is to overthrow the Communist Party and the present government. The situation became stable for a time, but the disturbances started up again following the talk or article of a certain person from the central authorities. After it subsided a little, it started up again. Eventually, Beijing could not help but declare martial law.

Why has this situation emerged? Why has the capital gone out of control? Why have there been major demonstrations across the country? Why are the slogans they raise specially directed against the State Council? Some time ago, some old comrades of noble character and high prestige, such as Comrade Chen Yun, Comrade [Li] Xiannian, Comrade Peng Zhen, Comrade Xiaoping, Comrade Wang Zhen, and Sister Deng Yingchao, were very worried about this and asked why the situation had developed to such an extent. After analyzing the development of things, they drew this conclusion: The events are happening among the students, but the root is in the party. That is to say, there are two voices, two different voices in the Standing Committee of the Politburo. As summarized by Comrade Xiannian, there are two headquarters.

Two Headquarters in the Standing Committee of the Politburo

The spirit of the April 26 editorial was to resolutely oppose disturbances. This was discussed and decided by the Standing Committee. At that time, Comrade

Ziyang was not in Beijing, but in [North] Korea. A cable was sent to Comrade Ziyang, informing him of the Standing Committee's decision and Comrade Xiaoping's view. He cabled a reply, saying that he agreed and completely supported this. However, when he returned on April 29, he was the first to say that the tone of the editorial was too shrill and that its nature was not correctly determined. The editorial dealt with the question of opposing the disturbance, pointing out that the disturbance was organized and planned, and that its purpose was to negate socialism and the Communist Party. In his view, however, it was a patriotic student movement. He did not recognize this as a disturbance. As soon as he returned, he wanted the party Central Committee to do as he said and announce that the editorial was erroneous. Thus, another voice among the five Standing Committee members was heard. He spoke several times. The first time was his May 3 speech marking the May 4th Movement. At that time, it could not be discerned clearly. He talked at great length about the disturbance, saying that our country could not tolerate it. That was good. But he also said that the student movement was still patriotic. It was most obvious in a speech delivered at a meeting with the board of governors of the Asian Development Bank. You should read the speech carefully; in it he says that the students' action is a patriotic one and understandable. Then, he pointed out that we indeed have many corrupt phenomena, that we are identical with the students in thinking, and that we should solve these questions through democracy and the legal system. In his speech, he did not say whether the April 26 editorial was correct or not; he just skirted the issue. But he did talk about the disturbance. This was quite an important speech. That is why Chairman Deng said that the student rioting has experienced several relapses and that two voices have emerged. This precisely refers to Comrade Zhao Ziyang's speech. It was a turning point. With the exposure to the students of the different views among the Standing Committee members of the Politburo of the CPC Central Committee, the students became even more vigorous, and thus, such slogans as "Support Zhao Ziyang," "Down with Deng Xiaoping," and "Down with Li Peng" emerged.

A Situation Similar to the Cultural Revolution Has Emerged

During this period, the Standing Committee of the Politburo of the CPC Central Committee held many meetings, saying that the tone should no longer be changed. But he [Zhao] stuck to his view. Even when Comrade Xiaoping attended the meeting, he also stuck to his view, saying that he was unconvinced and that on the question of the nature of the student movement, he could not maintain unanimity with the arguments of Comrade Xiaoping and other comrades of the Standing Committee. He therefore asked to resign, saying that he could no longer work. Later, I told him that the issue was so great that if the nature were changed, we would all collapse. The vast numbers of school teachers, presidents, and active students would be slapped in the face and could not have a foothold, and the vast numbers of student party members, cadres, and university presidents, who had been working hard among the students, would be overthrown. By this time, the students said they wanted to set up their own new student federation to oppose the original, old student federation. Moreover, they wanted to hold their own elections. A situation similar to that of the Cultural Revolution also emerged in Beijing. At Beijing University, for example, the school broadcasting station was occupied and the nameplate of the student union was smashed. Similar events also happened at the University of Political Science and Law. Cases of seizing broadcasting stations occurred in some universities, and some students even entered the stations by breaking through windows. The present problem is that two different voices in the party have been completely exposed in society. The students feel that there is a person in the party Central Committee who supports them and, therefore, they stir up greater trouble, calling for an emergency meeting of the National People's Congress [NPC] Standing Committee or an emergency session of the NPC. Their objective is clearly to use these organizations to pass a resolution to negate the April 26 editorial, and, in line with their argument, affirm that the student movement is a spontaneous patriotic, democratic movement. Please think it over; if the NPC Standing Committee makes such a resolution, does this not mean that the aforesaid editorial would be negated? Now they are energetically carrying out this work and initiating a signature campaign. In the face of this situation, what should we do? Comrades Chen Yun and Xiannian have hurriedly returned to Beijing, saying that it is absolutely necessary to hold a meeting to define a policy on what should be done. Naturally, other comrades, such as Peng Zhen, Wang Zhen, Sister Deng, and the two old marshals, are also very concerned about the situation. Shall we retreat or not? If we retreat, we shall have to recognize what they want; if we don't, we should unswervingly carry out the principle of the April 26 editorial.

This was the first time that these octogenarians had gotten together to discuss central affairs in many years. Xiaoping, Chen Yun, Peng Zhen, Big Sister Deng, and Wang Zhen all felt that there was no way to retreat, because a retreat would indicate our collapse and the collapse of the PRC, and this would mean a comeback for capitalism, just as former U.S. Secretary of State Dulles—who said that our socialism would become liberalism through a number of generations—had hoped. Comrade Chen Yun made a very important statement. He said that the People's Republic was built through decades of war, and that the achievements won with the blood of tens of millions of revolutionary martyrs could be ruined overnight, and that this would be equal to the negation of the CPC. Comrades in Beijing clearly heard what Comrade Ziyang said on the morning of May 19 when visiting the hunger strikers in Tiananmen Square. Any person of sensibility could discern that his words were unreasonable. First, he said that we had come too late, and then he began to cry. Second, he said that the events were very complicated and that many things could not be solved at that moment, but that things could eventually be solved in time. He told the students that they were still young and had a long way to go, but that we are old so it does not matter. It was a low-key speech full of compunction. It seemed that he had a great deal of pain and difficulty that could not be clearly expressed. After hearing what he said, most cadres in Beijing said that he simply had no sense of organization or discipline. On the same evening, we held a meeting of party, government, and military cadres in Beijing, and he was also asked to attend this meeting. However, he suddenly decided not to attend this meeting shortly before the meeting was opened. Without the participation of the general secretary, people could immediately discern the problem. According to the original agenda, he was supposed to make a speech at the meeting. So when the time for the meeting was up, we still had to wait for him. At that moment, the troops were moving toward Beijing. It was planned to declare the imposition of martial law at midnight on May 21, because under such circumstances, martial law had to be imposed. As a result, martial law was imposed on May 20. According to the original agenda, I was not required to make a speech. However, I could not help but make an impromptu speech, because the military vehicles were blocked there. How could I not say something to explain this? So, I said that the troops were ordered to move into Beijing to maintain law and order, and they were absolutely not aimed at the students. If you do not believe this, just see what happens in the next few days.

Zhao Wrote a Letter of Resignation to Deng

Materials compiled by several research institutes were circulated in society. They were even printed under the name of a *Renmin ribao* extra issue. Five points were mentioned in them. The General Political Department will reprint these materials for your reference. According to these materials, the several points presented by Comrade Zhao Ziyang were all vetoed by the Political Bureau Standing Committee, but this was absolutely untrue. For example, the point that problems should be solved along the course of democracy and the legal system was endorsed by all of the people. It was also agreed that a meeting of the National People's Congress Standing Committee would be held after Comrade Wan Li returned home. For a period of nearly one month, all of the comrades tried to persuade Zhao, telling him that the April 26 editorial should not be negated; otherwise our position would become untenable, but he refused to accept this. After Comrade Xiaoping and other elders decided that no concession could be made, he wrote a letter to Comrade Xiaoping, saying that he would not continue to work, because "my idea is different from yours and I cannot go along with your decision; if I continue to work with the Standing Committee, I might be an obstacle to the Standing Committee's implementation of the idea of several senior comrades, including Chairman

Deng." At the same time, however, he also agreed that making a decision is better than making no decision. He then said that he was willing to follow the principle of the minority being subordinate to the majority. He said that what Comrade Xiaoping said was correct and this was a principle of the organization's discipline. Finally, he resigned.

Therefore, as I have told you, the root cause of the problem lies within the party. On this issue, Comrade Xiaoping has spoken twice. The first time, he mentioned the economic disorder, inflation, and the overheated economy which appeared five years ago and has become more and more serious in the past three years since there have been no effective countermeasures. The second time, on April 25, he said that there were different opinions within the party. On the issue of opposing bourgeois liberalization, Zhao's attitude was the same as Hu Yaobang's. If the struggle against bourgeois liberalization had been carried out thoroughly, the current events would not have happened. In particular, the struggle against spiritual pollution was carried out for only twenty days. The current events are related to the failure to thoroughly carry out the struggle against bourgeois liberalization and the failure to oppose spiritual pollution. Therefore, the character of Comrade Ziyang's words is the same as that of Comrade Hu Yaobang's refusal to oppose liberalization. This thus thoroughly reveals the nature of things. On another occasion, Comrade Xiaoping told some foreign visitors that the greatest error of the past ten years has been our failure to attach importance to education. Then he said that we had not done painstaking work to advocate a hard-working spirit or to carry forward fine traditions. Here, he mentioned two points: First, the problem of education; and second, spiritual civilization. He did not only say that the education budget was insufficient. Comrade Xiaoping's thought is consistent. That is, the four cardinal principles must be maintained, and citizens should have the "four good things."

The Leader Must Be Changed if He Refuses to Carry Out Instructions

As we are now facing such a problem, how shall we solve it? Today I want to first talk to you, comrades in various major military units. The central comrades have considered again and again and found that it is necessary to change the leader, because he has refused to implement the central instructions and has stuck to his own ideas. He has tried to achieve his purpose through legislative procedures, because his opinion was opposed by most comrades in the Political Bureau and he could have only one vote in the Standing Committee. After Zhao Ziyang's resignation request was passed on to outside people, rumors circulated and people doubted that these old people in their seventies and eighties could properly solve problems. Here I would like to say that this question can be answered very easily. The decision was made by the majority of the Standing Committee members. The many old comrades enjoy the highest prestige inside the party, because they have the highest seniority in the party and have made major contributions to the party and the state. We do not need to mention that Comrade Xiaoping, Xiannian, Chen Yun, Marshal Nie [Rongzhen], Marshal Xu [Xiangqian], Big Sister Deng, Peng Zhen, and Wang Zhen have all made important contributions to the party. At such a critical juncture of the party and the state, how could they remain silent? They could not just sit there and see our state being brought to the verge of destruction. As Communist Party members, it was their duty to do something. Some people have spread the rumor that there is no party now and that only one person made the decision. This is completely wrong. The current events were handled correctly according to the decision made by the majority of comrades in the Politburo and its Standing Committee. The revolutionaries of the older generation, including Chen Yun, Xiannian, and Comrade Xiaoping, completely supported this correct decision. During Gorbachev's visit to China, Zhao Ziyang told Gorbachev of Comrade Xiaoping's historical position, which was proper of him to do. However, Zhao talked about this for a long time as soon as the talks began. He said that all major issues were decided by Comrade Xiaoping. Any comrade with a sober head could discern that Zhao was trying to shirk responsibility by saying this. He pushed Comrade Xiaoping to the forefront to bear the responsibility for all errors. I believe that you have also discerned Zhao's recent maneuvers.

Now, the whole party must be united and implement the April 26 editorial wholeheartedly. We can no longer retreat and must launch an offensive. Today I just want to tell you about this so that you can prepare yourself mentally. In particular, the army must be consolidated, and this is of vital importance. Have all the military personnel been convinced? This will depend on your work. I think that there is no problem among the comrades at the level of the major military regions. But are there any problems among the officers and men at and below the army corps level? Now some people ask: As there are three chairmen in the Central Military Commission, how could Deng Xiaoping alone order the movement of the troops responsible for enforcing martial law? These people do not understand the military service in our country at all, and can only deceive some students. In our army, we pursue a commander responsibility system. Such people as I only play a counseling role in assisting the chairman. When he made the decision, he had not only talked with me, but had also talked with [Hong] Xuezhi, [Liu] Huaqing, and Minister Qin [Jiwei] as well. Why could he not issue the order? Now I pass on this information to you, and I hope that you will not be too surprised if there is a change in the party's top leading body. Frankly speaking, we gave too much credit to Comrade Ziyang for his work in the past. The achievements of the past few years were in fact made collectively by the Politburo according to the instructions of

Comrade Xiaoping. Zhao was only responsible for implementing these decisions.

Now you are invited to this meeting, because we want you to do some work.

If the Troops Do Not Obey Orders, Commanders Will Be Punished According to the Military Law

First, you must clearly understand all this.

Second, you should hold party committee meetings after you return to your own units and clearly explain the situation to your comrades. This can be conveyed to cadres at the regiment level.

Third, all party committees should unify the thinking of their members and bring their thinking into line with the position of the central leadership. In particular, if any troops do not obey orders, I will punish those responsible according to the military law.

Fourth, you must pay special attention to the military academies. Cadres, instructors, and professors should effectively educate the cadets, who must not be allowed to join any demonstration or support activity.

Fifth, the troops that have arrived in the predetermined areas should now immediately settle down and take a good rest. Then the troops should be fully mobilized. Clear explanations should be given to the grass-roots cadres.

Before I came to this meeting, Chairman Deng gave me an idea. He said that military cadres should be organized to conduct propaganda among students and citizens. They should tell the masses (in various neighborhoods) and the students why the army has come here. Today is the fifth day of martial law. In the past five days, not a shot has been fired nor has anyone been beaten up. All citizens are clear about this. So we need to carry out propaganda work patiently.

In addition, we should also give explanations to retired comrades. We should notify them of this separately. This is an important job, and we must take it on immediately. After this meeting, we will see how the situation develops. You should submit a brief report about the general situation a few days from now. The central decision will be carried out through your work.

51
Solve the Current Problems in China Along the Track of Democracy and the Legal System

YAN JIAQI AND BAO ZUNXIN

Source: *Ming pao* (Enlightenment) (Hong Kong) (May 26, 1989): 2; FBIS, May 26, pp. 11–12.

The student movement currently happening in China has developed into a nationwide all-people protest movement. This is an epoch-making major event in modern China, and its irresistible force has greatly promoted the democratic process in China. The student movement has announced to the whole country the basic principle of democratic politics, namely, all the power of the country belongs to the people. The power of the ruling party which organizes the government and the government itself is not inherent, but comes from the people. The people have the power to overthrow the government which is not trusted by the people. The student movement has issued to the whole country the slogan "Down with Li Peng!" For a long period of time in the past, propaganda machines in our country regarded the criticism of the party and government leaders as "attacking the party and government leadership." The student movement has completely discarded such an outmoded idea, so that Li Peng and others cannot invent any excuse to prohibit people from condemning the perverse acts of the government. If a head of the government, who has been discarded by the people, refuses to resign of his own accord, people can dismiss him through the stipulations contained in the Constitution.

The First Step to Overthrow the Li Peng Government

According to Article 57 of the Constitution, the National People's Congress (NPC) is the highest organ of state power, and it has the power to recall or remove from office the premier of the State Council. The NPC Standing Committee, as the permanent body of the NPC, has the power to abrogate the administrative decrees and regulations, decisions and orders issued by the State Council which run counter to the Constitution and the laws.

The current problem is that we must take the first step. We must hold an urgent meeting of the NPC Standing Committee to make decisions on the following two issues: (1) abrogating the "State Council's Order on Imposing Martial Law in Some Areas of the Beijing Municipality"; and (2) Holding an urgent session of the NPC in the near future.

The order issued by the State Council on imposing martial law in some areas of the Beijing Municipality has been executed for five days. During the past five days, "social order in Beijing has been the same as usual, and the life of the residents has been roughly the same"; "in the areas designated by the municipal government where the martial law is imposed, no unusual situation different from the previous one has occurred," and "social order in Beijing is continuing to develop toward the direction of stability." However, (unlike what *Renmin ribao* has described above), after the proclamation of the martial law order, students and residents are extremely worried about the present situation. To block the troops which are advancing toward the city, at crossings of all roads leading toward the suburbs, Beijing residents set up roadblocks. Facts over the past five days have fully proved that it is unnecessary for the State Council to proclaim the martial law order. Furthermore, due to the resolute resistance of students and residents, and the common views shared by soldiers, students and residents, it has been impossible to execute the martial law order.

The Second Step to Overthrow the Li Peng Government

According to Article 29 of the Constitution, our country's armed forces belong to the people. They can be used only when the state is facing a foreign invasion, or a serious armed riot has occurred in our country. Now Beijing Municipality is not invaded by foreign armed forces, and no armed riot has occurred either; sending troops to the municipality to undertake the "task of martial law" is an act which violates the Constitution. Therefore, we strongly urge the NPC Standing Committee to hold an emergency meeting immediately to abrogate the martial law order.

Over the past month, Li Peng, as the prime minister of the State Council, has made very serious mistakes or has even committed crimes in the following two issues: First, he turned a blind eye to the petition of more than 3,000 students on a hunger strike, and more than 1,000 students fainted because of the hunger strike. In the history of the whole world, not a single government can turn a blind eye to several thousand students who are staging a hunger strike. This fact has fully shown that Li Peng has become a prime minister who has completely lost all his human nature.

Second, on May 20, Li Peng, as the prime minister of the State Council, issued the martial law order to be executed in some areas in Beijing to deal with students who were holding a peaceful petition, and those unarmed residents. This has enraged residents of the whole Beijing Municipality and people throughout the country. This has also been condemned by public opinion of the whole country and the whole world. Li Peng has used the troops to deal with the unarmed students and residents. This is an act seriously violating the Constitution.

Democratic politics is responsible politics. Article 61 of the Constitution stipulates: "A session of the NPC may be convened at any time the standing committee deems this necessary, or when more than one-fifth of the deputies to the NPC so propose." We strongly demand that the NPC session will be held as early as possible to examine the acts of Li Peng in April and May this year, which have betrayed and opposed the people, and to dismiss him from his post of prime minister.

Calling on People's Deputies to Cast Their Sacred Votes

Over a long period of time in the past, due to the fact that the government is replaced by the party, and the fact that the party is not differentiated from the government administration, the stipulation that the NPC is the highest organ of state power has remained an empty word. Now it is time for us to completely change the situation that the party is placed above the highest organ of state power. As long as the reasons for holding an NPC session comply with the stipulations contained in the Constitution, the session can be held without the approval of Li Peng who has held several party and government leading posts, and other persons. Must a meeting of the NPC Standing Committee aimed at abrogating the martial law order, and an NPC session aimed at dismissing Li Peng from the post of the prime minister be held with the approval of Li Peng, or some other persons? At present, the serious economic crisis in our country can only be solved along the track of democracy and a legal system. Therefore, we call on each and every people's deputy to cast his or her sacred vote to abrogate the martial law order and to dismiss Li Peng from his post as prime minister. When the Chinese people see that the NPC has become the true highest organ of state power, our people's deputies will realize that they have made an unprecedentedly great and historical contribution to the building of the democratic politics in China.

If Li Peng Resorts to Violence, He Will Be Brought to Trial

At present, the NPC Standing Committee meeting has not been held, and the martial law order has not been abrogated. The power is still in the hands of Li Peng. When Chairman Wan Li issues an appeal on solving the current problems in China along the track of democracy and the legal system, Li Peng and others might resort to violence to suppress the people. If the NPC Standing Committee meeting and the NPC session cannot be held, and if massive bloodshed occurs because of the suppression, Li Peng will further commit unpardonable crimes in addition to his previous two mistakes. This will bring Li Peng as the prime minister to trial in accordance with the law. We wish to offer a piece of advice to Li Peng: Your wisest choice is to resign of your own accord to reduce the catastrophe brought to the country and the people. If Li Peng resigns of his own accord, and if he does not commit further mistakes and crimes, we propose that we refrain from investigating and affixing his responsibility for the serious mistakes of dealing with students on hunger strike in an inhuman way, and of proclaiming the martial law order on May 20. What course to follow—it is now the time for Li Peng to make his final choice. If Li Peng resorts to violence to quell the student movement, and if he truly resorts to arms to maintain his tottering rule, millions upon millions of the Chinese people will establish democracy in China with their own blood and lives.

52
Speech to CPC Central Advisory Commission Standing Committee

CHEN YUN

Source: Beijing Television Service, May 26, 1989; FBIS, May 26, pp. 14–15.

["Important News"; announcer-read report over still photos of Chen Yun, chairman of the Central Advisory Commission, seated in a chair behind a desk, with two microphones in front; Chen Yun, seated, and Song Renqiong, vice-chairman of the Central Advisory Commission, standing next to a table applauding; Bo Yibo seated with an unidentified person; long shot of committee members voting by a show of hands.]

Comrade Chen Yun, chairman of the Central Advisory Commission, today presided over a meeting of the Standing Committee of the Central Advisory Commission and made an important speech at the meeting.

The meeting relayed and studied the guidelines of the series of instructions of the party Central Committee and the State Council on opposing turmoil and safeguarding social stability. The participating comrades unanimously expressed resolute support for Comrade Chen Yun's important speech; resolute support for speeches made by Comrades Li Peng and Yang Shangkun at the meeting of central and Beijing municipal party, government, and army cadres; and resolute support for the correct policy decisions and decisive measures taken by the party Central Committee and the State Council to stop the turmoil and stabilize the situation.

Everyone believed that the Chinese revolution went through decades of hard struggle and saw the sacrifice of more than twenty million people, and only then was the People's Republic of China founded. The victory has not come easily. We are all veteran comrades who have struggled for more than several decades for the founding and construction of the Republic. If the turmoil created by a very, very few people is not resolutely put down, then there will be no peace in the party and the country.

Not only is there the danger of losing the achievements of ten years of reform, but there is also the danger of losing all the fruits of revolution, which were won with blood, and all the achievements of the socialist construction. Therefore, in such a critical moment, we the veteran comrades must step forward boldly and, together with comrades of the whole party, resolutely expose the schemes and intrigues of the very, very few people who have created the turmoil and resolutely wage a struggle against them. We must never make concessions. There should be no slightest amount of vagueness.

At the same time, we should strictly distinguish between the extremely few people and the vast numbers of young students and resolutely protect the ardent patriotism of young students. This is the responsibility of each of us old comrades.

All believed that our party and government are able and have the means to stop the turmoil and will definitely act in accordance with the common wish of the people of all nationalities in China to carefully and successfully handle the problems confronting us. The comrades noted that it was by no means accidental that the turmoil occurred as it did. One of the major reasons is that, for a considerable length of time, we have relaxed our efforts in Marxist ideological education and relegated the party's ideological and political work. Facts once again tell us that, to safeguard the stability and unity in society and guarantee smooth sailing for the drive for socialist modernization and the cause of socialist reform, it is imperative to firmly adhere to the four cardinal principles.

All unanimously agreed that the ardent patriotism of the vast numbers of the students is very commendable and must be fully affirmed. Their demand to promote democracy and rectify corruption is in accord with the wishes of the party and the government and must be heeded earnestly to actively improve the work of the party and government.

At the same time, everyone sincerely hoped that the students would carry forward their spirit of loving the party and the country, take the interests of the whole situation into consideration, and quickly return to their schools to resume study to strive to learn good skills so as to shoulder the important task of building the future of the motherland assigned them by history.

All comrades attending the meeting also extended greetings and expressed gratitude to all workers, peasants, intellectuals, medical personnel, and office cadres who are remaining steadfast at their production and work posts and making contributions in improving the economic environment, rectifying the eco-

nomic order, and deepening the reform and in stopping the turmoil and safeguarding order in society; extended greetings and salute to the commanders and
fighters of the People's Liberation Army who are strictly observing discipline
and actively fulfilling their duty to enforce martial law; and extended greetings
and salute to the vast numbers of public security cadres and police and commanders and fighters of the armed police force.

Those attending the meeting included the vice-chairmen of the Central Advisory Commission, Bo Yibo and Song Renqiong; and Central Advisory Commission Standing Committee members Wang Ping, Wang Shoudao, Wu Xiuquan,
Liu Lantao, Jiang Hua, Yang Dezhi, Xiao Ke, Yu Qiuli, Song Shilun, Zhang
Jingfu, Lu Dingyi, Chen Pixian, Chen Xilian, Hu Qiaomu, Duan Junyi, Geng
Biao, Ji Pengfei, Huang Zhen, and Kang Shien. Comrade Huang Huoqing also
attended today's meeting. Five of the members of the Standing Committee requested leave because of illness or matters at hand. Comrade Cheng Zihua made
a telephone call to the meeting to express his firm support for the correct policy
decision and other measures adopted by the party Central Committee and the
State Council for the purpose of stopping the turmoil.

53
"Full Text" of Speech to Li Peng and Yao Yilin [May 31, 1989]

DENG XIAOPING

Source: *Tung fang jih pao* (Eastern daily) (Hong Kong) (July 14, 1989): 5; FBIS, July 17, pp. 15–17.

It is necessary to stress to the end that the policy of reform and opening will
remain unchanged and that it will remain unchanged for several decades. People
at home and abroad are very concerned about this issue. It is necessary to
implement the line, principles, and policies laid down since the third plenary
session of the Eleventh CPC Central Committee. Even the wording should remain unchanged. Having been approved by the party congress, not a character in
the political report of the Thirteenth Party Congress should be changed. I have
solicited the views of Comrades [Li] Xiannian and Chen Yun on this issue and
they have agreed.

Following this turmoil, we indeed have some matters to explain to the people.

After the turmoil is put down, it is necessary to make an account for this. There are chiefly two points:

First, we should change the leading group, and the new leading body should enable the people to sense a new outlook, realizing that this is a reform and a promising outlook. This is a most important point, an opportunity to declare our positions to the people! The people want to see practical things. Otherwise, we shall never have any tranquil days. If we present a lineup which the people think is a rigid, conservative leading body or a mediocre leading body which cannot reflect China's future, there will still be a lot of trouble in the future. The current event, on the whole, is not over yet! The students have not returned to classes yet, and, even if they return to classes, they will still take to the streets. One point that should be affirmed is that workers, peasants, intellectuals, and students will long for reform. This time, even the slogan of Down with Deng Xiaoping has been raised, but there is no slogan about overthrowing the reform. However, the name of the so-called "reform" advocated by some people should be changed to something else. It should be called liberalization, namely, capitalist liberalization. The heart of their "reform" is to turn toward capitalism. Our reform is different from theirs, and this question should still be continuously debated. In short, having a new, reform outlook is a very important issue in determining the members of the new leading body. This is not an important, but a very important issue. We should be able to see the overall situation.

Second, it is necessary to do several things in a down-to-earth manner to show that we are genuinely and not falsely opposed to corruption. We have been opposed to corruption. I am also very discontented with the corrupt phenomena! It is necessary to oppose corruption and do several things in a down-to-earth manner. For several years, I have been talking about this; you have also heard me talk on numerous occasions. I also frequently check on whether some people in my family have violated law and discipline. By grasping corrupt phenomena at random we can get hold of important cases. The problem is that we often do not have the determination to set about doing it. This has lost popular sympathy, making people think that we are shielding corruption. We must pass this barrier and make good our words. We should investigate and deal with the cases as they should be. We must establish credibility among the people.

A good leading body committed to reform and opening up should clearly do several things on opening up. If we meet such opportunities, we should not miss them. We should stick to and set about grasping them. We should reflect reform and opening up and open up wider. I have said in the past that we should build several Hong Kongs, which means that we should open up rather than close, and that we should open up wider than before. If we do not open up, it will be impossible to develop. We have little capital, but we can get some money by taking advantage of opening up, the labor force, taxation, and land; spur the development of other trades; increase financial revenue; and receive benefits.

Take Hong Kong as an example. It is advantageous to us. If we do not have Hong Kong, at the least we would have no access to information. In short, we should be bolder in reform and opening up.

I ask you to come here today to see whether this argument is correct. One is to form a leading body having the image of reform and opening up to put people at ease. This is the first point in establishing credibility among the people. The second is to carry out some practical work, punish corruption, and establish credibility among the people. We should genuinely do several things to show that not only will we not change our policy of reform and opening up, but we will also continue deepening the reform and opening up. We should present the people with facts so that the people can calm down. Otherwise, some people will take to the street today; others will do so tomorrow. If we do not consider this issue from a broader angle, it will be impossible to retain calm for one month, two months, and three months. This is the overall situation.

Comrades in our Politburo, Standing Committee of the Politburo, and Secretariat are all people administering important matters. When considering a problem, we should set our eyes on long-term interest and the overall situation. Many small situations must be subordinated to the overall situation. This is a crucial issue. All people have shortcomings. The three of us present here have shortcomings. Each has his own accounts and each has his own weak points. Naturally, some shortcomings are big and some are small; some people have many shortcomings and some have few. No people have no shortcomings.

Undoubtedly, as far as our experience in entering politics and engaging in struggle goes, our leading bodies have weak points. This is a fact. Starting from Mao Zedong, Liu Shaoqi, Zhou Enlai, and Zhu De, the Chinese party genuinely formed a tangible leadership. The previous leaders were not very stable, nor were they very mature. From Chen Duxiu to the Zunyi meeting, no leaders were genuinely mature. For a long time, we stressed the leadership of the working class by making, with difficulty, some workers leaders; in the Red Army, we also selected a group of workers to serve as commissars. In the history of our party, it was from the generation of Mao Zedong, Liu Shaoqi, Zhou Enlai, and Zhu De that a tangible leadership genuinely took shape. The early period of this generation was good, but it later became a disaster when the Great Cultural Revolution was launched. Hua Guofeng was only a transition, and his period could not be regarded as a generation. He himself did not have an independent thing, and he only had "two whatevers."[1] The second generation is our generation. Now it is the third generation. Genuine efforts should be made to establish

---

[1]"Whatever Mao said must be followed; whatever Mao decided must be upheld." Hua Guofeng's endorsement of this 1977 slogan identified his faction as the "Whateverists" during the post–Gang of Four power struggle with Deng Xiaoping's "Practice" faction.

new leadership in the third generation. This leadership should establish credibility among the people and win the trust of the party and the people. I do not mean that people are satisfied with all the people in the leading body, but are satisfied with this collective. People may have this or that opinion about everyone in this leading body. It is all right if they are satisfied with the collective as a whole. In our second generation, I can be regarded as a leader, but we are still a collective. The people are basically satisfied with this collective of ours, although some people have now promoted the slogan of pulling me down.

People are basically satisfied with this collective of ours chiefly because we have conducted reform and opening up, pushed the line of the four modernizations, and have performed actual deeds. The leadership of the third generation should likewise establish credibility among the people and perform actual deeds. It won't do to close the door. China cannot possibly return again to the previous closed era. The closed method also brought about disasters, such as the Great Cultural Revolution. Given that situation, the economy could not develop, the people's livelihood could not be improved, and the state's power could not be strengthened. Now the world is developing by leaps and bounds, and is changing every day. It is difficult to catch up with them, in science and technology, in particular.

The leadership of the third generation should establish credibility among the people and win the people's trust in this collective so that the people can rally around the leading collective—the CPC Central Committee—they believe in. There should be no wavering in opposing bourgeois liberalization and upholding the four cardinal principles. On this count, I have never made any concessions at any time. Can China not engage in the four adherences? Can the people be without the people's democratic dictatorship? Whether or not we adhere to Marxism and socialism is a fundamental issue.

In forming this new leading body, we should have very broad visions and be very broad-minded. This is a most fundamental requirement for our young leaders of the third generation. In the early period, the leaders of our first generation were broad-minded, and the leaders of our second generation are basically so. It is necessary to set such a demand on the leaders of the third generation, as well as the fourth and fifth generations in the future. Those entering the Political Bureau and the Secretariat, especially the Standing Committee of the Political Bureau, should be selected from the angle of reform and opening up. The new leading body should persist in doing something about reform and opening up to prove that at least you persist in reform and opening up and that you are genuinely implementing the policy of reform and opening up laid down since the third plenary session of the Eleventh CPC Central Committee. In this way, the people will feel at ease.

The people we are employing should now give up all prejudices and look for those who the people believe uphold the line of reform and opening up. It is necessary to give up personal feelings in selecting people. Those who have opposed us should also be used. For a long time in the past, Chairman Mao dared to use the opposition faction. It is also necessary to deepen the angle of taking people into consideration. This is also a reform, an ideological reform. I sincerely hope that, on the question of selecting people, we pay attention to public opinion rather than acting impetuously. We should deal with this question in the manner of a politician. We now should select people who are universally accepted as upholding the line of reform and opening up and have performed actual deeds. We should boldly put them in the new leading body so that the people feel that we sincerely want to conduct reform and opening up. All people have shortcomings and they can continue to improve after entering the leading body.

In punishing corruption, we should genuinely grasp several things and use facts to establish credibility among the people. We should grasp a dozen or so things, such as corruption, embezzlement, bribe taking, and reselling at a profit. Some are on a provincial scale and some are on a national scale. It is necessary to grasp them vigorously and speedily. We should make them public and act according to the law. Those who should be punished should invariably be punished no matter who they are. Hu Lijiao's son has been sentenced to death, but there have been few such things before. First, we should now employ universally accepted reformers and, second, the new leading body should carry out a few acts of reform and opening up to show to all people. In a matter of three to six months, our image can be fostered. The students have only voiced the demand to continue the reform, but we genuinely put it into effect. In this way we can work in harmony and the feelings of estrangement can be removed. Such feelings of estrangement cannot be removed by writing articles or engaging in debates. A reason for the emergence of this trouble is the multiplication of corrupt phenomena, which make some people lose confidence in the party and the government. Therefore, we should first straighten out our mistakes and take an accommodating attitude toward some actions of the masses. They should be dealt with appropriately and the scope of people involved should not be too wide.

All members entering the top central leadership are no longer their previous selves. They should no longer stay at the previous levels, because their responsibilities are different. From their own angles, including their work styles, there should be changes and there should be conscious changes. It is not easy to lead such a country as this! The responsibility is different! The most important point is to be broad-minded. It is necessary to have the whole world and the future in view; in having the present in view, we should also have all aspects in view. People can change. If we look at problems from the overall situation, what grievances cannot be removed?

There is still another issue: No matter what we do, we should not form small factions or small coteries. Strictly speaking, there has never been this or that faction in our party. During the Jiangxi period, people said that I belonged to the Mao faction. There was no such thing. There was not a Mao faction. A crucial problem is to be able to tolerate and unite with all quarters. Judging by myself, I am not a perfect man; I have also made many mistakes. I am not a person who has not made any mistakes, but I have a clear conscience. There is one point, however, that is, I have never formed a small coterie. When transferred to this or that job in the past, I went alone, not taking even an odd-jobman. Small coteries do people great harm! Many faults come from this, and errors derive from this. You are to work in the frontline; therefore I talk about this today.

When the new leading body has gained prestige, I will resolutely withdraw and not interfere with your work. It is hoped that all people can very satisfactorily consider Comrade Jiang Zemin as the core and unite. Do not take it amiss with each other and consume each other's strength. If we do not trust each other, make allowances for each other, make some concessions to each other, and fail to make necessary compromises, a small difference will develop into a major conflict. So long as this leading collective is united and we persist in reform and opening up, there will also be fundamental changes in China even if we are to steadily develop for several decades. I ask both of you to take my words to all comrades who will work in the new leading body. This can be regarded as my political justification.

VIII

Premonitions of Violence

This section begins with the government's reaction to yet another student "insult" to the Communist state: the erection of the "Goddess of Democracy" statue in Tiananmen. Crafted at the Central Arts Academy, this newly proclaimed symbol of democracy in China was to be the students' last defiant act before vacating the square. According to the June 1 *People's Daily* article (Doc. 54), however, their action was actually a "serious disruption of democracy and freedom." As in the CPC's response to the Democracy Wall movement of the late 1970s, the Communist leadership now decided to turn the students' advocacy of democracy against them. Two days later, the same paper published a long accusatory article against the students (Doc. 55), partially comprised of Li Ximing's May 19 briefing (Doc. 45 above). Although this *People's Daily* article contains no attribution, Beijing citizens could now read Li's views on the nefarious "plots" of the "very few" who indicated their incredible deviousness by actually chanting progovernment slogans such as "support the CPC."[1] In this sense, China's hard-line leaders once again resorted to Cultural Revolution–style rhetoric by accusing the students of a contemporary version of "waving the Red Flag, to oppose the Red Flag" (that is, Red Guard factions who had purportedly quoted Mao to actually attack him).

The June 3 article also reinforced the image of a crisis out of control by claiming that crime in Beijing was now rampant, though the examples given here—for instance, the theft from a milk truck—are not very persuasive.[2] The city was purportedly in "chaos," with "pandemonium" threatening the entire

---

[1]The published selections of Li Ximing's speech contain some interesting additions and deletions. Additions include his claim that Beijing University posters had attacked Mao Zedong, while the most interesting deletion is Li's accusation that the Bush administration had interfered in the demonstrations.

[2]The article also contradicts sympathetic Chinese and foreign observations that life in Beijing had actually become more civil during the movement, with even petty thieves

country. But even this article had to address the question being asked by the city's populace: "Because normal order has been largely restored in Beijing, why is martial law still necessary?" The answer, *People's Daily* claimed, was simple: the chaos had not, in fact, ended, as the locations of the Central Committee and the State Council were purportedly "surrounded." The conspiracy of the "extremely small number of people" to "fight the government" had not abated, as evidenced by the fact that "sixty martial law soldiers had [already] been wounded."[3] The students, the government seemed to admit, had won the people's hearts, but the secretive enemy manipulating the entire affair behind the scenes had to be "eliminated." For most residents of Beijing, this picture of reality was enormously distorted, but for the Communist Party readers of *People's Daily* throughout the country, it laid the political groundwork for the lethal force that was about to be unleashed.

On the same day, Wu'er Kaixi was interviewed by a Hong Kong journalist just hours before the young student leader had to flee the military assault on Tiananmen (Doc. 56). Remarkably free of invective toward the government, Wu'er Kaixi praised Hu Yaobang as a "democratic leader," but he bemoaned the Chinese people's lack of a "consciousness of democracy," which derived, he argued, from the country's "5,000-year history" and its large population. The authoritarian character of the Communist government simply reflected the "backward" political consciousness of the population—an argument modern Chinese intellectuals have made ever since the 1919 May Fourth Movement. While criticizing the excessively centralized authority in the Chinese government where "everything is decided by one person" (a fact revealed, he says, by Li Peng, not Zhao Ziyang), Wu'er Kaixi also criticized the prodemocracy movement, including the demonstrators' chanting of simplistic slogans and the "bureaucratic style" of some student leaders. He also derided Chinese intellectuals as "generally weak and prone to compromise," and too supportive of the kind of incremental reform favored by the government. "What China needs is revolution," the student leader asserted, though not a "violent" one.

---

promising to halt their activities. See Suzanne Ogden et al., eds., *China's Search for Democracy: The Student and Mass Movement of 1989* (Armonk, N.Y.: M. E. Sharpe, forthcoming).

[3]Virtually no foreign journalist reported assaults on soliders before June 3. CCTV, in fact, carried only one piece of film footage of a soldier who received a cut on his face, and that was broadcast after June 4.

54
What Does the Statue of the "Goddess of Democracy" which Appeared in Tiananmen Square Indicate?

WU YE

Source: *Renmin ribao* (People's daily) (Beijing) (June 1, 1989): 1; FBIS, June 1, p. 28.

Some people erected a statue of the "Goddess of Democracy" without authorization in dignified Tiananmen Square and this evoked various comments among the people. According to the people's common sense, the erection of any monument in Tiananmen Square must first be approved by the government and must be based on a relevant government decree.

In the square the Tiananmen rostrum, the flagpoles, the Monument to the People's Heroes, the memorial hall, the museum, and the Great Hall of the People are all built in good order and the layout is serious and solemn. The square is a site to hold grand ceremonies and major state activities and is an important place for domestic and foreign tourists to visit with reverence. It is the heart of the People's Republic and is the focus of the world's attention.

All citizens have the duty to cherish and protect Tiananmen Square. This is equal to cherishing and protecting our motherland and our nation and to cherishing and protecting our own rights. The square is sacred. No one has the power to add any permanent memorial or to remove anything from the square. Such things must not be allowed to happen in China. Even in foreign countries, including some Western countries, similar things are not permitted.

The feelings of the young students who hope to promote the construction of democracy are understandable. Advancing socialist democratic politics is also the hope of all people throughout the country and the objective of the party and government's efforts. The positive demands raised by the young students play a role in promoting the realization of this objective. However, the erection of a statue of the "Goddess of Democracy" by some people in Tiananmen Square was not a positive action in seeking freedom and democracy; instead, it was a serious distortion of freedom and democracy and showed disrespect for other people's free and democratic rights. Freedom can only exist within the limits permitted by the law. When a citizen exercises his rights and uses his freedom he must not impair state, social, or collective interests and must not infringe upon other citizens' freedom and rights. No one should be able to act as perversely as one likes.

55
Recognize the Essence of Turmoil and the Necessity of Martial Law

PROPAGANDA DEPARTMENT,
BEIJING MUNICIPAL PARTY COMMITTEE

Source: *Renmin ribao* (People's daily) (Beijing) (June 3, 1989): 1–2; FBIS, June 5, pp. 13–19.

The April 26 *Renmin ribao* editorial, as well as Comrade Li Peng's important speech made on behalf of the party Central Committee and the State Council on May 19, explicitly called for taking a clear-cut stance in opposing and halting turmoil. Hence, the State Council on May 20 issued an order to enforce martial law in some districts in Beijing Municipality and moved some troops into Beijing to work together with armed police units, public security personnel, and the large numbers of ordinary people and students in maintaining the capital's public security and restoring its normal production, work, teaching, research, and living order.

Quite a few people and students still do not thoroughly understand all of this, and a few ideological "knots" remain to be untied. Some people would ask: Why did we say turmoil has occurred and why is it necessary to move in the liberation army since the students are patriotic? In the final analysis, this is because they have failed to thoroughly understand the seriousness of this political struggle and the necessity of enforcing martial law. Therefore, it is necessary to give a clear account of the actual situation to the masses and students.

Why Did We Say Serious Turmoil Has Occurred in Beijing?

Above all, we want to say that the party and the government have fully confirmed the patriotic passion of the large number of students all along and never said they were stirring up turmoil. The April 26 *Renmin ribao* editorial, Comrade

Li Peng's speech on behalf of the party Central Committee and the State Council, talks by Marshals Xu Xiangqian and Nie Rongzhen, Comrade Deng Yingchao's letter, Comrade Chen Yun's speech at a meeting of the Central Advisory Commission's Standing Committee, Comrade Li Xiannian's speech at a chairmanship meeting of the National Committee of the Chinese People's Political Consultative Conference [May 27], Comrade Peng Zhen's speech at a forum of responsible persons of some democratic parties [May 26], and Comrade Wan Li's written statement [May 27] have repeatedly and explicitly pointed out that the students' demands for promoting democracy, eliminating corruption, rectifying "official profiteering," and overcoming bureaucracy are identical with the aspirations of the party and the government, and that the students' demands have exerted a positive influence on solving these problems. This suffices to explain that the party and the government have never said that the large number of students were stirring up turmoil. At the same time, the party and the government have invariably drawn a clear line of demarcation between conspiracy to stir up turmoil by the very few people and the patriotic passion of young students.

How, then, did the very few people stir up turmoil by manipulating the good wishes of young students, ideological confusion among some people, certain errors of the party and the government, and problems we encountered in the course of advance? A review of a series of very abnormal incidents, that happened recently, will easily provide a correct conclusion.

First, the very few people had long premeditated the turmoil.

As early as the end of last year and early this year, the very few people had plotted, inside and outside some schools of higher learning, to take the opportunity of the seventieth anniversary of the "May 4th Movement," fortieth national founding anniversary, and the bicentennial of the French Revolution to incite student unrest and make trouble.

In early March this year, some anonymous big- and small-character posters appeared in Beijing University, Qinghua University, and other schools of higher learning, directly attacking the party's leadership and the socialist system. A small-character poster, entitled "Grieve for the Chinese people," described the current government as "dictatorship" and called on people to "fight for freedom." A big-character poster, entitled "The call of the times," raised the questions of "whether or not there is still reason for the existence of socialism," and "what philosophical system should substitute for Marxism." A "Letter to the masses of students," posted at the triangle on Beijing University campus, called for fighting for "democracy, freedom, and human rights" under the leadership of a certain scholar who had advocated bourgeois liberalization. Meetings were held frequently by some active people of society. This scholar praised the meetings for "adopting a totally resistant and critical attitude toward the authorities" and "having a strong smell of gunpowder," and predicted that "after three successive meetings, [people] will take to the streets." When Comrade Hu Yaobang passed away on April 15, some people, believing that the time had come, were determined to indulge in creating disturbances.

Second, the political aim of the very few people is to negate the CPC's leadership and the socialist system.

A "Letter to young students all over the country," signed by "Nankai University," called for "establishing a committee for revising the Constitution to eliminate the 'upholding' of 'principles,' which the people detest." In a speech on Tiananmen Square, Ren Wanding, a responsible person from the "League of Human Rights," a defunct outlaw organization, said, "If the four cardinal principles are not deleted, the Constitution . . . will surely be placed above the people's interest." He went on that "the false relaxation, harmony, stability, and unity seen in Chinese society have been won at the price of imposing a high-handed policy on all people and sacrificing the blood, lives, freedom, and health of millions of brilliant personnel." A big-character poster in Beijing University said: "Marxism is tantamount to utopia; Mao Zedong is an out-and-out scoundrel, and without total repudiation of Mao Zedong, reform will be devoid of practical meaning." "The hope of China—a declaration of private ownership system," signed by a "doctoral student" and posted on Beijing Aerospace University campus, attacked China's socialist system of public ownership for "going faster than the law of historical development" and for "restricting the expansion of productive forces," because it is "the soil for the growth of bureaucratism" and a "hotbed for corruption" and a "cradle for centralized dictatorship." It also called for "sounding the death knell of the public ownership system to usher in the Republic's tomorrow."

Ignoring the fact of the fruitful achievements scored in China's decade-long reform, the articles and the small- and big-character posters written by the very few people vilified our socialist country as "pitch-dark" and "having entered into the most perilous moment," where "official profiteering and corruption have spread unchecked, and morality has declined and lost"; they said: "China is dying, its people are degenerating, and everything is perishing," and called for toppling China's socialist system.

A "Letter to all compatriots," posted in the Beijing Aerospace University, demanded that "the Communist Party be abolished and a multiparty system introduced," and that "party branches and political work cadres in all institutions, schools, and units be abolished." Some big-character posters openly called for "disbanding parties and getting rid of the four principles." Others attacked the CPC as a "treacherous party of the generation," "which is concerned only about its status, not the future of the country and the people." They said that "the CPC today is an organization heading toward imminent crumbling and fall," and even slandered that "the Communist Party has done nothing good since its founding, and has only committed corruption, autocracy, and national betrayal." Some big-character posters attacked the CPC for "having forfeited the role of the vanguard consisting of the so-called proletarian advanced elements" and for "representing only another group of rulers in the disguised form of China's 1,000-year-old feudal dictatorship." Some people openly called for toppling the CPC's "dictatorial rule." Others wanted to "invite the Guomindang to return to the mainland to set up bipartisan politics."

These very few people have consistently directed the spearhead of attack on Comrade Deng Xiaoping, using extremely vicious and even dirty language to slander him in a frenzied manner because he has all along upheld the four cardinal principles and persisted in opposing bourgeois liberalization and because, as the chief architect of China's reform, opening to the outside world, and modernization drive, he enjoys high prestige inside and outside the party, at home and abroad.

The four cardinal principles are the cornerstones of our country. Should the four cardinal principles be abandoned and CPC leadership be abolished, is there another road, aside from capitalism, for us to take?

Third, the turmoil has been meticulously plotted by the very few people, with the participation of various political forces at home and abroad.

Actions, slogans, and demands in every stage of the turmoil over the past month were carefully conceived and meticulously carried out.

At the beginning of the turmoil, the very few people plotted the trick of shooting arrows simultaneously in confusion, and launched an all-out attack on the four cardinal principles and every party and government leader by name. About April 18 or 19, around the time of the storming of Zhongnanhai, the spearhead of the attack was targeted at Comrades Deng Xiaoping and Li Peng. Following the April 26 *Renmin ribao* editorial's exposure of the essence of the turmoil plotted by the very few people, they made a 180 degree turn in their strategy by flaunting such slogans as "Support the CPC," "Support socialism," and "Support the Constitution." Later as they saw the party and the government exercising utmost restraint, they retrieved these slogans of "support." After May 4 the situation deteriorated and they again changed their slogans; the slogan "Down with Deng Xiaoping" blotted out the sky and caused a temporary clamor. Following Comrade Li Peng's important speech on May 19, they called for toppling both Deng Xiaoping and Li Peng, but subsequently readjusted the slogans, urging to "Refrain from shouting radical slogans, especially against Deng Xiaoping" in a vain hope of "Winning Deng Xiaoping over for the benefit of the next-stage struggle." Hence, they concentrated efforts on clamoring about "Down with Li Peng and the puppet government."

Some people hold that if the central leaders had conducted dialogue with the students earlier, problems would not have become so serious. However, this is not the case. Under the instigation of the very few people, organizers of the student unrest expressed willingness to hold dialogue with the government, on the one hand, but put forth various preconditions on the other. At the same time, they spread rumors that the government lacked sincerity. As a matter of fact, they obstructed dialogue and did their utmost to create obstacles to holding a dialogue. First, they demanded to send 20 representatives to attend the dialogue, to which the government agreed. Then, they demanded to send 200 people, but lied that the government only allowed them to send 20. Thus, the scheduled dialogue was aborted. On the morning of May 13, the General Offices of the party Central Committee and the State Council notified them that the dialogue would be held on May 15. On the one hand, they favored a dialogue, but on the other, they hurriedly released the "Declaration of Hunger Strike," which they had long prepared, falsely alleging that the government's refusal of dialogue forced some students to go on the front line of fasting.

During the student unrest, a handful of people who had access to top secrets of the central authorities went so far as to send personnel to some schools of higher learning and Tiananmen Square to divulge secret information to stir up trouble. At the time, information about discussion from a Standing Committee meeting of the Political Bureau of the CPC Central Committee was spread to some college campuses within a few short hours after the meeting, before it was officially reported. With an ulterior motive, this small handful of people also spread, and exposed to the masses, differences of opinion at the top leadership level regarding the student unrest, thereby creating serious ideological confusion.

During the student unrest, various political forces at home and abroad meddled in the unrest and worked concertedly in offering all kinds of advice and suggestions. On April 22, Hu Ping, Chen Jun, and other members of the reactionary organization "China Democratic League" jointly sent an "Open Letter to College Students in China" from New York, which was posted in Beijing's schools of higher learning. It urged organizers of student unrest to "consolidate the organizational ties established in the current activity and strive to carry out effective operations as a strong colony," and said that at the present, "it is necessary to achieve a breakthrough in totally negating the 1987 movement against liberalization," "to step up contacts with various mass media," and "to strengthen ties with all circles of society . . . to win their support for and participation in the movement." Wang Bingzhang and Tang Guangzhong, two chieftains of the "China Democratic League" hurriedly flew to Tokyo from New York in an attempt to rush back to Beijing to take direct part in the turmoil. Some former "China Spring" members, who are residing in the United States, set up a "China Democratic Party," and issued an "Appeal to All Compatriots" in some universities in Beijing on April 16, inciting students to "demand the resignation of conservative bureaucrats" and "urge the Chinese Communists to end their dictatorial rule."

Does not all of this suffice to explain that the very few people established illicit ties at home and abroad, at upper and lower levels, and carefully and deliberately plotted the turmoil? The large number of students and masses of people should never deal with this extremely complicated political struggle with their good intentions.

Fourth, extremely few people have constantly worsened the situation by resorting to some extremely despicable means such as spreading rumors.

Since the beginning of the student unrest, Beijing Municipality has been plagued by all kinds of rumors. What deserves our profound consideration is the fact that every time the government took measures to relax the student unrest and the feelings of the large number of students were calming down, some people were bound to spread new rumors and agitate anew to escalate the student unrest.

After Comrade Hu Yaobang's death on April 15, some people spread the rumor that "Li Peng scolded Hu Yaobang at a meeting of the Political Bureau, and Hu died of choked resentment."

On April 20, Xinhua Gate was stormed. At daybreak, some people who had gathered in front of Xinhua Gate were brought into large buses by policemen standing guard and sent back to school. Both sides engaged in scuffling. This led some people to spread the rumors that "the police at Xinhua Gate beat up people, including students, workers, women, and children," and that "more than 1,000 scientists and technicians were lying in pools of blood." They also fabricated the so-called April 20 tragedy. There were also rumors that a police car had run over and killed a Normal University student. All this aroused the sympathy and indignation of students who did not understand the truth.

On April 22, after the memorial service for Comrade Hu Yaobang ended, some people spread the rumor to the students in Tiananmen Square saying, "Premier Li Peng has agreed to receive students at 12:45 P.M." This was entirely untrue. After that, the rumors had it that Li Peng "deceived the students," which led to a class boycott by 60,000 students and escalated the student unrest.

On April 23, students of some colleges and universities in the capital boycotted classes, and an extremely few people, for the sake of inciting workers to create trouble, made up leaflets signed the "Beijing Municipal Federation of Workers" and circulated them everywhere.

After the publication of the *Renmin ribao* editorial on April 26, an extremely few people spread the rumors saying "Comrade Chen Yun has issued an 8-point instruction on the current student unrest, holding the general secretary and the premier responsible," and "the president of Beijing University has resigned." Some people even spread the rumor that "all banks in the world have stopped extending loans to China."

On May 13, some college students of Beijing came to Tiananmen Square to make a petition by staging hunger strikes. An extremely few people, for the sake of aggravating the situation, spread rumors everywhere saying "Workers of Beijing Municipality have staged a general strike."

On May 20, after the State Council issued the order to impose martial law in some parts of Beijing, some people spread the rumor that "Li Peng presided over a meeting which made a 4-point decision: (1) The nature of the current students' movement is determined and the movement is called turmoil; (2) The 200,000 students in Tiananmen Square should be suppressed; (3) Large prisons in the capital should be evacuated to make room for the students; and (4) All sanitation workers should be mobilized to clean up Tiananmen Square early in the morning after the suppression takes place." Later it was rumored that army units would be "air-dropped" and would use "gas weapons." These were meant purposely to agitate students and city residents and set them against the liberation army.

An extremely few people have fabricated these rumors to deceive the masses and create turmoil. Once their rumors were exposed by facts, they would dish out new ones in different forms. The large number of kind-hearted people and students should guard against these despicable tactics and should not be taken in easily.

Fifth, an extremely few people have wantonly trampled democracy and the legal system underfoot, and thereby have created serious confusion in social order.

Under the agitation of an extremely few people, some people have disregarded the ten-point regulations of the Beijing Municipal People's Congress Standing Committee on holding marches and demonstrations in the past few months. Without approval, they have organized marches, demonstrations, sit-ins, and hunger strikes at will, and have occupied Tiananmen Square for a long period of time, making it impossible to conduct the Sino-Soviet summit and other major state activities as scheduled, and forcing the cancellation of some activities. This has seriously damaged our country's image and reputation.

Since the beginning of May, these demonstrations had grown in size, from tens of thousands to hundreds of thousands to well over a million. Normal order in production and work, as well as social order in Beijing Municipality, was seriously disturbed and disrupted. Some people encircled and stormed the offices of the party Central Committee and the State Council, as well as the residences of central leading comrades. Late at night, some hooligans went to the gates of the municipal party committee and the municipal government to cause disturbance by shouting abuse in extremely vulgar language. Public transportation in the downtown area sustained great damage and was paralyzed for some time. Raw and semifinished materials for industrial use could not be shipped in promptly and products could not be shipped out in good time. The delivery of cooking gas, vegetables, and grain was obstructed. Shops and enterprises could not promptly deliver payments to the banks. Without authorization, some people deprived public security and traffic police of their power of directing traffic, stopped vehicles at will, and illegally checked pedestrians' certificates. Some lawbreakers even willfully abused, beat up, and injured public security and traffic police. Because of the growing seriousness of the state of anarchism, it became more difficult for public security cadres, police, and armed police forces in Beijing Municipality to assume the heavy task of safeguarding normal order in the capital. There were reports of beating, smashing and looting in many places. Some lawless people seized the opportunity to rob banks. Dozens of people looted the Huiyuan Department Store located on Dongsida Street. Some 3,800 bottles of milk were robbed from a Guanganmen Dairy Products delivery truck. A route 54 bus was smashed at the Yongdingmen railway station. Six bandits robbed peasants coming to Beijing from Hebei Province via Fangshan-Liangxiang highway, saying, "We heard Beijing is in chaos; we would like to have some spending money." During the period of demonstrations, some bandits went to the Wangfujing and Qianmen business districts and waited for the right moment to commit crimes. Thanks to the preparedness of public security cadres, police, and shop assistants, the bandits did not dare to make a move.

Even more serious is the fact that the situation in Beijing Municipality has affected other parts of China, resulting in chaos in many cities. In some places, local leading party and government organs were frequently stormed, and cases of beating, smashing, looting, arson, and other serious and illegal acts were reported. The trunk transport line of the country was obstructed. Students in many places have forced their way onto trains to come to Beijing, or even lay on railway tracks to stop the trains. A total of more than 200,000 people have come to Beijing. They rode trains without tickets, and ate their meals without paying money, very much in the style of people establishing mass connections during the period of the "Great Cultural Revolution."

Sixth, an extremely small number of people attempted to seize power during the turmoil.

Under the instigation of an extremely small number of people, some universities openly declared the abolition of associations of undergraduate and graduate students, which were formed through election, replaced them with so-called autonomous student organizations, and seized a student broadcasting station. These organizations then joined forces and formed a front-line headquarters to command the student strike.

The development of the situation became increasingly serious before the imposition of martial law. Some units plotted to demand that the leading authorities "hand over the power." Certain personnel of some State Council departments demanded some ministers to step down. Some people gave out handbills, declaring the formation of the "Preparatory Committee for the Conference of Representatives of People of All Circles in Beijing" to replace the Beijing Municipal People's Congress. They also advocated the formation of a "Beijing regional government" to replace the lawful Beijing municipal people's government. Some people slung mud at the State Council, which was formed lawfully through elections, saying that it is a "bogus government," and claimed that the Ministry of Foreign Affairs and a dozen or so other central departments had "declared independence" from the State Council. They also claimed that over thirty countries in the world had already severed diplomatic relations with China. Some people proclaimed that "Deng Xiaoping had stepped down" and that a "new government" would be formed three days later.

Meanwhile, an extremely small number of people had assembled some hoodlums and ruffians and formed a "Flying Tiger Squad" composed of over 100 motorcycles. They also organized a "Dare-to-Die Corps" with over 1,000 bicycles and demanded that the bicyclists "stage an uprising" and "attack the Bastille" like the French people did during the French Revolution. They even threatened to put party and state leaders under "house arrest."

Is it possible that all these acts still do not constitute a serious upheaval? Under such a highly chaotic situation, it was absolutely necessary for the State Council to come up with the decision to impose martial law in some parts of Beijing in accordance with constitutional provisions to maintain Beijing's public order, protect the lives and property of the people, protect public property from being violated, and make sure that central state organs and the Beijing Municipal Government can continue to carry out their official business normally. If it did not take decisive measures and let the chaos continue instead, there would be even greater turmoil in the capital and pandemonium in the country. In that case, can there be still any future for our reforms and four modernizations? It is obvious that this is a situation which the 1.1 billion people in the country do not want to see.

Some Questions Have Been Asked Concerning the Imposition of Martial Law

Some of the masses ask: Because the students on the hunger strike at Tiananmen Square had already declared on the evening of May 19 that they would stop the hunger strike, why was it still necessary to impose martial law on May 20?

There are two points here that have to be explained:

First, the imposition of martial law in some parts of Beijing is for the purpose of stopping upheaval, stopping the serious anarchic state, restoring normal order in the capital, and preventing an even greater upheaval, and not for stopping the hunger strike among some students.

Second, after the State Council decided to impose martial law in some parts of Beijing, the news of this decision leaked out quickly. An extremely small number of people immediately plotted to substitute the hunger strike with sit-ins to deal with us. This shows that it was a tactic plotted by an extremely small number of people.

Some of the masses ask: Because normal order has been largely restored in Beijing, why is martial law still necessary?

First of all, it should be pointed out that, under the extremely difficult conditions of the past month, the vast number of workers, peasants, commercial workers, teachers, medical workers, neighborhood cadres, party and government personnel, public security personnel, and armed police have been performing their duties responsibly on their respective posts, and they have contributed significantly to ensuring normal production and work order in the capital. Their work was particularly difficult after martial law was declared and the martial law troops arrived in Beijing. The current situation precisely shows the result of the efforts exerted by the vast number of cadres and people to stop the turmoil.

We must also realize, however, that, despite our efforts, Beijing's tumultuous situation has yet to calm down. During the first two days after martial law was imposed, all intersections were blocked, and 227 buses were commandeered and used as road blocks. Military vehicles were not permitted to enter the urban areas, and the delivery of official documents between government organs was also disrupted for a time. Even now, unauthorized parades, demonstrations, and sit-ins are still continuing. The district where the party Central Committee and the State Council are located is still being surrounded. Agitative speeches can still be heard everywhere. Rumor-mongering handbills are also everywhere. Classes have not yet been resumed in most schools of higher education. An extremely small number of people are still conspiring to fight the government through to the end. This shows that stopping the turmoil and restoring the capital's normal order remains an extremely formidable task.

Some of the masses maintain that when the students began their hunger strike, if the government had shown them some warmth and loving care and done some more work with them, the tension might have been alleviated and martial law might not have been needed.

The fact is, as soon as the hunger strikers entered Tiananmen Square, the party and the government anxiously did all they could to enlist the efforts of all quarters to dissuade the students from staging the hunger strike. First of all, faculty members of various schools and leading cadres at various levels, including party and state leaders, visited the hunger strikers on many occasions and tried to talk them out of the hunger strike. Then, they helped the Red Cross Society mobilize over 100 ambulances and hundreds of medical workers to keep watch on the hunger strikers around the clock. To ensure that medical care and treatment were available for the students in case they might go into shock or contract other illnesses because of fasting, 52 hospitals vacated nearly 2,000 sickbeds for their use. Then, to minimize the agony of hunger strikers and ensure their safety, all types of supplies were brought in. The Beijing municipal party committee and the municipal government also selected cadres, workers, and vehicles to deliver drinking water, salt, and sugar to the hunger strikers around the clock through the Red Cross Society. The Environmental Protection Bureau sent in watering cars, washing basins, and towels so that the hunger strikers could wash up and brush their teeth. Pharmaceutical companies brought in an ample supply of medicines for preventing sunstroke, cold, diarrhea, and gave them to the Red Cross Society for distribution. Food departments supplied large quantities of beverages and bread for emergency uses. Commercial departments brought in 6,000 straw hats and the Beijing Military Region sent in 1,000 cotton quilts for the students so that they would not get sunstroke during the day or catch cold at night. To maintain sanitation of the site of the hunger strike, temporary latrines were built. At night, sanitation workers also carried out general cleanups of the site. Prior to the downpour of May 18, the Municipal Public Transportation Company sent in seventy-eight large buses and the Supplies Bureau delivered more than 400 boards to shelter the students from rain and moisture. All this shows that the party, government, and the whole society do care about the students and have acted in a very responsible manner. It also shows that it is not the party and government that do not care about the students, but rather it is an extremely small number of people who have tried to use the students as hostages to force the government to accept their political terms. The development of the situation fully testifies to this.

Some of the masses think that the martial law troops were sent in to suppress the students and the people. This is simply a misconception.

Since the imposition of martial law, the martial law troops, armed police units, and public security personnel have always observed strict discipline. Even under circumstances in which they are misunderstood, humiliated, beaten up, and badmouthed by some people, they still exercise a high degree of restraint and tolerance. Since the imposition of martial law, not one single student has been arrested, but over sixty martial law soldiers, and hundreds of public security personnel and armed policemen have been wounded. They have proved with their actual deeds that they are the children of the people and soldiers who serve the people wholeheartedly, and that they are in the capital to enforce martial law and not to suppress the masses or the students. Because of their conduct, the martial law units, armed police forces, and public security personnel have received understanding from an increasing number of people and students and warm attention and support from the masses.

Unite All the Forces that Can Be United and Expose the Extremely Few People Who Incite and Create Turmoil

Within a month's time, large numbers of students have participated in marches, demonstrations, and sit-ins, while others have participated in fasting. Large numbers of city residents, workers, and even office workers have joined the processions and supported activities. The enthusiasm of the large number of patriotic students should be fully affirmed, and the concern and sympathy of the broad masses of people toward the students should be understandable. At present, however, some students and people are afraid that later on they may be accused of "participating in turmoil." Here, we would like to make it clear to all:

First, the party and government resolutely protect the patriotic enthusiasm of the large number of young students, and resolutely and strictly distinguish them from an extremely few people who create turmoil. The students will not be held accountable even if they have made extremist remarks or taken extremist actions during the student unrest. The party and government will widely and actively conduct dialogues at all levels, through all channels, and in all forms, with the large numbers of students and people in all circles, including those students who have joined processions, demonstrations, boycotted classes, and staged hunger strikes, and will listen fully to opinions from all quarters. Reasonable requests made by the students will be given explicit replies, and reasonable criticisms and suggestions offered by them, including those that deal with promoting democracy, punishing bureaucratic racketeers, eliminating corruption, overcoming bureaucratism, and others, will be earnestly heeded and adopted to effectively improve the work of the party and the government.

Second, because of their dissatisfaction with corruption and bureaucratic racketeering, and out of their sympathy toward the fasting students, some workers, city residents, and office cadres, who did not understand the complicated background, have taken part in the support activities and joined the processions. Some even went too far in their words and deeds. Once they understand the truth, they will support the policy decisions made by the central authorities and the State Council. They are also welcomed, and will not be held accountable.

Third, our armed police and public security cadres and policemen should closely cooperate with the martial law enforcement troops, and rely on the support of the large number of city residents and young students to deal resolute blows on those lawless people who engage in beating, smashing, and looting. The "Flying Tiger Team," "Death-Defying Team," and other political gangs of hooligans should be resolutely eliminated.

Fourth, it is imperative to resolutely expose the extremely few people who incite and create turmoil.

Fifth, the large number of Communist Party members, Communist Youth League members, and the masses should closely rally around the party Central Committee, uphold the four cardinal principles, uphold the reform and open policy, take a clear-cut stand in opposing and ending turmoil, strictly observe laws and discipline, strive to do well in production and work, and contribute their best at their own workposts to ending turmoil and stabilizing the situation.

56
Wu'er Kaixi Says, "We Must Face Reality"—China's Democratic Movement Might Retrogress

Source: *Ming pao* (Enlightenment) (Hong Kong) (June 17, 1989): 1, based on interview of June 3; FBIS, June 20, pp. 24–27

The most conspicuous leader of the student movement on the mainland, Wu'er Kaixi, was interviewed by another student movement leader on June 3, one day before the bloody suppression by the troops in Beijing. The tape recording of the interview was broadcast by the ABC Radio Network. The following text of the interview has been compiled from the tape recording for our readers' reference.

In the interview, Wu'er Kaixi talked about his main motives for participating in the student movement, and the development and prospects of the democracy movement.

After the bloody suppression of the democracy movement in the small hours of June 4, the whereabouts of this 21-year-old student of Beijing Normal University are unknown. However, our reporter has learned that he is still alive, having concealed his identity and gone underground.

Q: It seems that the situation in Beijing is fairly dangerous. So I would like to talk with you, and hope that this is not the last opportunity.

Wu'er Kaixi, what are the main motives that drive you to actively participate in the student movement and become its leader? What is your practical experience in this regard?

A: I have been paying attention to democratic developments on the Chinese mainland for many years. I have written some articles, although they have not been published. I buried myself in writing those articles. Now I believe that the current movement will become a great student movement, and that I have my own enthusiasm and capability in this regard. Therefore, I step forward bravely to participate in the student movement, and become its leader.

Q: What is your view on the death of Hu Yaobang?

A: The death of a Communist Party member or of a common person on the mainland must not produce such great repercussions. This matter itself is a problem, that the death of a democratic leader could cause such a great turmoil. This shows that the Chinese people are extremely dissatisfied with the current situation in their country.

Q: What did you expect to get when you first joined the movement?

A: I expected improvement in the following two aspects. First, as far as democratic consciousness was concerned, I hoped that we could get the same effects of enlightenment as those of the May 4 Movement. Actually, although the Chinese people strongly desire democracy, they lack consciousness of democracy, and do not understand democracy. I hope that through the student movement, we will make progress in our work toward enlightening the people. Second, I hoped that we could set a good example with regard to the skills for promoting democracy. At the beginning, I hoped that our Students' Self-Government Federation's legal status would be recognized, and could play its role in government administration as an opposition group.

Q: To your mind, what mistakes has the government made in dealing with the student movement? What basic problems have these mistakes reflected?

A: For example, before the massive demonstration on April 22, the majority of young students, who are only 18 or 19 years old, presented a petition (to the government). At that time, students only lodged their appeal. There was no organization. The government could have taken the initiative to solve the problem. The government could have easily disposed of and handled the student movement.

Q: If the government had handled the student movement at that time, what results would you expect?

A: This would have been determined by the efforts made by us. I didn't think that the situation would become so chaotic.

Q: What was the second mistake of the government in its policy?

A: On April 22, the government sent public security police and soldiers to beat students. Actually, force has enabled the students to become more united, and given rise to the establishment of the temporary students' federation. On April 27, I initiated the establishment of the federation. As a result, the student movement is greatly different from the past. Massive student organizations have been formed.

Q: To your mind, what problems have the government's mistakes reflected? Did you expect these problems? What will you expect in the future?

A: I think that the key to all these mistakes is that the government is not democratic. The government is not accustomed to listening to opinions.

Basically speaking, it is not accustomed to such democratic actions as demonstrations, sit-ins, and so on. The decision-making process of the government itself is not democratic. Actually, in the government everything is decided by one person. Li Peng himself has said: In our government, actually it is only Deng Xiaoping who has the final say. Lacking democracy and being unaccustomed to democratic life are the main factors contributing to the current situation. In the meantime, the quality of many high-ranking officials of the government is too poor. This is also a problem.

Q: What are your main motives for leading the student movement? What theories and convictions do you follow to understand democracy and the current situation of Chinese society?

A: Actually, my motives are very simple. I am very dissatisfied with the society. I study the science of education. When I assess education in China, I discover that the problems of education are very serious. At first, my attention was focused on education. After thinking over the matter further, I realized that it is the political system which blocks the improvement of education. Therefore, my first purpose in establishing a students' federation was to actively promote political reform, to protect citizens' rights and freedom contained in the Constitution, and to ensure that economic reform can be truly implemented. In addition, freedom of the press is, of course, also my goal. I believe that the main reasons contributing to the many problems in China's system, including corruption, bureaucracy, undemocratic practices, and so on, lie in the fact that the people cannot independently exercise their political rights, or exercise control over their own political and economic life. . . . Actually, we can say that it is a democratic movement of human rights.

Q: Through constant dialogue with the government and participating in such a massive social movement, do you think that you have enhanced your understanding, or accumulated more experiences?

A: Of course, I have. In particular, as far as I myself am concerned, I have greatly enhanced my capability to think over and to observe things. What I have learned in this regard is greater than what I had achieved in the classroom on the mainland. I understand the practical problems of the government and the society. People in general cannot understand this. One of the things which I have realized is that consciousness of democracy is inseparable from the environment and the people. Just as I said in the past, the greatest obstacle to reform in China is its population of one billion and its 5,000-year history.

Q: According to the organizational and political experiences you have gained from participating in the current student movement, what will be the main problems facing China on its path toward democracy?

A: There are mainly two problems in this regard. First, consciousness of democracy by the masses. When we are promoting the democracy movement, people are shouting their slogan of overthrowing Li Peng. This shows that we are unable to promote democratic ideas. This is a great obstacle to the consciousness of democracy. Second, the system itself is also an obstacle. If the government persists in the system of prohibiting the existence of an opposition party, and if there are no real checks and balances, there will be no hope of success for the reform and democracy in China.

Q: If your idea can be smoothly spread throughout the society, what will be the response of the government? How high will be the percentage of success?

A: I think that we will succeed. It is difficult to predict the result in the short run. However, in the long run, democracy in China will gradually advance. Our actions are speeding it up. At present, we are not powerful enough, and we must exert greater efforts.

Q: As far as the system is concerned, what obstacles will you encounter?

A: In view of the situation in Beijing over the past two days, no one is too optimistic about it. We must face reality. As far as the development of democracy in China is concerned, retrogression might possibly occur.

Q: As for myself, whether or not the government takes drastic actions to suppress the movement, or tries to suppress it, and whether or not Li Peng or some other people are in power, I believe that things will completely change in the coming two to five years. If this proves true, and if you can freely act at that time, what do you think that you will do?

A: I think that I will develop a balanced political power. I will contribute to such development. I agree with your analysis. Another possibility is that Li Peng might step down, and there will be a purge inside the party.

Q: Apart from the obstacles erected by the government, do you think that there are also problems with regard to the students and the masses who participate in the movement?

A: We lack the experience in fighting for democracy. In the meantime, we ourselves are maliciously poisoned by the bureaucratic system. Actually, many student leaders are also influenced by bureaucratic style. This is a very big obstacle.

Q: Now I want to ask you: How much do you understand the nature of the previous political movements over the past forty years in China? Let us take the May 4 democratic wall movement [*sic*] in 1986 and 1987 as an example. Can you compare it with the current movement, and tell us their similarities and differences?

A: I think that basically speaking, there is no difference between the previous student movements and the current one. However, the previous student movements lacked organization. They did not extensively involve people at various layers, and fewer people participated in them. In the meantime, they did not evoke the common understanding and response of the masses.

The greatest success of the current movement is that it has evoked the common understanding and response of Beijing residents. An organized and powerful opposition force has been developed. Although we are not completely satisfied with it, it is hard to come by. Even if we fail in our action, I believe that a greater student or social movement will occur soon. At that time, we will achieve greater success.

People of our generation have witnessed the opening up in China, and the contributions made by Hu Yaobang and others have further enlightened us ideologically. I believe that through the current democratic movement, university students of the 1990s will have a stronger consciousness of democracy.

Q: From newspapers I learn that many noted intellectuals have supported you. They are also active in disseminating their political ideas. I do not know whether you have contacted them. If you have, what is your appraisal of them? Can you tell me the similarities and differences between you and them?

A: In China, a small number of persons have made very great contributions to democracy. We should say that at least they have made great efforts in this regard. I believe that the quality of people of the younger generation is better than that of people of the older generation. Young people are also purer. Due to the restrictions of the environment and feudal system which lasted several thousand years, Chinese intellectuals are generally weak and prone to compromise. Yet, many of their proposals, we can also say that they are protests, are worth mentioning. Now in China what we need is to strengthen the consciousness of individuals as citizens. Apart from talking, each and every person must also act. I believe that people of the younger generation are purer and stronger than people of the older generation.

Q: I favor your view completely. Over the past ten years, I have been paying close attention to intellectuals, and the trends of intellectuals who demand democracy, freedom and cultural value in particular. I believe that every one of us must consider things in an all-round way in terms of theories, political reality and historical conditions. Do you think that their political and democratic ideas are disconnected with our social foundation?

A: What you say is right. Very often their theories are attached to the so-called reformists. But I believe that what we need is not reform. The reformist movement has been in effect for a long time. It started in the Qing dynasty, but it has never truly succeeded. Experiences have told us that reform is useless in foreign countries [as published]. However, our intellectuals have continued to stick to reform. I believe that what China needs is revolution. Of course, I do not favor violent revolution. What I mean is that some people believe that power only resides in the highest stratum. But I don't think that it resides in the highest stratum alone. It also resides in the people.

Q: I wish to ask you: What are the differences between your concept of people and that of the government? How do you define the word "people"?

A: First of all, people must not be regarded as an organic whole. They are individuals, or a group of citizens. According to the old concept, people are regarded as a pile of monotonous beings. This is actually an insult to the people. People are complicated. Regarding people as being one billion individual citizens is different from regarding them as an organic whole.

IX

The Aftermath

A Nation Divided

For two days after the massacre, China's government was curiously quiet. Rumors abounded in Beijing and abroad that Deng Xiaoping was incapacitated (or dead), and that a civil war between contending armies—the 38th and the notorious 27th (which carried out most of the killing on June 3–4)—was imminent.[1] In the city, government authority, except in areas controlled by the troops, was nonexistent, as posters and signs went up in neighborhoods describing the violence of the crackdown and estimating casualties. But finally, on June 7, the government responded to events when State Council spokesman Yuan Mu, joined by a military commander, convened a news conference to "explain" the crackdown of June 3–4 (Doc. 57). The army had simply responded, Yuan argued, to the giant conspiracy of "a very few thugs [who] engineered a counterrevolutionary rebellion." Three hundred people had died, he estimated, including many soldiers and "bad elements who deserve this because of their crimes."[2] But virtually no one had been killed or run over in Tiananmen, Commander Zhang Gong then reported, because

---

[1]Clashes between soldiers were reported in the Xuanwu district of Beijing, though Yang Shangkun quickly renounced such "rumors." Foreign military attachés in Beijing also noted the defensive positions assumed by tanks. Other armies taking part in enforcing martial law, such as the 40th Army from the Northeast, were praised by local residents in Dongzhimen for their restraint in not firing on the citizenry.

[2]That Yuan smiled when giving the casualty count especially outraged Beijing residents. His count of 300 dead (including only 23 students) is not shared by Western human rights organizations, which have given figures between 700 and 3,000. Amnesty International, *People's Republic of China: Preliminary Findings of Killings of Unarmed Civilians, Arbitrary Arrests and Summary Executions since June 3, 1989* (New York: August 1989).

the troops had exercised enormous restraint in checking the students' tents and sleeping bags before the oncoming tanks and APCs cleared the square.[3] Students had not left the square under the threat of brute force, Zhang claimed, but were persuaded to vacate by "our powerful and repeated propaganda work." Zhang also denied certain "rumors" that individual soldiers had been killed by average Beijing citizens after committing horrendous acts of violence. In fact, Zhang asserted, one soldier in question—thrown off a pedestrian overpass and then burned in Beijing's Chongwenmen area—was another example of the "heavy casualties" sustained by the PLA at the hands of "ruffians" who "used extremely inhuman means."[4] As for the genuinely innocent bystanders killed in the crackdown, the government now apologized, though it also claimed that the minds of many innocent bystanders had been "poisoned" by the counterrevolutionary conspirators.

On June 9, Deng reappeared, putting to rest rumors of his death or incapacitation. In a speech congratulating martial law troops (Doc. 58), Deng reinforced his air of prescience by asserting that "the storm was bound to come" largely because of the "major international climate" (namely, the intervention of foreigners) and "China's own minor climate." Deng admitted to internal opposition to the use of such heavy-handed violence—"some comrades do not understand"—but stood by the decision, praising the army as "a most lovable people" while complaining "how cruel our enemies are."[5] But just to make sure that conservatives did not use this political victory to scuttle the reforms, Deng defended his program, though he supported a return to "plain living" and a shift of economic investment to "basic industries" like transportation and energy. Political reform, however, was clearly dead, with Deng once again attacking his favorite whipping horse, the "American system of separation of powers."

In the second speech (Doc. 59), Deng unveiled Jiang Zemin as the new general secretary. He also joined in laying responsibility for the "rebellion" squarely on Zhao Ziyang by asserting that with a united CPC Politburo Standing Committee, the party could "quell all disturbances." The peasants, workers, and PLA—

---

[3]Contrary to the official account, Robin Munro, an eyewitness on the square, reported that no soldiers walked in front of the tanks, which ran over tents and sleeping bags, while one student was saved at the last minute from being bayonetted in his tent. Robin Munro, "The Real Story of the Slaughter in Beijing," *The Nation,* June 11, 1990.

[4]Zhang disclaimed the contention, reported in the foreign press and widely believed in Beijing, that the soldier had been killed after unmercifully shooting three innocent women.

[5]The next day, June 10, a secret party document—read to party members over the phone to insure against its duplication—claimed that Zhao Ziyang had planned to use 4,000 troops at his personal command to stage a coup, to which the crackdown was only a response. Zhao was also reportedly offered military support by Minister of Defense Qin Jiwei but he turned it down.

though clearly not intellectuals—were all "reliable," but stability could be easily destroyed if "central authorities are thrown into confusion." Deng also promised finally to retire (curiously, one of the anddemonstrators' demands)[6] warned his successors of the dangerous international situation in which Western countries were plotting to "force various socialist countries to give up their socialist road." Even before the dramatic collapse of the regimes in Eastern Europe, Deng, like Fidel Castro, promised that China would not waver from socialism. He also again allayed fears that the PRC would isolate itself from the world.

After June 4, any open challenge in China to Yuan Mu's and Deng's version of the massacre was impossible. But in Hong Kong, the local Communist press was livid in its condemnation of the Chinese government's brutality. The articles presented here (Docs. 61–65) describe the battle in the streets of Beijing not as between heroic, restrained troops and "inhuman thugs," but as an overwhelming military assault by a professional army on an unarmed civilian population. Responsibility for the violence, they argue, rested squarely with the government, which had "furtively" sent the army into the city, just as Japanese troops had raided villages during the Resistance War. Although these articles employ inflated rhetoric strikingly parallel to the official CPC version of events—though with the "good" and "bad" forces completely reversed—these press accounts also convey the Beijing population's enormous loss of faith in the government. China's leaders will confront, the articles predict, the same fate of other national leaders, most notably South Korea's Chun Doo Hwan, who, after massacring their own people, were decisively defeated. Some of these Hong Kong reporters have nothing but "hatred for a handful of beasts who have betrayed the people." But others are left with an unanswerable question: "When the leadership of our country is controlled by a group of butchers, what should we do?"

---

[6]Deng acted on his promise by resigning his last formal positions in the party and state Central Military Commissions, which have since been assumed by Jiang Zemin. Yet Deng left open the option of continuing to provide advice, and, indeed, he played a central role in meeting with American representatives sent by President Bush to the PRC in July and December 1989.

57
State Council Spokesman Yuan Mu
Holds News Conference

Source: Beijing Television Service, June 6, 1989; FBIS, June 7, pp. 12–19

[Video opens with a caption board reading "Yuan Mu Hosts News Conference," then cuts to a close-up of Yuan Mu speaking.]

[Yuan Mu:] Today we are holding a news conference for domestic journalists, not for [overseas] Chinese and foreign journalists. The main reason for doing this is that since the early hours of the morning of June 3, a shocking counterrevolutionary rebellion, unprecedented in the history of the Republic, has occurred in the capital. It has caused great concern to the media at home and abroad. Everybody is concerned about the event. Thus, the State Council asked Comrade Zhang Gong, political commissar and director of the Political Department of a certain martial law unit [video cuts to Zhang Gong in uniform]; Comrade Yuan Liben, secretary general of the Beijing Municipal Party Committee; Comrade Ding Wenjun, deputy secretary general of the Beijing municipal government [video cuts to Ding Wenjun], and myself to give to you information about this matter. [Video shows people seated at long tables in rows, cuts to show Yuan Liben seated on Yuan Mu's right. Camera moves to close-up of Yuan Mu.] After this, you may ask questions if you have any, and we will answer them as completely as possible according to what we know about the situation. To begin with, I would like to say a few things:

First, the current situation is that a very few thugs engineered a counterrevolutionary rebellion in the early hours of the morning of June 3, but because of the valiant struggle of the People's Liberation Army, they were not entirely successful—their plot for rebellion was not entirely successful. We have achieved the initial—or shall we say first-step—victory in crushing the rebellion. The rebellion has not been completely quelled, however. The situation in the capital remains very grim. This is a general description of the current situation after our study.

Second, after the rebellion took place, people of all walks of life in society, including journalistic units, may have become very concerned about the casualties in this rebellion. The State Council is also very concerned with this matter and has instructed all departments concerned to investigate the actual state during the past couple of days. Current statistics are incomplete because the situation is still unstable and confused, and order has not yet been normalized in various channels. At the time of my arrival here, the incomplete statistics, which I have verified several times, are roughly as follows:

Over 5,000 officers and men of the PLA have been wounded. Over 2,000 civilians, including the handful of lawless ruffians and the onlooking masses who do not understand the situation, have been wounded. As for the number of people who have died, our preliminary statistics, which are incomplete as I just said, show that nearly 300 people have died. This includes soldiers, bad elements who deserve this because of their crimes, and people who were killed by mistake.

Moreover, over 400 PLA officers and men are still missing. These figures are acquired from various martial law units. Their whereabouts are still unknown. We do not know whether they are dead or alive. As time goes on, or when the situation stabilizes, we may, through further investigation, establish that some are still alive and that some may have sacrificed themselves.

This is the general situation. I have repeatedly stated that these figures may not be very accurate. However, one figure is relatively accurate because it has been obtained from various colleges—we checked all colleges, one by one: As of now, twenty-three college students have been reported dead. This figure is more specific. All other figures are not very specific. They are just rough figures. They are not very accurate. I expect possible changes to these figures when things become clearer as the situation further develops or stabilizes. Since it is a question in everyone's mind, I therefore have opted to inform you comrades first.

[Video cuts back to a medium close-up of Yuan Mu.] Another issue is the clean-up in Tiananmen for which I will give the floor to Comrade Zhang Gong in a short while as he was there when the troops cleaned up Tiananmen Square. There is also a tape recording which you can also view. The basic situation of the students' withdrawal from Tiananmen Square was peaceful [pauses, smiles, and chuckles]. Yes, a peaceful withdrawal.

[Interrupted by voice from off camera.] Voluntary withdrawal? [Yuan Mu half-turns to his left, smiles.]

[Yuan Mu:] Yes, voluntary withdrawal. Peaceful withdrawal. But the students maintained that their withdrawal was peaceful. It was possible that both sides [words indistinct]. As for the specific conditions, Comrade Zhang Gong will brief you later on.

Another point is that the State Council maintains that the situation facing the capital is still very grim. Stabilizing the overall situation and the further restoration of public order are primary concerns regarding the capital's overall situation. The capital has a population of over ten million. If the situation further worsens and public order cannot be restored, it would give the extremely few rebels, the thugs, the extremely few thugs or bad people an opportunity which they can exploit to their advantage. [Attendant leans in front of camera, apparently placing microphone before Zhang Gong.]

According to the information gathered so far, they are still carrying on with various kinds of sabotage activities including beating, smashing, looting, and burning. [Video cuts to wide shot of hall, showing attendant moving microphones around Yuan Mu's table.] Buses are continuously being burned; roadblocks are being set up constantly. What is particularly serious is that we have been informed that they are planning to cut off the water and electric supply and further paralyze transportation. [Video cuts back to same medium close-up view of Yuan Mu.]

These activities are going on in some areas. If the situation is not improved, the immediate problem would be that the lives of the 10 million residents in the capital would not return to normal. We have already experienced difficulties in supplies, particularly in nonstaple foodstuff and vegetables. If the supply of coal, gas, liquified gas, and electricity is interrupted or stops and if public transportation is further paralyzed, the situation would become even more severe.

Therefore, we hope that all residents of the capital will join comrades of the PLA, armed police, public security cadres, and policemen in quickly restoring normal order to the capital. Some comrades have suggested that we may now raise a slogan saying that we should safeguard our life and safety. If our daily activities cannot be carried out as usual, the people's interests would be more difficult to protect. If the situation gets worse, if the conspiracies of those scoundrels who have harbored all kinds of hatreds against socialism and our country should succeed, and if these scoundrels do overturn the People's Republic of China by taking advantage of the current chaotic situation, then the problem would be more grave. I feel that there should not be any basic conflict of interest between our comrades of the PLA, armed police personnel, public security cadres and policemen, and the vast number of the masses. Their interests should be in line with each other's. Therefore, we hope our public media units, considering the overall situation, will do their best to prevent our internal problems from getting worse.

Let us join our efforts in maintaining order. By so doing, those illegal and riotous acts may be more clearly exposed and better handled, and social order may be restored more quickly. I wish to make it clear that we should not have mercy for those who planned the riots and those behind-the-scenes organizers of the riots, because the contradictions between them and us are of an antagonistic nature. If this is not clearly understood, and if this problem is not resolved, the interests of the great majority of the people cannot be safeguarded. I think the vast numbers of the masses, including the vast numbers of students, have expressed their support for communism and socialism since the beginning of the student strike. I think our country would not have a future if it does not have the leadership of the communists and if it does not take the socialist path. I think the great majority of the people of Beijing and the whole country have a common understanding of this.

Therefore, I hereby urge the public media to do their best to convey this signal in order to defuse all kinds of misunderstandings and to ease as many contradictions as they can. Let us join forces to achieve these goals. As I have said, the precondition for this is that the people, the military, the armed police, and public security personnel must unite. The most urgent thing, as mentioned in the Beijing municipal government's emergency notice, is that, in order to improve the current situation, the vast numbers of Beijing residents should not go out to the streets as onlookers in the current chaotic situation. They should just go to work and go home as usual, stick to their own posts, and should not stay too long in the streets. This is not a restriction of the people's freedom. The purpose of enforcing martial law is to restore normal order. Under the current conditions, the situation could be stabilized sooner if this advice is followed. If the situation is not stabilized, many things will be very difficult to carry out. Our reforms, construction, efforts to improve the economic environment and rectify the economic order, and our efforts to deepen reforms would become empty talk. So, we must first stabilize the situation. It is very, very important that everyone stay at his or her post, and do his or her share.

Here I have to say that there is one thing that leading comrades of the State Council had told me repeatedly before this news conference and wanted me to stress here: Once the general situation is stabilized—that is, when the order has returned to normal in the capital and the general situation is fairly stable—the dialogue between the government and the people of all walks of life, including the vast number of students, will continue at various levels and in various ways and forms. As for the suggestions previously made by people from all walks of life, including young students, regarding punishing bureaucrat profiteering, overcoming corruption, promoting democracy, and so forth, the government will continue to give them serious consideration and earnestly take the advice from various circles through dialogue. Since the current situation is so grim, the processes of a number of things that we had already begun considering have been interrupted, and they cannot be carried out for the time being. In the future, I think, we shall have to make up for this loss. We should stabilize the situation as soon as possible and overcome at an early date the various shortcomings in our party and government work that should be overcome. This is perhaps also the desire of the broad masses. I have said this. Will Comrade Zhang Gong give a brief account on what has happened at Tiananmen, the work done to clean up Tiananmen Square, the enforcement of martial law by PLA units, and other things related to the martial law troops.

[Zhang Gong:] I am Zhang Gong.

[Unidentified voice:] How do you write your name?

[Zhang Gong:] Zhang is the character composed of *gong* [bow] and *chang* [long], and Gong is the same character as used in the term *gongren* [workers]. First, I wish to explain a question to our comrades in the journalistic circles in a responsible manner. Through you, I also wish to see to it that the people in the capital and all other parts of the country can clearly understand the question I am going to explain. Between 4:30 A.M. and 8:30 P.M. on June 3, that is, at the time when our martial law unit was carrying out the task of cleaning up Tiananmen Square, the unit absolutely did not kill one single student or individual. No one was killed at that time. Nor was there a single person killed or injured because he was run over by our vehicle.

[Yuan Mu interposes as video shows him:] That is to say, no tank or military vehicle was used to run over people.

[Zhang Gong:] No, not a single person was killed or injured because he was run over by our vehicle. At present, an allegation is being circulated in society; that is there was a so-called bloodbath at Tiananmen Square when the liberation army was cleaning up the square. Also, there is another allegation that many people were shot to death, and the corpses were burned in Tiananmen Square. This is a sheer rumor. Nothing like that has ever happened. I think this perhaps was fabricated by a very few people with ulterior motives. I hope that you will not believe this rumor.

[Zhang smiles, picks up a folded page from table, and unfolds it, and refers to the page.] Now there are many rumors. Incidentally, when I entered this hall a while ago, I was told that there is now a rumor which claims that our 38th Army Group and the 27th Army Group have been engaged in a vigorous fight for the Nanyuan Airport, that the fight has been continuing since last night, and that even artillery has been employed. [Turns to look behind, over his left shoulder] I can tell you all that the 38th Army Group and the 27th Army Group are simply not at the Nanyuan Airport. [Turns again to look at same spot behind him, over left shoulder.] There is no such place [*sic*]. Rumors like this are total nonsense, designed to fool people.

In addition to these problems, I also want to brief you on the operation to clean up Tiananmen Square.

At about 1:30 P.M. on June 4 [1630 GMT June 3], the martial law units arrived in Tiananmen Square to enforce the martial law order and clean up the square. After we arrived, we spent several hours—about three hours or so—repeatedly broadcasting the urgent announcement of the Beijing municipal government and the Headquarters of the Martial Law Units, pointing out that a serious counter-revolutionary rebellion had taken place since the early morning of June 3, and requesting the citizens and students still in the square to leave there as soon as possible. After our repeated broadcast, most of the onlookers and other masses gradually moved out of the square. Only some people still remained around the Monument to the People's Heroes.

[Zhang continues to read from page before him on table.] We again broadcast the urgent announcement, so that more people could leave the square before the troops formally cleaned up the square. As a result of our repeated broadcasts, some representatives of the student organizations asked our martial law units whether the students could peacefully or voluntarily withdraw from the square. The martial law units promptly accepted their request and, through loudspeakers, again explained to the students that their request had been accepted. [Again looks back, over left shoulder.] In our broadcasts we kept asking the students to leave the square voluntarily and peacefully. Thus, quite a number of students began to leave the square from the southeast exit.

When we began to clean up the square, there were not many people there. When the cleanup began, the troops moved from north to south, moving from the Tiananmen tower toward the monument. As they moved, they left an opening through which the students and the masses in the square could leave voluntarily. After all the students and masses had left, the officers and men of our troops began to examine the tents they left behind to see if there were still people inside. We examined each and every tent. After making sure that there were no more people inside those tents, we used vehicles to knock down those make-shift tents and piled them up into one place. We also knocked down barricades, including things like the so-called goddess statue.

[Zhang continues to read from page on table before him.] During the cleanup process, seven people—some were on a vehicle with two tanks of gasoline, and some were carrying glass bottles of gasoline—headed by a ringleader from the illegal organization, the Self-Government Union of College Students, attempted to burn and blow up our military vehicles. [Again looks back, over left shoulder.] They also threatened to burn down the Tiananmen Tower. When our cadres and fighters discovered them, they tried to escape with the bottles, heading in the direction of [words indistinct]. We caught them, so they did not achieve their scheme. Thus we can say that the entire cleanup process was basically one of peaceful withdrawal under our powerful and repeated propaganda work.

It is quite clear that during the course of withdrawal, not a single person was killed or crushed. [Zhang again looks over his left shoulder, then smiles. He briefly sits quietly, before suddenly continuing.]

[Yuan Mu, interrupting:] Can we show the video? [Yuan's hand seen, gesturing, between camera and Zhang.]

[Zhang Gong:] This is roughly what happened. [Yuan Mu's hand is seen gesturing with index finger extended, pointing.]

[Yuan Mu:] We have a video film about the withdrawal.

[Video shows a television monitor, showing a column of people, holding banners and streamers, slowly walking down side of an avenue toward the camera. Film on monitor cuts to shots of a large crowd, carrying banners and streamers, moving toward camera, intercutting with other views of crowd moving toward camera. Last shots are of crowd moving away from camera. The film lasts about two minutes.]

[Yuan Mu:] Comrade Zhang Gong, please continue.

[Zhang Gong:] One more thing that I would like to say is that, since the imposition of martial law on April 20 [date as heard], all the officers and men of the martial law enforcement troops have exercised maximum restraint vis-à-vis the crowd that encircled the PLA fighters and cadres. Many among the crowd were, certainly, bad elements. For a considerably long period, we adopted the policy of not talking back when abused and not hitting back when hit. Therefore, our troops were pinned down for three nights and days in the area between Gucheng and Bajiao. They were unable to have decent means. They were abused, beaten, and grabbed. Even army commanders and political commissars, encircled and pushed and shoved by the crowd, were forced to stand there for 5 hours. Under these conditions, they exercised great restraint all along. During the period from the night of June 3 to the early morning of June 4—we arrived at Tiananmen at 1:30, as was said just now—we were under the frenzied attacks of the ruffians as we marched toward Tiananmen. You just saw a film. As a matter of fact, we were unable to shoot many of the scenes; there was not enough time for that.

According to the reports from the troops, the weapons used by the ruffians were steel bars, big wooden sticks with nails at the end, molotov cocktails— many cars and armored vehicles were burned by them. They threw many rocks, bricks, and bottles. Some units said these things were thrown at their heads like falling raindrops. Fortunately, our soldiers are helmeted. Therefore, when the soldiers arrived at Tiananmen . . . [changes thought]. Now, when we speak of the number of soldiers injured, we do not include light wounds. They are not counted. Some bad elements wrested guns from the soldiers and shot them then and there. As Comrade Yuan Mu just said, casualties among the soldiers are quite heavy. We already gave you the figures. You already saw the end that came to that officer. In addition to that, a soldier was carried to, to . . .

[Yuan Mu, interrupting:] An overpass.

[Zhang Gong:] An overpass in Chongwenmen. They lifted him and threw him down from the overpass. After killing the soldier by throwing him, they poured gasoline on the body and burned it. They then hoisted the charred body for others to see. We did not record this scene. [Zhang again looks back over his left shoulder.] It took place in Chongwenmen. Many people saw it. In addition to the rather heavy casualties, which Comrade Yuan Mu has already given an account of, our equipment was also greatly damaged. All kinds of military vehicles have been burned. According to preliminary, incomplete figures, hundreds of vehicles have been burned.

[Yuan Mu:] According to our latest statistics, 590 . . . 90 . . . [hesitates]. How many? [Yuan Mu turns to ask Yuan Liben.]

[Zhang Gong:] All vehicles, including buses.

[Yuan Mu:] Tell us the total figure.

[Yuan Liben, referring to a paper on the table:] Some statistics are still not in—some incidents of burning took place relatively far away. The total number as of now is 568, including 364 military vehicles and 102 buses. The rest are vans, trucks, and so forth. Another 202 buses are now being used as barricades in the middle of the roads.

[Zhang Gong:] In the area east of Junbo alone, more than 100 armored and other military vehicles were burned. They lie there. We want to remove them but it is rather difficult. They are all burned and it is difficult to move them. They still lie there. Hundreds of guns have been snatched. We don't have an exact figure. It is hard to get the figure in a short time. Now the ruffians are armed with guns. Our patrols saw them riding on bicycles carrying submachines. I got this message on my way here. [Takes a folded piece of paper from his inside breast pocket, unfolds it, and hesitates as he refers to it.]

At 1:00 this morning, at the interchange in Fuxingmen—we had set up a checkpoint there to ensure that troop patrols will be able to move around unimpeded and to restore traffic order in the capital—the checkpoint was attacked by two groups of armed ruffians. They attacked the troops with guns [pauses and looks over his left shoulder] . . . guns. Their chieftain is now under arrest. His name is Zhang Jun, twenty-two years of age, a worker at the Chongguang Machinery Plant in Beijing. He lives [words indistinct].

[Unidentified male voice from off-camera:] What is the name?

[Zhang Gong:] Chong—Guang [names Chinese characters] Machinery Plant.

[Unidentified male voice asks question from off-camera:] [Words indistinct.]

[Zhang Gong:] [Looks to his left, apparently to address questioner, checks paper in his hand.] The name of the plant where he worked is called Chongguang Machinery Plant. He is twenty-two years old. His residence is in Shijingshan, and I can't remember the name of the street where his house is located. If you want the details, I can give them to you later [pauses].

According to him, they still have four of our soldiers—one officer and three soldiers. He now refuses to speak and we don't know how credible his words are. We only know from him that one officer and three of our soldiers are in their custody. I think these facts can fully explain two things: First of all, what has happened in our capital is indeed a very serious counterrevolutionary rebellion. These ruffians cannot be more arrogant now. This has been proven by facts. Second, it shows that our troops were overly afraid of hurting the masses and the onlookers, many of whom were agitated and had come to believe the hearsay, and so they always exercised great restraint. If we did not exercise restraint, there simply could not have been that many casualties among us and so much of our equipment destroyed. This is ample proof of facts. There couldn't be so many officers and men who have died or been wounded, nor could there have been so many weapons and equipment destroyed or robbed from them. This is something anyone with some common sense can understand. If the troops, who had weapons in their hands, did not exercise restraint [Zhang smiles], then we would not have needed that many troops and we could have completely . . . [Zhang again looks back over his left shoulder, then changes thought, without finishing the sentence]. The current situation would not have happened. Thus, I think we exercised great restraint.

Our troops did not take actions to defend themselves until the counterrevolutionary rebellion took place on the evening of June 2 and the early morning of June 3. Our self-defense was [words indistinct] something which we took when we could not afford not to. But we still did our best to exercise restraint. This is because our troops are children of the people. Their goal is to serve the people wholeheartedly. In fact, when our cadres and fighters could not distinguish who was a rebel and who was just an ordinary civilian, they simply could not pull the trigger. If they had not exercised restraint, our equipment could not have been destroyed like that. Take a look at our armored vehicles [words indistinct]. The fact that so much equipment has been destroyed and so many cadres and fighters have been beaten up or killed can also account for our troops' restraint. This is all I want to say.

[Yuan Mu:] Now I would like to ask Comrade Yuan Liben to report on the losses that Beijing has suffered from the rebellion. Now there are still some problems in our society. Some ruffians are still hatching all types of plots. He will brief you on what he knows. [Video cuts to medium close-up of corner of table, showing Yuan Mu seated at head of table, on right, and Yuan Liben seated on the side, to his right, consulting pages on table.]

[Yuan Liben, reading from notes on table:] Let me give you a brief description of the situation. The things I am going to tell you cannot represent the whole picture because conditions are relatively difficult at present and because the general situation is still very grim.

[Video zooms to medium close-up of Yuan Liben, reading from notes, glancing up occasionally. As Yuan continues to speak, he removes his glasses and seems to stare into space, seeming to avoid looking at the camera. He holds the glasses up to his eyes periodically to read from notes.]

The situation in the capital is still severe since the initial victory was won in our counterattack against the counterrevolutionary rebellion. The thugs have changed their tactics. They have not reconciled themselves to their defeat and are still carrying out furious counterattacks. Their activities generally include the following.

First, they continue spreading rumors to poison the people's minds and incite those people who do not know the facts, and they continue to oppose the government and the people. We have certain difficulties in trying to clarify the truth because of the limited means available to us at the moment. For instance, we were unable to deliver the newspapers yesterday and today.

[Yuan Mu:] We have not read the newspapers for the past two days.

[Yuan Liben, reading from notes without looking up:] Therefore, we earnestly hope that the reporters here, for the sake of Beijing's peace and stability as well as the overall interests of the state and the people, will spread the truth to society. Currently, the rumor-mongers are pandering to the tastes of the masses and what they spread is very poisonous. In particular, when the masses' emotions are worked up, it is hard for them to consider problems with a cool head. For instance, a PLA fighter was thrown over the railing of an overpass close to the Chongwen Gate to the street below, where he was burned alive. Even in such a situation, there were still people who were spreading the rumor that the fighter was beaten to death by the masses in anger because he killed three residents.

This was out-and-out fabrication. Yesterday morning, we received a telephone call from a woman comrade who lives in the Chongwen Gate area telling us the whole story about the incident. She said that, being a conscientious citizen, she wanted to tell us the true story about the burned fighter at Chongwen Gate, which she witnessed with her own eyes. A rumor is going around among thousands of people that the fighter had beaten three people to death, including an old lady who knelt in front of him to beg for her life. Comrades, do you think that such a thing could actually happen? The woman comrade said that at around 5:00 A.M. on June 4, when three motor vehicles, one of which was a trailer loaded with vegetables, were passing through Chongwen Gate, many people threw stones and bottles at them. Two of the vehicles made a U-turn and sped away, while the third car could not make a U-turn in time because of the trailer. It was immediately hit with stones, which fell like raindrops. At first, the woman thought that there was no one else in the car except for the driver. But actually there were eleven people aboard. They could have opened fire on the crowd, but they did not. What she saw was them jumping down from the vehicle and running toward a nearby alley. However, whether they opened fire while running, she did not see. It seems that they carried firearms, but not many. One of them failed to escape and was beaten, thrown from the Chongwenmen overpass, and drenched with gasoline and burned. He was dead.

This man had never beaten anyone. If he had had a gun, he would have been entirely able to defend himself and would not have met his death in such a manner. After the innocent fighter was burned alive, it was still rumored this happened because he had killed three people. That was a total injustice. Even after his death, he was spurned by so many people. She hoped that her story would prompt the martial law units to clarify the case by further investigation. But under the present circumstances, it is very difficult to conduct a thorough investigation. [Stops reading from notes and looks up.]

The rumor-mongers are of course very detestable. But those who spread rumors can always make a rumor sound as if it were 100 percent true. If someone should ask them, "Did you see or just hear it?" they would say that they are not sure. But rumors like that can really poison the people's mind.

Some comrades were indeed brutally murdered. Just now you comrades have seen the video picture. Of course there are other materials and they can all be made public in the future. This is the first point. I believe, as can be seen from the video, the great majority of them were innocent bystanders who went there simply to watch the excitement, not to act against the PLA nor to take part in the riot. Not everyone who appeared in the video is a rioter. In such a chaotic condition where good and bad people were intermingled and right and wrong were mixed up, the PLA, driven beyond the limits of forbearance, was forced to take some drastic measures. As a result, some people were accidentally killed. To those comrades who were accidentally killed, before I came here, the leading comrade of the State Council told me to express, well, deep regrets. In addition, in the future when it is found out which units or organizations they belong to—some have already been identified. . . .

[Unidentified male voice interrupts from off-camera. Words indistinct.]

[Yuan Mu:] . . . some have already been identified—the units will be instructed to make satisfactory, appropriate arrangement for their funerals. I hope that the journalistic circles will also relay this attitude of the State Council to everyone.

Of course, there are people who, under the influence of the thugs, did not know the truth and who had misunderstandings of one kind or another about martial law and felt rather sulky about it from the start. When the time came, these people also took to the streets, throwing some stones at the PLA or beating them in some small way. I said that such things could also happen. Therefore, I do not believe that whoever took part in the attack against the PLA are all thugs. I do not see things in this way. I believe that the vast number of students must be separated from the thugs. The bystanders and people who do not know the truth must also be separated from the very few traitors [Yuan Mu immediately correcting], thugs and ruffians. Whom we call thugs and ruffians and those who masterminded the counterrevolutionary rebellion are still those who are described in the letter of the CPC Central Committee and the State Council sent to all party members and the people throughout the country. They are the schemers and organizers behind the scene: people who colluded with overseas hostile forces, people who leaked important, high-level party and state secrets to illegal organizations, and people who conspired and plotted behind the scene. These people did not necessarily go to the streets to do the beating. They might have stayed behind, plotting other things. Strikers, smashers, and looters, those hooligans and gangs, those released from reeducation through labor, and those released from prison after serving their terms without being successfully reformed—these are the people we are talking about, and they include those who came to Beijing from elsewhere to commit crimes.

There is absolutely no intention to indiscriminately call everyone who took to the streets as thugs. I do not recognize this idea. It is also wrong to do so. Precisely in this sense, I said from the very beginning that the current incident is a counterrevolutionary rebellion in nature. The reason it is called a counter-revolutionary rebellion is that there are a very few thugs and ruffians who used extremely cruel, extremely inhuman means against our people's soldiers. I believe that those bystanders, those who generally did not know the truth, could not possibly use that kind of cruel and brutal means against our own troops. They threw the bodies high from the overpass bridge. On top of it, they burned them with gasoline. Their intestines were taken out. Men were beaten to death and the bodies were hung up to show to the public. Men were hit inside the vehicles, and stones were thrown at them even after they were dead. No one could do such a thing unless he harbored deep-seated hatred toward the PLA and the Communist Party. Such people are absolutely very, very few in our country.

Thus, we still have to, first of all, make clear that this rebellion was certainly a counterrevolutionary act, a very serious rebellion. You can see that the methods used were [words indistinct]. Even the personal insult and abuse they heaped against the liberation army were not ordinary abuse. Their cruelty and inhumanity has developed to such an extent. What is more, in just one or two days, more than 500 vehicles were burned, exploded, or destroyed. If a vehicle costs approximately 100,000 yuan, 500 vehicles would cost some 50 million yuan. They had not the least feeling of affection for the state property, the public property. This was absolutely not what the general people could do. They captured ammunition and guns. This was a very clear [distinction?]. Some students in schools have handed over the ammunition and guns of their own accord. One school has handed over more than forty guns. If the students of this school were thugs, how could they have handed over the guns? Certainly not. However, there certainly are some guns still scattered in society. Some people have swaggered around flagrantly, carrying submachine guns, and there have been instances of people shooting people from hiding. I do not mean to say—I do not mean it at all—that all people wounded by mistake were shot from hiding. That would not be seeking truth from facts. However, there were certainly such instances as shooting from hiding. There were certainly the instances where people were shot from hiding and then put the blame on the liberation army. Therefore, the only course for us kindhearted and good people to take is to unite to deal with the very few thugs.

We sincerely appeal to all people to understand that, first, this was indeed a shocking counterrevolutionary rebellion, and, second, there are certainly cruel and inhuman thugs in our capital. These thugs are beyond the general imagination of we kindhearted people. Some kind and honest people and some of the masses might not quite understand the fact that the liberation army entered the city to carry out the task of enforcing martial law. We cannot blame these people. Perhaps, there was not enough work of propaganda and explanation, and these people could not understand the theory about this matter and were unclear about the situation. But definitely we cannot view them as thugs. We should isolate the thugs. That is, we should stop the rebellion. We should not be soft-hearted in dealing with them, but should resolutely strike at them. As for the masses, we should side with them as our people. We should side with the liberation army so as to guarantee that they can carry out the normal task of enforcing martial law. We should neither interfere with them nor upset them nor stir up incidents. If so, I think it will be much easier to stabilize the situation.

For a period, class struggle was not stressed at all and even political struggle was not stressed. It was said that they were all gone, that people were all brothers and sisters, and that the world was full of love [laughs]. People were all like this. I did not say that we do not need love. Neither did I say that among our comrades people should all live in harmony, unite and help each other [as heard]. However, our society is complex. There exist indeed in our society a number of bad people. This is an objective fact. [Video shows Yuan Mu gesturing to emphasize the point.] There exist these people who are dissatisfied with our social system. Of course, I should also mention that these are indeed mistakes in our work. There are many things in our work that the party and the government did not do well. However, do the mistakes reach the extent that the people simply must destroy our People's Republic? [Video shows Yuan Mu gesturing to emphasize the point.] I feel that this is not the case. This is absolutely not the case. This is not so. However, there are at present some people who exploit this and use it to instigate people. [Video shows Yuan Mu laughing.]

On top of it, as Comrade [Yuan] Liben said just now, they mean to create all kinds of rumors to confuse and poison people's minds. Therefore, they simply feel that they must use the originally normal dissatisfaction over certain things in our work, for example, bureaucratic profiteering and corruption, to instigate and lead people to the extent that they simply must overthrow the Communist Party and negate the system from the root. This is unacceptable. I want to say again, and very unequivocally, that people who, as a result of their dissatisfaction of one kind or another, became the object of other people's instigation—these comrades are still good. They are the masses who simply do not know much about the truth, and [laughs] this requires us to work patiently on them.

Here I also want to make one more point, that is, with regard to current international opinion. [Video shows Yuan Mu gesturing to emphasize.] At present, there are different opinions. It should be said that the current international opinion is not quite uniform with regard to the counterrevolutionary rebellion in China's capital and the struggle to put down the rebellion. There are already people openly condemning us. In addition, there are people who have said that they are not going to give us this or that, that they are going to set this restriction or that, and that they are going to sanction us.

With regard to this point, before I came here I also asked the leading comrade of the State Council [Li Peng] for instruction. He asked me to make two points clear through the media. First, we are not afraid. [Video shows Yuan Mu gesturing to emphasize the point.] No matter what kind of means they use, whether condemnation or sanction, the Chinese people will never permit their intervention in China's internal affairs. Even if we encounter some temporary difficulties as a result of their actions, we must also cope with them. This is because the current struggle to put down the rebellion is one of life-and-death for the party and the state. If you cannot cope with these minor issues, you simply dare not proceed in this way [laughs]. "The State Council and the People's Republic will all be overturned. What is the use of asking for loans or aid from him?" This is the first attitude. [Video shows Yuan Mu appearing defiant.] Second, we also hope to tell, through the media, the international media, foreign statesmen, and the governments that they must not be too short-sighted and that they need to have a somewhat broader point of view. Even though we face difficulties at the present and are in a grim situation and the party and the state can be said to be in a quite critical moment, China's party and government have the ability, methods, and determination to pull through these difficulties. If they approach the problems with a broader point of view, I do not think they will go as far as acting in a way that will solely upset the Chinese government and people, nor do we want to see this happen. [Video ends with shot showing Yuan Mu looking down at the table, followed by the caption: "Central Television Station."]

58
June 9 Speech to Martial Law Units

DENG XIAOPING

Source: Beijing Domestic Television Service, June 27, 1989; FBIS, June 27, pp. 8–10.

["Text" of speech delivered by Deng Xiaoping while receiving cadres of the martial law units in the capital at and above the army [corps?] level on June 9—read by announcer; from the "News" program.]

Comrades, you have been working very hard. First, I express my profound condolences to the commanders and fighters of the People's Liberation Army

[PLA], commanders and fighters of the armed police force, and public security officers and men who died a heroic death; my cordial sympathy to the several thousand commanders and fighters of the PLA, commanders and fighters of the armed police force, and public security officers and men who were injured in this struggle; and cordial regards to all commanders and fighters of the PLA, commanders and fighters of the armed police force, and public security officers and men who took part in this struggle. I propose that we all rise and stand in silent tribute to the martyrs.

I would like to take this opportunity to say a few words.

This storm was bound to come sooner or later. This is determined by the major international climate and China's own minor climate. It was bound to happen and is independent of man's will. It was just a matter of time and scale. It is more to our advantage that this happened today. What is most advantageous to us is that we have a large group of veteran comrades who are still alive. They have experienced many storms and they know what is at stake. They support the use of resolute action to counter the rebellion. Although some comrades may not understand this for a while, they will eventually understand this and support the decision of the Central Committee.

The April 26 *Renmin ribao* editorial ascertained the nature of the problem as that of turmoil. The word turmoil is appropriate. This is the very word to which some people object and which they want to change. What has happened shows that this judgment was correct. It was also inevitable that the situation would further develop into a counterrevolutionary rebellion.

We still have a group of veteran comrades who are alive. We also have core cadres who took part in the revolution at various times, and in the army as well. Therefore, the fact that the incident broke out today has made it easier to handle.

The main difficulty in handling this incident has been that we have never experienced such a situation before, where a handful of bad people mixed with so many young students and onlookers. For a while we could not distinguish them, and as a result, it was difficult for us to be certain of the correct action that we should take. If we had not had the support of so many veteran party comrades, it would have been difficult even to ascertain the nature of the incident.

Some comrades do not understand the nature of the problem. They think it is simply a question of how to treat the masses. Actually, what we face is not simply ordinary people who are unable to distinguish between right and wrong. We also face a rebellious clique and a large number of the dregs of society, who want to topple our country and overthrow our party. This is the essence of the problem. Failing to understand this fundamental issue means failing to understand the nature of the incident. I believe that after serious work, we can win the support of the overwhelming majority of comrades within the party concerning the nature of the incident and its handling.

The incident became very clear as soon as it broke out. They have two main slogans: One is to topple the Communist Party, and the other is to overthrow the socialist system. Their goal is to establish a totally Western-dependent bourgeois republic. The people want to combat corruption. This, of course, we accept. We should also take the so-called anticorruption slogans raised by people with ulterior motives as good advice and accept them accordingly. Of course, these slogans are just a front: The heart of these slogans is to topple the Communist Party and overthrow the socialist system.

In the course of quelling this rebellion, many of our comrades were injured or even sacrificed their lives. Their weapons were also taken from them. Why was this? It also was because bad people mingled with the good, which made it difficult to take the drastic measures we should take.

Handling this matter amounted to a very severe political test for our army, and what happened shows that our PLA passed muster. If we had used tanks to roll across [bodies?], it would have created a confusion of fact and fiction across the country. That is why I have to thank the PLA commanders and fighters for using this attitude to deal with the rebellion. Even though the losses are regrettable, this has enabled us to win over the people and made it possible for those people who can't tell right from wrong to change their viewpoint. This has made it possible for everyone to see for themselves what kind of people the PLA are, whether there was bloodbath at Tiananmen, and who were the people who shed blood.

Once this question is cleared up, we can seize the initiative. Although it is very saddening to have sacrificed so many comrades, if the course of the incident is analyzed objectively, people cannot but recognize that the PLA are the sons and brothers of the people. This will also help the people to understand the measures we used in the course of the struggle. In the future, the PLA will have the people's support for whatever measures it takes to deal with whatever problem it faces. I would like to add here that in the future we must never again let people take away our weapons.

All in all, this was a test, and we passed. Even though there are not very many senior comrades in the army and the fighters are mostly children of 18 or 19 years of age—or a little more than 20 years old—they are still genuine soldiers of the people. In the face of danger to their lives, they did not forget the people, the teachings of the party, and the interests of the country. They were resolute in the face of death. It's not an exaggeration to say that they sacrificed themselves like heroes and died martyrs' deaths.

When I talked about passing muster, I was referring to the fact that the army is still the People's Army and that it is qualified to be so characterized. This army still maintains the traditions of our old Red Army. What they crossed this time was in the true sense of the expression a political barrier, a threshold of life and death. This was not easy. This shows that the People's Army is truly a great wall of iron and steel of the party and state. This shows that no matter how heavy our losses, the army, under the leadership of the party, will always remain the defender of the country, the defender of socialism, and the defender of the public interest. They are a most lovable people. At the same time, we should never forget how cruel our enemies are. We should have not one bit of forgiveness for them.

The fact that this incident broke out as it did is very worthy of our pondering. It prompts us cool-headedly to consider the past and the future. Perhaps this bad thing will enable us to go ahead with reform and the open policy at a steadier and better—even a faster—pace, more speedily correct our mistakes, and better develop our strong points. Today I cannot elaborate here. I only want to raise a point.

The first question is: Are the line, principles and policies adopted by the third plenary session of the Eleventh CPC Central Committee, including our three-step development strategy, correct? Is it the case that because of this rebellion the correctness of the line, principles, and policies we have laid down will be called into question? Are our goals leftist ones? Should we continue to use them as the goals for our struggle in the future? We must have clear and definite answers to these important questions.

We have already accomplished our first goal, doubling the GNP. We plan to take twelve years to attain our second goal of again doubling the GNP. In the next fifty years we hope to reach the level of a moderately developed nation. A 2 to 2.9 percent annual growth rate is sufficient. This is our strategic goal.

Concerning this, I think that what we have arrived at is not a "leftist" judgment. Nor have we laid down an overly ambitious goal. That is why, in answering the first question, we cannot say that, at least up to now, we have failed in the strategic goals we laid down. After sixty-one years, a country with 1.5 billion people will have reached the level of a moderately developed nation. This would be an unbeatable achievement. We should be able to realize this goal. It cannot be said that our strategic goal is wrong because this happened.

The second question is: Is the general conclusion of the Thirteenth Party Congress of one center, two basic points correct? Are the two basic points—upholding the four cardinal principles and persisting in the open policy and reforms—wrong?

In recent days, I have pondered these two points. No, we have not been wrong. There is nothing wrong with the four cardinal principles. If there is anything amiss, it is that these principles have not been thoroughly implemented: They have not been used as the basic concept to educate the people, educate the students, and educate all the cadres and Communist Party members.

The nature of the current incident is basically the confrontation between the four cardinal principles and bourgeois liberalization. It is not that we have not talked about such things as the four cardinal principles, work on political concepts, opposition to bourgeois liberalization, and opposition to spiritual pollution. What we have not had is continuity in these talks, and there has been no action—or even that there has been hardly any talk.

What is wrong does not lie in the four cardinal principles themselves, but in wavering in upholding these principles, and in very poor work in persisting with political work and education.

In my CPPCC talk on New Year's Day in 1980, I talked about four guarantees, one of which was the enterprising spirit in hard struggle and plain living. Hard struggle and plain living are our traditions. From now on we should firmly grasp education in plain living, and we should grasp it for the next sixty to seventy years. The more developed our country becomes, the more important it is to grasp the enterprising spirit in plain living. Promoting the enterprising spirit in plain living will also be helpful toward overcoming corruption.

After the founding of the People's Republic, we promoted the enterprising spirit in plain living. Later on, when life became a little better, we promoted spending more, leading to waste everywhere. This, together with lapses in theoretical work and an incomplete legal system, resulted in breaches of the law and corruption.

I once told foreigners that our worst omission of the past ten years was in education. What I meant was political education, and this does not apply to schools and young students alone, but to the masses as a whole. We have not said much about plain living and enterprising spirit, about the country China is now and how it is going to turn out. This has been our biggest omission.

Is our basic concept of reform and openness wrong? No. Without reform and openness, how could we have what we have today? There has been a fairly good rise in the people's standard of living in the past ten years, and it may be said that we have moved one stage further. The positive results of ten years of reforms and opening to the outside world must be properly assessed, even though such issues as inflation emerged. Naturally, in carrying out our reform and opening our country to the outside world, bad influences from the West are bound to enter our country, but we have never underestimated such influences.

In the early 1980s, when we established special economic zones, I told our Guangdong comrades that they should conduct a two-pronged policy: On the one hand, they should persevere in reforms and openness, and the other they should severely deal with economic crimes, including conducting ideological-political work. This is the doctrine that everything has two aspects.

However, looking back today, it appears that there were obvious inadequacies. On the one hand, we have been fairly tough, but on the other we have been fairly soft. As a result, there hasn't been proper coordination. Being reminded of these inadequacies would help us formulate future policies. Furthermore, we must continue to persist in integrating a planned economy with a market economy. There cannot be any change in this policy. In practical work we can place more emphasis on planning in the adjustment period. At other times, there can be a little more market regulation, so as to allow more flexibility. The future policy should still be an integration of a planned economy and a market economy.

What is important is that we should never change China into a closed country. There is not [now?] even a good flow of information. Nowadays, do we not talk about the importance of information? Certainly, it is important. If one who is involved in management doesn't have information, he is no better than a man whose nose is blocked and whose ears and eyes are shut. We should never again go back to the old days of trampling the economy to death. I put forward this proposal for the Standing Committee's consideration. This is also a fairly urgent problem, a problem we'll have to deal with sooner or later.

This is the summation of our work in the past decade: Our basic proposals, ranging from our development strategy to principles and policies, including reform and opening to the outside world, are correct. If there is any inadequacy to talk about, then I should say our reforms and openness have not proceeded well enough.

The problems we face in the course of reform are far greater than those we encounter in opening our country to the outside world. In reform of the political system, we can affirm one point: We will persist in implementing the system of people's congresses rather than the American system of the separation of three powers. In fact, not all Western countries have adopted the American system of the separation of three powers.

America has criticized us for suppressing students. In handling its internal student strikes and unrest, didn't America mobilize police and troops, arrest people, and shed blood? They are suppressing students and the people, but we are quelling a counterrevolutionary rebellion. What qualifications do they have to criticize us? From now on, we should pay attention when handling such problems. As soon as a trend emerges, we should not allow it to spread.

What do we do from now on? I would say that we should continue to implement the basic line, principles, and policies we have already formulated. We will continue to implement them unswervingly. Except where there is a need to alter a word or phrase here and there, there should be no change in the basic line and basic principles and policies. Now that I have raised this question, I would like you all to consider it thoroughly.

As to how to implement these policies, such as in the areas of investment, the manipulation of capital, and so on, I am in favor of putting the emphasis on basic industry and agriculture. Basic industry includes the raw material industry, transportation, and energy. There should be more investment in this area, and we should persist in this for ten to twenty years, even if it involves debts. In a way, this is also openness. We need to be bold in this respect. There cannot be serious mistakes. We should work for more electricity, more railway lines, more public roads, and more shipping. There's a lot we can do. As for steel, foreigners think we'll need some 120 million metric tons in the future. We are now capable of producing about 60 million metric tons, about half that amount. If we were to improve our existing facilities and increase production by 20 million metric tons, we would reduce the amount of steel we need to import. Obtaining foreign loans to improve this area is also an aspect of reform and openness. The question now confronting us is not whether or not the reform and open policies are correct or whether we should continue with these policies. The question is how to carry out these policies: Where do we go and which area should we concentrate on?

We must resolutely implement the series of line, principles, and policies formulated since the third plenary session of the Eleventh CPC Central Committee. We should conscientiously sum up our experiences, persevere with what is correct, correct what is wrong, and do a bit more where we have lagged behind. In short, we should sum up the experiences of the present and look forward to the future.

59
Full Text of Gists of Deng Xiaoping's Speech to Members of New Politburo Standing Committee [June 16, 1989]

Source: *Tung fang jih bao* (Eastern daily) (Hong Kong) (July 15, 1989): 6; FBIS, July 18, pp. 13–15.

From now on, we must establish a leadership collective of the third generation in the history of the CPC. Before the Zunyi meeting [1935], there was no mature Central Committee in our party. During the periods of Chen Duxiu, Qu Qiubai, Xiang Zhongfa, Li Lisan, and Wang Ming, no capable central leadership was established. The leadership collective of our party started after the Zunyi meeting. It consisted of Mao [Zedong], Liu [Shaoqi], Zhou [Enlai], and Zhu [De]. Later, Comrade Ren Bishi was included in it. After the death of Comrade Bishi, Comrade Chen Yun joined in the leadership collective. At the Eighth CPC National Congress, a six-member Standing Committee consisting of Mao, Liu, Zhou, Zhu, Chen, and Deng was formed. Later, Lin Biao was also included in it. This leadership collective existed until the Great Cultural Revolution. During the long history before the Great Cultural Revolution, a leadership collective with Comrade Mao Zedong as its core was always maintained, whether our party committed this or that kind of mistake, or whether changes took place in our party membership. This was our party leadership of the first generation.

At the third plenary session of the Eleventh CPC Central Committee, our party's new leadership collective, namely the leadership collective of the second generation, was established. In this collective, I was actually in a key position. Once this collective was established, I was engaged in making arrangements for my successor. Although the two candidates failed to stand their ground, at that time we could only select them, considering their experiences in struggle, their achievements in work, and their political and ideological level. In the meantime, men are always changing.

There should be a core in any collective. A leadership without a core is unreliable. The core of the leadership collective of the first generation was Chairman Mao. With the chairman as the core of the leadership, the Communist Party could not be overthrown during the Great Cultural Revolution. In the leadership collective of the second generation, I am actually the core. Although the two leaders have changed, our party leadership has not been affected. It has always been stable. In the leadership of the third generation, there should also be a core. The comrades present must understand and handle this issue with their high level of consciousness. They must make conscious efforts to uphold such a leadership core. This leadership core is Comrade Jiang Zemin, whom we agreed to select. When doing things, it is necessary for us to make a comparison. Now it is our turn to select Comrade Jiang Zemin. We must make clear the purpose and main theme from the very beginning. Our new Standing Committee starts work today. It must pay attention to establishing and safeguarding the core of the leadership. As long as we have a good Politburo, and a good Standing Committee in particular which unites as one, works hard and lays an exemplary role in carrying out the hard struggle and opposing corruption, we can quell all disturbances. From the current incident, we find that the working class is reliable. Peasants are reliable, and the People's Liberation Army [PLA] is also reliable. However, if the central authorities are thrown into confusion, it is hard to predict their fate. This is the most crucial issue. The fate of our country, party and people has determined that such leadership is needed.

When I talked with Comrades Li Peng and Yao Yilin, I stressed that after the new leadership establishes its working order, I will refrain from bothering about, or interfering in their work. I once said that this is my political task. Of course, if you want to discuss something with me, I will not refuse you. But I will not do as I did in the past. I don't think that it is necessary to announce my role after the establishment of the new Political Bureau and the new Standing Committee. Why? This is not because I am too modest, or something else. Now it is obvious that if I play too great a role, this will be harmful to our country and party. This will be dangerous some day. The U.S. policy for China is based on whether I fall ill, or die. Many countries in the world also base their policy for China on my life. I realized this problem several years ago. It is unhealthy and dangerous to base the fate of a country on the prestige of one or two persons. It is all right when nothing has happened. However, when something has happened, there will be a hopeless mess. Once the new leadership is established, it must assume responsibility. It is all your matter whether you have done something wrong, or something right, or rendered great service. In such a way, you will go ahead boldly with your work. This will also be good for the self-tempering of the new collective. The previous method was not so successful. I am eighty-five now. Any person at such an advanced age must be aware of all this. What we should mainly consider is the general situation. If individual factors affect the stability of the situation, or the healthy development of matters, it will be difficult to solve problems. If something has happened, I can give you indirect help. But I don't want any official titles.

Things which happened currently have shown that persisting in the socialist road and party leadership is the crux. The entire imperialist and the Western world intend to force various socialist countries to give up their socialist road, so that they will be eventually placed under the rule of the international monopoly capital, and be included in the tract of capitalism. Now we must resist such a trend, and take a clear-cut position to oppose it. If we fail to persist in socialism, we will eventually become a dependency. It will then be difficult to develop ourselves. Now the international market has been fully occupied, and it is not easy for us to enter into it. Only socialism can save China, and only socialism can develop China. As far as this matter is concerned, the current rebellion has given us some enlightenment. This is very important. It has enabled us to keep a clear head. If we fail to take the socialist road, there will be no hope for China. There won't even be a great triangle consisting of China, the United States, and the Soviet Union. China is a poor country. Why can such a great triangle exist? It is because China is an independent country with the initiative in its own hands. Why do we say that China is an independent country with the initiative in its own hands? It is because we persist along the socialist road. Otherwise, we can only behave in accordance with the expression on the face of the Americans, or developed countries. It will then be impossible for us to talk about independence! Now international public opinion is putting pressure on us. We have an easy conscience, and will never play into their hands. However, we must do our own work well. The current incident has fully exposed our mistakes and defects. We truly have mistakes and defects! They are not trivial, or insignificant!

Now I am going to talk about the work we must grasp. We must not wait until the complete suppression of the rebellion. While suppressing the rebellion, we must find out where our previous mistakes or defects lie, and study ways to correct them. We must also find out the problems which must be urgently solved. Now there is a lot of work which must be done. It is impossible for us to fully grasp it all. If we now hold a theoretical discussion to discuss problems such as market, planning, and so on, this might not be beneficial to stabilizing the situation. On the contrary, it will hold things up. Now it is necessary for us to do something which will satisfy and gladden the people. In the meantime, we must pay attention to those things which will harm our progress.

The first thing for us to do is that we must prevent our economy from declining. We must actively strive for a faster speed within our power. Of course, we must not set an excessively high demand as we did in the past. At present, the main problem facing us is that our basic industry is weak, and that we lack electric power and raw and processed materials. In the process of distributing raw and processed materials, big enterprises suffer a great deal from the small ones. This has caused a great loss to the state. Now when solving the problem of economic decline, we must know the problem which must be urgently solved. We must accelerate our efforts to solve problems which must be solved, just like cutting a tangled skein of jute with a sharp knife. A dilatory style of work will not do. Otherwise, things will be held up. We must avoid endless quibbling over the question of responsibility. All questions regarding responsibility can be discussed only after two or three years. There is no need for us to make such great efforts to do such a thing. We must be precise in our judgments and actively do things which are beneficial to the development of our cause. Once we grasp the essential point, we can start our work immediately.

In the coming eleven and a half years, we must strive for a more satisfactory speed of development. Even if we cannot attain the objective of 7 percent increase, 6 percent is acceptable. An average of 9 percent increase was needed for the first doubling of our gross industrial and agricultural production output value, whereas 6 percent increase is enough for the second doubling. If we can double again our gross industrial and agricultural production output value without any exaggeration, the people will then perceive the prosperity of our country and socialist cause. With regard to those township and town enterprises which waste electric power and raw and processed materials, we must take resolute actions to close them. Comrades in localities must guarantee to do so with their party character. The CPC Central Committee and the State Council must have their own authority and capability. They cannot work without authority. I suggest that we establish a study group responsible for studying strategy for development and plans for fifty years into the next century. It must mainly work out a plan for development involving basic industry, communications, and transportation. We must take forceful measures to ensure that our development can be sustained, and that it will be full of vigor and vitality. Without basic industry, it is impossible to ensure that our economic development will be full of vigor and vitality. Economic chaos, stagnation, or even retrogression might occur sooner or later. We must devise some methods for dealing with the problem of communications. This problem must be solved. We must also study the problems of steel products, wood, and plastic industries. To solve these problems, we can absorb foreign capital. This also means opening up. Now there are second-hand equipment and

facilities in developed countries. We must be well-informed, and take the opportunity to buy them to reform our old enterprises. We must concentrate our minds
on dealing with these problems. We must specially study these problems, and
fish for information, and speed up the work.

I once said that after the occurrence of the incident, we can only review the
past and look forward to the future. Our future development might be more
stable, better, and even faster. There is the possibility for turning such a bad
thing into a good one. We must also study agricultural problems. We must
eventually solve the problem through science. Rice output in Hunan increased by
15 to 20 percent. Now there is a new method for increasing it by another 20
percent. This shows that the potentials are great. Science is a magnificent thing,
and we must attach importance to it.

The second thing which we must do is something with which the people will
be satisfied. Our efforts must be exerted toward the following two major aspects.
First, we must carry out reform and opening up in a bolder way. Second, we
must firmly grasp the work of handling cases of corruption and punishing those
involved in them.

The work of reform and opening up should be carried out mainly by the State
Council. It must do several things. It must promptly flaunt the banner of opening
up.

Some courage is needed in order to do so. Generally speaking, taking losses
must be allowed. We must not be afraid of taking losses for the sake of big gains
in the future. We must do more things beneficial to reform and opening up.
Cooperation with foreign capital in operations, and development zones in various localities must be carried on. We must absorb more foreign capital. It is true
that foreign businessmen will be benefited, but we will also eventually receive
benefits. We must levy some tax. There must be more service trades for foreign
businessmen. We may also promote some profitable undertakings. In so doing,
our economy will be enlivened.

Now the international community is worried about the possibility that we will
again close our door against the world. We must do something to show that our
policy of reform and opening up will remain unchanged, and that we will further
implement the policy. As far as reform of the political structure is concerned, our
greatest aim is to create a stable environment. I told the Americans that stability
is in the highest interest of China. Things which are beneficial to stability in
China are good things. Regarding the four cardinal principles, I have never made
any concession. We must never give up the people's democratic dictatorship.
However, we must talk less about dictatorship, or only carry it out without
talking about it. The Americans swear at us and fabricate rumors. There is no
terrible problem here. Dealing with the issue of overstaffed government organs,
punishing those involved in corruption, and strengthening the legal system all
mean reform.

To punish those involved in corruption, we must conscientiously grasp several important matters and work must be done for at least ten or twenty years. We must make the matter known to the public. Recently, I have been thinking why we continue to fail in solving this problem. Probably those cases of corruption have involved our senior cadres, or their family members. We have discussed this issue repeatedly in the past, and have been mentioning it for several years. Why did we achieve little? The reasons probably lie inside the party, or the highest leadership stratum. To solve this problem, we must reduce the obstacles. It is advisable for us to work out a policy, stressing that if those who are guilty of corruption can return their illicit money within a certain time limit they will be exempted from prosecution, and treated leniently. Within a certain time limit, they can be given a chance for confessing their crimes. We must persuade them to do so. In the meantime, the reporting of crimes must also be encouraged. We must formulate a temporary policy. I believe that the number of such cases is very large. If the cases below the county level are included, the number will be larger. We must conscientiously handle these cases without any delay. In the current incident, there were no slogans opposing reform and opening up. The slogans were concentrated on opposing corruption. Of course, these slogans only served as a foil. They tried to use the slogans to incite people. However, as far as we are concerned, we must consolidate our party organizations well. If we fail to punish those guilty of corruption, and especially those inside the party, we will truly face the danger of being defeated. Therefore, the slogans of opposing corruption in the incident must be accepted in spite of the fact that they only served as a foil. We must solve the problem of corruption. The new leadership must, first of all, grasp this issue. We must enact a policy to solve the problem smoothly. We must achieve something in this regard. This is a problem inside the party, and an important content of the party consolidation as well. Some people are struggling hard, but some other people are involved in the cases of corruption. How can we tolerate this? I hope that you will especially discuss the problem of punishing those who are guilty of corruption.

While grasping reform and opening up with one hand, we must grasp the work of punishing those guilty of corruption with the other. When we put these two matters together, our policy will become more distinct and explicit. Thus it will enjoy more support.

The third thing for us to do is that we must carry the work of suppressing rebellion through to the end. This is a good chance for us to ban illegal organizations at one go. This is really a good thing. We can win a great victory provided that we can handle the matter well. We must not be soft on those who are guilty of the most heinous crimes. Of course, they must be treated in light of the seriousness of their crimes. Everything must be based on facts and laws. There must be a limit for killing those criminals. We must stress the policy of leniency to confessors and severity to resistors. Many ways can be followed to reflect our policy.

We must now concentrate our efforts on doing the three things which I mentioned above. All disputes, or arguments, are not allowed for at least two years. The line, guiding principles, and policies of the Thirteenth CPC National Congress remain unchanged. Some improper words must not be repeated. There is one more point I want to stress—that is, comrades of the Standing Committee must concentrate their minds on grasping construction. The party must grasp it. Things will not proceed without grasping construction well.

60
Why Good Intentions May Lead to Turmoil and Riot

Source: *China Daily* (Beijing—in English) (June 23, 1989).

Now that the riot in Beijing has been largely quelled, people are beginning to think twice about why the students' good intentions and justifiable aspirations for democracy eventually led to turmoil and riot. A *People's Daily* article tries to offer an answer. Excerpts follow:

Most of the students were unaware that from the very beginning their good intentions were shaped to the ends of a handful of conspirators whose goal is to negate the leadership of the Chinese Communist Party.

In fact, as early as the beginning of 1989, these people began planning to fan disturbances through the opportunities offered by the seventieth anniversary of the May 4th Movement and the fortieth anniversary of the founding of the People's Republic of China. They advocated the "overthrow of the socialist system," and "ending the rule of the Chinese Communist Party." They said that Marxism was totally utopian.

When the April 26 editorial of the *People's Daily* pointed out that their true purpose was to create chaos, they cloaked their ulterior motives by claiming they "opposed corruption."

Whenever the students seemed to calm down, these people tried to rekindle their agitation.

They egged the students on to stage strikes, hunger strikes and stop army trucks. They were actually taking the striking students hostage to pressure the government to agree to their terms.

Most of the students were unaware of the scheme. But once they were unknowingly manipulated, their aspirations and enthusiasm turned to something that stripped them of their senses and reason. As a result, they were pulled farther and farther away from their original hopes. The government tried to give them an out again and again, but in vain.

Why have the students been caught in such a dilemma? The crux of the matter is that they have cast to the wind the notion of class struggle. Even the phrase "political struggle" jars on their ears. As a result, they refused to accept the stark fact that the demonstrations were being shaped to the ends of a handful of bad elements.

This is a lesson to be learned.

Students called their demonstrations "a movement for democracy." But from the very beginning they turned to means beyond the law.

On the one hand they called for "maintaining the dignity of the Constitution." On the other hand, they turned a blind eye to constitutional articles and local regulations concerning putting up posters and holding demonstrations. On the one hand, they asked for equal dialogue with the government. On the other hand, they dictated to the government who should participate in the dialogue and what questions must be answered.

The students have revealed immaturity and superficiality over the last two months.

To begin with, their idea about the basic approach to found democratic politics in China is only skin-deep. They don't understand that China, with its long feudal traditions, underdeveloped economy and alarmingly high illiteracy rate, has a long way to go in bringing about highly developed democracy and that, therefore, only initial steps should be taken in this regard. Grafting Western-style democracy to the Chinese reality is but a fantasy.

Students have had much access to Western ideas since the implementation of the open-door policy, but have failed to digest them. They hold in high esteem Western representative institutions and the practice of checks and balances in government. At the same time, corruption among party and government officials and the defects in China's political set-up caused confusion in their beliefs. Moreover, the political education of the party and Youth League among students became lax, which failed to drive home the truth: only socialism can save China. As a result, many students turned to Western democracy.

Apart from students themselves, we should study the reality in China today to find other causes which helped give rise to the chaos.

A poor country like China, which is going all out to develop its economy, faces a major problem: premature needs for material and political luxuries.

The students' pressing aspiration for democracy is the chief expression of premature political needs. Guided in a correct direction, their enthusiasm could become a driving force for the country's construction of democratic politics. Misled or pressed over-anxiously, their enthusiasm becomes a destabilizing factor. In the absence of restraint, it could go to extremes. Under such circumstances, nothing short of a fresh start can satisfy students' cravings. When things have gone that far, students' passions can be easily used by a handful of conspirators to achieve their ends. This has been borne out by the events over the past two months.

In light of this, the party and government should open up more channels for the people, students in particular, to voice their views on politics and democracy in a positive and reasonable way guaranteed by normal procedures. This will help regulate contradictions in their psychology and reinforce their capability to withstand social changes.

61
Newsletter from Beijing: Beijing Crisis Worsens Under the Violence

HUA MING

Source: *Ta kung pao* (Hong Kong) (June 4, 1989): 2; FBIS, June 5, pp. 32–33.

Violent Incidents Intensify the Contradictions

Martial law enforcement troops, who tried to move to Tiananmen Square, were held back by citizens and students in Beijing and could not enter the square. This unexpected development once again shocked the city of Beijing, which had gradually calmed down in the past few days. On Saturday afternoon, in the Liubukou area of Western Chang'an Avenue, the armed police force used tear gas and electric prods to beat up and clear away citizens and students. The violent incidents thus sharply intensified the contradictions.

On the early morning of Saturday, June 3, when most citizens stepped out of their houses and prepared to go to work, the first message they got was that plainclothes troops who tried to enter the city were held back by the common people, and some people were knocked down and killed by a military vehicle in the Muxudi area. Then, the citizens saw that many military vehicles were surrounded by students and citizens in many intersections along Chang'an Avenue. On top of these vehicles could be seen metal helmets, rifles, daggers, hardtack, and other military equipment and materials. Some college students stood on the tops of these vehicles and told the onlookers about the uses of these military materials which were to be used to "protect the people."

After the troops entered the city and used violence against the people, the attitude of the citizens toward the government and the army changed several times in ten-odd hours. The public order in Beijing was gradually recovered due to the efforts of various circles, and the citizens in Beijing were not as enthusiastic about supporting the students who continued the sit-in as in mid-May. People did not always concentrate their talks on the issue of student unrest. Moreover, as various documents and leaders' speeches were being relayed, many citizens realized that the key issue was to solve the contradictions inside the party through changing some leaders.

However, two or three days ago, some counties and districts in the outer suburbs of Beijing began to organize "anti-turmoil parades" by means of giving money to lure marchers. People were disgusted with this trick and many people asked: Is there any difference between this trick and that of inciting the masses to struggle against each other during the "Cultural Revolution"? Does this mean that the marches organized by the authorities will not affect transportation and production? Can this be described as the proverb goes: "The magistrates were allowed to burn down houses, while the common people were forbidden even to light lamps"? In these circumstances, when seeing the troops who disguised themselves with plain clothes and the weapons in the vehicles, the first reaction of the citizens was surprise and indignation.

Who Were the Weapons Used Against?

The government continuously said through its propaganda that the martial law enforcement troops came to Beijing only to maintain public order and they were never aimed at the citizens and students. However, why did they enter the city furtively at night to perform their aboveboard duties? Why did they transport so many weapons secretly into the city? Did they prepare to fight against the people?

Between 7:00 and 8:00 in the morning, millions of citizens walked out of their houses and went to various intersections to see the military vehicles being surrounded by the masses. Many people persuaded the soldiers inside the vehicles not to suppress students and the people. More people loudly cursed the government, saying that the government did not act in an aboveboard manner and was totally perfidious. An old worker said: Why did the open and aboveboard People's Liberation Army sneak into the city like the Japanese invaders who sneaked into the villages to raid the villagers? Those who planned this action really brought shame on the People's Liberation Army.

The People's Indignation and Distress

Such anger and puzzlement were immediately turned into hostility and despair when the armed policemen used tear gas and electric prods indiscriminately against the innocent people, including old people, women, and children. Hundreds of thousands of people then dashed to Chang'an Avenue and Tiananmen Square by bicycle or on foot. The fury and indignation of the citizens were all expressed in their words and actions. Women reproached some soldiers wearing helmets and holding clubs: Don't you have brothers and sisters? How could you so brutally beat up the masses who feed you? How could you be so merciless? Some old people sighed with bated breath: China has been liberated for forty years, but the country has not changed. How could this government still be called the people's government? Some people remember a popular song named "The Sky of the Liberated Areas" in the early period after liberation and could not help shedding tears when thinking of the words of this song: "The sky of the liberated areas is clear and the people in the liberated areas are joyful. The democratic government loves the people. We can never say enough about our gratitude to the Communist Party."

In the early evening, the radio and television in Beijing broadcast an urgent circular, demanding that the citizens not go into the streets from now on and stay at home in order to ensure their personal safety and prevent unnecessary losses. This was a warning which hinted that violence would be used. This caused fears and worries to the citizens! They feared that something unhappy would occur and some people would meet with misfortunes. They were worried that the students and citizens in Tiananmen Square and Chang'an Avenue would meet with misfortune. Indignation, hostility, terror, and apprehension mixed in the minds of the citizens. They were extremely anxious and could not get to sleep.

Acting Peremptorily to Maintain Authority

When facing the obstruction and condemnation of the masses, what action will the martial law enforcement troops take? It seems that they will inevitably enter the city tonight. In order to maintain the authority of the army and to implement the government's hard-line policy, the troops will certainly resume the action of entering the city. They will not hesitate to injure more people as bloody conflicts have occurred. The riot police force, who conserved strength and stored up energy inside Zhongnanhai, will once again set out with their electric prods to show their strength.

It will not be too hard for the army and the armed police force, especially the riot police force outside the Xinhua Gate, to deal with bare-handed students and citizens. No people can resist the heavy prods. The government should reconsider its plan in order to properly handle citizens and students in Tiananmen Square and Chang'an Avenue. Otherwise, more serious and even unimaginable consequences will be caused and the crisis will be aggravated.

62
The Judgment of History
Will Be Severe

KUNG YAO-WEN

Source: *Ta kung pao* (Hong Kong) (June 4, 1989): 2; FBIS, June 5, pp. 23–24.

Gunshots finally were heard in Tiananmen Square, Beijing, last night. The triggers were pulled by the troops enforcing martial law, the so-called "People's Army." Initial reports indicate that scores of people, students and Beijing citizens, were shot dead. Here is the iron-clad evidence: The Chinese people in Tiananmen Square shed blood, when ruthless bullets pierced the bodies of students and citizens. Alas! Things should have worsened to such a condition! The day June 3, 1989, is one that all Chinese nations wept for the tragedy that took place in Tiananmen and will go down in Chinese history. Those who have committed this error will come under the judgment of history.

Guns were fired, and batons, tear gas, and armored vehicles were used. We can well imagine what a scene it was!

Disregarding objective facts, turning a blind eye on the reality in which a million of Beijing's residents, out of indignation, dashed ahead regardless of their safety to protect the students on consecutive evenings, the Beijing authorities insist that "a small group of people have premeditated to create disturbances to expand turmoil." They have even said that "the graveness of the behavior of a small group of people violating the law has gone beyond our endurance. . . ." In line with this tone, a murderous note could keenly be felt in the June 3 urgent circular issued by the headquarters of the troops enforcing martial law, and the curse between their teeth: "Nobody should illegally stop military vehicles under whatever pretext, obstruct and besiege the People's Liberation Army, or prevent the troops enforcing martial law from exercising their duties. . . . Should anyone pay no heed to our persuasion, cling obstinately to his course, and defy the law, the troops enforcing martial law, public security cadres and police, and the Armed Police Corps are authorized to adopt all measures to deal with him by force; the organizers and trouble-makers will have to bear responsibility for all consequences." It actually means: "Kill on the spot with the authority of the law."

Anyone who is objective and knows something about Beijing's situation cannot but pose the question: Was it necessary to dispatch the troops enforcing martial law? Who is exercising dictatorship on whom? The majority of the students in Tiananmen Square have pulled out in recent days. Remaining there were only some 3,000 students from other provinces. Furthermore, students from other provinces were continuously leaving Beijing. Traffic in Beijing was back to normal, while schools had resumed in some institutes of tertiary education. Teachers and personages of various circles were appealing to the students to leave the square as soon as possible. All signs showed that the situation was tending to be pacified. But on the evening of June 2, close to 10,000 troops exercising martial law made a sudden move to storm the square in two flanks from the east and west. This action promptly stirred up the wrath of Beijing's citizens. One million people swarmed into the streets on their own to put up roadblocks to stall the troops upon hearing the news. The troops were eventually forced to halt. Even many old ladies and housewives could not help themselves from arguing with the officers and men, and pointed out that they had been fooled to come to the capital to suppress the students. Some young soldiers were torn by their own mental conflict and could not help crying. Viewing the on-the-spot pictures taken by reporters, the soldiers exercising martial law were expressionless, but their heartache could hardly be concealed. In the bus transporting soldiers, the students found tommy guns, machine guns, bullets, daggers. . . . At whom would those weapons be aimed?

According to Beijing government media reports over the past month or so, when a news blackout for all other media was enforced, some 1 million Beijing citizens and the public of all parts in the country who support the students are regarded as "an extremely small group," and they have slandered the students by saying that they have initiated another "Cultural Revolution." But Beijing citizens have answered their accusation in voices and actions with righteousness. The people know very well who are in the "extremely small group" and "little handful" behind the scene. Today, it is simply impossible for anyone to conceal the fact from the public, should he want to extend inner-party struggle to the masses.

The blind faith in force and the barrels of the guns are no longer suitable to today's conditions. The strong current of the world today as well as the current of reform in East European socialist countries have all demonstrated that only by following the popular will to conduct democratic political structural reform will there be a way out, while the order to impose martial law, witchhunts, and massacres can only rouse more people to oppose the power that be. The example of Poland has illustrated that point. The suppression of students, workers, and citizens, and the arbitrary apprehension of political offenders under martial law would only end in acknowledging the people's strength and conducting dialogues with the people. Take other examples: [South Korean President] Chun Doo Hwan massacred students in Kwangju and Marcos suppressed the masses by sending the army and police. In the end, both lost their power and failed to protect their own "tiny handful."

Today, Chinese compatriots at home and overseas have to utter their loudest appeal, to demand that the Beijing authorities replace their agitated sentiment with reason and intuitive knowledge and immediately halt the military suppression!

Some one million citizens and students and the support of the whole nation are by no means "an extremely small group." Definitely, the shooting by the troops exercising martial law was an unforgivable error.

It is China's misfortune that on the fortieth anniversary of the founding of the PRC, it will be forced to come to a standstill and even a retrogression. The "June 3" gunshots have announced that the ten-year reform and opening up have suffered irredeemable harm. The achievements of the "one country, two systems," and "the reunification between Taiwan and the mainland" scored only after tremendous efforts are likely to go down the drain. The investments of and talks with foreign businessmen will have to be shelved. In short: Who is to take the blame?

"When the people show no fear of death, will it be effective to scare them with death?" The indomitable spirit of Beijing's citizens and students facing the armed forces day in and day out has fully evidenced this point. The current patriotic student movement fighting for democracy has roused the support of all descendants of the Chinese nation worldwide as well as the intellectuals, workers, and citizens nationwide. Should the Beijing authorities fail to wake up and escape disaster at the last moment, nobody can tell what will happen to them tomorrow. When the people's wrath bursts into a fire, can anyone tell who will be the last victor?

He who has won the people's faith in him will prosper, and he who has lost the people's faith in him will perish. This is a truth that all those who are in power, Chinese or foreign alike, should bear in mind. The Beijing authorities should think twice before taking further action!

63
Statement Issued by Zhongguo Tongxun She Employees

Source: Zhongguo Tongxun She (China news organization) (Hong Kong) (June 5, 1989); FBIS, June 5, p. 94.

[The following statement issued by "some" Zhongguo Tongxun She employees was transmitted in big characters.]

What an unheard-of injustice! What an extremist means!

Indignantly denouncing the fascist bloody atrocities.

Expressing sorrow over the fallen compatriots in Beijing.

By some employees of Hong Kong Zhongguo Tongxun She.

June 5, 1989

64
Wen Wei Po Does Two Things to Mourn Beijing Victims

Source: *Wen wei po* (Hong Kong) (June 5, 1989): 1; FBIS, June 5, p. 94.

All staff at *Wen wei po*, who were extremely indignant at the savage act of the Chinese Government, which massacred the patriotic students and residents in Beijing, held an emergency meeting last night. They first stood in silent tribute for the compatriots who had been killed and then decided to take the following two actions:

1. A flag will be lowered to half staff and a strip of black gauze will be hung on the door to mourn the dead.

2. There will be a charity sale by *Wen wei po* today, and the funds thus raised will be donated to the Chinese Red Cross Society to save the students and residents who have been wounded in this incident.

At the same time, an elegiac couplet will be hung on the gate of our office building today. It reads: Grief over the death of thousands of people in Beijing who have been savagely massacred while striving for democracy; hatred for a handful of beasts who have betrayed the people and who should pay their blood debt.

65
Denouncing the Li-Yang Clique, Traitors to the People

Source: *Wen wei po* editorial (Hong Kong) (June 5, 1989): 2; FBIS, June 5, pp. 8–9.

June 4 was a bitter day of wholesale massacre in Beijing. Flying in the face of the will of the people and dispatching tanks, armored cars, and machine guns under the public gaze, the Li-Yang [Li Peng–Yang Shangkun] clique carried out a bloody suppression of the unarmed students and residents striving for democracy, resulting in a major tragedy in which over 1,000 people were killed and over 10,000 people were wounded. Under these circumstances, what lies before the Chinese people is no longer a question of calling for their downfall but for a public trial of this group of traitors to the people.

In modern history, Beijing city has undergone numerous calamities, none of which has been as tragic as this. When Japan invaded China and entered Beijing city, it did not carry out a massacre like this. In the later period of the civil war, Beijing city was peacefully liberated. The liberation army entering the city did not fire a single shot. Neither during the invasions of foreign enemies or during the civil wars did a real war bring massacres of such scale to Beijing. However, such a tragedy has happened on the 40th anniversary of the founding of the PRC. This has bitterly disappointed all good and honest people, but is not understood by the vast numbers of CPC members and soldiers.

The people cannot forgive the Li-Yang clique because the people have given them many opportunities that they have rejected. They have entirely changed into the opposite of the people and taken a path alienating themselves from the people.

When the student movement started, the students did not make excessive demands. Out of the need to create party strife, however, the Li-Yang clique intentionally procrastinated and refused to accept the students' demands. This tended to intensify the students' attitude. When the situation grew more serious, people from all circles in society stepped forward to mediate. Some members of the National People's Congress Standing Committee also issued a call. But they were also rejected by the Li-Yang clique. Thus, the Li-Yang clique missed the opportunity.

Zhao Ziyang's speech on May 4 was well received by the people of the country. The students also wanted to return to school and, while resuming classes, continue to hold dialogues with the government. However, out of the need to create party strife, the Li-Yang clique again gave up this chance by categorically rejecting it.

During the hunger strike held by the students, over 3,000 people fainted and were sent to hospitals. Judging from whatever angle, this is a tremendous calamity. In fact, the Li-Yang clique could have used humanitarianism (didn't Li Peng pay lip service to humanitarianism when meeting the students at the Great Hall of the People?) to extricate themselves from an awkward position. But they refused to do so. When General Secretary Zhao Ziyang met the students, the students agreed to stop fasting and the dawn of a solution appeared. It is a pity that at this moment the Li-Yang clique decided on a crackdown.

The soldiers were fearlessly held back by good and honest people. The fact that the unarmed people used their flesh and blood to resist the fully-armed troops can completely explain the problem. People with a little sensibility should have been able to see the will of the people and rein in at the brink of the precipice, thus preventing the disaster. But the Li-Yang clique again gave up this chance. The good and honest people never expected the clique to be so cold-blooded.

The Li-Yang clique is also a clique telling shameless lies. When meeting the students in the Great Hall of the People, Li Peng solemnly vowed that the party and state never said that the student movement was a disturbance. Less than twenty-four hours later, however, in his speech on May 19, the self-same Li Peng defined the student movement as a counterrevolutionary disturbance. How can the premier of a dignified republic go back on his word in such a way! At the May 19 meeting, Yang Shangkun also solemnly pledged to all the people that the troops would not be used to suppress the students and said that all people would be able to see this clearly in a few days' time. In his numerous talks later, he repeatedly stressed this point. However, the fact is that the president of a republic has employed troops to massacre the people of the republic. Is the Li-Yang clique still qualified to hold the premiership and presidency of the republic? Their remaining in office represents the greatest humiliation to the republic.

Since the student movement started, this paper has always used press reports and commentaries to persuade the authorities to hold sincere dialogues with the students to avoid the worsening of the situation. After the sabre-rattling May 19 speech, in the face of great risks, this paper continuously cautioned the authorities to use restraint and not to intensify the contradictions. The Chinese people in the mainland, Hong Kong, Macao, and abroad have also made similar great efforts. It is a pity that the kind-hearted admonitions of the people cannot prevent the atrocities of a handful of people. This cannot but set people thinking: What has gone wrong with our system? We should also ponder this question: When the leadership of our country is controlled by a group of butchers, what should we do?

Glossary of Important Figures, Recurrent Terms, and Abbreviations

Bao Tong (1934–)—personal secretary to Zhao Ziyang and major theorist for economic and political reforms. Reportedly arrested; mentioned in Chen Xitong's report as a main instigator of student unrest. Former positions: member, CPC Central Propaganda Group; director of Political Structure Reform Research Center; on board of directors for CITIC's Institute for International Studies.

Bao Zunxin (1937–)—research fellow at CASS Institute of History; organizer of the Autonomous Intellectuals' Union and signature campaign in support of students.

Bei Dao (1949–)—leading contemporary poet; initiated "Petition of 33."

Bo Yibo (1909–)—party elder; CPC Central Advisory Commission vice-chairman; former Politburo member; economic specialist.

bourgeois liberalization—term used by the party to describe the ideas, such as democracy and free speech, advocated by students and intellectuals after December 1986. Initial campaign culminated in removal of Hu Yaobang as CPC general secretary and dismissal of Liu Binyan, Wang Ruowang, and Fang Lizhi from party.

CASS—Chinese Academy of Social Sciences; established July 1977.

CCTV—China Central Television

Chai Ling (1966–)—graduate student in psychology at Beijing Normal University; student leader of Tiananmen Square Headquarters; on government's "twenty-one most wanted" list; now living in exile in France.

Chen Xitong (1930–)—one of chief exponents of the crackdown; mayor of Beijing; CPC Central Committee member; deputy secretary of Beijing Party Committee; State Council councilor; delivered major report on crisis.

Chen Yun (1905–)—party elder; former Politburo Standing Committee member; current chairman of CPC Central Advisory Commission; specialist in economic affairs and party disciplinary work.

CITIC—China International Trust and Investment Corporation; established July 1979.

CPC—Communist Party of China (often given as CCP in the West).

CPCCC—Central Committee of the Communist Party of China; most recent elected at Thirteenth Party Congress (1987); 175 members, 110 alternates.

CYL—Communist Youth League.

Deng Pufang (1943–)—Deng Xiaoping's son; pushed out a window by Red Guards during the Cultural Revolution, making him a paraplegic; director of China Welfare Fund for the Handicapped; criticized for undue influence in allocation of state funds.

Deng Xiaoping (1904–)—China's preeminent leader; chairman of CPCCC Military Commission from 1981 to 1989; Long March veteran; exponent of economic reform, open-door policies, and need to combat bourgeois liberalization.

Deng Yingchao (1904–)—Mme. Zhou Enlai; party elder; former Politburo member and Sixth CPCCC chair; resigned in 1985.

Elders/Octogenarians—Bo Yibo, Chen Yun, Deng Yingchao, Li Xiannian, Nie Rongzhen, Peng Zhen, Song Renqiong, Wang Zhen, and Xu Xiangqian.

Fang Lizhi (1936–)—astrophysicist; leading exponent of political reform and democracy; dismissed from CPC and vice-presidency of University of Science and Technology in Hefei, Anhui Province, early in 1987; became a leading Chinese dissident; after June 4, officials condemned him as a main instigator of the student movement, obtained refuge in U.S. Embassy with his wife Li Shuxian. Now living in England.

Federation for a Democratic China (FDC)—founded in Paris September 1989 by leading dissidents.

Four cardinal principles—adherence to socialism, the dictatorship of the proletariat, the leadership of the CPC, and subscribing to Marxism–Leninisn–Mao Zedong Thought; first articulated by Deng Xiaoping in March 1979.

Four modernizations—formulated by Premier Zhou Enlai in 1975: the goals of modernizing agriculture, industry, science and technology, and national defense.

Gang of Four—Jiang Qing (Mao's widow), Wang Hongwen (CPC vice-chair), Yao Wenyuan (vice-premier), and Zhang Chunqiao (vice-premier); arrested in 1976, soon after the death of Mao Zedong, as instigators of the Cultural Revolution.

He Dongchang (1923–)—State Education Commission vice-minister, CPCCC member.

Hou Dejian (1957–)—Taiwanese popular singer who defected to China in 1983; one of four people who began hunger strike June 1.

Hu Jiwei (1917–)—vice-chair of NPC Committee on Education, Science, Culture, and Public Health; Sixth NPC Standing Committee member; director and chief editor of *People's Daily* until 1983; former president of All-China Federation of Journalists; in May 1989, initiated campaign to convene emergency NPC session to challenge martial law.

Hu Qili (1929–)—former Politburo Standing Committee member and head of CPC Central Propaganda Group; retained membership on CPC Central Committee but dismissed from posts in June 1989.

Hu Yaobang (1915–1989)—former CPC general secretary; replaced by Zhao Ziyang in 1987 after student demonstrations; April 15 death was catalyst for Beijing Spring student movement.

Jiang Zemin (1926–)—Shanghai party secretary who replaced Zhao Ziyang as CPC general secretary in June 1989; replaced Deng as CPC Military Commission chair in November.

Li Peng (1928–)—Politburo Standing Committee member; State Council premier; Central Foreign Affairs Group head; minister in charge of State Commission for Restructuring the Economic System; announced martial law on May 19–20, 1989.

Li Ruihuan (1934–)—Politburo member; Tianjin mayor; party secretary; promoted in June to Politburo Standing Committee and put in charge of propaganda and ideological work.

Li Tieying (1936–)—Politburo member; State Council councilor; State Education Commission minister.